AF559728

ROQUE MESQUITA

MADHVA'S QUOTES FROM THE PURĀṆAS AND THE MAHĀBHĀRATA

MADHVA'S QUOTES FROM THE PURĀṆAS AND THE MAHĀBHĀRATA

AN ANALYTICAL COMPILATION OF UNTRACEABLE SOURCE-QUOTATIONS IN MADHVA'S WORKS ALONG WITH FOOTNOTES

ROQUE MESQUITA
University of Vienna

ADITYA PRAKASHAN
Delhi 2008

First English version: 2008

ISBN: 978-81-7742-082-1

Published by Aditya Prakashan, Delhi – 110 009,
and printed at Rajkamal Electric Press, Delhi – 110 033.

TABLE OF CONTENTS

INDICES

PREFACE TO THE ENGLISH EDITION

My original collection of all untraceable quotations from the Purāṇic and Epic literature in Madhva's different works was published along with its German translation in the Publications of the De Nobili Research Library, Vienna 2007. The present English version complies with the wish of several Indologists to make it accessible also to English-speaking scholars. At present I am not in a position to submit an English translation of the said quotations, which remains a long-term project for the future. The present English version contains, however, some changes and several additions. Two of these deserve a special mention, namely the lively discussion of the avatārahood of Madhva in a recent study 'Gomañjarī' by a Madhvite author,[1] with its nexus to the restoration of the lost texts (*śāstra*) in the Kaliyuga by Madhva and the critical appraisal of the discussion initiated by DEEPAK SARMA about the so called "insider epistemology".

The project aimed at collecting all untraceable quotations ascribed to the Purāṇic and Epic literature, which are found all over the works of Madhva, had its origin in connection with my preliminary enquiries into the text-materials for the first monograph on Madhva's unknown literary sources (German edition 1997 – English version 2000).

The present collection, comprising more than 1.960 *śloka*s, constitutes a supplement to the aforesaid monograph and it should serve as working materials for future studies. The majority of these quotations can be found in Madhva's commentaries on Prasthānatraya, Bhāgavatapurāṇa and on Mahābhārata. His procedure is based mainly on the interpretation of these basic texts in close relationship to his original teachings, which are not traceable to a particular *guruparaṃparā*.[2] Accordingly, Madhva pursues, like many other Vedānta commentators before him, the aim of explaining the basic texts artificially within the lines of his own system. In this case, the following statement of W.

---

[1] Gomañjarī authored by Śrī Dvārakānāthācārya, A critique of the Māṇikya Mañjarī of Raghunātha Sūri, Compiled and edited with a foreword in Sanskrit by Śrī Śrīnivāsachārya Tāmraparṇī, Banashankari prakashana, Bangalore 2004. The Study has fourteen chapters. The longest among them is the fifth chapter: *Śrīmadhvasya vāyutvasamarthanam.* I am sincerely grateful to Mr. H.P. Raghunandan (IBM certified Project Manager, Pune), who brought to my attention this recent publication and sent to me a copy of the same.

[2] Cf. MESQUITA 2000_1: 18; 77ff. (= 1997: 16f.; 61ff.) and below GarP 36.

RAU on Śaṅkara's method of interpretation is applicable to Madhva even in a much stronger sense: "His (Śaṅkara's) defective philological dexterity produced lapses and obscurities ... his philosophy drove him into a cage of preconceived ideas and forced him to base his doctrinal convictions or beliefs on texts which at the utmost comprised merely germs of a philosophical system which Śaṅkara himself, born (centuries later after the text of BĀU was composed), thought to be destined to lead them to completion. Therefore, we cannot accept Śaṅkara as an interpreter of BĀU. We would understand the text of BĀU rather by ourselves and without his help than under his guidance" [RAU 1960: 299].

Besides, the passages of the basic texts commented upon by Madhva deviate in several cases from the transmitted text. The publisher of the Sarvamūlagrantha-edition has noted down all the variant readings in the footnotes. As a matter of fact, the Bhāgavatapurāṇa used by Madhva has not only a different numbering of *adhyāya*s and *śloka*s but also a different text-tradition with additional *śloka*s and variant readings. According to HAZRA (1987: 54), "textual problems relating to Bhāgavata had already begun in Madhva's time." Furthermore, Madhva introduces silently minor amendments and adjustments in the *śruti* and *smṛti* passages, while commenting on them. One example among many others is *atat tvam asi* (ChU VI 1f.).[3] Frequently, Madhva puts forward teachings which have nothing to do with the text he comments upon.[4]

A detailed discussion on all the text-critical and philosophical points or a precise reconstruction of the background of numerous mythological elements, theological dogmas and other particular teachings[5] is not attempted here, since it would go beyond the scope of this

---

[3] Cf. MESQUITA 2000: 126ff.; 140ff. and MESQUITA 2000_1: 107f.; 108n. 204; 237n. 278; 143ff. [= 1997: 85f.; 87n. 194; 110n. 267; 115f.]; MESQUITA 2007: 9 [= 2007_1: 434]; LORENZ 2005: 28ff.; see also below BhāgP 5.

[4] Cf. v.g. BhāgP 5; BhaviṣP 5; 7; see also GHATE 1981: 27; 30 [= MESQUITA 2000_1: 19n. 15; 25n. 27 (= 1997: 17n. 8; 22n. 20)].

[5] Cf. LORENZ's study (2003): Mahidāsa Aitareya in the work of Madhva, "... what Madhva and his quoted sources say about Mahidāsa reveal one statement that stands out ... : Mahidāsa is Viṣṇu. This seems to be Madhva's most urgent message" (p. 34). LORENZ comes also to the conclusion that all the sources and passages adduced by Madhva in support of this teaching are untraceable, and furthermore, that they are authored by Madhva himself; cf. also below BrāṇP 95[23-27]; BrahP 16 and VarP 51[5-7]. This conclusion is valid also for my paper (MESQUITA 2003), where I have elaborated Madhva's doctrine of the Rank and Function of God Vāyu in the Philosophy of Madhva, as well as for my paper on "*jīvanmukti* in the Philosophy of

collection. As far as the close context of the unknown or untraceable quotations was available through Madhva's other quite similar passages or inasmuch as it has been discussed by me in my previous publications, I have referred to them in the footnotes.

It is my hope that the venture started here with this huge collection of untraceable quotations may encourage lovers of Madhva's philosophy and provide them with initial materials and ideas for further research in this area. For this purpose, I have appended three lists of the remaining untraceable or unknown quotes with indication of their precise location in the works of Madhva. I collected three hundred and fifty five sources. Most of them are named after the names of Vedic schools or after famous Vedic teachers. Some of these titles are quite strange. Many of them appear also in variant readings of the editor under different names. The choice of the source title seems to follow the rule *nomen est omen* [MESQUITA 2000_1: 32 [= 1997: 48f.]. It is striking that some of them are quoted only once, and very often in a single work.

I took over the lists prepared by GLASENAPP [1923: 21* (= 1992: 24)] with some major changes. In contrast to him, I have arranged these lists in an alphabetical sequence, together with their precise location, according to pages, in Madhva's different works in order to enable the research scholars to carry out a detailed investigation into them. With this aim in mind, I have also added a *pāda*-index of all untraceable or unknown quotations of the Purāṇic and Epic literature collected here.

As a matter of fact, Madhva's untraceable sources comprise a whole class of literary works with countless different titles. The assumption of Madhva's followers that some manuscripts of the old texts, which are reported to be existent, though inaccessible, may provide evidence for the veracity of Madhva's quotations in the near future [SHARMA 2000: 88] is nothing but a conjecture, or wishful thinking at best [MESQUITA 2003_1: 196f.], as it was in the case of Brahmatarka, whose alleged authenticity could be definitively proved to be false [ibid. p. 198f. and MESQUITA 2000_1: 93n. 162 [= 1997: 74n. 151]). Even the general attitude of Jayatīrtha – who was the "next lodestar

Madhva" (MESQUITA 2007 [= 2007_1]). HOUBEN (1999: 156f.) also draws the same conclusions in his study of *yajñapaśu*: "It is worthwhile noting in this context that Madhva often gives quotations from sources which are not only unknown to us, but which were already unknown (or allegedly 'lost') in his own time"; see also below BrāṇP 35 and VarP 39.

after Madhva in the firmament of Dvaita Vedānta" and "who gave final shape and form to Madhva's concepts and categories" – "to the numerous authorities cited by Madhva was one of respectful acquiescence; but for his own part he relies more on extant texts."[6]

Another common assumption of followers of Madhva is that the unknown or untraceable sources "are not wanting in the Bhāṣyas of Śaṅkara, Rāmānuja and Śrīkaṇṭha and that the charge against Madhva alone, savours of nothing but prejudice ... and that Vijayīndra has given crushing replies to this charge" (SHARMA 2000: 404f.), this too is unwarranted. As a matter fact, Vijayīndra could name in his polemical pamphlet *madhvatantramukhabhūṣaṇa* against Appaya Dīkṣita only three untraceable sources in Śaṅkara's BSūBh (*ad* III,2,18); in Rāmānuja's BSūBh (*ad* I,1,26) and in Śrīkaṇṭha's BSūBh.[7] In comparison with the large number of Madhva's untraceable sources these passages are a minute fraction, and they therefore constitute a sheer negligible number.

One more instance of assumption that "the appeal to [untraceable] texts occurs only in respect of purely theological issues and interpretations of disputed texts. But this does not affect the metaphysical bases of his thought, or his ontology and theory of knowledge,"[8] is out-

---

[6] Cf. SHARMA 2000: 244 and also p. 241. SHARMA himself, although he defended the veracity of Madhva's sources, concludes his comments with a mild statement (p. 89): "We must, therefore, concede that there must have been some basis for these sources utilized by Madhva."

[7] Śaṅkara's untraceable quote in defence of *nirviśeṣa*-Brahman: ... mokṣaśāstreṣu –

yathā hy ayaṃ jyotir ātmā vivasvān
apo bhinnā bahudhaiko 'nugacchan /
upādhinā kriyate bhedarūpo
devaḥ kṣetreṣv evam ajo 'yam ātmā // *iti.*

Rāmānuja's unknown source regarding a four-footed *gāyatrī* metre runs:

indraḥ śacīpatir balena pīḍitaḥ /
duścayavano vṛṣā samitsu sāsahiḥ // *iti.*

Apart from a short passage: *yaś caṇḍālaḥ śiva iti vācaṃ vadet* ..., no other particulars are given regarding this quote in Śrīkaṇṭha's Bhāṣya. For other details see my Rejoinder: Madhva's unknown Sources in MESQUITA 2003_1: 197f.

[8] Cf. SHARMA 2000: 86; see also ibid. (Appendix XX): "However in discussing the question it would be proper to keep in mind that the logical and metaphysical foundations and the superstructure built up by Madhva do not at all depend on these, untraceable sources, but have the full support of the existing sources of Śrutis and Smṛtis. The untraceable sources relate mainly to the theological aspects of the system with which Modern Scholars need have no concern. It would thus appear that it would be blowing an irrelevant issue beyond all proportions, to denigrate Madhva's system – which can stand on its own inherent logical and metaphysical strength."

right unjustified on account of the fact that the contents of the untraceable sources, as the collection of these sources below clearly shows, comprise all areas of Madhva's thought, conspicuously including also realms of ontology and theory of knowledge. In fact, Madhva bases his theory of knowledge on an unknown and untraceable source, namely Brahmatarka. It is therefore a text dealing with *tarka*, meaning that it was concerned also with epistemology. This source is introduced by Madhva as *tarkaśāstra*: *brahmatarkas tarkaśāstraṃ viṣṇunā yat samīritam.*[9]

Finally, the assumption that "the attempt to discredit the sources of Madhva is of much later origin, springing from the days of Appaya Dīkṣita" [SHARMA 2000: 87] ignores the fact that serious criticism of Madhva's unknown sources was articulated already during the time of Madhva himself.[10]

---

[9] Cf. NārP 48; see also below Introduction n. 55. Over and above that, Madhva remarks that his two other epistemological works, Mānalakṣaṇam and Kathālakṣaṇam are based on Brahmatarka, cf. MESQUITA 2000_1: 90-92n. 160 [= 1997: 72-73n. 149]; see also VTN pp. 17,1-18,11; BĀUBh pp. 269,14-270,18; see also MESQUITA 2000: 339ff.

[10] Cf. below Introduction n. 15. While referring to the problem of sources, SHARMA [2000: 85f.] wholly abstains from discussing the aspect of Madhva's *avatāra*-claim under the pretext that the point in question is too sensitive to be discussed: "But this discussion should be in a balanced way, [...] without straying into sensitive issues relating to the Avatarhood of the person concerned"; cf. SHARMA 2001: 7f. and MESQUITA 2003_1: 211f. As far as I know, the only place where SHARMA refers to Madhva as *avatāra* of Vāyu, the son of Viṣṇu, without however going into details, is the Madhva comics! (Amar Citra Katha No. 579; see also below Introduction n. 37).

The *prācīnaṭīkākāras*, as Trivikramapaṇḍitācārya as well as other later commentators like Jayatīrtha etc. (cf. Introduction nn. 16 and 36), on the contrary, had no reservations about discussing this issue. Trivikramapaṇḍitācārya carefully considered the details of this most important teaching in the system of Madhva in his subcommentary on Madhva's BSūBh, namely in the Tattvapradīpikā and underlined Madhva's special character as an omniscient author and as one who does not deceive: *... ācāryaḥ svoktārthe svayam eva pramāṇaṃ sarvajñatvād avipralaṃbhakatvāc ca ... sarvajñātvaṃ tāvac chrutisiddham* (= ṚV I 141,1-5; see also Introduction nn. 44f.). Within the framework of this doctrine falls also Trivikramapaṇḍitācārya's famous Stotra, Vāyustuti praising the triple incarnations of Vāyu, as Hanumān, Bhīma and Madhva. Probably, SHARMA could not follow this line of argumentation, since omniscience does not match with ignorance of Pāṇini's rules. Every now and then, SHARMA speaks of several weaknesses of Madhva, for instance that "The rules of Pāṇini are frequently violated in the AV and other works of Madhva" (SHARMA 2000: 242; 253; 256) or of his "disconnected and 'laboured' explanations of texts" and of his "apparently, piecemeal and uncoordinated treatment of the so-called Advaita śrutis, resting ... on corroborative evidences of a large body of non-extant texts" (ibid. p. 241). At

I wish to express my gratitude to students of mine who attended my seminars on Madhva's philosophy and his scientific methodology (between winter-term 1996 and summer-term 2002). I am indebted to them in particular for checking and verifying the quotations collected by me, with the help of existing Śloka-indices of the Purāṇas and the Mahābhārata. For any lapses in this aspect I alone shoulder the responsibility.

I am greatly indebted to Prof. Dr. George Chemparathy, Emeritus Professor of Indian Philosophy at the University of Utrecht, for his useful remarks and improvements to the English expression of this paper. Thanks also to Himal Trikha for his valuable suggestions regarding the electronical designing of the manuscript and to Christian Ferstl for preparing the camera-ready copy of the book.

Last but not least I am most thankful to my family specially to my wife for her constant encouragement. It is to her that this book is lovingly dedicated.

---

the same time, SHARMA speaks of Jayatīrtha with high-flown expressions of praise, which by implication seems also to point out the deficiences of Madhva, as when he writes: "He gave final shape and form to its (dvaita's) concepts and categories, standardized their definitions, formulated new ones where none had been given by Madhva ..." (ibid. p. 335). ... "This shows boldness and originality to go ahead of Madhva (without prejudice of the Siddhānta) and explore fresh lines of thought and interpretation ... Jayatīrtha displays consummate skill in detecting hidden significance in the all but too brief utterances of Madhva ..." (ibid. p. 239). "He is ready with suitable defences of the grammatical 'lapses' of Madhva" (ibid. p. 256). "He does not hesitate to differ from the interpretations of his own school ..." (p. 244). This remark may refer also to *jīvanmukti* which Madhva clearly defends. He not only uses the technical term 'for liberation while living' but also explains it quoting profusely several unknown and untraceable sources (cf. MESQUITA 2007: 1n. 4 [= 2007_1: 1n. 4]; see also Introduction n. 30).

BIBLIOGRAPHY AND ABBREVIATIONS

AgniP — Agnipurāṇa, ed. by KH. KRSNADASA. Delhi 1985.

AiU — Aitareyopaniṣad.

AiUBh — Madhva, Aitareyopaniṣadbhāṣya, see Anuv.

Anuv — Madhva, Anuvyākhyāna. [Works of Sri Madhwacharya]. In: Sarvamūlagranthāḥ-Prasthānatrayī, saṃpuṭa 1, ed. by B. GOVINDACHARYA. Udipi 1969.

AWASTHI 1992 — A.B.L. AWASTHI, Purāṇa Index. New Delhi 1992.

BĀU — Bṛhadāraṇyakopaniṣad.

BĀUBh — Madhva, Bṛhadarāṇyakopaniṣadbhāṣya, see Anuv.

BhāgP — Bhāgavatapurāṇa with Sanskrit Commentary Bhāvārthabodhinī of Śrīdhara, ed. by J.S. SHASTRI. Delhi 1983.

BhāgTN — Madhva, Bhāgavatatātparyanirṇaya. [Works of Sri Madhwacharya]. In: Sarvamūlagranthāḥ – Purāṇaprasthāna, saṃpuṭa 3, ed. by B. GOVINDACHARYA. Udipi 1980.

BhaviṣP — Bhaviṣyatpurāṇa, ed. by KH. KRSNADASA. Delhi 1984.

BhaviṣPV — Bhaviṣyatparvan.

BrahP — Sanskrit Indices and Text of the Brahmapurāṇa by P. SCHREINER and R. SÖHNEN. [Purāṇa Research Publication, Tübingen, ed. by H. VON STIETENCRON, 1]. Wiesbaden 1987.

BrahVP — Brahmavaivartapurāṇa, ed. by J.L. SHASTRI. Delhi 1983.

BrāṇP — Brahmāṇḍapurāṇa, ed. by K.V. SARMA. Varanasi 1983.

BSū	Brahmasūtras.
BSūBh	Madhva, Brahmasūtrabhāsya, see Anuv.
CHANDRAVASU 1910	Chhandogya Upaniṣad with the Commentary of Madhvāchārya, transl. S. CHANDRAVASU. [Sacred Books of the Hindus, ed. by B.D. BASU, Vol. III, Part II]. Allahabad 1910.
ChU	Chāndogyopaniṣad.
ChUBh	Madhva, Chāndogyopaniṣadbhāṣya, see Anuv.
DASGUPTA 1975	S. DASGUPTA, A History of Indian Philosophy (First Indian Edition), Vols. 1-5. Delhi 1975.
FRAUWALLNER 1973	E. FRAUWALLNER, History of Indian Philosophy. Translated from original German into English by V.M. Bedekar. Delhi 1973, vols I-II.
GarP	Garudapurāṇa, ed. by KH. KRSNADASA. Delhi 1984.
GHATE 1981	V.S. GHATE, The Vedānta. A Study of the Brahma-Sūtras with the Bhāṣyas of Śaṃkara, Rāmānuja, Nimbārka, Madhva, and Vallabha. [Bhandarkar Oriental Research Institute: Government Oriental Series Class B. No. 5]. Poona 1981.
Gī	Bhagavadgītā.
GīBh	Madhva, Bhagavadgītābhāṣya, see Anuv.
GīT	Madhva, Bhagavadgītātātparya, see Anuv.
GK	Gauḍapādakārikā.
GLASENAPP 1992	H. VON GLASENAPP, Philosophy of the Vishnu Faith translated by SH.B. SHROTHRI, ed. by K.T. PANDURANGI [Dvaita Vedanta Studies and Research Foundation]. Bangalore 1992.
GRIFFITH 1987	R.T.H. GRIFFITH, Hymns of the Ṛgveda. Translated with a Popular Commentary, Vols. I-II. New Delhi 1987.
HACKER 1958	P. HACKER, Ānvīkṣikī, WZKSO 2 (1958), 54-83.

HACKER 1959 — Prahlāda. Werden und Wandlungen einer Idealgestalt. Beiträge zur Geschichte des Hinduismus. TeilI: Die Entstehung der Legende. Die Prahlāda-Legende des Viṣṇupurāṇa und des Bhāgavatapurāṇa. [Abhandlungen der Geistes- und Sozialwissenschaftlichen Klasse, Jg. 1959/9]. Wiesbaden 1959.

HACKER 1960 — Zur Entwicklung der Avatāralehre. WZKSO 4 (1960), p. 47-70.

HACKER 1985 — Grundlagen indischer Dichtung und indischen Denkens. [Publications of the De Nobili Research Library 11]. Wien 1985.

HALBFASS 1991 — W. HALBFASS, Tradition and Reflection in Indian Thought. New York 1991.

HarV — The Harivaṃśa Being the Khila or Supplement to the Mahābhārata, for the first time crit. ed. by P.L. VAIDYA, 2 vols. Poona 1969/1971.

HAZRA 1987 — R.C. HAZRA, Studies in the Purānic Records on Hindu Rites and Customs (reprint). Delhi 1987.

HEIMANN 1922 — Madhva's (Ānandatīrtha's) Kommentar zur Kāṭhaka-Upaniṣad. Sanskrit-Text in Transskription nebst Übersetzung und Noten. Hrsg. von BETTY HEIMANN. Leipzig 1922.

HOFSTÄTTER 2000 — E. HOFSTÄTTER, Zitate und Zitierweise in Madhva's Bhagavadgītabhāṣya (Diplomarbeit). Wien 2000.

HOHENBERGER 1965 — A. HOHENBERGER, Metren der Kunstdichtung in den Purāṇen. WZKSO 9: 48-97.

HOHENBERGER 1967 — Das Bhaviṣyapurāṇa. [Münchener Indologische Studien 5]. Wiesbaden 1967.

HOUBEN 1999 — JAN E.M. HOUBEN, To Kill or Not to Kill the Sacrificial Animal (*yajña-paśu*)? Arguments and Perspectives in Brahminical Ethical Philosophy. In: Violence Denied. Violence, Non Violence and the Rationalization of Violence in South Asian Cultural History, ed. by JAN E.M.

	HOUBEN and KAREL R. VAN KOOIJ. Leiden 1999 [Brill's Indological Library 6].
ĪśU	Īśopaniṣad.
ĪśUBh	Madhva, Īśopaniṣadbhāṣya, see Anuv.
KathU	Kathopaniṣad.
KathUBh	Madhva, Kathopaniṣadbhāṣya, see Anuv.
KeU	Kenopaniṣad.
KeUBh	Madhva, Kenopaniṣadbhāṣya, see Anuv.
KIRFEL 1954	W. KIRFEL, Das Purāṇa vom Weltgebäude. Die kosmographischen Traktate der Purāṇas. Versuch einer Textgeschichte. Bonn 1954.
KhN	Madhva, Kaṇḍārthanirṇaya, see ṚgBh.
KūrP	Kūrmapurāṇa, ed. by KH. KRSNADASA. Delhi 1983.
LORENZ 2003	E. LORENZ, Mahidāsa Aitareya in the Work of Madhva (Kandidatexamen). Stockholms universitet 2003.
LORENZ 2005	Genuine Ancient Source, Deliberately Fabricated Material, or Divine Revelation? An Analysis of Selected Quotes that Madhva Ascribes to the Brahmatarka (Magisterexamen). Stockholms universitet 2005.
MāṇU	Māṇḍūkyopaniṣad.
MāṇUBh	Madhva, Māṇḍūkyopaniṣadbhāṣya.
MārkP	Mārkandeyapurāṇa, ed. by KH. KRSNADASA. Delhi 1984.
MatsyaP	The Matsyapurāṇa. Text in Devanagari and Notes in English. Foreword by H.H. WILSON, Part I-II. Delhi 1983.
MBh	Mahābhārata, crit. ed. by V.S. SUKTHANKAR etc. Poona 1933ff.
MBhTN	Madhva, Mahābhāratatātparyanirṇaya. [Works of Sri Madhwacharya]. In: Sarvamūlagranthāḥ

– Itihāsaprasthāna, sampuṭa 2, ed. by B. GOVINDACHARYA. Udipi 1971.

MESQUITA 1989 Yāmunācārya's Lehre von der Größe des Ātmans, WZKS 33 (1989) 129-150.

MESQUITA 1990 R. MESQUITA, Yāmunācāryas Philosophie der Erkenntnis. Eine Studie zu seiner Saṃvitsiddhi. [SbÖAW 563 = Veröffentlichungen der Kommission für Sprachen und Kulturen Südasiens 24]. Wien 1990.

MESQUITA 1994 Die Idee der Erlösung bei Kumārilabhaṭṭa [Festschrift für G. Oberhammer]. WZKS 38 (1994): 451-484.

MESQUITA 1997 Madhva und seine unbekannten literarischen Quellen. Einige Beobachtungen. [Publications of the De Nobili Research Library, ed. by G. OBERHAMMER, Vol. XXIV]. Wien 1977.

MESQUITA 2000 Madhva, Viṣṇutattvanirṇaya. Der Nachweis des wahren Wesens Viṣṇus. Annotierte Übersetzung mit Studie. [Publications of the De Nobili Research Library, ed. by G. OBERHAMMER, Vol. XXVIII]. Wien 2000.

MESQUITA 2000_1 Madhva's Unknown literary sources. Some observations. Delhi 2000.

MESQUITA 2003 The Rank and Function of God Vāyu in the Philosophy of Madhva. Indo-Iranian Journal 46 (2003): 97-117.

MESQUITA 2003_1 Rejoinder: Madhva's unknown Sources. Asiatische Studien 57 (2003): 195-212.

MESQUITA 2007 The Concept of Liberation while still alive in the Philosophy of Madhva. Delhi 2007.

MESQUITA 2007_1 Die Idee der Erlösung bei Lebzeiten im System Madhvas. In: Expanding and Merging Horizons. Contributions to South Asian and Cross-Cultural Studies in Commemoration of Wilhelm Halbfass, ed. K. PREISENDANZ, Wien:

Verlag der Österreichischen Akademie der Wissenschaften, 2007, pp. 433- 454.

MSū — Mīmāṃsāsūtras.

MTM — Appayadīkṣita, Madhvatantramukhamardana [mit dem Autokommentar] Madhvamatavidhvaṃsana, [zusammen mit] Ṭippaṇa Sandarbhavivaraṇa [von] Chinnasvāmi Sāstri, ed. by RAMANATHA DIKSITA. Kāśī 1941.

MuU — Muṇḍakopaniṣad.

MuUBh — Madhva, Muṇḍakopaniṣadbhāṣya, see Anuv.

NārP — Nāradīyapurāṇa, ed. by KH. KRSNADASA. Delhi 1984.

NSū — Nyāyasūtras.

NyāV — Madhva, Nyāyavivaraṇa, see Anuv.

OBERHAMMER 1971 — G. OBERHAMMER, Yāmunamunis Interpretation von Brahmasūtram 2,2,42-45. Eine Untersuchung zur Pāñcarātra-Tradition der Rāmānuja-Schule. [Sb ÖAW 274 = Veröffentlichungen der Kommission für Sprachen und Kulturen Südasiens 10]. Wien 1971.

OBERHAMMER 1983 — Inklusivismus: Eine indische Denkform. Hrsg. von G. OBERHAMMER. [Publications of the De Nobili Research Library, Occasional Papers 2]. Wien 1983.

OBERLIES 1998 — TH. OBERLIES, Die Religion des Ṛgveda. Erster Teil: Das Religiöse System des Ṛgveda. [Publications of the De Nobili Research Library, ed. G. OBERHAMMER, Vol. XXVI]. Wien 1998.

PadP — Padmapurāṇa, ed. KH. KRSNADASA. Delhi 1984.

PANDURANGI 1989 — K.T. PANDURANGI, Aitareyopaniṣad with Engl. Transl. and Notes According to Śrī Madhvacharya's Bhashya … . Chirtanur 1989.

PANDURANGI (Bāu) Bṛhadaraṇyakopaniṣad with Engl. Transl. and Notes according to Śrī Madhvacharya's Bhashya .... Chirtanur (no date of publication).

PANDURANGI 1993 Mahābhāratatātparyanirṇayaḥ, transl. by K.T. PANDURANGI [First Volume: First three Chapters, S.M.S.O. Sabha Publication 21]. Chirtanur 1993.

PANDURANGI 1997-2002 Brahmasūtra Bhāṣyam of Śrī Ānandatīrtha with the commentaries of Śrī Trivikrama Paṇḍita and Śrī Jayatīrtha, with sub-commentaries of Śrī Vādirājatīrtha, Śrī Raghūttamatīrtha, Śrī Rāghavendratīrtha, Śrī Tāmraparṇi Śrinivāsa; Śrī Pāndurangi Śrīnivāsa, Śrīnivāsatīrtha and Śarkara srīnivāsa. Vols. 1-7 edited by K.T. PANDURANGI. Bangalore 1997-2002.

PraśU Praśnopaniṣad.

PraśUBh Madhva, Praśnopaniṣadbhāṣya, see Anuv.

RAO 1960 C.R.K. RAO, Madhva and Brahmatarka. Udipi 1960.

RAO/SHARMA 2003 SHRISHA RAO und B.N.K. SHARMA, Madhva's Unknown Sources: A Review. Asiatische Studien / Études Asiatiques 57 (2003): 181–194.

RAU 1960 W. RAU, Bemerkungen zu Śaṅkaras Bṛhadaraṇyakopaniṣadbhāṣya. Paideuma 7 (1960): 293-299.

ṚgBh Madhva, Ṛgbhāṣya. [Works of Sri Madhwacharya]. In: Sarvamūlagranthāḥ – Śrutiprasthāna, samputa 4, ed. by B. GOVINDACHARYA. Udipi 1973.

ROCHER 1986 L. ROCHER, The Purāṇas. [A History of Indian Literature, ed. by J. GONDA II/3]. Wiesbaden 1986.

RUKMANI 1970 T.S. RUKMANI, A Critical Study of the Bhāgavata Purāṇa (With special reference to Bhakti). Varanasi 1970.

SARMA 1999 — DEEPAK SARMA, Regulating Religious Texts. Access to Texts in Mādhva Vedānta. Journal of Indian Philosophy 27 (1999): 584-634.

SARMA 2005 — DEEPAK SARMA, Epistemologies and the Limitations of Philosophical Inquiry. Doctrine in Mādhva. Vedānta. Routledgecurzon Hindu Studies Series. London and New York 2005.

SCHREINER 1977 — P. SCHREINER, Schau Gottes. Ein Leitmotiv indischer Religionsgeschichte. In: Nārāyaṇīya Studien. Wiesbaden 1977: 159-196.

SHARMA 1986 — B.N.K SHARMA, Philosophy of Śrī Madhvācārya. Delhi 1986

SHARMA 2000 — B.N.K. SHARMA, Dvaita School of Vedānta and its Literature. From the Earliest Beginnings to Our Own Times (rev. edition). Delhi 2000.

SHARMA 2001 — Brahmatarka and Other Unknown Source Books of Madhva. In: My latest four Research Papers. Mumbai 2001: 7-34.

SIAUVE 1957 — S. SIAUVE, La voie vers la connaissance de Dieu (*Brahma-Jijñāsā*) selon L'Anuvyākhyāna de Madhva. Pondichéry 1957.

SIAUVE 1968 — La Doctrine de Madhva. Dvaita-Vedānta. [Publications de l'Institut Francais d'Indologie 38]. Pondichéry 1968.

SIAUVE 1971 — Les Hiérarchies Spirituelles. Selon l'Anuvyākhyāna de Madhva. Textes choisis et traduits par S. SIAUVE. [Publications de l'Institut Francais d'Indologie 43]. Pondichéry 1971.

SkaP — Skandapurāṇa, ed. by KH. KRSNADASA. Delhi 1986.

SÖHNEN 1985 — R. SÖHNEN, Zur Metrik der Kaṭha-Upaniṣad, Festgabe für Karl Hoffmann. Münchener Studien zur Sprachwissenschaft 44 (1985): 215- 238.

STEPHAN 2002 — P. STEPHAN, Erlösung im Spannungsfeld von aktivem Leben und Entsagung. Eine Studie zu

Śaṅkaras Exegese der Bhagavadgītā. Aachen 2002.

SYED 2003 — R. SYED, Tṛtīyā Prakṛti: Das "Dritte Geschlecht" im Alten Indien. Asiatische Studien 57 (2003): 64-120.

TAGARE 1979 — The Bhāgavata-Purāṇa, transl. and annotated by G.V. TAGARE. Delhi 1979.

TaiU — Taittirīyopaniṣad.

TaiUBh — Madhva, Taittirīyopaniṣadbhāṣya, see Anuv.

TphSI — Terminologie der frühen philosophischen Scholastik in Indien: Ein Begriffswörterbuch zur altindischen Dialektik, Erkenntnislehre u. Methodologie, hrsg. von G. OBERHAMMER, Bd. 1 u. 2 [ÖAW Denkschriften, Bd. 223 und 248, Beiträge zur Kultur- und Geistesgeschichte Asiens 9 und 17]. Wien 1991 u. 1996.

TSa — Madhva, Tattvasaṃkhyāna, see VTN.

UKh — Madhva, Upādhikhaṇḍana [with] Ṭīkā by Jayatīrtha [Daśaprakaraṇāni, prathamo bhāgaḥ, ed. by P.P. LAKSHMININARAYANA UPADYAYA. Madras 1969].

Upagī — Upagītā.

Vāda — Madhva, Vāda, see VTN.

VāmP — Vāmanapurāṇa, ed. by KH. KRSNADASA. Delhi 1983.

VarP — The Varāha Purāṇa, crit. ed. by A.S. GUPTA. Varanasi 1981.

VāyuP — Vāyupurāṇa, ed. by KH. KRSNADASA. Delhi 1983.

ViṣDhP — [Viṣṇudharmapurāṇa =] Viṣṇudharmāh: Precepts for the Worship of Viṣṇu, Parts I-III, hrsg. von R. GRÜNENDAHL. Wiesbaden 1983-1989.

ViṣDhUP — Śrīviṣṇudharmottarapurāṇa, ed. by KH. KRSNADASA, vols. I-II. Delhi 1985.

ViṣP	a) The Critical Edition of the Viṣṇupurāṇa vols. I-II, ed. by M.M. PATHAK (Oriental Institute). Vadodara (India) 1997.
	b) Viṣṇupurāṇa [mit dem Kommentar] Śrīviṣṇucittīya, ed. by P. ANNANGARACARYA. Kañcipuram 1972.
VTN	Madhva, Viṣṇutattvanirṇaya. [Works of Sri Madhwacharya]. In: Sarvamūlagranthāḥ – Saṅkīrṇagranthāḥ, saṃpuṭa 5, ed. by B. GOVINDACHARYA. Udipi 1974.

INTRODUCTION

The present collection of all untraceable and unknown quotations from the Purāṇic and Epic literature, which Madhva cites as evidence for his special teachings, serves as a supplement to my already published studies on unknown sources of Madhva. References to only a few identifiable quotations have been mentioned in the short introductory section, always at the beginning of the Purāṇa and Mahābhārata-Text.

This collection, the first of its kind, substantiates the results arrived at in my two previous publications: in the first place, the untraceable quotations have an intimate connection with the original and peculiar teachings of Madhva; secondly, he considers such passages as a kind of a secondary textual extension of the literary works transmitted in the tradition, such as Purāṇas, or in many cases he presents them merely as anonymous citations with *iti* or *iti ca*.[1] While quoting from his untraceable sources, Madhva follows a particular scheme; for these are introduced only after he brings forward his point of view by a personal statement. The aim of this scheme is to show that the particular doctrine is definitely embedded in an existing tradition.[2] In order to underline the agreement of the contents of the untraceable source quotations with Madhva's teachings, text-quotations have been reproduced below together with the introductory remarks of Madhva. References to other quotes in the collection with identical or similar contents have been given in the footnotes.

The textual origin of the Purāṇic and Epic literature implies a manifold historical development, in which a single text takes shape slowly over centuries through the redaction of several authors, in such a manner that one could theoretically assume that Madhva might have had knowledge of textual portions unknown to us. However, an analysis of the untraceable and fictitious passages has shown that Madhva himself composed them as befitted the occasion. For it is highly unlikely that the textual tradition of the Purāṇas reads differently as it was opportune to Madhva, in order to support his new doctrine. In any case, the additions of texts from the Purāṇas which were introduced by

---

[1] Cf. MESQUITA 2000_1: 21f.; 99; 139; 152f.; 172ff. (=1997: 18f.; 79; 112; 122f.; 139ff.).

[2] Cf. MESQUITA 2000_1: 175; see also pp. 21f.; 63ff.; 118ff. (= 1997: 142; cf. 18f.; 51ff.; 95ff.); see also MESQUITA 2000: 32ff. and MESQUITA 2003_1: 196f.

Madhva in conformity with his doctrines did not find acceptance of the *śiṣṭāḥ* beyond Madhva's own tradition.[3]

The untraceable quotations collected here belong on the whole to the Purāṇas. However, there are no quotes from LiṅgaP and ŚivaP. On the other hand, Upapurāṇas are also, although sparsely, represented, namely ĀdiP (once); ĀdityaP (twice); Upanāradīya (once); Upagīta [?] (once) and NarasiṃhaP (once). Thirty-seven quotes are attributed to Harivaṃśa, which is accepted in the tradition as a supplement to the Mahābhārata, but is not included in the count of the eighteen Purāṇas, though it is to be taken as a genuine Purāṇa.[4] The Mahābhārata as the only epic text, with forty-seven quotations, was included in this collection.

It is surprising that in this collection the highest number of quotes are assigned precisely to two Śaiva-Purāṇas, namely PadP and SkaP.[5] Madhva designates them *mohaśāstrāṇi.* He considers both these Purāṇas as partially trustworthy, since they have been composed by Śiva on the command of Viṣṇu.[6] With the help of the principle of inclusivism, which consists in including in one's doctrine what really belongs to an alien sect, namely to the texts of Śivaism,[7] Madhva attempts to defend not only the authoritativeness of his own teaching, but also that of the sources which proclaim it.

The central topics of these untraceable quotations are always the same. They are focussing on the supreme transcendence of Viṣṇu or His divine creatorship and His incomprehensible almighty power. This latter implies that He could even violate the principle of contradiction; for otherwise it would follow as a logical consequence that He is not almighty.[8] These topics appear in a variety of different aspects, since the relationship of Viṣṇu to the world and to the human beings can be seen under different aspects and degrees. The thematic classification of

---

[3] MESQUITA 2000_1: 21f.; 27f.; 109f.; 174f. (= 1997: 18f.; 23f.; 87; 141f.). It is worthwhile noting, that even the followers of the Gauḍīya Vaiṣṇava sect who – in order to reject the accusation that they had no proper *saṃpradāya*, accepted Madhva-*saṃpradāya* as their own – were aware of the fact that Madhva's unknown sources were of dubious character (cf. LORENZ 2005: 13f.; 58f.).

[4] Cf. ROCHER 1986: 31f. and 80f.

[5] Cf. below pp. 234-262 and 262-299 respectively.

[6] Cf. below MārkP 1; see also MESQUITA 2000_1: 157ff. (= 1997: 127ff.).

[7] Cf. MBhTN I 52:

skānde 'py uktaṃ śivenaiva ṣaṇmukhāyaiva sādaram /
śivaśāstre 'pi tad grāhyaṃ bhagavacchāstrayogi yat //

see also MESQUITA 2000_1: 160ff. [= 1997: 127ff.].

[8] Cf. e.g. BrāṇP 69; KūrP 1; see also BrahP 62.

the unknown quotations has been assembled in an alphabetical list in the Appendix. This classification comprises references which are related in each case to a certain topic in its different variations. To simplify matters all references to a particular topic with more than five entries have been gathered under one single unknown source-quotation. This quotation is referred to in every other unknown quotation broaching the same or similar subject. The Pāda-index also comprises other relevant references to the different topics of untraceable quotations.

The present collection of all untraceable or unknown quotations provides support for another observation of mine, namely, that these quotes, under different titles and sometimes also anonymous, are not identical in all their contents, although they are adduced as a proof for a particular teaching. Apart from some common features, these quotations have sometimes complementary, but sometimes also contrary or even contradictory elements, so that they necessarily give the impression that by no means one single person could be the author of these quotations.[9] As an interesting example, among many others, an unknown quote ascribed to BrāṇP 53 could be mentioned, where Madhva, in conformity with the teaching of some Purāṇic texts,[10] puts forward the doctrine of liberation through hatred (*vairayuktayāpy anucintayā tam āpuḥ*). According to this belief, one who is seething inwardly with hatred towards Viṣṇu attains also liberation for the simple reason that He is the focus of his sole attention and thoughts. In contrast to it, another untraceable quote attributed also to this Puṛāṇa ranks this teaching with heresies: *samyagbhaktim ṛte muktir viṣṇau taddveṣatas tathā.*[11] Another example of an untraceable quotation with contradicting contents referring to the qualities of the released souls is presented by Madhva in his BĀUBh, first in a long passage and then in a shorter passage. They belong to one and same Purāṇa, namely VāyuP.[12] Whereas in the first passage, Madhva declares that, like Brahmā, all

---

[9] Cf. MESQUITA 2000$_1$: 22; 100n. 178; 160n. 330 [= 1997: 19; 80n. 167; 129n. 319].

[10] Cf. ViṣP IV 15,11 and BhāgP VII 1,25-27/29-30; see also BrāṇP 53n. 4; BrahVP 10[3f.]; SkaP 65.

[11] Cf. BrāṇP 12n. 3; BrahP 79:

śubhecchārahitānāṃ ca dveṣiṇāṃ ca ramāpatau /
nāstikānāṃ ca vai puṃsāṃ sadā muktir na jāyate /
iti niṣedhād brāhme;

see also BhaviṣPV 29[46b]: *vimuktir vidyayā tathā*; ibid. 30[85cd]: *sneho bhaktir iti proktas tayā muktir na cānyathā*; HarV 5[6c]: *viṣṇubhaktiyuto muktiṃ yāti nānyaḥ kathaṃcana*; MESQUITA 2000$_1$: 169f. [= 1997: 137f.].

[12] Cf. VāyuP 1 and 2$_1$; see also BrahPV 30.

released souls possess the same qualities such as happiness with the exception of sovereign power (*ānandena ... sarve te brahmaṇas tulyāḥ ... ādhipatyam ṛte*), in the second passage he states explicitly that the released souls are devoid of happiness (*ānandena vinā*) but that they possess, exactly like Brahmā, the sovereign power (*sarve te brahmaṇas tulyā ādhipatyena caiva hi*).[13]

One can legitimately assume that the untraceable literary texts and sources quoted by Madhva in his different literary compositions are by no means treatises or books as a whole, like Purāṇic and Epic texts, but mere fictitious work-titles which Madhva uses as 'hanger' for text-passages composed *ad hoc* by him.[14]

On further consideration of all untraceable and fictitious source quotations, new arguments could be found to maintain the view that Madhva's unknown and fictitious quotes cannot be taken as old but rather as lost literary compositions, as Madhva's followers assert, nor are they fraudulent literary compositions (*svamātrakalpita/svakapola-kalpita*), as Madhva's adversaries claim,[15] but 'texts' which Madhva

---

[13] Cf. also GarP 44 and 34. Both these quotes assert that the worship of idols, inasmuch as *devas* are believed to reside in them, is to be approved (*... devāś ca na śilāmātrāḥ kiṃtu tatrāntarāsthitāḥ*). In BrahP 58 it is declared that only ignorant persons (*aprabuddhānām*) cultivate this kind of worship.

[14] Cf. MESQUITA 2000_1: 99f. [= 1997: 79f.].

[15] Madhva's untraceable or unknown sources gave rise to very strong criticism already at the time of Madhva himself, and not just in the 16th century when Appayadīkṣita launched an attack on Madhva, as it is claimed by the followers of Madhva. In reality, the first critics were contemporaries of Madhva and of his disciples, namely the adherents of Viśiṣṭādvaita, Varadaguru and Veṅkaṭanātha. They took Madhva to task, without mentioning him by name, which does not mean that their criticism has not been acknowledged by other contemporaries of Madhva. While Varadaguru names the unknown sources as a 'fantasy' of Madhva (*svakapolakalpita*), Veṅkaṭanātha describes Madhva's *modus operandi*, when he remarks: "There are other passages which are not found in acknowledged Vedas and *smṛtis*. Sinful people ... first interpolate them and then claim to find them in some Purāṇas that are not well known, or whose collections are lost, or whose beginnings and ends are not determined ..." (cf. MESQUITA 2000_1: 27f. [= 1997: 22f.] and MESQUITA 2003_1: 205ff.). Some decades of years later, another Vedānta author (*svābhāvikabhedābhedavādin*), namely Nimbārka, expresses his criticism, mentioning Madhva by name, in his pamphlet called 'Madhvamukhamardana'. This short treatise (paper MS of nine pages) is deposited in the Madan Mohan Library, Benares and is mentioned also in the Catalogue of Sanskrit Manuscripts in the private libraries of the North Western Provinces (Part I, pp. 274-277, Benares 1874). It is specially interesting that the column with remarks of this catalogue bears the following note: "Criticism of Madhvāchārya's religion. The followers of Madhvāchārya do not lend it to any one. The MS examined is old and apparently correct". DASGUPTA (1975, Vol. III, pp. 400f.) was aware of this

himself composed as *aṃśāvatāra* of Viṣṇu, and therefore in sincere obedience to His impelling force and which in a special way can be attributed to Viṣṇu himself as their author.[16] For, Madhva ascribes to Viṣṇu not only his own compositions and his special doctrine (*bhagavadrāddhānta*) or his logical arguments in defence of his teachings

---

MS in Madan Mohan Library and N.W.P. Catalogue. He conveys in his own words also the remark referred to: "This manuscript is not procurable on loan and has not been available to the present writer. But the account of the authors of the *Catalogue* is to be believed." Basing on these facts DASGUPTA fixed the date of Nimbārka after Madhva and after Sāyaṇa Mādhava since he does not mention Nimbārka's system in his Sarvadarśanasaṃgraha. It is noteworthy, that the title of Appayadīkṣita's polemical pamphlet against Madhva, namely Madhvatantramukhamardana deviates only slightly from Nimbārka's title. It is amazing that B.N.K. SHARMA mixes up Nimbarka's critical document with Appayadīkṣita's pamphlet when he reports on the dating of Nimbārka by DASGUPTA: "The last point (= the existence of a work called Madhvamatamukhamardana (*sic*) attributed to Nimbārka ...) is evidently due to a mistaken ascription, the work mentioned being presumably the same as that of Appaya Dīkṣita. It is unlikely that N. would have so aggressively criticized Madhva or that it would have remained unrefuted by Madhva's followers" (SHARMA 2000: 97n. 3). On account of this confusion we can assume that SHARMA himself did not have a look at this critical document of Nimbārka.

[16] The immediate disciples of Madhva, known also as *prācīnaṭīkākāras*, were aware of this teaching. Trivikramapaṇḍitācārya, for instance, considers carefully the details of this teaching while discussing the Baḷitthāsūkta (= Ṛgveda I 141,1-3) and other unknown sources quoted by Madhva in order to substantiate his own claim of being a partial incarnation of Viṣṇu (cf. MESQUITA 2000_1: 54f. [= 1997: 43f.]). One of his short statement in this connection in Tattvapradīpikā (cf. PANDURANGI 1997-2002, Vol. I, pp. 4,16-19; 52,15f.) runs: ... *ācāryaḥ svoktārthe svayam eva pramāṇaṃ sarvajñatvād avipralaṃbhakatvāc ca ... sarvajñatvaṃ tāvac chrutisiddham* (= ṚV I 141,1-5); see also ibid. Vol. 7, p. 350 and MESQUITA 2000_1: 54f.; 177n. 374 [= 1997: 43f.; 143n. 360.] Another statement Trivikrama's that ultimately Viṣṇu is behind the works of Vyāsa (ibid. p. 54,8-10) ... *sūtrakartā bhagavān vyāsa eva purāṇādikartāpi / na ca tadvākyaṃ kvacid apramāṇam āśaṅkyam / āptisāmyāt / sarvatra bhagavatpramāṇā bhagavadvacanaprāmāṇyā* | iti mūlaśruti – is also valid for Madhva (*āptisāmyāt*), since he too is the author of all classical literary works by the favour of Viṣṇu (*viṣṇuprasādāt*) (cf. MESQUITA 2000_1: 63f. [= 1997: 51f.]). Madhva has attested this claim, also on the basis of Ṛgveda I 141,1-5, for himself in a statement at the end of his commentary on Mahābhārata; cf. MBhTN XXXII 157-165 and MESQUITA 2003_1: 203f.; see also MESQUITA 2000_1: 14f.; 46ff.; 70ff. [= 1997: 12; 38ff.; 57ff.]. The untraceable or unknown source (with two different sections) quoted by Madhva to substantiate his claim of being a partial incarnation of Viṣṇu based on the prophecy in Baḷitthāsūkta is attributed to *sadbhāva* (cf. MESQUITA 2000_1: 54f. [= 1997: 43f.). Strangely enough, Trivikramapaṇḍitācārya attributes the first section to *bhāvavṛtta* (not found among Madhva's untraceable sources) and the second section to *yajuḥsaṃhitā* (this untraceable source is quoted by Madhva three times, but only in his TaiUBh, without, however, referring to Madhva's partial incarnation).

(*yuktayo nirṇayasyaiva svayaṃ bhagavatoditāḥ*) but also his unknown sources.[17] As a matter of fact, Madhva is sincerely convinced of his mission, for again and again he refers to his divine charisma (*viṣṇuprasādāt/viṣṇvājñayaiva*) not only to proclaim new texts, but also to supplement or modify the transmitted ones, such as the Purāṇa-texts.[18]

The analytical compilation of the untraceable quotations does not comprise source-references under collective names like *śrutismṛtītihāsapurāṇeṣu* which can be identified[19] and also those under generic title references which cannot not be localized, as for instance: *ityādīni ca vākyāni purāṇeṣu pṛthak pṛthak or pāñcarātroktaṃ purāṇeṣv anumoditam* or *śrutipurāṇoktibalataḥ.*[20] In the same way, the great number of anonymous *iti* and *iti ca* quotes[21] have not been included in this list, as well as the numerous quotations attributed to a fictitious treatise called Brahmatarka,[22] since these have been collected, sorted out according to their different topics and published by A. NARAYANA TANTRY, regrettably, without a Pāda-index.[23] A precise study of all these texts on the basis of historico-philological method is pending.

It is striking that the highest number of untraceable source quotations from the Purāṇic and Epic literature is found in the BhāgTN and in BSūBh. This can be accounted for by the large size of both these compositions. On the other hand, quotations from the ViṣP are very rare, only three in GīBh and six in GīT, and no quotes at all in the BhāgTN, although BhāgP has taken over many legends from ViṣP.[24] Madhva quotes in BhāgP only once from ViṣDhP, and likewise once from ViṣDhUP.

There are some metrical lapses, namely a surplus and minus of syllables.[25] They are indicated with signs +/– on the right margin of the

---

[17] Cf. MESQUITA 2000_1: 80ff.; 172f. [= 1997: 64f.; 139f.].

[18] Cf. MESQUITA 2000_1: 61ff. [= 1997: 51ff.] and MESQUITA 2000: 385f.

[19] Cf. for instance BĀUBh p. 341,22.

[20] Cf. MBhTN I 109-120; 126 and Anuv pp. 194,23-195,16.

[21] Cf. MESQUITA 2000_1: 20f. [= 1997: 17f.].

[22] Cf. above n. 20.

[23] Cf. RAO 1960: 11-15; see also LORENZ 2005 [Appendix A: All Brahmatarka quotes in the works of Madhva]. This collection is also without an alphabetical Pāda-index. LORENZ has translated and commented in this excellent study some selected quotations attributed to Brahmatarka.

[24] Cf. HACKER 1960: 98; RUKMANI 1970: 4.

[25] Appayadīkṣita (cf. MTM p. 6,3f.) criticised Madhva's metrical lapses as follows: *prayeṇāsādhubhir eva ca śabdair vyavahāraḥ / ślokaracanāyāṃ tv anvayāsaṃbhavo vṛttānyathābhāvaś cādhikaḥ / sarvam etat tadīyabhāṣyānuvyākhyānabhāratatātparyasāṅgrahādidarśināṃ spaṣṭam eva.* However, it should be said in defence of

Sanskrit-text. Finally, it should be mentioned that some quotations close the text with a Purāṇa-reference composed also in Śloka-metre, for instance: ... *ityādi kathitaṃ sarvaṃ brahmāṇḍe hariṇā svayam.*[26] This fact seems to indicate that the author of the closing remark was identical with the author of the quotation, namely Madhva.

While several studies of mine on Madhva's philosophy have found a wide acceptance of Indological research scholars, the Madhva followers acknowledged the results of my research with sharp criticism.[27] The stumbling-block was my detailed discussion on the *avatāra*-claim of Madhva through the intermediate agency of God Vāyu based on unequivocal statements of Madhva.[28] As a matter of fact, it was a scholar of the Madhva-tradition, ŚRISA CHANDRA VASU, who, about hundred years ago, was the first to draw attention to Madhva's *avatāra*-claim and also to its similarity with Christian ideas: "Before closing this introduction, I may mention a point on which perhaps Madhva is unique, namely, his claim that he is an incarnation of Vāyu. The Vāyu, called also Prāṇa, is the highest being next to God. He is called 'the beloved son of God', the 'servant of God', the 'mediator between God and man', the 'saviour'. The functions assigned by Śrī Madhva to Vāyu correspond very closely to the Christ principle of the Christian theology. I have, therefore, not hesitated in translating Vāyu and Prāṇa by Christ. Some may think that Madhva's idea of Vāyu is not the same as the Christian idea of Christ. No one can expect exact similarities in such cases, but the approach is still remarkable. But even more remarkable than this, is the claim of Madhva that he is an incarnation of Vāyu. Other authors have been more modest, and left it to their disciples to deify them, but Madhva, like Jesus, boldly lays claim to be the incarnation of Vāyu, the son of God."[29]

Unfortunately, the Madhva-*saṃpradāya* was reluctant to adopt this and other important teachings of its founder, like the doctrine of *jīvanmukti*.[30]

Madhva, that such kind of metrical lapses are not wanting in the classical texts which have been accepted as falling within the limits of metrical licence (cf. SÖHNEN 1985: 215-238 and HOHENBERGER 1965: 48-97).

[26] Cf. e.g. BrāṇP 94; 95; MārkP 2; NārP 48; SkaP 122; 123; 124; 126.

[27] Cf. RAO/SHARMA 2003 and Sharma 2001. For my response to their criticism see MESQUITA 2003_1: 195-212 and MESQUITA 2003: 97-117.

[28] Cf. MESQUITA 2003_1: 212n. 49; MESQUITA 2003: 107ff.

[29] Cf. CHANDRA VASU 1910: XV.

[30] Cf. MESQUITA 2007: 7n. 4 [= 2007_1: 433n. 4]; SHARMA (1986: 440n. 7) while referring to the term *jīvanmukti* used by Vyāsatīrtha in his Nyāyāmṛtam (IV 4)

And the modern Madhvites reject Madhva's teachings which are clearly based on his own statements. This line of thought was pursued also by the well known traditional Madhva-scholar B.N.K. SHARMA, who in one of his latest papers attracted the attention of the readers with a cautious statement about the authorship of Madhva's untraceable and unknown sources and quotes: "The Gītā says God descends on earth in all Yugas and surely some of the gods too do so with Him. The BV Bhavan, Mumbai has published a volume of Vedic Sūktas conforming to Rgvedic prototype in language, idiom and accentuation, tested by experts. If a gifted genius *of our own times* can do this, why disbelieve the ability of a great thinker like M to be able to *recapture lost sakhas* by his Yogic spiritual power, centuries ago, for the benefit of posterity?"[31]

SHARMA refers here to an old traditional teaching which he wrongly ascribes to Sāyana (14th cent.).[32] In fact, it was known already to Śaṅkara (circa 7th cent.) who traced it back to a mythical author, named Vedavyāsa: *vedavyāsaś caivam eva smarati ...* .[33] In contrast to it, Madhva developed, in order to defend his claim as the author of all classical texts, another theorem in the context of *aṃśāvatāra*, namely that he is the third incarnation of Vāyu (*tṛtīyā bhaumī tanur marutaḥ*).[34] And this would imply that the lost teaching "recaptured" by Madhva is nowhere recorded than in the text passages produced by Madhva himself. A thorough consideration of this theory has been pertinaciously rejected by SHARMA.[35]

---

seems to be unware of the fact that Madhva was the first to introduce this doctrine in his school; see also SHARMA (2000: 240) "Doctrines of Advaita, like ... Jīvanmukti ... *not* discussed (*sic*) by Madhva, are examined by Jayatīrtha, on his own initiative". Trivikramapaṇḍita too accepted this doctrine in Tattvapradīpikā (cf. PANDURANGI 1997-2002, Vol. IV, p. 154,9f. and Vol, V, p. 149,9-10).

[31] Cf. SHARMA 2001: 21; see also MESQUITA 2003$_1$: 211f.; 203n. 28.

[32] Cf. SHARMA 2001: 20.

[33] Cf. MESQUITA 2003$_1$: 203n. 28 and MESQUITA 2000: 62n. 39; 380n. 391-392.

[34] Cf. MESQUITA 2000$_1$: 63ff. [= 1997: 51ff.].

[35] Cf. MESQUITA 2003$_1$: 212n. 49. Another madhvite scholar, Prof. Dr. D.N. SHANBHAG also played down the avatārahood of Madhva in the introduction of his edition to Pūrṇaprajña-Darśana (Bangalore 1992, p. 4), where he remarks: "Madhavācārya *is believed to be* [italics are mine] the third incarnation of Vāyudeva or Wind-god, the first two being the forms of Hanuman and of Bhīma." SHANBHAG gives in this connection the opinion of the author of Sarvadarśanasaṃgraha that "Madhvācārya considers himself to be the third incarnation of Vāyu" (ibid. p. 72). In Sāyana Mādhavācārya's wording the text reads as follows: *etac ca rahasyaṃ pūrṇaprajñena madhyamandireṇa vāyos tṛtīyāvatāraṃ manyena nirūpitam*: "And this mys-

The uncritical judgements on Madhva's *avatāra*-doctrine in general circulation among Madhva-followers now-a-days[36] cannot be a basis for a serious discussion, such as the following statement of L.V. RAO, who dismisses Madhva's concept of *aṁśāvatāra* as trifling, with a casual and insignificant remark: "The idea of Avatar is not acceptable as such, but, the insider's view, was simply, 'like to & so', not be taken too seriously in simple English, it should be understood as 'God's gift'."[37]

A similar statement, based also on the so called insider epistemology, is made by another Madhvite, DEEPAK SARMA, in connection with the unknown sources of Madhva: "Many of the *Purāṇas* that Madhvācārya cites in his corpus are not extant and some have argued that they never existed and were mere fabrications.[38] *If they did not exist, then this may indicate that Madhvācārya had relied on other ways to*

---

tery has been discussed by Pūrṇaprajña Madhyamandira, thinking himself to be the third incarnation of Vāyu." SHANBHAG avoids, however, to discuss this topic here on the basis of Madhva's statements quoting Baḷitthāsūkta (see MESQUITA 2000_1: 54ff. [= 1997: 43ff.]), as Madhva's immmediate disciples and the later commentators of his works have profusely argued (see below n. 36 and above n. 16 and Preface n. 10).

[36] There are however a few exceptions among the modern madhvites, for instance CANDRA VASU (see above n. 29), who was well versed by study and experience in Madhva's doctrinal tradition. His superb English translations of Madhva's works reveal that he was definitely well aware of the fact that the teaching of Madhva's avatārahood, as *aṁśāvatāra* of Vāyu, was taught and discussed not only by Madhva's immediate disciples like Trivikramapaṇḍitācārya in his commentary of BSūBh, namely Tattvapradīpikā (see above n. 16 and Preface n. 10) but also by later commentators like Jayatīrtha, known as Ṭīkācārya, in his Tattvaprakāśikā (*ad* BSū IV 4,23) as well as by other subcommentators of Tattvaprakāśikā as Vādirājatīrtha (Gurvarthadīpikā); Raghūttamatīrtha (Bhāvabodha), Rāghavendratīrtha (Bhāvadīpa), Tāmraparṇī Srīnivāsa (Vākyārthamuktāvalī), Panduraṅgi Śrīnivāsacārya (Tattvasubodhinī), Śrīnivāsatīrtha (Vākyārthavivaraṇa) and Śarkarā Śrīnivāsa (Vākyārthamañjarī). All these commentators base their statements on the presumed prophecy in Baḷitthāsukta (Ṛgveda I 141,1-3) which Madhva adduced at the end of his works in order to substantiate his claim of being partial incarnation of Vāyu (cf. MESQUITA 2000_1: 54 ff. [= 1997: 43ff.]).

[37] Cf. Deccan Herald [Feb52006/artic_15468200622.asp]: Madhvacharya in the 21st century – Was Madhva inspired by Christianity and other religious existing at that time? L.V. RAO finds out more about the saint.

[38] Cf. SARMA (2005: 26n. 15: see Mesquita 1997) refers here to my first monograph on Madhva's unknown sources (in German), however without giving the details of my argumentation or its location. SARMA was also unaware that an English version of this monograph was available in India since 2000.

conceal and protect his doctrines, namely to refer to texts that could never be discovered" (italics are mine).[39]

---

[39] Cf. SARMA 2005: 26. The discussion that "the Mādhva School of Vedānta is founded upon such an unusually strict insider epistemology that it prohibits outsiders from accessing its texts altogether", initiated by DEEPAK SARMA, has a rather artificial character, since Madhva's texts have been read and criticized already at Madhva's time by his outsider contemporaries, as Varadaguru, Venkaṭanātha (13th cent.), Sāyana Mādhava (14th cent.), Nimbārka (end of the 14th cent. or beginning of the 15th cent.), Appayadikṣita (16th cent.), Gauḍīya Vaiṣṇava authors (from 16th to 18th cent.), Vīraśaivite Nīrvāṇa (18th cent.); see above nn. 15 and 3. Even the famous madhvite scholar, B.N.K. SHARMA (2000: 233) declares that the immediate disciples of Madhva like Trivikrama, Padmanābha and Narahari "spread the message of Madhva to a wider circle of adherents and popularized it in the country. They widened the ambit of its religious, secular and political influence ... The period of Madhva and his immediate disciples may therefore, be described as the seed-time of Dvaita-thought. The cc. of Padmanābha and others were merely content with a faithful rendering of the originals." We can be sure that all the works of Madhva were available to the outsiders all the time. Sāyana Mādhava, for instance, relates in his "Sarvadarśanasaṃgraha: Pūrṇaprajñadarśana" the teaching of Madhva faithfully on the basis of quotations found in Madhva's works. He not only cites from the works of Madhva but also adduces his unknown sources, like *śrutis*, as well as his untraceable quotes ascribed to the Purāṇas, exactly as Madhva himself refers to the teachings of his several adversaries in order to criticize them and quotes from the works of the advaita authors like Ānandabodha, Anubhūtisvarūpa, Citsukha, Maṇḍanamiśra, Prakāśātman (cf. MESQUITA 2000: 533-536 [Index of Authors]) as also from Sarvajnātman's Saṅkṣepaśaraka (ibid. p. 332f.; see also MESQUITA 2003_1: 209n. 42) and from Vimuktātman's Iṣṭasiddhi (cf. MESQUITA 2000: p. 118nn. 198-206; 208n. 433), as well as from the works of buddhist authors, like Nāgārjuna (see MESQUITA 2000: 220n. 474 and p. 168n. 344; see also below BrahVP 42; PadP 2; SkaP 39). In view of this fact, it is not possible that Madhva was arguing against his Vedānta, or Buddhist-adversaries merely '*via vitaṇḍā*', as SARMA asserts (cf. 2005: 61; 63). Moreover, while explaining this point SARMA overlooked also a specific circumstance that the famous debate between Madhva and Māyāvādin Trivikramapaṇḍitācārya referred to in the Sumadhvavijaya, (authored by Trivikramapāṇḍitācārya's son Nārāyaṇa Paṇḍitācārya), did not take place '*via vitaṇḍā*', that means "only by showing the incoherence of the position of one's opponent and neither presenting nor exposing, one's own position for judgement", but on the basis of a real disputation, which lasted fifteen days (*saptāṣṭāni dināny evaṃ vādaṃ kṛtvā*); cf. ibid. XV 69. Another particular circumstance which also deserves to be specially mentioned, is that the debate began with an exposition of Madhva's Brahmasūtrabhāṣya (cf. ibid. XV 1f.; 71ff.), which – according to SARMA – was a restricted root text and as such the Māyāvādin Trivikramapaṇḍitācārya, an outsider, was not allowed to hear or read!

Therefore, the following statement of SARMA is absolutely senseless in this context: "One must give Madhvācārya the benefit of the doubt and presume that he was arguing *via vitaṇḍā*. For, if he were not, then he would be willingly revealing restricted doctrines to those who were ineligible." The fact that Trivikramapaṇḍitācārya, after

his defeat in the debate, begged to be admited as a disciple of Madhva, cannot substantiate the thesis of the insider epistemology.
This is also a clear indication that Madhva himself did not have the intention of prohibiting outsiders from reading and commenting on his works. DEEPAK SARMA ignores this fact altogether throughout his investigation and claims that the root texts of Madhva-School have been made accessible to the outsiders only in the 19th century: "When (MAX) MÜLLER and others made this hidden text (= Vedas) available for public consumption, the traditions of Vedānta such as Madhvācharya's were simply unable to maintain such strong restrictions as they had in the past" (cf. p. 64). No wonder, that DEEPAK SARMA could provide no evidence whatsoever for his statements in favour of the insider epistemology in such statements as "The Mādhva school of Vedānta is based on an insider epistemology. Its founder, Madhvācārya, employed strategies to exclude outsiders and unauthorized readers from accessing the root texts and from obtaining oral commentary from living virtuosos. Madhvācārya's regulations are so thorough that the truth of his doctrine can neither be questioned nor refuted by outsiders. Madhvācārya thus successfully insulated his position from criticism and evaluation" (o.c. pp. 10; 53). Since the basic premise of the insider epistemology is fundamentally flawed, the entire interpretation of the same can also be considered as essentially faulty and therefore artificial in its character. As a matter of fact, not only the Vedāntins mentioned above questioned Madhva's teachings and expressed disapproval of them, but also living insiders like B.N.K SHARMA. He criticized not only Madhva's frequent violations of the rules of Pāṇini but also Madhva's treatment of the so-called Advaita *śrutis*, which according to him, was piecemeal and uncoordinated; resting on corroborative evidences of a large body of non-extant texts (!); (cf. above Preface n. 10). See also criticism of Madhva's unknown sources by VEKANTASUBBIAH; BHANDARKAR, KANE and GHATE, in: MESQUITA 2000_1: 20n. 16; 25n. 27 [= 1997: 17n. 9; 22n. 20.]. In this context, it is noteworthy to mention that D. SARMA too, in contradiction to the principles of insider epistemology, acknowledged that there were Vedāntins at Madhva's time who criticised his teachings (see D. SARMA's Response to Robert Zydenbos' Review of An Introduction to Mādhva Vedānta in Philosophy, Philosophy East & West Vol. 56, p. 674n. 3): "... Although Mesquita is the first to write about it (= M's unknown and fictitious texts) extensively for a Western audience, he is, by no means, the first to have addressed the issue. Veṅkatanātha, a contemporary of Madhvācārya, noted the same in the thirteenth century C.E."
The fact that the outsiders, according to DEEPAK SARMA, are excluded "from obtaining oral commentary from living virtuosos" could not hinder them from doing precise studies on Madhva's doctrine. The oral commentaries, if they really exist, may be useful for the religious training of young Madhvites; they could even be an indispensable help to insiders with no or only deficient knowledge of Sanskrit (cf. p. 74) in order to understand Madhva's works. Nevertheless, indologists with solid knowledge of Sanskrit and trained in philological and historical method of text-interpretation do not require secret oral or written commentaries from living virtuosos in order to study the classical texts of the Madhva-School. Its meaning is to be unlocked by grammatical and philological keys. DEEPAK SARMA is the first Madhvite to lay claim to the existence of secret commentaries, prohibited to outsiders. B.N.K SHARMA is silent on them in his Study: Dvaita School of Vedānta and its Literature. And no serious scholar will accept the view proposed by DEEPAK SARMA that the correct inter-

As far as I see, this statement makes no sense, to say that Madhva hid his sources in order to conceal and protect his doctrines. Actually, his particular teachings, although these are attributed to the untraceable quotes from known and unknown texts, were accessible to his contemporaries and cleary stated, so that no one could misuse or misinterpret them. Why should Madhva hide his sources when he was empowered by virtue of divine charisma (*viṣṇuprasādāt*) to proclaim all canonical works in the name of Viṣṇu in the *kali*-age and as such a divinely authorized spokesman for God Viṣṇu?[40] Prof. SHARMA, a true insider, *nolens volens* accepted that Madhva recaptured the lost *śākhās* by his spiritual power, centuries ago, for the benefit of posterity.[41] In contrast to Prof. SHARMA, a recent study in Sanskrit "Gomañjarī" by Dvārakānāthācārya[42] discusses profusely the avatārahood of Madhva, quoting from older sources, specially from Vādirājatīrtha's (1480-1600) Yuktimallikā and from Vaiśvanāthinārāyaṇapaṇḍitācārya's (1600-1660)[43] Vyākhyāna (= Sumadhvavijayabhāvaprākāśikā) and from his Madhvamantramañjarī interpreting also the Baḷitthasūkta (Ṛgveda I 141,1-3) as Madhva did[44] as well as several other passages of the Ṛgveda in sup-

---

pretation of Madhva's Sanskrit-texts is not possible without the help of these secret commentaries insofar as "sanskrit can never be fully translated into any other language" (pp. 67f.). As a matter of fact, western scholars have worked out thorough philological studies in almost all fields of Madhva's philosophy, as also in the realm of ontology and soteriology, which – according to DEEPAK SARMA – were prohibited to outsiders (p. 10). SARMA did not disclose the authorities behind this prohibition.

See, for instance, SUZANNE SIAUVE, La Doctrine de Madhva. Dvaita-Vedānta ... . (Pondichéry 1971); Le Hiérarchies Spirituelles. Selon l'Anuvyākhyāna de Madhva (Pondichéry 1971); Les Noms Védiques de Viṣṇu. Dans L'Anuvyakhyāna de Madhva ... (Pondichéry 1959); ROQUE MESQUITA, Madhva, Viṣṇutattvanirṇaya ... (Vienna 2000); Madhva's Unknown Sources ... (Delhi 2000); The concept of Liberation while still alive in the Philosophy of Madhva (Delhi 2007). DEEPAK SARMA referred to most of these studies in his books without, however, quoting from them or commenting upon them.

Taking all these points into consideration, we could say that the statement of DEEPAK SARMA: "The schools of Vedānta all followed insider epistemologies forbidding outsiders from studying root texts and Madhvācārya's restrictions were identical with his counterparts", is, owing to the absence of arguments in both cases, absolutely unwarranted, and therefore the theory of insider epistemology, as *svakapolakalpita*, belongs to the realm of pure imagination.

[40] Cf. MESQUITA 2000_1 : 10f. and 63ff. [= 1997: 51f.].

[41] See above n. 31f.

[42] Cf. Preface n. 1.

[43] Cf. SHARMA 2000: 413 and 432ff.

[44] Cf. MESQUITA 2000_1: 54ff. [= 1997: 43ff.]; see also Śrīdvārakānāthācārya 2004: Gomañjarī pp. 63ff. [= Preface n. 1].

port of this belief.[45] The author of Gomañjarī has displayed only sixty nine such passages out of numerous others quoted by Vaiśvanāthinārāyaṇapaṇḍitācārya in his Bhāvaprākāśikā. As a matter of fact, these vedic passages are not commented upon in their literal sense, but according to thought "of the traditional belief in Madhva's being an Avatāra of Vāyu".[46] One among them, exciting a special attention, is Ṛgveda III 8,1,[47] as far as its commentary by Vaiśvanāthinārāyaṇapaṇḍitācārya links up the last part of this passage with the unknown sources of Madhva:

upasthe paramātmopadeśārthaṃ sūryeṇa sarve 'pi devādayo mumukṣuvargā vāyuṃ prārthayanta iti yāvat / vānarāṇāṃ prārthanā hanumantaṃ prati / pāṇḍavānāṃ ca prārthanaṃ bhīmasenaṃ prati / tathaiva jñānināṃ ca prārthanaṃ śrīmadhvācāryaṃ prati / purāṇādiṣu prasiddhā / atra -

evaṃ dharmeṣu naṣṭeṣu śāstreṣu ca kalau yuge /
devair vijñāpito viṣṇur vāyum ājñāpayiṣyati //
uddharasva mahābāho mama dharmān sanātanān /
ity ājñapto bhagavatā kalau vāyur bhaviṣyati //
madhvanāmā yatir asau sacchāstrāṇi kariṣyati /
gītāyāś copaniṣadāṃ bhāṣyāṇi ca kariṣyati //
nirasiṣyati pāṣaṇḍān sacchāstrāṇi mahāmatiḥ /
sthāpayiṣyati saddharmān sacchāstraṃ vyākariṣyati //

---

[45] Cf. Śrīdvārakānāthācārya 2004: Gomañjarī (p. 174,6f.): *evaṃ bhāvaprakāśikāyāṃ paṇḍitācāryair ādipādena sūcitānīmāni vedavākyāni pūrvaiḥ śrīvādirājatīrthair vaiśvanāthinārāyaṇapaṇḍitaiḥ sūcitamārgānusāreṇātra niveśitāni / eteṣām eva sūktānāṃ grahaṇe madhvapadapratyakṣaśrutir eva nidānam / sudhiya idaṃ mahāsāhasaṃ kṣāmyantu / śrīvādirājatīrthaiḥ svagranthe yuktimallikāyāṃ tathā ca vaiśvanāthinārāyaṇapaṇḍitācāryair madhvamantrārthamañjarināmake grantha imāni vākyāni vyākhyātāni / teṣāṃ vākyānāṃ paryālocanaṃ kṛtvātra samyak śrimadhvācāryaparatayā yojanā kṛtā ...* ; see also ibid. p. 146,3f.: *evaṃ vedavākyeṣu madhvācāryasya vāyvavatāratve siddhe tadanukūlapurāṇavacanāny api santi / tasmāt śrīmadhvācāryasya vāyurūpatvāt taduktam eva grāhyam iti siddham / pratyuta śaṅkarācāryasya daityasvarūpatvabodhakāny api anekavākyāni santi ...* .

[46] Cf. SHARMA 2000: 443 and MESQUITA 2000_1: 57- 60 [= 1997: 45ff.].

[47] Cf. Śrīdvārakānāthācārya 2004: Gomañjarī (pp. 99f.):

añjanti tvām adhvare devayanto
vanaspate madhunā daivyena /
yadūrdhvastiṣṭā draviṇeha dhattād
yadvā kṣayo mātur asyā upasthe /

Transl. GRIFFITH (1987): "God-serving men, O Sovran of the Forest, with heavenly meath at sacrifice anoint thee. Grant wealth to us when thou art standing upright as when reposing on this Mother's bosom."

śroṣyanti munayaḥ sarve śukādyāḥ devarūpiṇaḥ |
ityādivacanāni kūrmapurāṇasthāni pramāṇāni bhavanti |

The explanation of *upasthe* (= on this Mother's bosom) is: "All gods etc. together with Sūrya, belonging to the class of beings striving after emancipation, asked God Vāyu for the meaning of the teaching of the supreme Spirit (Viṣṇu). The request of the apes was addressed to Hanumān [the first *avatāra* of Vāyu], while the petition of the descendants of Pāṇḍu was addressed to Bhīmasena [the second *avatāra* of Vāyu], likewise the wish of the people endowed with knowledge was directed to Madhvācārya [the third *avatāra* of Vāyu]." This is recorded in the Purāṇas. The following statements of the KūrP are a corroborating evidence [for the teaching above]: "As the prescribed good works and the sacred books of divine authority were lost in the Kali-age,[48] the supreme God Viṣṇu was solicited by gods for ordering God Vāyu [as follows]: 'Oh long-armed, please rescue my eternal good works'. On account of this order of the venerable [God Viṣṇu], Vāyu will appear/come in the Kali-age as an ascetic called Madhva with the purpose of rescuing the true sacred books and [also] with the purpose of commenting upon the Bhagavadgītā and the Upaniṣads. He will annihilate the heretics [= Advaitins]. The great-minded [Madhva] will restore the true sacred books [likewise] the true good works and write commentaries on sacred books [like Bhagavadgītā etc.]. All sages like Śuka etc., appearing as gods, will hear [his divine message]."

Another Veda-word in the commentary of Vaiśvanāthinārāyaṇapaṇḍitācārya, deserving our attention, is *kṣayaḥ* (= dwelling place), which means: Vāyu dwells in this world in the form of three *aṃśāvatāras* (= *kṣayo nivasasy avatārarūpair iti yāvat kṣiṅ adhīvase*). In this connection, Vaiśvanāthinārāyaṇapaṇḍitācārya underlines the role of Madhva dwelling in the famous Badarī-Āśrama, mentioned by Madhva

---

[48] Madhva used this motif also elsewhere, cf. GīBh p. 1,4: *naṣṭadharmajñānalokakṛpālubhir brahmarudrendrādibhir arthito jñānapradarśanāya bhagavān vyāso 'vatatāra ...* ; see also below NārP 30.
Surely the statement on the recovery of the lost texts is based on the traditional teaching mentioned by Saṅkara in his Brahmasūtrabhāṣya (*ad* Sū. I 3,29) that Mahariṣis restore the Veda together with the Itihāsas hidden at the end the age through the power of their religious austerities:

vedavyāsaś caivam eva smarati –
yugānte 'ntarhitān vedān setihāsān maharṣayaḥ |
lebhire tapasā pūrvam anujñātāḥ svayaṃbhuvā ||

cf. MESQUITA 2003_1: 203n. 28; see also MESQUITA 2000_1: 130n. 255 [= 1997: 105n. 245].

as the place of his spiritual instruction by Viṣṇu (*nārāyaṇenābhihitaḥ*): *tasmād evānandatīrthasya badarikāśramapraveśa ity evocyate.* In support of this statement Vaiśvanāthinārāyaṇapaṇḍitācārya adduces a quote from the SkaP:

> *sa yogī mātariśvāṃśo madhvo dhvastadurāgamaḥ /*
> *svayam abhyarcya devāṃśaḥ kṛṣṇaṃ kalimalāpaham //*
> *navamyāṃ prātar evāsau māghe makarage ravau /*
> *pratipede badarikāṃ śuklapakṣe satāṃ gatiḥ //*
> *ityādi skāndapurāṇavacanāni cātra pramāṇāni bhavanti /*

"The ascetic Madhva, the *aṃśāvatāra* of Vāyu, wiped out the wicked scriptures. As himself being an *aṃśāvatāra* of God [Vāyu] he worshiped Kṛṣṇa, who destroyed the impurities of the Kaliyuga. He (i.e. Madhva) – the refuge of the honest people – entered the Badarikā [-hermitage] in the month Māgha (January-February) on the ninth day of the lunar halfmonth in the bright half exactly at the daybreak, when the sun was in the sign of Capricornus." These statements out of SkaP are an unfailing proof [for the teaching above].

Strangely, both these quotes are untraceable and they are also not found in the works of Madhva. But their contents correspond to the teaching of Madhva:

> *ānandatīrthākhyamuniḥ supūrṇa-*
> *prajñābhidho grantham imaṃ cakāra /*
> *nārāyaṇenābhihito badaryāṃ*
> *tasyaiva śiṣyo jagadekabhartuḥ //*[49]
> *yas tatprasādād akhilāṃś ca vedān*
> *sapañcarātrān sarahasyasaṅgrahān /*
> *vedetihāsāṃś ca purāṇayuktān*
> *yathāvad anyā api sarvavidyāḥ //*

Furthermore, Madhva refers in this connection also to the commentaries he wrote:

> *vyāsājñayā bhāṣyavaraṃ vidhāya*
> *pṛthak pṛthak copaniṣatsu bhāṣyam /*
> *kṛtvākhilān yaṃ puruṣottamaṃ ca*
> *hariṃ vadantīti samarthayitvā //*

---

[49] See also Trivikramapaṇḍita's Tattvapradīpikā, in: PANDURANGI 1997-2002, Vol. I, p. 6,1ff.

tanus tṛtīyā pavanasya seyaṃ
sadbhāratārthapratidīpanāya /
granthaṃ cakāremam udīrṇavidyā
yasmin ramante haripādabhaktāḥ //[50]

As a matter of fact, the canonical texts mentioned above cover the domain of all the untraceable source-quotations Madhva cites in his works. This would imply that the traditional works lost in the Kali-age and recaptured by Madhva are nowhere recorded but in the text passages produced by Madhva himself. This assumption is strongly backed up by a clear assessment made by Madhva's immediate disciple Trivikramapaṇḍitācārya, for instance in his commentary Tattvapradīpikā, discussing Madhva's BSūBh *ad* II 1,14. Madhva refutes here the Advaita teaching of absolute identity based on MuU III 2,7: *karmāṇi vijñānamayaś cātmā pare' vyaye sarva ekībhavantīti.*[51] After confirming Madhva's arguments against the absolute identity (*karmāṇi vijñānamayaś cety atra na svarūpaikatvam ucyate / karmaṇāṃ tadanabhyupagamāt*), Trivikramapaṇḍitācārya remarks that Madhva himself (*eva*) treated these arguments at length again in the Tattvanirṇaya: *prapañcitaṃ caitat tattvanirṇaye bhagavatpādair eva*[52] *– svarūpaikyābhiprāye karmāṇi vijñānamayaś ceti na yujyate / na hi tatpakṣe 'pi karmaṇāṃ brahmaikyaṃ muktāv asti / nivṛttyabhiprāye pañcadaśakalānām api samatvādityādi.* Tattvanirṇaya, being an unknown and untraceable source, is clearly ascribed by Trivikramapaṇḍitācārya to Madhva as its author, in the same way as Trivikramapaṇḍitācārya refers to Madhva while quoting from his real works.[53] Tattvanirṇaya has also another distinguishing mark of Madhva's unknown sources which I discussed extensively elsewhere[54], namely that these sources as well as the real

---

[50] Cf. MBhTN XXXII 157f.; see also ibid. IX 116ff. and MESQUITA 2000_1: 10f. and 63ff. (= 1997: 51f.]; see also MESQUITA 2003_1: 203n. 26 and 28.

[51] Cf. PANDURANGI o.c. Vol. III, p. 87,18f.

[52] Cf. PANDURANGI o.c. Vol. I, p. 2, v. 8:

so 'yaṃ guṇāmṛtamahabdhir ihāvatīrṇā-
nandatīrthabhagavān paramo gurur me /
yatpādapadmarajasā śirasā dhṛtena
sadyaḥ prayānti pariśuddhim aśeṣalokāḥ //

ibid. p. 52,15f.: ... *ācāryaḥ svoktārthe svayam eva pramāṇaṃ sarvajñatvād avipralaṃbhakatvāc ca ... sarvajñatvaṃ tāvat śrutisiddhaṃ baḷitthā tad vapuṣe dhāyi darśatam iti* (Ṛgveda I 141,1-5); see also above n. 16.

[53] Cf. PANDURANGI o.c. Vol I, p. 53,2f.: *pratyakṣam eva caitallakṣaṇaṃ dṛṣyate bhagavati bhāṣyakāre ...* ; Vol. II, p. 247,21-22: *uktaṃ ca ... iti bhagavataivānubhāṣye.*

[54] Cf. MESQUITA 2000_1: 77ff. [= 1997: 61ff.].

works of Madhva are said to be authored also by Viṣṇu. In this sense, Madhva introduces this source as '*viṣṇukṛte tattvanirṇaye*'.[55] Taking all these points into consideration, we could justly postulate that this line of reasoning should also be *mutatis mutandis* applied to the whole class of Madhva's unknown sources.

As the untraceable text passages collected here are, as a whole, supportive of the typical teaching of Madhva and therefore only traceable from Madhva onwards, this means that these passages were not transmitted from generation to generation and accepted by *śiṣṭa*s before Madhva's time and the question of credibility implied here is to be solved within the framework of *aṃśāvatāra* of Madhva.[56] Madhva draws a clear line between traditional literary sources which have been wrongfully modified or where an unauthorized deliberate change has taken place, and his own works or his sources quoted therein. Any traditional source which has been deliberately changed due to carelessness or due to any other reasons, they are to be considered as falsified. The trustworthiness of Madhva's sources depends above all on the fact, that they, on the one hand, are firmly established in the untainted original literaly tradition, acknowledged as such by Madhva under the guidance of Viṣṇu, and that they, on the other hand, have been proclaimed or composed by Madhva on command of Viṣṇu, in order to restore the original doctrine lost in the Kali age. One can be sure that Madhva, with the allusion to the huge loss of the original sources (*koṭyaṃśo 'pi na vartate*), has felt called upon to restore in a divine mission also the lost portions of the traditional texts. In this sense, Madhva appears as a self-confident literary author with divine warrant not only of his own original and other commented works, but also of all other literary texts which in the tradition are known as works of Viṣṇu or of Vyāsa. His model of truthfullness and realization of his divine task is Vyāsa (*yathā sa bhagavān vyāsaḥ sākṣān nārāyanaḥ prabhuḥ / jagāda bhāratādyeṣu tathā vakṣye ...*). Madhva underscores in this fact the difference between himself and Vyāsa. Whereas Viṣṇu is identical with Vyāsa, he is only present in Madhva due to the illumination (*jñānadīpana*), i.e. due to the taking possession (*āveśa*) through Viṣṇu. With the help of this double-track which allows to put Viṣṇu's presence in Madhva and

---

[55] Cf. BhāgTN p. 199,4-7; see also MESQUITA 2000: 316-318; 163n. 333 and 228n. 493. I have collected about nineteen quotations of this unknown source cited in the different works of Madhva (see the Index of untraceable source-quotations). All of them are composed in *śloka*. However, the quote referred to by Trivikramapaṇḍitācārya is in prosa. Unfortunately it escaped my attention.

[56] Cf. MESQUITA 2000_1: 48ff. [= 1997: 39ff.].

Viṣṇu's identity with Vyāsa side by side, Madhva can show in an emphatic way that in both cases Viṣṇu alone is ultimately the proclaimer of all canonical texts.[57]

[57] Cf. MESQUITA 2000_1: 77f. [= 1997: 61f.].

MADHVA'S
UNTRACEABLE SOURCE-QUOTATIONS

SANSKRIT-TEXT

Ādipurāṇa (ĀdiP)

[ĀdiP deals primarly with the story of Kṛṣṇa and appears in the first place in most of the lists of UpaP, and it is very often confused with BrahP (cf. HAZRA 1987: 90f.; ROCHER 1986: 133f.).]

1) MBhTN (XI 93):
Subject matter: Rāma-Avatāra

viddhavan mugdhavac caiva keśavo vedanārtavat |
darśayann api mohāya naiva viṣṇus tathā bhavet |
evam ādipurāṇotthavākyād rāmaḥ sadā jayī | (1)

(1) Cf. BhaviṣPV 26; 29[37f.]; BhaviṣP 9; BrahP 16; 32; 35; BrahVP 4; 5; 17; BrāṇP 27; 39; 52; 60; 65; 95; 105; GarP 18; 49; KūrP 2; 3; 7; 17; MBh 42; MatsyaP 14; NārP 35; PadP 21; 25; 38; 50; 55_1; 77, 79; SkaP 5; 6; 12_1; 20; 30; 31; 36; 37; 45; 64; 73; 84; 111; VahniP 1; VāmP 31; VarP 3; 11; 22; 25; 51; see also MESQUITA 2000_1: 35ff. [= 1997: 29ff.].

Ādityapurāṇa (ĀdityaP)

[ĀdityaP is frequently quoted by the Nibandhakāras on a large variety of topics: death and ritual for the dead, impurity, marriage and duties of married life, donations, *vratas* and festivals (cf. ROCHER 1986: 134).]

1) AiUBh (p. 186,25-26) = BSūBh (p. 35,2-3) = GīBh (p. 29,15-16):
Subject matter: Jīvanmukti / Videhamukti

bahunātra kim uktena yāvac chvetaṃ na gacchati |
yogī tāvan na muktaḥ syād eṣa śāstrasya nirṇayaḥ ||
ity ādityapurāṇe (1)

(1) In this quote *jīvanmukti* is also implied (GīBh p. 29,17-18): *ye tv atraiva bhagavantaṃ praviśanti* (= jīvanmukti) *te 'pi paścāt tatra yānti* (= videhamukti); cf. BSūBh (p. 34,24f.): ... *brahmavid āpnoti param* ... (TaiU II 1,1) *ityādinā tasyaiva muktaprāpyatvavyapadeśāt* ... ; KathUBh (p. 484,25f.):

vimukto nirabhimānāt pūrvam evāparokṣavit |
mukhyato mucyate paścād duḥkhādyabhāsahānataḥ |
iti ca (untraceable source);

see also BhaviṣPV 5; 31; BhaviṣP 5; BrahP 82; BrāṇP 76; GarP 19; 21; 42; 44; 45; 47; MBh 29; PadP 74; SkaP 47; 109; VarP 54; VāyuP 12 and MESQUITA 2007: 12n. 15 [= 2007_1: 435n. 15].

2) GīBh (p. 107,17-18):
Subject matter: Prakṛti

[avyaktasyānantatvād eva mahato mahattve 'parimeyatvaṃ siddhyati]

mahāntaṃ ca samāvṛtya pradhānaṃ samavasthitam /
anantasya na tasyāntaḥ saṅkhyānaṃ cāpi vidyate /
ity ādityapurāṇe (1)

(1) Cf. ibid. l. 19: *tāni caikaikāni rūpāṇy anantānīti caikatra bhavanti*; see also AgniP 25.

Agnipurāṇa (AgniP)

[AgniP was originally a work of the Pañcarātras. It is for this reason that Viṣṇu's incarnations are narrated at the very outset. The Purāṇa is a sort of an encyclopedia in miniature. Sometimes it is confused with VahniP (cf. HAZRA 1987: 134ff.; ROCHER 1986: 134f.; see also below VahniP). It is quoted twice in BĀUBh; eleven times in BhāgTN; thrice in BSūBh, and eleven times in GīT.]

1) BĀUBh (p. 272,26-27)
Subject matter: True Brahma-knowledge

tattvavid devagauḥ prokto naragauś cāpy atattvavit /
tasmād devās tattvavide priyaṃ kurvanty atandritāḥ /
ity āgneye (1)

(1) Cf. ibid. l. 28: *tasya ha na devāś ca nābhūtyā īśata iti* (BĀU I 4,10) *devānāṃ tattvajñānaṃ priyam ity uktaṃ ca*; see also AgniP 9.

2) BĀUBh (p. 274,19-20):
Subject matter: Murder of a Brāhmana

svato 'dhikaguṇaṃ hatvā sākṣāc ca pitaraṃ punaḥ /
kṣatrasya brāhmaṇaṃ hatvā tāvān doṣo bhaved dhruvam /
ity āgneye (1)

(1) Cf. VāmP 2 [6cd-7ab].

3) BhāgTN (p. 93,4-5):
Subject matter: Characteristics of Hari

hareḥ śmaśrvāśrayā vidyucchilālohā nakhāśrayāḥ /
ity āgneye (1)

(1) Cf. PadP 20.

4) BhāgTN (p. 138,8):
Subject matter: Manifestation of Viṣṇu (*vyakti*)

> *na dehayogo hi janir viṣṇor vyaktir janiḥ smṛtāḥ /*
> ity āgneye (1)

(1) Cf. ibid. (p. 288,6-7):
> *utpattir harirūpāṇāṃ vyaktir eva na saṃśayaḥ /*
> *utpattir eva jīvānāṃ dehotpattir udīyate /*

see also BrahVP 8; 32; BrāṇP 105[4]; GarP 18; HarV 21; 29; MBh 25; 32; PadP 50; 63; SkaP 15;VarP 2; 11; 55 and MESQUITA 2000: 230n. 496; 492n. 644-645.

5) BhāgTN (p. 140,6):
Subject matter: Similarity of evolutes to its root principle

> *uttamaiḥ sarvataḥ sāmyaṃ kiṃcit sāmyam udīritam /*
> ity āgneye (1)

(1) Cf. BrahP 5 and MESQUITA 2000: 149f.; 475f.; 494f.; 530f.

6) BhāgTN (p. 144,12-13):
Subject matter: Viṣṇu – Jīvādhipati / Viṣṇu's supreme transcendence

> *paramātmā yato jīvaṃ mene 'santam aśaktataḥ /*
> *asann asau tato nityaṃ satyajñāno yato hariḥ /*
> ity āgneye (1)

(1) Cf. ibid. l. 9: *ātmanāṃ vibhuḥ jīvādhipatiḥ*; see also AgniP 7; BhavisPV 3; 6; BhaviṣP 6; BrahP 1_2; 1_4; 23; 56; BrahVP 2; 15; 16; 20; 22; 23; 33; BrāṇP 3; 32; 40; 47; 61; 62; 85; 90; 91; 92; GarP 40; HarV 3; 7; 12; 21; KūrP 3; 5; 14; 18; 29; 30; MBh 7; 8_1; 20; 22; 34; 35; 38; 40; 41; 43; 44; 45; MatsyaP 4; 11; 18; NārP 6; 7; 11; 31; 42; PadP 3; 3_1; 6; 21; 21_1; 24; 26; 48; 58; 59; 63; 81; SkaP 9; 14; 15; 51; 67; 68; 80; 91; 92; 93; 110; 129; VāmP 9; 23; 28; 30; 33; 42; VarP 6; 27; 29; 47; 50; 52; 55; ViṣP 4; 8 and MESQUITA 2000: 459ff.

7) BhāgTN (p. 183,3-4):
Subject matter: Viṣṇu, the supreme Creator of the universe

> *kartā ca karaṇaṃ caiva karma caiva svayaṃ hariḥ /*
> *ātmano bahudhābhāve prakṛtes tu svatantratā /*
> ity āgneye (1)

(1) Cf. NārP 11; BhāgTN (p. 131,11): *kartṛtvāt tu sakarmāsau niṣphalatvād akarmaka iti ca* (untraceable source); see also AgniP 6; 12 and MESQUITA 2000: 470ff.

8) BhāgTN (p. 222,2):
Subject matter: Flight of jackals (birth of Hiraṇyākṣa etc.)

nāśas tatra sṛgālānāṃ śivānāṃ cānyathāsvare /
ity āgneye (1)

(1) Cf. ibid. l. 1: *ṭhaṅkāro 'py anukāraśabdaḥ* / *sṛgālāḥ puṃsāṃsaḥ*; ibid. p. 221n. 13: *gomāyuṣu pumāṃsaḥ sṛgālāḥ* / *striyaḥ śivāḥ* / *ṭhaṅkāraiḥ ninditānukārasvarair* ity anantatīrthāḥ; see also BrāṇP 38.

9) BhāgTN (p. 274,4-5):
Subject matter: Means/Ways of liberation (*śravaṇa, manana, nididhyāsana, darśana*)

punaḥ punaḥ kathāḥ prāhur abhyāsād uttamaṃ phalam /
vijñāpayitukāmās tu vidvāṃsas tatra tatra ha /
ity āgneye (1)

(1) Cf. AgniP 1; 14; 15; 19; 20; 21; 26: BrahP 21; 55; 74; 77; BrahVP 3; 38; 39; BrāṇP 80; GarP 7; MBh 27; NārP 19; 26; 36_1; PadP 72; SkaP 65; 120; 121; VarP 43; 59; MESQUITA 2007: 16n. 25 and p. 21f. [= 2007_1: 437n. 25 and p. 441f.].

10) BhāgTN (p. 415,3-6):
Subject matter: Death of Vṛtra

sandhitaḥ samayenendro vṛtreṇātho karagrahaḥ /
samudratīre vicaran phenena vadham asya tu /
narmaṇā jahi pheneti vācayitvā sureśvaraḥ /
pādasparśavivādaṃ ca kṛtvā yuddhāya daṃsitaḥ /
phene vajraṃ samāveśya viṣṇuyuktaṃ vyasarjayat /
apānudac chiras tasya dhyāyato vatsareṇa saḥ /
ity āgneye (1)

(1) Cf. Ṛg V 30,8; VIII 14,13; OBERLIES 1998: 219-220; 247-250; see also BhaviṣPV 12; BrāṇP 3[1].

11) BhāgTN (p. 517,6-7):
Subject matter: Attributes of Viṣṇu

aguṇo 'guṇadehatvāt saguṇo guṇadhāraṇāt /
aiśvaryādiguṇatvād vā vāsudeva udīryate //
ity āgneye (1)

(1) Cf. ibid. l. 5: *aguṇaś cet kathaṃ guṇaiḥ sṛṣṭyādikṛd iti tadāśrayatvād iti*; see also BrāṇP 69 and MESQUITA 2000: 429ff.

12) BhāgTN (p. 527,4-5):
Subject matter: Prime cause of the universe (*mūlakāraṇa*)

viśvasya tadadhīnatvāt viśvaṃ viṣṇur udīryate /
mūlahetutvato hetuḥ kartā prātisvikaṃ kṛteḥ /
ity āgneye (1)

(1) Cf. AgniP 7; BhaviṣPV 8; 10; 16; BhaviṣP 3; 12; 13; BrahP 44; BrahVP 1; 21; BrāṇP 8; 70; 72; HarV 12; 33; KūrP 11; 30_5; MBh 9; 16; MatsyaP 8; 16; NārP 3; 10; 11; 22; 41; 42; PadP 12; 16; 37; 64; 66; SkaP 87; 93; 100; 118; 127; VarP 36 and MESQUITA 2000: 473n. 605.

13) BhāgTN (p. 536,3-4):
Subject matter: Viṣṇu, the Judge of honest and wicked men

asatāṃ ca satāṃ caiva harir evānuśāsakaḥ /
satāṃ tu śreyase saiva hy anuśāstir bhaviṣyati /
asatāṃ viparītāya laṅghayitvānuśāsanam /
ity āgneye (1)

(1) Cf. AgniP 6 and MESQUITA 2000: 492ff.

14) BSūBh (p. 153,4-6):
Subject matter: Brahma-Knowledge

āgneye ca –
yathā nadīnāṃ salilaṃ śakye sāgaragaṃ bhavet /
evaṃ vākyāni sarvāṇi puṃśaktyā brahmavittaye /(1)

(1) Cf. ibid. ll. 3: *yathā sarvaṃ salilaṃ samudraṃ gacchati evaṃ sarvāṇi vacanāni brahmajñānārthānīti niyamaḥ*; see also Agni 9; BrahP 22.

15) BSūBh (p. 177,11+178,3):
Subject matter: Means/Ways of liberation

yasya jñānaṃ tasya mokṣa iti nātra vicāraṇā /
tasya śāntyādayo 'ṇgāni tasmāt teṣām anuṣṭhitiḥ /
avaśyakaraṇīyā syād anyathālpaphalaṃ bhavet /
iti cāgneye (1)

(1) Cf. ibid. ll. 7: *yady api jñānenaiva mokṣo niyataḥ tathāpi jñānī śamadamādyupetaḥ syāt*; see also AgniP 9.

16) BSūBh (p. 198,10-11):
Subject matter: Liberation

yathāśleṣo vināśaś ca muktasya tu vikarmaṇaḥ /
evaṃ sukarmaṇaś cāpi patatas tamasi dhruvaḥ /
iti cāgneye (1)

(1) Cf. ibid. l. 9: *puṇyasyāpy evam asaṃśleṣaḥ pāte / tuśabdo 'nutthānavācī*; see also AgniP 18; BhaviṣPV 10; 25; 28; 31; BhaviṣP 1; 4; 8; BrahP 14; 54; 75; BrahVP 27; 28; 29; 31; 36; 37; 40; BrāṇP 6; 20; 24; 26; 27; 28; 43; 58; 87; GarP 11; 15; 47; 48; HarV 2; 18; KūrP 30; MBh 5; MārkP 1; NārP 4; 8; 45; 46; 47; 54; PadP 42; 56; 75; 87; 88; SkaP 41; 72; 112; VāmP 6; 13; 16; VarP 56; 57; VāyuP 1; 2_1; 12; MESQUITA 2007: 39f. [= 2007_1: 450f.] and MESQUITA 2000: 517ff.

17) GīT (p. 24,12-13):
Subject matter: Vaiṣṇava Dharma

prārambhamātram icchā vā viṣṇudharme na niṣphalā /
na cānyadharmākaraṇād doṣavān viṣṇudharmakṛt /
ity āgneye (1)

(1) Cf. AgniP 9; 20; 28; BrahP 28; BrahVP 38; NārP 2[9]; PadP 2[3ab].

18) GīT (p. 42,27-28):
Subject matter: Liberation

viṣṇuprasādād ratimāṃs tṛpto viṣṇuprasādataḥ /
viṣṇāv evātitṛptaś ca mukto 'sau vidhyagocaraḥ /
ity āgneye (1)

(1) Cf. ibid. l. 26: *tṛptisantoṣaśabdayoḥ paryāyatve 'pi paramātmanā tṛptaḥ paramātmani tṛpta iti viśeṣaḥ*; see also AgniP 16.

19) GīT (p. 50,23-25):
Subject matter: True Brahma-knowledge

jānanto 'pi viśeṣārthajñānāya sthāpanāya vā /
pṛcchanti sādhavo yasmāt tena pṛcchasi pāṇḍava /
ity āgneyavacanān *nārjuno bhagavantaṃ na jānāti* /(1)

(1) Cf. AgniP 1; 9.

20) GīT (p. 52,28-30):
Subject matter: Worship of Viṣṇu / Bhakti / Upāsana

anyadaivatapūjāpi yasminn ante samarpitā /
svargādiphalahetuḥ syān nānyathā taṃ bhajed dharim /
ity āgneye (1)
sattvasattvādhikarajorajobhis tamasā tathā /
varṇā vibhaktāś catvāraḥ sāttvikā eva vaiṣṇavāḥ /
iti ca (2)

(1) Cf. ibid. ll. 26f.: *anyadevatāyājinām api matsamarpaṇena vaiṣṇavamārgānuvartanenaiva samyak phalaṃ bhavati* and Gī VII 20-23; IX 23; for particulars of the mode

of thought of inclusivism cf. OBERHAMMER 1983 ... ; see also AgniP 9; 17; 23; 26; BhaviṣPV 20; 23; 30[92f.]; BrahP 58; 74; BrahVP 35; 38; 41; BrāṇP 80; 99; GarP 1; 34; 34_1; 44; 51; 52; 53; 55; HarV 5; 13; KūrP 30_1; MBh 4; NārP 16; 38; 43; 57; NarsiṃP 1; PadP 39; 43; 51; 55; 89; 101; SkaP 24; 57; 95; 106; VāmP 2; 8; 36; 42; VarP 26; 28.
(2) Cf, BrāṇP 13; NārP 52.

21) GiT (p. 59,28-29):
Subject matter: Means of liberation / Renunciation

mokṣopāyo yoga iti tadrūpo nyāsa eva tu /
viṣṇvarpitatayā bhadro nānyo nyāsaḥ kathaṃcana /
ity āgneye (1)

(1) Cf. AgniP 9; BrahP 77; NārP 36_1 and MESQUITA 2007: 17f. [= 2007_1: 438f.].

22) GīT (p. 80,23-24):
Subject matter: Difference of Jīva from Īśvara

jīvadharmān īśvare tu yo jīveṣv aiśvarān api /
vidyāj jīveśvaraikyaṃ vā dvandvamohī sa ucyate /
ity āgneye (1)

(1) Cf. ibid. ll 18f.: *dvandvamoho mithyājñānam ... jīveśvarādikaṃ dvandvam / tad-viṣayo moho dvandvamohaḥ / sammohas tadāgrahaḥ* ... ; AgniP 6; 24; BhāgP 3; BhaviṣPV 14; BrāṇP 61; GarP 30; 40; HarV 11; KūrP 10; 30_3; NārP 32; PadP 41; SkaP 98; VāmP 12; VarP 23; VāyuP 3_1.

23) GīT (p. 93,28+94,25):
Subject matter: Viṣṇu's Bhakti / Pūjā

ananyadevatāyāgād bhaktyudrekād akāmanāt /
sadā yogāc ca vaiśiṣṭyaṃ traividyād vaiṣṇavād api /
syād dhi bhāgavatasyaiva tena brahmādayo 'khilāḥ /
aśvamedhādibhir yajñair api keśavayājinaḥ /
vaiṣṇavā iti buddhyaiva mānayanty anyadevatāḥ /
ity āgneye (1)
samyag guṇagaṇajñānād upāsā paryupāsanā /
iti ca.

(1) Cf. AgniP 20.

24) GīT (p. 108,28+109,28):
Subject matter: Beatific vision of Viṣṇu / Liberation

trilokeṣu sthitair bhaktair arjunāya pradarśitam /
dṛṣṭaṃ viṣṇor viśvarūpaṃ svayogyatvānurūpataḥ /
prāyaḥ sahaiva pārthena prāyo bhītāś ca te 'khilāḥ /
darśanābhyāsato dṛṣṭir ānandodrekadā bhavet /
tasmin kāle tu bhūmeś ca bhārahārārtham udyamāt /
ugratvam iva sarvatra na bhītir brahmadarśinām /
arjunād adhikā ye tu teṣāṃ bhītir na cābhavat /
śrībrahmarudrapūrvāṇāṃ kṛṣṇāyā bhīmarāmayoḥ /
ity āgneyavacanam (1)

(1) Cf. BhaviṣPV 21; BhaviṣP 8; BrāṇP 80; BrahP 22; KūrP 30_4; KūrP 30_4; MBh 27; NārP 36; 39; 40; see also AgniP 16; MESQUITA 2000: 506ff.; MESQUITA 2007 39f. [= 2007_1: 450f.] and SCHREINER 1977: 159-196.

25) GīT (p. 118,23):
Subject matter: Śrī, the Immovable

na calet svāt padād yasmād acalā srīs tato matā /
ity āgneye (1)

(1) Cf. ĀdityaP 2; AgniP 27; BhaviṣPV 8; 24; BrāṇP 70; 89; BrahP 21; BrahVP 9; GarP 35; HarV 9; 29; MBh 14; 36; MatsyaP 20; NārP 4; 23; 41; 56; PadP 53; 63; 84_1; SkaP 9; SkaP 9; 91; 129; VāmP 32; ViṣP 8 and MESQUITA 2000: 415ff.

26) GīT (p. 150,20-21):
Subject matter: Vaiṣṇava rites

sāttvikaṃ mokṣadaṃ karma rājasaṃ sṛtiduḥkhadam /
tāmasaṃ pātadaṃ jñeyam tat kuryāt karma vaiṣṇavam /
ity āgneye (1)

(1) Cf. ibid. (p. 149,27-28): *tadarthatvena phalānabhisandhipūrvakakarmaṇa eva sāttvikatvāc ca / tadbhaktyā tatsmaraṇapūrvakam eva karma sat anyad asad eveti bhāvaḥ / rājasasyāpy asadantarbhāva eva / viṣṇuśraddhārahitatvāt*; see also AgniP 17; 20.

27) GīT (p. 162,13-14):
Subject matter: Viṣṇuloka / Vaikuṇṭha

śrīr eva lokarūpeṇa viṣṇos tiṣṭhati sarvadā /
ato hi vaiṣṇavā lokā nityās te cetanā api /
ity āgneye (1)

(1) Cf. ibid. ll. 12: *śāśvataṃ sthānaṃ vaikuṇṭhādi*; see also BhaviṣPV 9; BhaviṣP 4; 9; BrahP 12; 60; BrāṇP 27; 30; 51; HarV 1_1; MatsyaP 8; 13; NārP 46; 49; VāmP 6; 12; 15; VarP 4.

Bhāgavatapurāṇa (BhāgP)

[BhāgP is the most popular and also the most famous of all Purāṇas, which has influenced Indian thought and religion more deeply than any other composition of this genre, not only in the past but also at the present time. One of the best indicators of its influence is the fact that there have been a number of translations and adaptations in the vernaculars and also that it has been commented on by authors belonging to different schools of thought, each of them trying to demonstrate that the Purāṇa exhibits the views of his particular school. It is therefore not surprising that Madhva considered this text as the Purāṇa *par excellence*, which he very often names as a *śruti* (cf. Anuv. p. 54,15f.; 74,21f.; NyāV p. 208,23-24; see also MESQUITA 2000_1: 131f. [= 1997: 105f.].

The BhāgP is divided into 12 Skandhas, with a total of 335 Adhyāyas and 18.000 Ślokas (cf. HAZRA 1987: 52ff; ROCHER 1986: 138ff.). Madhva refers to the size of this Purāṇa, somewhat diverging from the current opinion, in an untraceable quote ascribed to GarP 8: *dvādaśaskandhayukto 'yaṃ śatavicchedasaṃyutaḥ grantho 'ṣṭadaśasāhasraḥ*. The text of BhāgP Madhva comments upon in his BhāgTN deviates heavily from the traditional version, not only with regard to the number of Adhyāyas but also as regard the number of Ślokas and to the text itself. HAZRA remarks appealing to Madhvavijaya (IV 49-52) of Nārāyaṇa Paṇḍitācārya, son of a direct pupil of Madhva that the textual problems relating to the BhāgP had already begun in Madhva's time. The editor indicates in the footnotes several variant readings. He points out to ślokas which are quoted and commented on only by Madhva (cf. e.g. MBh 14; see also BhāgP 5n. 1 and BhaviṣP 7n. 1). Madhva's commentary (BhāgTN), comprising 3.600 *granthas*, is based on a selected number of 1.600 ślokas out of a total of 18.000 ślokas of BhāgP.

For establishing his basic teachings such as the supreme transcendence of Viṣṇu or *creatio ex nihilo*, Madhva relies upon BhāgP (cf. MESQUITA 2000: 415f.; 425n. 492; 461f.). It is significant that, out of a total of 52 quotes from BhāgP, which Madhva ascribes by name to this Purāṇa in his different works, only five are authored by Madhva himself (see below). And this stands in flagrant contrast to the quotes attributed to other Purāṇas, in so far as they are traceable, that is to say, in a very few cases. More often Madhva quotes from BhāgP either as iti śrībhāgavate (v.g. GīBh p. 12,16) or as iti bhāgavate (v.g. ibid. p. 32,22-23). Some of these quotes either differ only slightly [*] from the traditionally transmitted text, whereas other differ substantially from it [**]. In several other cases, they are identical [=] with the transmitted reading. In five cases the quotes are either not traceable at all or can be identified only partially (see below BhāgP 1; 4). Sometimes, these quotes are indicated by bhagavadvacanāt. By bhagavadvacana/bhagavadrāddhānta or by bhagavatā uktam/kathitam/abhihitam etc. Madhva cites also very often Gī (v.g. AiUBh p. 187,11; Vāda p. 48,17; ChUBh p. 441,16) or Brahmasūtras (v.g. ChUBh p. 400,17; 442,27; GīT p. 131,25; PraśUBh p. 507,14; TaiUBh p. 537,4) and also MBh (BSūBh p. 162,22-23). All identified quotes as far as they are cited under the name of BhāgP are listed below with their precise location: *AiUBh* (p. 217,20 = III 2,11*; p. 240,24 = II 4,20*); *Anuv* (p. 54,16-18 = III 26,10-11; p. 194,16-17 [BSūBh p. 12,16-17] = IV 1,15**); *BĀUBh* (p. 260, 10-13 [GīT p. 162,13-14] = II 9,9f.**; p. 266,8 = V 11, 12-13**; p. 305,18-19 = XI 7,17cd); *BSūBh* (p. 11,2-3 [GīBh p. 25,8f.] = BhāgP XI 21,42cd-43ab*; p. 18,14 = II 10,6cd; p. 74,1-4 = BhāgP I 10,22, II 5,14; p. 94,7-9 = III 5, 49cd-50* p. 95,26 = X 71.8*; p. 117,14 = III 26,43cd; p. 134,4 = I 9,42cd); *ChUBh* (p. 406,27-28= III

19,22cd*); *GīBh* (p. 12,16 = I 2,30cd; p. 23,16 = IV 18,3cd; p. 25,13-14 = V 11,3*; p. 27,10-11 = XI 3,46d*/ = XI 21,23d; p. 32,22f. = BhāgP XI 8,20*; p. 39,20-21 = V 11,3; p. 84,12 = III 5,45f.*; p. 90,3 = VI 4,48*; p. 90,14 = II 5,14 / II 10,12; p. 95,6 = VI 3,22 / III 25,44**, p. 96,19 = XI 2,42*; p. 97,27 [GīT p. 34,23] = XI 19,36*; 98,10 = III 21,49cd; 107,23 = X 16,31*; p. 111,21 = XI 15,15ab**; p. 111,25 = XI 3,38*;118,1-2 = III, 26,10; 127,6 = III 26,8; p. 139,7-8 = VIII 17,27*; p. 139,9 = XI 28,17a; p. 146,2 = VI 1,40); *GīT* (p. 14, 1-6 = II 9, 10-12**; p. 22,27f. = II 10,14 / II 5,14; p. 25,24 = XI 18,30*; 34,23 = XI 19,36; p. 65,28f. = XI 19,36*; p. 73,23 = VI 14,5*;124,25f. = V 11,12-13**; 156,28 = XI 13,5*; 158,18 = XI 19, 30*); *KhN* (p. 218,13-14 = III 32,13cd; p. 239,1-2 = IV 3,22); *MBhTN* (I 27a = IX 4,56b; I 27b = VIII 12,10a**;II 124-125 = V 19,5-6**); *MuUBh* (p. 495,22-23 = III 9,24); *ṚgBh* (p. 6,9-10 = II 7,11cd; *TaiUBh* (p. 536,11 = X 87,22).]

1) Anuv (p. 194,14-17):
Subject matter: Epithets of Viṣṇu

om ātmā bhagavān viṣṇur ātmānando 'kṣaraḥ svarāṭ /
viśvatrātā nṛsiṃho 'jo nārāyaṇa urukramaḥ /
anasūyā tathaivātrer jajñe putrān akalmaṣān /
dattaṃ durvāsasaṃ somam ātmeśabrahmasaṃbhavān /
iti bhāgavate (1)

(1) Madhva's *siddhānta* is that all persons seeking release should worship Viṣṇu as *ātman* following the teaching of BSū (IV 1,3). He brings forward this premise quite spontaneously and thereafter he quotes untraceable source-references from Piṅga and Paramaśruti (MESQUITA 2000_1: 175f. [= 1997: 141f.]), introducing a quote from BhāgP. The first Śloka is freely invented. The second Śloka corresponds, with some alterations, to BhāgP (IV 1,15): (*atreḥ patny anasūyā trīñ jajñe suyaśasaḥ sutān / dattaṃ durvāsasaṃ somam ātmeśabrahmasaṃbhavān*). The last part of this Śloka is also cited by Madhva, in identical wording and in the same context, in BSūBh (p. 12,16-17) and in ChUBh (p. 440,21-22); see also Anuv (193,26-194,17):

ātmeti nāma kathitaṃ sakṣān nārāyaṇasya hi /
ātmā brahma mahāṃstāraḥ parameśaḥ śuciśravāḥ /
viṣṇur nārāyaṇo 'nanta iti śrīpatir īryate /
iti piṅgaśrutiś *caiva tathaiva* paramaśrutiḥ /(untraceable source)
...
iti bhāgavate *caiva tasmād ātmā janārdanaḥ /*
tasmād upāsyo viṣṇur iti jñātavyaḥ sajjanaiḥ sadā /

cf. BrahP 57; BrāṇP 4; 81; GarP 5; KūrP 25; MBh 33; PadP 1_1 [= BrahVP 23]; SkaP 11; 21; 66; 107; VāmP 1; VarP 52; 53; 55[4]; see also BrāṇP 68.

2) BSūBh (p. 23,12):
Subject matter: Viṣṇu, the supreme guiding Spirit

saṃvic chāstraṃ paraṃ padam /
iti hi bhāgavate (1)

(1) Cf. ibid. l. 11: *śāstraṃ antaryāmī*; see also BhāgP 5; BhaviṣPV 3; 4; BhaviṣP 6; BrahP 15; 22_1; 25; 30; 84; BrahVP 2; 11; 17; BrāṇP 3; GarP 14; HarV 4; 14; 19; MBh 2; 6; 30; MatsyaP 12; NārP 42; PadP 44; 57; 92; SkaP 28; VāmP 7; 11; 40; VarP 5.

3) GīBh (p. 13,11-12):
Subject matter: Jīva, the reflection of Viṣṇu

pratipattau vimokṣasya nityopādhyā svarūpayā /
cidrūpayā yuto jīvaḥ keśavapratibiṃbakaḥ /
iti bhagavadvacanāt (1)

(1) Cf. ibid. ll. 9f: *na hy upādhibiṃbasannidhyanāśe pratibiṃbanāśaḥ sati ca pradarśake / svayam evātra pradarśakaḥ / cittvāt / nityaś copādhiḥ kāścid asti*; see also AgniP 22; BrahVP 4; BrāṇP 71; HarV 34; KūrP 32 [12f.]; PadP 11; SkaP 54; VarP 35; 41; 57 and MESQUITA 2000: 497ff.

4) GīBh (p. 39,19):
Subject matter: Indifference to wordly objects and life (*vairāgya*)

karmabhiḥ śuddhasattvasya vairāgyaṃ jāyate hṛdi /
iti bhāgavate (1)

(1) Cf. ibid. l. 18: *akāmakarmaṇāṃ antaḥkaraṇaśuddhyā jñānān mokṣo bhavati / yac coktam ...* ; see also AgniP 9. The quote is not traceable. It is followed by the statement: *viraktānām eva ca jñānam ity uktam* – and a traceable quote from (BhāgP V 11,3). The untraceable quote above could be a paraphrase of BhāgP III 32.23:
vāsudeve bhagavati bhaktiyogaḥ prayojitaḥ /
janayaty aśu vairagyaṃ jñānaṃ yad brahmadarśanam //
see also MESQUITA 2007: 20 [= 2007_1: 439].

5) GīBh (p. 118,3-4):
Subject matter: Brahman / Vāsudeva

ānandam ānandamayo vasāne sarvātmake brahmaṇi vāsudeve /
iti bhāgavate (1)

(1) Cf. ibid. l. 3: *paraṃ tu brahma na hi bhagavato 'nyat ...* ; see also BhāgP II 2,31:
tenātmanātmānam upaiti śāntam ānandam ānandamayo 'vasāne /
etāṃ gatiṃ bhāgavatīṃ gato yaḥ sa vai punar neha viṣajjate 'ṅga //
Madhva re-shaped this verse also in *triṣṭubh*-metre (= Upajāti) in the sense of identity (*sarvātmaka* / Brahman = Vāsudeva). In this re-shapement he replaces *avasāne* (= in/ after the death) through *vasāne* (= taking outward appearance). It is strange, however, that Madhva in BhāgTN (p. 78,1-7 *ad* II 3,34c) holds on to the traditional reading (*avasāne*) and mixes up the *pādas* (II 3,34d; ibid. p. 78n. 3: *etau ślokau kiṃcid vyatyāsena ... paṭyate*). Furthermore, the supplementary line (II 2,33b: *sanātano 'sau bhagavān anādiḥ*) is mentioned only by Madhva, and the re-shapment spoken of above by Madhva: *sarvātmake brahmaṇi vāsudeve* is not found in other editions. For Madhva's

technique of textual composition (see MESQUITA 2000_1: 172f.[1997: 139f.]; see also BhāgP 1; MESQUITA 2000: 33n. 12 and MESQUITA 2000_1: 35ff. [= 1997: 29ff.]).

Bhaviṣyatparvan (BhaviṣPV)

[BhaviṣPV is either identical with Bhaviṣyapurāṇa or with the homonymous last chapter of Harivaṃśa. As a matter of fact, BhaviṣPV predicts the birth of Madhva as a divine incarnation (*aṃśāvatāra*) in the Kali-era, and thus it alludes to the context of prophecy (BhaviṣPV = a text about future events awaiting their fulfilment!). In contrast to the transmitted Purāṇas the title BhaviṣPV has been coined by Madhva himself in agreement with his particular teaching implied here. (cf. MESQUITA 2000_1: 53f. [= 1997: 43f.]). BhaviṣPV is the second most important fictitious work of Madhva after Brahmatarka (ibid. p. 89ff. [= p. 71ff.]) propounding Madhva's particular doctrines (ibid. p. 169ff. [= p. 137ff.]). Madhva's authorship of the work is also clear from the fact that sometimes the verses attributed to both these texts end with a reference composed in Śloka-metre, indicating that the author of the closing remark is identical with the author of the quotation itself (BhaviṣPV 29; 30 and 31; 32[112ab]; see also BrāṇP 94[3ab]; 95; 96 and 101). It is notewhorthy that neither of these two works has been quoted at all in GīBh, which is supposed to be Madhva's first composition. Quotes from from BhaviṣPV are to be found in AiUBh (once); BĀUBh (thrice); BhāgTN (nine times); BSūBh (twelve times); GīT (thrice); KathUBh (once); MBhTN (four times). In Anuv and VTN, which are taken as Madhva's last works, only Brahmatarka is quoted. Metrical lapse is to be found in BhaviṣPV 12cd which is indicated also by the editor (BhāgTN p. 429n. 3: *prācīnapāṭha ekākṣaranyūnaḥ pādaḥ*).]

1) AiUBh (184,33-185,2):
Subject matter: Universe with its five-fold difference (*pra-pañca*)

jīveśvarabhidā caiva jīvabhedaḥ parasparam /
jaḍeśvarabhidā caiva jaḍabhedas tathaiva ca /
jaḍajīvabhidā caiva satyo 'yaṃ bhedapañcakaḥ /
na kadācin nivartyo 'yaṃ muktau saṃsāra eva vā /
ya etadanyathā brūyus te hi yānty adharaṃ tamaḥ /
iti bhaviṣyatparvaṇi (1)

(1) Cf. ibid. ll. 30f.: *yadi bhedasya pūrvam api mithyātvam aṅgīkriyate tarhi bhūmidānādisarvakarmaṇāṃ manvāditvasyāpi mithyātvāt ahaṃ manur abhavam ityādi sarvam anarthakam eva bhavati* ... ; see also BrahP 2; 53; BrāṇP 103; GarP 6; MatsyaP 7; VarP 27 and the detailed discussion on this topic in MESQUITA 2000_1: 104 ff. [= 1997: 83ff.]; MESQUITA 2000: 192n. 396.

2) BĀUBh (p. 268,24-269,13):
Subject matter: Prāmāṇya of the Vedas and the Sadāgamas

uktaṃ ca bhaviṣyatparvaṇi –
yenoktam āgamāmātvaṃ kutas tad iti taṃ vadet /
pratyakṣāder yadi brūyāt tanmātvaṃ kveti taṃ vadet / [1]
tat svataś ced āgamasya prāmāṇyaṃ na svataḥ kutaḥ /
parataś cet pramāṇasya na kasyāpi sthitir bhavet / [2] (1)
aṅgīkṛtaṃ ca prāmāṇyaṃ sarvair apy āgamasya tu /
yataḥ svapakṣaprāmāṇyaṃ virodhe 'py akṣajādinā / [3]
aṅgīkurvanti tatpakṣaḥ pratyakṣādivirodhakaḥ /
śūnyatā kṣaṇikatvaṃ ca jñānamātratvam eva ca / [4]
bhāvābhāvātmatā sākaṃ śarīrātmatvam eva ca /
pratyakṣeṇa viruddhyante maddeha iti darśanāt / [5]
bhāvarūpasthiratvāder jñānād bhedasya darśanāt /
dehabhedo yady amukhyo dehaikye mukhyatā kutaḥ / [6]
jātismṛtipramāṇāc ca na yuktā deharūpatā /
anuṣṭhāya ca śāstrārthaṃ phalabhogasya darśanāt / [7]
pratyakṣāder viruddhatvāt saugatādyā durāgamāḥ /
bahvāgamavirodhāc ca duṣṭatvaṃ teṣu saṃsthitam / [8]
prāmāṇyaṃ svīkṛtaṃ yais tu vedānām āgamā hi te /
śatakoṭayaḥ pañcarātraṃ purāṇaṃ tāvad eva ca / [9]
rāmasya caritaṃ tāvat tāvad anyac ca sarvaśaḥ /
anantāś ca tathā vedāḥ sāṅgopāṅgāś ca sarvaśaḥ / [10]
sarvādhikyaṃ yatra viṣṇos tātparyāt samudīryate /
viṃśad eva sahasrāṇi ślokānāṃ samudīritam / [11]
bārhaspatyaṃ tathā bauddhaṃ bhāvābhāvamataṃ tathā /
śivaśaktyādikaṃ yac ca kiṃcit prāmāṇyasaṃyutam / [12]
triṃśatkoṭy eva tat sarvam ato mānaṃ na tat smṛtam /
bahumānaviruddhaṃ yan na tanmānaṃ vido viduḥ / [13] (2)
guṇasāmye 'pi kimuta guṇādhikavirodhi yat /
yathā bahūnāṃ jñānānāṃ samānāṃ guṇato 'pi ca / [14]
virodhy ekaṃ tu yajjñānaṃ na mānatvaṃ gamiṣyati /
pratyakṣādau hi bahubhiḥ samair ekam apodyate / [15]
tasmād vedāḥ pramāṇaṃ syur bāhulyād eva kiṃ punaḥ /
adoṣatvād guṇāc caiva balavatkāryasādhanāt / [16]
vedoktakarmayuktānāṃ tathā siddhimatām api /
vedabāhyakriyāyogān na bādhaḥ kvāpi dṛśyate / [17]
vedoktakarmasiddhānāṃ na bādhyaṃ dṛśyate kvacit /
asādhyaṃ vā tato vedāḥ prāmāṇyaṃ niścayād gatāḥ / [18]
iti (3)

(1) Cf. ibid. l. 23f.: *atas teṣāṃ pratyakṣavad anumānavac cāṅgīkartavyam āgamaprāmāṇyam* ... ; BrāṇP 11.
(2) Cf. BhaviṣPV 3n. 7; see also MESQUITA 1990: 184ff.

(3) Cf. the fictitious quote from Brahmatarka (BĀUBh 269,14+270,5-18) and MESQUITA 2000: 51n. 13; 57n. 25; 280f.; 384f.

3) BĀUBh (p. 270,25-271,30):
Subject matter: Viṣṇu, the supreme guiding Spirit / Syllabus of right and heretical doctrines

yad āhur brahmavijñānāt samagratvaṃ yiyāsavaḥ /
brahmajñānāt samagratvaṃ nānyataś ceti niścayāt / [1]
tatra kecin manuṣyās tu manyante brahma kiṃmateḥ /
samagrabhāvam agamad iti brūyāc ca tān iti / [2]
brahmāpi sarvadātmānam aheyaṃ guṇabṛṃhitam /
sarvadāstīti meyaṃ ca vijānāti tathaiva tu / [3] (1)
ata eva samagratvaṃ svata evāsya sarvadā /
tadaheyaṃ paraṃ brahma yo yo 'ved guṇabṛṃhitam / [4]
sarvadāstīti meyaṃ ca sa sa yāti samagratām /
mukhyaṃ samagraṃ tad brahma jñānasyāpi samagrataḥ / [5]
kiṃcit samagratāṃ devās teṣāṃ jñānaṃ hi tādṛśam /
āpus tato 'dhamāṃ jñānatādṛktvād ṛṣayo 'pi tu / [6]
ṛṣibhyo 'py adhamāṃ prāpur mānuṣāś ca samagratām /
aheyaṃ ca guṇaiḥ pūrṇaṃ nityāstijñānagocaram / [7]
brahma paśyan vāmadevaḥ sūktam etad dadarśa ha /
ahaṃ manuḥ sūrya iti svāntaryāmivyapekṣayā / [8] (2)
ahaṃśabdo yato viṣṇau tataś cottamapuruṣāḥ /
vartante 'bhavam ityādyāḥ sarvāntasthe janārdane / [9]
manur eṣo 'vabodhatvān manvantastho janārdanaḥ /
sa hy ācārān uvāceśaḥ prerayan manumānasam / [10]
sa eva sūribhiḥ prāpyaḥ sūryāntastho mumukṣubhiḥ /
sa eva kakṣagaiḥ sevyaḥ kakṣīvati samāsthitaḥ / [11]
sa eva śukrasaṃsthas tu nītīḥ kavayati svayam /
yataḥ kaviḥ sa kāmasya preraṇād uśanā smṛtaḥ / [12]
sa eva śaṃbarapuro bibhedendre vyavasthitaḥ /
sarvāntaryāmikatvāt tu sarvakarmā sa eva hi / [13]
tataḥ sūkte tathovāca vāmadevaḥ śriyaḥ patim /
yo yo 'heyaṃ paraṃ brahma sadaivāstīti mānagam / [14] (3)
idānīm api jānāti svayogyāṃ sa samagratām / (4)
prāpnoti tasya devāś ca nābhūtiṃ kartum īśate / [15]
ātmā hi viṣṇur devānāṃ teṣu vyāpto yataḥ sadā /
niyoktṛtvena kāryeṣu tajjño yasmāc ca sādhakaḥ / [16] (5)
yasya prīto harir nityaṃ tasya prītāś ca devatāḥ /
prītiyogān naiva tasya viruddhaṃ kartum īśate / [17]

evaṃ vilakṣaṇaṃ devam upāste jīvarūpiṇam /
aheyo 'stīti meyo 'nyo 'thānyo 'sau harir ity api / [18]
na sa veda paraṃ viṣṇuṃ jīvarūpeṇa vetti yat /
nāheyatvaṃ ca vedāsya tasmāt paśuvad īritaḥ / [19]
devānāṃ paśuvac cāsau yo vedāheyarūpiṇam /
paśavo bahavo yadvat puruṣaṃ bhojayanty uta / [20]
tattvajñaḥ puruṣas tadvad eko 'pi bahugā yathā /
devān bhojayati jñānasampattyā viṣṇusaṃśrayāt / [21]
svīkāre tu paśoḥ prītir ekasyāpi bhaviṣyati /
bahūnāṃ hi gavāṃ lābhe parā prītiś ca kiṃ punaḥ / [22]
tasmāt subahugorūpe devānāṃ tattvavedini /
bhaved abhyadhikā prītir viṣṇvaheyatvavedanāt / [23]
nityāheyas tathaivānyas tadanyo viṣṇur ity api /
devānām apriyaṃ jñānaṃ naivaṃ vidyād ataḥ pumān / [24]
viṣṇor aheyatāṃ caiva nityatvaṃ pūrṇatām api /
yo na veda tathā yaś ca jīvair aikyaṃ harer vadet / [25]
yaś cāsatyaṃ jagad brūyāt sarve te tamasi sphuṭam /
majjanti sarvavedair hi guṇaiḥ sarvair harir yataḥ / [26]
pūrṇo nityam apūrṇāś ca jīvā muktā api sphuṭam /
niḥśeṣaduḥkhamokena sukhaikānubhavas tu yaḥ / [27]
mokṣa ity ucyate vedais te 'pi muktā hariṃ sadā /
upāsate jagac caitat sarvadādyantavarjitam / [28]
na kadācij jagan nāśo na kadācit tad anyathā /
jagat pravāharūpeṇa sarvadaiva vyavasthitam / [29] (6)
jñānataḥ karmato vāpi tapasā śaktito 'pi vā /
na kasyāpy anyathā bhāvyaṃ jagad etat kadācana / [30]
satyo viṣṇuḥ śrīś ca satyā jīvāḥ satyā jaḍaṃ tathā /
asatyaṃ nāsti kiṃcic ca sarveṣāṃ jñānagocaram / [31]
jñātvā viṣṇum ato muktiṃ prāpnuyāt puruṣottamam / [32ab] (7)
iti bhaviṣyatparvaṇi (8)

(1) In several passages and in untraceable quotes Madhva explains or defends the supreme transcendence of Viṣṇu as *ens a se* or as *actus purus* since there are no limitations (*na hīyate*) and no additions (*na vardhate*) to His Being; moreover, there are no positive potentialities in His Being which are not actualized. Therefore Viṣṇu is always *guṇapūrṇa*; cf. ṚgBh (p. 76,8-10): *pūrṇam adaḥ pūrṇam idaṃ pūrṇāt pūrṇam udacyate* [BĀU I 1,1] *heyopādeyarahitaguṇapūrṇo hariḥ sadā / anugrahavyaktir eva tadguṇānāṃ na cānyathā ityādivedavākyebhyo naiva vṛddhir hareḥ kvacit*; see also AiUBh (p. 189,14f.) and MBh 35: *yasya divyaṃ hi tad rūpaṃ hīyate vardhate na ca.* Thus, Madhva excludes in Viṣṇu the six-fold change of beings, taught by Yāska in his Nirukta (crit. ed. by M. J. BHAKSHI, Delhi 1982: 9f. [I 1.3]): *ṣaḍ bhāvavikārā bhavantīti vārṣyāyaṇiḥ / jāyate 'sti vipariṇamate vardhate 'pakṣīyate vinaśyatīti / jāyate iti*

pūrvabhāvasyādim ācaṣṭe; see also BrahP 1_4; BrahVP 2; 29; BrāṇP 3n. 3; 85; MESQUITA 2000: 423ff.; 490f.; below n. 3; AgniP 6 and MESQUITA 2000: 142f.; 162f.
(2) Cf. Ṛg IV 26,1 = BĀU I 4,10; see also BhāgP 2.
(3) Cf. BĀUBh (p. 258,14f.): *aham aheyaṃ brahma paripūrṇam asmi sarvadāstīti meyam ity etair viśeṣaṇair ātmānaṃ svarūpam evāvet / yady ahaṃśabdo 'smacchabdārthavācī, asmiśabdaś cottamapuruṣe tadātmānam iti vyarthaṃ syāt / ato 'hamasmiśabdāv uktārthāv eva / agre anādikālata eva vidyamānam ātmānaṃ jānāti ca tad brahmety arthaḥ*; see also MBh 8_1; GīT (p. 15,11f.): *aheyatvād ahaṃnāmā bhagavān harir avyayaḥ.*
(4) Cf. MESQUITA 2000: 506ff.
(5) Cf. ibid. 489f.; 516ff.
(6) Cf. ibid. p. 467f.; 186ff. and MESQUITA 2000: 192n. 397.
(7) Cf. BhaviṣPV 2; 29; 30; BrahP 43; 48; BrahVP 42; BrāṇP 12; 43; 57; PadP 94; SkaP 39; 40; 55; 69; 122; see also MESQUITA 2000_1: 169f. [= 1997: 137f.] and MESQUITA 2000: 528f.
(8) Cf. BĀUBh (p. 271,31f.): *idam ity ātmano yogyaṃ sarvaṃ samagraṃ bhavati / nirduḥkhānandasyāpekṣitatvān manasi sthitatvenedam iti yujyate / tat sarvam abhavat / sarvaṃ bhaviṣyanta ity ādinā samagrabhāvasya prastutatvāt ....*

4) BĀUBh (p. 276,19-29):
Subject matter: Viṣṇu, the resting-place and the supreme guiding Spirit of all beings and worlds

so 'yaṃ sarveṣu jīveṣu niyāmakatayā sthitaḥ /
sa viṣṇur āptakāmatvād ātmety evocyate budhaiḥ / [1] (1)
sa lokaḥ sarvabhūtānāṃ sa hi jīveṣu saṃsthitaḥ /
vaiśvadevādikān homān yajñāṃś ca kurute vibhuḥ / [2]
kāruṇyāt sarvadeveṣu tena devāśrayo hariḥ /
ṛṣīṇām āśrayaś cāpi svādhyāyeṣv ṛṣisaṃsmṛteḥ / [3]
sa hi jīveṣu saṃviṣṭhaḥ piṇḍaṃ putrajaniṃ tathā /
yat karoti pitṝṇāṃ ca saṃśrayas tata eva saḥ / [4]
tṛṇodakādidānena paśūnāṃ annato nṛṇām /
upakārāc ca sarveṣāṃ prāṇinām āśrayo hariḥ / [5]
yajñādīn devatādīnām annatvena puraiva yat /
brahmādyair arthitaḥ prādāt kṣīrābdhes taṭa uttare / [6]
ataś ca sarvalokānām āśrayo viṣṇur eva saḥ /
evaṃ yo vetti viṣṇos tu sarvādhāratvam uttamam / [7]
sarvāṇy api hi bhūtāni tasyecchanty avināśitām /
svāśrayasya yathā nityam anāśaṃ prārthayanti hi / [8]
rājāder api tāny evam uttamāśrayavedinaḥ /
tad etad vāsudevasya sarvādhāratvam uttamam / [9]
viditaṃ sarvavedaiś ca mīmāṃsābhiś ca niścitam / [10ab]
iti bhaviṣyatparvaṇi (2)

(1) Cf. HarV 26.

(2) Cf. ibid. l. 18: *etābhyāṃ rūpābhyāṃ sahitaṃ hi brahmābhavat / svaṃ lokaṃ svāśrayam*; see also BhāgP 2; PadP 3_1 and MESQUITA 2000: 141n. 274; 162f.

5) BhāgTN (p. 51,2-3):
Subject matter: Jīvanmukti / Prārabdhakarman

mahatā kāraṇenaiva prārabdhāny api kānicit /
karmāṇi kṣayam āyānti brahmadṛṣtim ataḥ kvacit /
iti bhaviṣyatparvaṇi (1)

(1) Cf. ibid. l. 1: *jñāninām prārabdhasyaiva nirmathanam / yogasyaiva ...* ; see also ĀdityaP 1; BrahP 10 and MESQUITA 2007: 32n. 67 [= 2007_1 446n. 66].

6) BhāgTN (p. 85,6-8):
Subject matter: Viṣṇu's supreme transcendence

yadadhīnā yasya sattā tat tad ity eva bhaṇyate /
vidyamāne vibhede 'pi mitho nityaṃ svarūpataḥ /
iti bhaviṣyatparvaṇi (1)

(1) Cf. AgniP 6 and MESQUITA 2000: 455ff.

7) BhāgTN (p. 240,1):
Subject matter: Vedic rites

ānuśravikakarmāsau śrutyuktaṃ yo na laṅghayet /
iti bhaviṣyatparvaṇi (1)

(1) Cf. VarP 61.

8) BhāgTN (p. 243,10-12):
Subject matter: Viṣṇu, the supreme Creator of the universe

brahmādibhiḥ sargakarī śrīr viṣṇubalasaṃśrayāt /
sukhaduḥkhaprado viṣṇuḥ svayam eva sanātanaḥ /
kartṛtvaṃ sukhaduḥkhānām anyeṣāṃ ca tadājñayā /
bhoktṛtvaṃ sukhaduḥkhānāṃ karoty eko hariḥ svayam /
bhoktṛtvamātrahetutvaṃ jīve nānyatra kutracit /
iti bhaviṣyatparvaṇi (1)

(1) Cf. AgniP 12; 25; BrāṇP 51 and MESQUITA 2000: 460f.; 470ff.

9) BhāgTN (p. 302,9-11):
Subject matter: The heaven of Brahmā

ādhipatyam anityaṃ tu dhruvalokasya yad dhruve /
na tu tatsthānagantṛṇāṃ yatīnāṃ gatir uttamā /
tasyāpi muktir niyatā niyataṃ cāpi tatpadam /
tathāpi kāmanānindā dhruveṇa sukṛtā bata /
iti bhaviṣyatparvaṇi (1)

(1) Cf. ibid. n. 6: *yad dhruve dhruvalokasyādhipatyaṃ tad anityam antavat / sādhanena tallokaṃ prāptā yatayas tu punar nāvartante saṃsārāya* (BhāgP IV 9,25) */ kiṃtu muktim evādhitiṣṭhanti / tataś ca tatsthānagantṛṇāṃ yatīnām uttamā gatir nityā mukter nityatatvāt ... na hi mukter nityatvam atra niṣidhyate / kiṃtv ādhipatyasya nityatvam eva*; see also AgniP 27; KūrP 16.

10) BhāgTN (p. 303,7-8):
Subject matter: Definition of liberation

harau niyatacittatvād grahavat tatpraveśanāt /
mokṣaṃ tādātmyam ity āhur na tadrūpatvataḥ kvacit /
iti bhaviṣyatparvaṇi (1)

(1) Cf. AgniP 16 and MESQUITA 2000: 524f.

11) BhāgTN (p. 401,2-3):
Subject matter: Viṣṇu, the supreme Creator of the universe

vibhaktyarthasya kālasya prakārāṇāṃ ca kāraṇam /
eka eva paro viṣṇuḥ sarvasattāpradatvataḥ /
iti bhaviṣyatparvaṇi (1)

(1) Cf. ibid. l. 1: *saptavibhaktyarthasya kālasya prakārasya ca hetur brahmaiva*; see also AgniP 12 and MESQUITA 2000: 227n. 493; 460f.; 470ff.

12) BhāgTN (p. 429,4-5):
Subject matter: Punishment of the demons

bādhyādistho harir nityaṃ bādhyatādi gatety api /
gīyate na tu bādhyatvādidoṣayutatvataḥ / -1
iti bhaviṣyatparvaṇi (1)

(1) Cf. ibid. n. 3: *prācīnapāṭha ekākṣaranyūnaḥ pādaḥ*; see also AgniP 10; BhaviṣPV 15; 19; BrahP 68; 73; 79; BrahVP 10; 42; BrāṇP 22; 38; 42; 58; HarV 30; NārP 44; 50; VāmP 43; see also BrāṇP 53 and MESQUITA 2000: 527f.

13) BhāgTN (p. 613,7-11):
Subject matter: Hierarchy of disciples searching for liberation

bahvapekṣo hi jijñāsur ato dehādivṛttaye /
kiṃcitsatsv api saṅgī syād aśakye sati vartane /
kṛtakṛtyas tyajet saṅgaṃ sadā gurusurādiṣu /
saṅgī syān na hi tatsaṅgaṃ vinā tu sukhabhāg bhavet /
tasmād anādyanantaiva saktir gurusurādiṣu /
anyatra kṛtyāpekṣā syād iti saṅgavinirṇayaḥ /
iti bhaviṣyatparvaṇi (1)

(1) Cf. BhavişPV 15 and GarP 37.

14) BSūBh (p. 101,4-6):
Subject matter: Spiritual nature of the Jīvas

bhaviṣyatparvaṇi ca –
bhinnā jīvāḥ paro bhinnas tathāpi jñānarūpataḥ /
procyante brahmarūpeṇa vedavādeṣu sarvaśaḥ /
iti (1)

(1) Cf. ibid. l. 3f.: *jñānānandādibrahmaguṇā evāsya yataḥ sārasvarūpam ato 'bheda-vyapadeśaḥ / yathā sarvaguṇātmakatvāt sarvātmatvaṃ brahmaṇa ucyate sarvaṃ khalv idaṃ brahmeti* (ChU III 14,1) ... ; see also AgniP 22 and BraṇP 71.

15) BSūBh (p. 103,2-6):
Subject matter: Hierarchy of the spiritual beings

bhaviṣyatparvaṇi ca –
nityānandajñānabalā devā naivaṃ tu dānavāḥ /
duḥkhopalabdhimātrās te mānuṣās tūbhayātmakāḥ /
teṣāṃ yad anyathā dṛśyaṃ tadupādhikṛtaṃ matam /
vijñānenātmayogyena nijarūpe vyavasthitiḥ /(1)
samyagjñānaṃ tu devānāṃ manuṣyāṇāṃ vimiśritam /
viparītaṃ ca daityānāṃ jñānasyaivaṃ vyavasthitiḥ /
iti (2)

(1) Cf. MESQUITA 2000: 506f.
(2) Cf. ibid. p. 102,20f.: *vyaktyanaṅgīkāre devānāṃ nityopalabdhir ānandādīnām asurāṇāṃ nityānupalabdhir manuṣyāṇāṃ nityopalabdhyanupalabdhī ca prasajyate / nityānando nityajñāno nityabalaḥ parātmā naivam asurā evam anevaṃ ca manuṣyāḥ / ity āgniveśyaśrutiḥ* ... (untraceable source); see also BhavişPV 13; 30[86f.]; BrahP 4; 24; BrahVP 35; BrāṇP 15; 48; 88; GarP 33; 36; 37; HarV 22; 34; PadP 70; 71; 82; 103; 104; SkaP 32; 53; 54; VāmP 17; 41; VarP 10; 41; 42; 44; 46 and MESQUITA 2000: 492ff.

16) BSūBh (p. 104,9-10):
Subject matter: Viṣṇu, the supreme Creator of the universe

pūrvakarma prayatnaṃ ca saṃskāraṃ cāpy apekṣya tu /
īśvaraḥ kārayet sarvaṃ tac ceśvarakṛtaṃ svayam /
anāditvād adoṣaś ca pūrṇaśaktitvato hareḥ / (1)
iti bhaviṣyatparvaṇi (2)

(1) Cf. MESQUITA: 2000: 467f.
(2) Cf. ibid. l. 7f.: ... *kṛtaprayatnāpekṣatvāt tatprerakatvasya* ... ; see also AgniP 12; BhaviṣP 12 and MESQUITA 2000: 486f.

17) BSūBh (p. 108,12-13):
Subject matter: Eternity of breath of life / Sense organs (*prāṇa*)

nopādānaṃ hīndriyāṇām ato 'nutpattir iṣyate /
upādānakṛtā sṛiṣṭiḥ sarvalokeṣu dṛśyate /
iti hi bhaviṣyatparvaṇi (1)

(1) Cf. ibid. l. 10f.: *prāṇā evedam agra āsuras tebhyo bhūtāni jajñire bhūtebhyo 'ṇḍam aṇḍasyāntas tv ime lokā atha prāṇā evānādayaḥ prāṇā nityā iti* kāṣāyaṇaśrutau (unknown source) *prāṇānām anutpattiḥ pratīyate* ... ; see also MESQUITA 2000: 99n. 143; MESQUITA 2003: 101f. and BhaviṣPV 18; 18_1; BrahP 42; 67; BrahVP 13; 18; 34; BrāṇP 73; GarP 12; 32; HarV 6_1; 24; 25; KūrmP 23; MBh 11; 12; 17; 23; NārP 17; PadP 18; 19; SkaP 25; 46; 103; VāyuP 3_5; 4; 7; 8; 9; 10.

18) BSūBh (p. 109,2-3):
Subject matter: Eternity of sense organs

nityāny etāni saukṣmyeṇa hīndriyāṇi tu sarvaśaḥ /
teṣāṃ bhūtair upacayaḥ sṛṣṭikāle vidhīyate /
pareṇa sāmyasaṃprāpteḥ kasya syān mukhyanityatā /
iti bhaviṣyatparvaṇi (1)

(1) Cf. ibid. p. 108, 17: *anāditvaśrutir gauṇānaditvāpekṣayā / mukhyāsaṃbhavāt* ... ; see also BhaviṣPV 17; MatsyaP 5.

18_1) BSūBh (p. 110,9-10):
Subject matter: Twelve sorts of breath of life (*prāṇa*)

sapta prāṇās tv avagateḥ pañca prāṇāś ca karmaṇaḥ /
evaṃ prāṇadvādaśakaṃ śarīre nityasaṃsthitam /
iti bhaviṣyatparvavacanaṃ caśabdāt (1)

(1) Cf. ibid. l. 8: *jñānendriyāpekṣayā saptatvam / guhāśayāṃ nihitāḥ sapta sapta* (MuU II 1,8) *iti viśeṣaṇāt* ... ; see also BhaviṣPV 17.

19) BSūBh (p. 121,12-13):
Subject matter: Hell

tiryakşu narake caiva sukhaleśo vidhīyate /
nāndhe tamasi magnānāṃ sukhaleśo 'pi kaścana /
iti bhavişyatparvaṇi (1)

(1) Cf. BrahP 68; KūrP 26; MBh 26; NārP 50; PadP 93_1; SkaP 104; VāmP 19; see also BhavişPV 12 and MESQUITA 2000: 527ff.

20) BSūBh (p. 155,11-12):
Subject matter: Upāsana

guṇaiḥ sarvair upāsyo 'sau brahmaṇā parameśvaraḥ /
anyair yathākramaṃ caiva mānuṣaiḥ kaiścid eva tu /
iti bhavişyatparvaṇi (1)

(1) Cf. ibid. l. 10: *yujyate copasaṃhāro 'nupasaṃhāraś ca yogyatāviśeṣāt* ... ; see also AgniP 20; MESQUITA 2000: 519f. and MESQUITA 2007: 25 [= 2007_1: 442f.]

21) BSūBh (p. 171,26-172,6):
Subject matter: Doctrines of liberation according to Vyāsa

vijñātam etat sarveṣāṃ munīnāṃ tattvadarśanāt /(1)
syād eva mokṣo nānyasmād iti tatrāpi citratā /[1]
svargādayaḥ karmaṇaiva nānyenety apare viduḥ /
jñānenādhikyam ityāhur jaiminyādyās tu kecana /[2] (2)
adṛṣtam eva jñānena dṛṣṭaṃ naivopalabhyate /
iti kecid vidaḥ prāhur vyāsaśiṣyā ime 'khilāḥ /[3]
yasmād vyāsamataṃ sarvaṃ satyam eva tato 'khilam /
yathākāśas tv ananto 'pi vyāmo hastāvadhis tathā /[4]
prādeśo 'pi hi satyena tathaiteṣāṃ matāni tu /
svayaṃ tu bhagavān vyāso vyāptajñānamahāṃśumān /[5]
anantākāśavat paśyan nikhilaṃ puruṣottamaḥ /
jñānenaivāpyate sarvaṃ karmaṇā tv adhikaṃ bhavet /[6]
iti prāha mahāyogī pumarthānāṃ vinirṇayam /[7ab]
iti bhavişyatparvaṇi (3)

(1) Cf. AgniP 24.
(2) Cf. MESQUITA 1994: 451-484.
(3) Cf. ibid. l. 25: *rājasūyādikṛtāv akṛtau ca samam eva teṣāṃ jñānam* ... ; BhavişPV 29[42]; BrahP 1_5; 9_1; 51; 18; 63; BrahVP 39[1]; BrāṇP 86[5]; 95[9f.]; KūrP 2; PadP 23; 61; SkaP 12_1; 23; 78; 89; see also BrāṇP 14; GarP 9 and MESQUITA 2003_1: 206f.

22) BSūBh (p. 182,3-4):
Subject matter: Viṣṇu, the world-Ruler

asurān damayan viṣṇuḥ svapadaṃ ca surān nayan /
punaḥ punar mānuṣāṃs tu sṛtāv āvartayaty asau /
iti bhaviṣyatparvaṇi (1)

(1) Cf. ibid. p. 181,13f.: *śṛṇve vīra ugram ugraṃ damāyann anyam anyam atinenīyamānaḥ / edhamānadvilubhayasya rājā coṣkūyate viśa indra manuṣyān iti viśeṣānugrahaṃ ca darśayati deveṣu parameśvarasya* (Ṛg VI 47,16?) ... ; see also BhāgP 2; BhaviṣPV 12; BhaviṣP 3 and MESQUITA 2000: 510ff.

23) BSūBh (p. 194,3-4):
Subject matter: Upāsana

ātmety upāsanaṃ kāryaṃ sarvathaiva mumukṣubhiḥ /
nānākleśasamāyukto 'py etāvan naiva vismaret /
iti bhaviṣyatparvaṇi (1)

(1) Cf. ibid. p. 193,14: *ātmety upadeśa upāsanaṃ ca mokṣārthibhiḥ sarvathā kāryam eva* ... ; see also AgniP 20.

24) BSūBh (p. 211,15-17):
Subject matter: The three-fold infinity of Viṣṇu

deśataḥ kālataś caiva samā prakṛtir īśvare /
ubhayor apy abaddhatvaṃ tadabandhaḥ parātmanaḥ /
svata eva pareśasya sā copāste sadā harim /
prakṛteḥ prākṛtasyāpi ye guṇās te tu viṣṇunā /
niyatā naiva kenāpi niyatā hi harer guṇāḥ /
iti hi bhaviṣyatparvaṇi (1)

(1) Cf. ibid. l. 14: *atas tasya ye viśeṣaguṇās teṣām anupamardenaiva sāmyam* ... ; see also AgniP 25; BrahVP 12_1; BrāṇP 51;MBh 34; and MESQUITA 2000: 416ff.; 421n. 486.

25) GīT (p. 43,24-25):
Subject matter: Liberation / Pāṇḍavas

brahmaniṣṭhā brahmaratā brahmajñānasutarpitāḥ /
pāṇḍavānāṃ ca muktānām antaraṃ kiṃcid eva hi /
iti bhaviṣyatparvavacanāt (1)

(1) Cf. AgniP 16; 18; BrahVP 39; MatsyaP 15; SkaP 22; 33.

26) GīT (p. 90,28+91,31):
Subject matter: Doctrine of Avatāras

brahmarudraramādīnāṃ sāmyadṛṣṭir ananyatā /
prādurbhāvagatasyāpi doṣadṛṣṭir apūrṇatā /
dharmadehāvatārāder bhedadṛṣṭiś ca saṅkaraḥ /
avatāreṣv iti jñeyam avajñānaṃ janārdane /
sarvaṃ moghaṃ śubhaṃ tasya yo 'vajānāti keśavam / (1)
adharaṃ yāti ca tamaḥ prādurbhāvagato 'py ataḥ /
jñeyaḥ kevalaciddeho nirdoṣaḥ pūrṇasadguṇaḥ /
iti bhaviṣyatparvaṇi (2)

(1) Cf. Gī IX 11-12.
(2) Cf. ĀdiP 1; MESQUITA 2000_1: 35ff. [= 1997: 29ff.] and MESQUITA 2000: 415ff.

27) GīT (p. 96,23-27):
Subject matter: Doctrine of transmigration

pāpādikāritāś caiva puṃsāṃ svābhāvikā api /
vipratvādyās tatra puṇyāḥ svābhāvyā eva muktigāḥ / (1)
yānti strītvaṃ pumāṃso 'pi pāpataḥ kāmato 'pi vā / (2)
na striyo yānti puṃstvaṃ tu svabhāvād eva yāḥ striyaḥ /
puṃsā sahaiva puṃdehasthitiḥ syād varadānataḥ /
tajjanmani varāḥ pāpajātābhyo nijasatstriyaḥ /
sarveṣām api jīvānām antyadeho yathā nijaḥ /
muktau ca nijabhāvaḥ syāt karmabhogāntato 'pi ca /
iti bhaviṣyatparvavacanāt pāpayonayaḥ puṇyā iti viśeṣaṇam

(1) Cf. MESQUITA 2000: 506ff.
(2) The comments of Madhva are original and strange. They differ from other traditional commentaries. While Śaṅkara and Rāmānuja apply *pāpayonayaḥ* as in Gītā (IX 32) only to women, Vaiśyas and Śūdras, Madhva seems to relate the Pratīka also to the third-sex (*tṛtīyā prakṛti*) [eunuchs]. It deals with men who rejected the roles prescribed for them by the society and behave like women (*strīceṣṭitākāra*) as well as to those women who behave like men (*puruṣavat/naraceṣṭitā*); cf. SYED 2003: 64-120; see also BrāṇP 5; 33; 70; GarP 4.

28) KathUBh (p. 484,21-23):
Subject matter: Liberation

sarveṣāṃ jñāninām ātmā devānāṃ ca viśeṣataḥ /
mukto vāyuś ca sādṛśyam eva viṣṇos tu gacchati /
na tu tadrūpatāṃ yāti kimv anye devamānuṣāḥ /
ābhāsābhāsarūpās tu vāyor devasya sarvaśaḥ /
iti bhaviṣyatparvaṇi (1)

(1) Cf. ibid. ll. 19f.: ... *vijānato muner ātmā vāyur api tādṛg eva bhavati / na tu sa eva bhavati / kimv anye jīvāḥ* ... ; AgniP 16; MESQUITA 2003: 105f. and MESQUITA 2000: 495ff.

29) MBhTN (I 30-47):
Subject matter: Pañcamaveda / Syllabus of right and heretical doctrines

ṛgādayaś ca catvāraḥ pañcarātraṃ ca bhāratam /
mūlarāmāyaṇaṃ brahmasūtraṃ mānaṃ svataḥ smṛtam / [30]
aviruddhaṃ ca yat tv asya pramāṇaṃ tac ca nānyathā /
etadviruddhaṃ yat tu syān na tanmānaṃ kathaṃcana / [31]
vaiṣṇavāni purāṇāni pañcarātrātmakatvataḥ /
pramāṇāny eva manvādyāḥ smṛtayo 'py anukūlataḥ / [32]
eteṣu viṣṇor ādhikyam ucyate 'nyasya na kvacit /
atas tad eva mantavyaṃ nānyathā tu kataṃcana / [33]
mohārthāny anyaśāstrāṇi kṛtāny evājñayā hareḥ /
atas teṣūktam agrāhyam asurāṇāṃ tamogateḥ / [34]
yasmāt kṛtāni tānīha viṣṇunoktaiḥ śivādibhiḥ /
eṣāṃ yan na virodhi syāt tatroktaṃ tan na vāryate / [35]
viṣṇvādhikyavirodhīni yāni vedavacāṃsy api /
tāni yojyāny ānukūlyād viṣṇvādhikyasya sarvaśaḥ / [36] (1)
avatāreṣu yat kiṃcit darśayen naravad dhariḥ / (2)
tac cāsurāṇāṃ mohāya doṣā viṣṇor na hi kvacit / [37]
ajñatvaṃ pāravaśyaṃ vā vedhabhedādikaṃ tathā /
tathā prākṛtadehatvaṃ dehatyāgādikaṃ tathā / [38]
anīśatvaṃ ca duḥkhitvaṃ sāmyam anyaiś ca hīnatām /
pradarśayati mohāya daityādīnāṃ hariḥ svayam / [39]
na tasya kaścid doṣo 'sti pūrṇākhilaguṇo hy asau /
sarvadehastharūpeṣu prādurbhāveṣu ceśvaraḥ / [40]
brahmādyabhedaḥ sāmyaṃ vā kutas tasya mahātmanaḥ /
yad evaṃ vācakaṃ śāstraṃ tad dhi śāstraṃ paraṃ matam / [41]
nirṇayāyaiva yat proktaṃ brahmasūtraṃ tu viṣṇunā /
vyāsarūpeṇa tad grāhyaṃ tatroktāḥ sarvanirṇayāḥ / [42]
yathārthavacanānāṃ ca mohārthānāṃ ca saṃśayam /
apanetuṃ hi bhagavān brahmasūtram acīklṛpat / [43]
tasmāt sūtrārtham āgṛhya kartavyaḥ sarvanirṇayaḥ /
sarvadoṣavihīnatvaṃ guṇaiḥ sarvair udīrṇatā / [44]
abhedaḥ sarvarūpeṣu jīvabhedaḥ sadaiva ca /
viṣṇor uktāni sūtreṣu sarvavedeḍyatā tathā / [45]
tāratamyaṃ ca muktānāṃ vimuktir vidyayā tathā /
tasmād etadviruddhaṃ yanmohāya tad udāhṛtam / [46]

tasmād ye ye guṇā viṣṇor grāhyās te sarva eva tu /
ityādyuktaṃ bhagavatā bhaviṣyatparvaṇi *sphuṭam* / [47] (3)

(1) Cf. MESQUITA 2000_1: 164f. [= 1997: 132f.]; see also BhaviṣP 10 and BrāṇP 11.
(2) Cf. BhāgTN p. 837,4-6 (= iti ca unknown source); ĀdiP 1 and MESQUITA 2000_1: 37ff. 153ff. [= 1997: 31ff.; 123ff.].
(3) Cf. BhaviṣPV 3n. 7.

30) MBhTN (I 78-99):
Subject matter: Syllabus of right doctrines

viṣṇur hi dātā mokṣasya vāyuś ca tadanujñayā / (1)
mokṣo jñānaṃ ca kramaśo muktigo bhoga eva ca // [78]
uttareṣāṃ prasādena nīcānāṃ nānyathā bhavet / (2)
sarveṣāṃ ca harir nityaniyantā tadvaśāḥ pare // [79]
tāratamyaṃ tato jñeyaṃ sarvoccatvaṃ hares tathā /
etad vinā na kasyāpi vimuktiḥ syāt kathaṃcana // [80]
pañcabhedāṃś ca vijñāya viṣṇoḥ svābhedam eva ca / (3)
nirdośatvaṃ guṇodrekaṃ jñātvā muktir na cānyathā // [81]
avatārān harer jñatvā nāvatārā hareś ca ye /
tadāveśāṃs tathā samyag jñātvā muktir na cānyathā // [82]
sṛṣṭirakṣāhṛtijñānaniyatyajñānabandhanān /
mokṣaṃ ca viṣṇutas tv eva jñātvā muktir na cānyathā // [83] (4)
vedāṃś ca pañcarātrāṇi setihāsapurāṇakān /
jñātvā viṣṇuparān eva mucyate nānyathā kvacit // [84]
māhātmyajñānapūrvas tu sudṛḍhaḥ sarvato 'dhikaḥ /
sneho bhaktir iti proktas tayā muktir na cānyathā // [85]
trividhā jīvasaṅghās tu devamānuṣadānavāḥ / (5)
tatra devā muktiyogyā mānuṣeṣūttamās tathā / [86]
madhyamā mānuṣā ye tu sṛtiyogyāḥ sadaiva hi /
adhamā nirayāyaiva dānavās tu tamolayāḥ / [87]
muktir nityā tamaś caiva nāvṛttiḥ punar etayoḥ /
devānāṃ nirayo nāsti tamaś cāpi kathaṃcana / [88]
nāsurāṇāṃ tathā muktiḥ kadācit kenacit kvacit /
mānuṣāṇāṃ madhyamānāṃ naivaitad dvayam āpyate / [89]
asurāṇāṃ tamaḥprāptis tadā niyamato bhavet /
yadā tu jñānisadbhāve naiva gṛhṇanti tat param / [90]
tadā muktiś ca devānāṃ yadā pratyakṣago hariḥ /
svayogyayopāsanayā tanvā tadyogyayā tathā / [91]
sarvair guṇair brahmaṇā tu samupāsyo hariḥ sadā / (6)
ānando jñāḥ sadātmeti hy upāsyo mānuṣair hariḥ / [92]
yathākramaṃ guṇodrekāt tadanyair ā viriñcataḥ /

brahmatvayogyā ṛjavo nāma devāḥ pṛthaggaṇāḥ / [93]
tair evāpyaṃ padaṃ tat tu naivānyaiḥ sādhanair api /
evaṃ sarvapadānāṃ ca yogyāḥ santi pṛthag gaṇāḥ / [94]
tasmād anādyanantaṃ hi tāratamyaṃ cidātmanām /
tac ca naivānyathā kartuṃ śakyaṃ kenāpi kutracit / [95]
ayogyam icchan puruṣaḥ pataty eva na saṃśayaḥ /
tasmād yogyānusāreṇa sevyo viṣṇuḥ sadaiva hi / [96]
acchidrasevanāc caiva niṣkāmatvāc ca yogyataḥ /
draṣṭuṃ śakyo hariḥ sarvair nānyathā tu kathaṃcana / [97]
niyamo 'yaṃ harer yasmān nollaṅghyaḥ sarvacetanaiḥ /
satyasaṅkalpato viṣṇur nānyathā ca kariṣyati / [98] (7)
dānatīrthatapoyajñapūrvāḥ sarve 'pi sarvadā / (8)
aṅgāni harisevāyāṃ bhaktis tv ekā vimuktaye /
bhaviṣyatparvavacanam *ity etad akhilaṃ param* / [99] (9)

(1) Cf. AiUBh (p. 181,21; 233,21); MESQUITA 2000_1: 169ff. [= 1997: 137ff.] and MESQUITA 2003: 106ff.
(2) Cf. MESQUITA 2000: 498f.
(3) Cf. BhaviṣPV 1; see also MESQUITA 2000_1: 104ff. [= 1997: 83ff.] and MESQUITA 2003: 429 ff.
(4) Cf. MESQUITA 2000_1: 171n. 348 [= 1997: 139n. 335] and BhaviṣP 1.
(5) Cf. GarP 37 and MESQUITA 2000: 492ff.
(6) Cf. AgniP 20; BhaviṣPV 20.
(7) Cf. MESQUITA 2000: 512n. 673.
(8) Cf. NārP 36 and MESQUITA 2007: 21f. [= 2007_1: 440f.]
(9) Cf. BhaviṣPV 3n. 7.

31) MBhTN (I 127-129):
Subject matter: Jīvanmukti

yadā muktipradānasya svayogyaṃ paśyati dhruvam /
rūpaṃ hares tadā tasya sarvapāpāni bhasmasāt / [127]
yānti pūrvāṇy uttarāṇi na śleṣaṃ yānti kānicit /
mokṣaś ca niyatas tasmāt svayogyaharidarśane / [128]
bhaviṣyatparvavacanam ity etat sūtragaṃ tathā | [129] (1)

(1) Cf. ĀdityaP 1; AgniP 16 and MESQUITA 2007: 32n. 66; 40n. 87 [= 2007_1: 446n. 65; 450n. 86]

32) MBhTN (II 112-123):
Subject matter: Madhva, the third *avatāra* of Vāyu

bhaviṣyatparvagaṃ *cāpi vaco vyāsasya sādaram* /
vāsudevasya mahimā bhārate nirṇayoditaḥ / [112]
tadarthās tu kathāḥ sarvā nānyārthaṃ vaiṣṇavaṃ yaśaḥ /

tatpratīpaṃ tu yad dṛśyen na tan mama manīṣitam / [113]
bhāṣās tu trividhās tatra mayā vai saṃpradarśitāḥ /
ukto yo mahimā viṣṇoḥ sa tūkto hi samādhinā / [114]
śaivadarśanam ālaṃbhya kvacic chaivī kathoditā /
samādhibhāṣayoktaṃ yat tat sarvaṃ grāhyam eva hi / [115]
aviruddhaṃ samādhes tu darśanoktaṃ ca gṛhyate / (1)
ādyantayor viruddhaṃ yad darśanaṃ tad udāhṛtam / [116]
darśanāntarasiddhaṃ ca guhyabhāṣānyathā bhavet /
tasmād viṣṇor hi mahimā bhāratokto yathārthataḥ / [117] (2)
tasyāṅgaṃ prathamaṃ vāyuḥ prādurbhāvatrayānvitaḥ / (3)
prathamo hanumān nāma dvitīyo bhīma eva ca /
pūrṇaprajñas tṛtīyas tu bhagavatkāryasādhakaḥ / [118]
tretādyeṣu yugeṣv eṣa sambhūtaḥ keśavājñayā /
ekaikaśās triṣu pṛthag dvitīyāṅgaṃ sarasvatī / [119]
śaṃrūpe tu rater vāyau śrīr ity eva ca kīrtyate /
saiva ca draupadī nāma kālī candreti cocyate / [120]
tṛtīyāṅgaṃ hareḥ śeṣaḥ prādurbhāvasamanvitaḥ /
prādurbhāvā naraś caiva lakṣmaṇo bala eva ca / [121]
rudrātmakatvāc cheṣasya śuko drauṇiś ca tattanū /
indre narāṃśasaṃpattyā pārtho 'pīṣat tadātmakaḥ / [122]
pradyumnādyās tato viṣṇor aṅgabhūtāḥ krameṇa tu /
caritaṃ vaiṣṇavānāṃ tad viṣṇūdrekāya kathyate / [123]

(1) Cf. BhaviṣPV 29[30-36]; BrahVP 30; see also bhāṣāviveka (untraceable source) BhagTN (p. 767,11-768,3) and MESQUITA 2000_1: 157-164 [= 1997: 127-132].
(2) Cf. MESQUITA 2000: 402ff.
(3) Cf. MESQUITA 2000_1: 46ff. [= 1997: 38ff.] and MESQUITA 2003: 105ff.

Bhaviṣyatpurāṇa (BhaviṣP)

[As the title reveals, this Purāṇa comprises predictions of future events (*bhaviṣya*). Fifteen quotes from it are spread over BhāgTN (eight); BSūBh (six) and BĀUBh (one). Everywhere it appears as Bhaviṣyatpurāṇa, and not in its current designation, namely as Bhaviṣyapurāṇa. Possibly, Madhva has borrowed this title, which actually implies a *contradictio in terminis*, from Āpastambadharmasūtra (cf. ROCHER 1986: 86). The main topic of its untraceable quotes is the supreme being of Viṣṇu and liberation. BhaviṣP 5 not only speaks of 'liberation while still living' as *terminus technicus* but also gives its clear definition. This is the only place where Madhva unambiguously speaks of a *jīvanmukta* (cf. MESQUITA 2007: 10 [= 2007_1: 434]). Surprisingly, the quotes are completely silent on the prophecies, although Pratisargaparvan (III 8,1-12; 19,48-66; 21,61-63) reports on the mythological birth of Madhva:

...
vṛndāvane mahāramye janayiṣye kalau bhaye //
sa dvijaḥ sūryarūpaś ca devakāryaṃ kariṣyati /

mādhvasya dvijasyaiva tanayaḥ sa bhaviṣyati ||
madhur nāma mahābhāgo devamārgaparāyaṇaḥ |
...
madhvācārya iti khyātaḥ prasiddho 'bhūt mahītale |
...

(cf. HAZRA 1987: 169): "The Pratisargaparvan, though nominally mentioned in Bhav[iṣya] I 2,2-3, is practically a new work. It narrates stories about Adam, Noah ... and fabricates myths about the births of Varāhamihira, Śaṅkarācārya, Rāmānuja, Nimbārka, Madhva ... It even knows the British rule in India and names Calcutta and the Parliament (aṣṭa-kauśalya). Thus its contents betray its late composition." See also ROCHER 1986: 151-154 and HOHENBERGER 1967.]

1) BĀUBh (p. 265,18-19):
Subject matter: Liberation

abhedam īśarūpāṇāṃ bhedaṃ jīveśayor api |
yaḥ paśyet sthirayā buddhyā bhaktimān sa vimucyate |
iti bhaviṣyatpurāṇe (1)

(1) Cf. ibid. l. 17: *yadā hy evaiṣa etasminn udaram antaraṃ kurute* (TaiU II 7) *ity atrāpi etasminn iti viśeṣaṇāt svagatabhedaniṣedha eva*; see also AgniP 16 and MESQUITA 2000: 437ff.

2) BhāgTN (p. 119,5-10):
Subject matter: Human body and its birth

aśarīrasya jīvasya śarīrotpattikāraṇam |
īśvarecchā prāthamikā tāṃ vinā na hi kiṃcana | [1] (1)
dvitīyā prakṛtiḥ proktā tadrūpā hi guṇās trayaḥ |
teṣāṃ saṃpātajo bhāvo mamāham iti yā matiḥ | [2]
dehāt parasya dehitvam ahaṃbhāvam ṛte kutaḥ |
yathā rajastamobhāvair vinā svāpno na jāyate | [3]
nidrākāmādyabhāvena tadvad dehaḥ kva tān vinā |
tasmāt prakṛtyaiva pumān mānuṣādivihārayā | [4]
mānuṣādir ivābhāti nityacaitanyarūpavān |
yadā svarūpaṃ jānāti kālaprakṛtivarjitam | [5]
vāsudevaprasādena tadā mukto bhavaty asau | [6ab]
iti bhaviṣyatpurāṇe (2)

(1) Cf. ibid. ll. 3f.: ... *yato bhagavaduktaṃ pramāṇam atas taduktaṃ purāṇaṃ tvatpraśnānām uttaratvena vakṣye* ... ; see also BrāṇP 33 and MESQUITA 2000: 484f.

3) BhāgTN (p. 134,4-5):
Subject matter: Viṣṇu, the Cause of transmigration and liberation

pratiṣedhāya bandhasya jīvānāṃ parameśituḥ /
svecchayaiva tu kartṛtvaṃ nityārūḍhaṃ cidātmakam /
iti bhaviṣyatpurāṇe (1)

(1) Cf. ibid. l. 3: *janmakarmāṇi vidhīyata iti kriyāviśeṣaṇam*; see also BhaviṣPV 22; 30[78]; BrahP 50; 53; KūrP 27; 28; SkaP 70; 81; 116; 121; MESQUITA 2000_1: 171n. 348 [= 1997: 139n. 335] and MESQUITA 2000: 511ff.

4) BhāgTN (p. 207,1-2):
Subject matter: Abode and functions of the released souls

muktāś caivādhikārasthā dvedhā vaikuṇṭhalokagāḥ /
amuktānāṃ bhramaḥ kvāpi na muktānāṃ kvacid bhavet /
iti bhaviṣyatpurāṇe (1)

(1) Cf. AgniP 16; 27; BhaviṣP 4; 5; 15; KūrP 16; VāyuP 1; 2_1; VarP 49 and MESQUITA 2000: 519ff.

5) BhāgTN (p. 280,13-281,4):
Subject matter: Jīvanmukti / Gods and their activities

ābrahmā sthitadhīr jīvanmuktaś cety abhidhīyate /
yas tasya na nivṛttaṃ ca pravṛttaṃ karma ceṣyate /
yat tu devāḥ prakurvanti sa mahāniyamaḥ smṛtaḥ /
svargādyarthaṃ pravṛttaṃ syān nivṛttaṃ muktaye tu yat /
sa mahāniyamo nāma karma yat tv ādhikārikam /
mahato niyamād viṣṇoḥ prītyā muktau sukhonnatiḥ /
kecin nivṛttam ityāhur mahāniyamam apy uta /
iti bhaviṣyatpurāṇe (1)

(1) Cf. ibid. l. 12: *ābrahmaṇi samyagjñānini ...* ; cf. also Gītā (II 54-56):
arjuna uvāca –
sthitaprajñasya kā bhāṣā samādhisthitasya keśava /
sthitadhīḥ kiṃ prabhāṣeta kim āsīta vrajeta kim //
prajahāti yadā kāmān sarvān pārtha manogatān /
ātmany evātmanā tuṣṭaḥ sthitaprajñas tadocyate //
duḥkheṣv anudvignamanā sukheṣu vigataspṛhaḥ /
vītarāgabhayakrodhaḥ sthitadhīr munir ucyate //
cf. also GarP 21; MESQUITA 2007: 8f. [= 2007_1: 434f.]; see also ĀdityaP 1; BhaviṣP 4; 11; BrahP 37; 70; BrāṇP 9; 96; 98; 99; GarP 24; 26_1; 34; KūrP 16; NārP 44; PadP 80; 90; 93; 101; SkaP 53; 62; 69; VāmP 27; VarP 49; VāyuP 1; 2_1.

6) BhāgTN (p. 294,6-8):
Subject matter: Antaryāmin

antaryāmisvarūpeṇa brahmarudrādyabhinnatā /
na tu jīvasvarūpeṇa jīvā bhinnā yato hareḥ /
viśeṣābhedavacanaṃ sannidhānaviśeṣataḥ /
sannidhānaṃ tu tat proktaṃ sāmarthyavyañjanaṃ hareḥ /
iti bhaviṣyatpurāṇe (1)

(1) Cf. ibid. n. 5: *atra* vīrarāghavo *'py āha – aham eka eva maccharīrabhūtabrahmarudrākhyajīvānupraveśena jagat sṛjāmi saṃharāmi svāvatārarūpeṇa pālayāmi*; see also AgniP 6; BhāgP 2 and MESQUITA 2000: 162n. 333; 226n. 493; 489f.

7) BhāgTN (p. 311,13-312,4):
Subject matter: Demons

ahaṃ brahmeti venas tu dhyāyan nāpādharaṃ tamaḥ /
tadrāddhānto mahīṃ vyāpto bheryā khyāpayato 'niśam /
asurā rākṣaśāś caiva piśācās tatpathi sthitāḥ /
bhūmau tat pṛthunā sarvaṃ nirastaṃ mahitātmanā /
punaḥ kaliyuge prāpta aṣṭāviṃśatime manoḥ /
vaivasvatasya samaye jātāḥ krodavaśā bhuvi /
khyāpayanti durātmāno maṇimāṃs tatpuraḥsaraḥ /
iti bhaviṣyatpurāṇe (1)

(1) This untraceable quote has no relation whatever to the basic text. This fact is confirmed also by the editor who remarks that Madhva is using here other sources (n. 8): *mūle 'vyaktam anuktaṃ ca venasaṃbandhaṃ prameyajātaṃ bhāṣyakāraḥ pramāṇāntareṇa saṅgṛhṇāti*; see also BhaviṣPV 12 and BrāṇP 42.

8) BhāgTN (p. 523,7-8):
Subject matter: True knowledge of Viṣṇu / Liberation

bhagavaddarśanād yasya virodhād darśanaṃ pṛthak /
pṛthagdṛṣṭiḥ (1) *sa vijñeyo na tu sadbhedadarśanaḥ /*
iti bhaviṣyatpurāṇe (2)

(1) Cf. ibid. n. 2: *bhagavaddarśanād yasya darśanaṃ pṛthag anyādṛśam / kutaḥ virodhāt / tathā ca ayathāvaddarśanaṃ pṛthagdṛśiḥ / taddarśino viparītajñāḥ pṛthagdṛśaḥ / na hi santaṃ bhedaṃ yathāvat paśyan pṛthagdṛṣṭir bhavati.*
(2) Cf. the following untraceable iti ca-quote:

svarūpabhedo hi parajīvayor jīvago mithaḥ /
paraspareṇa vastūnāṃ viśeṣaḥ śāstradarśitaḥ /
sadbhedo 'yaṃ samuddiṣṭhas tv asadbhedaṃ ca me śṛṇu /
svarūpāṇāṃ guṇānāṃ ca viṣṇor bhedaḥ parasparāt /
sarvasyāviṣṇutantratvaṃ śatrumitrādibheditā /
yac cānyac chāstravidviṣṭam asadbhedaḥ sa īritaḥ /
sadbhedadarśanān mokṣas tv asadbhedāt tamo vrajet /

sadbhedādarśanāc caiva tamo mokṣas tathetarāt /
iti ca;
see also AgniP 1; 16; 24; BrāṇP 10; MESQUITA 2000_1: 169ff.;104-126 [= 1997: 137ff.; 84-101] and MESQUITA 2000: 429ff.

9) BhāgTN (p. 637,3-5):
Subject matter: Kṛṣṇa-Avatāra

vatsarāṇāṃ śataṃ caiva ṛtūnāṃ pañcaviṃśakam /
avatīrṇasya kṛṣṇasya yadā prāgāt tadā harim /
svasthānagamanāpekṣī brahmā tuṣṭāva sāmaraḥ /
saṃvatsaradvayaṃ caiva paścāt sthitvā janārdanaḥ /
abhipede paraṃ sthānaṃ caturmāsādhikaṃ punaḥ /
iti bhaviṣyatpurāṇe (1)

(1) Cf. ĀdiP 1; AgniP 27.

10) BSūBh (p. 60,3-8):
Subject matter: Pañcamaveda / Svataḥprāmāṇya

bhaviṣyatpurāṇe ca –
ṛgyajuḥsāmātharvākhyā mūlarāmāyaṇaṃ tathā /
bhārataṃ pañcarātraṃ ca vedā ity eva śabditāḥ /
purāṇāni ca yānīha vaiṣṇavāni vido viduḥ /
svataḥ prāmāṇyam eteṣāṃ nātra kiṃcid vicāryate /
yady eṣūktaṃ na dṛśyeta pūrvakarmātra kāraṇam /
nāprāmāṇyaṃ bhaved eṣāṃ dṛśyate hy adhikārataḥ /
itaḥ prāmāṇyam anyeṣāṃ na svatas tu kathaṃcana /
adṛśyoktau tatas teṣām aprāmāṇyaṃ na saṃśayaḥ /
iti (1)

(1) Cf. ibid. p. 59,3f.: *naivaṃ śrutes tadanusārismṛteś ca taduktānupalabdher aprāmāṇyam / vilakṣaṇatvāt / nityatvāt / tadanusāritvāc ca / na hi nitye doṣaḥ kalpyāḥ / svataś ca prāmāṇyam / anyathānavasthiteḥ ... adhikāriṇāṃ phalam ...* ; see also BrāṇP 104; KūrP 30_2; NārP 30; SkaP 99; 108; 126; UpanārP 1 and BrāṇP 11; MESQUITA 2000_1: 131ff.; 159f. [= 1997: 105ff.; 128f.] and MESQUITA 2000: 378ff.

11) BSūBh (p. 62,7-9):
Subject matter: Presiding Deities

bhaviṣyatpurāṇe ca –
pṛthivyādyabhimāninyo devatāḥ prathitaujasaḥ /
acintyāḥ śaktayas tāsāṃ dṛśyante munibhiś ca tāḥ /
tāś ca sarvagatā nityaṃ vāsudevaikasaṃśrayāḥ /
iti (1)

(1) Cf. ibid. l. 4f.: *mṛdādyabhimānidevatā tatra vyapadiśyate / tāsāṃ cetarebhyo viśiṣṭaṃ sāmarthyam anugatiś ca sarvatra / atas tāsāṃ sarvam uktaṃ yujyate ... tāsāṃ sāmarthyaṃ mahadbhiḥ* ... ; see also BhavişP 5; BrahP 20; 38; 67; 82; BrahVP 37; BrāṇP 1; 9; 13; 41; 83; 104[7]; GarP 57; NārP 1; 2; 47; PadP 22; 28; SkaP 102; VāmP 2; 17; 20.

12) BSūBh (p. 70,14-16):
Subject matter: Requital for good or evil deeds / Viṣṇu, the supreme All-creator

bhaviṣyatpurāṇe ca –
puṇyapāpādikaṃ viṣṇuḥ kārayet pūrvakarmaṇā /
anāditvāt karmaṇaś ca na virodhaḥ kataṃcana /
iti (1)

(1) Cf. ibid. l. 14 ... *tasyāpi pūrvaṃ karma kāraṇam ity anāditvāt karmaṇaḥ* ... ; BhaviṣPV 16; BrāṇP 100; MBh 15; SkaP 123; see also AgniP 12 and BhaviṣP 12.

13) BSūBh (p. 94,25-26):
Subject matter: Viṣṇu's unconceivable almighty power (*acintyaśakti / līlā*)

kartā sarvasya vai viṣṇur eka eva na saṃśayaḥ /
itareṣāṃ tu sattādyā yata eva tadājñāyā /
iti ca bhaviṣyatpurāṇe (1)

(1) Cf. ibid. l. 22f.: *brahmaivedam agra āsīt tadāpo 'sṛjata tad idaṃ sarvam iti śruter agner āpa ity ukte 'pi brahmaṇa evāpādisṛṣṭiḥ* ... ; BrahVP 20; BrāṇP 8; HarV 33; MatsyaP 14; NārP 42; PadP 65;79; SkaP 12; 50; 78; VāmP 39; VarP 19; ViṣṇP 3; see also AgniP 12; BrāṇP 69 and MESQUITA 2000: 188n. 390; 460n. 579-581; 484f.

14) BSūBh (p. 98,13-14):
Subject matter: Viṣṇu, the supreme meaning of the Vedas / Sarvanāmatva

ekaśabdaiś dviśabdaiś ca bahuśabdaiś ca keśavaḥ /
eka evocyate vedais tāvatā nāsya bhinnatā /
iti ca bhaviṣyatpurāṇe (1)

(1) Cf. BrāṇP 2; 82 and MESQUITA 2000: 227n. 493.

15) BSūBh (p. 221,12-14):
Subject matter: Bliss in liberation

bhaviṣyatpurāṇe ca –
muktāḥ prāpya paraṃ viṣṇuṃ tadbhogān leśataḥ kvacit /

bahiṣṭhān bhuñjate nityaṃ nānandādīn kathaṃcana /
iti (1)

(1) Cf. BSūBh (p. 221,9): *ye bhogāḥ paramātmanā bhujyante ta eva muktair bhujyante* ... ; see also BrahVP 29; BrāṇP 28; 48[3]; HarV 2; KūrP 30; NārP 37; PadP 95; 103; SkaP 2; 8; SkaP 2, 8; VarP 42; 57; VāyuP 1; 2_1 and MESQUITA 2000: 522f.

Brahmāṇḍapurāṇa (BrāṇP)

[BrāṇP and VāyuP were originally to a large extent identical, and they took their individual shape only at a later date. Even as separate Purāṇas their contents remained the same. In almost all the lists of Mahāpurāṇas, the BrāṇP is assigned, though it is one of the oldest of the extant Purāṇas, to the eighteenth place (cf. ROCHER 1986: 156-160; HAZRA 1987: 17f.). In Madhva's works, BrāṇP with 107 quotes stands close to the SkaP with 132 quotes and PadP with 110 quotes and find an important place after Brahmatarka and Bhaviṣyatparvan. The 107 different quotes from the BrāṇP are to be found in AiUBh (seven times); BĀUBh (thirtheen times); BhāgTN (fortyfive times); BSūBh (sixteen times); ChUBh (four times); GīT (four times); ĪśuBh (three times); KathUBh (once); MBhTN (three times); MāṇUBh (once); MuUBh (twice); NyāV (once); RgBh (once); TaiUBh (once); Vāda (once); VTN (four times). These quotes are sometimes very extensive, and they render all the typical doctrines of Madhva exactly as the two above mentioned fictitious works, Brahmatarka and Bhaviṣyatparvan. Only half a Śloka BrāṇP III 4,55ab: *niruktam asya yo veda sarvapapaiḥ pramucyate* (= GīT p. 1,15-16; MBhTN II 10cd = MBh I 1,209) could be indentified. In MBhTN I 48-50ab Madhva attributes to BrāṇP two verses found in VārP 70 35f.: *iti vārāhavacanaṃ brahmāṇḍoktaṃ tathāparam*, which are not traceable in that Purāṇa. But in BSūBh (p. 7,12f.) and in GīBh (p. 35,22-24; MBhTN XX 152-153) Madhva ascribes these Ślokas exclusively to VārP (see also MESQUITA 2000_1: 153f. [= 1997: 123f.]). For the composition of BrāṇP 3, Madhva seems to have used BrāṇP II 47,45-52ab as literary basis. It is interesting to note that in BrāṇP 12 Madhva refers to a section of this Purāṇa dealing with doctrines and heresies, namely Tattvanirṇayagītā.

The verses are throughout epic Ślokas. Sometimes, even the reference at the end of the quotation (cf. BṛāṇP 94[3ab]; 95; 96; 101; see also BhāviṣPV 29; 30; and 32[112ab]) is arranged in Śloka-metre. BrāṇP 57[3]), however, has a triṣṭubh metre. There are a few metrical lapses v.g. BrāṇP 3[3cd]; 9[2ab]; 12[7ab]; 18ab; 48[6cd]; 64[7ab] and 3[29ab]. BrāṇP 96 has two different metres, Upajāti and Indravajrā, and 96 [1c] has a surplus syllable. The *pādas* of BrāṇP 100 with eleven syllables each are difficult to assign to any particular metre. BrāṇP 99 has also some metrical irregularities.]

1) AiUBh (p. 176,28-30):
Subject matter: Specific activities of the Deities with regard to the human beings

mānuṣāṇāṃ tu yat karma na devotpattikāraṇam /
daivatair upakāras tu kriyate narakarmaṇā /

devānāṃ karmaṇaivaite jāyante sarvamānuṣāḥ /
pradhānatvān na devānāṃ nṛkarmotpattikāraṇam /
iti ca brahmāṇḍe (1)

(1) Cf. BhaviṣP 5; 11.

2) AiUBh (p. 181,13-19):
Subject matter: Viṣṇu's Sarvanāmatva

dvāu ātmānau hi vedeṣu dvau prāṇau dvau ca cetanau /
ajñānābhibhavāspṛṣṭau vāyur nārāyaṇaś ca tau / [1]
tadanye cetanāḥ sarve prāṇāś cātmāna eva ca /
ajñānābhibhavaspṛṣṭās tasmāt te hy adhamāḥ śrutāḥ / [2]
madhyamo vāyur evaika uttamaḥ kevalo hariḥ /
sarvaśabdoditau tasmād etau dvāv eva nāparaḥ / [3]
anye caiva mitaiḥ śabdair ucyante nāmitaiḥ kvacit /
śrīr apy akhilaśabdoktā viṣṇuvan na tu mukhyataḥ / [4]
tasmād amitanāmānāv api tau mitanāmavat /
śrīś ca vāyuś ca viṣṇus tu mukyokter amitābhidhaḥ / [5]
anantanāmakatvāc ca so 'nantaguṇa īritaḥ /
pṛthaṇnāmāni yasmāt tadguṇān eva pracakṣate / [6]
ityādi brahmāṇḍe (1)

(1) Cf. ibid. ll. 11f.: ... (BĀU II 2,1) *vāyor viśeṣaṇād uttamaḥ prāṇo viṣṇur iti ca siddham* ... ; see also Gī XV 16f.; AgniP 25; BrahVP 23; BrāṇP 3; 25; KūrP 21; 22; MBh 2; MatsyaP 12; PadP 34; 52; 57; 91; SkaP 31; 71; 86; VāmP 35; 37; MESQUITA 2000: 162ff.; 227f. and MESQUITA 2003: 108n. 27.

3) AiUBh (p. 181,23+182,30):
Subject matter: Viṣṇu's Sarvanāmatva / Viṣṇu, the Antaryāmin

vṛtraṃ hatvā purendras tu mahendratvābhipattaye /
mahāvrataṃ karma cakre hautraṃ cakre 'tra kauśikaḥ / [1] (1)
bhṛgur adhvaryur abhavad brahmā brahmābhavat svayam /
udgātā vāyur abhavat svayaṃ nārāyaṇaḥ prabhuḥ / [2]
sādasyam akarot tatra tadanye 'nye 'pi cartvijaḥ / (2)
bṛhatīsahasraṃ śaṃsiṣyan yadā sasmāra keśavam / [3] + 1
vāyunā saha deveśas tadā vāsavam āviśat /
āviṣṭo viṣṇunāthendro vāyunā saha kauśikam / [4]
śaṃsety uktvā niṣaṇṇo 'bhūd idam annaṃ taveti saḥ /
ṛksāhasraṃ śaśaṃsātra yajñāṅgatvena bhaktitaḥ / [5]
tacchrutvā tuṣṭim agamat keśavo vāyusaṃyutaḥ /
dvitīyavāraṃ śaṃseti prāha taṃ ca janārdanaḥ / [6]

prītyaiva śakram āviṣṭo viśvāmitraḥ śaśaṃsa tat /
atipriyatvād bhagavān punar apy āha kauśikam / [7]
tṛtīyaṃ ca śaśaṃsāsau viṣṇor annaṃ prakalpya tat /
tato 'tituṣṭo bhagavān dadāni varam ity amum / [8]
ūce sa prathame tv eva nijasālokyam īśvaraḥ /
prādād dvitīye sāmīpyaṃ tṛtīye punar eva ca / [9]
varaṃ dadānīty uktaḥ san muniḥ prāha janārdanam /
samyak tvām eva jānīyām iti mokṣe sukhoccatām / [10]
icchaṃs taṃ prāha bhagavān indrastho vāyusaṃyutaḥ /
sarvanāmāham asmy eka iti jñānaṃ mamottamam / [11]
yasmāt sarvaguṇatvaṃ syāt sarvanāmatva eva tu /
na hi doṣābhidhāyīni viṣṇor nāmāni kānicit / [12]
adoṣatvān mahāviṣṇor na sāmānyavacāṃsy api /
sarvottamaguṇātmatvāt sadā nārāyaṇasya hi / [13]
sarvottamaguṇān eva nāmāny ācakṣate hareḥ /
yāvaj jñānena mokṣaḥ syāt tāvaj jñātvāpi kauśikaḥ / [14]
adhikajñānalabdhyarthaṃ mokṣe 'dhikasukhāptaye /
jānīyāṃ tvām iti prāha tasmā āha sa keśavaḥ / [15]
indrāviṣṭaḥ prāṇanāma tathānyāś cābhidhāḥ prabhuḥ /
prakṛṣṭānandarūpatvāt prāṇa ity abhidhīyate / [16]
aheyatvād ahaṃnāmāsmy asanān minuter api /
tato vetteti ca tvaṃ sa pūrṇatvāt sarvanāmakaḥ / [17] (3)
sarvāṇi bahurūpatvāt sarvarūpeṣu pūrtitaḥ /
prabhūtatvād bhūtānāmā sarvarūpaprabhūtataḥ / [18]
bahurūpaḥ sa bhūtānīty ukto viṣṇuḥ sanātanaḥ /
sarvaiśvaryasvarūpatvād eṣa ity abhidhīyate / [19]
sa eva sūryasaṃsthaḥ san lokaṃ tapati kesavaḥ /
sarvanāmavatas tasya mamānnaṃ mitram ucyate / [20]
annābhimāninī sākṣāc chrīr eva pramadottamā /
sānnam ity ucyate viṣṇor bhogyatvān mitram eva ca / [21]
dakṣabhāgasthitenatvād dakṣiṇaṃ nāma socyate /
tasyā ino hi viṣṇuḥ sa dakṣabhāge sthitaḥ sadā / [22] (4)
yasyābhimāniny annasya lakṣmīḥ sā devatottamā /
vaiśvāmitraṃ tadannaṃ tu ṛksahasrātmakaṃ matam / [23]
viśvāmitreṇa dṛṣṭatvād vaiśvāmitraṃ tadīryate /
indrāviṣṭaḥ ko 'yam iti śaṅkāṃ pariharan hariḥ / [24]
ādityasaṃsthito viṣṇus tapann asmīti cocivān /
tvāṃ jānīyām iti praśnaṃ viśvāmitrasya kurvataḥ / [25]
abhiprāyadvayaṃ hy asti śakrāviṣṭo na cāparaḥ /
harer iti tu me tarkas tejobāhulyato 'janiḥ / [26]
tasya tarkasya satyatvaṃ jñātavyaṃ prathamaṃ mama /

dvitīyaṃ yadi viṣṇuḥ syāj jñātavyo me viśeṣataḥ / [27]
ity abhiprāyam asyaiva jñātvā viṣṇuḥ sanātanaḥ /
abhiprāyadvayasyāpi parihāraṃ harir dadau / [28]
prāṇo vāham ityādi nāmasandarbham uktavān / -1
viśeṣajñānasiddhyarthaṃ nāmnām uktiḥ parātmanaḥ / [29]
indrāviṣṭaḥ ko 'yam iti śaṅkānuttyartham eva ca /
tapann evāsmīty avadat tapantaṃ veda so 'pi hi / [30]
nārāyaṇaṃ sūryagataṃ gāyatryopāsako hi saḥ / [31ab]
ityādi brahmāṇḍe (5)

(1) Cf. AgniP 10.
(2) Cf. BrāṇP II 3, 47,45-52ab:
tatas teṣām anumate munīnāṃ bhāvitātmanām /
hayamedhaṃ mahāyajñam āhartum upacakrame /
saṃbhritya sarvasaṃbhārānair vādyaiḥ sahito nṛpa /
viśvāmitrabharadvājamārkaṇḍeyādibhis tathā /
teṣām anumate kṛtvā kāśyapaṃ gurum ātmanaḥ /
vājimedhaṃ tato rājann ājahāra mahākratum /
tasyābhūt kāśyapo 'dhvaryur udgātā gautamo muniḥ /
viśvāmitro 'bhavad dhotā rāmasya viditātmanaḥ /
brahmatvam akarot tasya mārkaṇḍeyo mahāmuniḥ /
bharadvājāgniveśyādyā vedavedāṅgapāragāḥ /
munayaś cakrur anyāni karmāṇy anye yathākramam /
putraiḥ śiṣyaiḥ praśiṣyaiś ca sahito bhagavān bhṛguḥ /
sādasyam akarod rājann anyaiś ca munibhiḥ saha /
sa taiḥ sahākhilaṃ karma samāpya bhṛgupuṃgavaḥ /
brahmāṇaṃ pūjayāmāsa yathāvad guruṇā saha /
(3) Cf. GiT (p. 15,10f.):
aheyatvād ahaṃnāmā bhagavān harir avyayaḥ /
brahmāsau guṇapūrṇatvād asmy asāv asanān miteḥ /
asanād asināmāsau tejastvāt tvam itīritaḥ /
sarvaiḥ kriyāpadaiś caiva sarvair dravyapadair api /
sarvaguṇapadaiś caiva vācya eko hariḥ svayam /
yuṣmatpadaiḥ prātiyogyāt tadyutaiś ca kriyāpadaiḥ /
asmatpadair āntaratvāt kriyārthaiś ca tad anvayaiḥ /
parokṣatvāt tatpadaiś ca mukhyavācyaḥ sa eva tu /
[iti];
see also BĀUBh (p. 25f.): ... *ata ahaṃ brahmāsmītyādiṣv apy ahaṃśabdo 'heyavācīti siddham / anyathā katham ahaṃ vijānātīti yujyeta / etāvad vijñātuḥ paramātmano vijñānādikam evaṃ hy amṛtatvaṃ mokṣaḥ*; also AiUBh (p. 189,14f.) and MESQUITA 2000: 162ff; 425n. 492: *aheyam guṇabṛṃhitaṃ sarvadāsti meyam*; and ibid. 455ff.; PANDURANGI (Bāu), p. 51: *aham – aheyaṃ sarvaniyantṛtayā sarvagatvena ca kenāpi hātum aśakyam, brahma – pūrṇam, asmi – astīti meyaṃ jñeyam ity ātmanam avet*; (PANDURANGI 1989: 65f): ... *asanāt doṣādinirasanāt minuter jñānāc ca asmi nāmā, tattvād vetṛtvāt tvaṃ nāmā, pūrṇatvāt sarvanāmakaḥ, sarvarūpeṣu prabhūtatvād bhūtāni, sarvaiśvaryasvarūpatvād eṣanāmā.*
(4) Cf. HarV 1.

(5) Cf. ibid. ll. 21f.: *tasmād bṛhatīsahasraṃ sarvaṃ mukhyato nārāyaṇasyānnam / tadājñayā vāyoś ca / tasmāt tacchaṃsanena bhagavān vāyuś cātiprīta iti darśayati – viśvāmitraṃ hy etad ahar ityādinā*; see also BhāgP 2; BhavişPV 3n. 2; BrāṇP 2; GarP 1; 2.

4) AiUBh (p. 203,18-19):
Subject matter: Ātman, Viṣṇu's specific appellation

ātmaśabdaḥ pare viṣṇau nānyatra kvacid iṣyate / (1)
guṇapūrtyabhidhāyī sa nānyasya guṇapūrṇatā /
amukhyātmāna evāto brahmādyāḥ sarva eva hi /
ityādi ca brāhmāṇḍe (2)

(1) metri causa *pare* for *parasmin*!
(2) Cf. ibid. ll. 14f.: ... *na ca laukikastrīpuruṣasaṃbandhamātram atrocyate / aprastutvāt tasya / bhagavān eva hy atra prastutaḥ / asāv ātmety* (MaitrāyaṇyU V 5) *ātmaśabdāc ca bhagavān eveti jñāyate* ... ; Anuv *ad* BSū IV 1,5; see also BhāgP 1; BrahVP 19 and MESQUITA 2000: 142n. 279.

5) AiUBh (p. 207,26-27):
Subject matter: Viṣṇu's Strīpuṃrūpa

strīpuṃrūpadvayī viṣṇor na tṛtīyaṃ kathaṃcana /
sākṣān napuṃsakas tasmān muktibhāgī na tu kvacit /
iti ca brahmāṇḍe (1)

(1) Cf. ibid. ll. 23f.: *na ca napuṃsakarūpaṃ bhagavataḥ kutracid uktam / prasiddham eva ca rūpadvayam / ato napuṃsake vadann api na vadatīti na tadvad anuṣajjate / napuṃsakarūpe pramāṇābhāvād eva / laukikastrīpuṃvilakṣaṇatvād astrīpumān ity api vadann iti bhavati ... napuṃsakaśabdamātreṇa rāvaṇādayo napuṃsakā bhavanti* ... ; on 'third-sex' cf. SYED 2003: 64-120, pp. 100f.: Die göttliche Zweigeschlechtlichkeit; see also BhavişPV 27n. 2; BrāṇP 70; GarP 4.

6) AiUBh (p. 220,19-22):
Subject matter: Liberation – Videhamukti

anārabdhaphalānāṃ ca prārabdhānāṃ ca sarvaśaḥ /
karmaṇāṃ dāha evāyaṃ muktir ity abhidhīyate /
sa tu muktas tato dehād udgacchati parātmanā /
prerito viṣṇulokaṃ ca prāpya bhogān avāpya ca /
bhuṅkte viṣṇuprasādena na viṣṇor avaśaḥ kvacit /
viṣṇutantrā ime sarve muktā api yato 'khilāḥ /
iti brahmāṇḍe (1)

(1) Cf. AgniP 16 and AgniP 27; see also MESQUITA 2007: 12n. 15; 41n. 89 [= 2007_1: 435n. 15; 450n. 88].

7) AiUBh (p. 238,16-17):
Subject matter: Dream as cause of death

bṛhattaraṃ madhu yadi sahāpūpaṃ prabhakṣayet /
svapne tasyācirān mṛtyū raktābje vā śirodhṛte /
iti brahmāṇḍe (1)

(1) Cf. BrahVP 27; BrāṇP 7; 74; 97; GarP 54; MārkP 3; PadP 54; VarP 23; 40; 58 and MESQUITA 2000: 202; 250n. 27.

8) BĀUBh (p. 246,22-26):
Subject matter: Viṣṇu, the supreme Creator of the universe

aichad viṣṇur adehaḥ san dehavān syām iti prabhuḥ /
yato deha idaṃ sarvaṃ tasya viṣṇor adehinaḥ /
tadvaśatvāt svayaṃ devaś cidānandaśarīrakaḥ / (1)
so 'tmānam arcann acarad apsṛṣṭyarthaṃ janārdanaḥ /
yat kurvan yat sṛjed īśas tad bhaved dhi tadātmakam /
ato 'rcato yato jātā āpo 'to 'rcanasādhanāḥ /
anyathākartum īśo 'pi krīḍayā tattadātmakam /
kartuṃ tattatpravṛttiḥ saṃs tat karoti svayaṃ prabhuḥ /
iti brahmāṇḍe (2)

(1) Cf. VarP 55; MESQUITA 2000_1: 39nn. 48-49 [= 1997: 32nn. 40-41.]
(2) Cf. ibid. ll. 19f.: *tat tata eva mano 'kuruta yataḥ svayam evāsīn nānyat / ātmavān syām ity aicchat / śarīravān syām iti / apsṛṣṭyarthaṃ mano 'kuruta* ... ; see also AgniP 12 and MESQUITA 2000: 485ff.

9) BĀUBh (p. 259,19-260,9):
Subject matter: Creation / Presiding Deities / path of liberation

tejo'bhimānavān brahmā vāyuś cābabhimānavān /
rudraḥ kṣityabhimānī cāpy etanmayam idaṃ jagat / [1]
abhimanyamānasahitās traya ete 'bhimāninaḥ / +1
viṣṇor jātāḥ krameṇaiva pūrvasmād uttarottaram / [2]
tejo 'bannābhidhā tasmād eṣām eva prakīrtitā /
ete ca trīṇi rūpāṇīty abhidhāgocarāḥ surāḥ / [3]
brahmavāyugirīśebhyas tebhyo jātam idaṃ jagat /
ato 'gnisūryasomānām api rūpaṃ tadudbhavam / [4]
ato 'gnisūryasomānāṃ nāmāpy eṣāṃ prakīrtitam /
sādanād yamanāc caiva satyam eṣāṃ trayaḥ surāḥ / [5]
teṣāṃ satyaṃ hariḥ sākṣād yatas teṣāṃ niyāmakaḥ /
pradhāne satyaśabdo 'yaṃ śrutibhiḥ samudāhṛtaḥ / [6]
yathaiva sarvalohānāṃ pradhānaṃ kāṃcanaṃ smṛtam /

yathā mṛtpiṇḍasadṛśā mṛnmayāḥ sarva eva ca / [7]
yathā kārṣṇāyasaṃ sarvaṃ samaṃ kārṣṇāyasāntare /
evaṃ sarvasya jagataḥ sadṛśaḥ śreṣṭha eva ca / [8] (1)
haris tena tu tajjñānāj jagaj jñātam ivākhilam /
sa sraṣṭā caiva saṃhartā niyantā rakṣitā hariḥ / [9]
tena vyāptam idaṃ sarvam aitadātmyam ato viduḥ /
sa ātmā pūrṇaguṇataḥ sa sūkṣmaḥ sarvagaḥ sadā / [10]
sarvottamatvāt satyaṃ tajjīvābhinnaṃ tadāsurāḥ / (2)
vidur na tvaṃ tathā viddhi śvetaketo kadācana / [11]
kiṃtu viṣṇuḥ pṛthak sarvadevadeveśvaraḥ prabhuḥ /
pṛthag evāham atyalpaśaktijñānasukhādikaḥ / [12] (3)
ity eva viddhi satatam ato mokṣam avāpsyasi /
sarvottama iti jñāto viṣṇur mokṣam imaṃ nayet / [13]
jīvarūpatayā jñātas tamo 'dhaṃ prāpayet prabhuḥ /
viṣṇor dāsatayā viṣṇoḥ sāmīpyaṃ mokṣa ucyate / [14] (4)
na viṣṇutvaṃ tu mokṣaḥ syād eṣo 'ham iti cāsmṛteḥ /
saṃsārasāgarāt tīrṇo mukto 'ham iti cāsmṛtiḥ / [15]
yadā tadā vimokṣeṇa kiṃ phalaṃ jñānino bhavet /
yathā madhukarair nānāvidhapuṣparasaḥ saha / [16]
madhutvaṃ prāpitaḥ saṃvidabhāvān na sukhī bhavet /
yathā nadyo na muktā hi samudraṃ prāpitā api / [17]
iyam asmīti cājñānād yathā supto na mucyate /
pralaye 'pi hariṃ prāptaḥ pṛthaktvajñānavarjanāt / [18]
evaṃ jīveśayor bhedajñānād viṣṇoḥ sadocyatām /
jñātvaiva mucyate tasmād evaṃ jānīhi putraka / [19]
ityādi brahmāṇḍe (5)

(1) Cf. MESQUITA 2000: 147ff.; 475f.
(2) Cf. ibid. p. 528f.
(3) Cf. BrāṇP 61; SkaP 67; ViṣP 4; MESQUITA 2000: 166-168; 371f.
(4) Cf. MESQUITA 2000: 175n. 365 and p. 524f.
(5) Cf. ibid. l. 17: *sṛṣṭikathanaṃ ca prādhānyārtham / trīṇi rūpāṇīty eva satyam ity api prādhānyārtham eva abhimānidevatāpekṣayā* ... ; see also BhaviṣP 5; 11.

10) BĀUBh (p. 264,23-24):
Subject matter: Indivisibility of Viṣṇu's nature

bhedena darśanād vāpi bhedābhedena darśanāt /
viṣṇor guṇānāṃ rūpāṇāṃ tadaṅgānāṃ mukhādinām /
tathā darśanakālāt tu kṣipram eva tamo vrajet /
iti brahmāṇḍe (1)

(1) Cf. ibid. ll. 20f.: *svagatabhedāvivakṣāyām iheti viśeṣaṇaṃ vyarthaṃ syāt nān eveti bhedābhedanirākaraṇārtham ... parvateṣu durge parvatāgre vṛṣṭaṃ yathādho vidhāvati evaṃ pṛthag dṛṣṭān dharmān anv eva tadanantaram evādho 'ndhe tamasi vidhāvati* ... ; see also BhavisP 8; BrahP 71; GarP 13; 43; MatsyaP 17; NārP 27; PadP 99; SkaP 58; VarP 51; MESQUITA 2000_1: 35f.;121f. [= 1997: 29f.; 97f.] and MESQUITA 2000: 429ff.

11) BĀUBh (p. 268,17-18):
Subject matter: Sadāgamas/Durāgamas

viṣṇoḥ sarvottamatvasya jñānārthaṃ śāstram iṣyate /
atas tatsādhakaṃ śāstraṃ duḥśāstraṃ tadvirodhi yat /
iti brahmāṇḍe (1)

(1) Cf. BhavisPV 2; 29; BhavisP 10; BrāṇP 21; 82; 94; 103_1; 104; GarP 50; NārP 34; 48; 58; PadP 2; 3; SkaP 126; VarP 24; 30; 61; 62; MESQUITA 2000_1: 126f. [= 1997: 101ff.] and MESQUITA 2000: 378ff.

12) BĀUBh (p. 273,2+274,11):
Subject matter: Syllabus of all right and heretical doctrines

tiryaṅmānuṣadevādiviṣṇurūpeṣv aśaktatā /
yasmin kasmiṃś ca viṣaye duḥkhitvaṃ bhinnatāpi vā / [1]
prakṛter vikāratā vāpi cchedabhedavraṇādi vā / + 1
ajñānaṃ nāśitā vāpi janma jīvair abhinnatā / [2]
prakṛtyabhinnatā vāpi jīvābhedaḥ parasparam /
jaḍābhedo 'thavā viṣṇor mithyātvaṃ jagato 'pi vā / [3] (1)
aguṇatvam adehatvam akartṛtvaṃ tathā hareḥ / (2)
samyagbhaktim ṛte muktir viṣṇau taddveṣatas tathā / [4] (3)
muktāv abhogo jīvānāṃ muktau sāmyaṃ tathaiva ca /
arūpatvaṃ ca jīvānāṃ muktānāṃ bandhinām api / [5]
nāmatīrthādibhir muktis tattvajñānaṃ vināpi tu / (4)
viṣṇoḥ sakāśāt prakṛter brahmaṇo 'nantarudrayoḥ / [6]
garuḍendrasūryavighnāder agnisomaguhādinām / +1
pradyumnasyāniruddhasya devaviprādinām api / [7]
yaiḥ kaiś cāpi guṇair viṣṇoḥ sakāśād varatā tathā /
yadā kadāpi yatnair vā varaśāpādināpi vā / [8]
tapasā vāpy upāyair vā yogajñānādināpi vā /
sāmyaṃ vā viṣṇvadhīnatvād anyathaiṣāṃ sthitiḥ kṛtiḥ / [9]
asaṃsāritvam eṣāṃ cāpy eṣām īśvaratāpi vā /
vinā viṣṇuprasādena muktir eṣāṃ sakāśataḥ / [10]
viṣṇoḥ prayojanāvāptir viṣṇor doṣaś ca kaścana /
viṣṇoḥ sarveṣu rūpeṣu saṃpūrṇaguṇahīnatā / [11]
bhedo vā viṣṇurūpeṣu viśeṣo vā guṇeṣu ca /

śriyaḥ sakāśād ādhikyaṃ brahmādeḥ sāmyam eva vā / [12]
brahmavāyvor anantasya rudrasya garuḍasya ca /
tebhyaś caivendrasūryāder viprabhūpādināṃ tataḥ / [13]
baddhānāṃ muktigānāṃ vā daityāder mokṣa eva ca /
sarvaṃ mohārtham uddiṣṭaṃ vedeṣu hariṇāpi vā / [14]
brahmaṇā vātha rudreṇa devaiś ca munibhis tathā /
yathā surāṇāṃ sujñāne tātparyaṃ sarvadā śruteḥ / [15]
tathā durjñānajanane tātparyam asureṣu ca /
evam eva ca devānāṃ viṣṇubrahmādinām api / [16]
viṣṇoḥ sarvaguṇaiḥ pūrtir api matsyādirūpiṇaḥ /
ajeyatvam abhedyatvam acchedyatvaṃ ca sarvaśaḥ / [17]
sarvāvatārarūpāṇām api citsukharūpatā /
śrībrahmarudrādyādhikyaṃ sarveśatvaṃ svatantratā / [18]
sarvaśaktis tatprasādān mokṣo brahmādinām api /
tadbhaktyaiva vimokṣaś ca bhedo jīveśayor api / [19]
śrībrahmarudraśakrādeḥ krameṇaiva nijā guṇāḥ /
sarvadoṣavyapetatvaṃ viṣṇoḥ sarvatra sarvadā / [20]
etat sarvaṃ sarvavedair viṣṇvādyair devatāgaṇaiḥ /
ṛṣibhiḥ kṣatriyādyaiś ca samyak tātparyataḥ sadā / [21]
uktaṃ sarveṣu śāstreṣu tasmād grāhyaṃ bubhūṣubhiḥ /
idaṃ satyam idaṃ satyam idaṃ satyaṃ na saṃśayaḥ / [22] (5)
koṭibhiḥ śapathaiś cāpi nirṇītaṃ devatāgaṇaiḥ /
anādikālataś cāyaṃ śāstrārtho nānyathā kvacit / [23]
punaś cānantakālīna eṣa eva na saṃśayaḥ /
jñātavyaś caiṣa evārthaḥ sarvadaiva bubhūṣibhiḥ / [24]
evaṃ tu sthirayā buddhyā jñātvā yāsy atha tatparam /
evaṃ te haṃsarūpeṇa viṣṇunā devatāgaṇāḥ / [25]
brahmādyā bodhitāḥ sarve tathā jñātvā paraṃ gatāḥ /
sākṣād viṣṇur haṃsarūpa uktvaivaṃ tu divaukasām / [26]
vāsudevākhyarūpeṇa tena sarvahṛdi sthitaḥ /
saṅkarṣaṇākhyarūpeṇa viveśānantam eva ca / [27]
taṃ dhyāyati sadānantas tasmān muktipadecchayā /
pradyumnākhyena rūpeṇa kāmam eva viveśa saḥ / [28]
haṃsas taddhyānato muktiṃ kāma icchati sarvadā /
aniruddhākhyarūpeṇa so 'niruddhaṃ viveśa ha / [29]
haṃsas taddhyānato muktim aniruddhas tathecchati / [30ab] (6)
ityādi brahmāṇḍapurāṇe tattvanirṇayagītāyām | (7)

(1) Cf. MESQUITA 2000_1: 104f. [= 1997: 83f.].
(2) Cf. BrāṇP 8[2ab].
(3) Liberation through hatred is considered by Madhva as a heresy (cf. also HarV 5 [6cd]; BhāgP (V 1,25-26/29), whereas ViṣP (IV 15,11) does accept liberation through

hatred as a correct teaching on the ground that a person seething with hatred thinks intensively of Viṣṇu as God and that these intensive thoughts bring about the liberation. Surprisingly, in his commentary on BhāgP Madhva adopts also this view (ibid. p. 435,5f.): *vairayuktayāpy anucintayā tam āpuḥ / anucinteti tām āhur bhaktipūrvaṃ tu yā smṛti* iti ca (untraceable). Moreover, he adduces, in support of this opinion, also other untraceable quotes from BrāṇP 53 and SkaP 65; see also BrahVP 10[3f.].
(4) Cf. NārP 36 and MESQUITA 2007: 441n. 40.
(5) The threefold repetition of a solemn declaration endows it with the meaning and power of a swear or oath, cf. MESQUITA 2000: 166n. 341.
(6) Nowhere in the religious literature could I find a supporting reference for this singular mythical belief belonging to the theology of Pāncarātra (cf. OBERHAMMER 1971: 41ff.); see also BrāṇP 12 [7]; 15[4]; GarP 47; VarP 51[8].
(7) Cf. BhaviṣPV 3n. 7.

13) BĀUBh (p. 275,20+276,17):
Subject matter: The four castes and their presiding Deities

bṛhattvāt sarvavarṇānāṃ brāhmaṇaḥ parikīrtitaḥ /
kṣatatrāṇāt kṣatriyaś ca triṣūnatvāt viśaḥ smṛtāḥ / [1]
ūnavācī hi viṭśabdaḥ śubhe datte tribhir yataḥ /
ramate sa tataḥ śūdraḥ sa brāhmaṇyābhimānavān / [2]
brahmāgninā sahaivāste deveṣv atha nareṣu ca /
brāhmaṇena sahaivāste brahmā śubhacaturmukhaḥ / [3]
kṣatrajātyabhimānī tu pavano devarājabhiḥ /
suparṇaśeṣarudrādyair mānuṣeṣu ca rājabhiḥ / [4]
vaiśyajātyabhimānī ca nāsikyo vāyur ūrjitaḥ /
vasvādibhiḥ sahaivāste deveṣv atha nareṣu ca / [5]
viḍbhiḥ śūdrābhimānī ca nirṛtir devatāsu ca /
nāsatyayoḥ pṛthivyāś ca śūdreṣv eva tu mānuṣe / [6]
yasmād agnau viśeṣeṇa brahmaṇaḥ sannidhir bhavet /
ato 'gnāv eva devānāṃ sarveṣāṃ niyamād dhaviḥ / [7]
hutvā lokān prārthayanti tathā vipre ca mānuṣe /
sarvajātyuttamo brahmā yato viprāgnisaṃsthitaḥ / [8]
tasmād viprāṃs tathaivāgniṃ tarpayed brahmatuṣṭikṛt /
tuṣṭe brahmaṇi viṣṇuś ca tuṣṭo lokān pradāsyati / [9]
agniviprārcako 'py evaṃ yo na veda hariṃ param /
āśrayaṃ sarvajīvānāṃ haris taṃ naiva bhojayet / [10]
yathānadhīto vedas tu yathā karmākṛtaṃ tathā /
na samyak phalado viṣṇur ajñāto jagadīśvaraḥ / [11]
yady avettā mahad api hayamedhādikaṃ hareḥ /
kuryāt kṣayiṣṇuphalavān sa bhaven nātra saṃśayaḥ / [12]
āptakāmatayātmeti yo viṣṇuḥ samudīritaḥ /
sarvāśrayam upāsīta tam eva puruṣaḥ sudhīḥ / [13]

viṣṇuṃ sarvāśraya iti sadopāste ya ātmavān /
kṣīyante nāsya karmāṇi śubhāny eva kadācana / [14]
upāsanābalān mukto bhogān karmaphalān sadā /
bhuṅkte viṣṇoḥ samīpasthaḥ sarvadoṣavivarjitaḥ / [15]
iti brahmāṇḍe (1)

(1) Cf. ibid. ll. 19f.: *naiva vyabhavad iti parivārabahutvena yad viśiṣṭatvaṃ tan nābhavad ity arthaḥ* ... ; see also AgniP 20; BhaviṣP 11; HarV 26; NārP 2; VāmP 2.

14) BĀUBh (p. 298,21-22):
Subject matter: Kṛṣṇadvaipāyana

pārāśaryo jātukarṇyaḥ parāśarasutāv ubhau /
viprāyām eva bhāryāyāṃ tṛtīyaḥ kṛṣṇa eva ca /
iti brahmāṇḍe (1)

(1) Cf. BrahP 1_5; 18; BrāṇP 21[2]; 95 [24]; PadP 23; 61; VāyuP 13; see also BhaviṣPV 21.

15) BĀUBh (p. 306,26+307,23):
Subject matter: Hierarchy of the released souls

uktaṃ ca –
āpibanty akhilān bhogān ity āpaś cakravartinaḥ /
muktās teṣāṃ vāyusutaś cakro nāma vyapāśrayaḥ / [1]
muktas tasya ca muktas tu marud gandharvanāmavān /
suto vāyos tatsukhānāṃ mauktānām antarikṣagāḥ / [2]
marutām eka evāsāv antarikṣaś ca vāyujaḥ /
tatsukhānāṃ ca mauktānām ānandāḥ sūryarūpakāḥ / [3]
saurāṇāṃ cāpi muktānām ānandāś candrarūpakāḥ /
āhlādanāc candranāmā devo 'sāv aniruddhakaḥ / [4]
sa eva candram āviśya sthitas tannāmako 'pi saḥ /
aniruddhasukhānāṃ ca mauktānām indra āśrayaḥ / [5]
nakṣatranāmavān indro naivānyaḥ kṣatriyo 'sya hi /
vidyate triṣu lokeṣu brahmādyās tūrdhvalokagāḥ / [6]
ānandānāṃ tathaindrāṇāṃ mauktānāṃ deva āśrayaḥ /
deveti liṅganāma syāl liṅgātmā rudra ucyate / [7]
indrāśrayaḥ śivasyāpi sukhānāṃ muktigāminām /
śivo hīśvaranāmā syāt tatpāramyāt sarasvatī / [8]
indrety uktā tatsukhānāṃ brahmādhirmuktigāminām /
tatsukhānāṃ paraṃ brahma muktigānāṃ parāśrayaḥ / [9]
evam eva ca saṃsāre biṃbatvād uttarottaram / (1)
na parabrahmaṇaḥ kaścid āśrayaḥ svāśrayaṃ yataḥ / [10]

tasyāśrayo 'sti vety evaṃ pṛcchato 'pi śiraḥ sadā /
bhidyate parvatair andhe tamasi sthasya daivataiḥ / [11]
tasmād brahma paraṃ nityaṃ jñeyaṃ pūrṇam anāśrayam / [12ab]
iti brahmāṇḍe (2)

(1) Cf BhāgP 3 and MESQUITA 2000: 497ff.
(2) Cf ibid. ll. 20f.: *muktānāṃ tāratamyaṃ gārgibrāhmaṇenocyate / lokā iti muktānām ānandānubhavāḥ svarūpabhūtāḥ / apsu vāyāv iti svarūpasyaiva prastutvāt anatipraśnyāṃ vai devatām atipṛcchasīti* (BĀU III 6,1) *devatāsvarūpapraśnasyaivāvagamyamānatvāc ca / na coparitanalokeṣv adhastanā lokā āśritāḥ / na ca vāyur gandharvalokāśritaḥ / ... vāyvāśrayatvaśruteḥ sarvalokānām ... na cānatipraśnyatvaṃ lokamātrasyāsti / adhastaneṣu coparitanā lokās tiṣṭhanti / na ca marutām eko 'pi gandharvalokād avaro vidyate* ... ; see also BhaviṣPV 15.

16) BĀUBh (p. 313,21-23):
Subject matter: Flaw in the argument by which a disputant is put down in argument (*nigraha*)

punaruktiḥ śabdadoṣo nyūnādhikyādikaṃ tathā /
na jigīṣukathāyāṃ tu kāraṇaṃ syāt parājaye /
kvacid vidyādhikasyāpi skhalanaṃ saṃbhaved yataḥ /
tattvanirṇayavailomyaṃ vilambo vā muhūrtataḥ /
vidyādaurbalyahetuḥ syād atas tasmin parājayaḥ /
iti brahmāṇḍe (1)

(1) Cf. ibid. l. 24: *atas tattvanirṇayavirodhi punaruktyādi nigrahaḥ*; see also TphSI: *adhikam, nyūnam* and *nigrasthānam* and MESQUITA 2000: 96n. 132.

17) BĀUBh (p. 320,20-21):
Subject matter: Dialogue between Śakalya and Yājñavalkya

neti netyādirūpeṇa vijñāpitaguṇo 'pi tu /
viśeṣāpekṣayā pṛṣṭo na śākalyo viveda tam /
iti brahmāṇḍe (1)

(1) Cf. BrāṇP 19; SkaP 10; VarP 1.

18) BĀUBh (p. 323,19-20)
Subject matter: Definition of Pañcarātra

amitākṣaraṃ pañcarātraṃ vidyety āhur manīṣiṇaḥ / + 1
mitākṣaraṃ ślokavācyam ubhayaṃ veda īryate /
iti brahmāṇḍe (1)

(1) Cf. MESQUITA 2000_1: 131f. [= 1997: 105f.].

19) BĀUBh (p. 337,19-20):
Subject matter: Dialogue between Janaka and Yājñavalkya

rahasyam asyāyogyaṃ ca yadi mām eṣa pṛcchati /
datto varo mayāsyeti vaktavyaṃ me bhaviṣyati /
iti bhīto 'bhavad rājño yājñavalkyaḥ sumedhayā /
iti brahmāṇde

20) BĀUBh (p. 355,19-20):
Subject matter: Liberation / Kramamukti

pravahaṃ vāyuputraṃ ca sūryasomau ca vidyutam /
prāpya pradhānavāyuṃ ca yāti tat paramaṃ padam /
iti brahmāṇḍe (1)

(1) Cf. AgniP 16; BrahP 82; MESQUITA 2003: 106f. and LORENZ 2005: 41ff.

21) BhāgTN (p. 5,21-6,5):
Subject matter: Veda-tree

uktaṃ ca brahmāṇḍe –
dharmapuṣpas tv arthapattraḥ kāmapallavasaṃyutaḥ /
mahāmokṣaphalo vṛkṣo vedo 'yaṃ samudīritaḥ /
śātitāni phalānīha kṛṣṇadvaipāyanena tu / (1)
bhāratākhyāni yānīha tathā bhāgavataṃ bhuvi /
ārdrīkṛtāni tānīha śukaprabhṛtibhir janaiḥ /
khyāpayadbhir guruproktān vedārthān granthaniṣṭhitān /
kānicid darśayāmāsa vṛkṣasyāgre phalāni tu /
vyācakṣamāṇo vedārthaṃ bhagavān lokapūjitaḥ /
eteṣām atha teṣāṃ vā rasān pibata sajjanāḥ /
ā mokṣān mahatī tṛptir aho me paśyato bhavet /
iti (2)

(1) Cf. BrāṇP 14 and GarP 9.
(2) Cf. ibid. l. 21: *nigamakalpataror iti / bhagavatā galitam / śukena dravīkṛtam* ... ; see also BrāṇP 11.

22) BhāgTN (p. 19,12-14):
Subject matter: Avatāras

mohanārthaṃ dānavānāṃ bālarūpī pathi sthitaḥ /
putraṃ taṃ kalpayāmāsa mūḍhabuddhir janaḥ svayam /
tataḥ saṃmohayāmāsa jinādyān asurāṃśakān /

bhagavān vāgbhir ugrābhir ahiṃsāvācibhir hariḥ /
iti brahmāṇḍe (1)

(1) Cf. ĀdiP 1 and BhaviṣPV 12; BrahP 43.

23) BhāgTN (p. 43,1-3):
Subject matter: Death of Dhṛtarāṣṭra

brahmāṇḍe ca –
dhṛtarāṣṭre mṛte sūtaḥ sañjayaḥ pāṇḍusūnave /
gatiṃ śaśaṃsa kuntyāś ca gāndhārīdhṛtarāṣṭrayoḥ /
ityādi

24) BhāgTN (p. 60,11):
Subject matter: Liberation

svato manasthitir viṣṇau brahmabhāva udāhṛtaḥ /
iti brahmāṇḍe (1)

(1) Cf. AgniP 15 and 16.

25) BhāgTN (p. 69,6-7):
Subject matter: Viṣṇu's Sarvanāmatva

sarvanāmā yato viṣṇus tadanyārthān na tu smaret /
smaraṃs tu yāvadarthaḥ syād anyathā so ātmahā smṛtaḥ /
iti brahmāṇḍe (1)

(1) Cf. ibid. l. 5: *eṣa hariḥ / yadapārthair dhyāyati tatrārthān na vindate* ... ; see also BrāṇP 2.

26) BhāgTN (p. 75,2-3):
Subject matter: Liberation

vaiśvānare dyunadyāṃ vā sūrye vā deha eva vā /
vidhūya sarvapāpāni yānti kiṃstughnakeśavam /
iti brahmāṇḍe (1)

(1) Cf. ibid. l. 1: *hareḥ śaiśumāraṃ cakram / vaiśvānarodastāt*; see also AgniP 16; BrāṇP 27.

27) BhāgTN (p. 77,3-4):
Subject matter: Path of liberation

aśeṣajagadādhāraḥ śiṃśumāro hariḥ paraḥ /

sarve brahmavido natvā taṃ yānti paramaṃ padam /
iti brahmāṇḍe (1)

(1) Cf. AgniP 16; 27; BrahP 38; BrāṇP 26; 52; 95[25]; MatsyaP 13; VarP 51[5cd-7]; see also ĀdiP 1.

28) BhāgTN (p. 80,17-81,2):
Subject matter: Liberation

vāsudevāśritā devā brahmādyā muktabandhanāḥ /
bhedadṛṣṭyābhimānena cāvṛttiṃ naiva yānti te /
bhuñjate tu pṛthag bhogān nānandaṃ tatsvarūpakam /
svarūpaṃ ca pṛthak tv eṣām āviṣṭagrahavad bhavet /
iti brahmāṇḍe (1)

(1) Cf. ibid. ll. 14f.: *matisthena tena manasthena ca saha vijñānatattvaṃ yāti / guṇasannirodhaṃ nirguṇaṃ vāsudevam / etāṃ gatiṃ gato na viṣajjate* ... ; see also AgniP 16; BrahVP 17.

29) BhāgTN (p. 91,10-12):
Subject matter: Cosmic egg / Creation / Viṣṇu, the supreme Creator of the universe

kālakarmasvabhāvastho vāsudevaḥ paraḥ pumān /
akarod aṇḍam udvṛddham ātmaprasavakāraṇam /
iti brahmāṇḍe (1)

(1) Cf. ibid. ll. 7f. *kālakarmasvabhāvasthaḥ ajīvaḥ parameśvaraḥ ajīvaṃ svātmānam ajījanat / tadaṇḍaṃ yathā svātmānaṃ prasūte tathā cakāra* ... ; BrahP 13; 19; 20; 22; 22_1; 25; 61; 66; 72; BrahVP 6; 21; BrāṇP 31; 37; GarP 17; 19; HarV 34; KūrP 8; NārP 2; 24; PadP 21; 30; 31; 98; SkaP 7; 26; 27; 75; 101; VarP 1; VāyuP 3_3; 11; see also AgniP 12.

30) BhāgTN (p. 95,8-12):
Subject matter: Viṣṇu's abodes

anantāsanavaikuṇṭhanārāyaṇapurāṇi tu /
trīṇi dhāmāni vai viṣṇos trilokād bahir eva hi /
adāyadās tu putrāṇām udriktajñānacakṣuṣaḥ /
nārāyaṇaparā devā eva tāny āpnuvanti ca /
sa evānyasvarūpeṇa śakralokasamīpagaḥ /
ijyo yajñapumān nāma jñāninām gṛhiṇāṃ padam /
yatīnāṃ dhruvalokastho vaninām merumadhyagaḥ /
ādityamaṇḍalasthas tu jñāninām bramacāriṇām /
iti brahmāṇḍe (1)

(1) Cf. AgniP 27 and MatsyaP 8.

31) BhāgTN (p. 98,3-4):
Subject matter: Brahmā / Vāyu in possession of higher knowledge than the individual souls

sarvajīvanikāyeṣu brahmavāyū harer vidau /
na cānyas tādṛśo vettā yāvad vetti hariḥ svayam /
tāvat tāv api no viṣṇuṃ jānīto lokavanditau /
iti brahmāṇḍe (1)

(1) Cf. BrāṇP 29; MESQUITA 2000: 498f. and MESQUITA 2003: 98f.

32) BhāgTN (p. 115,5-6):
Subject matter: Viṣṇu's supreme transcendence (*svatantra/svayaṃbhū*)

sattādir yat svato viṣṇos tasmād anyaḥ sa sarvataḥ /
yat sattādir ato 'nyasya nānyatvaṃ bhedino 'pi tu /
iti brahmāṇḍe (1)

(1) Cf. AgniP 6; VarP 52 also MESQUITA 2000: 460ff.; 530f.

33) BhāgTN (p. 154,14-155,3):
Subject matter: Error, the cause of transmigration

aluptabodharūpatvān nāsau prākṛtadehavān / (1)
na ca sṛṣṭyādikaṃ bhrāntir bhrāntivādā hi dānavāḥ /
ato bhrāntyā hi saṃbandho nāsya kvacana yujyate /
bhrāntyā jīvasya saṃsāra īśajñānād vilīyate /
bhrāntir hi dehābhimatir ato jñānād vinaśyati /
iti brahmāṇḍe (2)

(1) Cf. BrāṇP 8[2ab];12[18ab].
(2) Cf. BhavișPV 27; BhavișP 2; BrahP 76; GarP 32; HarV 20; MatsyaP 6; NārP 29; 33; PadP 13; VarP 34; 37; 38; VāyuP 6 and MESQUITA 2000: 528f.

34) BhāgTN (p. 160,4-5):
Subject matter: Creation

muktavāyvādibhir viṣṇum vṛtaṃ brahmā dadarśa ha /
tadanyābhāvato nānyad atas tat sraṣṭum aicchata /
iti brahmāṇḍe (1)

(1) Cf. ibid. l. 3: *sūryenduvāyvagnyādibhis tridhāmnos viṣṇor agacchadbhiḥ prādhanikaiḥ* ... ; see also BrāṇP 29.

35) BhāgTN (p. 180,1-5):
Subject matter: Sacrificial victims (animals)

aṣṭāviṃśad viśeṣeṇa yajñeṣūpakṛtaṃ yataḥ /
tiraścāṃ tāvad etasmād gaṇyate śāstravedibhiḥ /
gaur ajo mahiṣaḥ kṛṣṇaḥ sūkaro gavayo ruruḥ /
avyuṣṭrau ca kharāśvau ca tathaivāśvataro 'paraḥ /
gauraś ca śarabhaś caiva camarī śvasṛgālakau /
vṛko vyāghraś ca mārjāro hariś ca śaśaśalyakau /
kapir gajaś ca godhādyā jalajāḥ pakṣiṇas tathā /
iti brahmāṇḍe (1)

(1) Cf. ibid. l. 6: *kūrmo jalajatvenāṣṭaviṃśatsv antarbhūto 'pi pañcanakhatvapradarśanārthaṃ pṛthag uktaḥ.* The animal species named by Madhva deviates slightly from the species mentioned in BhagP (III 10,20-24 [Madhva's count III 11, 20-24]). Like the previous commentators of the Vedānta-Sūtras, Madhva too approves, in accordance with BSū (III 1,26), animal sacrifice. He supports this teaching on the basis of an untraceable quotation from VarP 39; cf. HOUBEN 1999: 157. HOUBEN overlooked another supportive evidence of the untraceable quote from BrāṇP 35.

36) BhāgTN (p. 190,1-2):
Subject matter: Kālaśuddhi

nirmalena samoṣṇena nityasūryāṃśuvāriṇā /
pravāhagena kāryā syāt kālaśuddhiḥ sadaiva tu /
iti brahmāṇḍe (1)

(1) Cf. PadP 33.

37) BhāgTN (p. 197,4-6):
Subject matter: Cosmic egg

ekam aṇḍaṃ bahutvena pratyekaṃ romakūpagam /
brahmāpaśyat tathātmānaṃ hares teṣu pṛthak pṛthak /
iti brahmāṇḍe (1)

(1) Cf. BrāṇP 29.

38) BhāgTN (p. 204,8-205,1):
Subject matter: Hiraṇya-Daitya

brahmajas tu hiraṇyākhyaḥ prathamaṃ daṃṣṭrayā hataḥ /
sa eva pārṣadāviṣṭo dvitīyaṃ karṇatāḍanāt /
pūrvaṃ layodake magnāṃ dvitīyaṃ tena majjitām /
bhuvam uddharataivāsau hariṇā kroḍamūrtinā /
iti brahmāṇḍe (1)

(1) Cf. BhāgP (III 13,32-33) = Madhva's count (III 15,33-34); see also BhaviṣPV 12; 17.

39) BhāgTN (p. 223,7-10):
Subject matter: Viṣṇu's Avatāras

akṣataḥ kṣatavad viṣṇur asamaḥ samavat tathā /
ajito jitavac caiva jño 'jñavac ca prakāśayet /
sarvarūpeṣv ananto 'pi brahmādyāś caiva tanmateḥ /
anusāritayā brūyuḥ kuryuś ca na sa duḥkhabhāk /
iti brahmāṇḍe (1)

(1) Cf. ĀdiP 1 and MESQUITA 2000_1: 35ff. [= 1997: 29ff.].

40) BhāgTN (p. 239,7-8).
Subject matter: Viṣṇu's supreme transcendence

ekaḥ pūrṇo haris nānyas tadanye tadvaśā matāḥ /
iti jñānaṃ sthiraṃ yat tadaikātmyajñānam ucyate /
iti brahmāṇḍe (1)

(1) Cf. AgniP 6.

41) BhāgTN (p. 298,11-14):
Subject matter: Presiding Deities

yatra devaiḥ kṛte vighne khaṇḍito na pumān bhavet /
tatra tadyaśase vighnaṃ kuryur na tu vighātane /
yatra khaṇḍitatā tatra khaṇḍanāyaiva kevalam /
satyakāmā yato devās te cittādyabhimāninaḥ /
ato vimohanāyaiva prāpnuyus te parājayam /
teṣām aśaktatoktiś ca vimohāya suradviṣām /
iti brahmāṇḍe (1)

(1) Cf. BhaviṣP 5; 11.

42) BhāgTN (p. 325,4-5):
Subject matter: Vena and Pṛthu

venastho rājaso jīvaḥ pṛthunā svargatiṃ gataḥ /
svayaṃ tu tama evāpa sāttvikaḥ pṛthutām agāt /
iti brahmāṇḍe (1)

(1) Cf. ibid. l. 3: *aho vayam ityādi tatsthaparameśvarāpekṣayā / yo brahma kṣatram āviśyeti vacanāt*; see also BhaviṣPV 12; BhaviṣP 7; BrahP 39; BrahVP 42; BrāṇP 44; 53; GarP 26; KūrP 13; NārP 15; PadP 10; SkaP 52; VāmP 22.

43) BhāgTN (p. 328,3-4):
Subject matter: Liberation

bhidā yadi na dṛśyeta jīvātmaparamātmanoḥ /
muktau tadā vimokṣāya ko yatnaṃ kartum arhati /
iti brahmāṇḍe (1)

(1) Cf. ibid. p. 327,13f.: *dagdhāśayaḥ / bījāśayanāśe tadguṇānāṃ jñānādīnām abhāvān na kiṃcid vicakṣīta / parātmanos yadā vyavadhānaṃ saṃsārāvasthāyāṃ tadā svapna ivety etāvat / bījahṛdayanāśe tv apuruṣa eva / ātmanāśa evety arthaḥ / ataḥ saṃsārāvasthaivottamā syāt* ... ; cf. GīBh (p. 14,32f.); see also AgniP 16; 22; BhaviṣPV 3n. 7; SkaP 54 and MESQUITA 2000: 171n. 356

44) BhāgTN (p. 334,7-8):
Subject matter: Pṛthu

guruvipreṣu bhaktyā ca pareṣāṃ hitakṛtyayā /
praśrayeṇa ca kīrtyā ca pṛthū rāmam anuvratah /
iti brahmāṇḍe (1)

(1) Cf. BrāṇP 42.

45) BhāgTN (p. 344,1-3):
Subject matter: Correct performance of ritual works

yathāvat karma kartus tu jñānasāhāyyakārakam /
anyathā kurvataḥ karma nirayāya bhaviṣyati /
tathāpi karma nindanti na yataḥ kartum añjasā /
śakyaṃ jñānaphalasyāpi bahutvān mohanāya vā /
iti brahmāṇḍe (1)

(1) Cf. ibid. n. 2: *añjasā kartuṃ na śakyam iti kleśahetutvāt karma nindanti / jñānaphalasya bahutvāt tadapekṣayā karmaṇo 'lpāsthiraphalatvāc ca nindanti / kvacin mohanāya vā nindanti*; see also AgniP 20; BrāṇP 77.

46) BhāgTN (p. 353,8-9):
Subject matter: Protection of the earth

mānuṣāṇāṃ vatsarāṇāṃ lakṣadvādaśakaṃ purā /
pracetobhir iyaṃ pṛthvī pālitāvyāhatendriyaiḥ /
iti brahmāṇḍe (1)

(1) Cf. ibid. l. 7: *divyavarṣasahasrāṇām iti sahasraśabdo bahuvācī* ... ; see also BhaviṣPV 1.

47) BhāgTN (p. 361,3-4):
Subject matter: Viṣṇu's supreme transcendence

nāsti viṣṇoḥ sama iti jānanto 'py ṛṣayaḥ sadā /
tajjñāpanāya lokānām anye ca prārthayan samam /
iti brahmāṇḍe (1)

(1) Cf. ibid. n. 3: ... *evam anye 'pi atrikaśyapaprabhṛtayas dattavāmanādīn viṣṇusadṛśān eva putrān prārthayanta / kiṃ kāraṇaṃ tajjñāpanāya lokānām / viṣṇoḥ samo 'nyo nāstīti lokānām api jñāpayitum* ... ; see also AgniP 6.

48) BhāgTN (p. 366,8-367,3):
Subject matter: Hierarchy of the individual souls

mahaiśvaryasvarūpo 'pi bhagavān ṛṣabho virāṭ /
naiśvaryāṇi svakīyāni khyāpayāmāsa sarvavit / [1]
uttamānāṃ jñāpanārthaṃ dharmatattvasya keśavaḥ /
teṣām aiśvaryabhogo hi manaḥ saktiṃ vrajed yadi / [2]
ānando muktigo hrāsaṃ vikarmakaraṇād vrajet /
dharmādharmavihīno 'pi bhagavān ṛṣabhas tataḥ / [3]
teṣāṃ dharmajñāpanārthaṃ nāviścakre parāṃ sthitim /
devānāṃ nāśubhād dhrāsaḥ śubhāt kācit sukhonnatiḥ / [4]
ādhikārikajīvānām evam anyeṣu tu dvayam /
alpādhikāriṇāṃ tatra hrāso 'pi bhavati dhruvam / [5]
aśubhābhāvajonnāho mahādhikāriṇām api /
aśubhe kṛte na bhavati tāratamyāc ca sa smṛtaḥ / +1 [6]
prajāpāś ca tathā devā mahādhikāriṇaḥ smṛtāḥ /
ṛṣyaśītis tathā sapta pitaro 'psarasāṃ śatam / [7]
gandharvāṇāṃ tathā rājnāṃ viṃśad anyāsu jātiṣu /
alpādhikāriṇaḥ proktā anadhikāriṇaḥ pare / [8]
iti brahmāṇḍe (1)

(1) Cf. BhaviṣPV 15.

49) BhāgTN (p. 370,3-4):
Subject matter: Bhārata – Karmabhūmi

viśeṣād bhārate puṇyaṃ careyuḥ pāpam apy atha /
tathaiva bhagavadbhaktiṃ pṛthivyāṃ nānyavarṣagāḥ /
iti brahmāṇḍe (1)

(1) Cf. SkaP 76 and ROCHER 1986: 131.

50) BhāgTN (p. 385,2-4):
Subject matter: Purāṇic world-conception

yathā bhāgavate tūktaṃ bhauvanaṃ kośalakṣaṇam /
tasyāvirodhato yojyaṃ sarvagranthāntarasthitam /
maṇḍode (1) *pūraṇaṃ caiva vyatyāsaṃ kṣīrasāgare /*
rāhusomaravīṇāṃ ca maṇḍalād viguṇoktitām /
vinaiva sarvam unneyaṃ yojanābhedato 'tra tu /
iti brahmāṇḍe (2)

(1) *metri causa* for *maṇḍodake* or *dadhimaṇḍode*; BhāgP V 1,33.
(2) Cf. ibid. n. 2: ... *atra tu kṣīrodaḥ pañcamaḥ dadhimaṇḍodaḥ ṣaṣṭha iti vyatyāsena paṭhyate / tathāhi śruyate – kṣārodekṣurasodasurodadhṛtodakṣīrodadadhimaṇḍodaśuddhodāḥ saptajaladhayaḥ* (ibid. V 1,33) iti prathamādhyāye / *so 'yaṃ maṇḍode kṣīrasāgare ca vyatyāsaḥ / tad etad anyagranthānusārena bhāgavatam eva vyatyasya yojanīyam / dadhipadena kṣīragrahaṇaṃ kṣīrapadena dadhigrahaṇaṃ ceti / upapattiṃ tu svayam ācārya upariṣṭād vakṣyati / maṇḍode pūraṇam ity aparo 'ṃśaḥ nātisphuṭārthaḥ*; see also AWASTHI 1992: 42f. and KIRFEL 1954: 1*ff.

51) BhāgTN (p. 389,1-2):
Subject matter: Viṣṇu / Śrī

kāmadevasthitaṃ viṣṇum upāste śrī ratisthitā /
kāmadevaṃ ratiś cāpi viṣṇos tu prākṛtāṃ tanum /
iti brahmāṇḍe (1)

(1) Cf. AgniP 25 ; BhavişPV 8; BrāṇP 2 [4f.]; GarP 35; HarV 1; SkaP 9; 129; VāmP 29; VarP 13 and MESQUITA 2000: 421ff.

52) BhāgTN (p. 393,7-394,1):
Subject matter: Dolphin, the Avatāra of Viṣṇu

jñānānandātmake viṣṇau śiṃśumāravapuṣy atha /
ūrdhvalokeṣu saṃvyāpta ādityādyāḥ samāśritāḥ /
iti brahmāṇḍe (1)

(1) Cf. BrāṇP 27 and ĀdiP 1.

53) BhāgTN (p. 435,6-13):
Subject matter: Liberation through hatred / Viṣṇu's Kāruṇyatva

snehād annaṃ dadātīti svākarṣaṇabhaye 'pi ca /
vidyamāne 'py alpakope saṅgatisnehatas tathā /[1] (1)
peśaskṛdrūpatāṃ kīṭo yathā yāti tathaiva tu /
caidyādayo 'surāveśād dharau dveṣayutā api /[2]
nijasvabhāvayā bhaktyā nītā harisarūpatām /(2)

tathā hi karuṇo viṣṇur anyāveśād yadi dviṣan / [3]
hīyate kiṃ mamānena nityānandasvarūpiṇaḥ /
dehabandhayutānāṃ hi dveṣiṇāpakṛtaṃ bhavet / [4]
mama ko hy aparādhyeta nirdoṣaśubharūpiṇaḥ /
ato mayy aparādhas tu svasminn eva na me bhavet / [5] (3)
ato yady asurāveśāt kṛtam anena duṣkṛtam /
anādibhakto yasmān me mocayiṣye tatas tv aham / [6]
iti matvā mocayati caidyādīn api keśavaḥ / [7ab]
iti brahmāṇḍe (4)

(1) Cf. ibid. p. 433,8f.: *yoga snehaḥ / saṃraṃbhayayuktasnehena.*
(2) Cf. BhāgP VII 1,27 (= VII 1,28).
(3) Cf. BhāgTN (p. 433,9-10: *yasmād evaṃ ko 'py upadravo nāsti bhagavatas tasmād evaṃ dveṣādinā mano yoktuṃ śakyate / tad eva cintayati ca / anyathātmano duḥkhakāraṇaṃ dveṣādikaṃ kathaṃ sarvaniyāmako harir utpādayeta.*
(4) Cf. ibid. ll. 5: *vairayuktayāpy anucintayā tam āpuḥ / anucinteti tām āhur bhaktipūrvaṃ tu yā smṛti* iti ca (untraceable source). Madhva gives here a completely new interpretation to the idea of liberation through hatred, diverging from the doctrine of ViṣP (IV 15,11) and BhāgP VII 1,25-27 [= VII 1,26-28]; 29-30 [= 30-31]; III 2,24 [= III 3,24; see also BrahVP 10), that a person seething with hatred thinks intensively of Viṣṇu as God and that these intensive thoughts characterized by constant hostility bring about the liberation:

tasmād vairānubandhena nirvaireṇa bhayena ca /
snehāt kāmena vā juñjyāt kathaṃcin nekṣate pṛthak //
yathā vairānubandhena martyas tanmayatām iyāt /
na tathā bhaktiyogena iti me niścitā matiḥ //
kīṭaḥ peśaskṛtā ruddhaḥ kuḍyāyāṃ tam anusmaran /
saṃraṃbhabhayayogena vindate tatsarūpatām //
kāmād dveṣād bhayāt snehād yathā bhaktyeśvare manaḥ /
āveśya tadaghaṃ hitvā bahavas tadgatiṃ gatāḥ //

(cf. also BhāgP X 29,15 and HACKER 1959: 106f.). In contrast to it, Madhva shifted his focus towards the idea that the members of the Cedi-family are by nature fond of Viṣṇu and that only after their possession by Asuras (see also PadP 43 and BrahVP 10) or on account of a curse (*śāpābalād eva* [GīBh p. 91,25]) they changed their behaviour completely and felt hatred towards Viṣṇu. This act or state of being possessed is compared with "worm-wasp", since the worm shut up by a wasp in its hole thinks again and again so intensively through hatred and fear of wasp that it gets the same shape as wasp. It is noteworthy that in the course of this re-arrangement of the doctrine of liberation through hatred, Madhva traces back even the "hatred thinking" (*vairayuktayāpi anucintayā*) ultimately to Bhakti (*bhaktipūrvam*). In support of this interpretation he cites untraceable sources or quotations. The first source is an anonymous Smṛti followed by an unknown source called Prakāśikā (p. 438, 13-14): *vairānubandho vairayuktā bhaktiḥ – anubandhas tu bhaktiḥ syād bandhaḥ snehaḥ udāhṛtaḥ* iti. Strangely, in BrāṇP 12[4cd] Madhva ranks this teaching among the heresies: *samyagbhaktim ṛte muktir viṣṇau taddveṣatas tathā.* In addition, the idea of *vairayuktā bhaktiḥ* is in clear contradiction to Madhva's doctrine of *saṃyagbhaktiḥ*, which is specified in several other untraceable quotes as *sneho bhaktir iti proktas tayā*

muktir na cānyathā (BhavişPV 30[85cd]) or as *kāmayuktā sadā bhaktir ... ato mokṣe'pi ... kāmo bhaktyānuvartate* (SkaP 65[3cd-4ab]). The last Purāṇa-quote speaks also of liberation through hatred, and BhāgP (VII 1,25/30 = VII 1,26/31) mentions along with Bhakti and hatred other ways of concentration of one's mind on Him as causes of liberation; also ViṣP IV 15,11: *ayaṃ hi bhagavān kīrtitaś ca saṃsmṛtaś ca dveśānubandhenāpi akhilasurāsurādidurlabhaṃ phalaṃ prayacchati kimuta samyagbhaktimatām iti.* It is also strange that Madhva has reservations about the teaching that Bhakti is equal to other ways of concentration of mind, as hatred etc. (BhāgP VII 1, 25 = 26/28: *kathaṃcin nekṣate pṛthak* = 'he sees no difference among them'), insofar as he remarks (BhāgTN p. 432,5f.), that the said teaching is rather based on an impulsive feeling than on God's precept (*svabhāvakathanaṃ na vidhiḥ*), and he brings forward in this connection many quotes dismissing that doctrine. All those quotations with the exception of the last one (p. 432,7-17), which seems to have been authored by Madhva himself, are genuine (= MBh XII 334,5cd-6ab and Gī XVI 19-20; IX 11-12; BhāgP VII 10,15cd/17ab and IV 21,47 = ViṣP I 20,21cd/24cd). In GīBh (*ad* IX 11-12) this doctrine is also dismissed as false on the basis of the above quoted BhāgP IV 21,47 (cf. p. 91,13-92,9): *bhagavaddveṣibhir āśāsitam āmuṣmikaṃ na kiṃcid āpyate / yajñādikarmāṇi ca teṣāṃ vṛtthaiva / jñānaṃ ca ...* (= MBh XII 334,5cd-7ab) ... In GīBh (*ad* IX 12) Madhva broaches again this subject. However, he admits (GīBh p. 91,21f.) in reference to BrāṇP 53 that Viṣṇu confers upon the Cedi-kings etc. – who were followers of Viṣṇu from the beginning and who became his enemies only after a curse (*śāpabalād eva*) or after their possession by Asuras – liberation, out of compassion, after turning away from their hatred, as reward for their erstwhile affection (*dveṣiṇām api dveṣam anirūpya pūrvatanabhaktiphalam eva dadāti*). Other beings full of hate persevere in their hatred forever (*dveṣabhāvināṃ dveṣa eva bhavantīti hi yuktam*). Another similar doctrine held in BhāgP (cf. above VII 10,15cd and also IV 21,46-47; BrāṇP 42), that Hiraṇyakaśipu attained liberation on account of affection of his son Prahlāda for Viṣṇu (*sunoḥ prahlādasyānubhavataḥ*), is ruled out by Madhva on the ground that only very few traditional texts support it, whereas other weighty sources reject it (*bahuṣu grantheṣu niṣedhaḥ kutracid eva taduktir iti viśeṣaḥ*).
In BhāgTN (p. 440,5-7) Madhva refers to a doctrine, which he ascribes to an unknown source, that all statements about happiness experienced by beings who attained their liberation only through hatred for Viṣṇu, has been merely taught for the sake of bewilderment of human beings (... *viṣṇvādidveṣataś caiva sukhavācas tathākhilāḥ / mohanārthāḥ samuddiṣṭās tathārthadyotakāḥ sadā* / iti prakāśasaṃhitāyām). This teaching is confirmed also by another untraceable quote ascribed by Madhva to BrahVP 10[3f.]. In view of these facts, we can assume that Madhva definitely rejected the doctrine of liberation through hatred taught in BhāgP: *ato na bhagavaddveṣiṇāṃ kācid gatir iti siddham.* This opinion is supported also by other untraceable quotes of Madhva like BrahP 79; BrāṇP 12[4cd] and HarV 5[6c]; see also BrahVP 10; BrāṇP 56; 59[2cd]; GarP 29; 33; HarV 19_1. For the conception of *āveśa* (Madhva's being possessed by Viṣṇu) cf. MESQUITA 2000_1: 71ff. (= 1997: 57ff.).

54) BhāgTN (p. 448,6-7):
Subject matter: Asuras

madhukaiṭabhayoś caiva hiraṇyādes tathaiva ca /
nānyo brahmapadaṃ vāñchaty ṛjūn yogyān vinā kvacit /

tataḥ śreyāṃsi vāñchanti na tu tatpādam āptave / (1)
iti brahmāṇḍe (2)

(1) *āptave* (=Ved. infinitive dative case)
(2) Cf. ibid. l. 5: *bhavāya śreyase / na kaścit tadapekṣate*; see also BhavişPV 12; BrāṇP 53n. 3.

55) BhāgTN (p. 463,3-6):
Subject matter: Prahlāda

adṛṣṭāśrutapūrvatvād anyaiḥ sādhāraṇair janaiḥ /
nṛsiṃhaṃ śaṅkiteva śrīr lokamohāya no yayau /
prahlāde caiva vātsalyadarśanāya harer api / (1)
jñātvā manas tathā brahmā prahlādaṃ preṣayat tadā / (2)
ekatraikasya vātsalyaṃ viśeṣād darśayed dhariḥ /
avarasyāpi mohāya krameṇaivāpi vatsalaḥ /
iti brahmāṇḍe (3)

(1) Cf. ibid. n. 1: *na kevalaṃ mohāya / kiṃtu prahlāde harer vātsalyātiśayapradarśanāyāpi.*
(2) Cf. ibid. n. 2: *aḍbhāvena / apreṣayat ... śriyo harer api tathāvidhaṃ mano 'bhiprāyaṃ jñātvā brahmā prahlādaṃ preṣayāmāsa*; see also BrāṇP 53; 56.
(3) Cf. BhāgP VII 9,1f.; see also BrāṇP 53; 56; SkaP 63 and HACKER 1959: 117f.

56) BhāgTN (p. 493,10-494,1):
Subject matter: Bali

balir apy asurāveśāt stuvann api janārdanam /
ākṣipaty antarā kvāpi prahlādo nityabhaktimān /
iti brahmāṇḍe (1)

(1) Cf. BrahVP 17 and BrāṇP 53; 55; 59[2cd].

57) BhāgTN (p. 516,5-9):
Subject matter: Heresy of identity between Īśvara and Jīva

praviṣṭatvāc charīreṣu jīva eveti durdhiyaḥ /
manyante paramātmānaṃ na tanmatam anuvrajet /
vedavādavirodhitvād anuyātā tamo viśet /
tataḥ paryaṅkaśayana āha viṣṇuḥ sanātanaḥ /
idaṃ jagat sarvam athedṛśāni
bhūrīṇi vā mām abhiyānti saṅkhye /
dhānyāni yadvat khalagāni martyaḥ
sañcūrṇayiṣyāmy aham eka eva /
ityādi brahmāṇḍe (1)

(1) Cf. ibid. ll. 1f.: *paramātmano 'pi śarīre sannidhānād abuddhair asvavyatirekato jñāyase / yathānukūlavādaṃ vedavacanaṃ vinā pravartanān na tanmanīṣitaṃ samyak* ... ; see also BhaviṣPV 3n. 7; 12 and MESQUITA 2000: 528f.

58) BhāgTN (p. 523,2-4):
Subject matter: Liberation

devo 'haṃ mānuṣo veti viśeṣaṃ tatra cāpi tu /
tathaiva paramātmānaṃ viśeṣaṃ brahmajīvayoḥ /
samyag bhedena yaḥ paśyet sa hanty ajñānasaṃbhavāḥ /
yātanāḥ paramātmānaṃ tatprasādāc ca gacchati /
iti brahmāṇḍe (1)

(1) Cf. ibid. l. 1: *dehinām ajñānaprabhavā yātanāḥ svapareti bhidā hanti* ... ; see also AgniP 16.

59) BhāgTN (p. 530,8-531,1):
Subject matter: Subhari's curse / Tāratamya

viṣṇunā viṣṇubhaktaiś ca brahmaśāpo 'nuvartyate /
brāhmaṇānām apīḍāyai balibhiḥ kṣatriyādibhiḥ /
viṣṇoś ca viṣṇubhaktānāṃ śāpād vyaiti tapo 'khilam /
athāpi cāsurāveśāc chapeyur harim apy aho /(1)
atas tu saubhareḥ śāpaṃ nātyavartat khageśvaraḥ /
anyathā tūttamānāṃ hi nādhamaiḥ śāpa iṣyate /
varo 'pi dattas tv adhikair nādhamādhikyakāraṇam /
viṣṇor api varas tasmān nādhikyaṃ saṃprayacchati /
kramaśaḥ śrīviriñcādeḥ kathaṃcit kenacit kvacit /
na ca dadyād dharis tādṛg dattaṃ vā bāhyam eva tu /
iti brahmāṇḍe (2)

(1) Cf. BrahVP 17; BrāṇP 53; 56; GarP 34; SkaP 59.
(2) Cf. ibid. p. 431n. 1: *tādṛgādhikyādirūpaṃ kiṃcid abhīṣṭaṃ na dadyād eva / yatra kvacid dattaṃ dṛśyate tad api bāhyam āveśādinimittaṃ na svarūpabhūtam iti*; see also BhaviṣPV 15; NārP 12; PadP 14; SkaP 33; 34; 59; 78[2f.]; VarP 16.

60) BhāgTN (p. 550,1-4):
Subject matter: Doctrine of Avatāra

jānan sālvakṛtāṃ māyām ajānann iva keśavaḥ /
anvavartata kiṃcit tu tatas tām aharad vibhuḥ /
evam eva tu sarvatra paramātmā sanātanaḥ /
viddhaś ca rudhirasrāvī kathaṃcid ajayat param /
ityādi darśayed viṣṇur mohayan māyayā jagat /

cidānandaghanasyāsya kuto vedhādi sadgateḥ /
iti brahmāṇḍe (1)

(1) Cf. ĀdiP 1; BrāṇP 69.

61) BhāgTN (p. 553,1-2):
Subject matter: Viṣṇu's supreme transcendence

alpasaṃpūrṇaśaktitvād alpapūrṇasukhatvataḥ /
alpasaṃpūrṇadarśitvān na sāmyaṃ jīvakṛṣṇayoḥ /
iti brahmāṇḍe (1)

(1) Cf. AgniP 6; 22 and MESQUITA 2000: 166-168; 371ff.

62) BhāgTN (p. 583,11-15):
Subject matter: Viṣṇu's supreme transcendence

svatantro nāparaḥ kaścid viṣṇoḥ prāṇapateḥ prabhoḥ /
yathā prāṇāt paro nāsti svatantro jagati kvacit /
tathā prāṇo ramā caiva na viṣṇoḥ pṛthag īśvarau /
yady ucyante prāṇatantrā bahavaḥ puruṣā iti /
satyam eva hy asaṅkhyātā na niyamyaniṣedhikāḥ /
ekādvitīyaśrutayaḥ kiṃtv īśāntaravārakāḥ /(1)
tathā svagatabhedasya tadatantraniṣedhakāḥ /
iti brahmāṇḍe (2)

(1) Cf. ChU VI 2, 1.
(2) Cf. ibid. ll. 1f.: *yasya paramasya te kaścid aparaḥ svatantro nāsti / anaparasya prāṇottamasya / ... yathā prāṇasya nāparaḥ svatantras tadvat prāṇaḥ śrīr anyo vā tvāṃ vinā svatantro nāsti ... kiṃtu svagatabhedasya īśvarāntarasya atattantrasya ca niṣede* ... ; see also AgniP 6; KūrP 18 and MESQUITA 2003: 98n. 7.

63) BhāgTN (p. 600,5-6):
Subject matter: Hari's love / affection

na snehabhaṅgo devyās tu na bhayaṃ keśavasya ca /
snehabhīta ivāthāpi noce rugmivadhe hariḥ /
iti brahmāṇḍe (1)

(1) Cf. ibid. n. 2: ... *syāle rugmaṇi balarāmeṇa nihate sati / hariḥ sādhv asādhu vā nābravīt / sādhu kṛtam ity ukte rugmaṇī na snihyati / asādhu kṛtam ity ukte balarāmaḥ krudhyatīti*; see also BrāṇP 51.

64) BhāgTN (p. 613,14-614,9):
Subject matter: Śraddhā

śraddhā bhāgavate tantre vede bhāratapañcame /
viṣṇor avyavadhānena vaktṛtvāt sarvathā bhavet / [1]
kalāvidyāsv anindā ca vyavadhānena keśave /
praveśād yatibhiḥ kāryā hy anyathā nirayaṃ vrajet / [2]
śraddhā tv āstikyabuddhiḥ syāt sā caiva dvividhā matā /
atroktam astīty ekā tu mamātrāsti prayojanam / [3]
ity anyā tatra pūrvā tu yateḥ kāryā kalāsv api /
dvitīyā tu na kartavyā pañcarātravirodhiṣu / [4]
sadaiva nindā sarvaiś ca brahmādisthāvarāntakaiḥ /
samyak kāryā tad vinā ca tamo yāti viniścayāt / [5]
kurvanty eva surās tatra tadanyeṣāṃ tamo bhavet /
pañcarātraṃ ca vedāś ca mūlarāmāyaṇaṃ tathā / [6]
purāṇaṃ bhāgavataṃ caiva bhārataṃ ca na bhidyate / +1
eteṣv api yathā viṣṇor ādhikyapratipādanam / [7]
tadbhaktānāṃ ca kramaśaḥ sa evārtho na cāparaḥ /
anyathā dṛśyamānaṃ tu mohāyaiva vinirdiśet / [8]
tasmāt sarveṣu śāstreṣu viṣṇor ādhikyam eva tu /
krameṇa ca tadīyānāṃ pratipādyaṃ na cāparam / [9]
iti brahmāṇḍe (1)

(1) Cf. BhaviṣP 10; BrāṇP 101; HarV 23 and MESQUITA 2000_1: 140ff. [= 1997: 112ff.].

65) BhāgTN (p. 839,5-7):
Subject matter: Doctrine of Avatāra

jīvaviṣṇvor abhedaś ca dehayogaviyojane /
viṣṇor duḥkhaṃ vraṇitvādi parābhāvas tathaiva ca /
asvātantryaṃ ca vedādāv uktavad bhāsate vibhoḥ /
kvacit kvacit vimohāya daityādīnāṃ durātmanām /
iti brahmāṇḍe (1)

(1) Cf. ĀdiP 1; see also MBh 42n. 6 and MESQUITA 2000: 231n. 498.

66) BSūBh (p. 17,9-10):
Subject matter: Bhedābheda

ananyo 'py anyaśabdena tathaiko bahurūpavān /
procyate bhagavān viṣṇur aiśvaryāt puruṣottamaḥ /
iti brahmāṇḍe (1)

(1) Cf. ibid. l. 8: *rasaśabdena viśeṣaṇāt tattatsārabhūtaṃ cinmātram evocyate / idam iti ca sadṛśyamānasannihitvāt* ... ; see also BrāṇP 69 and MESQUITA 2000: 429ff.

67) BSūBh (p. 23,19-20):
Subject matter: Viṣṇu's Mahidāsa-Avatāra, the proclaimer of the Vaiṣṇava doctrine

mahidāsābhidho jajña itarāyās tapobalāt /
sākṣāt sa bhagavān viṣṇur yas tantraṃ vaiṣṇavaṃ vyadhāt /
iti ca brahmāṇḍe (1)

(1) Cf. ĀdiP 1; BrahP 16; BrāṇP 95[26]. For the teaching of Mahidāsa-Avatāra see LORENZ 2003.

68) BSūBh (p. 35,8-14):
Subject matter: Etymologies of the Names of Viṣṇu

brahmāṇḍe ca –
rujaṃ drāvayate yasmād rudras tasmāj janārdanaḥ /
īśanād eva ceśāno mahādevo mahattvataḥ /
pibanti ye narā nākaṃ muktāḥ saṃsārasāgarāt /
tadādhāro yato viṣṇuḥ pinākīti tataḥ śrutaḥ /
śivaḥ sukhātmakatvena śarvaḥ śaṃrodhanād dhariḥ /
kṛttyātmakam imaṃ dehaṃ yato vaste pravartayan /
kṛttivāsās tato devo viriñcaś ca virocanāt /
bṛṃhaṇād brahmanāmāsāv aiśvaryād indra ucyate /
evaṃ nānāvidhaiḥ śabdair eka eva trivikramaḥ /
vedeṣu sapurāṇeṣu gīyate puruṣottamaḥ /
iti (1)

(1) Cf. ibid. ll. 5f.: ... *so 'ntakaḥ sa rudra ... ityādinā prāṇagranthirudratvāder viṣṇor evoktvāt* ... ; BrahP 1_1; 49; 61; BrāṇP 68; PadP 46; SkaP 4; 90; VāmP 37; see also BhāgP 1 and MESQUITA 2000: 141n. 276.

69) BSūBh (p. 51,15-16):
Subject matter: Viṣṇu's contradictory attributes

dhyāyati dhyānarūpo 'sau sukhī sukham atīva ca /
paramaiśvaryayogena viruddhārthatayeṣyate /
iti brahmāṇḍe (1)

(1) Cf. AgniP 11; BrahP 40; 59; 62; 65; BrahVP 5; BrāṇP 66; GarP 13; 46; HarV 10; KūrP 1; NārP 21; see also BhavişP 13 and MESQUITA 2000: 443n. 540.

70) BSūBh (p. 52,5-7):
Subject matter: Viṣṇu, the supreme cause of the Universe

vyavadhānena sūtis tu puṃstvaṃ vidvadbhir ucyate /
sūtim avyavadhānena strītvam āhur manīṣiṇaḥ /
ubhayātmakasūtitvād vāsudevaḥ paraḥ pumān /
prakṛtiḥ puruṣaś ceti śabdair eko 'bhidhīyate /
iti brahmāṇḍe (1)

(1) Cf. ibid. ll. 3f.: *avyavadhānenotpattidvāratvaṃ ca prakṛtitvam / tac cāsyaiva gīyate yad bhūtayoniṃ paripaśyanti dhīrā iti* (= MuU I 2,6); BrāṇP 5; GarP 4; see also AgniP 12; 25 and MESQUITA 2000: 470ff.

71) BSūBh (p. 98,24-25):
Subject matter: Atomic size of Jīva

aṇumātro 'py ayaṃ jīvaḥ svadehaṃ vyāpya tiṣṭhati /
yathā vyāpyaśarīrāṇi haricandanavipluṣaḥ /
iti bramāṇḍapurāṇe (1)

(1) Cf. ibid. l. 22: *aṇor api jīvasya sarvaśarīravyāptir yujyate / yathā haricandana-vipluṣa ekadeśapatitāyāḥ sarvaśarīravyāptiḥ* ... ; see also BhāgP 3; BrahVP 19; BrāṇP 61; GarP 25; HarV 26; KūrP 10; MBh 19; 21; 49; 50; NārP 53; PadP 65; 67; 86; SkaP 26; 54; 97; 128; VarP 14; 33; 34; VāyuP 3_3 ; MESQUITA 1989: 129-150 and MESQUITA 2000: 136n. 257.

72) BSūBh (p. 115,8-10):
Subject matter: Viṣṇu, the Creator of the wordly Vyavahāra

trivṛtkriyā yato viṣṇo rūpaṃ ca tadapekṣayā /
rūpāpekṣaṃ tathā nāma vyavahāras tadātmakaḥ /
ato nāmnaś ca rūpasya vyavahārasya caikarāṭ /
harir eva yataḥ kartā pitāto bhagavān prabhuḥ /
iti ca brahmāṇḍe (1)

(1) Cf. ibid. l. 6: ... *trivṛtkurvata iti hetugarbhaḥ / trivṛtkaraṇāpekṣatvān nāmarūpayoḥ* ... and ChU VI 3,3-4; see also AgniP 12; PadP 66.

73) BSūBh (p. 118,2-4):
Subject matter: Breath of life / Sense organs (*prāṇa*)

brahmāṇḍe ca –
mṛtikāle jahaty enaṃ prāṇā bhūtāni pañca ca /
bhāgato bhāgatas tv enam anugacchanti sarvaśaḥ /
iti (1)

(1) Cf. BhaviṣPV 17; MatsyaP 5; see also MESQUITA 2003: 104f.

74) BSūBh (p. 128,13-16):
Subject matter: Dream and waking state

brahmāṇḍe ca –

manogatāṃs tu saṃskārān svecchayā parameśvaraḥ /
pradarśayati jīvāya sa svapna iti gīyate /
yadanyathātvaṃ jāgratvaṃ sma bhrāntis tatra tatkṛtā /
anabhivyaktarūpatvān nānyasādhanajaṃ bhavet /
iti (1)

(1) Cf. ibid. l. 12: *manogatān saṃskārān svecchāmātreṇa pradarśayati nānyena sādhanena samyag anabhivyaktvāt*; see also BrāṇP 7 and MESQUITA 2000: 202; 250n. 27.

75) BSūBh (p. 138,16-17):
Subject matter: Viṣṇu, the supreme Creator of the universe

sṛṣṭiṃ ca pālanaṃ caiva saṃsāraṃ niyamaṃ tathā /
eka eva karotīśaḥ sarvasya jagato hariḥ /
iti brahmāṇḍe (1)

(1) Cf. ibid. ll. 13f.: *uktaṃ sṛṣṭisaṃhārakartṛtvamātraṃ pratiṣidhya tato 'dhikaṃ bravīti / naitāvadenā paro anyad asty ukṣā sa dyāvāpṛthivī bibhartīti* (= Ṛg X 31,8) *caśabdāt smṛtiś ca* ... ; see also AgniP 12 and MESQUITA 2000: 109n. 172; 486f.

76) BSūBh (p. 158,21-23):
Subject matter: Liberation

kadācit karma kurvanti kadācin naiva kurvate /
nityajñānasvarūpatvān nityaṃ dhyāyanti keśavam /
tīrṇatartavyabhāgā ye prāptānandāḥ parātmanaḥ /
pratyavāyasya bandhasyāpy abhāvāt svecchayā bhavet /
iti hi brahmāṇḍe (1)

(1) ibid. l. 20: *bandhapratyavāyābhāve hi mokṣasyārthavattvam / anyathā mokṣatvam eva na syāt* ... ; see also AgniP 16; BrahVP 29 and MESQUITA 2000: 520f.

77) BSūBh (p. 180,3-4):
Subject matter: Liberation

jñānān mokṣo bhavaty eva sarvākāryakṛto 'pi tu /
ānando hrasate 'kāryāc chubhaṃ kṛtvā ca vardhate /
iti ca brahmāṇḍe (1)

(1) It means that the execution of the ritual rites plays only a secondary role (ibid. p. 179,13f.): *yathā rājñaḥ sahakāry eva mantrī tathāpy ṛte taṃ kṣitipaḥ kāryam ṛcchet /*

evaṃ jñānaṃ karma vināpi kāryaṃ sahāyabhūtaṃ na vicāraḥ kutaścid iti kamaṭha-śrutau (unknown source) *sahakāritvokteś ca*; see also AgniP 16; BrahVP 29; BrāṇP 45 and MESQUITA 2007: 17ff. [= 2007_1: 438ff.].

78) BSūBh (p. 184,6-7):
Subject matter: Liberation (according to the individual Yogyatā)

na devapadam anvicchet kuta eva harer guṇān /
icchan patati pūrvasmād adhastād yatra notthitiḥ /
iti brahmāṇḍe (1)

(1) Cf. ibid. ll. 3f.: *na ca paramātmaiśvaryādikam ākāṅkṣyam / brahmādīnām api nākaṅkṣyaṃ kimu parasyeti sūcayitum api śabdaḥ / caśabdas tu jñānārthināṃ pūrvoktād itthaṃbhāvāntarasūcakaḥ / anyogyam āroṇḍhuṃ prayatan patan hi dṛśyate / evam ayogyasya paramātmaiśvaryasya brahmādipadasya vākaṅkṣāyāṃ patanam anumīyate* ... ; see also AgniP 16 and BhavisṣPV 15; BrahP 36.

79) BSūBh (p. 197,9-10):
Subject matter: Body-postures in meditation

acalaṃ cec charīraṃ syān manasaś cāpy acālanam /
calane tu śarīrasya cañcalaṃ tu mano bhavet /
iti ca brahmāṇḍe (1)

(1) Cf. VarP 45.

80) BSūBh (p. 197,24-26):
Subject matter: Means of liberation

śṛṇuyād yāvad ajñānaṃ matir yāvad ayuktatā /
dhyānaṃ ca yāvad īkṣā syān nekṣā kvacana bādhyate /
dṛṣṭatattvasya ca dhyānaṃ yadā dṛṣṭir na vidyate /
bhaktiś cānantakālīnā parame brahmaṇi sphuṭā /
ā vimukter vidhir nityaṃ svata eva tataḥ param /
iti ca brahmāṇḍe (1)

(1) Cf. ibid. l. 21: *yāvan mokṣas tāvad upāsanādi kāryam* ... ; see also AgniP 9; 20 and MESQUITA 2007: 15n. 23; 27ff. [= 2007_1: 437n. 23; 443ff.].

81) BSūBh (p. 221,5-6):
Subject matter: Epithets of Hari

parañjyotiḥparaṃbrahmaparamātmādikā giraḥ /
sarvatra harim evaikaṃ brūyur nānyaṃ kataṃcana /
iti ca brahmāṇḍe (1)

(1) Cf. ibid. l. 4: *parañjyotiḥśabdena paramātmaivocyate / tatprakaraṇatvāt* ... ; see also BhāgP 1.

82) ChUBh (p. 400,23-27):
Subject matter: Viṣṇu, the supreme meaning of all Vedas

viṣṇur uktaḥ sarvavedair mantreṣu tu viśeṣataḥ /
āraṇyake viśeṣeṇa naivānyat kiṃcid ucyate /
karmārthaṃ ca brāhmaṇaṃ syād amukhyārthavivakṣayā /
mukhyato viṣṇur evaiko brāhmaṇeṣv api kathyate /
āraṇyakeṣv ṛte viṣṇuṃ naivānyat kiṃcid ucyate /
sūtrātmā tūcyate viṣṇos tadviśiṣṭatvavittaye /
kutracit tadupāstiś ca tasyādhyarddhatanutvataḥ / (1)
tasmin viṣṇor upāstyarthaṃ nānyathā kiṃcid ucyate /
iti brahmāṇḍe (2)

(1) *adhyardha* (= *pavate/pavana*) cf. BĀU III 9,9 and ChUBh (p. 400,20f.):
vede rāmāyaṇe caiva purāṇe bhārate tathā /
ādāv ante ca madhye ca viṣṇuḥ sarvatra gīyate /
nāmāni sarvāṇi yam āviśanti tam vai viṣṇuṃ paramam udāharantītyādeś ca / upaniṣattvāc ca viśeṣato na yat kiṃcid ucyata iti vaktuṃ yuktam ... ; see also MESQUITA 2000_1: 44n. 59; 49n. 76 [= 1997: 36n. 51; 40n. 68] and MESQUITA 2003: 101f.
(2) Cf. BhaviṣP 14; BrāṇP 11; 84; 103_1; HarV 27; NārP 58; PadP 3; 60; 62; SkaP 110; VarP 15; 24; 62; MESQUITA 2000_1: 133ff. [= 1997: 107ff.] and MESQUITA 2003: 102n. 14.

83) ChUBh (p. 436,25-26):
Subject matter: Presiding Deities

tejo 'bhimāninī lakṣmīḥ prāṇas tv ababhimānavān /
annābhimānī rudraś ca tisras tā devatāḥ purā /
iti ca brahmāṇḍe (1)

(1) Cf. ibid. l. 4: *prāthamyāc ca teja ādyā lakṣmyādaya iti siddham* ... ; see also BhaviṣP 11.

84) ChUBh (p. 442,25-26):
Subject matter: Viṣṇu's supreme transcendence

mahātatparatā viṣṇor utkarṣe 'vāntarā tataḥ /
anyatra sarvavākyānāṃ yuktīnāṃ ca viśeṣataḥ /
iti brahmāṇḍe (1)

(1) Cf ibid. ll. 21f.: ... *yasyotkarṣaprasiddhyarthaṃ sarvavedāś ca yuktayas / jñatvā ca yadutkarṣaṃ mucyante sa hariḥ paraḥ / adyā tamasya mahimānamāyavo 'nuṣṭuvanti*

pūrvathā – ity ādiśrutiś ca viṣṇor utkarṣe mahātātparyaṃ kathayati ... ; see also AgniP 6; BrāṇP 82; SkaP 127n. 1 and MESQUITA 2000: 107n. 167; 402f.

85) ChUBh (p. 443,20-23):
Subject matter: Viṣṇu's supreme transcendence

> *haṃnāma hanyamānatvāj jīvasya samudāhṛtam /*
> *jīvād anyo yato viṣṇur ahaṃnāmā tataḥ smṛtaḥ /*
> *smīti jīvaḥ samuddiṣṭaḥ smītyalpaṃ sumitatvataḥ /*
> *pūrṇatvād asmināmāsau pūrṇapūrṇatvahetutaḥ /*
> *brahmāsmīty ucyate viṣṇur bṛhatpūrṇo yataḥ sadā /*
> *asau sūryagato viṣṇur dūrasthatvāt prakīrtitaḥ /*
> *ahaṃnāmā jīvagato nityāheyatvahetutaḥ /*
> iti brahmāṇḍe (1)

(1) Cf. AgniP 6; BrahVP 2; BrāṇP 92 and MESQUITA 2000: 141n. 274; 162n. 330-333; p. 406f.

86) GīT (p. 1,12-17):
Subject matter: Etymology of the Mahābhārata

> *śāstreṣu bhārataṃ sāraṃ tatra nāmasahasrakam /*
> *vaiṣṇavaṃ kṛṣṇagītā ca tajjñānān mucyate 'ñjasā /* [1]
> *na bhāratasamaṃ śāstraṃ kuta evānayoḥ samam /*
> *bhārataṃ sarvavedāś ca tulām āropitāḥ purā /* [2]
> *devair brahmādibhiḥ sarvair ṛṣibhiś ca samanvitaiḥ /*
> *vyāsasyaivājñayā tatra tv atyaricyata bhāratam /* [3]
> *mahattvād bhāravattvāc ca mahābhāratam ucyate /*
> *niruktam asya yo veda sarvapāpaiḥ pramucyate /* [4]
> *svayaṃ nārāyaṇo devair brahmarudrendrapūrvakaiḥ /*
> *arthito vyāsatāṃ prāpya kevalaṃ tattvanirṇayam /* [5]
> *cakāra pañcamaṃ vedaṃ mahābhāratasañjñitam /* [6ab]
> iti brahmāṇḍe (1)

(1) Cf. BrāṇP 95[9-10]; KūrP 30_2 ; SkaP 126 and MESQUITA 2000_1: 143ff. [= 1997: 115ff.].

87) GīT (p. 109,29):
Subject matter: Liberation

> *praveśo nirgamaś caiva muktānāṃ svecchayā bhavet /*
> iti brahmāṇḍe (1)

(1) Cf. ibid. l. 29: *muktāḥ surasaṅghā viśanti* ... ; see also AgniP 16 and MESQUITA 2000: 520ff.

88) GīT (p. 115,24-26):
Subject matter: Gradation (*tāratamya*) in the state of liberation

viśvarūpaṃ prathamato brahmāpaśyac caturmukhaḥ /
tacchatāṃśena rudras tu tacchatāṃśena vāsavaḥ /
yathendreṇa purā dṛṣṭam apaśyat so 'rjuno 'pi san /
tadanye kramayogena tacchatāṃśādidarśinaḥ /
iti brahmāṇḍe (1)

(1) Cf. ibid. l. 22f.: *tvadanyena na dṛṣṭapūrvam* (Gī XI 47d) *ity anena tenaivendraśarīreṇa dṛṣṭam iti jñāyate / tvadanyeneti tvad avarāpekṣayā / tair api tadvan na dṛṣṭam ity eva*; see also BhaviṣPV 15.

89) GīT (p. 117,27-30):
Subject matter: Śrī = Prakṛti

śrīḥ sutuṣṭā hares toṣaṃ gamayet kṣipram eva tu /
atuṣṭā tadatuṣṭiṃ ca tasmād dhyeyaiva sā sadā /
avyaktaṃ prakṛtiṃ prāhuḥ kūṭasthaṃ cākṣaraṃ ca tām /
pradhānam iti ca prāhur mahāpuruṣa ity api /
tāṃ brahma mahad ity āhuḥ paraṃ jīvaṃ parāṃ citim /
tasyās tu paramo viṣṇur yo brahma paramaṃ mahat /
iti brahmāṇḍavacanāc (1)

(1) Cf. ibid. l. 23: *sādhananirṇayo 'tra*; see also AgniP 25 and MESQUITA 2000: 421f.; 508ff.

90) ĪśUBh (p. 509,11-14):
Subject matter: Viṣṇu's supreme transcendence

svāyaṃbhuvaḥ svadauhitraṃ viṣṇuṃ yajñābhidhaṃ manuḥ /
īśāvāsyādibhir mantrais tuṣṭāvāvahitātmanā /
rakṣobhir ugraiḥ saṃprāptaḥ khāditum mocitas tadā /
stotraṃ śrutvaiva yajñena tān hatvāvadhyatāṃ gatān /
prādād dhi bhagavāṃs teṣām avadhyatvaṃ haraḥ prabhuḥ /
tair vadhyatvaṃ tathānyeṣām ataḥ ko 'nyo hareḥ prabhuḥ /
iti brahmāṇḍe (1)

(1) Cf. ibid. l. 10: *svāyaṃbhuvo manur etair mantrair bhagavantam ākūtisūnuṃ yajñanāmānaṃ viṣṇuṃ tuṣṭāva ...* ; see also AgniP 6; NārP 13.

91) ĪśUBh (p. 510,10-14):
Subject matter: Viṣṇu's supreme transcendence

anejan nirbhayatvāt tad ekaṃ prādhānyatas tathā /
samyag jñātum aśakyatvād agamyaṃ tat surair api /
svayaṃ tu sarvānugamāt pūrvam eva svabhāvataḥ /
acintyaśaktitaś caiva sarvagatvāc ca tat param /
dravato 'tyeti santiṣṭhat tasmin karmāṇy adhān marut /
māruty eva yataś ceṣṭā sarvā tāṃ haraye 'rpayet /
iti brahmāṇḍe (1)

(1) Cf. ibid. l. 15: *tad ejati tata ejaty anyat / tad svayaṃ naijati ...* ; see also AgniP 6.

92) ĪśUBh (p. 511,27+512,9):
Subject matter: Viṣṇu's supreme transcendence

pātraṃ hiraṇmayaṃ sūryamaṇḍalaṃ samudāhṛtam /
viṣṇoḥ satyasya tenaiva sarvadāpi hitaṃ mukham /
tat tu pūrṇatvataḥ pūṣā viṣṇur darśayati svayam /
satyadharmāya bhaktāya pradhānajñānarūpataḥ / (1)
viṣṇur ekarṣir jñeyo yamo niyamanād dhariḥ /
sūryaḥ sa sūrigamyatvāt prajāpatyaḥ prajāpateḥ /
viśeṣeṇaiva gamyatvād ahaṃ cāsāv aheyataḥ /
asmi nityāstitāmānāt sarvajīveṣu saṃsthitaḥ /
svayaṃ tu sarvajīvebhyo vyatiriktaḥ paro hariḥ /
sa kratur jñānarūpatvād agnir aṅgapraṇetṛtaḥ /
iti brahmāṇḍe (2)

(1) Cf. ibid. p. 512,10f.: *satyaṃ brahma hṛdaye dhārayatīti satyadharma / eko 'sauśabdaḥ prāṇe sthita iti / yasmin prāṇe sthitaḥ so 'py amṛtaḥ / kimu paraḥ / aḥ brahmaiva nilayanaṃ yasya vāyoḥ so 'nilam ....*
(2) Cf. BhaviṣPV 3; BrāṇP 85; see also AgniP 6 and BhāgP 2.

93) KathUBh (p. 478,23-24):
Subject matter: Antaryāmin

guhyaṃ tat paramaṃ brahma mriyamāṇaśarīriṇam /
saṃprāptam api jīveṣu jāgarti svapiteṣv api /
iti brahmāṇḍe (1)

(1) Cf. ibid. l. 22: *mṛtajīve sthito muktajīve sthitaś cobhayātmako bhagavān vivakṣita ity etasmāc cāvirodhaḥ ...* ; see also BhāgP 2; BrāṇP 7.

94) MBhTN (I 48-51):
Subject matter: Durāgamas

eṣa mohaṃ sṛjāmy āśu yo janān mohayiṣyati /
tvaṃ ca rudra mahābāho mohaśāstrāṇi kāraya /

atatthyāni vitatthyāni darśayasva mahābhuja /
prakāśaṃ kuru cātmānam aprakāśaṃ ca māṃ kuru /
iti vārāhavacanaṃ brahmāṇḍoktaṃ *tathāparam /*
amohāya guṇā viṣṇor ākāraś ciccharīratā /
nirdoṣatvaṃ tāratamyaṃ muktānām api cocyate /
etadviruddhaṃ yat sarvaṃ tanmohāyeti nirṇayaḥ / (1)

(1) Cf. BrāṇP 11; SkaP 122a. For a detailed analysis of this topic see MESQUITA 2000_1: 153f. [= 1997: 123f.].

95) MBhTN (II 9-49ab):
Subject matter: Sadāgamas / Doctrine of Avatāras

bhārataṃ sarvavedāś ca tulām āropitāḥ purā /
devair brahmādibhiḥ sarvair ṛṣibhiś ca samanvitaiḥ /
vyāsasyaivājñayā tatra tv atyaricyata bhāratam / [9]
mahattvād bhāravattvāc ca mahābhāratam ucyate /
niruktam asya yo veda sarvapāpaiḥ pramucyate / [10] (1)
nirṇayaḥ sarvaśāstrāṇāṃ sadṛṣṭānto hi bhārate / (2)
kṛto viṣṇuvaśatvaṃ hi brahmādīnāṃ prakāśitam / [11]
yataḥ kṛṣṇavaśe sarve bhīmādyāḥ samyag īritāḥ /
sarveṣāṃ jñānado viṣṇur yaśodāteti coditam / [12]
yasmād vyāsātmanā teṣāṃ bhārate yaśa ūcivān /
jñānadaś ca śukādīnāṃ brahmarudrādirūpiṇām / [13]
brahmādhikaś ca devebhyaḥ śeṣād rudrād apīritaḥ /
priyaś ca viṣṇoḥ sarvebhya iti bhīmanidarśanāt / [14]
bhūbhārahāriṇoḥ viṣṇoḥ pradhānāṅgaṃ hi mārutiḥ / (3)
māgadhādivadhād eva duryodhanavadhād api / [15]
yoya eva balajyeṣṭhaḥ kṣatriyeṣu sa uttamaḥ /
aṅgaṃ ced viṣṇukāryeṣu tadbhaktyaiva na cānyathā / [16]
balaṃ naisargikaṃ tac ced varāstrādes tadanyathā /
anyāveśanimittaṃ ced balam anyātmakaṃ hi tat / [17]
deveṣu balinām eva bhaktijñāne na cānyathā /
sa eva ca priyo viṣṇor nānyathā tu kathaṃcana / [18]
tasmād yoyo balajyeṣṭhaḥ sa guṇajyeṣṭha eva ca /
balaṃ hi kṣatriye vyaktaṃ jñāyate sthūladṛṣṭibhiḥ / [19]
jñānādayo guṇā yasmāj jñāyante sūkṣmadṛṣṭibhiḥ /
tasmād yatra balaṃ tatra vijñātavyā guṇāḥ pare / [20]
deveṣv eva na cānyeṣu vāsudevapratīpataḥ /
kṣatrād anyeṣv api balaṃ pramāṇaṃ yatra keśavaḥ / [21]
pravṛtto duṣṭanidhane jñānakārye tad eva ca /
anyatra brāhmaṇānāṃ tu pramāṇaṃ jñānam eva hi /

kṣatriyāṇāṃ balaṃ caiva sarveṣāṃ viṣṇukāryatā / [22]
kṛṣṇarāmādirūpeṣu balakāryo janārdanaḥ /
dattavyāsādirūpeṣu jñānakāryas tathā prabhuḥ / [23]
matsyakūrmavarāhāś ca siṃhavāmanabhārgavāḥ /
rāghavaḥ kṛṣṇabuddhau ca kṛṣṇadvaipāyanas tathā / [24]
kapilo dattavṛṣabhau śiṃśumāro rūceḥ sutaḥ /
nārāyaṇo hariḥ kṛṣṇas tāpaso manur eva ca / [25]
mahidāsas tathā haṃsaḥ strīrūpo hayaśīrṣavān /
tathaiva baḍavāvaktraḥ kalkī dhanvantariḥ prabhuḥ / [26]
ityādyāḥ kevalo viṣṇur naiṣāṃ bhedaḥ kathaṃcana /
na viśeṣo guṇaiḥ sarvair balajñānādibhiḥ kvacit / [27] (4)
śrīr brahmarudrau śeṣaś ca vīndredrau kāma eva ca /
kāmaputro 'niruddhaś ca sūryaś candro bṛhaspatiḥ / [28]
dharma eṣāṃ tathā bhāryā dakṣādyā manavas tathā /
manuputrāś ca ṛṣayo nāradaḥ parvatas tathā / [29]
kaśyapaḥ sanakādyāś ca brahmādyāś caiva devatāḥ /
bharataḥ kārtavīryaś ca vainyādyāś cakravartinaḥ / [30]
gayaś ca lakṣmaṇādyāś ca trayo rohiṇinandanaḥ /
pradyumno raugmiṇeyaś ca tatputraś cāniruddhakaḥ / [31]
naraḥ phalguna ity ādyā viśeṣāveśino hareḥ /
vālisāṃbādayaś caiva kiṃcidāveśino hareḥ / [32]
tasmād balapravṛttasya rāmakṛṣṇātmano hareḥ /
antaraṅgaṃ hanūmāṃś ca bhīmas tatkāryasādhakau / [33]
brahmātmako yato vāyuḥ padaṃ brāhmam agāt purā /
vāyor anyasya na brāḥmaṃ padaṃ tasmād sa eva saḥ / [34]
yatra rūpaṃ tatra guṇā bhaktyādyāḥ striṣu nityaśaḥ /
rūpaṃ hi sthūladṛṣṭīnāṃ dṛśyaṃ vyaktaṃ tato hi tat / [35]
prāyo vettuṃ na śakyante bhaktyādyāḥ strīṣu yat tataḥ /
yāsāṃ rūpaṃ guṇās tāsāṃ bhaktyādyā iti niścayaḥ / [36]
tac ca naisargikaṃ rūpaṃ dvātriṃśallakṣaṇair yutam /
nālakṣaṇaṃ vapurmātraṃ guṇahetuḥ kathaṃcana / [37] (5)
āsurīnāṃ varādes tu vapurmātraṃ bhaviṣyati /
na lakṣaṇāny atas tāsāṃ naiva bhaktiḥ kathaṃcana / [38]
tasmād rūpaguṇodārā jānakī rugmiṇī tathā /
satyabhāmetyādirūpā śrīḥ sarvaparamā matā / [39]
tataḥ paścād draupadī ca sarvābhyo rūpato varā /
bhūbhārakṣapaṇe sākṣād aṅgaṃ bhīmavad īśituḥ / [40]
hantā ca vairahetuś ca bhīmaḥ pāpajanasya tu /
draupadī vairahetuḥ sā tasmād bhīmād anantarā / [41]
baladevas tataḥ paścāt tataḥ paścāc ca phalgunaḥ /
narāveśād anyathā tu drauṇiḥ paścāt tato 'pare / [42]

rāmavaj jāmbavatyādyāḥ ṣaṭ tato revatī tathā /
lakṣmaṇo hanumatpaścāt tato bharatavālinau /
śatrughnas tu tataḥ paścāt sugrīvādyās tato 'varāḥ / [43]
rāmakāryaṃ tu yaiḥ samyak svayogyaṃ na kṛtaṃ purā /
taiḥ pūritaṃ tat kṛṣṇāya bīmatsvādyaiḥ samantataḥ / [44]
adhikaṃ yaiḥ kṛtaṃ tatra tair ūnaṃ kṛtam atra tat /
karṇādyair adhikaṃ yais tu prādurbhāvadvaye kṛtam /
vividādyair hi taiḥ paścād vipratīpaṃ kṛtaṃ hareḥ / [45]
prādurbhāvadvaye hy asmin sarveṣāṃ nirṇayaḥ kṛtaḥ /
naitayor akṛtaṃ kiṃcic chubhaṃ vā yad ivāśubham /
anyatra pūryate kvāpi tasmād atraiva nirṇayaḥ / [46]
paścāttanatvāt kṛṣṇasya vaiśeṣyāt tatra nirṇayaḥ /
prādurbhāvam imaṃ yasmād gṛhītvā bhārataṃ kṛtam / [47] (6)
uktā rāmakathāpy asmin mārkaṇḍeyasamāsyayā /
tasmād yad bhārate noktaṃ taddhi naivāsti kutracit /
atroktaṃ sarvaśāstreṣu na hi samyag udāhṛtaṃ / [48] (7)
ityādi kathitaṃ sarvaṃ brahmāṇḍe *hariṇā svayam* / [49ab] (8)

(1) Cf. BrāṇP 86[4]; see also MESQUITA 2000$_1$: 143ff. [= 1997: 115ff.].
(2) Cf. MESQUITA 2000: 51n. 13.
(3) Cf. ĀdiP 1 and MESQUITA 2000$_1$: 46ff. [= 1997: 38ff.].
(4) Cf. ibid. 36f. [= 29f.]; MESQUITA 2000: 429ff. and MESQUITA 2003: 111.
(5) Cf. MESQUITA 2000: 381ff.; MESQUITA 2003: 100n. 9.
(6) Cf.BrāṇP 14.
(7) Cf. MBh I 56,33cd.
(8) Cf. BrāṇP 11; SkaP 38; see also BhaviṣP 10.

96) MBhTN (II 159-161):
Subject matter: Birth of the Deities ·

uktaṃ purāṇe brahmāṇḍe brahmaṇā nāradāya ca –
yasyāḥ prasādāt paramaṃ vidanti
śeṣaḥ suparṇo giriśaḥ surendraḥ /
mātā ca yaiṣāṃ prathamaiva bhāratī
sā draupadī nāma babhūva bhūmau / +1
yā mārutād garbham adhatta pūrvaṃ
śeṣaṃ suparṇaṃ giriśaṃ serendram /
caturmukhābhāṃś caturaḥ kumārān
sā draupadī nāma babhūva bhūmau / (1)

(1) Cf. BhaviṣP 5.

97) MāṇUBh (p. 516,10-15):
Subject matter: State of *turīya*

viṣṇus turīyarūpeṇa dvādaśānte vyavasthitaḥ /
muktānāṃ prāpyarūpo 'sau vyavahāre na dṛśyate /
samyak samāhitānāṃ tu prāptānāṃ ṣoḍaśīṃ kalām /
aparokṣadṛśāṃ kvāpi turīyaṃ dṛśyate padam / (1)
antar bahiś ca sauptaṃ ca samādhijñānam eva ca /
bahiḥśabdādikaṃ jānan paśyan svapnaṃ tathaiva ca /
yadā bhavati sāvasthā hy ubhayajñānaśabditā /
etat sarvaṃ turīyeṇa rūpeṇa na karoty ajaḥ /
sarvajñānapradaś cāpi muktasyaiva turīyakaḥ /
iti brahmāṇde (2)

(1) Cf. MESQUITA 2000: 174n. 362; HACKER1985: 131f.
(2) Cf. ibid. l. 15f.:
amuktasya tv adṛśyatvāt ṣoḍaśīṃ vā kalāṃ ṛte /
turīyo 'dṛṣṭa ity ukto grahaṇāder agocaraḥ /
vinā muktiṃ yatas tenāvyavarhārya itīritaḥ /
jāgradādipravṛttis tu lakṣaṇaṃ hy anumāpakam /
alakṣaṇas tadrāhityād acintyas tata eva ca /
tata eva hy anirdeśyaś cidānandaikalakṣaṇaḥ /
muktasya sarvavyāpārahetur eva turīyakaḥ /
...
iti māhātmye (unknown source);
see also BrāṇP 7.

98) MuUBh (p. 490,10-12):
Subject matter: Birth of the Deities and Rākṣakas

manor vaivasvatasyādāv atharvā brahmaṇo 'jani /
mitraś ca varuṇaś cātho prahetir hetir eva ca /
brahmaṇaḥ prathame kalpe śivaḥ prathamajaḥ sutaḥ /
sanakādyās tu vārāhe brāhmā viṣṇoḥ suto 'grajaḥ /
iti brahmāṇḍe (1)

(1) Cf. BhavisP 5.

99) MuUBh (p. 493,21-23):
Subject matter: Worship of Viṣṇu and Deities

evaṃ vāyoḥ pitaraṃ viṣṇum eva
yajanti devaiḥ saha ye kṛte janāḥ /+1
evaṃ tretāyāṃ kecid anye pṛthak
tān iṣṭvā viṣṇāv arpayante na cānye /+1

iti ca brahmāṇḍe (1)

(1) Cf. ibid. l. 17: *tretāyāṃ bahudhā santatāni / kṛte tv ekaprakāreṇaiva santatāni* ... ; see also AgniP 20; BhaviṣP 5; PadP 101 and MESQUITA 2003: 108f.

100) NyāV (p. 127,21-24):
Subject matter: Requital for actions

karmāṇy anantāni yatheṣṭam īśaḥ
saṃpādya teṣāṃ phalam icchayaiva /
kva cid dadāti kva ca no dadāti
na hy ānantyāt karmāṇāṃ bhoganāśaḥ /
svātantryaṃ cet karmāṇāṃ sarvabhogaḥ
syān na hy evaṃ kvāpi tat kenacit syāt /
ato 'pi sa svecchayā kiṃcid eva
phalaṃ kuryād viphalaṃ prāyaśaś ca /
kvacij jñānaṃ janayan basma kuryāt
svecchāvṛttis tasya viṣṇoḥ sadaiva /
iti brahmāṇḍe (1)

(1) Cf. ibid. l. 20: *na ca karmānvayavyatirekāt phalasyeśvaraḥ phaladāteti pralobhamātram / tasyaiva svātantryāt* ... ; see also BhaviṣP 12; MESQUITA 2000: 485f. and MESQUITA 2007: 25f. [= 2007_1: 442f.].

101) ṚgBh (p. 6,10-7,1):
Subject matter: Revelation of the Vidyās

brahmāṇḍe 'pi tathāparam –
hayagrīvādimā vidyāḥ śvasitatvena niḥsṛtāḥ / (1)
brahmaṇā svīkṛtās tāś ca rudraśeṣavipā api /
dakṣādyāḥ sanakādyāś ca śakrādyā manavas tathā /
jagṛhus te ca viśvasmiṃś cakrur vyāptā tato 'khilāḥ / (2)

(1) Cf. ibid. ll. 8f.:
munis tu sarvavidyānāṃ bhagavān puruṣottamaḥ /
viśeṣataś ca vedānāṃ yo brahmāṇam iti śrutiḥ / (= ŚvU VI 18)
ṛgvedādikam asyaiva śvasitaṃ prāha cāparā / (= BĀU IV 5,11)
vāco babhūvur uśatīr hayagrīvād iti sphuṭam /
vaco bhāgavate *'py asti* ... (= II 7,11cd).
(2) Cf. BrahP 21; 27; 34; 81; BrāṇP 64; GarP 7; PadP 102; VarP 30; 61; MESQUITA 2000: 71n. 63 and HACKER1985: 43ff.

102) TaiUBh (p. 536,22-24):
Subject matter: Definition of the Śrotriya

yasya śrutiphalaṃ pūrṇaṃ sa śrotriya udāhṛtaḥ /
sa hi mukto 'kāmahataḥ sa hi kāmair na hanyate /
yasya kāmās tu satyāḥ syuḥ sa hi kāmair na hanyate /
na hy akāmaḥ kvacit kaścid dṛśyate śrūyate 'pi vā /
iti brahmāṇḍe (1)

(1) Cf. ibid. l. 20: *na hy amuktasyākāmahatvaṃ mukhyaṃ bhavati / na ca mukhyā śrotriyatā* ... ; see also MBh 5.

103) Vāda (p. 47,8-10):
Subject matter: Real existence of the universe

na ca māyāvinā māyā dṛśyate viśvam īśvaraḥ /
sadā paśyati tenedaṃ na māyety avadhāryatām /
aparokṣadṛśo mithyādarśanaṃ na kvacid bhavet /
sarvāparokṣavid viṣṇur viśvadṛk tan na tanmṛṣā /
iti ca brahmāṇḍe (1)

(1) Cf. ibid. l. 5f.: *pratyakṣabādhitaṃ ca jaganmithyātvam / sad iti pratīyamānatvāt / na ca pratyakṣasiddham anyena kenāpi bādhyaṃ dṛṣṭam / candraprādeśatvādiviṣayatvaṃ tu dūrasthatvādidoṣayuktavād apaṭu / na ca jagatpratyakṣasyāpaṭutve kiṃcin mānam / na ca jagato 'jñānajanyatve kiṃcin mānam* ... ; see also BhaviṣPV 1 and MESQUITA 2000: 101n. 149f.; 157n. 314f.; 210n. 437f.; 326n. 233.

103_1) VTN (p. 11,5-8):
Subject matter: Sadāgamas

ṛgādyā bhārataṃ caiva pañcarātram athākhilam /
mūlarāmāyaṇaṃ caiva purāṇaṃ caitadātmakam /
ye cānuyāyinas tv eṣāṃ sarve te ca sadāgamāḥ /
durāgamās tadanye ye tair na jñeyo janārdanaḥ /
jñeya etaiḥ sadā yuktair bhaktimadbhiḥ suniṣṭhitaiḥ /
na ca kevalatarkeṇa nākṣajena na kenacit /
kevalāgamavijñeyo bhaktair eva na cānyathā /
iti brahmāṇḍe (1)

(1) Cf. ibid. l. 2f.: *sadāgamaikavijñeyam ... nārāyaṇam* ... ; see also BrāṇP 11; 82 and MESQUITA 2000: 51-56.

103_2) VTN (p. 12,16-19):
Subject matter: Mahāpuruṣalakṣaṇa

uktaṃ ca brahmāṇḍe –
viṃśallakṣaṇato 'nūnas tapasvī bahuvedavit /
veda ity eva yaṃ paśyet sa vedo jñānadarśanāt / iti (1)

(1) Cf. ibid. ll. 14f.: *na ca svayaṃpratibhātavedair dṛṣṭam avedavākyaṃ bhavati / paraṃparāsiddhavedavākyānusāritvāt / vedadraṣṭṝṇām uktaguṇavattvāc ca teṣām* ... ; see also VāyuP 3; 3_4; MESQUITA 2000: 63; 381ff.

104) VTN (p. 14,7-15,5):
Subject matter: Pañcamaveda

nityā vedāḥ samastāś ca śāśvatā viṣṇubuddhigāḥ /
sarge sarge 'munaivaita udgīryante tathaiva ca // [1]
tatkrameṇa ca tair varṇais taiḥ svarair eva nānyathā /
ataḥ śrutitvam etāsāṃ śrutā eva yato 'khilaiḥ // [2]
janmāntare śrutās tās tu vāsudevaprasādataḥ /
munīnāṃ pratibhāsyanti bhāgenaiva na sarvaśaḥ // [3]
yatas tā hariṇā dṛṣṭāḥ śrutā evāparair janaiḥ /
śrutayo dṛṣṭayaś ceti tenocyante purātanaiḥ // [4]
tadutpattivacaś caiva bhaved vyaktim apekṣya tu /
cetanasya janir yadvad ucyate sarvalaukikaiḥ // [5]
purāṇāni tadarthāni sarge sarge 'nyathaiva tu /
kriyante 'tas tv anityāni tadarthāḥ pūrvasargavat // [6]
vedānāṃ sṛṣṭivākyāni bhaveyur vyaktyapekṣayā /
avāntarābhimānānāṃ devānāṃ vā vyapekṣayā // [7] (1)
nānityatvāt kutas teṣām anityatvaṃ sthirātmanām / [8ab]
iti brahmāṇḍe (2)

(1) Cf. GīBh (p. 87,9): *abhimānidevatāś cāgnyādayaḥ*; see also BhaviṣP 11.
(2) Cf. ibid. (p. 13,14f.): ... *ato 'pauruṣeyavākyenaiva dharmādisiddheḥ sarvavādinām api tadaṅgīkāryam / tatprāmāṇyaṃ ca siddham* ... ; see also BhaviṣPV 1; BhaviṣP 10; BrāṇP 11; MESQUITA 2000_1: 126f. [= 1997: 101ff.] and MESQUITA 2000: 71f.; 378ff.

105) VTN (p. 42,10-43,2):
Subject matter: Doctrine of Avatāras

nityapūrṇo 'khilaguṇo vidoṣaḥ sarvadaiva yaḥ /
svatantraḥ sa paro viṣṇur janmamṛtyādivarjitaḥ / [1]
śrīnārada uvāca –
nirdoṣaś cet kathaṃ viṣṇur mānuṣeṣūdapadyata /
cintāśramavraṇājñānaduḥkhayug dṛśyate katham / [2]
eṣa me saṃśayo brahman hṛdi śalya ivārpitaḥ /
anuddhāryo 'parair martyaiḥ sūktiśaktyā tam uddhara / [3]
brahmovāca –
strīpuṃmalābhiyogātmadeho viṣṇur na jāyate /
kiṃtu nirdoṣacaitanyasukhāṃ nityāṃ svakāṃ tanum / [4]
prakāśayati saiveyaṃ janir viṣṇor na cāparā /

tathāpy asuramohāya pareṣāṃ ca kvacit kvacit / [5]
duḥkhājñānaśramādīn sa darśayec chuddhasadguṇaḥ /
kva vraṇādi kva cājñānaṃ svatantrācintyasadguṇe / [6]
daurlabhyāyaiva mokṣasya darśayet tāny ajo hariḥ /
mithyādarśanadoṣeṇa tena muktiṃ na yāti ca / [7]
tamo yāti ca tenaiva tasmād doṣavivarjitam /
prādurbhāvagataṃ caiva jānīyād viṣṇum añjasā / [8]
iti brahmāṇḍe (1)

(1) Cf. ibid. l. 9f.:
varjitaḥ sarvadoṣair yo guṇasarvasvamūrtimān /
svatantro yadvaśāḥ sarve sa viṣṇuḥ paramo mataḥ /
iti mahopaniṣadi (untraceable source);
see also ĀdiP 1; AgniP 4.

Brahmapurāṇa (BrahP)

[BrahP contains several passages which correspond to the portions transmitted in other Purāṇas, as ViṣṇuP; MārkP; SāmbaP; VāyuP; HarV and MBh (cf. HAZRA 1987: 145-157; ROCHER 1986: 154-156; also P. SCHREINER and R. SÖHNEN, Introduction, in: Sanskrit Indices and Text of Brahmapurāṇa. Wiesbaden 1987). The unknown quotes attributed to this Purāṇa are to be found in BhāgTN (fifty-seven times); BĀUBh (four times); BSŪBh (twenty times); GīBh (seven times); in GīT; IśUBh and Vāda each one-time. The verse on the Saptarṣis (BrahP 83) is recorded in a different wording than in BrahP (III 8-9ab) or in MBh (XII 201,4). For metrical lapses see BrahP 30ab; 34ab and BrahP 43[2ab].]

1_1) BĀUBh (p. 246,17-18):
Subject matter: Etymology of Hari

aśanaṃ jagad etad yan nayaty ātmecchayā hariḥ /
aśanāyā tataḥ prokta udanyā karmanāyakaḥ /
iti brāhme (1)

(1) Cf. ibid. l. 16: *layakāle paramātmanaivāvṛtam āsīt* ... ; see also BrāṇP 68 and PANDURANGI (Bāu) p. 10f.

1_2) BĀUBh (p. 264,18-19):
Subject matter: Viṣṇu, one without a second (*advitīya*)

eka evādvitīyo 'sau tadatantrasya varjanāt /
tatsamasyādhikasyāpi hy abhāvāt puruṣottamaḥ /
iti ca brāhme (1)

(1) Cf. ibid. l. 6: *yathaikam uttamapuruṣam apekṣya tasmin pure sa eka eva nānyo 'stīty ukte 'pi tatsadṛśas tadadhiko vānyo nāstīty uktaṃ bhavati* ... ; see also AgniP 6 and MESQUITA 2000: 190n. 394; 455ff.

1_3) BĀUBh (p. 267,18-20):
Subject matter: The real meaning of a sentence (*siddhārtha*) as against *kāryārtha*

sukhasādhanam evaikaṃ nṛṇāṃ vedaḥ pradarśayet /
na kurvati naraṃ kvāpi prerayaty atra kañcana /
sukhasādhanatājñānāt sukhaprāptyartham icchayā /
pravartate tato vedaḥ siddhasyaiva pradarśakaḥ /
na tu kārakatāṃ kvāpi vedaḥ prāpnoti kasyacit /
iti brāhme (1)

(1) Cf. ibid. ll. 15f.: *vyutpattir api siddhe sāṅgulinirdeśādinā yujyate / na ca kutracit sukhasādhanaṃ vinā kāryānvitaṃ vidyate / liṅgādyartho 'pi sukhasādhanatvam eva / na ca kāryānvita eva tātparyam ity atra kiṃcinmānam* ... ; see also BrahVP 30; HarV 6 and MESQUITA 2000: 77n. 79; 389ff.; also ibid. p. 394f.

1_4) BĀUBh (p. 272,3-4):
Subject matter: Viṣṇu's supreme transcendence

brahma paśyan vāmadevo brahmaṇo 'heyatāṃ sadā /
manvādibhiḥ sarvajīvaiḥ pratipede hi mantradṛk /
iti brāhme (1)

(1) Cf. ibid. p. 271,31f.: *idam ity ātmano yogyaṃ sarvaṃ samagraṃ bhavati / nirduḥkhānandasyāpekṣitatvān manasi sthitatvenedam iti yujyate / tat sarvam abhavat /* (BĀU I 4,10) *sarvaṃ bhaviṣyanta ity ādinā samagrabhāvasya prastutvāt / brahma paśyan vāmadevo brahmaṇo manvādijīvair aheyatvaṃ pratipede* ... ; see also AgniP 6; BhaviṣPV 3[7-9]; BrahVP 2; and MESQUITA 2000: 425n. 492.

1_5) BhāgTN (p. 6,16-18):
Subject matter: Omniscience of Kṛṣṇadvaipāyana / Bādarāyaṇa

uktaṃ hi brāhme
dvaipāyanena yad buddhaṃ brahmādyais tan na buddhyate /
sarvabuddhaṃ sa vai veda tadbuddhaṃ nānyagocaram /
iti (1)

(1) Cf. ibid. l. 16: *yāni bhagavajjñātāni tāny anyair apy ṛṣibhir jñāyante / tāni vettha* ... ; see also BhaviṣPV 21; BrāṇP 14.

2) BhāgTN (p. 17,2-3):
Subject matter: Origin of the visible world

brāhme ca –
yacchaktyekāṃśasaṃbhūtaṃ jagad etac carācaram /
iti (1)

(1) Cf. ibid. l. 1: *nidhānam atraikībhavanty anta iti* / *aṃśāṃsena sāmarthyair ekadeśena* ... ; see also BhavișPV 1.

3) BhāgTN (p. 17,5-7):
Subject matter: Sanatkumāra

kumāro nāma bhagavān svayaṃ svasmād ajāyata /
dideśa brahmaṇe brahma brahmacarye sthito vibhuḥ /
yasmāt sanatkumāraś ca brahmacaryam apālayat /
yaḥ sthāṇoḥ sthāṇutāṃ prādād bhagavān avyayo hariḥ /
iti brāhme (1)

(1) Cf. ĀdiP 1; SkaP 74.

4) BhāgTN (p. 20,4-5):
Subject matter: Hierarchy of the human beings

trividhāḥ puruṣā loke nīcamadhyavidāsinaḥ /
iti brāhme
caturdhā varṇarūpeṇa jagad etad vidāsitaṃ / (1)
iti ca (2)

(1) The BhāgP-text (I 3,26) used by Madhva reads *yathā vidāsinaḥ* (adj. of *vidasyati* = to be wanting; to become exhausted). Other editions however read *yathā avidāsinaḥ* = not drying up; perennial. Nevertheless, Madhva interprets *vidāsinas* in the sense of *avidāsinaḥ*; cf. BhāgTN p. 20,3: *vidāsinaḥ unnatāt bhinnād vā*!
(2) Cf. BhavișPV 15.

5) BhāgTN (p. 23,4-5):
Subject matter: Similarity and subservience of all beings to Viṣṇu

sāmyam īśvararūpeṣv sarvatra tadadhīnatām /
paśyati jñānasaṃpattyā vinidro yaḥ sa yogavit /
iti brāhme (1)

(1) Cf. ibid. l. 3: *nirvikalpakaḥ* / *madīyaṃ tadīyam iti bhedam apahāya sarvam īśvarādhīnam iti sthitaḥ* ... ; see also AgniP 5 and MESQUITA 2000: 323f.; 475f.; 496.

6) BhāgTN (p. 26,1-2):
Subject matter: Bad states of mind

atuṣṭir aprasādaś ca khedo 'tṛptis tathaiva ca /

analatvaṃ vadanty ete sarve paryāyavācakāḥ /
iti hi brāhme (1)

(1) Cf. ibid. (p. 25,15): *khedo 'nalaṃbuddhiḥ ... manyamānasya svecchayā.*

7) BhāgTN (p. 34,7-8):
Subject matter: Spies in the secret service of a King

amātyā mantriṇo dūtāḥ śreṇayaś ca purohitāḥ /
puraṃ janapadaṃ ceti sapta praṇidhayaḥ smṛtāḥ /
iti brāhme (1)

(1) In contrast to Madhva Kauṭilya mentions nine different classes of spies, cf. Arthasāstra I 11,1f.: *upadhābhiḥ śuddhāmātyavargo gūḍhapuruṣān utpādayet kāpaṭikodāsthitagrahapatikavaidehatāpasavyañjanān śattritīkṣṇarasadabhikṣukīś ca*; see also R.P. KANGLE, The Kauṭilya Arthaśāstra (Delhi 1986) Part III, 205-207.

8) BhāgTN (p. 38,4-5):
Subject matter: Dṛṣṭāntābhāsa

vyatyāso 'nanvayaś caiva prasiddho 'bhūta eva ca /
sarvasaṃhārikaś ceti dṛṣṭāntaḥ pañcadhā smṛtaḥ /
iti brāhme (1)

(1) Cf. ibid. l. 3: *tadāśrayā buddhiḥ / tajjñāninām api prakṛtisthānāṃ na tatsaṅgaḥ / kimu tasyeti vyatyāsadṛṣṭāntaḥ* ... ; ibid. n. 5; NSū (I 1. 5): *laukikaparīkṣakānāṃ yasminn arthe buddhisāmyaṃ sa dṛṣṭāntaḥ* and TphSI s.v.; see also BrahP 9 and MESQUITA 2000: 356f.

9) BhāgTN (p. 39,1-2);
Subject matter: Adhikadṛṣṭānta

ūrṇanābhyādiko viṣṇor viṣṇur viṣṇos tathaiva ca /
viṣṇur jīvasya dṛṣṭāntā ūnasāmyādhikāḥ kramāt /
iti brāhme

(1) Cf. ibid. (p. 38,12): *rāmo dāśarathir yathā / adhikadṛṣṭāntaḥ*; see also BrahP 8.

9_1) BhāgTN (p. 45,7-9):
Subject matter: Reversion of normal course of time

vyāsādayo vartamānam atītānāgate tathā /
vyatyasyāpi vadanty addhā mohanārthaṃ durātmanām /
paurvāparyaṃ yato naiva sadaiva parivartanāt /

ataś ca vyatyayād etad vadanti jñānacakṣuṣaḥ /
iti brāhme (1)

(1) Cf ibid. l. 3: *āsta ityādyatītārthe* ... ; ĀdiP 1 and MBhTN IX 125:
kvacin mohāyāsurāṇāṃ vyatyāsaḥ pratilomatā /
uktā grantheṣu tasmād dhi nirṇayo 'yam kṛto mayā /
see also BhaviṣPV 21; KūrP 2; MBh 42n. 6; NārP 9 and MESQUITA 2000_1: 48n. 72-73 [= 1997: 39n. 64-65].

10) BhāgTN (p. 51,13-14):
Subject matter: Prārabdhakarma and true knowledge of Brahman

bhagavantaṃ vinānyatra pravṛttyādiprakāśanam /
prārabdhakarmaṇaiva syāt kadācij jñāninām api /
tāṃ dvaitadṛṣṭiṃ me deva cchindhi jñānavarāsinā /
iti brāhme (1)

(1) Cf. ibid. l. 12: *brahmasampattir avagatiḥ* ... ; ĀdityaP 1; AgniP 1; BhaviṣPV 5; BrahVP 7; BrāṇP 6; MESQUITA 2000_1: 104f. [= 1997: 84f.] and MESQUITA 2007: 36n. 78 [= 2007_1: 448n. 77].

11) BhāgTN (p. 73,11-12):
Subject matter: Sense organs

cinmātrāṇīndriyāṇy āhur muktānām anyadaiva tu /
tāny eva jaḍayuktāni hy abhinnāni svarūpataḥ /
iti brāhme (1)

(1) v.l. *vibhinnāni*; ibid. n. 5: *vibhinnānīti pāṭhe – anyadā amuktidaśāyāṃ tāni cinmātrāṇīndriyāṇi jaḍendriyayuktāny eva bhavanti ity ekaṃ vākyam / tāni ca jaḍendriyāṇi vibhinnāni svarūpata ity aparam iti bhinnavākyatayā yojanīyam*; see also BhaviṣPV 17. For Madhva's doctrine of two-fold *manas* cf. MESQUITA 2000: 272f.

12) BhāgTN (p. 77,6-7):
Subject matter: Maharloka / Janarloka / Brahmaloka

manvantarāyuṣaḥ svargyā maharloke tu kālpikāḥ /
ābrahmaṇo janādyās tu maharloke 'pi ye varāḥ /
iti brāhme (1)

(1) Cf. ibid. l. 5: *tad viṣṇor viśvādhārarūpaṃ pratipadya yatra kalpāyuṣas taṃ maharlokam upaiti* ... ; see also AgniP 27.

13) BhāgTN (p. 92,9-10):
Subject matter: Brahmā-Jīva

brāhmaṇo mukham ity eva mukhāj jātatvahetutaḥ /

yathāvadac chrutau tadvaj jīvo brahmeti vāg bhavet /
iti brāhme (1)

(1) Cf. ibid. n. 5: *śukadevo 'py āha – brahma brāhmaṇaḥ puruṣasya mukhaṃ mukhajam / kṣatraṃ kṣatriyaḥ bāhava bāhujam iti*; see also BrāṇP 29.

14) BhāgTN (p. 93,10-11):
Subject matter: Mokṣa (synonyms)

mokṣaḥ śāntiś ca śaraṇaṃ nirvāṇaṃ cābhidhīyate /
iti brāhme (1)

(1) Cf. AgniP 16.

15) BhāgTN (p. 100,7-9):
Subject matter: Antaryāmin

kālo vastusvabhāvaś ca prakṛtiḥ prāṇa eva ca /
manaś ca pañca bhūtāni vikārastriguṇā api /
na svarūpaṃ harer etat tathāpy eṣu hariḥ sthitaḥ /
iti brāhme (1)

(1) Cf. ibid. l. 5: *puruṣa evādyo 'vatāraḥ / kālādayo rūpavat asvarūpam api priyatvāt* ... ; see also BhāgP 2; PadP 21.

16) BhāgTN (p. 106,1-2):
Subject matter: Mahidāsa

aitareyo hariḥ prāha nāradāya svakāṃ tanum /
yat prāpur vaiṣṇavā nānye yadṛte na sukhaṃ param /
iti brāhme (1)

(1) Cf. BhāgTN (p. 17,10-11):
avatāras tṛtīyo 'sya devarṣiḥ prathito divi /
mahidāsas tv aitareyo yas tantraṃ nārade 'vadat /
iti ca (unknown source);
cf. ĀdiP 1; AgniP 16; BrāṇP 67; 95[26] and LORENZ 2003: 25; 28f.; see also MESQUITA 2000: 522ff.

17) BhāgTN (p. 108,5-6):
Subject matter: Rāmāvatāra

rāma eko hy anantāṃśas tatra rāmābhido hariḥ /
śuklakeśātmakas tiṣṭhan ramayāmāsa vai jagat /
iti brāhme (1)

(1) Cf. ĀdiP 1 and MESQUITA 2000_1: 40f. [= 1997: 33f.].

18) BhāgTN (p. 118,1-2):
Subject matter: Vyāsa

bālo'pi sa gurutvena munibhyo brahmaṇā yataḥ /
datto 'to brahmarāteti nāma vaiyāsiker abhūt /
iti brāhme (1)

(1) Cf.BhaviṣPV 21; see also BrāṇP 14 and MESQUITA 2000_1: 42ff. [= 1997: 35ff.].

19) BhāgTN (p. 137,7):
Subject matter: Brahmā / Śrī

padmo brahmā samuddīṣṭaḥ padmā śrīr api cocyate /
iti brāhme (1)

(1) Cf. AgniP 25; BrāṇP 29; 51.

20) BhāgTN (p. 145,6-7):
Subject matter: Brahmā, the presiding Deity

kālajīvaguṇādīnām abhimānī caturmukhaḥ /
sarvajīvābhimānitvād aṃśa ity eva cocyate /
iti brāhme (1)

(1) Cf. ibid. l. 5: *aṃśo jīvaḥ* ... ; see also BhaviṣP 11; BrāṇP 29.

21) BhāgTN (p. 146,9-10):
Subject matter: Brahmavidyā

brahmavidyā hareś chāyā tadāṃśā hi sureṣv api /
sarvavidyāḥ śriyaḥ proktāḥ pradhānāṃśaś caturmukhe /
iti brāhme (1)

(1) Cf. AgniP 9; 14; BrāṇP 51; 101.

22) BhāgTN (p. 153,2-3):
Subject matter: Brahmā / Śiva

guṇapūrter ātmaśabdo brahmāhīnatvato haraḥ /
ahaṃśabdas tathāpy etau na jānīto hariṃ param /
iti brāhme (1)

(1) Cf. ibid. l. 1: *ātmā na veda brahmā / ahaṃ rudraḥ* ... ; AgniP 24[4c]; BhaviṣPV 26; BhaviṣP 6; BrahP 30; 34; BrahVP 14; 15; 39; BrāṇP 15[7]; 95; GarP 20; PadP 86; SkaP 13; 62; 68; 105; VāmP 10; 20; VarP 51; see also BrāṇP 29 and GarP 17.

22_1) BhāgTN (p. 156,16):
Subject matter: Viṣṇu, the supreme guiding Spirit

brahmāṇaṃ prāviśad viṣṇuḥ sahasrākṣaḥ sahasrapāt /
iti brāhme (1)

(1) Cf. ibid. l. 15: *virājaṃ brahmāṇam* ... ; see also BhāgP 2; GarP 17.

23) BhāgTN (p. 159,1):
Subject matter: Viṣṇu's supreme transcendence

pradhānavācakās tv ekaś cānanyaḥ kevalaḥ svayam /
iti brāhme (1)

(1) Cf. ibid. n. 1: ... *svayam iti sarvapradhāno bhagavān / tato bhavatīti svayambhūr iti / ata eva tantranyāyenātrodājahāra*; see also AgniP 6; VarP 52 and MESQUITA 2000: 424ff.

24) BhāgTN (p. 177,9-178,5):
Subject matter: Gradation in the creation

sthāsnubhir niyamān mukhyā sthiter gatir avāpyate /
prāyaḥ paropakartṛtvāt te mukhyasrotasas tataḥ / [1] (1)
nādho nordhvaṃ tiraścāṃ tu punas tatraiva yajjaniḥ /
yajñopayogaṃ ca satām upakāraṃ vināpi vā / [2]
tiryaksrotasa ity eva procyante jñānibhis tataḥ /
prāyo 'dhogamanaṃ yasmāt prayatnena vinā bhavet / [3]
arvāksrotasa ity eva mānuṣāḥ parikīrtitāḥ /
niyamād ūrdhvagantāro devā mokṣaikabhāginaḥ / [4]
ūrdhvasrotasa ity eva tasmāt te parikīrtitāḥ / [5ab]
iti brāhme
tiraścām sthāvarāṇāṃ ca buddhipūrvapravṛttinām /
asurāṇāṃ rakṣasāṃ ca piśācānāṃ tathaiva ca / [6]
arvāksrotastvam uddiṣṭaṃ niyamād asurādinām / [7ab]
iti ca (2)

(1) Cf. ibid. (178,6f.): *mukhyasrotasa ity asyārtha utsrotasa iti – ūrdhva ity eva yaḥ sūccatamaḥ saivābhidhīyate / ūrdhvasrotasa etasmād devā eva na tatpare / ucchabda uccamātre 'pi tasmāt sthāsnuṣu bhaṇyate* | iti ca (untraceable source).
(2) Cf. ibid. n. 3: *manuṣyāḥ ūrdhvagamanaṃ prati prayatnena vinādhogantāra ity arvāksrotasaḥ / asurādayaś ca prayatnenāpy adhogantāra iti te niyamenārvāksrotasaḥ*; see also BhaviṣPV 15; PadP 32.

25) BhāgTN (p. 185,14-15):
Subject matter: Antaryāmin

devyāṃ kālādirūpiṇyāṃ sthitaṃ brahmāpi sarvagam /
ucyate 'nanyagaṃ yasmād ātmavat sā harer vibhoḥ /
mahadādigataṃ yat tu tadanyagatam ucyate /
iti brāhme (1)

(1) Cf. ibid. l. 12f.: *sarvagatasyāpi brahmarūpasya kālādirūpayā prakṛtyā samavyāptāv api dārṣṭāntikāntarbhāvāt tadanyasminn anavasthānāc ca svarūpāvasthitasyety uktam*; see also AgniP 25; BhāgP 2; BhaviṣP 2[5]; BrahP 26; 30; 71; BrahVP 12_1; BrāṇP 29; 51; GarP 6[2cd]: HarV 32; KūrP 23; PadP 28; SkaP 21: VarP 53; ViṣP 1.

26) BhāgTN (p. 195,5):
Subject matter: Night (before creation)

brahmaṇā kālanāmnā tu saha śete harir niśi /
iti brāhme (1)

(1) Cf. BrahP 25; see also BrāṇP 29.

27) BhāgTN (p. 202,5-6):
Subject matter: Sacred syllable Om

praṇavaḥ pūrvavaktreṇa bhūrādyāś ca mukhatrayāt /
pradakṣiṇam avartanta vedāś caivāśramās tathā /
iti brāhme (1)

(1) Cf. ibid. l. 4: *praṇavaḥ pūrvavāktrāt*; see also BrāṇP 101.

28) BhāgTN (p. 225,1):
Subject matter: Dharma

dharmaḥ satya iti prokto dharmaś cāpi hareḥ priyaḥ /
iti brāhme (1)

(1) Cf. AgniP 9; 17; MBh 31; PadP 73; see also HarV 16 and MBh 15; 31.

29) BhāgTN (p. 227,5):
Subject matter: Nourishment of Deities and Ancestors

ūrjaṃ sārānnam uddiṣṭhaṃ tad devapitṛbhakṣaṇam /
iti brāhme (1)

(1) Cf. also BhaviṣP 5.

30) BhāgTN (p. 245,1-2):
Subject matter: Antaryāmin

puruṣo hṛdisthaḥ paramaḥ kālaḥ sarvagato hariḥ /+1

athavā rudradehastho hariḥ kāla itīritaḥ /
iti brāhme (1)

(1) A surplus syllable in the first Pāda or *paramaḥ* should be replaced by *paraḥ*; cf. BhāgP 2; BrahP 25; ViṣP 1.

31) BhāgTN (p. 252,6):
Subject matter: Satkāryavāda

asad avyaktanāma syād vyaktaṃ sad iti cocyate /
iti brāhme (1)

(1) Cf. ibid. l. 5: *sadviśeṣaṇaṃ viśeṣeṇa vyaktatvam*; see also MESQUITA 2000: 321f.

32) BhāgTN (p. 271,10-11):
Subject matter: Viṣṇu's Avatāras

matsyakūrmādirūpaṃ ca viṣṇor jñānaikamātrakam /
tan manyante bhautikaṃ tu ye gacchanty adharaṃ tamaḥ /
iti brāhme (1)

(1) Cf. ĀdiP 1; GarP 34 and MESQUITA 2000_1: 34ff. [= 1997: 29ff.].

33) BhāgTN (p. 277,1-2):
Subject matter: Viṣṇu's supreme transcendence

yathākāśe vimānādirūpabhedaḥ pratīyate /
tathā harau jagad idaṃ tatsāmarthyāt pratīyate /
iti brāhme (1)

(1) Cf. ibid. (p. 276,14): *khe rūpabhedo vāyvādikaḥ yathākāśasthito nityam ityādi ca* ... ; see also AgniP 6.

34) BhāgTN (p. 280,1-2):
Subject matter: Nārāyaṇa, the first / original Teacher

sanakādayo rudraśiṣyās teṣām anye tu yoginaḥ /+1
brahmaśiṣyās tathā rudro brahmā nārāyaṇasya ca /
iti brāhme (1)

(1) Cf. ibid. (p. 279,8f.): *brahmarasāsavārthibhiḥ śiṣyāṇāṃ mano 'libhiḥ* ... ; see also BrāṇP 101.

35) BhāgTN (p. 283,3-5):
Subject matter: Hara's Avatāras

vīrabhadrākhyarūpeṇa svena pūrvaṃ yayau haraḥ /

mūlarūpeṇa paścāt tu gatvā dakṣam athāvadhīt /
tatropendreṇa hariṇā jito dharmātmajena ca /
anyān jigāya prayayau kailāsam svaniveśanam /
iti brāhme (1)

(1) Cf. ĀdiP 1.

36) BhāgTN (p. 285,7-8):
Subject matter: Intrinsic aptitude (*yogyatā*) of Jīvas / Viṣṇu, the supreme guiding Spirit

kriyante stutayo 'nyatra tadantaryāmyapekṣayā /
na jīveṣu guṇāḥ pūrṇā yathāyogyā hi tadgatāḥ /
iti brāhme (1)

(1) Cf. ibid. l. 6: *antaryāmyapekṣayā śakteḥ śivasya ca param iti* ... ; see also BhāgP 2; BhaviṣPV 15; 30[86f.]; NārP 18; 20; 52; PadP 82; SkaP 60.

37) BhāgTN (p. 298,4-5):
Subject matter: Power of Deities

nāśakyaṃ devatānāṃ tu yadanyaiḥ śakitaṃ kvacit /
śaktā api na kurvanti yad anyavihitaṃ buddhāḥ /
iti brāhme (1)

(1) Cf. ibid. l. 3: *tasyaiva yogyatvāt lokapālānāṃ duṣkaram* ... ; see also BhaviṣP 5.

38) BhāgTN (p. 309,8-9):
Subject matter: Presiding Deity of Kalpas

kalpaḥ kalpābhimānī saṃchiṃśumārānugaḥ sthitaḥ /
vatsaro rājyam akarot pitrā dattaṃ mahābalaḥ /
iti brāhme (1)

(1) Cf. BhaviṣP 11; BrāṇP 27; PadP 37.

39) BhāgTN (p. 314,11-12):
Subject matter: Possession / seizure (*āveśa*) by Viṣṇu-Janārdana

vainye pṛthau sannihito rājarūpī janārdanaḥ /
iti brāhme (1)

(1) Cf. ibid. l. 7: *tatra sannihitaḥ sākṣād bhagavān* ... ; see also ĀdiP 1; BhāgP 2; BrahVP 17 and BrāṇP 42.

40) BhāgTN (p. 317,6-7):
Subject matter: Two types of Guṇas

guṇāḥ svarūpabhūtāś ca bāhyāś ceti dvidhā matāḥ /
svarūpabhūtā vyajyante harer bāhyān duhuḥ payaḥ /(1)
iti brahme (2)

(1) *duhuḥ* for *duduhuḥ*, metri causa (*lopaḥ samāne*).
(2) Cf. BrāṇP 69; 70 and MESQUITA 1990: 208n 603; 214f.; see also MESQUITA 2000: 239ff.

41) BhāgTN (p. 337,1-2):
Subject matter: Agni and the princess Śukī

rājaputrīṃ śukīm agnir āvartantīṃ pradakṣiṇam /
ādāyāntaradhād dānasamaye manmathāturaḥ /
iti brāhme

42) BhāgTN (p. 351,8-10):
Subject matter: Organs of life, perception and action

prāṇendriyāntaḥkaraṇabhedena trividhaṃ matam /
pañcapañcaiva te sarve prāṇā buddhīndriyāṇi ca /
karmendriyāṇi ca tathā tasmāt pañcavidhaṃ smṛtam /
liṅgaṃ ṣoḍaśakaṃ prāhur manasā saha tat punaḥ /
iti brāhme (1)

(1) Cf. BhaviṣPV 17 and MESQUITA 2000: 272.

43) BhāgTN (p. 369,6-15):
Subject matter: Heretics and the doctrine of Jainas

jñānānandātmako deha ṛṣabhasya mahātmanaḥ /
tādṛśenaiva manasā kramaṃs tu kuṭacācale /[1] (1)
davāgnim anupraviśyātha tatrasthaḥ prādahaj jagat /+ 1
evam agner abhivyaktas tatstho viṣṇuḥ sanātanaḥ /[2]
ṛṣabhatvena saṅgopya dharmān adyāpi tatragaḥ /
āste sa vāsudevātmā vāsudevo 'ham ity ajaḥ /[3]
sadā sthitaḥ sthitiṃ tāṃ tu śuśrāvārho durātmavān /
pūrvaṃ tu pauṇḍrako nāma vāsudevaḥ sudurmatiḥ /[4]
jātismaro dvidhā śāstraṃ pāṣaṇḍaṃ nirmame nṛpaḥ /
ekaṃ tu vāsudevākhyaṃ vāsudevo 'ham ity api /[5]
kutsitaṃ vāsudevatvapratipādakam ātmanaḥ /
lokārthe cāparam iti cakārārhatanāmakam /[6]

tatpraśiṣyaḥ krumur nāma na jānaṃs tanmataṃ param /
vāsudevātmatāṃ sarvajīvānām avadat kudhīḥ / [7]
krumbākhyaṃ śāstram akarod abhedapratipādakam /
kuśāstraṃ sarvavedānāṃ viruddhaṃ tāmasālayam / [8]
taddṛṣṭyādyāpi vartante vartiṣyanti tathā kalau /
aśaucā avratācārā vāsudevo 'ham ity api / [9]
iti brāhme (2)

(1) For *kuṭakācala.*
(2) Cf. ibid. l. 5: *abhimānābhāsena abhito jñānaprakāśena* ... ; see also BhavișPV 3n. 7; BrāṇP 22; GarP 28 and RUKMANI 1970: 34f.

44) BhāgTN (p. 441,5-6):
Subject matter: Hari, the supreme Creator of the universe

viprayajñādi mūlaṃ tu harer ity āsuraṃ matam /
harir eva hi sarvasya mūlaṃ samyaṅmater nṛpa /
iti brāhme (1)

(1) Cf. ibid. l. 2f.: *liṅgavān iva jīva iva –*
asamaṃ samatām eti bhrāntidṛṣṭyaiva kevalam /
jīvena brahma na samaṃ tattvaddṛṣṭyā kathaṃcana /
iti ṣāṅguṇye (untraceable source);
see also AgniP 12.

45) BhāgTN (p. 489,9-10):
Subject matter: Churning of the ocean

anantoḍho mandaras tu yadā vaivasvatāntaram /
amṛtārthaṃ suparṇoḍho raivatasyāntare manoḥ /
iti brāhme (1)

(1) Cf. ibid. n. 4: *vaivasvatamanvantare anantākhyena garuḍena ūḍhaḥ / raivatamanvantare tu suparṇākhyena / tathāhi*; MBhTN X 6: ... *yo 'nantanāmā garuḍas tadāṃsake / utpāṭya caikena kareṇa mandaro nidhāpatiḥ* ... iti |

46) BhāgTN (p. 508,8-9):
Subject matter: Viṣṇu's boat

bhagavatpadanaukā yā neyaṃ naukopamā bhavet /
tayā tīrtvā tu tām eva prāpya tiṣṭhanti tatra yat /
iti brāhme (1)

(1) Cf. VāmP 25.

47) BhāgTN (p. 517,3-4):
Subject matter: Viṣṇu, the supreme Creator of the universe

anīho 'kliṣṭakāritvāt tathāvikṛta eva san /
sarvaṃ kṛṇoti tad yuktam aiśvaryāt pūrṇaśaktitaḥ /
iti brāhme (1)

(1) Cf. AgniP 12 and MESQUITA 2000: 473f.

48) BhāgTN (p. 522,5-8):
Subject matter: Heretical doctrine that the world is illusory – a product of *māyā*

ahaṃ brahmāsmi devo 'smi nāsmi kevalamānuṣaḥ /
jāto 'smi varddhe dhanavān mriya ityādikaḥ sadā / [1]
dehādiṣu ca deveṣu parabrahmaṇi cābhidā /
mohād yanmāyayā nityaṃ dṛśyate 'dhamamadhyame / [2]
sa īśo na viparyeti sarveśatvāt kadācana /
putrādikaṃ viparyeti pitrādiś ca yato bhavet / [3]
iti brāhme
tallakṣaṇair vihīnāś ca brahma devo 'smi ceti tu /
asurāḥ pratipadyante janyādiṃ mānuṣā janāḥ / [4]
iti ca
parabrahmaṇa ekasya brahmāsmīti vicintanam /
paraṃ brahmeti rāmādīn lakṣaṇair avadhārayet / [5]
devo 'smīti ca devānāṃ tac ca jñeyaṃ svalakṣaṇaiḥ /
martyānāṃ mānuṣo 'smīti pratipattir vidhīyate / [6]
anyathā pratipattyā tu tamo yānti viniścayāt /
anyathā pratipadyanta āsurā niyataṃ janāḥ / [7]
ghoraṃ tamaś ca te yānti yathā jñānāt paraṃ surāḥ / [8ab]
iti ca (1)

(1) Cf. ibid. ll. 1f.: *ayam ātmā paramātmā / yataḥ paramātmano 'nekavidham aikyaṃ viparītajñānena yataś ca saṃsṛtir na nivartate sa eva na viparyeti / putrādikaṃ tu viparyeti tasmāt tasminn eva sthitiṃ kṛtvā mānuśoca ...* ; BhaviṣPV 3n. 7; see also ĀdiP 1.

49) BhāgTN (p. 540,4-5):
Subject matter: Etymology of *janārdana* and *rākṣasa*

ādino rākṣasāḥ proktās tadantatvāj janārdanaḥ /
ādyanta iti vijñeyaḥ pareśo brahmaṇīśanāt /
iti brāhme (1)

(1) Cf. BrāṇP 68.

50) BhāgTN (p. 582,6-7):
Subject matter: Viṣṇu, the Grantor of liberation

ātmānaṃ muktidaṃ viṣṇur yadi puṃsa udīkṣayet /
suprasannas tadā bandhas tata eveti setsyati /
iti brāhme (1)

(1) Cf. BhaviṣP 3.

51) BhāgTN (p. 598,11-13):
Subject matter: Veda, the supreme means of knowledge

kathāḥ kathayatīśasya vyāsasyānte sa nāradaḥ /
stutyarthaṃ tasya devasya jñāpanāya na tu kvacit /
pūrṇajñānāmṛtasyāsya na tu jñaptiḥ parād bhavet /
ṛṣiṣu prīyate viṣṇuḥ svayam eva janaiḥ śrutaḥ /
iti brāhme (1)

(1) Cf. BhaviṣPV 21; BrāṇP 82; MESQUITA 2000_1: 126 ff. [= 1997: 101ff.] and MESQUITA 2000: 402f.

52) BhāgTN (p. 624,4-5):
Subject matter: Trimūrti

brahmaṇi stho 'sṛjad viṣṇuḥ sthitvā rudre tv abhakṣayat /
pṛthak sthitvā jagat pāti tad brahmādyāhvayo hariḥ /
iti brāhme (1)

(1) Cf. AgniP 12; see also BrahVP 14; PadP 11; SkaP 29; VāmP 4; 10; 14.

53) BhāgTN (p. 774,2-4):
Subject matter: Viṣṇu, the Grantor of liberation / Doctrine of Pañcabheda

puruṣākhyo hṛdgatas tu viṣṇur jīvavibodhakaḥ /
phaladātrā tu bāhyena ya īśena bhidāṃ vadet /
tathaivānyasvarūpeṣu viṣṇor yo bhedadarśakaḥ /
yaś ca jīveśvarābhedaṃ paśyet te 'narthabhāginaḥ /
iti brāhme (1)

(1) Cf. BhaviṣPV 1; BhaviṣP 3 and MESQUITA 2000_1: 104ff. [= 1997: 83ff.].

54) BhāgTN (p. 808,4-5):
Subject matter: Liberation

sattvād guṇāj jātam api vyavadhānaṃ vinaiva tu /
muktidaṃ nirguṇaṃ proktaṃ vyavadhānena sāttvikam /
iti brāhme (1)

(1) Cf. ibid. (p. 807,6f.):
parokṣajñānam ātmottham āparokṣyeṇa darśanam /
viṣṇvāśrayaṃ sukhaṃ nityaṃ gamayet tatprasādataḥ /
na tu viṣṇoḥ svarūpaṃ tu sukhaṃ kenacid āpyate /
tasyaiva viṣayatvāt tu tatsukhaṃ ceti bhaṇyate /
parokṣajñānage yasmād viṣayaḥ svamanogataḥ /
ata ātmottham ity eva sukham āhur vipaścitaḥ /
iti ca (untraceable source);
see also AgniP 16 and 24.

55) BhāgTN (p. 833,5-6):
Subject matter: Brahmātmavid

brahmaṇāttam idaṃ sarvaṃ yat kiṃcit sacarācaram /
iti paśyeta yo vidvān sa hi brahmātmavin mataḥ /
iti brāhme (1)

(1) Cf. AgniP 9.

56) BSūBh (p. 8,2-3):
Subject matter: The supreme transcendence of Viṣṇu

śvapacād api kaṣṭatvaṃ brahmeśānādayaḥ surāḥ /
tadaivācyuta yānty eva yadaiva tvaṃ parāṅmukhaḥ /
iti brāhme ca (1)

(1) Most probably this quote is assigned to two sources, namely śaive ca skānde ... : cf. below SkaP 80; see also AgniP 6.

57) BSūBh (p. 21,7-8):
Subject matter: The epithets of Viṣṇu

ananto bhagavān brahma ānandetyādibhiḥ padaiḥ /
procyate viṣṇur evaikaḥ pareṣām upacārataḥ /
iti ca brāhme (1)

(1) Cf. BhāgP 1.

58) BSūBh (p. 24,3-5):
Subject matter: Upāsana (according to the *yogyatā* of the individual souls)

keṣāṃcit sarvagatvena keṣāṃcid hṛdaye hariḥ /

keṣāṃcid bahir evāsāv upāsyaḥ puruṣottamaḥ /
iti brāhme
agnau kriyāvatāṃ viṣṇur yogināṃ hṛdaye hariḥ /
pratimāsv aprabuddhānāṃ sarvatra viditātmanām /
iti ca (1)

(1) Cf. ibid. l. 2: *tattadupāsanāyogyatayā ca puruṣāṇāṃ* ... ; see also AgniP 20; BrahP 36; GarP 34; 44.

59) BSūBh (p. 27,13-15):
Subject matter: The attributes of Viṣṇu

pṛthag vaktuṃ guṇās tasya na śakyante 'mitatvataḥ /
yato 'to brahmaśabdena sarveṣāṃ vacanaṃ bhavet /
etasmād brahmaśabdo 'yaṃ viṣṇor eva viśeṣaṇam /
amitā hi guṇā yasmān nānyeṣāṃ tam ṛte vibhum /
iti brāhme (1)

(1) Cf. ibid. l. 16: *na ca jīve samanvayo 'bhidhīyate*; see also BhāgP 1; BrāṇP 40; 69.

60) BSūBh (p. 32,21-33,3):
Subject matter: Viṣṇu, the last Refuge

tathā ca brāḥme –
yathaiva pauruṣaṃ sūktaṃ nityaṃ viṣṇuparāyaṇam /
tathaiva me mano nityaṃ bhūyād viṣṇuparāyaṇam / (1)

(1) Cf. ibid. l. 21: *caśabdena sakaladevatantrapurāṇādiṣu viṣṇuparatvaṃ puruṣasūktasya darśayati* ... ; see also AgniP 27; SkaP 64.

61) BSūBh (p. 35,20-21):
Subject matter: The epithets of Brahmā and Śiva

caturmukhaḥ śatānando brahmaṇaḥ padmabhūr iti /
ugro bhasmadharo nagnaḥ kapālīti śivasya ca /
viśeṣanāmāni dadau svakīyāny api keśavaḥ /
iti ca brāhme (1)

(1) Cf. BrahP 66; BrāṇP 29; 68 and SkaP 90.

62) BSūBh (p. 37,7-8):
Subject matter: The contradictory attributes of Viṣṇu

asthūlānaṇurūpo 'sau sa viśvo 'viśva eva ca /
viruddhadharmarūpo 'sāv aiśvaryāt puruṣottamaḥ /
iti brāhme (1)

(1) Cf. ibid. ll. 5f.: *asthūlam anaṇu ityādinā sthūlāṇvādīnām anyavastusvabhāvānāṃ vyāvṛtteś ca / asthūlo 'naṇur amadhyamo madhyamo 'vyāpako vyāpako yo 'sau harir ādir anādir aviśvo viśvaḥ saguṇo nirguṇa ityāder viṣṇor eva te dharmāḥ* ... ; see also BrāṇP 69 and MESQUITA 2000: 436ff.

63) BSūBh (p 42,20-21):
Subject matter: Omniscience of Vyāsa

sarvajñasyaiva kṛṣṇasya tv ekadeśavicintitam /
svīkṛtya munayo brūyus tanmataṃ na virudhyate /
iti ca brāhme (1)

(1) Cf. ibid. l. 19: *uktaphalānadhikāramātraṃ jaiminimatam / ato na matavirodhaḥ* ... (BSū I 3,31/33); see also BhaviṣPV 21.

64) BSūBh (p. 43,4):
Subject matter: Citraratha, the Kṣatriya's mark

rathas tv aśvatarīyuktaś citra ity abhidhīyate /
iti brāḥme (1)

(1) Cf. ibid. l. 3: *ayam aśvatarīratha iti citrarathasaṃbandhitvena liṅgena pautrāyaṇasya kṣatriyatvāvagateś ca* ... ; see also BrahVP 24 and SARMA 1999: 606.

65) BSūBh (p. 44,23-24):
Subject matter: Viṣṇu's namelessness and formlessness

anāmā so 'prasiddhatvād arūpo bhūtavarjanāt /
iti hi brāhme (1)

(1) Cf. BrāṇP 69.

66) BSūBh (p. 114,22-23):
Subject matter: Brahmā, the Creator (etymology)

yasmād virecayet sarvaṃ viriñcas tena bhaṇyate /
eko hi kartā jagato brahmaiva ca caturmukhaḥ /
iti ca yuktir brāhme (1)

(1) Cf. ibid. ll. 21f.: *viriñco vā virecayati vidadhāti brahmā vāva viriñca etasmād dhīme rūpanāmanīti* gaupavanaśrutiḥ (untraceable source); see also BrāṇP 29.

67) BSūBh (p. 117,23-24):
Subject matter: Vital airs (*prāṇa*) at the time of death

puruṣasya mṛtau brahman prāṇā bhāgata eva tu /

adhidaivaṃ prāpnuvanti bhāgato 'nuvrajanti tam /
punaḥ śarīrasaṃprāptau tam evānuviśanti ca /
iti brāḥme (1)

(1) Cf. ibid. l. 22: *yatrāsya puruṣasya mṛtasyāgnim vāgapy eti vā taṃ prāṇaḥ* (BĀU III 2,13) *ity ādiśruter na prāṇānaṃ jīvena saha gatir iti cet / na / bhāgato 'gnyādiprāpteḥ* ... ; see also BhavisPV 17.

68) BSūBh (p. 121,15-16):
Subject matter: Torments of hell

atipriye yathā rājā na duḥkhaṃ sahate kvacit /
atyapriye sukham api tathaiva parameśvaraḥ /
iti hi brāhme (1)

(1) Cf. ibid. l. 14: *lokasiddhaṃ ca / caśabdāl lokasiddhir api smārtety āha* ... ; see also BhavisPV 12; 19.

69) BSūBh (p. 124,4-7):
Subject matter: Transmigration / Origin of human life

sthāvarāṇi divaḥ prāptaḥ sthāvarebhyaś ca pūruṣam /
puruṣāt striyam āpannas tato dehaṃ yathākramam /
dehena jāyate jantur iti sāmānyato janiḥ /
viśeṣajananaṃ cāpi procyamānaṃ nibodha me /
sthāsnuṣv athāpi puruṣe pramadāyām athāpi vā /
garbhe vā bahir evātha kvacit sthānāntareṣu vā /
iti ca brāhme (1)

(1) Cf. ibid. (p. 123,9f.): *pitṛśarīrān mātṛyonim anupraviśya tata eva śarīraṃ prāpnoti ... divaḥ sthāsnūn gacchati sthāsnubhyaḥ pitaraṃ pitur mātaraṃ mātuḥ śarīraṃ śarīreṇa jāyata iti saṃmitam athāsaṃmitaṃ sthāsnubhyo jāyate pitur mātur antare vā garbhe vā bahir veti* pauṣyāyaṇaśruteḥ (untraceable source); see also BrahP 76 and BrāṇP 33.

70) BSūBh (p. 138,2-3):
Subject matter: Reward of the Deities

sādhanasyottamatvena sādhyaṃ cottamam āpnuyuḥ /
brahmādayaḥ krameṇaiva yathānandaḥ śrutau śrutaḥ /
iti ca brāhme (1)

(1) Cf. ibid. (p. 137,9f.): *tasya ca bhaktijñānāder vṛddhihrāsabhāktvaṃ vidyate / brahmādīnām uttamānāṃ sarveṣāṃ bhaktatve 'ntarbhāvāt / evaṃ bhaktyādiviśeṣāṅgīkārād eveśvarasya brahmādīn anyān prati ca sāmañjasyaṃ bhavati* ... ; see also BhavisP 5; 15 and MESQUITA: 2007: 11 [= 2007_1: 435].

71) BSūBh (p. 139,29-30):
Subject matter: Attributes of Viṣṇu are identical with His nature

ānandena tv abhinnena vyavahāraḥ prakāśavat /
kālavad vā yathā kālaḥ svāvacchedakatāṃ vrajet /
iti brāhme (1)

(1) Cf. ibid. ll. 27f.: *prakāśavat kālavad vā yathāṅge śayanādikam* / *brahmaṇaścaiva muktānām ānando 'bhinna eva tv* iti nārāyaṇādhyātme (untraceable source); see also BrahP 25 and MESQUITA 2000: 429ff.

72) BSūBh (p. 175,10-11):
Subject matter: Brahmā's freedom during the creation

svecchayaiva pravṛttis tu brahmaṇo vidhicoditā /
nāśaṅkyaṃ tanmataṃ kvāpi viṣṇoḥ pratyakṣacodanā /
itareṣāṃ na vihitā svecchāvṛttiḥ kathaṃcana /
iti hi brāhme (1)

(1) Cf. ibid. ll. 8f.: ... *yathā vedadhāraṇaṃ traivarṇikānāṃ vihitaṃ nānyeṣāṃ* / *evaṃ svamatānusāriṇī pravṛttir jñānināṃ vihitā na tatrādharmāśaṅkā kāryā nānyeṣām iti vā* ... ; see also BrāṇP 29.

73) BSūBh (p. 182,8):
Subject matter: Asuras

asurā bahulā yasmāt tasmān na janatām iyāt /
iti ca brāhme (1)

(1) Cf. ibid. ll. 6f.: *devabhāgād asurabhāga eva bahulaḥ* (BĀU I 3,10) *tasmān na janam iyād iti liṅgāt* / *caśabdāt tataḥ kānīyasā eva devā jyāyasā asurā iti* śruteś *ca* (BĀU I 3,1) ... ; see also BhaviṣPV 12.

74) BSūBh (p. 194,4-6):
Subject matter: Meditation as means of liberation

ātmā viṣṇur iti dhyānaṃ viśeṣaṇaviśeṣyataḥ /
sarveṣāṃ ca mumukṣūṇām upadeśaś ca tādṛśaḥ /
kartavyo nāsya hānena kasyacin mokṣa iṣyate /
iti ca brāhme (1)

(1) Cf. ibid. (p. 193,14f.): *ātmety upadeśa upāsanaṃ ca mokṣārthibhiḥ sarvathā kāryam eva* / *nānyaṃ vicintaya ātmānam evāhaṃ vijānīyām ātmānam upāsa ātmā hi mamaiṣa bhavati* / *iti hy upagacchanti* ... ; see also AgniP 9; 20; BrahVP 19.

75)BSūBh (p. 213,3-4):
Subject matter: Attributes of the released souls

muktānāṃ satyakāmatvaṃ sāmarthyaṃ ca parasya tu /
kāmānukūlakāmatvaṃ nānyat teṣāṃ vidhīyate /
iti hi brāhme (1)

(1) Cf. ibid. l. 2: *tat parameśvarakāmādyavibhāgenaiva teṣāṃ satyakāmatvam* ... ; see also AgniP 16; BhaviṣP 15; HarV 26; VāyuP 1; 2_1 and MESQUITA 2000: 519f.

76) GīBh (p. 39,10-12):
Subject matter: Transmigration

jīvaṃś caturdaśād ūrdhvaṃ puruṣo niyamena tu /
strī vāpy anūnadaśakaṃ dehaṃ mānuṣam ārjate /
caturdaśordhvajīvini saṃsāraś cādivarjitaḥ /
ato 'vittvā paraṃ devaṃ mokṣāśā kā mahāmune /
iti brāhme (1)

(1) Cf. GīBh (p. 39,6-9): *pratijanma kṛtānām anantakarmaṇāṃ bhāvāt / na ca sarvāṇi (karmāṇi) bhuktāni / ekasmiñ charīre bahūni hi karmāṇi karoti / tāni caikaikāni bahujanmaphalāni kānicit / tatraikaikāni karmāṇi bhuñjan prāpnoty eva śeṣeṇa mānuṣyam / tataś ca bahuśarīraphalāni karmāṇīty asamāptiḥ / tac coktam* ... ; see also BSūBh (p. 118,24-27): *tataḥ śeṣeṇemaṃ lokam āyāti punaḥ karma kurute punar gacchati punar āgacchatīti śruteḥ /*
bhuktaśeṣānuśayavān imām prāpya bhuvaṃ punaḥ /
karma kṛtvā punar gacchet punar āyāti nityaśaḥ /
ā caturdaśamād varṣāt karmāṇi niyamena tu /
daśāvarāṇāṃ dehānāṃ kāraṇāni karoty ayam /
ataḥ karmakṣayān muktiḥ kuta eva bhaviṣyati /
ityādismṛteś *ca śeṣavān evāyāti* (unknown source).
See also BrahP 80, BrāṇP 33 and MESQUITA 2007: 35n. 76 [= 2007_1: 448n. 75].

77) GīBh (p. 58,14-15):
Subject matter: Samnyāsa

saṃnyāse tu turīye vai prītir mama mahīyasī /
yeṣām atrādhikāro na teṣāṃ karmeti niścayaḥ /
ityādeś ca brāhme (1)

(1) Cf. NārP 36_1; see also AgniP 9 and 21.

78) GīBh (p. 67,4-8):
Subject matter: Predestination

svataḥ sarve 'pi cidrūpāḥ sarvadoṣavivarjitāḥ /
jīvās teṣāṃ tu ye doṣās ta upādhikṛtā matāḥ /

sarvaṃ ceśvaratas teṣāṃ na kiṃcit svata eva tu /
samā eva hy ataḥ sarve vaiṣamyaṃ bhrāntisaṃbhavam /
evaṃ samā nṛjīvās tu viśeṣo devatādiṣu /
svābhāvikas tu niyamād dharer eva sadātanaḥ /
asurādes tathā doṣā nityāḥ svābhāvikā api /
guṇadoṣau mānuṣāṇāṃ nityau svābhāvikau matau /
guṇaikamātrarūpās tu devā eva sadā matāḥ /
iti brāḥme (1)

(1) Cf. ibid. ll. 2f.: ... *cidrūpā eva hi jīvāḥ / viśeṣas tv antaḥkaraṇakṛtaḥ / sarveṣāṃ ca sādhutvādikaṃ sarvam īśvarakṛtam eva svato na kiṃcid api / uktam caitat sarvam* ... AgniP 12; BhaviṣP 3 and MESQUITA 2000: 510ff.

79) GīBh (p. 71,4-5):
Subject matter: Damnation of evil souls

śubhecchārahitānāṃ ca dveṣiṇāṃ ca ramāpatau /
nāstikānāṃ ca vai puṃsāṃ sadā muktir na jāyate /
iti niṣedhād brāhme (1)

(1) Cf. ibid. l. 3: *na kadācit svayam eva mano niyamyate* ... ; see also BhaviṣPV 12; 19; BrahVP 10[3f.]; BrāṇP 53n. 4; SkaP 65.

80) GīBh (p. 78,4-5):
Subject matter: Liberation

tac coktaṃ brāhme –
janmabhir bahubhir jñātvā tato māṃ pratipadyate /
iti (1)

(1) Cf. ibid. l. 4: *bahunāṃ janmanām ante jñānavān bhavati* ... ; AgniP 16; BrahP 76; BrahVP 31 and MESQUITA 2007: 33f. [= 2007_1: 447f.]

81) GīBh (p. 83,23-24):
Subject matter: The omniscient author of the Vedas

tvaṃ kaviḥ sarvavedānāt /
iti ca brāhme (1)

(1) Cf. ibid. l. 23: *dhyeyam āha kavim iti / kaviṃ sarvajñam / "yaḥ sarvajñaḥ"* iti śrutiḥ (= MuU I 1,9); see also BrāṇP 101 and MESQUITA 2000: 156n. 308.

82) GīBh (p. 87,10):
Subject matter: Liberation / Kramamukti

divādidevatābhis tu pūjito brahma yāti hi |
iti hi brāhme (1)

(1) Cf. ibid. l. 9: *abhimānidevatāś cāgnyādayaḥ | katham anyathā ahna āpūryamāṇa-pakṣam iti* (ChU IV 15,5) *yujyate*; see also ĀdityaP 1; BrahVP 37; BrāṇP 20; GarP 42; 44; 45; 57; NārP 47; VarP 20; 38; 54 and MESQUITA 1994: 463f.

83) GīT (p. 98,6):
Subject matter: Saptarṣi

marīcir atryaṅgirasau pulastyaḥ pulahaḥ kratuḥ |
vasiṣṭhaś ca mahātejāḥ pūrve saptarṣayaḥ smṛtāḥ |
iti brāhme (1)

(1) This Śloka has been handed down with different variants (= BrahP III 8-9ab):
marīcir atrir bhagavān aṅgirāḥ pulahaḥ kratuḥ |
pulastyaś ca vasiṣṭhaś ca saptaite brahmaṇaḥ sutāḥ |
uttarasyāṃ diśi tathā dvijāḥ saptarṣayas tathā |
In GīBh (p. 98,5-6) it has been transmitted in the wording of GīT (p. 97,30f.) *pūrve sapta ṛṣayaḥ – marīcir atryaṅgirasau pulastyaḥ pulahaḥ kratuḥ | vasiṣṭhaś ca mahātejā iti* mokṣadharmoktāḥ = MBh (XII 201,4/322,27; I 59,10) ending with: ... *te hi sarva-purāṇeṣūcyante*; see also KūrP 30_3; PadP 47; SkaP 78[2f.]; ViṣP 7.

84) ĪśUBh (p. 509,17-19):
Subject matter: Viṣṇu, the supreme guiding Spirit (*antaryāmin*) of Prakṛti

svataḥ pravṛttyaśaktatvād īśāvāsyam idaṃ jagat |
pravṛttaye prakṛtigaṃ yasmāt sa prakṛtīśvaraḥ |
tadadhīnapravṛttitvāt tadīyaṃ sarvam eva yat |
taddattenaiva bhūñjīthā ato nānyaṃ prayācayet |
iti brāhme (1)

(1) Cf. ibid. ll. 15f.: *īśasya vāsayogyam īśāvāsyam | jagatyāṃ prakṛtau | tena īśena tyaktena dattena bhuñjīthāḥ* ... ; see also AgniP 25; BhāgP 2; BrāṇP 51.

85) Vāda (p. 50,18-19):
Subject matter: Exegetical principles of Āgama

viruddhavat pratīyanta āgamā yatra vai mithaḥ |
tatra dṛṣṭānusāreṇa teṣāṃ artho 'nvavekṣyate |
iti brāhmavacanāc ca (1)

(1) Cf. ibid. ll. 16f.: *evaṃ pratyakṣānumānāgamaviruddhatvād abhedaviṣayavat pra-tīyamānāny api vākyāni sādṛṣyādyarthāny eva yojanīyāni*; see also BrahVP 30; MES-QUITA 2000_1: 155ff. [= 1997: 125ff.] and MESQUITA 2000: 174n. 361.

Brahmavaivartapurāṇa (BrahVP)

[BrahVP is dedicated to Kṛṣṇa because in it Brahman is fully revealed by Kṛṣṇa. BrahVP explains its title as follows (I 1,58cd-59ab):

vivṛtaṃ brahmakārtsnyaṃ ca kṛṣṇena yatra śaunaka /
brahmavaivartakaṃ tena pravadanti purāvidaḥ /

(cf. ROCHER 1986: 160-164; HAZRA 1987: 166f.). The quotes attributed to it appear in AiUBh (twice); BhāgTN (nineteen times); BSūBh (ten times); ChUBh (once); GīBh (seven times); GīT (five times); KathU (once); VTN (once). Their topics are the usual ones, namely the supreme transcendence of Viṣṇu, *avatāra*-doctrine; liberation, creation etc., but there is not a single quote referring directly to Kṛṣṇa. I could find only two indirect references to him in BrahVP 6[2d] and 39 [2a]. Some quotes seem to belong to Brahmatarka (cf. v.g. GīBh p. 67,13-15 = BrahVP 35n. 1). One quote is ascribed to BrahP and BrahVP at the same time (cf. below BrahPV 20). Another quote reference (BrahVP 34), beginning with *uktaṃ ca* and ending with ityādi brahmavaivarte, is in reality a collection of several different quotes. I could identify only one of them (MBh XIII 295*; MaitrU VI 34). It seems that the remaining quotes have been authored by Madhva himself, as his interpretation of Gī VI 6 shows (cf. also BrahVP 34n. 2). The first part of the said quote seems to follow Upendravajrā. I was unable to assign the last part with twelve syllables to any known metre. The verses in-between are Ślokas. There are some metrical lapses in BrahVP 34 (last but one) and in BrahVP 38[14cd] or BrahVP 43cd.]

1) AiUBh (p. 214,26-27):
Subject matter: Viṣṇu, the supreme Creator of the universe

bhūtebhyo 'nantaraṃ tv aṇḍaṃ sṛṣṭvā viṣṇuḥ purā prabhuḥ /
lokabhedāṃś ca cakre 'tra paścād brahmā viśeṣataḥ /
samyak cakāra lokāṃs tān lokakartā tataḥ sa ca /
iti brahmavaivarte (1)

(1) Cf. AgniP 12; MatsyaP 5.

2) AiUBh (p. 217,26-27):
Subject matter: Viṣṇu's supreme transcendence / Antaryāmin

aheyatvād ahaṃ viṣṇuḥ sa tu sarvāntaratvataḥ /
asy asmītyādibhiḥ śabdair ucyate 'nyo 'pi jīvataḥ /
iti brahmavaivarte (1)

(1) Cf. ibid. ll. 24f.: ... *janma jānann api devānāṃ / duḥkhādiheyarahitatvena vyajānām ity arthaḥ / tasmād ahaṃ manur abhavam ityādāv aheyaguṇaṃ bhagavantam evāhaṃśabdo vakti / sarvāntaratvāt tasminn evābhavam ity uttamapuruṣaśabdo 'pi sarvo vartate* ... ; see also AgniP 6; BhāgP 2; BhaviṣPV 3n. 1 and 3; BrahP 1_4; BrāṇP 3n. 3; 85 also MESQUITA 2000: 162n. 330.

3) BhāgTN (p. 7,3-5)
Subject matter: Liberation by means of Abhyāsa

uktaṃ ca brahmavaivarte –
śārīrād vācikābhyāso vācikān mānaso bhavet /
mānasād vivaśān mucyen nānyathā muktir iṣyate /(1)

(1) Cf. ibid. l. 3: *vivaśaḥ bahvabhyāsāt* ... ; AgniP 9; GarP 3.

4) BhāgTN (p. 20,9-10):
Subject matter: Doctrine of Avatāra

jīvās tatpratibiṃbāṃśā varāhādyāḥ svayaṃ hariḥ /
dṛśyate bahudhā viṣṇur aiśvaryād eka eva tu /
iti brahmavaivarte (1)

(1) Cf. ibid. l. 8: *ete proktāvatārāḥ / mūlarūpī svayam eva* ... ; see also ĀdiP 1; BhāgP 3.

5) BhāgTN (p. 36,9-10):
Subject matter: Attributes of Viṣṇu

sāttvataḥ sāttvikasnehāt satvo hy ānandarūpataḥ /
iti brahmavaivarte (1)

(1) Cf. ibid. l. 7: *sāttvikānām anugrāhaka.* I prefer the reading *satya* to *satva* as in Tantrabhāgavata:

dhārakatvād dharmarūpo hy aiśvaryāder bhago hy asau /
satya ānandarūpatvād ṛto jñānasvarūpataḥ /
yaśo hy alaṃ prasiddhatvād dayā hi karuṇākaraḥ /
iti tantrabhāgavate (untraceable source-quotation);

see also ĀdiP 1; BrāṇP 69; NārP 21.

6) BhāgTN (p. 45,12-46,3):
Subject matter: Viriñca / Brahmā

vijñānātmā viriñco 'yaṃ yas tasmin līyate jagat /
yādāṃsi sāgare yadvat sa kṣetrajñe janārdane /
hṛdisthe 'tha sa ca vyāpte svātmany ekībhavaty uta /
pralayau bhedavantau tau pūrvoktau brahmakṛṣṇayoḥ /
antasthasya bahiṣṭhe tu tasya tasminn abhedataḥ /
iti brahmavaivarte (1)

(1) Cf. BrāṇP 29.

7) BhāgTN (p. 51,10-11):
Subject matter: Prārabdhakarma and knowledge of liberation

jñānādivyaktir avyaktiḥ sukhaduḥkhādikaṃ tathā /

sudṛṣṭabrahmatattvānāṃ bhavaty ārabdhakarmaṇā /
iti brahmavaivarte (1)

(1) Cf. ibid. l. 9: *tamādirodhaś ca prārabdhakarmaṇaiva* ... ; see also ĀdityaP 1; cf. BrahP 10 and MESQUITA 2007: 36n. 78 [= 2007_1: 448n. 77].

8) BhāgTN (p. 67,9-10):
Subject matter: Viṣṇu's Body

śilāvat tasya deho 'yam āṇḍakośas tu sāvṛtiḥ /
tattantratvān na tatsaṃsthaduḥkhabhogena tu kvacit /
iti brahmavaivarte (1)

(1) Cf. ibid. l. 8: *yādṛśīty asya viśeṣa ityādi / viśeṣa āṇḍakośaḥ* ... ; see also AgniP 4, GarP 34.

9) BhāgTN (p. 87,7-8):
Subject matter: Viṣṇu's supreme transcendence

nityaṃ gṛhītāḥ sattvādyā sthityādiṣu viśeṣataḥ /
yugapat kramaśaś caiva gṛhṇāti bhagavān hariḥ /
iti brahmavaivarte (1)

(1) Cf. ibid. l. 6: *yugapat kramaśo 'pi vety asya parihāraḥ / sattvaṃ rajas tama iti* ... ; n. 4: *nirguṇasya guṇebhyo 'tikrāntasya adhīnā ye guṇās te trayo 'pi sthitisarganirodhalakṣaṇavyāpārārthaṃ māyayā prakṛtyā saha gṛhītā vyāpāravantaḥ kṛtāḥ / māyayā svecchayā vā / sṛṣṭisthityādīnāṃ kramikatvāt guṇānāṃ krameṇa pravartanam īśaḥ karotīti bhāva* iti prācīnaṭīkā; see also AgniP 6.

10) BhāgTN (p. 139,6-11):
Subject matter: Asuras

asurā api ye viṣṇuṃ śaṅkhacakradharaṃ raṇe /
bhaktipūrvam avekṣante jñeyā bhagavatā iti /
vidviṣanti tu ye viṣṇum ṛṣiputrā api sphuṭam /
asurās te 'pi vijñeyā gacchanti ca sadā tamaḥ /
jīvadvayasamāyogād dhiraṇyakamukhāḥ pare /
bhaktidveṣayutāś ca syur gatis teṣāṃ yathānijam /
kaṃsapūtanikādyāś ca bāndhavādiyutā yataḥ /
jīvadvayasamāyogād gatidvayajigīṣavaḥ /
sarvathā bhaktito muktir dveṣāt tama udīritam /
niyamas tv anayor nityaṃ mohāyānyad vaco bhavet /
iti brahmavaivarte (1)

(1) Cf. BhāgP III 2,24 (= III 3,24) and BrahP 79; BrāṇP 53n. 4; GarP 29; see also BhaviṣPV 12.

11) BhāgTN (p. 161,3-4):
Subject matter: Antaryāmin

eko 'pi sthānanānātvān nāneva harir īyate /
sarvāntaryāmiṇas tasya na bhedo vidyate kvacit /
iti brahmavaivarte (1)

(1) Cf. ibid. l. 1: *svato nāsti / tadadhīnaṃ vidyamānam apy aśuddham / yac ca nānātvaṃ tadapi sthānabhedād asad eva bhāti* ... ; see also BhāgP 2.

12) BhāgTN (p. 170,12-13):
Subject matter: Viṣṇu's supreme transcendence

sarvato 'pi priyo hy ātmā tasyāpi priyatāṃ hariḥ /
āpādayati yat tasmāt svātmano 'pi priyo hariḥ /
iti brahmavaivarte (1)

(1) Cf. ibid. n. 8: *kalatraputrādiṣu prītir dehasaṃbandhena / dehe prītir jīvātmasaṃbandhena / jīvātmani prītiḥ paramātmasaṃbandheneti / paramātmany eva prītiḥ svābhāvikī*ti viśvanāthacakravartī; see also AgniP 6.

12_1) BhāgTN (p. 186,10-182,2):
Subject matter: Viṣṇu's three-fold infinity

deśataḥ kālataś caiva vastutas tu tridhā hareḥ /
yathānantyaṃ na cānyasya prakṛter deśakālataḥ /
tathā śabdasya kālasya deśānantyaṃ ca kālataḥ /
kālaśabdātmikā saiva tathāpi tu hareḥ sadā /
nāsyāḥ sāmarthyaleśo 'pi jñānānandaguṇeṣv api /
jñeyas tadavaro vāyuḥ śesavīndraharās tataḥ /
avarās tata indrādyā guṇaiḥ sarvair na saṃśayaḥ /
iti brahmavaivarte (1)

(1) Cf. ibid. ll. 8f.: *svarūpāvasthitasya kaivalyam aviśeṣo nirantara ity etāni viśeṣaṇāni krameṇa paramamahataḥ kālasyāpy atroktāni* ... ; see also AgniP 25; BhaviṣPV 24; MBh 34; MESQUITA 2000: 415ff.; 494ff. and MESQUITA 2003: 98f.

13) BhāgTN (p. 251,1-3):
Subject matter: God Vāyu

prāpnoti vāyuḥ sarvaṃ tu svata eva hares tathā /
ataḥ prāptir iti prāhur vāyuṃ bhūtapatiṃ prabhum /
pradhānavāyur anyeṣu nityāviṣṭo yatas tataḥ /

tadguṇās teṣu cocyante nīcatā nāsya tatkṛtā /
iti brahmavaivarte (1)

(1) Cf. BhaviṣPV 17; KūrP 23 and MESQUITA 2003: 103.

14) BhāgTN (p. 274,11-275,2):
Subject matter: Trimūrti

brahmasthaś caiva rudrasthaḥ svayaṃ cāpi hariḥ prabhuḥ /
prajāṃ tripūruṣasamāṃ yacchatv ity atrir aicchata /
tasmāt sa brahmarudrābhyāṃ saha viṣṇur jagatpatiḥ /
āgatya tu trimūrtyaṃśān putrān prādāj janārdanaḥ /
bhāvitvāc caiva kāryasya lokānāṃ mohanāya ca /
iti brahmavaivarte(1)

(1) Cf. BhāgTN (p. 275n. 1): *avaśyaṃ bhāvitatvāt dattadurvāsaḥsomānām avatārakāryasya ... tena trayāṇām apy aikātmyaṃ jagadīśvaratvaṃ ceti duṣṭānāṃ mohanāya ca*; see also BhāgP 1 and BrahP 52; 83; ViṣP 7.

15) BhāgTN (p. 279,4):
Subject matter: Viṣṇu's supreme transcendence

rudreṇa dhīyate viṣṇur viṣṇor dhyeyo na kaścana /
iti brahmavaivarte (1)

(1) Cf. ibid. l. 3: *viśeṣeṇa dhīyate cintyate ...* ; see also AgniP 6.

16) BhāgTN (p. 284,6-7):
Subject matter: Viṣṇu's supreme transcendence

nāhaṃ nendro na caivānye yat tattvaṃ na viduḥ param /
tasya viṣṇor vaśe rudro mama vāyor athāpi vā /
nānyasya kasyacit puṃsas tasyetthaṃ vaḥ kutaḥ kṛtam /
iti brahmavaivarte (1)

(1) Cf. ibid. ll. 3f.: *yajña indraḥ – yajño yajñapatis tv indraḥ puruhūtaḥ puruṣṭuta* iti abhidhānam (unknown source) *tasyātmatantrasya / tasya viṣṇor manovaśagasya ...* ; see also AgniP 6.

17) BhāgTN (p. 296,7-8):
Subject matter: Aṃśāvatāras and Avatāras

āviṣṭā hariṇā jīvā brahmā dakṣo manuḥ pṛthuḥ /
śakrādyā ṛṣayaś caiva matsyavyāsādayo hariḥ /
iti brahmavaivarte (1)

(1) Cf. ĀdiP 1; BhāgP 2; BhaviṣPV 30[82]; BrahP 39; BrāṇP 3; 28; 39; 53; 56; 59[2]; 95[17f.]; PadP 43; 50; SkaP 2; 52; VarP 51 and MESQUITA 2000_1: 42f. [= 1997: 35f.].

18) BhāgTN (p. 419,10-11):
Subject matter: Sense organs

dravyātmakaḥ sthūladehaḥ kriyā karmendrīyāṇi ca /
jñānendriyāṇi ca mano jñānātmakam udāhṛtam /
iti brahmavaivarte (1)

(1) Cf. BhaviṣPV 17.

19) BhāgTN (p. 446,8-12):
Subject matter: Ātman's true nature

na hi dehādir ātmā syān na ca śatrur udīritaḥ /
ato daihikavṛddau vā kṣaye vā kiṃ prayojanam /
yas tu dehagato jīvaḥ sa hi nāśaṃ na gacchati /
ataḥ śatruvivṛddhau ca svanāśe śocanaṃ kutaḥ /
dehādivyatiriktau tu jīveśau pravijānatām /
ata ātmavivṛddhis tu vāsudeve ratiḥ sthirā /
śatrunāśas tathājñānanāśo nānyaḥ kathaṃcana /
iti brahmavaivarte (1)

(1) Cf. ibid. l. 7: *ka ātmā kaḥ para iti dehādyapekṣayā* ... ; BhaviṣPV 3[14f.]; BrahP 74; BrahVP 2; 26; BrāṇP 3[17]; 4; HarV 8; 26; MBh 35; PadP 56; VāmP 26; 34; VāyuP 3_3; see also BrāṇP 71.

19_1) BhāgTN (p. 516,11-12):
Subject matter: Liberation

aikātmyajñānato yānti tamo bhedāt paraṃ padam /
svātantryapāratantryādijñānaṃ bhedadṛśir bhavet /
iti brahmavaivarte (1)

(1) Cf. ibid. l. 10: *ceti phalato 'pi tamo yāntīti* ... ; see also AgniP 16.

20) BSūBh (p. 8,3-5):
Subject matter: Viṣṇu's unconceivable almighty power (*līlā*) / Viṣṇu's supreme transcendence

brāhme ca brahmavaivarte –
nāhaṃ na ca śivo 'nye ca tacchaktyekāṃśabhāginaḥ /
bālaḥ krīḍanakair yadvat krīḍate 'smabhir acyutaḥ /
iti (1)

(1) Cf. BSūBh (p. 67,12-14: *cetanatve 'py aśmādivadasvatrantatvāt svataḥ kartṛtvānupapattir jīvasya –*

yathā dārumayīṃ yoṣāṃ naraḥ sthirasamāhitaḥ /
iṅgayaty aṅgam aṅgāni tathā rājan imāḥ prajāḥ /
iti bhārate (= III 31,22; V 32,12ab):
puruṣo viceṣṭate sūtraprotā dārumayīva yoṣā

MBhTN II 72 (= MBh II App. I 1605f.; see below MBh 42n. 2):

aprameyo 'niyojyaś ca svayaṃ kāmagamo vaśī /
modaty eṣa sadā bhūtair bālaḥ krīḍanakair iva /

see also AgniP 6; BhavişP 13 and MESQUITA 2000: 487f.

21) BSūBh (p. 26,17-21):
Subject matter: Brahmā, the world-creator

nehāsīt kiṃcanāpy ādau mṛtyur āsīd dharis tadā / (1)
so 'tmano manasāsrākṣīd apa eva janārdanaḥ /
śayānas tāsu bhagavān nirmame 'ṇḍaṃ mahattaram /
tatra saṃvatsaraṃ nāma brahmāṇam asṛjat prabhuḥ /
tam attuṃ vyādadād āsyaṃ tadāsau virurāva ha /
atha tatkṛpayā viṣṇuḥ sṛṣṭikarma nyayojayat /
so 'sṛjad bhuvanaṃ sarvam ādyārthaṃ haraye vibhuḥ /
iti ca brahmavaivarte (2)

(1) Cf. MESQUITA 2000: 173.
(2) Cf. ibid. l. 15: *apsaṃvatsarasṛṣṭyādinā tatprakaraṇāc ca* ... ; see also AgniP 12 and BrāṇP 29.

22) BSūBh (p. 29,4-5):
Subject matter: Viṣṇu's supreme transcendence

lakṣaṇaṃ paramānando viṣṇor eva na saṃśayaḥ /
avyaktāditṛṇāntās tu vipluḍānandabhāginaḥ /
iti brahmavaivarte (1)

(1) Cf. ibid. l 3f.: (ChU IV 10,4; BĀU III 9,28; TaiU III 6): ... *ānando brahmeti vyajānāt ityādes tasyaiva tallakṣaṇam* ... ; see also AgniP 6 and MESQUITA 2000: 429n. 501.

23) BSūBh (p. 34,20-22):
Subject matter: Viṣṇu's supreme transcendence

ātmabrahmādayaḥ śabdās tam ṛte viṣṇum avyayam /
na saṃbhavanti yasmāt tair naivāptā guṇapūrṇatā /
iti hi brahmavaivarte (1)

(1) Cf. ibid. ll. 20f.: (MuU II 2,5) ... *ityātmaśabdād dyubhvādyāyatanaṃ viṣṇur eva* ... ; see also AgniP 6; BhāgP 1; BrahVP 19; BrāṇP 2; PadP 1_1 and MESQUITA 2000: 133ff. and p. 141n. 275.

24) BSūBh (p. 43,4-5):
Subject matter: Citraratha, the Kṣatriya's mark

> *yatra vedo rathas tatra na vedo yatra no rathaḥ* /
> iti brahmavaivarte (1)

(1) Cf. ibid. l. 3: *ayam aśvatarīratha iti citrarathasaṃbandhitvena liṅgena pautrāyaṇasya kṣatriyatvāvagateś ca* ... ; see also BrahP 64; SARMA 1999: 606.

25) BSūBh (p. 44,8-10):
Subject matter: Etymology of Viṣṇu's weapons

> *cakraṃ caṅkramaṇād eṣa varjanād vajra ucyate* /
> *khaṇḍanāt khaṅga evaiṣa hetināmā svayaṃ hariḥ* /
> iti hi brahmavaivarte (1)

(1) Cf. ibid. l. 5: *ejatīti kaṃpanavacanād udyutavajro bhagavān* ... ; see also BrahVP 10ab.

26) BSūBh (p. 138,26-27):
Subject matter: Viṣṇu's invisibility

> *na tam ārādhayitvāpi kaścid vyaktīkariṣyati* /
> *nityāvyakto yato devaḥ paramātmā sanātanaḥ* /
> iti brāhmavaivarte (1)

(1) Cf. ibid. l. 25: *ārādhane 'py avyaktam eva / jñānipratyakṣeṇetareṣām atisūkṣmatvaliṅgād anumānena* ... . For the doctrine of inferential proof Madhvas see also BrahVP 19; GarP 6; KūrP 20 and MESQUITA 2000: 339ff.

27) BSūBh (p. 225,13-16):
Subject matter: State of liberation

> brahmavaivarte ca –
> *svapnasthānāṃ yathā bhogo vinā dehena yujyate* /
> *evaṃ muktāv api bhaved vinā dehena bhojanam* /
> *svecchayā vā śarīrāṇi tejorūpāṇi kānicit* /
> *svīkṛtya jāgaritavad bhuktvā tyāgaḥ kadācana* / (1)

(1) Cf. AgniP 16; see also BrāṇP 7.

28) BSūBh (p. 226,4-7):
Subject matter: Videhamukti

brahmavaivarte ca —
jyotirmayeṣu deheṣu sveccchayā viśvamokṣiṇaḥ /
bhuñjate susukhāny eva na duḥkhādīn kadācana /
tīrṇā hi sarvaśokāṃs te puṇyapāpādivarjitāḥ / (1)
sarvadoṣanivṛttās te guṇamātrasvarūpiṇaḥ /
iti (2)

(1) v.l. : *nivṛttasarvadoṣās te puṇyapāpavivarjitāḥ.* Already Hṛṣīkeśatīrtha had pointed out this reading with quotation marks, cf. ibid. (p. 226n. 1).
(2) Cf. ibid. (p. 225,23): *suptau mokṣe vā tad ucyate* ... ; see also BrahVP 27.

29) BSūBh (p. 228,16-19):
Subject matter: Videhamukti

brahmavaivarte ca –
na hrāso na ca vṛddhir vā muktānāṃ vidyate kvacit /
vidvatpratyakṣasiddhatvāt kāraṇābhāvato 'numā /
harer upāsanā cātra sadaiva sukharūpiṇī /
na tu sādhanabhūtā sā siddhir evātra sā yataḥ /
iti (1)

(1) Cf. ibid. l. 16: *vidvatpratyakṣāt kāraṇābhāvaliṅgāc ca* ... ; see also AgniP 16; BhaviṣP 15; BrahP 14; 76-77; HarV 2; KūrP 30; SkaP 72.

30) ChUBh (p. 445,10-11):
Subject matter: Exegetical principles of the texts

brahmasūtrānusāreṇa vedādyaṃ sarvam eva ca /
yojyaṃ na brahmasūtrāṇi dṛśyamānārthato 'nyathā /
iti ca brahmavaivarte (1)

(1) Cf. ibid. ll 9f.: *jagadvyāpāravarjam – prakaraṇāt* ... (= BSūIV 4,17-18) *ityādinaiśvaryamaryādayā muktānāṃ brahmanaś ca bhedasyaiva nirṇītatvāc ca bhagavatā* ... ; see also BhaviṣPV 29 [42f.]; 32[112f.]; BrahP 1_3; 85; GarP 41; HarV 6; KūrP 24; SkaP 94; VarP 32; VāyuP 2_1 and MESQUITA 2000_1: 155ff. [= 1997: 125ff.].

31) GīBh (p. 36,8-9):
Subject matter: Videhamukti

bahujanmavipākena bhaktijñānena ye harim /
bhajanti tatsmṛtiṃ tv ante devo yāti na cānyathā /
ity ukter brahmavaivarte (1)

(1) Cf. ibid. l. 8: *na cānyeṣāṃ tadā smṛtir bhavati* ... ; see also AgniP 9; 16 , BrahP 80 and MESQUITA 2007: 34f. [= 2007_1: 448].

32) GīBh (p. 37,2-3):
Subject matter: Viṣṇu's body

deho 'yam me sadānando nāyaṃ prakṛtinirmitaḥ /
paripūrṇaś ca sarvatra tena nārāyaṇo 'smy aham /
ityādibhyo brahmavaivarte (1)

(1) Cf. ibid. (p. 36,33f.):
saddehaḥ sukhagandhaś ca jñānabhāḥ satparākramaḥ /
jñānajñānaḥ sukhasukhaḥ sa viṣṇuḥ paramo 'kṣaraḥ /
iti paiṅgikhileṣu (unknown source);
see also AgniP 4; MESQUITA 2000_1: 40f. [= 1997: 32f.] and MESQUITA 2000: 482f.

33) GīBh (p. 51,4-5):
Subject matter: Viṣṇu's supreme transcendence

īśebhyo brahmarudraśrīśeṣādibhyo yato bhavān /
varo 'ta īśvarākhyā te mukhyā nānyasya kasyacit /
iti brahmavaivarte
samartha īsa ity uktas tadvaratvāt tvam īśvaraḥ /
iti ca (1)

(1) Cf. ibid. l. 3: *īśvara īśebhyo varaḥ / tac coktam* ... ; see also AgniP 6.

34) GīBh (p. 66,6-9):
Subject matter: Internal organ (*manas*)

uktaṃ ca –
'manaḥ paraṃ kāraṇam āmananti'
'mana eva manuṣyāṇāṃ kāraṇaṃ bandhamokṣayoḥ' / (1)
'uddharen manasā jīvaṃ na jīvam avasādayet / (2)
jīvasya bandhuḥ śatruś ca mana eva na saṃśayaḥ' /
'jīvena buddhyā hi yadā mano jitaṃ tadā bandhuḥ /
śatrur anyatra cāsya tato jayed buddhibalo naras / +1
tad deve ca bhaktyā madhukaiṭabhārau' /
ityādi brahmavaivarte (3)

(1) Cf. MBh XIII 295*; MaitrāyaṇaU VI,34; see also BhaviṣPV 17.
(2) Cf. Gī VI 5: *uddhared ātmanātmānaṃ nātmānam avasādayet* / also MESQUITA 2000: 135n. 254.
(3) Cf. GīBh (p. 66,3f.): ... *kasya bandhur ātmeti / āha – bandhur ātmeti / ātmā manaḥ / ātmano jīvasya / ātmanā manasā / ātmānaṃ jīvam / ātmaiva manaḥ / ātmanā buddhyā jīvenaiva vā / sa hi buddhyā vijayati*; GīT (p. 65,31+66,29):

uddharetaiva saṃsārāj jīvātmānaṃ parātmanā /
viṣṇur bandhuḥ satāṃ nityaṃ parātmā hy asatām ariḥ /
tatprasādajayā bhaktyā jito yasya vaśe tv iva /
vartate tasya mitraṃ sa tadanyasya ca śatruvat /
iti ca (untraceable source).

35) GīBh (p. 67,12-14):
Subject matter: Pūjā

guṇānusāriṇīṃ pūjāṃ samāṃ dṛṣṭiṃ ca yo naraḥ /
sarvabhūteṣu kurute tasya viṣṇuḥ prasīdati /
vaiṣamyam uttamatvaṃ tu dadāti narasañcayāt /
pūjāyā viṣamā dṛṣṭiḥ samā sāmyaṃ viduḥkhajam /
iti brāhmavaivarte (1)

(1) Elsewhere (cf. GīBh [Pariśiṣṭam: Gītabhāṣyatātparyayoḥ prācīnapāṭhaḥ, p. 7]) this quote appears as belonging to Brahmatarka. Madhva presupposes here the sense of equanimity as taught in the Gī, which is based on three different types of equanimity, namely on the equanimity of a Yogin (like Gī VI 8), on the equanimity in respect to all human beings, regardless whether they are friends or foes (Gī VI 9) and on the equanimity based on the faith that Viṣṇu is always the same in all beings (Gī VI 29-31). Above all, the fact that all these types are mentioned one after another in the Gī VI implies that they are intimately connected. For a detailed account of this maxim of ethical conduct cf. HACKER 1959: 88f.; see also AgniP 9; 20; BrahVP 41; GarP 51; 52; HarV 22; MBh 6; NārP 43; PadP 82; SkaP 60; 69[4]; ViṣP 6 and BhāgTN 430,7f.

36) GīBh (p. 78,17-18):
Subject matter: Viṣṇu's Bhakta

avatāre mahāviṣṇor bhaktaḥ kutra ca mucyate /
ityādeś ca brahmavaivarte (1)

(1) Cf. AgniP 16; NārP 45.

37) GīBh (p. 87,13-15):
Subject matter: Liberation / Kramamukti

tac coktaṃ brahmavaivarte –
sāhnā madhyandinenātha śuklena ca sapūrṇimā /
saviṣvā cāyanenāsau pūjitaḥ keśavaṃ vrajet /
iti (1)

(1) Cf. ibid. l: 13: *ahar abhijitā śuklaṃ paurṇamāsyā ayanaṃ viṣuvā saha* ... ; see also ĀdityaP 1 and BrahP 82.

38) GīT (p. 24,13-31):

Subject matter: Vaiṣṇava Dharma

svocitenaiva dharmeṇa viṣṇupūjām ṛte kvacit /
nāpravṛttiḥ pravṛttir vā yatra dharmaḥ sa vaiṣṇavaḥ / [1]
enaṃ dharmaṃ ca devādyā vartante sāttvikā janāḥ /
eṣa kārtayugo dharmaḥ pāñcarātraś ca vaidikaḥ / [2]
tatprītyarthaṃ vinānyasmai nodabinduṃ na taṇḍulam /
dadyān nirāśī ca sadā bhaved bhaktaś ca keśave / [3]
naitatsame 'dhike vāpi kuryāc chaṅkām api kvacit /
jānīyāt tadadhīnaṃ ca sarvaṃ tat tattvavit sadā / [4]
yathākramaṃ tu devānāṃ tāratamyavid eva ca /
eṣa bhāgavato mukhyas tretādiṣu viśeṣataḥ / [5]
eṣa dharmo 'tiphalado viśeṣeṇa punaḥ kalau /
evaṃ bhāgavato yas tu sa eva hi vimucyate / [6]
traividyas tv aparo dharmo nānādaivatapūjanam /
tatrāpi viṣṇur jñātavyaḥ sarvebhyo 'bhyadhiko guṇaiḥ / [7]
samarpayati yajñādyam antatas tv eva viṣṇave /
traividyadharmaḥ puruṣaḥ svargaṃ bhuktvā nivartate / [8]
punaḥ kuryāt punaḥ svargaṃ yāti yāvad dharer vaśe /
sarvān devān pravijñāya tatkarmaiva sadā bhavet / [9]
samyak tattvāparijñānād anyakarmakṛter api /
svargādiprārthanāc caiva rāgādeś cāparikṣayāt / [10]
sadā viṣṇor asmaraṇāt traividyo nāpnuyāt param /
krameṇa mucyate viṣṇau karmāṇy ante samarpayan / [11]
yadi sarvāṇi niyamāj janmabhir bahubhiḥ śubhaiḥ /
paraṃ viṣṇuṃ na yo vetti kurvāṇo 'pi trayīkriyāḥ / [12]
nāsau traividya ity ukto vedavādī sa ucyate /
vādo vivādaḥ saṃprokto vādo vacanam eva ca / [13]
vedokte viṣṇumāhātmye vivādāt paṭhanād api /
athavā nirarthakāt pāṭhād vedavādī sa ucyate / [14] +1
vedavādarato na syān na pāṣaṇḍī na haitukī / (1)
tebhyo yāti tamo ghoram andhaṃ yasmān na cothitiḥ / [15]
anārambham anantaṃ ca nityaduḥkhaṃ sukhojjhitam /
vavraṃ yadvedagaditaṃ yatra yānty asurādayaḥ / [16] (2)
buddhir nirṇītatattvānām ekā viṣṇuparāyaṇā /
bahuśākhā hy anantāś ca buddhayo 'vyavasāyinām / [17]
iti brahmavaivarte(3)

(1) Cf. BhāgP (XI 18,30):
vedavādarato na syān na pāṣaṇḍī na haitukaḥ / = GīT (p. 25,24)
śuṣkavādavivāde na kaṃcitpakṣaṃ samāśrayet //

(2) Cf. Ṛg (VII 104,3a); see also BSūBh (p. 120,3-6) and MESQUITA 2000: 529n. 704.

(3) Cf. AgniP 17; 20; BrahVP 41; NārP 2[9].

39) GīT (p. 49,27+50,23):
Subject matter: Summary of Bhagavadgītā

brahmarudrendrasūryāṇāṃ yad dattaṃ viṣṇunā purā /
pañcarātrātmakaṃ jñānaṃ vyāso 'dāt pāṇḍaveṣu tat / [1]
teṣām eva ca vārṣṇeyaḥ senāmadhye 'rjunāya ca /
prādād gīteti nirdiṣṭaṃ saṅkṣepeṇāyuyutsave / [2]
yathā kurvanti karmāṇi yathā jānanti devatāḥ /
sarve kārtayugāś caiva nṛpāś ca manupūrvakāḥ / [3]
jñātavyaṃ caiva kartavyaṃ yathā sarvair mumukṣubhiḥ /
tretāditriṣu jātaiś ca gītāyāṃ tad udāhṛtam / [4]
pāṇḍavādyāḥ kṣemakāntāḥ kariṣyanti ca jānate /
tathaiva tena gītāyā nāsti śāstraṃ samaṃ kvacit / [5]
vedārthapūrakaṃ jñeyaṃ pañcarātraṃ yato 'khilam /
tatsaṅkṣepaś ca gīteyaṃ tasmān nāsyāḥ samaṃ kvacit / [6]
iti brahmavaivarte (1)

(1) Cf. ibid. l. 26: *uktayor jñānakarmaṇor ubhayor viśeṣavistārātmako'yam adhyāyaḥ* ... ; see also AgniP 9; KūrP 30_2 and MESQUITA 2000_1: 143f. [= 1997: 115f.].

40) GīT (p. 51,29-31):
Subject matter: Liberation

yeṣāṃ guṇānāṃ jñānena muktir uktā pṛthak pṛthak /
vedeṣu vetihāseṣu sā tu teṣāṃ samuccayāt /
evam eva śamādīnāṃ nānyathā tu kathaṃcana /
iti brahmavaivartavacanāt (1)

(1) Cf. AgniP 16 and MESQUITA 2007: 9n. 11 [= 1997_1: 434n. 11].

41) GīT (p. 55,29-30):
Subject matter: Pūjā

tenaiva taṃ pūjayed vā vihitair vānyasādhanaiḥ /
sa eva viṣṇor yajñaḥ syān mānaso vātha bāhyakaḥ /
iti brahmavaivarte (1)

(1) Cf. ibid. ll. 26f.: *daivaṃ viṣṇum eva yajña ity upāsane / svabhogyatvāt svayam eva yajñaḥ / brahmākhyāgnau kriyāyajñaṃ tenaiva yajñākhyena viṣṇunā samarpayanti / tatpūjātvena śrotrādisaṃyamaṃ kurvanti / tatpūjātvena viṣayān bhuñjate / tatpūjātvenendriyādisaṃyamaṃ kurvanti / yajñenaiveti sarvatrāpy anvīyate* ... ; see also AgniP 17; 20; BrahVP 35; 38.

42) GīT (p. 144,20-26):
Subject matter: Doctrines of Advaitins = Asuras

ye 'timānena manyante parameśo 'ham ity api /
mithyā jagad idaṃ sarvaṃ bhramajatvān na tiṣṭhati / [1]
mithyātvān neśvaro 'syāsti parebhyo na ca jāyate /
svasminn api tathānyasmin niyantānya itīrite / [2]
pradviṣanty asurās te tu sarve yānty adharam tamaḥ /
ayogyeśatvakāmatvāt lobhāc cātmasamarpaṇe / [3]
tattvavādiṣu kopāc ca tatas teṣāṃ na durlabham /
akṣānumāgamānāṃ ca svokter api virodhinaḥ / [4]
yasmāt te 'to 'surā jñeyā evam anye 'pi tādṛśāḥ /
ye tu viṣṇuṃ paraṃ jñātvā yajante 'nanyadevatāḥ / [5]
pratyakṣādyavisaṃvādijñānād eva vimuktigāḥ / [6ab]
iti brahmavaivarte (1)

(1) Cf. ibid. l. 19: *devāsuralakṣaṇam* ... ; see also BhavişPV 3n. 7; 12; SkaP 39; 40; 55 and MESQUITA 2000: 528f.

43) KathU (p. 479,16-17):
Subject matter: Heretical doctrine that there is no difference between Viṣṇu and individual souls

jīvānāṃ caiva viṣṇoś ca yo na vetti bhidāṃ pumān /
tadanuvratāś ca ye kecit teṣāṃ jñānaṃ na jāyate / + 1
iti brahmavaivarte (1)

(1) Cf. ibid. ll. 14f.: *anyo bhagavān anyo 'ham ity ajānann ananyaḥ / tena prokte gatir jñānaṃ nāsti proktānanyenaiva sujñānāya preṣṭha iti vākya śeṣāt*; ibid. (p. 479,7-8); see also BrahVP 42.

44) VTN (p. 36,19-37,1):
Subject matter: Theory of error

adhiṣṭhānaṃ ca sadṛśaṃ tathyavastudvayaṃ vinā /
na bhrāntir bhavati kvāpi svapnamāyādikeṣv api /
mānasyāṃ vāsanāyāṃ tu bahirvastutvakalpanam /
svāpno bhramaś ca māyāyāṃ kartṛdehādivastuṣu /
caturaṅgabalatvādikalpanaṃ bhrama iṣyate /
na bhrāntikalpitaṃ viśvam ato viṣṇubalāśrayam /
iti brahmavaivarte (1)

(1) Cf. ibid. l. 17: *māyāmayī sṛṣṭir api tatsadṛśasya satyasyānyasya vidyamānatva eva dṛṣṭā / dravyatvādisādṛśyayuktaṃ kiṃcid adhiṣṭhānam āśrityaiva ca* ... ; see also KūrP 20 and MESQUITA 2000: 202f.; 325ff.

Garuḍapurāṇa (GarP)

[GarP is a true encyclopedic Purāṇa like AgniP and MatsyaP (cf. HAZRA 1987: 141-145; ROCHER 1986: 175-179). One quote ascribed by Madhva to this Purāṇa (cf. GarP 8) describes the precise size and sections of BhāgP and defines it as quintessence (*sārarūpa*) of all the Purāṇas, proclaimed by Viṣṇu himself. This quote reproduces also an opinion based on an old tradition that BhāgP is *gāyatrībhāṣya* (cf. MESQUITA 2000_1: 90. 153f. [= 1997: 71n. 142]). It is remarkable that almost the half of the quotes (thirty-two) are adduced by Madhva in BhāgTN. The remaining ones are spread over AiUBh (five times); BĀUBh (twice); BSūBh (eight times); ChUBh (once); GīBh (eleven times); MānUBh (once).

Some metrical irregularities regarding the number of syllables are found in some quotes (cf. v.g. GarP 2ab; GarP 5[6ab]; GarP 45[6ab]; see also GarP 42[3ab] and GarP 54).]

1) AiUBh (p. 184,6-8)
Subject matter: Viṣṇu's Worship in the Ṛg-verses

mahāvrataniyuktaṃ yad ṛksahasraṃ hareḥ priyam /
tad uktham iti saṃproktaṃ tene yo viṣṇur eva hi /
tasmād ukthāyur ity ukta aiśvaryād indra ucyate /
tasmād ukthāyur indreti viṣṇur yajñeṣu pūjyate /
iti hi gāruḍe (1)

(1) Cf. ibid. l. 5: *ukthāyutvāc ca viṣṇur evātrokta ity avagamyate / bṛhatīsahasraṃ hy ukthanāmakaṃ mukhyataḥ*; see also AgniP 20 and LORENZ 2003: 16f.

2) AiUBh (p. 184,15-16):
Subject matter: Viśvāmitra

bṛhatīsahasre prathame sālokyaṃ pradadau hariḥ / +1
dvitīye svapuraprāptiṃ tṛtīye 'ntaḥpurasya ca /
tathā svaviṣayaṃ jñānaṃ viśvāmitre dadau prabhuḥ /
iti ca gāruḍe (1)

(1) Cf. ibid. ll. 14f.: *priyadhāmna upa samīpe gamanaṃ nāma taddhāmaprāptikāraṇa-bhagavatprasādaprāptiḥ / anyathopaśabdo vyarthaḥ syāt / na ca tadaiva bhagavataḥ priyaṃ dhāma viśvāmitreṇa prāptam* ... ; see also BrāṇP 3.

3) AiUBh (p. 189,12-13):
Subject matter: Abhyāsa

ekaprakārā bahuśo vāg abhyāsa itīritaḥ /
arthāntarārthā dvividhā prayukteti hi nirṇayaḥ /
iti hi gāruḍe (1)

(1) Cf. ibid. ll. 10f.: ... *caitro maitro maitraś caitra itivat / tatra hy ubhayasnehāpekṣayā punarvacanaṃ yujyate / abhyāsatve hy ekaprakāreṇa prayoga dṛṣṭaḥ / atra hi prayogadvaividhyaṃ dṛśyate* ... ; see also BrahVP 3; GarP 41.

4) AiUBh (p. 204,23-25):
Subject matter: Viṣṇu in the form of male and female (*strīpuṃrūpa*)

strīrūpaś caiva puṃrūpo yasmān nārāyaṇaḥ sthitaḥ /
pumān strī ceti vācyo 'to vailakṣaṇyān na cocyate /
viṣṇor napuṃsakākāro naivāsti kvacana prabhoḥ /
tathāpy arāgākṛṣṭatvāt tacchabdair api kathyate /
iti gāruḍe (1)

(1) Cf. ibid. ll. 20f.: ... *svatantro hi bhagavān tatprerita eva taṃ vadatīty abhiprāyaḥ / vadan vadati / vadann eva na vadati / bhavaty eva hi bhagavān strīrūpaḥ puṃrūpaś ca / tasmād vadaty eva / aprasiddhatvān na vadati ca*; see also BhaviṣPV 27n. 2; BrāṇP 5; 70; GarP 5 and MESQUITA 2000: 229n. 493.

5) AiUBh (p. 204,25-205,7):
Subject matter: Viṣṇu's outward appearances

nārāyaṇādirūpeṇa pañcadhaiṣa hariḥ sthitaḥ /
tannāmabhiś ca strīrūpaiḥ sameti svaiḥ sa keśavaḥ / [1]
yat syandanaṃ vahanty ete devā bhāryāsamanvitāḥ /
adhidaive tathādhyātme jīvadehātmakaṃ ratham / [2]
sa sūryaḥ sūryabhāryā ca cakṣurdvayasamāsthitau / (1)
vahato 'śvātmakau dehaṃ nārāyaṇarathātmakam / [3]
somaś ca rohiṇī caiva dakṣavāmaśrutisthitau /
ubhayoḥ pakṣayoḥ sthitvā vahato 'śvātmakau tayoḥ / [4]
uddhāraṇārtham eteṣām umā vāci samāsthitā /
nāgākāraiva raśmitvam agamad vaiṣṇave rathe / [5]
manasi sthitaḥ śivaś cātra manonāmā mahābalaḥ / +1
abhavat sārathir viṣṇor viṣṇur vāyuś ca taṃ ratham / [6]
prakṛṣṭānandarūpatvāt prāṇākhyāv adhitiṣṭhataḥ /
tāv eva cāśvināmānau hayāsyau jagadīśvarau / [7]
ityādi gāruḍe (2)

(1) Regarding the fire-doctrine cf. FRAUWALLNER 1973: I, 47f.
(2) Cf. BhāgP 1 and GarP 4.

6) BĀUBh (p. 272,31-273,2):
Subject matter: Doctrine of Pañcabheda / Liberation
bhedenaiva jagat sarvaṃ bhedeneśaṃ guṇaiḥ saha /
bhedena jīvān anyonyaṃ muktāḥ paśyanti sarvaśaḥ /

niḥśeṣaduḥkhahīnāś ca kevalaṃ sukhabhoginaḥ |
janmamṛtyuvihīnāś ca kālasaṃbandhavarjitāḥ |
rajastamaḥsattvahīnāḥ prakṛtyā ca vivarjitāḥ |
ityādigāruḍavacanān na jñānanivartyatā vaktuṃ yuktā | (1)

(1) Cf. ibid. ll. 29f.: (Gī XVI 8) – *yac ciketa satyamit tan na moghaṃ vasu spārham uta jeṭota dāta satyo jīveśayor bhedaḥ satyā viṣṇor guṇā api | satyaṃ jagad idaṃ sarvaṃ satyeśajagator bhidiḥ* | ityādeś ca (untraceable quote); see also AgniP 16; BhaviṣPV 1; BrāṇP 103; and MESQUITA 2000_1: 104ff. [= 1997: 83ff.]; MESQUITA 2000: 188n. 391.

7) BĀUBh (p. 298,21-23):
Subject matter: Brahmavidyā

parasya brahmaṇo viṣṇor hayaśīrṣād adhītavān |
brahmavidyām imāṃ brahmā tataḥ sanaka eva ca |
iti gāruḍe (1)

(1) Cf. AgniP 9; BrāṇP 101.

8) BhāgTN (p. 4,7-10):
Subject matter: Analytical account of BhāgP

uktaṃ ca gāruḍe –
artho 'yaṃ brahmasūtrāṇāṃ bhāratārthavinirṇayaḥ |
gāyatrībhāṣyarūpo 'sau vedārthaparibṛṃhitaḥ |
purāṇānāṃ sārarūpaḥ sākṣād bhagavatoditaḥ |
dvādaśaskandhayukto 'yaṃ śatavicchedasaṃyutaḥ |
grantho 'ṣṭādaśasāhasraḥ śrīmadbhāgavatābhidaḥ |
iti (1)

(1) Cf. ibid. l. 7: *brahmasūtramahābhāratagāyatrīvedasaṃbandhaś cāyaṃ granthaḥ* ... ; see also VāmP 3 and MESQUITA 2000_1: 90n. 153 [= 1997: 70n. 142].

9) BhāgTN (p. 5,11-13):
Subject matter: Puruṣārtha

gāruḍe ca –
dharmārthakāmamokṣāṇām ekam eva paraṃ padam |
avarodho hṛdīśasya pṛthag vakṣye na tān aham |
iti (1)

(1) Cf. ibid. l. 11: *kiṃ vā parair arthakāmādikathanaiḥ* ... ; see also. BhaviṣPV 21; BrāṇP 21[1]; 43; MBh 46; 48; PadP 8; SkaP 54; VarP 2 and MESQUITA 2000_1: 169n. 346 [= 1997: 137n. 333].

10) BhāgTN (p. 39,5):
Subject matter: Soma

pūrayanti diśaḥ somaṃ devā gāvaḥ sarasvatī /
iti gāruḍe

11) BhāgTN (p. 66,4-6):
Subject matter: Liberation of the Deities

ṛṣyuttamā devatāś ca vimuktau pariniścitāḥ /
tathāpy adhikasaukhyārthaṃ yatante śubhakarmasu /
vimuktās tu svabhāvena nityaṃ dhyānāditatparāḥ /
iti gāruḍe (1)

(1) Cf. ibid. l. 3: *pariniṣṭhito 'pi muktir asya bhaviṣyatīti niścito 'pi – udaraṃ saṃśayaḥ proktaḥ pariniṣṭhā viniścayaḥ* / ity abhidhāne (untraceable quote); see also AgniP 16 and BhaviṣP 5.

12) BhāgTN (p. 89,8-9):
Subject matter: Three-fold Ahaṃkāra

bhūtāni dravyanāmāni jñānaṃ jñānendriyāṇy api /
kriyā karmendriyāṇy āhus tanmūlatvād ahaṃ tridhā /
iti gāruḍe (1)

(1) Cf. ibid. n. 4 = Anantatīrtha's statement; see also BhaviṣPV 17.

13) BhāgTN (p. 93,18-19):
Subject matter: Indivisibility of Viṣṇu's nature

dehendriyādibhedena nirbhedo 'pi hariḥ svayam /
bhaṇyate kevalaiśvaryād anādyānandacidghanaḥ /
iti gāruḍe (1)

(1) Cf. BrāṇP 10; 69; MESQUITA 2000_1: 36n. 42 [= 1997: 30n. 35] and MESQUITA 2000: 445ff.

14) BhāgTN (p. 94,4):
Subject matter: Antaryāmin

vitastimātraṃ hṛdayam āsthāya vyāpnute jagat /
iti gāruḍe (1)

(1) Cf. ibid. ll. 3f.:
sarvaṃ puruṣa eveti bhaṇyate bhedavaj jagat /
tadadhīnaṃ tu sattādi yato hy asya sadā bhavet /

iti brahmatarke (fictitious source) ... ;
see also BhāgP 2 and MESQUITA 2000: 162f; 489f.

15) BhāgTN (p. 122,1-2):
Subject matter: Liberation

muktaih pārṣadaiḥ pūrvair brahmādyaiś caiva saṃyutam / -1 (1)
brahmā dadarśa tapasā bhagavantaṃ hariṃ prabhum /
iti gāruḍe (2)

(1) v.l. *svapārṣadaiḥ* (BhāgTN p. 122 n. 1 = ibid. II 9, 14d) attempts to fill the missing syllable.
(2) Cf. AgniP 16 and MESQUITA 2000: 62n. 39.

16) BhāgTN (p. 142,4-7):
Subject matter: Badarī, the sacred place of Viṣṇu's instruction

jñātvā katipayair varṣair pūrvam eva janārdanaḥ /
mausalaṃ jñānasantatyā uddhavaṃ badarīṃ nayat / (1)
sa jñānaṃ tatra vistīrya punar dvāravatiṃ yayau /
pūrvam evopadiṣṭo 'pi hariṇā jñānam uddhavaḥ /
svargārohaṇakāle tu punaḥ prapaccha keśavam /
punaḥ śrutvā badaryāṃ tu varṣatrayam uvāsa ha /
jñānaṃ saṃsthāpya paścāc ca svecchayā svargataḥ prabhuḥ /
iti gāruḍe (2)

(1) v.l. *nayan* and *anayat* (ibid. n. 4).
(2) Cf. ibid. l. 3: *ātmamāyāyāḥ – ātmasāmarthyasya gatiṃ pūrvam evāvalokya*; see also PadP 14; SkaP 34 and MESQUITA 2000_1: 64n. 107 [= 1997: 52n. 99].

17) BhāgTN (p. 156,16-18):
Subject matter: Creation of the Universe and of the caste system

anupraviśya brahmāṇaṃ prāṇaṃ daśavidhaṃ tathā /
indriyāṇīndriyārthāṃś ca varṇāṃś caivāsṛjad dhariḥ /
iti gāruḍe (1)

(1) Cf. BhaviṣPV 17; BrahP 22_1 and BrāṇP 29.

18) BhāgTN (p. 239,11-12):
Subject matter: Viṣṇu's divine body

śuklena janir anyeṣāṃ hareḥ svatanu vaiva tu /
nityoditajñānatanoḥ kutaḥ syāc chuklato janiḥ /
iti gāruḍe (1)

(1) Cf. AgniP 4; ĀdiP 1 and MESQUITA 2000_1: 37f. [= 1997: 31f.].

19) BhāgTN (p. 269,8-270,2):
Subject matter: Brahmā

brahmā devaiḥ parivṛtaḥ pralaye parameśvaram /
praviśya sarge tu punaḥ śvetadvīpe pramodate /
jñānadharmaphalāṃs tatra bhogān bhuktvā laye punaḥ /
nārāyaṇaṃ samāviśya jñānavyaktaṃ nijaṃ sukham /
bhuñjate tv evam evaiṣāṃ kāle saṃsarganirgamau /
nityau nityasukhaṃ caiva sṛṣṭau bhogās tathottamāḥ /
guṇavyatikarābhāve 'py uccanīcādi pūrvavat /
viṣṇoś caiva vimuktānāṃ na kadācana gacchati /
iti gāruḍe (1)

(1) Cf. ibid. l. 7: *guṇavyatikare asati / laye prāpte / punaḥ parameśvaram āyānti*; see also ĀdityaP 1; BrāṇP 29.

20) BhāgTN (p. 280,8-9):
Subject matter: Worship of Rudra

suparṇaśeṣaprāṇeśabrahmaviṣṇūn śriyaṃ giram /
ṛte namati no rudraṃ ka eva puruṣārthabhāk /
iti gāruḍe (1)

(1) Cf. ibid. l. 7: *brahmādayo brahmaputrāḥ*; see also BrahP 22.

21) BhāgTN (p. 281,5-6):
Subject matter: Liberation while living (*jīvanmukti*)

yadi devāś ca ṛṣyādyā nindyante yatrakutracit /
na tavatā guṇair hīnāḥ sthitaprajñā hi te matāḥ /
yathāyogyaṃ tu tātparyaṃ nindāyām anyad eva tu / (1)
iti gāruḍe (2)

(1) Cf. ĀdityaP 1 and MESQUITA 2007: 10f. [= 2007_1: 434f.].
(2) Cf. MESQUITA 2000: 506n. 663.

22) BhāgTN (p. 287,2-4):
Subject matter: Definition of the true doctrine

viṣṇvadhīnā jagatsattā pratītiś ceṣṭitaṃ gatiḥ /
iti yan niścitaṃ jñānam apṛthagdarśanaṃ matam / (1)
mithyājñānaṃ pṛthagjñānam iti vedavido viduḥ /

yathaivārthas tathā jñānam apṛthagdṛṣṭir ucyate /
iti gāruḍe (2)

(1) Cf. BhaviṣPV 3n. 7 and MESQUITA 2000_1: 170f. [= 1997: 138f.].
(2) Cf. MESQUITA 2000: 249ff.: *yathārthyam eva prāmāṇyam.*

23) BhāgTN (p. 292,6-9):
Subject matter: Theory of knowledge

pṛthagjñānaṃ tad ity āhur yatkiṃcid vīkṣyate 'nyathā /
jñānaṃ jñeyāvirodhena tv apṛthag vastuto dṛśiḥ /
kecid bhedaṃ vinindanti hy āsurajñānavṛttayaḥ /
nirākurvanty atho mandā bhedasya paramārthatām /
ye tu tattvavido mukhyā bhedaṃ brahmānyavastunoḥ /
paramārtham iti jñātvā nityaṃ viṣṇum upāsate /
iti gāruḍe (1)

(1) Cf. ibid. l. 5: *na pṛthag ya ātmanaḥ / anyathā yo na paśyati ...*
yathārthajñānino nānyaḥ priyo viṣṇos tu kaścana /
tathāpy adhikasantuṣṭyai prasīdaty arthanaṃ punaḥ /
iti ca (unknown source);
see also BhaviṣPV 1; KūrP 20 and MESQUITA 2000_1: 104ff. [= 1997: 83ff.].

24) BhāgTN (p. 295,1-2):
Subject matter: Deities, the holders of the true knowledge

harer vaśatvadṛṣṭis tu bhūtānām apṛthagdṛśiḥ / (1)
priyatvadṛṣṭir athavā brahmādīnāṃ viśeṣataḥ /
iti gāruḍe (2)

(1) Cf. MESQUITA 2000: 429ff.
(2) Cf. BhaviṣP 5.

25) BhāgTN (p. 309,4-5):
Subject matter: Deities and Pūrṇāvataras

bhinnasvarūpam abhidaṃ svarūpaṃ tu dvidhā hareḥ /
bhinnasvarūpaṃ brahmādyā matsyādyabhidam ucyate /
iti gāruḍe (1)

(1) Cf. ibid. l. 3: *svarūpaṃ jīvasya biṃbarūpaṃ paramātmānam ...* ; ĀdiP 1; BhāgP 3; BhaviṣP 5; BrāṇP 71 and MESQUITA 2000_1: 35ff. [= 1997: 29ff.].

26) BhāgTN (p. 312,12-14):
Subject matter: Vena / Pṛthu

pāparūpī pṛthagjāto niṣādo venadehataḥ /
yasmāt tasmāt pṛthoḥ putrād rajo veno divaṃ yayau /
iti gāruḍe (1)

(1) Cf. BhaviṣP 7; BrāṇP 42.

26_1) BhāgTN (p. 318,8-9):
Subject matter: Deities and Ṛṣis

devāḥ śaktāś ca mohāya darśayeyur aśaktavat /
ṛṣīṇāṃ caiva rājñāṃ ca na hi te devatāsamāḥ /
ājñayā vā hareḥ kvāpi kāryato vā kvacit kvacit /
iti gāruḍe (1)

(1) Cf. SkaP 53 and BhaviṣP 5. For the topic of bewilderment see MBh 42n. 6; NārP 9 and MESQUITA 2000_1: 37f. [= 1997: 31f.].

27) BhāgTN (p. 360,1-2):
Subject matter: Priyavrata

pūrvasṛṣṭān rathāvṛttyā sthūlāṃś cakre priyavrataḥ /
samudrāṃs te na tatkartety āhur enaṃ priyavratam /
iti gāruḍe (1)

(1) Cf. BrāṇP 29; HarV 14.

28) BhāgTN (p. 372,10-11):
Subject matter: Son of Ṛṣabha

tatkālasthitabhakteṣu mānuṣeṣv ṛṣabhātmajaḥ /
varo 'pi dhikkṛto rājñā suhṛdā vaiṣṇaveṣv api /
iti gāruḍe (1)

(1) Cf. ibid. l. 9: *aśeṣabhagavatpriyāṇāṃ niketaḥ sa eva bharato mānuṣāpekṣayā* ... ; see also BrahP 43.

29) BhāgTN (p. 438,10-12):
Subject matter: Hiraṇyakaśipu

hiraṇyakaśipur bhūtam apaśyata mṛtau harim /
ato bhayānako jātas tatra rājānam eva ca /
matvā rājaiva sañjātaḥ kṛṣṇaṃ cakrādilakṣaṇaiḥ /
mṛtikāle hariṃ caiva matvā bhaktyaiva kevalam /
dvāsthatāṃ harim āviśya prāpaiva manujo 'pi tu /(1)
iti gāruḍe (2)

(1) Cf. BrahVP 10.
(2) Cf. ibid. l. 13: *vairānubandho vairayuktā bhaktiḥ*; also BhāgP (VII 1,26):
tasmād vairānubandhena nirvaireṇa bhayena vā /
snehāt kāmena vā yuñjyāt kathaṃcin nekṣate pṛthak //
cf. BrāṇP 53; HarV19$_1$; SkaP 61; 65; see also BhavişPV 12 and HACKER 1959: 106f.

30) BhāgTN (p. 444,11-445,8):
Subject matter: Jīva's subordination to Viṣṇu / Viṣṇu's supreme transcendence

anyo jīvo 'cito dehāt tadvaśo deha ucyate /
paśyāmīty abhimāno 'sya cakṣurādyabhimānavān / [1]
na tadvaśāś cakṣurādyā na dṛṣṭyādau sa īśvaraḥ /
cakṣurādyā mano jīvo dṛṣṭyādiś cāpi yadvaśe / [2]
sa prāṇa iti vijñeyo jñātā mantā ca sa prabhuḥ /
tasyāpi jñātṛmantṛtvaṃ na svataḥ śakyate kvacit / [3]
yas tasya jñātṛmantṛtvadātā sa bhagavān hariḥ /
svato jñātā ca mantā ca dṛṣṭā śrotā ca keśavaḥ / [4]
jñātyādido na tasyānyaḥ sarvasya jñātido hariḥ /
sa dehān bhajate viṣṇuḥ svecchayaivotsṛjaty api / [5]
yāvad dehasthito viṣṇus tāvaj jīvo viparyayaḥ /
tāvat kleśādayaś cāsya vṛthā cendriyavṛttayaḥ / [6]
yadotsṛjati dehaṃ sa hariḥ sarvātmanā vibhuḥ /
tadā tadabhimānī tu jīvo mucyeta saṃsṛteḥ / [7]
atibhinnasvarūpau tau jīveśāv ekadehagau /
dehābhimānī tv eko 'tra na mānī mānadaḥ paraḥ / [8]
iti gāruḍe (1)

(1) Cf. ibid. ll. 8f.:
indriyādyabhimānena tadvān jīva udīryate /
atanmānād dhariḥ proktas tv adeho 'nindriyas tathā /
jīvānabhimate dehe na viṣṇur jīvati sthitaḥ /
ataś cādeha uddiṣṭaḥ paramātmā sanātanaḥ /
iti prakāśikāyām (unknown source);
see also AgniP 6; 22; BrāṇP 71 and MESQUITA 2000: 497ff.

31) BhāgTN (p. 495,5-496,5):
Subject matter: King Ambarīṣa

brahmādibhaktikoṭyaṃśād aṃśo naivāmbarīṣake /
naivānyasya ca kasyāpi tathāpi harir īśvaraḥ /
tātkālikopaceyatvāt teṣāṃ yaśasa ādirāṭ /
brahmādayaś ca tatkīrtiṃ vyañjayāmāsur uttamāḥ /
mohanāya ca daityānāṃ brahmāder nindanāya ca /

anyārthaṃ ca svayaṃ viṣṇur brahmādyāś ca nirāśiṣaḥ /
mānuṣeṣūttamatvāc ca teṣāṃ bhaktyādibhir guṇaiḥ /
brahmāder viṣṇvadhīnatvajñāpanāya ca kevalam /
durvāsāś ca svayaṃ rudras tathāpy anyāyyam uktavān /
tasyāpy anugrahārthāya darpanāśārtham eva ca /
iti gāruḍe (1)

(1) Cf. ibid. n. 3.

32) BhāgTN (p. 502,3-4):
Subject matter: Transmigration

daivagāndharvapitryeṣu mānuṣeṣv āsureṣu ca /
yatra yatra mano yāti tatra tatropajāyate /
svaguṇasyānusāreṇa sattvādivinibandhanaḥ /
iti gāruḍe (1)

(1) Cf. ibid. l. 1: *yatra yatra mano dhāvaty ātmapañcānāṃ madhye tatra tatra tad-adhīnena dehena sahānujāyate guṇānubaddhaḥ san* ... ; see also BhaviṣPV 17; BrāṇP 33.

33) BhāgTN (p. 521,4-7):
Subject matter: Hierarchy among the individual souls

pūtanākaṃsanarakaśiśupālādiṣu dvidhā /
jīvāḥ santas tv asantaś ca tatra bandhvādirūpiṇaḥ /
viṣṇoḥ santa iti jñeyā asantaḥ śatrurūpiṇaḥ /
śubhajīvaprakāśena kadācic chubhabuddhayaḥ /
viparyaye 'nyathā ca syuḥ śubhās tatra hariṃ yayuḥ /
aśubhāś ca tamo ghoraṃ yadi tatraiva madhyamāḥ /
madhyamāṃ gatim evāpur ekadehagatā api /
iti gāruḍe (1)

(1) Cf. BhaviṣPV 12; 15 and MESQUITA 2000: 506f.

34) BhāgTN (p. 547,5-8):
Subject matter: Tīrtha / Idols

prākṛtair dṛśyamānaṃ tu na dravaṃ tīrtham ucyate /
devāś ca na śilāmātrāḥ kiṃtu tatrāntarāsthitāḥ /
gurūpadeśaṃ tu vinā na te dṛśyāḥ kathaṃcana /
na jñāyate ca tadrūpam anyathājñāninām ca te /
kopāc chāpaṃ prayacchanti tasmād gurum upavrajet /

tasmāt tīrthāni devāś ca nityaṃ vidvatsu saṃsthitāḥ /
iti gāruḍe (1)

(1) Cf. ibid. ll. 3f: *aṃmayādyabhimānino'pi devā urukālenaiva punanti gurūpadeśaṃ prāpayitvā / bhedakṛtaḥ anyathājñāninaḥ / vipaścitas tu pratyakṣadarśanād anyathājñānam evāpagamayanti*; see also SkaP 69[3f.]. Madhva approves here the worship of idols. On the other hand, in BrahP 58[2ab] he takes it as a behaviour of ignorant persons (*aprabuddha*); also AgniP 20; BhaviṣP 5; BrahP 32; 58; BrahVP 8; GarP 44; NārP 1; SkaP 69[3f.].

34_1) BhāgTN (p. 580,7-581,3):
Subject matter: Upāsana

yathaiva kuṇḍalaṃ tyaktvā nādātuṃ kanakaṃ śakam /
tasyaiva tadavasthatvāt kevalābhedataḥ sphuṭam /
evaṃ surāsuranareṣv āsthito bhagavān hariḥ /
naiva bhedena mantavyo jīvabhede tu saty api /
ye tathābhinnam īśeśaṃ paśyanti paramarṣayaḥ /
ṛtaprāptiviruddhatvāt saṃsāranirṛteḥ śiraḥ /
agaṇayya padākramya vaiṣṇavaṃ nilayaṃ yayuḥ /
iti gāruḍe (1)

(1) Cf. ibid. ll. 1f.: *yathā kanakasya vividhakṛtaṃ kuṇḍalādi kanakaṃ vinā parityaktuṃ na śakyate tathā svakṛtaṃ jagadanupraviṣṭo bhagavān mūlarūpaṃ vinā tyaktuṃ na śakyaḥ / ātmatayā ekasvarūpatvāt / rasitam ātmanā prakāśitaṃ jagat praviṣṭaḥ / tasmāt sarvagato viṣṇur iti jñātavya ity arthaḥ / ithaṃ ye jñātvā paricaranti tava svarūpaṃ te ṛtātmakabrahmaprāptiviruddhatvān nirṛtyākhyasaṃsārasya śiraḥ padākramanti* –

svargaṃ ye prapaśyanti brahmānandam ajākṣaram /
ekam evādvayaṃ nityaṃ nirṛtes te śirogatāḥ /
iti saukarāyaṇaśruti (unknown source);

cf. BhāgP (X 94,27 = X 87,26f.); see also AgniP 20.

35) BhāgTN (p. 593,7-9):
Subject matter: Śrī / Prakṛti

svātantryāt prakṛtityāgakartā nārāyaṇaḥ paraḥ /
yady apy eṣā jīvasaṃsthā hantā ca bhagavān prabhuḥ /
iti gāruḍe (1)

(1) Cf. ibid. ll. 3f.: ... *yac cāyaṃ pumān ātta bhagāṃ tvayāpahṛtabhagāṃ prātisvikāṃ pūrvoktāṃ dvividhāṃ kaṣṭāṃ prakṛtiṃ jahāti hanti ca tad api tvam eva jahāsi jihāsi ca / uteti tyāgavadhayoḥ samuccayārthe* ... ; see also AgniP 25 and MESQUITA 2000: 473f; 478f.

36) BhāgTN (p. 596,11-598,3):
Subject matter: Hierarchy of the rational Beings

anye sarve śriyā baddhāḥ śrīr baddhā viṣṇunaiva tu /
bandhaś ca viṣṇutantratvaṃ muktānāṃ ca śriyas tathā / [1]
amuktānāṃ ca baddhatvaṃ janmamṛtyādiduḥkhitā /
heyo bandhaś ca saiva syān na tu svoccavaśe sthitiḥ / [2]
guṇātmikā ca sā devī nirguṇaḥ puruṣottamaḥ /
saiva viṣṇuṃ vijānāti jñeyo jñātā ca keśavaḥ / [3]
na tāv anye vijānanti vinā haṃsaparaṃparām / (1)
tayāpi naiva jānanti mānuṣā asūrās tathā / [4]
niṣphalaivāsure tasmāc chrutir bandhāya kevalam /
niṣedhavidhyutkramaṇāt tamasy eva vinikṣipet / [5]
niṣphalā saphalā caiva mānuṣāṇāṃ tu madhyataḥ / (2)
saphalaiva tu devānāṃ niyataṃ muktidāyinī / [6]
garuḍaḥ |
ke haṃsāḥ kaḥ paro haṃsaḥ ke ca pārāvatā gaṇāḥ /
ke ca tittirayas tatra ke śukāḥ ke ca vāyasāḥ / [7]
śrībhagavān uvāca |
paro haṃso 'ham evaiko haṃsā brahmāṇa eva tu /
pārāvatā devatās tu munayas tittirāḥ smṛtāḥ / [8]
mānuṣās tu śukāḥ proktā asurāś caiva vāyasāḥ /
prāpyaṃ prāptaṃ yato nityaṃ pūrṇaṃ sarvottamaṃ mayā / [9]
ataḥ paramahaṃso 'ham madanantaram eva tu /
yataḥ prāptam ivāśeṣaṃ sarvajīvottamaṃ śubham / [10]
ato brahmapade yogyā jīvā hamsāḥ prakīrtitāḥ /
teṣāṃ paraṃparāprāptaṃ yair jñānaṃ niyamena tu / [11]
te mucyante na caivānye gurur brahmā yato nṛṇām /
daivataṃ tv aham evaiko mām avittvā na mucyate / [12]
paraṃ prati yato nīcā brahmaṇaḥ sarvadevatāḥ /
pārāvatās tataḥ proktās tais tīrṇāḥ saṃsṛtir yataḥ / [13]
tittirā munayas tasmāt kāsukhatvāt tu mānuṣāḥ /
śukā iti samuddhiṣṭā vayomātrasukhitvataḥ / [14]
vayaso 'nte tu duḥkhitvād asurā vāyasāḥ smṛtāḥ /
evaṃ pañcavidhā jīvāḥ ṣaṣṭho 'haṃ parameśvaraḥ / [15]
na matsamo 'dhiko vāpi kaścid asti dvijottama / [16ab]
iti gāruḍe (3)

(1) In contradiction to the opinion of GLASENAPP [1992: 22f.] Madhva himself traced back his school to Haṃsaparamparā and not his disciples, as GLASENAPP asserts. See also HarV 3; BraṇP 12[25]; KūrP 32[1]; MBh 19.
(2) Cf. ibid. p. 597n. 5: *madhyataḥ madhyamatvāt / na nitarāṃ sāttvikaḥ / nāpi kevalaṃ tāmasaḥ / kiṃtu madhyagataḥ / sattvena tamasā cobhayataḥ saṃsṛṣṭaḥ madhyamena rajasopaplutaḥ.*
(3) Cf. BhaviṣPV 15; GarP 37.

37) BhāgTN (p. 612,6-613,7):
Subject matter: Hierarchy among the rational Beings

santas tu trividhāḥ proktā uttamā madhyamādhamāḥ /
uttamā devatās tatra ṛṣyādyā madhyamā matāḥ / [1]
adhamā mānuṣotkṛṣṭās te cāpi trividhā matāḥ / (1)
tatrādhameṣu yeṣāṃ tu saṅgo vighnāya vai bhavet / [2]
teṣām uttamasaṅgasya teṣāṃ saṅgaṃ parityajet /
ādau tu teṣām api ca saṅga uttamasaṅgateḥ / [3]
sādhanatvān na tu tyājyo yadi tyaktuṃ na śakyate /
tadā te 'pi tathā neyā yathā vighno na vai bhavet / [4]
taduccasaṅgateḥ kvāpi tadā doṣo na jāyate /
prayojanāya teṣāṃ tu saṅgaḥ sarvātmaneṣyate / [5]
sarvathā caiva deveṣu saṅgo munigaṇeṣu ca /
bhāvyo hi taṃ vinā naiva puruṣārthaḥ kvacid bhavet / [6]
viśeṣataḥ svottameṣu vinā saṅgaṃ na mucyate /
svanīceṣu tu deveṣu vinā saṅgaṃ na pūryate / [7]
tasmāt satsūttameṣv eṣu saṅgaḥ kāryo viśeṣataḥ /
anādyanantakāleṣu na ca hāpyaḥ kathaṃcana / [8]
satāṃ saduttameśeśe kimu viṣṇau parāyaṇe / [9ab]
iti gāruḍe (2)

(1) Cf. an untraceable quote Madhva attributes to Bhāgavatantra (BSūBh p. 4,2-7); see also BhavişPV 13; 30[86f.].
(2) Cf. BhavişPV 15 and MESQUITA 2000: 167n. 343; 507n. 663.

38) BSūBh (p. 2,17-3,11):
Subject matter: Explanation of the Pratīka [BSū I 1.1.: *athātas*]

uktaṃ ca gāruḍe –
athātaḥśabdapūrvāṇi sūtrāṇi nikhilāny api /
prārabhante niyatyaiva tat kim atra niyāmakam / [1]
kaś cārthas tu tayor vidvan katham uttamatā tayoḥ /
etad ākhyāhi me brahman yathā jñāsyāmi tattvataḥ / [2]
evam ukto nāradena brahmā provāca sattamaḥ /
ānantarye 'dhikārasya maṅgalārthe tathaiva ca / [3]
athaśabdas tv ataḥśabdo hetvarthe samudīritaḥ /
parasya brahmaṇo viṣṇoḥ prasādād iti vā bhavet / [4]
sa hi sarvamanovṛttiprerakaḥ samudāhṛtaḥ /
sisṛkṣoḥ paramād viṣṇoḥ prathamaṃ dvau viniḥsṛtau / [5]
oṃkāraś cāthaśabdaś ca tasmāt prāthamikau kramāt /
taddhetutvaṃ vadaṃś cāpi tṛtīyo 'ta udāhṛtaḥ / [6]

akāraḥ sarvavāgātmā parabrahmābhidhāyakaḥ / (1)
tathau prāṇātmakau proktau vyāptisthitividhāyakau / [7]
ataś ca pūrvam uccāryāḥ sarva ete satāṃ matāḥ /
athātaḥśabdayor evaṃ vīryam ājñāya tattvataḥ / [8]
sūtreṣu tu mahāprājñās tāv evādau prayuñjate / [9ab]
iti (2)

(1) Cf. MESQUITA 2000: 158n. 318.
(2) Cf. ibid. l. 17: *athaśabdo maṅgalārtho 'dhikārānantaryārthaś ca / ataḥśabdo hetvarthaḥ* ... ; see also SIAUVE 1957: 29ff.

39) BSūBh (p. 12,2-3):
Subject matter: Viṣṇu's inexpressibility in words

aprasiddher avācyaṃ tad vācyaṃ sarvāgamoktitaḥ /
atarkyaṃ tarkyam ajñeyaṃ jñeyam evaṃ paraṃ smṛtam /
iti gāruḍe (1)

(1) Cf. ibid. p. 11,11: *avācyatvādikaṃ tv aprasiddhatvāt –*
na tadṛg iti jñeyaṃ na vācyaṃ na ca tarkyate /
paśyanto 'pi na jānanti mero rūpaṃ vipaścitaḥ /
itivat;
see also AgniP 6 and BrāṇP 69.

40) BSūBh (p. 26,3-5):
Subject matter: Viṣṇu's supreme transcendence

uktaṃ hi gāruḍe –
sarvajñālpajñatābhedāt sarvaśaktyalpaśaktitaḥ /
svātantryapāratantryābhyāṃ saṃbhogo neśajīvayoḥ /
iti ca (1)

(1) Cf. ibid. l. 3: *jīvaparayor ekaśarīrasthatve samānabhogaprāptir iti cen na / sāmarthyavaiśeṣyāt* ... ; AgniP 6: 22; BrāṇP 61 and MESQUITA 2000: 167n. 343; p. 371f.

41) BSūBh (p. 116,8-11):
Subject matter: Repetition (*dviruktiḥ*)

gāruḍe ca –
adhyāyānte dviruktiḥ syād vede vā vaidike 'pi vā /
vicāro yatra sajyeta pūrvoktasyāvadhāraṇe /
anuktānāṃ pramāṇānāṃ svīkāraś ca kṛto bhavet /
vinindya cetarān mārgān saṃpūrṇaphalatā tathā /
iti (1)

(1) Cf. ibid. 1. 8: *sarvādhyāyārthāvadhāraṇārthādhyāyānte dviruktiḥ* ... ; see also GarP 3; BrahVP 30; VarP 32.

42) BSūBh (p. 122,1-5):
Subject matter: Kramamukti

gāruḍe ca –
dhūmādibhāvaprāptiś ca tadgatau gatir eva tu /
sthitau sthitiḥ praveśaś ca laghutvādis tathaiva ca /
na hy anyasyānyathābhāvo na ca tatpadam iṣyate /
vidyāgamyaṃ padaṃ yasmān na tat prāpyaṃ hi karmaṇā /
ekadeśasvabhāvena vāgbhedāpi yujyate /-1
yathā jīvaḥ paraṃ brahma brahmedaṃ jagad ity api /
iti (1)

(1) Cf. ibid. (p. 121,28f.): *dhūmādiṣu praviśya tadgatau gatiḥ sthitau sthitir ityādir eva tadbhāvāpattiḥ / na hy anyasyānyabhāvo yujyate / na ca tatpadaprāptiḥ* ... ; see also ĀdityaP 1; BrahP 82; GarP 44; 53n. 1 and MESQUITA 1994: 463.

43) BSūBh (p. 139,4-5):
Subject matter: Unity and indivisibility of Viṣṇu's nature

sthūlasūkṣmaviśeṣo 'tra na kvacit parameśvare /
sarvatraikaprakāro 'sau sarvarūpeṣv ajo yataḥ /
iti ca gāruḍe (1)

(1) Cf. BSūBh (p. 139,2): *agnyādivat sthūlasūkṣmatvaviśeṣābhāvāt*; see also BrāṇP 10; 69; KūrP 29.

44) BSūBh (p. 218,9-13):
Subject matter: Kramamukti

pratīkaṃ deha uddiṣṭho yeṣāṃ tatraiva darśanam /
na tu vyāptatayā kvāpi pratīkālaṃbanās tu te /(1)
apratīkā devatās tu ṛṣīṇāṃ śatam eva ca /
rājñāṃ ca śatam uddiṣṭaṃ gandharvādiśataṃ tathā /
ete 'dhikāriṇo vyāptidarśane 'nye na tu kvacit /
ayogyadarśane yatnād bhraṃśaḥ pūrvasya cāpi tu /
apratīkāśrayā ye hi te yānti param eva tu /
svadehe brahmadṛṣṭyaiva gacched brahmasalokatām /
brahmaṇā saha saṃprāpte saṃhāre paramaṃ padam /
iti gāruḍavacanāt (2)

(1) Cf. GHATE 1981: 148f. and Anuv (p. 194,22ff); see also BrahP 82, GarP 34.
(2) Cf. ĀdityaP 1; AgniP 20; GarP 34.

45) BSūBh (p. 226,19-227,9):
Subject matter: Jīvanmukti / Kramamukti / Videhamukti

gāruḍe ca –
ātmety eva paraṃ devam upāsya harim avyayam /
kecid atraiva mucyante notkrāmanti kadācana / [1] (1)
atraiva ca sthitis teṣām antarikṣe tu kecana /
kecit svarge maharloke jane tapasi cāpare / [2]
kecit satye mahājñānā gacchanti kṣīrasāgaram /
tatrāpi kramayogena jñānādhikyāt samīpagāḥ / [3]
sālokyaṃ ca sarūpatvaṃ sāmīpyaṃ yogam eva ca / (2)
imām ārabhya sarvatra yāvat sukṣīrasāgare / [4]
puruṣo 'nantaśayanaḥ śrīmān nārāyaṇābhidaḥ /
mānuṣā varṇabhedena tathaivāśramabhedataḥ / [5]
kṣitipā manuṣyagandharvā devāś ca pitaraś cirāḥ / +1
ājānajāḥ karmajāś ca tāttvikāś ca śacīpatiḥ / [6]
rudro brahmeti kramaśas teṣu caivottamottamāḥ /
nityānande ca bhoge ca jñānaiśvaryaguṇeṣu ca / [7]
sarve śataguṇodriktāḥ pūrvasmād uttarottaram /
pūjyante cāvarais te tu sarvapūjyaś caturmukhaḥ / [8]
svajagadvyāpṛtis teṣāṃ pūrvavat samudīritā /
sayujaḥ paramātmānaṃ praviśya ca bahirgatāḥ / [9]
tadrūpān prākṛtāṃś cāpi vinā bhogāṃs tu kāṃścana /
bhuñjate muktir evaṃ te vispaṣṭaṃ samudāhṛtā / [10]
iti (3)

(1) Cf. ĀdityaP 1; BrahP 82; see also MESQUITA 2007: 12n. 15 [= 2007_1 435n. 15]
(2) Cf. MESQUITA 2000: 524f.
(3) Cf. ibid. ll. 18f.: ... (TaiU I 5,3) *pratyakṣopadeśāj jagadaiśvaryam apy astīti cet / na / ādhikārikamaṇḍalādhipatir brahmā hi tatrocyate* ... ; see also AgniP 27; BrahP 82; VāyuP 1.

46) ChUBh (p. 458,10-11):
Subject matter: Contradictory attributes of Viṣṇu

suviruddhā aśrutāś ca guṇāḥ santy eva sarvaśaḥ /
doṣā api na santy eva śrutā api tu sarvaśaḥ /
iti gāruḍe (1)

(1) Cf. ibid. ll. 7f.: (ChU III 14,3) iti hṛdayāsthasyaivānutvamahatvokteś ca –
guṇāḥ śrutāḥ suviruddhāś ca deve santy aśrutā api naivātra śaṅkā /
cintyā acintyāś ca tathaiva doṣāḥ śrutāś ca nājñair hi tathā pratītāḥ /

iti ca śrutiḥ (unknown);
see also BrāṇP 69.

47) GīBh (p. 35,13-14):
Subject matter: Liberation while still alive (*jīvanmukti*)

sthitaprajño 'pi yas tūrdhvaḥ prāpya raudraṃ padaṃ tataḥ /
sāṅkarṣaṇaṃ tato muktim agād viṣṇuprasādataḥ /
iti gāruḍe (1)

(1) Cf. ibid. ll. 9f.: ... *jñāninām api sati prārabdhakarmaṇi śarīrāntaraṃ yuktam / bhogena tv itare iti hy uktam* (BSū IV 1,19) *santi hi bahuśarīraphalāni karmāṇi kānicit / saptajanmani vipraḥ syāt ityādeḥ* (Ṛg IX 67,190?) */ dṛṣṭeś ca jñāninām api bahuśarīraprāpteḥ* ... ; see also ĀdityaP 1 and 2007: 12n. 15f. [= 2007_1 435n. 15f.].

48) GīBh (p. 36,5-6):
Subject matter:Videhamukti

jñāninām karmayuktānāṃ kāyatyāgakṣaṇo yadā /
viṣṇumāyā tadā teṣāṃ mano bāhyaṃ karoti hi /
iti gāruḍe (1)

(1) Cf. ibid. ll. 3f.: *ato jñānināṃ bhavaty eva muktiḥ / bhīṣmādīnāṃ tu tatkṣaṇe yuktyabhāvaḥ / smaraṃs tyajatīti vartamānāpadeśo hi kṛtaḥ / tac coktam* ... ; see also ĀdityaP 1.

49) GīBh (p. 37,13-14):
Subject matter: Pūrṇāvatāras

paripūrṇāni rūpāṇi samāny akhilarūpataḥ /
tathāpy apekṣya mandānāṃ dṛṣṭiṃ tvām ṛṣayo 'pi hi /
parāvaraṃ vadanty eva hy abhaktānāṃ vimohane /
iti gāruḍe (1)

(1) Cf. ibid. l. 12: *yatra ca parāvarabhedo 'vagamyate tatrājñabuddhim apekṣyāvaratvam / viśvarūpam apekṣyānyatra / tac coktam* ... ; see also ĀdiP 1 and MESQUITA 2000_1: 35ff. [= 1997: 29ff.].

50) GīBh (p. 48,18-20):
Subject matter: Sadāgamas

apauruṣeyavedeṣu viṣṇuvedeṣu caiva hi /
sarvatra ye guṇāḥ proktāḥ saṃpradāyāgatāś ca ye /
sarvais taiḥ saha vijñāya ye paśyanti paraṃ harim /
teṣām eva bhaven muktir nānyathā tu kathaṃcana /
iti gāruḍe (1)

(1) Cf. ibid. ll. 15f.: *na ca tatra tatroktaikadeśajñānamātreṇa bhavati muktiḥ / sārvatrikaguṇopasaṃhāro hi bhagavatā guṇopasaṃhārapāde 'bhihitaḥ – ānandādayaḥ pradhānasyetyādinā* (= BSū III 3,12) / *tathā cānyatra* ... ; see also BhavișP 10; BrāṇP 11; MESQUITA 2000₁: 127ff. [=1997: 101ff.] and MESQUITA 2000: 51n. 13.

51) GīBh (p. 67,16-17):
Subject matter: Equanimity

yathā suhṛtsu kartavyaṃ pitṛśatrusu teșu ca /
tathā karoti pūjādiṃ samabuddhiḥ sa ucyate /
iti gāruḍe (1)

(1) Cf. ibid. l. 15: *suhṛdādiṣu śāstroktapūjādikṛtir anyūnādikā yā sāpi samatā / tad apy āha* ... ; see also BrahVP 35 and BhāgTN (p. 430,7- 431,5 = Brahmatarka [fictitious source]).

52) GīBh (p. 70,6-7):
Subject matter: Bhakti / Equanimity

sarvadā sarvabhūteșu samaṃ māṃ yaḥ prapaśyati /
acalā tasya bhaktiḥ syād yogakṣemavaho 'py aham /
iti gāruḍe (1)

(1) Cf. ibid. ll. 3f: *tasyāhaṃ na praṇaśyāmīti sarvadā yogakṣemavahaḥ syām ity arthaḥ / sa ca me na praṇaśyati sarvadā madbhakto bhavati / saty api svāminy arakṣaty anāthaḥ / evaṃ bhṛtye apy abhajaty abhṛtya iti hi prasiddhiḥ / uktaṃ ca* ... ; see also BrahVP 35.

53) GīBh (p. 72,13-14):
Subject matter: Excellence of Viṣṇu's meditation

kṛcchrāder api yajñāder dhyānayogo viśiṣyate /
tatrāpi śeṣaśrībrahmaśivādidhyānato hareḥ /
dhyānaṃ koṭiguṇaṃ proktam adhikaṃ vā mumukṣuṇām /
iti gāruḍe (1)

(1) Cf. ibid. ll. 12f.: *jñānibhyo yogajñānibhyaḥ / tapasvibhyaḥ kṛcchrādicāribhyaḥ / uktaṃ ca* ... This statement corresponds to the doctrine of Vedānta. For instance, Śaṅkara remarks in his (BSūBh *ad* I 1,4): *tathā ca yāgādyanuṣṭhāyinām eva vidyāsamādhiviśeṣād uttareṇa pathā gamanam / kevalair iṣṭāpūrtadattasādhanair dhūmādikrameṇa dakṣiṇena pathā gamanaṃ / tatrāpi sukhatāratamyaṃ tatsādhanatāratamyaṃ ca śāstrāt* (ChU V 10,5). Likewise Rāmānuja (*ad* I 1,4.): *tasmād dhyānaniyogena brahmaparokṣajñānaphalenaiva bandhanivṛttiḥ*; cf. also the commentaries of both authors *ad* Gī VI 46; see also AgniP 20; MBh 27; NārP 8.

54) GīBh (p. 75,21):
Subject matter: Three-fold state of consciousness

śārīras tu tridhā bhinno jāgrādiṣv avasthiteḥ / -1
iti vacanād gāruḍe (1)

(1) Cf. ibid. l. 21: *svapnādiś ca śārīra eva* ... ; see also BrāṇP 7.

55) GīBh (p. 77,29-78,1):
Subject matter: Bhakti

tac coktaṃ gāruḍe –
mayy eva bhaktir nānyatra ekabhaktiḥ sa ucyate /
iti (1)

(1) Cf. ibid. l. 29: *ekasminn eva bhaktir ity ekabhaktiḥ / tatra coktam* ... ; see also AgniP 20.

56) GīBh (p. 86,15-16):
Subject matter: Viṣṇu – Avyakta / Viṣṇu's supreme transcendence

avyaktaṃ paraṃ viṣṇum
iti prayogāc ca gāruḍe (1)

(1) Cf. ibid. l. 15: *avyakto bhagavān* ... ; see also AgniP 6 and BrahP 26; KūrP 29.

57) GīBh (p. 87,11-12):
Subject matter: Presiding Deity over solstice

tac coktaṃ gāruḍe –
pūjitas tv ayanenāsau māsaiḥ parivṛtena ha /
iti (1)

(1) Cf. ibid. l. 11: *māsābhimānibyo 'yanābhimānī ca pṛthak / tac coktam* ... ; see also BhaviṣP 11; BrahP 82.

58) MāṇUBh (p. 515,18-19):
Subject matter: Varuṇa

pramāṇasya pramāṇaṃ ca balavad vidyate mune /
brahmadṛṣṭān yato mantrān pramāṇaṃ salileśvaraḥ /
atra ślokā bhavantīti cakāraiva pṛthak pṛthak /
iti gāruḍe (1)

(1) Cf. HarV 32 [5ab]; PadP 100. The view that MāṇU was visioned by Brahmā has been suscribed to also by other Vedānta authors, CH. BOUY, La Māṇḍūkya-Upaniṣad et L'Āgamasāstra, concordances externes et citations, WZKS 41 (1997): 131f.

Harivaṃśa (HarV)

[It is worthy of note that HarV is quoted only from 3. Adhyāya in BĀUBh and that, apart from one single traceable quote (= III 132,95; cf. BSūBh p. 7,9; MuUBh p. 490,17-18; see also MESQUITA 2000₁: 20n. 16; 44n. 59; 133n. 266 [= 1997: 17n. 9; 36n. 51; 107n. 256), all others could not be identified. Out of a total of 37 references, twenty-five are found in BhāgTN; seven in BĀUBh; two in MāṇUBh and one each in AiUBh; BSūBh and TaiUBh. One metrical *lapsus* is to be found in HarV 34.]

1) AiUBh p. 183,29+184,1).:
Subject matter: Śrī – Wife of Viṣṇu

['me 'nnaṃ dakṣiṇam' ity uktatvāc ca viṣṇur eveti jñāyate | sa hi viṣṇur dakṣiṇāmitra ukto] <u>harivaṃśeṣu dhanyāścaryādhyāye</u> –
dakṣiṇābhiḥ sahaivaitan madadhastāj jagat sadā | (1)
dhanyāścaryo 'ham evaiko mitraṃ me dakṣiṇā rāmā |
ity avādīd dharir bhūpā dhanyo 'sītyudito mayā |
iti nāradavacanam (2)

(1) Cf. ibid. (p. 184,2): *na ca bṛhatīsahasrābhimāninīṃ devīṃ vinā cetanamātrasya mukhyamitratvaṃ yujyate* ... ; see also MBh 1; BrāṇP 3[21f.] and 51.
(2) This quote is not avalaible in Harivamśa and it might have been authored by Madhva himself. But he mentions the name of the chapter where, according to him, it has been handed down, namely *dhanyāścaryādhyāya*. Most probably he means by it *dhanyopākhyānam* (HarV 110): iti ... *harivaṃśe viṣṇuparvaṇi dhanyopākhyānaṃ nāma daśādhikaśatamo 'dhyāyaḥ*. In the critical ed. it was eliminated. Madhva could have used HarV 100, 21-29 as literal basis for the above quote.
so 'vagāhya narendrāṇāṃ madhyaṃ sāgarasaṃnibham |
āsanasthaṃ yaduśreṣṭham uvāca munir avyayaḥ ||
āścaryaṃ khalu devānām ekas tvaṃ puruṣottama |
dhanyaś cāsi mahābāho loke nānyo 'sti kaścana ||
evam uktaḥ smitaṃ kṛtvā pratyuvāca muniṃ prabhuḥ |
āścaryaś caiva dhanyaś dakṣiṇābhiḥ sahety aham ||
evam ukto muniśreṣṭhaḥ prāha madhye mahīkṣitām |
kṛṣṇa paryāptavākyo 'smi gamiṣyāmi yathāgatam ||
taṃ prasthitam ābhiprekṣya pārthivāḥ prāhur īśvaram |
guhyaṃ mantram ajānato vacanaṃ nāraderitam ||
āścarya ity abhihito dhanyo 'sīti ca mādhava |
dakṣiṇābhiḥ sahety evaṃ pratyukte 'pi ca nārade ||
kim etan nābhijānīmo divyaṃ mantrapadaṃ mahat |
yadi śravyam idaṃ kṛṣṇa śrotum icchāma tattvataḥ ||
tān uvāca tataḥ kṛṣṇaḥ sarvān pārthivapuṃgavān |
śrotavyaṃ nāradas tv eṣa dvijo vaḥ kathayiṣyāti ||
brūhi nārada tattvārthaṃ śrāvyantāṃ pṛthivīkṣitaḥ |
yat tvayābhihitaṃ vākyaṃ mayā ca pratibhāṣitam ||
see also BrāṇP 51.

1[1]) BĀUBh (p. 260,13-14):
Subject matter: Viṣṇuloka / Liberation

adarśayet svakaṃ lokaṃ brahmaṇe viṣṇur avyayaḥ /
yasmāt padāt paraṃ nāsti yatra muktā upāsate /
iti harivaṃśeṣu (1)

(1) Cf. BhāgP II 9,9f.; see also AgniP 16; 27.

2) BĀUBh (p. 265,15-16):
Subject matter: Liberation

narādibrahmaparyantaṃ vimuktānāṃ śatocchrayaḥ /
niḥśeṣaduḥkhahīnānāṃ nityānandaikabhoginām /
apy ānande mitho hy uktas tv adhvaryūṇāṃ śrutau pṛthak /
iti harivaṃśeṣu (1)

(1) Cf. ibid. ll. 12f.: *na cendrapadād viraktasyendrasamaṃ sukhaṃ brahmapadād viraktasya tatsamam ity atra kiṃcin mānam asti / dṛṣṭavastuni virāge āyāsābhāvāt kaścit sukhaviśeṣo dṛśyate / anyatra brahmapadād viraktasyendrādipadād viraktasya ca na hi kaścid viśeṣo dṛśyate / ato 'nubhavavirudhatvād yat kiṃcid etat*; see also AgniP 16; BhaviṣP 15; BrahPV 29.

3) BĀUBh (p. 265,28-266,5):
Subject matter: Viṣṇu's supreme transcendence

śarīrānabhimānī yo hṛdi saṃstho janārdanaḥ /
abhimānavato dehe jīvasya sa niyāmakaḥ /
sa eva sūryasaṃsthaś ca haṃsaḥ so 'ham iti śrutaḥ / (1)
hantṛtvād dhaṃsanāmāsau so 'haṃ cāsāv aheyataḥ / (2)
sa eva sūryasaṃsthena rūpeṇaivākṣiṇi sthitaḥ /
sūryasaṃsthād dhi rūpāt sa vibhakto 'kṣiṇi saṃsthitaḥ / (3)
gacchato mriyamāṇasya tāv ubhāv api dehataḥ /
tayor dehavihāne tu bhavetāriṣṭadarśanam /
tadā sañcintayed devaṃ tam eva puruṣottamam /
ityādi harivaṃśeṣu (4)

(1) For etymology of *haṃsaḥ* see M. WILLIAMS, A Sanskrit-English Dictionary, Oxford 1964 s. v.; see also GarP 36[4ab]; KūrP 32[1]; MBh 19; VarP 51[6].
(2) Cf. BhaviṣPV 3[3f.]; BrāṇP 3[17f.].
(3 Cf. GarP 5.
(4) Cf. AgniP 6.

4) BĀUBh (p. 266,8-9):
Subject matter: Antaryāmin

svecchayaivāvṛtto viṣṇur jīve tiṣṭhati nityadā /
yo 'sau niyāmayan jīvaṃ kṣetrajña iti śabditaḥ /
iti harivaṃśeṣu (1)

(1) Cf. BhāgP 2.

5) BĀUBh (p. 266,21-267,3):
Subject matter: Bhakti / Syllabus of heresies

sarvasmād uttama iti samyak snehayutā matiḥ /
susthirā bhaktir uddiṣṭā tayā mokṣo na cānyataḥ / [1]
tayā mokṣo bhavaty eva sā cet pūrṇā svayogyataḥ / (1)
aparokṣaḍṛśā yuktā sā pūrṇety abhidhīyate / [2]
aparokṣadṛśiś cāpi mahācāryoktadarśanam /
so 'pi yanmokṣaniyataṃ manasā samudīrayet / [3]
tasya darśanato yāti muktiṃ nāsty atra saṃśayaḥ /
dhyānaṃ ca guruśuśrūṣā nityanaimittikāḥ kriyāḥ / [4]
tīrthadānajapādyāś ca svādhyāyo harikīrtanam /
dvādaśyādivrataṃ caiva tulasyādyair athārcanam / [5]
sarvaṃ bhaktyartham uddiṣṭaṃ niṣphalaṃ tat tayā vinā /
viṣṇubhaktiyuto muktiṃ yāti nānyaḥ kathaṃcana / [6]
etadanyat tu yacchāstraṃ na tacchāstraṃ kuvartma tat /
viṣṇor bhaktim ṛte muktir jīvābhedo harer api / [7] (2)
śivabrahmādisāmyaṃ ca harer mohārtham ucyate /
daityānāṃ mohanārthāya viṣṇor anyasamānatā / [8]
hīnatā vocyate śāstrair na tad grāhyaṃ manīṣibhiḥ /
viṣṇuvāyugirīśendradevaviprāḥ kramāt sadā / [9]
sāmarthyato vihīnās tu guṇaiḥ sarvais tathaiva ca /
hīno viṣṇur na kasyāpi sarvataś cottamottamaḥ / [10]
etadanyat tu yac chāstraṃ tadāsuravimohanam /
tasmāt sarvottamaṃ viṣṇuṃ niścitya paramaṃ vrajet / [11]
iti harivaṃśeṣu (3)

(1) Cf. MESQUITA 2000: 506ff.; see also AgniP 24.
(2) Cf. BrāṇP 12n. 3.
(3) Cf. AgniP 6; 20; BhaviṣPV 3n. 7 and MBh 7.

6) BĀUBh (p. 267,30-268,2):
Subject matter: The real meaning of a sentence (*siddhārtha*), as against *kāryārtha*

upāsanāyāḥ kāryatve viṣṇor ātmatva eva ca /
ubhayatrāpi tātparyam ātmopāsādike vidhau /

tasmād asatyaṃ na dhyāyed dhyāyet tatsatyatāṃ yathā /
vicārya matimān vākyair bahubhiḥ svārthavācakaiḥ /
iti harivaṃśeṣu (1)

(1) Cf. ibid. ll. 25f.: *kartavyatāmātre vākyaprāmāṇyāṅgīkāre karmaprayojane pramāṇābhāvāt tatrāpi tātparyam aṅgīkartavyam eveti siddham eva siddhe tātparyam / citrāditārakādvandvaṃ yadā pūrṇendusaṃyutam / caitrādimāsā vijñeyā ity ādau vastuyāthārthye tathā jñāne cobhayatra tātparyadarśanāt / upāsanāvākyeṣv apy upāsanāyāṃ vastuyāthārthye cobhayatra tātparyaṃ yuktam / ...* (ibid. 268,3): *tasmād iṣṭasādhanajñānam eva sarvavākyārthaḥ*; see also BrahP 1_3; BrahVP 19; 30; HarV 27; NārP 58 and MESQUITA 2000: 389ff.

6_1) BĀUBh (p. 306,24):
Subject matter: God Vāyu

saptaskandhagato lokān yo bibharti mahābalaḥ /
iti ca harivaṃśeṣu (1)

(1) Cf. ibid. ll. 22f.: *na ca vāyur gandharvalokāśritaḥ / vāyvāśrayatvaśruteḥ sarvalokānām – vāyunā hi sarve lokā nenīyanta ityādinā ...* ; also HarV 34, 27:
yaḥ prāṇaḥ sarvabhūtānāṃ pañcadhā bhidyate nṛṣu /
saptaskandhagato lokāṃs trīn dadhāra cakāra ca //
see also BhaviṣPV 17; BrahVP 13 and MESQUITA 2003: 101f.

7) BhāgTN (p. 195,9-10):
Subject matter: Viṣṇu's supreme transcendence

nāyur mānaṃ bhagavataḥ kasmin rūpe 'pi vidyate /
anāditvād amadhyatvād anantatvāc ca so 'vyayaḥ /
iti harivaṃśeṣu

(1) Cf. AgniP 6 and MESQUITA 2000: 415ff.

8) BhāgTN (p. 198,2-3):
Subject matter: Synonyms of ignorance

tamo 'jñānaṃ viparyāso moho 'nye tu tadāgrahāḥ /
iti harivaṃśeṣu (1)

(1) The quote referred to comes after the following Śloka-text:
tamas tu śārvaraṃ proktaṃ mohaś caiva viparyayaḥ /
tadāgraho mahāmohas tāmisraḥ krodha ucyate /
maraṇaṃ tv andhatāmisram avidyā pāñcaparvikā /
iti bhārate.
The first part of the above Śloka is not available. The parts that follow deviates greatly from the traditional wording (MBh XIV 37,33):
tamo moho mahāmohas tāmisraḥ krodhasaṃjñitaḥ /
maraṇaṃ tv andhatāmisraṃ tāmisraṃ krodha ucyate /

cf. KūrP 6; MBh 13; 39; PadP 13; SkaP 12; 35; 38; 50; VarP 18.

9) BhāgTN (p. 244,1-4):
Subject matter: Prakṛti / Śrī

> *vyaktāvyaktātmakaṃ yat tad vidyāt sadasadātmakam /*
> *asargā kevalāvyaktā sisṛkṣur ubhayātmikā /*
> *vyaktāiva kāryarūpā tu prakṛtis trividhā matā /*
> *kāryataḥ sā pradhānatvāt pradhānam iti kīrtyate /*
> *aviśeṣā hy akāryatvāt sā ca śrīr viṣṇusaṃśrayā /*
> iti harivaṃśeṣu (1)

(1) Cf. AgniP 25 and MESQUITA 2000: 473ff.

10) BhāgTN (p. 244,11-12):
Subject matter: *nirguṇam* and *saguṇaṃ* Brahman

> *haris tu nirguṇaṃ brahma śrīr brahma saguṇaṃ smṛtā /*
> *tadaṅgajāni tattvāni tasmāt tadrūpam ucyate /*
> iti harivaṃśeṣu (1)

(1) Cf. AgniP 25; BrāṇP 69 and MESQUITA 2000: 438ff.

11) BhāgTN (p. 256,10-11):
Subject matter: Difference of Ātman from Paramātman

> *nityadṛk paramātmāsau mṛtavad yo na kiṃcana /*
> *jānāti jīvaḥ sa jñeyaḥ paramātmā tadāśrayaḥ /*
> iti harivaṃśeṣu (1)

(1) Cf. ibid. l. 9: *sāhaṅkāradravyaṃ jīvaḥ / tasyāvasthānam anugrāhakaś ca paramātmā* ... ; see also AgniP 22, GarP 40.

12) BhāgTN (p. 259,10-12):
Subject matter: Viṣṇu's supreme transcendence / Viṣṇu, the supreme Creator of the universe

> *durduḥkham iti vijñeyaṃ khaṃ sukhaṃ ca tayor yataḥ /*
> *pradātā paramo viṣṇus tasmād duḥkhadanāmavān /*
> iti harivaṃśeṣu (1)

(1) Cf. ibid. l. 10: *asatkartā tu jīvaḥ syāt satkartā parameśvara* iti śabdanirṇaye (unknown source); see also AgniP 6; 12 and MESQUITA 2000_1: 169n. 335 [= 1997: 139n. 335].

13) BhāgTN (p. 272,3-5):
Subject matter: Bhakti as means of liberation

jñānabhaktiṃ vinā naiva muktiḥ kasyāpi vidyate /
tayor ekatareṇaiva viṣṇugenobhayaṃ vinā /
evam apy etayor ekabhāve 'nyaniyater dhruvam /
ekenāpi bhaven muktis tadarthaṃ tv anyasādhanam /
iti harivaṃśeṣu (1)

(1) Cf. BhāgTN (p. 272n. 1 and 2): ... *tayor dvayor api jñānayogayor bhagavacchabdavācyaḥ paramātmaika evārthaḥ viṣayaḥ* ... *ubhayaṃ vinā tayor ekatareṇaiva naiva muktiḥ kasyāpi vidyate*; see also AgniP 20 and MESQUITA 2007: 28n. 58; 35ff. [= 2007_1 444n. 57; 447ff.].

14) BhāgTN (p. 297,1-2):
Subject matter: Viṣṇu, the supreme guiding Spirit (*antaryāmin*)

priyavratottānapādapramukheṣu hariḥ svayam /
āviṣṭaḥ sarvabhūteṣu vṛṣabhādyāḥ svayaṃ hariḥ /
iti harivaṃśeṣu (1)

(1) Cf. BhāgP 2; BrahVP 17; GarP 27.

15) BhāgTN (p. 303,3-4):
Subject matter: Viṣṇu's supreme transcendence / Viṣṇu, one without a second

dvitīyasya svatantrasya tv abhāvād dvayavarjitaḥ /
īśvaraś ceśitavyasya bhāvāt sa parameśvaraḥ /
iti harivaṃśeṣu (1)

(1) Cf. AgniP 6 and MESQUITA 2000: 438f.

16) BhāgTN (p. 319,1):
Subject matter: Upadharma

dharmopamas tv adharmo ya upadharmaḥ sa ucyate /
iti harivaṃśeṣu (1)

(1) Cf. AgniP 20 and BrahP 28.

17) BhāgTN (p. 324,4-5).
Subject matter: Viṣṇu – Brāhmaṇapriya

yatprasādena devendro vedoditayaśā abhūt /

so 'pi viṣṇur ameyātmā sadā brāhmaṇavatsalaḥ /
iti harivaṃśeṣu (1)

(1) Cf. ibid. l. 3: *harir indraḥ yaccaraṇābhivandanād anapāyinīṃ lakṣmīm avāpa so 'pi viṣṇur brāhmaṇapriyaḥ* ... .

18) BhāgTN (p. 352,1-2):
Subject matter: Liberation

dehādivyatirekeṇa cidrūpo 'ham iti sphuṭam /
sadaivānubhavo bhaktir viṣṇau taddarśanād anu /
yasyāsau mucyate kṣipraṃ saṃsārān nātra saṃśayaḥ /
iti harivaṃśeṣu (1)

(1) Cf. AgniP 16; see also MESQUITA 2007: 9n. 11 [= 2007_1: 434n. 11].

19) BhāgTN (p. 399,1-3):
Subject matter: Viṣṇu, the supreme guiding Spirit (*antaryāmin*)

yadoparāmo manasaḥ svapnasuptilayādiṣu /
tadāvasthāprabodhādikāraṇatvena keśavaḥ /
asvātantryāt tu jīvasya vidyate 'nyo niyāmakaḥ /
jīvapravṛttyanākulyāj jñāyate 'sau tadā prabhuḥ /
iti harivaṃśeṣu (1)

(1) Cf. ibid. (p. 398,8-9):*kevalayā svasaṃsthayā / svapnasuptyādau manauparamāj jīvasyāsvātantryadarśane 'pi svapnaprabodhādidarśanād anya īśvaras tanniyāmako 'stīti jñāyate / jīvecchābhāvāt kevalatvam* ... ; see also BhāgP 2; BrāṇP 7.

19_1) BhāgTN (p. 433,4-5)
Subject matter: Viṣṇu's adorers and foes

māgadhādyā yathā nityaṃ dveṣāḍ āgrahiṇo harau /
na tathāgrahiṇo bhaktā ṛte brahmāṇam avyayam /
iti harivaṃśeṣu (1)

(1) Cf. ibid. l. 3: *tanmayatāṃ manasas tatrābhiniveśam* ... ; cf. also BhāgP (VII 1,27 = VII 1,26):

yathā vairānubandhena martyas tanmayatām iyāt /
na tathā bhaktiyogena iti me niścitā matiḥ /

BhāgTN (p. 434,1-2): *tatraiva hetuḥ – yathā vairānubandheneti / yathā vairābhiniveśinas tathā bhaktyabhiniveśino na santi / tat katham / anyathā bhaktān eva bahūn hariḥ kuryād iti bhāvaḥ*; see also BhaviṣPV12; BrahVP 36; BrāṇP 53; GarP 28; 29; MatsyaP 3; NārP 45; SkaP 65.

20) BhāgTN (p. 602,1-4):
Subject matter: Transmigration

ātmano dehagehādi dvayaśabdena bhaṇyate /
avidyamānaṃ jīvasya pratibhāti tadīyavat /
jāgradvat tu yathā svapnaḥ pratibhāti manorathaḥ /
vidyamānavad evaivaṃ dehādīśavaśe sthitam /
vibhāti svavaśatvena saiṣa saṃsṛtir ucyate /
tasmāt tadviṣayaṃ tyaktvā mano viṣṇau niveśayet /
iti harivaṃśeṣu (1)

(1) Cf. ibid. (p. 602 n. 1): *ahaṃ rājā bhavānītyādimanorathamayaḥ svapno jāgradvat vidyāmānavad eva yathā pratibhāti tathā dehādīśavaśe sthitaṃ svavaśatvena vibhāti*; see also BrāṇP 7; 33.

21) BhāgTN (p. 602,11-12):
Subject matter: Viṣṇu's supreme transcendence

sarvaṃ harer vaśatvena śarīraṃ tasya bhaṇyate /
ananyādhipatitvāc ca tadananyam udīryate /
na cāpy abhedo jagatā viṣṇoḥ pūrṇaguṇasya tu /
iti harivaṃśeṣu (1)

(1) Cf. AgniP 4; 6 and MESQUITA 2000: 428n. 501.

22) BhāgTN (p. 607,2-3):
Subject matter: Tāratamya / Equanimity

na kvāpi jīvaṃ viṣṇutve saṃsṛtau mokṣa eva vā /
yaḥ paśyati surādiṃś ca yathotkarṣaṃ prapaśyati /
sa sarvabhūtasamadṛg viṣṇuṃ sarvottamaṃ smaran / (1)
iti harivaṃśeṣu (2)

(1) Cf. ibid. l. 1: *citte vidyamāne svātmani kevalātmabhāve mokṣe ca yasya jīva-parayor abhedo nāsti*; see also AgniP 16; BhaviṣPV 15; BrahVP 35.

23) BhāgTN (p. 614,10-12):
Subject matter: Fine Arts

gṛhiṇo 'py alpabhodasya na kalāsu prayojanam /
āvartayed vedatantrān mukhyokto harir atra hi /
iti harivaṃśeṣu (1)

(1) Cf. BrāṇP 64 and MESQUITA 2000_1: 140ff. [= 1997: 112ff.].

24) BhāgTN (p. 618,5-8):
Subject matter: Prāṇa

yathendriyagataḥ prāṇas teṣāṃ śaktyā vikalpyate /
dṛṣṭidaḥ śrutidaś ceti matido 'jñānadas tathā /
ityādibhedato vācya eka eva mahābalaḥ /
dṛṣṭyādiśaktis tasyaiva yato nānyasya kasyacit /
evaṃ sadrūpakaṃ brahma tattacchaktyā vikalpyate /
evam eva mahāśakti prāṇasyāpi balapradam /
iti harivaṃśeṣu (1)

(1) Cf. AgniP 12; BhaviṣPV 17; MESQUITA 2000_1: 171n. 248 [= 1997: 139n. 335] and MESQUITA 2003: 102n. 14.

25) BhāgTN (p. 619,5-10):
Subject matter: Prāṇa / Viṣṇu's supreme transcendence

dehād dehāntaragatau praviśet prāṇam eva tu /
jīvaḥ prāṇaḥ parātmānam evaṃ suptāv api sphuṭam /
tadanyā devatāḥ sarvāḥ prāṇasyaiva vaśe 'sthitāḥ /
īṣac ca suptavad yānti naiva mānuṣajīvavat /
svargasthānāṃ na tu svāpaḥ prāyo dehe 'pi nājñatā /
mṛtisuptiprabodhāder niyantā harir ekarāṭ /
tam ṛte naiva cāvasthā nāvasthāvān na ca smṛtiḥ /
tatas tu devadeveśaḥ prāṇaḥ prāṇeśvaro hariḥ /
na harer īśitā tv anyaḥ sa hi sarvādhiko mataḥ /
iti harivaṃśeṣu (1)

(1) Cf. ibid. ll. 3f.: *avanisthiteṣu svedajeṣu / bhūsvedena hi prāyo jāyante / tadā kūṭasthe paramātmany āsa jīvaḥ / yaṃ paramātmānam ṛte suptyanusmṛtir eva na ...* ; see also BhaviṣPV 17 and MESQUITA 2003: 104n. 18.

26) BhāgTN (p. 630,2-3):
Subject matter: Ātman

āptatvād ātmaśabdoktaṃ svasminn api pareṣu ca /
jīvād anyaṃ na paśyanti śrutvaivaṃ vidviṣanti ca /
etāṃs tvam āsūrān viddhi lakṣaṇaiḥ puruṣādhamān / (1)
iti harivaṃśeṣu (2)

(1) Cf. MESQUITA 2000: 527f.
(2) ibid. l. 1: *svātmānaṃ svasminn āptaṃ ca*; GīBh (p. 113,9-12): *pūrṇaś cāsau ātmā ceti mahātmā / ātmaśabdaś cokto* bhārate (= I 5. 24*) –
yac cāpnoti yad ādatte yac cātti viṣayān iha /

yac cāsya santato bhāvas tasmād ātmeti baṇyate /
iti;
see also AgniP 22; BhaviṣPV 4[1]; BrahVP 19; BrāṇP 13[13]; 71; VāmP 8.

27) BhāgTN (p. 678,3-4):
Subject matter: Viṣṇu, the supreme meaning of all Vedas

dugdhadohāṃ tu gāṃ rakṣet kṣīramātraprayojanaḥ /
yathā tadvad dhares anyad vāco dhāraṇam iṣyate /
iti harivaṃśeṣu (1)

(1) Cf. BhāgTN (p. 698 n. 4): *yathā kṣīramātraprayojano jano duḥkhamātraphalāya dugdhadohāṃ gāṃ rakṣet tadvat hariviṣayād vācaḥ anyad vāco dhāraṇaṃ duḥkhamātraphalam iṣyate* / *anyad anyasya vāca iti vā* / *kriyāviśeṣaṇaṃ vā* / *anyadanyaviṣayatvena* / *etenaiva adhenum iva rakṣata iti pūrvaśloko 'pi vyākhyātaḥ* / *adhenuṃ dugdhadohāṃ gāṃ iti* / *vedavācaḥ harer anyaviṣayatvena dhāraṇam iti ca*; see also BrāṇP 82.

28) BhāgTN (p. 715,6-10):
Subject matter: Eight yogic powers

śruteṣu tu yathāyogaṃ kṣipragrahaṇam eva tu /
uktaṃ prākāśyam anyeṣāṃ devānām aśruteṣv api /
ṛṣīṇāṃ miśrabhāvena bhāsate kiṃcid aśrutam /
viṣayebhyo 'dhikasukhavyaktiḥ prākāmyam eva tu /
itareṣāṃ surāṇāṃ tu niḥsīmānandabhojanam /
evam eva tu niḥsīmā devānām aṣṭasiddhayaḥ /
uttarottaram atrāpi yāvad viṣṇuḥ supūrṇabhuk /
iti harivaṃśeṣu (1)

(1) Cf. BhāgTN (p. 715n. 7): *viṣayebhyo yat sukhaṃ tato 'dhikasukhavyaktir viṣayān vināpīty arthaḥ*. The reference to Yoga in the above quote seems to be related with BhāgP (XI 15,8). It follows after a longer untraceable quotation with same contents (ibid. p. 713,5-715,6) which, however, clearly refers to the set of eight yogic powers (YSū III 45 = BhāgP XI 15,4f.):

...
etā niḥsīmakās teṣāṃ devānām aṣṭasiddhayaḥ /
ato 'ṣṭādaśasiddhīnāṃ tadantarbhāva iṣyate /
deveṣv indreśavāyuśrīviṣṇūnām uttarottaram /
siddhayaḥ paripūrṇās tu viṣṇor ekasya nānyagāḥ /
ity aiśvarye (unknown source);
see also KūrP 11;19; MBh 18; PadP 65.

29) BhāgTN (p. 717,8-9):
Subject matter: Production of / derivatives from Prakṛti

avyaktasyājanmavato vikāro janir ucyate /
iti harivaṃśeṣu (1)

(1) Cf. ibid. l. 6: *avyaktajanmanaḥ avyaktasyāpi kiṃcit sthūlatvasya kartuḥ ...*
tasmād avyaktam utpannaṃ triguṇaṃ dvijasattama /
iti mokṣadharmeṣu (= MBh XII 321,29ab) ... ;
see also AgniP 4; 25.

30) BhāgTN (p. 764,6-8):
Subject matter: Asuras

tāmaseṣu tu ye sattvā nirayapracurās tu te /
īṣatsvargādisaṃyuktā evaṃ niṣṭhāś ca te smṛtāḥ /
kevalaṃ niraye niṣṭhā ye te tāmasarājasāḥ /
andhe tamasi ye niṣṭhās te vai tāmasatāmasāḥ /
evaṃ tribhedayuktās tu yājñikā viṣṇuvarjitāḥ /
iti harivaṃśeṣu (1)

(1) Cf. ibid. l. 5: *tāmaseṣv eva rajaḥsattvatamoviśeṣāḥ*; also ibid n. 2: ... *yadi rajaḥsattvatamoniṣṭhā madupāsanaṃ kuryus tadā ayathā matsvabhāvam atikramya rudrādisāmyena mām upāsate / atas teṣām adhaḥpāta iti bhāvaḥ*; see also BhaviṣPV 12 and MESQUITA 2000: 527ff.

31) BSūBh (p. 178,13-14):
Subject matter: Good behaviour

atītānāgatajñānī trailokyoddharaṇakṣamaḥ /
etādṛśo 'pi nācāraṃ śrautaṃ smārtaṃ visarjayet /
iti harivaṃśeṣu (1)

(1) Cf. AgniP 20; VarP 12.

32) MāṇUBh (p. 513,22+514,5):
Subject matter: Pūrṇatva / Viṣṇu's supreme transcendence

pūrṇas tu harir evaiko nānyat pūrṇaṃ kadācana /
vinā ca prakṛtiṃ nānyat kālātītaṃ parātmanaḥ /
kālaś caiva diśo vedāḥ prakṛtyātmāna īritāḥ /
abhimānāt tu jīvānāṃ na kālātītatā bhavet /
muktānām api pūrvatra kālasaṃbandha īritaḥ /
pūrṇatvaṃ ca sadā viṣṇoḥ prasiddhaṃ sarvavedataḥ /
so 'yaṃ viṣṇū ramābrahmarudrānantādigaḥ sadā /
ādānādanakartṛtvād ātmā teṣām agocaraḥ /
iti maṇḍūkarūpī san dadarśa varuṇaḥ svayam /
iti harivaṃśeṣu (1)

(1) Cf. ibid. ll. 20f.: *śrībrahmādisakaladeheṣu sthitvādānādikartā yo 'yaṃ kaścit pratīyate / jīvānāṃ asvātantryadarśanāt so'pi sa eveti darśayati – ayam ātmā brahma iti* (ibid. l. 4); see also AgniP 6; GarP 58 and MESQUITA 2000: 421f.; 459ff.; 490f.

33) MāṇUBh (p. 515,21+516,10):
Subject matter: Viṣṇu, the supreme Creator of the universe

prabhavaḥ sarvabhāvānāṃ viṣṇur eva na saṃśayaḥ /
itthaṃ satāṃ niścayaḥ syād anyathā tv asatāṃ bhavet / [1]
sarvasya hi praṇetṛtvāt prāṇo nārāyaṇaḥ paraḥ /
tāṃ sṛṣṭiṃ bahudhā prāhur jñānino 'jñāninas tathā / [2]
viṣṇur vikṛtim āyāti mahadādisvarūpiṇīm /
tattadvividhabhūtis tu sṛṣṭiḥ proktā hy apaṇḍitaiḥ / [3]
svapnamāyāsarūpāṃ ca kecid ajñā janā viduḥ /
avikārasya cinmātrasvecchayaivākhilaṃ jagat / [4]
utpadyata iti prājñāḥ prāhur brahmādayo 'khilāḥ /
pūrṇaśakteḥ kuto māyā sārvajñyāt svapnavat kutaḥ / [5]
sarvadoṣavyatītasya vikāraḥ kuta iṣyate /
tasmād evāvikārasya viṣṇor icchāvaśād idam / [6]
yathārtham eva saṃbhūtam iti vedavaco 'khilam /
kecit kālata evaitāṃ sṛṣṭim āhur akovidāḥ / [7]
kecid rudrād brahmaṇaś ca pradhānād iti cāpare /
vimūḍhāḥ sarva evaite yato nārāyaṇaḥ paraḥ / [8]
sarvakartā sarvaśaktir eka eva na cāparaḥ /
pradhānakālabrahmeśamukhāḥ sarve 'pi tadvaśāḥ / [9]
tasyāpi viṣṇoḥ sṛṣṭiṃ tu kecid āhur anaipuṇāḥ /
atṛptasyaiva bhogārthaṃ krīḍārthaṃ tu vipaścitaḥ / [10]
sā ca krīḍā svabhāvo 'sya kuto 'tṛptyā spṛhā vibhoḥ / [11ab]
iti harivaṃśeṣu (1)

(1) Cf. AgniP 12; BhaviṣP 13; BrahVP 20; MESQUITA 2000: 467f.; 470ff. and MESQUITA 2003: 102n. 15.

34) TaiUBh (p. 542,5-8):
Subject matter: Brahmā / Tāratamya

viyudvan mānuṣā vidyuḥ sūryamaṇḍalavat surāḥ /
pratibiṃbavac ca giriśo brahmainaṃ paśyati sphuṭam / +1
brahmā hi sthiracidrūpo bahalātmā viśeṣataḥ /
anye kramād abahalās tathā cañcalacetanāḥ /
tasmāt samyaṅ na paśyanti hariṃ brahmā tu paśyati /
iti harivaṃśavacanāc ca brahmaivainaṃ samyag veda | (1)

(1) Cf. ibid. ll. 3f.: *prajāpatiḥ prathamajā ṛtasyātmanātmānam abhisaṃbabhūva* (Vājasaneyisaṃhitā X 19) *prajāpate ca na tvad etāny anyo viśvā jātāni paritā bhabhūva ityādinā viriñcasyaiva tad jñānam / anyo na paribhūveti niṣedhāt* ... ; see also BhaviṣPV 15; BrāṇP 29.

Kūrmapurāṇa (KūrP)

[KūrP seems to have belonged originally to the Pāñcarātras. Later it was appropriated by the Pāśupatas who added to it many new myths, legends, etc. So it presents a combination of Vaiṣṇava and Śaiva elements. Advaitic influence is also noticeable since "great emphasis is laid on the necessity of realizing the identity of *ātman* and *brahma*, along the lines of *māyāvāda*" and Viṣṇu is described with Advaitic characteristics as *nirguṇa, niṣprapañca, bhedābhedahīna* (cf.KūrP I 1,69-76; HAZRA 1987: 57-75; ROCHER 1986: 184-186). Among a total of 38 quotes, there are two genuine references to KūrP (I 4,13 and I 12,273). Both are referred to anonymously in BSūBh (p. 66,24-25 and p. 217,20-21), Most of the quotes (nineteen times) are adduced in BhāgTN (eleven times) in BSūBh, (five times) in GīBh; one each in ChUBh, KathUBh and ĪśUBh.]

1) BhāgTN (p. 16,3-6):
Subject matter: Viṣṇu's contradictory attributes

tathā ca kaurme –
asthūlaś cāṇuś caiva sthūlo 'ṇuś caiva sarvataḥ /
avarṇaḥ sarvataḥ proktaḥ śyāmo raktāntalocanaḥ /
aiśvaryayogād bhagavān viruddhārtho 'bhidhīyate /
tathāpi doṣāḥ parame naivāhāryāḥ kathaṃcana /
guṇā viruddhā api tu samāhāryās tu sarvataḥ /
iti (1)

(1) Cf. ibid. ll. 1f.: *ekam evādvitīyaṃ neha nanāsti kiṃcana* (ChU VI 2,1 / BĀU IV 4,19) *evaṃ dharmān pṛthak paśyan* ityādi ca (KathU IV 14) / *tasyaivāsthūlatvādyaiśvaryayogāt* ... ; see also BrāṇP 69 and ViṣDhUP 1.

2) BhāgTN (p. 19,4):
Subject matter: Vyāsa-Avatāra

tṛtīyaṃ yugam ārambhya vyāso bahuṣu jajñivān /
iti kaurme (1)

(1) Cf. ibid. l. 3: *rāmāt pūrvam apy asti vyāsāvatāraḥ*; ibid. (n. 1): *vaivasvatamanvatarasya tṛtīyaṃ dvāparam ārambhya bahuṣu / tṛtīyadvāpare, saptamadvāpare, ṣoḍaśadvāpare, pañcaviṃśadvāpare, aṣṭāviṃśadvāpare cety arthaḥ / tathā ca rāmāvatārāt pūrvaṃ caturvāraṃ vyāsāvatāra iti tasya pūrvaṃ nirdeśaḥ* ... ; see also ĀdiP 1; BrahP 9_1 and BhaviṣPV 21.

3) BhāgTN (p. 23,12-13):
Subject matter: Doctrine of Avatāras

sarvajño 'py ajñavad devaḥ sarvaśaktir aśaktivat /
pratyāyayati lokānām ajñānāṃ mohanāya ca /
iti kaurme (1)

(1) Cf. ibid. l. 11: *nityajñānasya ciradṛṣṭir lokadṛṣṭyapekṣayā*; ibid n. 5: ... *tathāhi* vijayadhvajatīrthīye – *sarvajñasya ciradhyānam ajñajanadṛṣṭyapekṣayā duṣṭamohanāya ceti*; see also ĀdiP 1; MBh 42n. 6 and MESQUITA 2000_1: 39ff. [= 1997: 33f.].

4) BhāgTN (p. 37,3-4):
Subject matter: Agni's sons

agniputrā mahātmānas tapasā strītvam āpire /
bhartāraṃ ca jagadyoniṃ vāsudevam ajaṃ vibhum /
iti mahākaurme (1)

(1) Cf. AgniP 16.

5) BhāgTN (p. 86,8):
Subject matter: Viṣṇu's supreme transcendence

tadvad eva sthitaṃ yat tu tāttvatas tat pracakṣate /
iti kaurme (1)

(1) Cf. ibid. l. 7: *paraḥ adhikaḥ* ... ; (ibid. n. 6): ... *vāsudeva eva sarvottama ity arthaḥ / tāttvato vāsudevasadṛśo vā nāstīty arthaḥ*; see also AgniP 6.

6) BhāgTN (p. 109,10-11):
Subject matter: Ignorance

yat tu sarvātmanājñānaṃ niśā sā parikīrtitā /
iti kaurme (1)

(1) Cf. ibid. l. 10: *anyathājñānahetur yā vāk sā jalpiḥ prakīrtitā* | iti tantramālāyām (unknown source); see also HarV 8.

7) BhāgTN (p. 216,1-3):
Subject matter: Doctrine of Avatāras

sarvottamo 'pi bhagavān viprādeḥ pūjanāya tu /
guṇalabdhiṃ tato brūte nityapūrṇaguṇo 'pi san /
brūyuś cānye kvacit tat tu tadukter anusārataḥ /
upādatte varāṃś cāpi lokānāṃ mohanāya vā /
iti kaurme (1)

(1) Cf. ĀdiP 1.

8) BhāgTN (p. 227,1-2):
Subject matter: Brahmā

vyasṛjan malavad dehaṃ bāhyaṃ na tu nijaṃ purā /
brahmā tac cāharāditvaṃ prāpa devābhidaivatam /
iti kaurme (1)

(1) Cf. BrāṇP 29; KūrP 16.

9) BhāgTN (p. 235,2):
Subject matter: Avatāra's outward appearances

vyakto bhaved dharis tatra yat sthānaṃ rucitaṃ satām /
iti kaurme (1)

(1) Cf. ibid. l. 1: *yāni yāni brahmādirūpāṇi rocante svajanānāṃ tāny eva te vyakty-artham abhirūpāṇi* ... ; see also ĀdiP 1.

10) BhāgTN (p. 242,1-2):
Subject matter: Difference between Viṣṇu and the individual soul

parasya janmamṛtyādyāḥ syuḥ svatantrasya kiṃ punaḥ /
jīvasyāpi yato bhrāntir janmamṛtyādisaṅgatiḥ /
iti mahākaurme (1)

(1) Cf. ibid. (p. 241,7-9): *sa hi paramo na jāyate na mriyeteti prasiddhaṃ hi / de-hādyupādhibhir āttataddharmo jīvo 'pi svapnavad bhrāntyaiva jāyate mriyate ca / bhrāntitvād dehātmatvasya / kimu sarvajñatvatantratvādivailakṣaṇyayukta īśvaraḥ* ... ; see also AgniP 22; BrāṇP 71.

11) BhāgTN (p. 257,1-2)
Subject matter: Viṣṇu, the supreme Cause of the Universe

sabījo vaiṣṇavo yogo nirbījas tv anyadaivataḥ /
bījaṃ viṣṇur hi jagataḥ śākhādyā anyadevatāḥ /
iti kaurme (1)

(1) Cf. AgniP 12 and HarV 28.

12) BhāgTN (p. 284,8-9):
Subject matter: Liberation through knowledge

mumukṣavo brahmaṇaś ca śivād indrādibhis tathā /
śrutvā jñānaṃ paraṃ guhyaṃ mucyante brahmaṇā saha /
iti kaurme (1)

(1) Cf. AgniP 16.

13) BhāgTN (p. 312,11-12):
Subject matter: Vena / Pṛthu

tryaṃśo vena uddiṣṭaḥ sattvāṃśaḥ pṛthutām agāt /
rajo 'ṃśas tridivaṃ prāpa niṣādas tāmaso 'bhavat /
svayaṃ venaś caturthas tu mahātamasi pātitaḥ /
iti kaurme (1)

(1) Cf. BrāṇP 42.

14) BhāgTN (p. 364,7):
Subject matter: Viṣṇu's supreme transcendence

nābhir ity atha nāma syād dhareḥ sarvāśrayo yataḥ /
iti kaurme (1)

(1) Cf. AgniP 6; SkaP 79 and MESQUITA 2000: 464ff.

15) BhāgTN (p. 367,8-9):
Subject matter: Viṣṇu's supreme transcendence

viṣṇoḥ kalevaratyāgo bhūtyāgo'nyo na vidyate /
kalevaratyāgo 'nyeṣāṃ pañcatvaṃ samudīritam /
iti kaurme (1)

(1) Cf. AgniP 6.

16) BhāgTN (p. 392,3-4):
Subject matter: Adhikāras of the Deities

anadhīkāriṇo devāḥ svargasthā bhāratodbhavam /
vāñchanty ātmavimokṣārtham udrekārthe 'dhikāriṇaḥ /
iti kaurme (1)

(1) Cf. BhaviṣPV 9; BhaviṣP 5; KūrP 8 and VāyuP 2_1 n. 1.

17) BhāgTN (p. 525,7-10):
Subject matter: Doctrine of the Avatāras

channo 'nyeṣāṃ na tu svasya bhagavān puruṣottamaḥ /
tasyāvatārā dehasthā adehasthā iti dvidhā /
antaryāmyādirūpāṇi dehasthāni vido viduḥ /
matsyakūrmādirūpāṇi na dehasthāni hṛtpateḥ /

anyātulyair atiśayair manaso niyamādibhiḥ /
jñāyante tāni rūpāṇi nityapūrṇāni sarvaśaḥ /
iti mahākaurme (1)

(1) Cf. ĀdiP 1 and MESQUITA 2000: 223ff; 416ff.

18) BhāgTN (p. 584,1-2):
Subject matter: Viṣṇu, one without a second

adhikasya samasyāpi svatantrasya ca varjanāt /
eka evādvitīyo 'sau na śāsyajanavarjanāt /
iti kaurme (1)

(1) Cf. BhāgTN (p. 583,4-7): *ekam evādvitīyam* (ChU VI 2,1) *ekaṃ paraṃjyotir* (ibid. VIII 3) *ananyam advayam* (?) *ityādi niyamo jīvānāṃ śāsyatā nety atra na hi / kiṃtu svagatabhedasya* (cf. MESQUITA 2000: 439ff.) *īśvarāntarasyātattantrasya ca niṣedhe / ato 'nyad ārtam* (BĀU III 4,2/5,1) *neha nānāsti kiṃcana* (KathU IV 11) *na tatsamaś cābhyadhikaś ca dṛśyata* (ŚvU VI 8ab; Gī XI 43cd) *ityādi tathā bruvate ca*; see also AgniP 6; BrahP 1_2; BrāṇP 62 and MESQUITA 2000: 227f.; 405ff.; 426f.

19) BhāgTN (p. 715,10-11):
Subject matter: Eight yogic powers

agnyādiśaktisaṃstambhas tv agnisaṃstambha iṣyate /
iti kaurme (1)

(1) Cf. YBh *ad* III 45; see also HarV 28; MBh 18.

20) BSūBh (p. 9,9-12):
Subject matter: Doctrine of valid means of knowledge (*pramāṇa*)

śrutisāhāyyarahitam anumānaṃ na kutracit /
niścayāt sādhayed arthaṃ pramāṇāntaram eva ca /
śrutismṛtisahāyaṃ yat pramāṇāntaram uttamam /
pramāṇapadavīṃ gacchen nātra kāryā vicāraṇā /
pūrvottarāvirodhena ko 'trārtho 'bhimato bhavet /
ityādyam ūhanaṃ tarkaḥ śuṣkatarkaṃ tu varjayet /
ityādi kaurme (1)

(1) Cf. ibid. ll. 8: *na cānumānasya niyataprāmāṇyaṃ* ... ; Madhva defends the validity of inference, which is based not only on the direct perception but also on the Vedas, which are said to be supreme means of knowledge. Madhva discusses this topic when he polemizes against the Jainas (cf. Anuv. p. 164,21-23):

viṣayān prati sthitaṃ hy akṣaṃ pratyakṣam iti gīyate /
pratyakṣaśabdānusārād anumeti prakīrtitā /
ā samantād gamayati dharmādharmau paraṃ padam /
yac cāpy atīndriyaṃ tv anyat tenāsāv āgamaḥ smṛtaḥ /

This definition of *āgamaḥ* is borrowed from Abhinavagupta (Īśvarapratyabhijñāvimarśinī II 3,2): *ā samantāt artham gamayatīti āgamasaṃjñakaṃ pramāṇaṃ sarvasya tāvat bhavati*; see also GarP 23; KūrP 24; MBh 8; NārP 58; VāmP 38; VarP 31; SkaP 83; VāyuP 2; MESQUITA 2000: 55f.; 369ff. and W. HALBFASS 1991: 145ff.

21) BSūBh (p. 28,14-15):
Subject matter: Viṣṇu's Sarvanāmatva

antaryāmiṇam īśeśam apekṣyāhaṃ tvam ity api /
sarvaśabdāḥ prayujyante sati bhede 'pi vastuṣu /
iti kaurme (1)

(1) Cf. ibid. l. 12: *cakṣurantastho viṣṇor eva / tripādasyāmṛtaṃ divi* (ChU III 12,6) *ityādinā tasyaivāmṛtatvādyupapatter brahmātmaśabdādyupapatteś ca / so 'ham asmītyādi* (BĀU I 4,1) *tv antaryāmyapekṣayā* ... ; see also BrāṇP 2 and MESQUITA 2000: 162f.

22) BSūBh (p. 52,12-15):
Subject matter: Viṣṇu's Sarvanāmatva

śamūnaṃ kurute viṣṇur adṛśyaḥ san paraḥ svayam /
tasmāc chūnyam iti proktas todanāt tuccha ucyate /
naiṣa bhāvayituṃ yogyaḥ kenacit puruṣottamaḥ /
ato 'bhāvaṃ vadanty enaṃ nāśyatvān nāśa ity api /
sarvasya tadadhīnatvāt tattacchabdābhidheyatā /
anyeṣāṃ vyavahārārtham iṣyate vyavahartṛbhiḥ /
iti kaurme (1)

(1) Cf. ibid. ll. 9f.: *etena sarve śūnyādiśabdā api vyākhyātāḥ – eṣa hy eva śūnya eṣa hy eva tuccha eṣa hy evābhāva eṣa hy avyakto 'dṛśyo 'cintyo nirguṇaś ceti hi* <u>mahopaniṣadi</u> (unknown source); see also BrāṇP 2; SkaP 4.

23) BSūBh (p. 93,17-20):
Subject matter: God Vāyu and eternal/temporal elements of the world

nityaḥ paramanityaś ca tathānityaḥ paras tathā
caturdhaitaj jagat sarvaṃ parānityaṃ tu pārthivam /
anityāni tu bhūtāni nityo vāyur udāhṛtaḥ /
paras tu nityaḥ puruṣaḥ prakṛtiḥ kāla eva ca /
etac catuṣṭayaṃ viṣṇuḥ svayaṃ nityaḥ parāt paraḥ /
prativyūhya vyūhya cāsāv atītya ca janārdanaḥ /
dhārayaty aniśaṃ devo nityānandaikalakṣaṇaḥ /
iti kaurme (1)

(1) Cf. ibid. l. 16: *etena mukhyāmukhyānutpattivacanena vibhaktatvāc ca vāyvanutpattiśrutir api vyākhyātā* ... ; see also BhavişPV 17; BrahP 25; BrahVP 13; HarV 6_1; MBh 23; MESQUITA 2003: 101ff.

24) BSūBh (p. 95,10-11):
Subject matter: Infallibility of the Vedas

> kaurme ca –
> *virodho vākyayor yatra nāprāmāṇyaṃ tad eṣyate* /
> *yathāviruddhatā ca syāt tathārthaḥ kalpya etayoḥ* /
> iti (1)

(1) Cf. ibid. ll. 7f.: ... *pṛthivī vānnam* (TaiU III 9) *tā āpo 'nnam asṛjanta* (BĀU V 5,1 [?]) *pṛthivī vānnam ityādiśabdāntarāc ca / ādiśabdād yuktir apauruṣeyatvenādoṣasya vākyasya nāprāmāṇyam ityādi* ... ; see also BhavişP 10; BrāṇP 11; BrahVP 30 and KūrP 20.

25) BSūBh (p. 98,19-20):
Subject matter: Epithets of Viṣṇu

> *ātmāmeyaḥ paraṃ brahma parānandādikābhidhāḥ* /
> *vadanti viṣṇum evaikaṃ nānyatrāsāṃ gatiḥ kvacit* /
> iti ca kaurme (1)

(1) Cf. ibid. ll. 16f.: *eṣo hyātmādhyudgato mānaśaktes tathāpy asau pramitiṃ yāti vedaiḥ / pūrṇo 'cintyaḥ sarvavedaikayoniḥ sarvādhīśaḥ sarvavit sarvakarteti vākyaśeṣa ātmaśabdonmānābhyāṃ ca* ... . KūrP (I 1,69-79) describes the nature of Viṣṇu with the help of several epithets. Some of them, like *nirguṇa, niṣprapañca, bhedābhedahīna*, are rejected outright by Madhva because of their Advaitic tradition; see also BhāgP 1; BrahVP 19; BrāṇP 69 and MESQUITA 2000: 429-454.

26) BSūBh (p. 121,23-24):
Subject matter: Three-fold hell

> *mahātamas tridhā proktam ūrdhvaṃ madhyaṃ tathādharam* /
> *śravaṇenaiva mūrcchādir adharasya yato bhavet* /
> *tasmān na vistareṇaitat kathyate rājasattama* /
> iti kaurme (1)

(1) Cf. ibid. l. 22: *tṛtīye tṛtīyatamasaḥ śravaṇād eva śabdānusāreṇa saṃśokajamohaprāptismaraṇāc ca* ... ; see also BhavişPV 19 and MESQUITA 2000: 529.

27) BSūBh (p. 132,4-5):
Subject matter: Viṣṇu, the cause of the transmigration and liberation

> *svapnādibuddhikartā ca tiraskartā sa eva ca* /

tadicchayā yato hy asya bandhamokṣau pratiṣṭhitau /
iti kaurme (1)

(1) Cf. ibid. l. 3: *bandhamokṣapradatvāt sa eva svapnatiraskartā* ... ; see also BhaviṣP 3; BrāṇP 7; MESQUITA 2000_1: 171n. 348 [= 1997: 139n. 355] and MESQUITA 2000: 224n. 480.

28) BSūBh (p. 133,20-21):
Subject matter: Viṣṇu, the cause of bewilderment and liberation

mūrcchā prabodhanaṃ caiva yata eva pravartate /
sa īśaḥ paramo jñeyaḥ paramānandalakṣaṇaḥ /
iti hi kaurme (1)

(1) Cf. ibid. ll. 15ff.: *mohāvasthāyāṃ parameśvare 'rdhaprāptir jīvasya* ... / *so 'pi tata eveti siddham* ... ; see also BhaviṣP 3; BrāṇP 7 and VarP 40.

29) BSūBh (p. 139,5-6):
Subject matter: Viṣṇu's supreme transcendence

avyaktavyaktabhāvau ca na kvacit parameśvare /
sarvatrāvyaktarūpo 'yaṃ yata eva janārdanaḥ /
iti ca kaurme (1)

(1) Cf. ibid. ll. 2f.: *agnyādivat sthūlasūkṣmatvaviśeṣābhāvāt* / *nāsau sūkṣmo na sthūlaḥ para eva sadā bhavati tasmād āhuḥ parama* iti māṇḍavyaśruteḥ (untraceable source); see also AgniP 6; GarP 43; 56.

30) BSūBh (p. 228,24-25):
Subject matter: State of the liberated individual souls

avṛddhihrāsarūpatvaṃ muktānāṃ prāyikaṃ bhavet /
kādācitkaviśeṣas tu naiva teṣāṃ niṣiddhyate /
iti ca kaurme (1)

(1) Cf. ibid. ll. 21f.: *na ca bhogāviśeṣādivirodhaḥ – etam ānandamayam ātmanam anuviśya na jāyate na mṛiyate na hrasate na vardhate yathākāmaṃ carati yathākāmaṃ pibati yathākāmaṃ ramate yathākāmam uparamata iti bhogamātrasāmyaliṅgāt* ...

pravāhatas vṛddhir vā hrāso vā naiva kutracit /
nāpriyaṃ kiṃcid api tu muktānāṃ vidyate kvacit /
kuta eva tu duḥkhaṃ syāt sukham eva sadoditam /
bhogānāṃ tu viśeṣeṣu vaicitryaṃ labhyate kvacit /
iti ca nārāyaṇatantre (unknown source);

see also AgniP 6; 16; BhaviṣP 15; BrahVP 29.

30_1) ChUBh (p. 420,20-21):
Subject matter: Vāmana / Viṣṇu

yatsthānatvād idaṃ cakṣur asaṅgaṃ sarvavastuṣu /
tasmai namo bhagavate vāmanāya parātmane /
iti ca mahākaurme (1)

(1) Cf. ibid. (p. 419,27f.): *asaṅgabhagavatsthānatvāc cakṣuṣo 'saṅgatvatam ucyate …*
cakṣuḥsthaṃ vāmanaṃ veda sa punar naiva jāyate /
mukto dustarasaṃsārād vāmanaṃ prāpnute 'cirāt /
iti ca (untraceable source);
see also ĀdiP 1 and VāmP 36:
yatsthānatvād idam cakṣur asaṅgaṃ sarvavastubhiḥ /
sa vāmanaḥ paro 'smākaṃ gatir ity eva cintaya /

30_2) GīBh (p. 4,6-7):
Subject matter: Eulogy of Mahābhārata

bhārataṃ sarvaśāstreṣu bhārate gītikā varā /
viṣṇoḥ sahasranāmāpi jñeyaṃ pāṭyaṃ ca tad dvayam /
iti mahākaurme (1)

(1) Cf. ibid. ll. 4f.: *tatra ca sarvabhāratārthasaṅgrahāṃ vāsudevārjunasaṃvādarūpāṃ bhāratapārijātamadhubhūtāṃ gītām upanibabandha / tac coktam …* ; see also BrahVP 39; BrāṇP 86; MārkP 2; NārP 30; PadP 27; SkaP 16; 17; 126; VāyuP 13 and MESQUITA 2000_1: 143ff. [= 1997: 115ff.].

30_3) GīBh (p. 29,4-5):
Subject matter: Ṛṣi-Vasiṣṭha

tā evāpo dadau tasya sa ṛṣiḥ śaṃsitavrataḥ /
iti mahākaurme samarthānaṃ bhedajñānāc ca (1)

(1) Cf. ibid. ll. 1f.: ... *ato jale jalaikībhāvavad ekībhāvaḥ / uktaṃ ca yathodakaṃ śuddhe śuddham* (KathU IV 15) *yathā nadyaḥ* (MuU II 2,8) *ityādau / tatrāpy anyonyātmakatve vṛddhyasambhavaḥ / asti ceṣat samudre 'pi dvāri / mahattvād anyatrādṛṣṭiḥ …* ; see also BrahP 83; ViṣP 7 and MESQUITA 2000: 132n. 243.

30_4) GīBh (p. 51,17-18):
Subject matter: Beatific vision of Viṣṇu

vedādyuktaṃ tu sarvaṃ yo jñātvopāste sadā hi mām /
tasyaiva darśanapathaṃ yāmi nānyasya kasyacit /
ity ukteś ca mahākaurme (1)

(1) Cf. ibid. l. 16: *pṛthaṅ muktyuktiḥ sarvajñānaniyamadarśanārtham / na tu tāvanmātreṇa muktir ity uktam …* ; see also AgniP 16 and 24.

30_5) GīBh (p. 82,19-21):
Subject matter: Viṣṇu, the supreme supreme Creator of the universe

mahākaurme ca –
adhyātmaṃ dehaparyantaṃ kevalātmopakārakam /
sadehajīvabhūtāni yat teṣām upakārakṛt /
adhibhūtaṃ tu māyāntaṃ devānām adhidaivatam / iti (1)

(1) Cf. below SkaP 114:
ātmābhimānādhikārasthitam adhyātmam ucyate /
dehād bāhyaṃ vinātīva bāhyatvād adhidaivatam /
devādhikāragaṃ sarvaṃ mahābhūtādhikāragam /
tatkāraṇaṃ tathā kāryaṃ adhibhūtaṃ tadantikāt /
see also AgniP 12; SkaP 106.

30_6) GīBh (p. 86,10-12):
Subject matter: Pralaya / Sarga

uktaṃ ca mahākaurme –
anekayugaparyantam ahar viṣṇos tathā niśā /
rātryādau līyate sarvam aharādau ca jāyate / iti (1)

(1) Cf. ibid. l. 10: *dviparārdhapralaya evātra vivakṣitaḥ / avyaktād vyaktayaḥ sarvā ity ukteḥ* (= Gī VIII 18ab); see also NārP 24 and VarP 7.

31) ĪśUBh (p. 511,16-26):
Subject matter: Upāsana

anyathopāsakā ye tu tamo 'ndhaṃ yānty asaṃśayam /
tato 'dhikam iva vyaktaṃ yānti teṣām anindakāḥ / [1]
tasmād yathāsvarūpaṃ tu nārāyaṇam anāmayam /
ayathārthasya nindāṃ ca ye vidus te hi sajjanāḥ / [2]
te nindayāyathārthasya duḥkhājñānādirūpiṇaḥ /
duḥkhājñānādisantīrṇāḥ sukhajñānādirūpiṇaḥ / [3]
yathārthasya parijñānāt sukhajñānādirūpatām /
yānty eva sṛṣṭikartṛtvaṃ nāṅgīkurvanti ye hareḥ / [4]
te 'pi yānti tamo ghoraṃ tathā saṃhārakartṛtām /
nāṅgīkurvanti te 'py evaṃ tasmāt sarvaguṇātmakam / [5]
sarvakartāram īśeśaṃ sarvasaṃhārakārakam /
yo veda saṃhṛtijñānād dehabandhād vimucyate / [6]
sukhajñānādikartṛtvajñānāt tadvyaktim āvrajet /
sarvadoṣavinirmuktaṃ guṇarūpaṃ janārdanam / [7]
jānīyān na guṇānāṃ ca bhāgahāniṃ prakalpayet /
na muktānām api hareḥ sāmyaṃ viṣṇor abhinnatām / [8]

naiva pracintayet tasmād brahmādeḥ sāmyam eva vā /
mānuṣādiviriñcāntaṃ tāratamyaṃ vimuktogam / [9]
tato viṣṇoḥ parotkarṣaṃ samyag jñātvā vimucyate / [10ab]
iti kaurme (1)

(1) Cf. AgniP 20.

32) KathUBh (p. 485,13-486,19):
Subject matter: Viṣṇu's supreme transcendence

nityaṃ hīno 'khilair doṣaiḥ sārarūpo yato hariḥ /
haṃsa ity ucyate tasmād vāyusthaḥ śuciṣan mataḥ / [1] (1)
varasur vasur ity uktaḥ sa evāpy antarikṣagaḥ /
hotā saś cendriyādistho vedyāṃ pūjyaś ca vediṣat / [2]
atyannaś cātithiḥ prokto yasmād annaṃ tham ucyate /
sa droṇakalaśe some sthita ukto duroṇasat / [3]
nṛṣu sthitaś ca deveṣu vareṣv api sa eva tu /
ṛtarūpe tathā vede vyomākhyaprakṛtāv api / [4]
vyotaṃ jagad idaṃ yasyāṃ sā vyoma śrīr udāhṛtā /
abjagojādrijeṣv eva āste abjādikas tataḥ / [5]
tathaivarteṣu mukteṣu gatās te viṣṇum ity ṛtāḥ /
vedair mukhyatayā prokta ṛtam ity eva cocyate / [6]
bṛhat pūrṇaguṇatvāc ca sa eva puruṣottamaḥ /
na kevalaṃ prāṇa eva cetanānāṃ vidhārakaḥ / [7] (2)
kiṃtu viṣṇuṃ samāśritya prāṇo jīvān bibharty ayam /
ato mukhyāśrayo viṣṇuś cetanānāṃ svatantrataḥ / [8]
agnir yathaiko lokeṣu praviṣṭo 'nyo na vidyate /
pākādikartāthāpy asya devasya pratirūpakāḥ / [9]
rūpaṃ rūpaṃ prati hy ete santy acetanavahnayaḥ /
evaṃ devo vāyur api dhārako 'nyo na vidyate / [10]
rūpaṃ rūpaṃ tathāpy asya pratyabhūt pararūpakaḥ /
acetanaḥ sparśagamyo yo 'yam eva janārdanaḥ / [11]
ekaḥ svatantro nānyo 'sti sarvajīvāntarasthitaḥ /
rūpaṃ rūpaṃ prati hy asya pratibiṃbākhyacetanāḥ / [12]
bāhyāś ca te tato nāsya svarūpaṃ te kathaṃcana /
anādipratibiṃbāś ca babhūvus te hy anantakāḥ / [13]
sūryo yathāntaraś cakṣuḥ pratibiṃbo 'sya bāhyakaḥ / (3)
bāhyacakṣur gatair doṣair antaś cakṣur na lipyate / [14]
antaś cakṣur devatā tu bāhyacakṣur acetanam /
evaṃ bāhyaḥ svatantratvāj jīvebhyaḥ puruṣottamaḥ / [15]
asvatantrasya jīvasya duḥkhair naiva hi lipyate /
cetanābhāsako jīvaḥ paramaś cetano hariḥ / [16]

svatantratvāt svatantro hi naiva doṣeṇa lipyate / [17ab]
iti mahākaurme (4)

(1) Cf. GarP 36[4f.]; HarV 3n. 1.
(2) Cf. MESQUITA 2000: 459n. 576; p. 490 and MESQUITA 2003: 103f.
(3) Cf. BhāgP 3 and MESQUITA 2000: 494ff.
(4) Cf. HEIMANN p. 47f.; see also AgniP 6 and MESQUITA 2000: 495f.

Mahābhārata (MBh)

[In the different works of Madhva there are about one hundert and thirty-eight quotes from MBh (most of them in GīBh [approximately thirty-seven] and in BhāgTN [approximately thirty-five]). Eighty-six out of them are traceable and fifty-one could not be identified. These are quoted in AiUBh (four times); BĀUBh (six times); BhāgTN (thirtheen times); BSūBh (five times); GīBh (ten times); GīT (two times); MBhTN (eight times); VTN (three times). Sometimes, only one part of the quote is not traceable whereas the following part could be identified, for instance. in BhāgTN (p. 198,1-2 = MBh XIV 37,33; see also HarV 8; MBh 39 and GīT p. 80,18f.); or the first part is transmitted (= MBh V 75,3) but the second part is untraceable (BhāgTN p. 730,1-3; deviating in MBhTN II 153 = MBh 46). One Śloka of Manusmṛti (= XII 89cd-90ab; cf. KūrP I 2,63f.) is ascribed by Madhva to MBh (cf. also BhāgTN p. 660, 5-6); however in the GīBh (p. 39,15-16) he attributes it explicitly to Manusmṛti, in MuUBh (p. 492,22-23) as well as to Vyāsasmṛti (see also MESQUITA 2003_1: 207n. 37). In another case, one reference of Rāmāyaṇa (= 6. App. No. 19,81f.) is attributed to MBh (cf. below MBh 50). The quotes deviate in several cases from the transmitted version (cf. also VarP 29). In the Critical Edition of the MBh, some deviating versions are recorded in the Appendix. It is notewhorty in this connection that the quotations from Gītā (cf. v.g. MBhTN II 82-100) are indicated accurately by Madhva. This perceptive observation has been recorded also by HOFSTÄTTER (2000: 19) regarding the entire text of the Gī in GīBh and GīT. The references are indicated in most of the cases with *iti mokṣadharme*, sometimes also with *iti bhārate* and *iti mahābhārate*, at times with *iti gītā* or *iti bhagavadvacanam* (cf. Anuv. 88,23 = MBh XII 63/67). In one case an untraceable quote is referred to in two different ways, namely as Vyāsayoga and Mokṣadharma (GīBh p. 85,4: <u>ityādi vacanāt vyāsayoge mokṣadharme ca</u>; cf. MBh 29). Occasionally, Madhva cites in MBhTN II,54f. anonymously verses from MBh, and comments on them. However, there is a general remark on MBh at the end of the second chapter of MBhTN:

pūrṇaprajñakṛteyaṃ saṅksepād uddhṛitiḥ suvākyānām /
śrīmadbhāratagānāṃ viṣṇoḥ pūrṇatvanirṇayāyaiva /

(cf. also MBhTN II 66). Most of these verses are not traceable (cf. below MBh 40-47). As already remarked, in contrast to MBh the quotes from the Gī are accurate. In this context it is specially interesting to note, that in one case (MBhTN II 69-81) Madhva has composed, simultaneuously with two transmitted Ślokas from MBh (MBhTN II 72-73/76 = below MBh 42), also verses clearly based on MBh as text-pattern (MBhTN II 74 = MBh II Appendix I 1605-11; V 66,14) and which tallies in content with the Ślokas attributed by Madhva to a ficitious source, namely Bhaviṣyatparvan (cf. MESQUITA 2000_1: 38n. 47; 40n. 51 [= 1997: 31n.; 39; 33n. 43]); see also MBhTN XI 93: ... <u>evam ādipurāṇotthavākyād</u> *rāmaḥ sadā jayī*; SkaP 20 and 36.

Apart from Śloka-quotes we find also Triṣṭubh/Upajāti-verses: MBh 49 and two Prosa quotes: MBh 34 and 36.]

1) AiUBh (p. 184,3-4):
Subject matter: Etymology of *mitra*

> *minoti trāyate ceti mitram ity abhidhīyate /*
> *tasmād yo yaṃ vijānāti sa mitraṃ tasya nānyathā /*
> iti hi bhārate (1)

(1) Cf. ibid. l. 2: *na ca bṛhatīsahasrābhimāninīṃ devīṃ vinā cetanamātrasya mukhyamitratvaṃ yujyate* ... ; see also Gī VI 5-6; 9; BrahVP 34; HarV 1 and NārP 55.

2) AiUBh (p. 185,11-12):
Subject matter: Antaryāmin

> uktaṃ ca bhārate –
> *sraṣṭṛtvāc caiva pātṛtvān niyamāc ca prakāśanāt /*
> *sarvatvam uktaṃ viṣṇos tu na tu sarvasvarūpataḥ /*
> iti (1)

(1) Cf. ibid. ll. 10f.: *tasmāt sarvāntaryāmitvāt sarvaguṇavattvāt sarvaśaktitvāc ca sarvanāmavattvam eva viṣṇor ucyate / na tu sarvasvarūpatvāt* ... ; see also BhāgP 2; BrāṇP 2; MBh 7; MatsyaP 12 and MESQUITA 2000: 455f.

3) AiUBh (p. 219,28-29):
Subject matter: Prajāpati's identity with Śiva

> *samam astv anayor yuddham iti prāha prajāpatiḥ /*
> *vākyaṃ śivasya tacchrutvā śakro nety āha satvaraḥ /*
> iti ca bhārate (1)

(1) Cf. ibid. ll. 25f.: ... *prajāpatiḥ śivaḥ / liṅgābhimānitvāt* ... ; see also BhāgP 1; BrahP 61; SkaP 6_1.

4) AiUBh (p. 226,12-13):
Subject matter: Bhakti

> *tadbhaktabhakteṣv api yo na kuryāt prītim añjasā /*
> *viṣṇur jahāti taṃ pāpam iha cāmutra ca prabhuḥ /*
> iti ca bhārate (1)

(1) Cf. ibid. ll. 10f.: ... (p. 225,4f.) *prāṇasya viṣṇoḥ priyatvaṃ tava na prāpsyatīti / nāśakaḥ sandhātum / mayā saha sandhānaṃ kartuṃ nāśakaḥ / mama prītiṃ kartuṃ nāśakaḥ* ... ; see also AgniP 20.

5) BĀUBh (p. 265,3-5):
Subject matter: Liberation

prāptaśrutiphalatvāt tu śrotriyāḥ prāptamokṣiṇaḥ /
ta eva cāptakāmatvāt tathākāmahatāḥ śrutāḥ /
iti bhārate (1)
brahmaṇo 'pi hy amuktasya nākāmahatatā parā /
yatas tasyāpi kāmasya kṣaṇavyavahitir bhavet /
iti ca

(1) Cf. ibid. l. 2: ... *na ca brahmāṇa eva kecanākāmahatāḥ kecana kāmahatā ity atra pramāṇam asti* / *tasmāc chrotriya iti prāptaśrutiphalatvān mukta ucyate* / *akāmahatatvaṃ ca mukhyaṃ muktasyaiva* ... ; see also AgniP 16 and BrāṇP 102.

6) BĀUBh (p. 266,13-14):
Subject matter: Antaryāmin

brahmādayo hi bhūtāni teṣām antargato hariḥ /
samaḥ sa sarvabhūteṣu ya evaṃ veda tattvavit /
iti bhārate (1)

(1) Cf. ibid. ll. 11f.: ... *eṣa ta ātmāntaryāmy amṛto* / *ato 'nyadārtam* (BĀU III 7,2 / III 4,2) *iti ca* / *na hi jīvād anyasyārtir upapadyate* / *sarveṣāṃ bhūtānām antarapuruṣaḥ sama ātmeti vidyād ityādiśrutibhyaś ca* (= AiU II 4,8); see also BhāgP 2 and BrahVP 35.

7) BĀUBh (p. 266,19-21):
Subject matter: Viṣṇu, the world-Ruler

puruṣa evedaṃ sarvaṃ bhūtaṃ bhavyaṃ bhavac ca yat /
ity ucyate tadīśatvān na tu sarvasvarūpataḥ /
bhūtabhavyādijātasya muktanām api ceśvaraḥ /
ity ucyate śrutau viṣṇuḥ sarvadā puruṣottamaḥ /
iti hi bhārate (1)

(1) Cf. ibid. ll. 17f.: *na cātraikyajñānam uktam* / *puruṣa evedaṃ sarvam ity atrāpi sarveśitṛtvam evoktam* / *utāmṛtatvasyeśānaḥ* / iti vākyaśeṣāt (ŚvU III 15 = Ṛg VIII 4,17 also AiUBh p. 185,13-14) ... ; see also AgniP 6; HarV 5 and MBh 2.

8) BĀUBh (p. 268,8-9):
Subject matter: Conclusive argument (*nirṇaya*)

nirṇayas tv āgamenaiva nānumāgamavarjitā /
kvacin nirṇītihetuḥ syād ataḥ śāstrād vinirṇayaḥ /
iti bhārate (1)

(1) Cf. BrahVP 30; KūrP 20; VāyuP 2.

8$_1$) BĀUBh (p. 272,10-12):
Subject matter: Liberation

abhāve pṛthagarthānāṃ vyākhyām abhyāsam eva vā /
kalpayen naiva tadbhāve vyākhyābhyāsaś ca yujyate /
iti bhārate
svarūpajñaṃ tathāheyaṃ nityaṃ ca brahma vetti yaḥ /
samagrabhāvaṃ gacchet sa tatprasādān na saṃśayaḥ /
iti ca (1)

(1) Cf. ibid. ll. 1f.: *'tat sarvam abhavat' 'sarvaṃ bhaviṣyantaḥ' ityādinā samagrabhāvasya prastutvāt / brahma paśyan vāmadevo brahmaṇo manvādijīvair aheyatvaṃ pratipede ... tad idaṃ brahma yo 'heyatvādiguṇam etarhy api / ahaṃśabdasyāheyatvānaṅgīkāre idaṃśabdo 'pi vyarthaḥ / sarvasvarūpatvaṃ hi durvidvadbhir aṅgīkriyate / idaṃśabdena parabrahmavivakṣāyāṃ brahmaśabdo vyarthaḥ / idaṃ yo 'ham iti vedety eva syāt / evaṃśabdaś ca vyarthaḥ / asmatpakṣe tu tadātmānam evāved ity api jñātavyam ity evaṃśabdārthaḥ / tatpakṣe tad api vyartham eva / na hi tatpakṣe tat svātmānaṃ vetti / vyākhyānavyākhyeyabhāvaś ca āgatikā gatiḥ*; see also AgniP 16; BhaviṣPV 3; BrāṇP 3[17].

9) BĀUBh (p. 301,26-27):
Subject matter: Viṣṇu, the supreme Creator of the universe

karmanāmā tu bhagavān phalakartṛtvato hariḥ /
pātanāt pāpanāmāsau punāteḥ puṇyanāmavān /
iti bhārate (1)

(1) Cf. ibid. ll. 22f.:

...
jñānasthitena rūpeṇa devānāṃ muktido hariḥ /
puṇyasthitena rūpeṇa svargaṃ nirayam anyagaḥ /
rahasyam etad devānāṃ viduḥ karmeti mānuṣāḥ /
tasmān naiva janeṣv etad viṣṇoḥ karma prakāśayet /
iti ca | (untraceable source) *ata eva yājñāvalkyo na janeṣūvāca ...* ;
see also AgniP 12 and BrāṇP 69.

10) BhāgTN (p. 62,10):
Subject matter: King Parīkṣit

gaṅgāyām udaka eva kiṃcid dakṣiṇabhāge prāsāde /
tathā hi mahābhārate (1)

(1) Cf. TAGARE 1979, Vol. I: 147n. 483: He [= Vijayadhvaja in Padaratnāvalī] states that Parīkṣit sat in a mansion on the bank of the Ganges .... .

11) BhāgTN (p. 73,4-5):
Subject matter: Breath of life

prāṇāpānāv iḍāyāṃ ca piṅgalāyāṃ ca vartataḥ /
vyānaḥ sandhiṣu sarvatra udāno brahmanāḍigaḥ /
sarvatraiva samānas tu samaṃ caritaḥ sarvagaḥ /
iti bhārate (1)

(1) Cf. ibid. l. 3: *udānagatyā brahmanāḍyā / athaikayordhva udānaḥ* iti śruteḥ (unknown) ... ; see also BhaviṣPV 17.

12) BhāgTN (90,7-8):
Subject matter: Prāṇa

sarvaceṣṭayitṛtvāt tu prāṇo 'bhibhavaśaktitaḥ /
ojas tv anabhibhāvyatvāt sahaś ca svecchayā kṛteḥ /
balaṃ vidhārakatvāc ca vidhṛtir vāyur ucyate /
iti ca bhārate (1)

(1) Cf. BhaviṣPV 17 and MESQUITA 2003: 101f.

13) BhāgTN (p. 254,11):
Subject matter: Synonyms of Ignorance

ajñānaṃ suptiśabdoktaṃ svapnaś caiva viparyayaḥ /
iti bhārate (1)

(1) Cf. HarV 8.

14) BhāgTN (p. 296,3):
Subject matter: Śrī

svāhādvāreṇa śarakānane caccharda /
iti bhāratokteḥ (1)

(1) I could not trace this Śloka (BhāgP IV 7,64), which is the basis for the above quote, in the several available editions of BhāgP. The editor remarks (p. 296n. 1): *ayaṃ śloko 'rvācīnakośeṣu na paṭyate / na vyākhyātaś ca śrīdharasvāmyādibhiḥ* and refers in this connection (ibid. n. 3) to MBh III 214,13-16ab, as a possible source; see also AgniP 25.

15) BhāgTN (p. 431,12-13):
Subject matter: Requital for Dharma and Adharma

niyamād bhujyate puṃbhir dharmādharmaphalaṃ mṛtau /
kaiścid atrāpi bhujyeta tasmān nādharmam ācaret /
iti bhārate (1)

(1) Cf. BhavişP 12 and BrahP 28.

16) BhāgTN (p. 639,5-7):
Subject matter: Viṣṇu, the supreme Creator of the universe / Liberation

svargādyāś ca guṇāḥ sarve doṣāḥ sarve tathaiva ca /
ātmanaḥ kartṛtābhrāntyā jāyante nātra saṃśayaḥ /
paramātmānam evaikaṃ kartāraṃ vetti yaḥ pumān /
sa mucyate 'smāt saṃsārāt paramātmānam eti ca /
iti bhārate (1)

(1) Cf. ibid. ll. 8f.: ... *idaṃ mayā kriyate idaṃ mayā na kriyate idaṃ mayā viparītaṃ kriyate iti buddhibhedaḥ rajastamoguṇanimitto bhramaḥ / sarvaṃ hi parameśvaraḥ karoti*; see also AgniP 12.

17) BhāgTN (p. 688,1-2):
Subject matter: Manas

manasi vyaktatāṃ yāmi tasmād vyaktir hi me manaḥ /
iti bhārate (1)

(1) Cf. ibid. (p. 687,4-5): ... *yathaikaṃ kalamādibījaṃ bhūmāv uptam bahvaṅkuraṃ bhavati / evaṃ paramātmānugṛhīto brahmāhaṅkārādiṣu bahudhā vyaktībhavati*; see also BhavişPV 17.

18) BhāgTN (p. 716,1-2):
Subject matter: Yogic powers

ekasmāt siddhayo viṣṇoḥ sthānabhedāt pṛthagvidhāḥ /
ekasthānagatād vā syuḥ susthiropāsanā yadi /
iti bhārate (1)

(1) Cf. HarV 28; KūrP 19.

19) BhāgTN (p. 718,12-13):
Subject matter: Jīva / Haṃsa

tyāgāt pūrvaśarīrāṇāṃ navānāṃ sañcayena ca /
jīvaṃ haṃsa iti prāhus taddhetutvād dhariṃ param /
iti bhārate (1)

(1) Cf. ibid. ll. 10f: *ākāśasyātmani / tatrākāśa upalabdhānāmā samantāt sthitānāṃ bhūtānāṃ vācaḥ / haṃsaḥ jīvaḥ* ... ; see also BrāṇP 71; GarP 36[4f.]; HarV 3n. 1.

20) BhāgTN (p. 742,9-10):
Subject matter: Viṣṇu's supreme transcendence

sattvaṃ svātantryam uddiṣṭaṃ tac ca kṛṣṇe na cāpare / (1)
asvātantryāt tadanyeṣām asattvaṃ viddhi bhārata /
iti bhārate (2)

(1) *apare* for *aparasmin.*
(2) Cf. ibid l. 8: *nas tattvānāṃ madhye yena yad yatra sthitvā ca syus tad eva sat* ... ; see also AgniP 6 and MESQUITA 2000: 460f.

21) BhāgTN (p. 792,3-4):
Subject matter: Nature of the individual soul

jīvasya sukharūpasya na duḥkhaṃ kvacid iṣyate /
ato mano 'bhimānena duḥkhī bhavati nānyathā /
iti bhārate (1)

(1) Cf. ibid. ll. 1f.: *na hy ātmanaḥ svabhāvād anyad bhavati / yadi dṛśyate tathāpi mṛṣā syāt / sukharūpaṃ duḥkhaṃ na bhavati / ato mana eva tathā darśayati*; see also BrāṇP 71.

22) BhāgTN (p. 815,1-2):
Subject matter: Viṣṇu's supreme transcendence

ekaṃ tu śubham uddiṣṭam aśubhaṃ dvaitam ucyate /
puṃso 'śubhasya kiṃ bhadraṃ kim abhadraṃ viśeṣataḥ /
sarvadāśubharūpatvād viśeṣo 'tyalpa eva hi /
iti bhārate (1)

(1) Cf. ibid. ll. 3f.: *dvaitasyāśubhasya puruṣasya kiyad atyalpam eva hi bhadram abhadraṃ vā svayogyād ādhikyena bhavati yatnavato 'pīty arthaḥ / atas tadviṣaye dhyātam uktaṃ ca śubham anṛtam eva* ... and BhāgTN (p. 653,1-13): *svādhīnaṃ sad iti proktam parādhīnam asat smṛtam* ... iti ca (unknown source); see also AgniP 6 and MESQUITA 2000: 455f.

23) BSūBh (p. 111,13-14):
Subject matter: Prāṇa / Vāyu

yadāśrayād asya ceṣṭhā so 'nyaṃ katham upāśrayet /
yathā prāṇas tathā rājā sarvasyaikāśrayo bhavet /
iti yuktir bhārate (1)

(1) Cf. ibid. ll. 14f.:
prāṇasyaitad vaśe sarvaṃ prāṇaḥ paravaśe sthitaḥ /
na paraḥ kañcidāśritya vartate paramo yataḥ /
iti ca paiṅgiśrutiḥ (unknown source);
see also BhavișPV 17 and MESQUITA 2003: 103f.

24) BSūBh (p. 115,13):
Subject matter: Āpa as *mahābhūta*

aṃmayaṃ tu yato māṃsam atas tṛptiś ca māṃsataḥ /
iti ca bhārate (1)

(1) Cf. ibid. ll. 11f.: *adbhyo hīdam utpadyata āpo vāva māṃsam asthi ca bhavaty āpaḥ śarīram āpa evedaṃ sarvaṃ* iti kauṇḍinyaśrutiḥ (unknown source); see also MatsyaP 5; 18; VāyuP 11.

25) BSūBh (p. 117,5-6):
Subject matter: Definition of Death

bhūtānāṃ vinivṛttis tu maraṇaṃ samudāhṛtam /
bhūtānāṃ saṃprayogaś ca janir ity eva paṇḍitaiḥ /
iti ca bhārate (1)

(1) Cf. ibid. l. 4: *tac ca maraṇe bhavati* ... ; see also AgniP 4; BrāṇP 33 and MESQUITA 2000: 493n. 645.

26) BSūBh (p. 120,8-10):
Subject matter: Seven hells

rauravo 'tha mahāṃś caiva vahnir vaitaraṇī tathā /
kuṃbhīpāka iti proktāny anityanarakāṇi tu /
tāmisraś cāndhatāmisro dvau nityau saṃprakīrtitau /
iti sapta pradhānāni balīyas tūttarottaram /
etāni kramaśo gatvaivāroho 'thāvarohaṇam /
iti ca bhārate (1)

(1) Cf. YBh (*ad* III 26): *tatrāvīcer upary upari niviṣṭāḥ ṣaṇmahānarakabhūmayo ghanasalilānalānilākāśatamaḥpratiṣṭhā mahākālāṃbarīṣarauravamahārauravakālasūtrāndhatāmisrāḥ / yatra svakarmopārjitaduḥkhavedanāḥ prāṇinaḥ kaṣṭam āyurdīrgham ākṣipya jāyante / tato mahātalarasātalātalasutalavitalatalātalapātālākhyāni sapta pātālāni*; see also BhaviṣPV 19.

27) BSūBh (p. 121,2-3):
Subject matter: Paths of liberation

vidyāpathaḥ karmapatho dvau panthānau prakīrtitau /
tadvarjitas tridhā yāti tiryag vā narakaṃ tamaḥ /
iti ca bhārate (1)

(1) Cf. ibid. l. 26: *vidyākarmāpekṣyaivaitad vacanam / tayor api prakṛtatvāt* ... ; see also AgniP 9; 24; BhaviṣPV 19 and GarP 53.

28) GīBh (p. 84,1-2):
Subject matter: Liberation

brahmā sthānu ity ārabhya –
tasya prasādād icchanti tadādiṣṭaphalāṃ gatim /
ityādi ca mokṣadharme (1)

(1) Cf. AgniP 16.

29) GīBh (p. 85,4):
Subject matter: Kramamukti

nirgacchaṃś cakṣuṣā sūryaṃ diśaḥ śrotreṇa caiva hi /
ityādivacanād vyāsayoge mokṣadharme ca (1)

(1) Cf. ibid. l. 3: *brahmanāḍīṃ vinā yady anyatra gacchati tarhi vinā mokṣaṃ sthānāntaraṃ prāpnotīti sarvadvārāṇi saṃyamya*; see also ĀdityaP 1.

30) GīBh (p. 88,20):
Subject matter: Antaryāmin

tvaṃ manastvaṃ candramāstvaṃ cakṣur ādityaḥ /
ityādeś ca mokṣadharme (1)

(1) Cf. ibid. ll. 15f.: *akṣeṣu indriyeṣu prati prati sthita iti pratyakṣaḥ / tathā ca śruti – yo vāci tiṣṭhan* (= BĀU II 7,17; III 7,16) *yaś cakṣuṣi tiṣṭhan ityādeḥ* (III 7,18) *ya eṣo 'ntarakṣiṇi puruṣo dṛśyata iti ca* (ChU IV 15,1) *aṅguṣṭhamātraḥ puruṣo 'ṅguṣṭhaṃ ca samāśrita iti ca* (MahānārayanaU XVI 5) ... ; see also BhāgP 2.

31) GīBh (p. 89,2):
Subject matter: Pṛthivī

pṛthivī dharmamūrdhani /
iti prayogān mokṣadharme (1)

(1) Cf. ibid. ll. 1: *dharmo bhagavān / tadviṣayaṃ dharmyam / sarvaṃ jagad dhatta iti dharmaḥ / ...* ; in MBh (VII 98,14cd) a similar text has been handed down: *pṛthivī dharmarājasya śamenaiva pradīyatam*; see also BrahP 28.

32) GīBh (p. 89,15):
Subject matter: Viṣṇu, the supreme Creator of the universe

mahāvibhūte māhātmyaśarīraḥ /
iti hi mokṣadharme (1)

(1) Cf. ibid. l. 15: *mamātmā deha eva bhūtabhāvanaḥ* / (= Gī IX 5d); see also AgniP 4; 12 and MESQUITA 2000: 482f.

33) GīBh (p. 91,10):
Subject matter: Attributes of Viṣṇu

> *brahmapurohita brahmakāyika mahārājika /*
> iti ca mokṣadharme (1)

(1) Cf. ibid. ll. 7f.: ... *bhūtaṃ mahadīśvaraṃ ceti bhūtamaheśvaram / tathā hi* bābhra-vyaśākhāyāṃ – *anādyanantaṃ paripūrṇarūpam īśaṃ varāṇāṃ api devavīryam* iti (untraceable sources); see also BhāgP 1.

34) GīBh (p. 102,16-17):
Subject matter: Viṣṇu's infinity

> *viśvarūpa anantagata anantabhāga anantagata ananta /*
> ityādi mokṣadharme (1)

(1) Cf. ibid. l. 16: *mayā vinā yad bhūtaṃ syāt tan nāsti* ... ; see also AgniP 6; BhaviṣPV 24; BrahVP 12_1 and MESQUITA 2000: 415ff.; 461f.

35) GīBh (p. 111,25-26):
Subject matter: Viṣṇu's supreme transcendence

> *yasya divyaṃ hi tad rūpaṃ hīyate vardhate na ca /*
> iti mokṣadharme (1)

(1) Cf. ibid. ll. 22f.: *pravṛddhaḥ paripūrṇo 'nādir vā ... na tu vardhanam – nāsau jajāna na mariṣyati naidhate 'sāv* iti bhāgavate (= XI 3,38); see also AgniP 6; BhaviṣPV 3n. 1 and MESQUITA 2000: 425f.

36) GīBh (p. 119,11-13):
Subject matter: Qualities of Prakṛti

> tathāhi mokṣadharme –
> *nārāyaṇaguṇāśrayād ajarād atīndriyād agrahyād asaṃbhavata asatyād ahiṃsrāl lalāmād dvitīyapravṛttiviśeṣād avairād akṣayād amarād akṣarād amūrtitaḥ sarvasyāḥ sarvakartuḥ śāśvatatamasaḥ* / iti (1)

(1) Cf. ibid. ll. 8f.: *uktaṃ ca* sāmavede kāṣāyaṇaśrutau (unknown source) – *nāsadāsīnno sadāsīt tadānīm iti / na mahābhūtaṃ nopabhūtaṃ tadāsīd ity ādyārambhya tama āsīt tamasā gūḍham agra iti tamo hy avyaktam ajaram anirdeśyam eṣā hy eva prakṛtir iti / sarvagācintyādilakṣaṇā ca sā* ... ; see also AgniP 25.

37) GīBh (p. 143,19):
Subject matter: Kāma

pātāla iva duṣpūro māṃ hi kleśayase sadā /
iti hi mokṣadharme (1)

(1) Cf. ibid. l. 19: *duṣpūro hi kāmaḥ*; see also BhaviṣPV 19.

38) GīT (p. 54,29):
Subject matter: Viṣṇu's supreme transcendence

ekaḥ svatantro bhagavāṃs tadīyaṃ tv anyad ucyate /
iti bhārate (1)

(1) Cf. ibid. ll. 27f.: *katham abhimānatyāgaḥ / brahmārpaṇam ityādi / brahmaṇy arpaṇaṃ brahmārpaṇam / brahmaṇo haviḥ / brahmaṇo 'gnau / brahmaṇaḥ karma / samādhinā saha / samādhir api tadadhīna ity artha* ... ; see also AgniP 6; NārP 53n. 1 and MESQUITA 2000: 455ff.

39) GīT (p. 80,19):
Subject matter: Synonyms of Tamas

tamas tu śārvaraṃ vidyān mohaś caiva viparyayaḥ /
iti ca bhārate (1)

(1) Cf. ibid. l. 18: *dvandvamoho mithyājñānam*; see also BhāgTN (p. 198,1f.): *tamas tu śārvaraṃ proktaṃ mohaś caiva viparyayaḥ* ... / (unknown) *tadāgraho mahāmohas tāmisraḥ* ... (= MBh XIV 37,33) and HarV 8.

40) MBhTN II 59:
Subject matter: Maṅgala-verse

sṛṣṭā brahmādayo devā nihatā yena dānavāḥ /
tasmai devādidevāya namaste śārṅgadhāriṇe /
(iti bhārate) (1)

(1) Cf. AgniP 6; BhaviṣPV 19.

41) MBhTN II 67:
Subject matter: Viṣṇu's supreme transcendence

satyaṃ satyaṃ punaḥ satyam uddhṛtya bhujam ucyate /
vedaśāstrāt paraṃ nāsti na daivaṃ keśavāt param /
(iti bhārate) (1)

(1) Cf. AgniP 6; MārkP 1n. 1 and MESQUITA 2000: 166n. 341.

42) MBhTN II 69-81:
Subject matter: Doctrine of Avatāras / Viṣṇu's inscrutability

smartavyaḥ satataṃ viṣṇur vismartavyo na jātucit /
sarve vidhiniṣedhāḥ syur etayor eva kiṃkarāḥ / [69]
ko hi taṃ vedituṃ śakto yo na syāt tadvidho 'paraḥ /
tadvidhaś cāparo nāsti tasmāt taṃ veda saḥ svayam / [70]
ko hi taṃ vedituṃ śakto nārāyaṇam anāmayam /
ṛte satyavatīsūnoḥ kṛṣṇād vā devakīsutāt / [71] (1)
aprameyo 'niyojyaś ca svayaṃ kāmagamo vaśī /
modaty eṣa sadā bhūtair bālaḥ krīḍanakair iva / [72] (2)
na pramātuṃ mahābāhuḥ śakyo 'yam madhusūdanaḥ /
paramāt param etasmād viśvarūpān na vidyate / [73] (3)
vasudevasuto nāyaṃ nāyaṃ garbhe 'vasat prabhuḥ /
nāyaṃ daśarathāj jāto na cāpi jamadagnitaḥ / [74] (4)
jāyate naiva kutrāpi mriyate kuta eva tu /
na vedhyo muhyate nāyaṃ baddhyate naiva kenacit /
kuto duḥkhaṃ svatantrasya nityānandaikarūpiṇaḥ / [75]
īśann api hi deveśaḥ sarvasya jagato hariḥ /
karmāṇi kurute nityaṃ kīnāśa iva durbalaḥ / [76] (5)
nātmānaṃ veda mugdho 'yaṃ duḥkhī sītāṃ ca mārgate /
baddhaḥ śakrajitetyādi līlaiṣāsuramohinī / [77]
muhyate śastrapātena bhinnatvagrudhirasravaḥ /
ajānan pṛcchati smānyāṃs tanuṃ tyaktvā divaṃ gataḥ / [78]
ityādyasuramohāya darśayāmāsa nāṭyavat /
avidyamānam eveśaḥ kuhakaṃ tad viduḥ surāḥ / [79] (6)
prādurbhāvā hareḥ sarve naiva prakṛtidehinaḥ /
nirdoṣā guṇasaṃpūrṇā darśayanty anyathaiva tu / [80]
duṣṭānāṃ mohanārthāya satām api tu kutracit /
yathāyogyaphalaprāptyai līlaiṣā paramātmanaḥ / [81]
(iti bhārate) (7)

(1) Cf. MBh IV 59,19a:
ṛte śāṃtanavād bhīṣmāt kṛṣṇād vā devakīsutāt /
(2) Cf. MBh II Appendix I 1605f.:
aprameyo 'niyojyaś ca yatrakāmagamo vaśī /
modate bhagavān bhūtair bālaḥ krīḍanakair iva //
see also BrahVP 20.
(3) Cf. MBh II App. I 1611-12:
na pramātuṃ mahābāhuḥ śakyo bhārata keśavaḥ /
paraṃ hy aparam etasmād viśvarūpān na vidyate //
(4) Cf. ibid. 1607-10:
naiṣa garbhatvam āpede na yonyām āvasat prabhuḥ /
ātmanas tejasā kṛṣṇaḥ sarveṣāṃ kurute gatim //
yathā budbuda utthāya tatraiva tu nilīyate /
carācarāṇi bhūtāni tathā nārāyaṇe sadā //

see also ĀdiP 1; BhaviṣPV 29; BrāṇP 105; PadP 79; SkaP 5; 111 and MESQUITA 2000_1: 37ff. [= 1997: 31ff.].
(5) Cf. MBh V 66,14:

īśann api mahāyogī sarvasya jagato hariḥ /
karmāṇy ārabhate kartuṃ kīnāśa iva durbalaḥ //

also ViṣDhP 1n. 1.
(6) Cf. BrahP 9_1; BrahVP 14; BrāṇP 22; 41; 60; 64; 94; 105; GarP 26_1; 31; 36; HarP 5[11]; KūrP 3; 7; NārP 9; 36; PadP 13; 17; 23; 50; 55_1; 77; SkaP 31; 36; 42; 43; 44; 115; 122; VarP 10; 15; 25 and MBhTN I 37-47: ... ityādy uktaṃ bhagavatā bhaviṣyat-parvaṇi sphuṭam = BhaviṣPV 29; see also ĀdiP 1.
(7) Cf. MBhTN II 66:

ādyantayor ity avadat sa yasmād vyāsātmako viṣṇur udāraśaktiḥ /
tasmāt samastā harisadguṇānāṃ nirṇītaye bhāratagā kathaiṣā /

43) MBhTN II 108:
Subject matter: Viṣṇu's supreme transcendence

brahmeśānādibhiḥ sarvaiḥ sametair yadguṇāṃśakaḥ /
nāvasāyayituṃ śakyo vyācakṣaṇaiś ca sarvadā /
(iti bhārate) (1)

(1) Cf. ibid. *tathaiva bhīmavacanaṃ dharmajaṃ praty udīritam* ... ; see also AgniP 6.

44) MBhTN II 111:
Subject matter: Viṣṇu's supreme transcendence

yathāśritāni jyotīṃṣi jyotiḥśreṣṭhaṃ divākaram /
evaṃ muktagaṇāḥ sarve vāsudevam upāśritāḥ /
(iti bhārate) (1)

(1) Cf. ibid.: *vacanaṃ caiva kṛṣṇasya jyeṣṭhaṃ kuntīsutaṃ prati* ... and App. IV 3383f.: *mamāśrayo na kaścit sarveṣām āśrayo hy aham / etan mayā proktaṃ rahasyam idam uttamam*; GīBh (p. 76,7-8): *tadanādhāratvam ucyate / uktaṃ ca –*

tadāśritaṃ jagat sarvaṃ nāsau kutracid āśritaḥ /
iti gītākalpe (unknown source);

see also AgniP 6 and MESQUITA 2000: 464f.

45) MBhTN II 149:
Subject matter: Viṣṇu's supreme transcendence

balam indrasya giriśo giriśasya balaṃ marut /
balaṃ tasya hariḥ sākṣān na harer balam anyataḥ /
(iti bhārate) (1)

(1) Cf. AgniP 6 and MESQUITA 2003: 103n. 17; 19.

46) MBhTN II 151-153:
Subject matter: Bhīma's distinctive qualities / Puruṣārtha

tattvajñāne viṣṇubhaktau dhairye sthairye parākrame /
vege ca lāghave caiva pralāpasya ca varjane /
bhīmasenasamo nāsti senayor ubhayor api /
pāṇḍitye ca paṭutve ca śūratve ca bale 'pi ca /
dharmaś cārthaś ca kāmaś ca mokṣaś caiva yaśo dhruvam /
tvayy āyattam idaṃ sarvaṃ sarvalokasya bhārata / (1)
(iti bhārate) (2)

(1) Cf. BhāgTN (p. 730,1f. [= MBh V 75,3ad]):
dharmo jñānaṃ tathā mokṣo yaśaḥ kīrtis tathaiva ca /
tvayy āyattam idaṃ sarvaṃ lokasyāpi na saṃśayaḥ /
iti bhārate;
see also GarP 9; MBh 48; SkaP 124; MESQUITA 2000: 108n. 169 and MESQUITA 2000_1: 169n. 346 [= 1997: 137n. 333].
(2) Cf. ibid. l. 11: *tathā yudhiṣṭhireṇāpi bhīmaṃ prati samīritam.*

47) MBhTN II 162-168:
Subject matter: Viṣṇu's supreme transcendence

yasyādhiko bale nāsti bhīmasenam ṛte kvacit /
na vijñāne na ca jñāna eṣa rāmaḥ sa lāṅgalī / [162]
yasya na pratiyoddhāsti bhīmam ekam ṛte kvacit /
anviṣyāpi trilokeṣu sa eṣa musalāyudhaḥ / [163]
anujñāto rauhiṇeyāt tvayā caivāparājitaḥ / (1)
sarvavidyāsu bībhatsuḥ kṛṣṇena ca mahātmanā / [164]
anveṣa rauhiṇeyaṃ ca tvāṃ ca bhīmāparājitam / (2)
vīrye śaurye 'pi vā nānyas tṛtīyaḥ phalgunād ṛte / [165]
adhijyam api yat kartuṃ śakyate naiva gāṇḍivam / (3)
anyatra bhīmapārthābhyāṃ bhavataś ca janārdana / [166]
dvāv eva puruṣau loke vāsudevād anantarau / (4)
bhīmas tu prathamas tatra dvitīyo drauṇir eva ca / [167]
akṣayāv iṣudhī divye dhvajo vānaralakṣaṇaḥ /
gāṇḍīvaṃ dhanuṣāṃ śreṣṭhaṃ tena drauṇer varo 'rjunaḥ / [168] (5)
(iti bhārate) (6)

(1) Cf. ibid (p. 28): *tathā yudhiṣṭhireṇaiva bhīmāya samudīritam.*
(2) Cf. MBh III 142,20:
saṃkarṣaṇaṃ mahāvīryaṃ tvāṃ ca bhīmāparājitam /
anujātaḥ sa vīryeṇa vāsudevaṃ ca śatruhā //
(3) Cf. MBhTN (p. 29) l. 1: *tathaiva draupadīvākyaṃ vāsudevaṃ pratīritam.*
(4) Cf, ibid. l. 4: *tathaivānyatra vacanaṃ kṛṣṇadvaipāyaneritam.*
(5) Cf. MBh II App. 39, 228 pr.: *gāṇḍīvaṃ ca dhanuḥśreṣṭham.*

(6) Cf. MBhTN II 169-171:

ityādyanantavākyāni santy evārthe vivakṣite /
kānicid darśitāny atra diṅmātrapratipattaye /
tasmād uktakrameṇaiva puruṣottamatā hareḥ /
anaupacārikī siddhā brahmatā ca vinirṇayāt /
pūrṇaprajñākṛteyaṃ saṅksepād uddhṛitiḥ suvākyānām /
śrīmadbhāratagānāṃ viṣṇoḥ pūrṇatvanirṇayāyaiva /

48) VTN (p. 19,19-20):
Subject matter: Liberation

anityatvāt saduḥkatvān na dharmādyāḥ paraṃ sukham /
mokṣa eva parānandaḥ saṃsāre parivartatām /
iti bhārate (1)

(1) Cf. ibid. l. 17: ... *mokṣo hi sarvapuruṣārthottamaḥ* and MESQUITA 2000: 108n. 169; see also AgniP 16 and GarP 9.

49) VTN (p. 25,18-19):
Subject matter: Individual soul, the conscious seat of the body

sukhasya cāpy āyatanaṃ śarīraṃ
duḥkhasya cāpy āyatanaṃ śarīram /
acetanaṃ prākṛtam etad āhur
bhoktā tayoś cetanakaḥ śarīrī /
iti ca bhārate (1)

(1) Cf. BrāṇP 71 and MESQUITA 2000: 139n. 266.

50) VTN (p. 38,21-22):
Subject matter: Refutation of the advaitic doctrine of Upādhis

udyatāyudhadordaṇḍāḥ patitasvaśirokṣibhiḥ /
paśyantaḥ pātayanti sma kabandhāpy arīn yudhi
iti bhāratavacanān *na viśleṣād viśeṣaḥ* (1)

(1) Cf. BhaviṣPV 3n. 7; SkaP 54. Madhva has used this quote in the same context also in another work of his, namely Vāda, MESQUITA 2000: 212n. 448-451.

Mārkaṇḍeyapurāṇa (MārkP)

[Possibly one of the oldest of the extant Purāṇas. Its first chapters are like a supplement to the MBh (cf. HAZRA 1987: 8ff.; ROCHER 1986: 192f.). According to MatsyaP (53,25-26) it has nine thousand verses:

yatrādhikṛtya śakunīn dharmādharmavicāraṇā /
vyākhyātā vai munipraśne munibhir dharmacāribhiḥ //

mārkaṇḍeyena kathitaṃ tat sarvaṃ vistareṇa tu /
purāṇaṃ navasāhasraṃ mārkaṇḍeyam ihocyate //

Only three untraceable quotes, one each in GīBh; MBhTN and MāṇUBh, are ascribed by Madhva to this Purāṇa.]

1) GīBh (p. 19,17-19):
Subject matter: Liberation

tatraiva śivaṃ prati mārkaṇḍeyavacanam –
saṃsārārṇavanirmagna idānīṃ muktim eṣyasi /
ityādi I pādme śaive mārkaṇḍeyakathāprabandhe śivān niṣidhya viṣṇor eva muktim āha –
ahaṃ bhogaprado vatsa mokṣadas tu janārdanaḥ / (1)

(1) Cf. ibid. ll. 16f.:
tatsamo 'bhyadhiko vāpi nāsti kaścit kadācana /
etena satyavākyena tam eva praviśāmy aham /
ityādy āha ... ;
see also Anuv (p. 167,25); AgniP 6 and MBh 41.

2) MBhTN (II 49cd-50):
Subject matter: Eulogy of Mahābhārata

mārkaṇḍeye 'pi kathitaṃ bhāratasya praśaṃsanam –
devatānāṃ yathā vyāso dvipadāṃ brāhmaṇo varaḥ /
āyudhānāṃ yathā vajram oṣadhīnāṃ yathā yavā /
tathaiva sarvaśāstrāṇāṃ mahābhāratam uttamam / (1)

(1) Cf. ibid. II 49ab:
...
ityādikathitaṃ sarvaṃ brahmāṇḍe hariṇā svayam (untraceable); VāyuP 13; see also MārkP I 4-8a:
tridaśānāṃ yathā viṣṇur dvipadāṃ brāhmaṇo yathā /
bhūṣaṇānāṃ ca sarveṣāṃ yathā cūḍāmaṇir varaḥ //
yathāyudhānāṃ kuliśam indriyāṇāṃ yathā manaḥ /
tatheha sarvaśāstrāṇāṃ mahābhāratam uttamam //
atrārthaś caiva dharmaś ca kāmo mokṣaś ca varṇyate /
parasparānubandhāś ca sānubandhāś ca te pṛthak //
dharmaśāstram idaṃ śreṣṭham arthasāstram idaṃ param /
kāmaśāstram idaṃ cāgryaṃ mokṣaśāstraṃ tathottamam //
caturāśramadharmāṇāṃ ācārasthitisādhanam /
MBh (I 1, 201-202; I 120* 4 pr.):
bhāratasya vapur hy etat satyaṃ cāmṛtam eva ca /
navanītaṃ yathā dadhno dvipadāṃ brāhmaṇo yathā //
hradānām udadhiḥ śreṣṭho gaur variṣṭhā catuṣpadām /
yathaitāni variṣṭhāni tathā bhāratam ucyate //
ibid. (IV 2,12-15):

sūryaḥ pratapatāṃ śreṣṭho dvipadāṃ brāhmaṇo varaḥ /
āśīviṣaś ca sarpāṇām agnis tejasvināṃ varaḥ //
āyudhānāṃ varo vajraḥ kakudmī ca gavāṃ varaḥ /
hradānām udadhiḥ śreṣṭhaḥ parjanyo varṣatāṃ varaḥ //
dhṛtarāṣṭraś ca nāgānāṃ hastiṣv airāvato varaḥ /
putraḥ priyāṇām adhiko bhāryā ca suhṛdāṃ varā //
yathaitāni viśiṣṭāni jātyāṃ jātyāṃ vṛkodaraḥ /
evaṃ yuvā guḍākeśaḥ śreṣṭhaḥ sarvadhanuṣmatām //

ibid. XIV 44,8cd:

hiraṇyaṃ sarvaratnānām oṣadhīnāṃ yavās tathā /
... ;

see also MBhTN II 148. One can find in this quote see a tangible redactional re-formulation by Madhva in order to eulogise the MBh as the best literary composition, incomparable in its genre to any other. For this purpose, he makes use of examples derived from the domains of gods, humans and other animate or inanimate beings, following exactly the intention of the quotations from MārkP 1,4-8a cited above. Among the four examples adduced in MārkP 2, only the second and the third are in fact handed down in this Purāṇa. Madhva has borrowed the fourth one from MBh. Moreover, he has adopted the first one with some changes: he replaces Viṣṇu by Vyāsa and *tridaśānāṃ* by *devatānāṃ*. While the last example is handed down in the classical literature, the first one is deeply rooted in the original Avatāra-doctrine of Madhva, according to which, God Viṣṇu at the request of Brahmā descends to earth taking the form of Vyāsa (*bhagavān vyāso avatatāra*), during the Dvāpara eon, which is characterized by a sudden decay of moral behaviour as well as a decrease in Vedic knowledge. Viṣṇu does so out of compassion for those in Saṃsāra, in particular for those who are not entitled to study of the Vedas, such as the women and the Śūdras. Vyāsa imparts to them the knowledge of the Veda, which is, as it were, a fifth Veda in other form (cf. MESQUITA 2000_1: 45ff. specially n. 61 [= 1997: 37ff. and n. 53]. In the form of Vyāsa he composes also the Brahmasūtras (*proktaṃ brahmasūtraṃ tu viṣṇunā vyāsarūpeṇa*) as well as MBh:

kṛṣṇadvaipāyanaṃ vyāsaṃ viddhi nārāyaṇaṃ prabhum /
ko hy anyaḥ puṇḍarīkākṣān mahābhāratakṛd bhavet //

(cf. MESQUITA o.c. 42; 95f. [= 35; 76f.). On the basis of these facts it is quite understandable why Madhva in connection with the eulogy of MBh (see ibid. p. 143ff. [= pp. 115ff.]) replaced Viṣṇu by Vyāsa in his untraceable quote MārkP 2; see also KūrP 30_2.

3) MāṇUBh (p. 515,13-16):
Subject matter: Catūrūpa Paramātman

paramātmā catūrūpaḥ sarvaprāṇiśarīragaḥ /
viśvaś ca taijasaḥ prājñas turīyaś ceti kathyate /
tāni rūpāṇi sarvāṇi pūrṇānandamayāni tu /
cetomukhāni sarvāṇi pūrṇajñānasvarūpataḥ /
mukhaśabdas tu sarvasya dehasyāpy upalakṣaṇaḥ /
tathāpi mukhaśabdo 'yaṃ pūrṇatvaṃ sūcayed vibhoḥ /
jñānasya mukhyavācitvān mukhavācy api san svataḥ /
iti mārkaṇḍeye (1)

(1) Cf. ibid. (p. 514,19f.): *ānandamayaḥ pūrṇānandaḥ / cetomukho jñānasvarūpamukhaḥ ... ānandamayaceto mukhasarvajñatvasarveśvarādicatuṣṭaye 'pi samaḥ / ... eṣa catūrūpa ātmā sarvajñatvasarveśvaratvādilakṣaṇaḥ* ... ; see also BhāgP 1; BrāṇP 7.

Matsyapurāṇa (MatsyaP)

[This Purāṇa is allegedly one of the oldest and the best preserved of the Purāṇas (cf. ROCHER 1986: 196f.). It is quoted by Madhva in BhāgTN (sixteen times), in BSūBh (three times) and one time in GīBh. Regarding the striking similarities with the chapters common to the BhaviṣP, BrāṇP and VāyuP, see HAZRA 1987: 26ff.]

1) BhāgTN (p. 16,15):
Subject matter: Definition of Sattva

> *balajñānasamāhāraḥ sattvam ity abhidhīyate /*
> iti mātsye (1)

(1) Cf. ibid. l. 14: *sattvaṃ jñānabalarūpam* ... ; see also VāmP 18.

2) BhāgTN (p. 18,8):
Subject matter: Ānvīkṣikī

> *ānvīkṣikī kutarkākhyā tathaivānvīkṣikī parā /*
> iti mātsye (1)

(1) Cf. ibid. l. 7: *ānvīkṣikīṃ tattvavidyāṃ*; see also ibid. n. 7: *anumānena kevalaṃ yatra tattvānīkṣyante sānvīkṣikī kutarkākhyā / vedādyanusāreṇa ca yatra tattvānīkṣyante sa sattarkavidyā mukhyānvīkṣikī*; and MESQUITA 2000: 339-378; HACKER 1958: 54-83.

3) BhāgTN (p. 24,11):
Subject matter: Viṣṇu's Adorer

> *śrutvā kathāṃ na tuṣyāmi harer avyaktakarmaṇaḥ /*
> iti mātsye
> *kaḥ prasanno bhaved divyāṃ kathāṃ śṛṇvan hareḥ parām /*
> iti ca (1)

(1) Cf. ibid. l. 10 and 12: *atoṣo 'nalaṃbudhiḥ ... aprasādaś ca saiva* ... ; see also HarV 19_1 and PadP 80.

4) BhāgTN (p. 85,15-16):
Subject matter: Viṣṇu's supreme transcendence

> *tvadadhīnā yataḥ sattā avarasyāpi keśava /*

ataḥ svarūpataḥ samyak sati bhede 'pi tad bhavān /
iti mātsye (1)

(1) Cf. ibid. n. 5: *kiṃcid apy anyataḥ na jāyate / atas tvam eva sarvakartety artha iti prācīnam*; see also AgniP 6; BhaviṣPV 6 and MESQUITA 2000: 460n. 579.

5) BhāgTN (p. 90,3):
Subject matter: Mahābhūtāni

pañcendriyābhimeyatvān mātrā guṇa itīritaḥ /
iti mātsye (1)

(1) Cf. BhaviṣPV 18; BrahVP 1; BrāṇP 73; MBh 24; MatsyaP 18; NārP 41; PadP 19 and SkaP 15; 25; VāmP 7; 20; VāyuP 8; 11.

6) BhāgTN (p. 91,3-4):
Subject matter: Transmigration

ākāśavāyū tv avyakte itare 'ṇḍe prakāśitāḥ /
tathātvād bāhyabhūtānām aṇḍasthānāṃ ca sā gatiḥ /
iti mātsye (1)

(1) Cf. ibid. ll. 1f.: *sadasattvaṃ vyaktāvyaktvam / naḥ / adaḥ brahmāṇḍam / brahmāṇḍaṃ hi vadanti jīvānāṃ bhayakāraṇam / tatra hi saṃsṛtiḥ* ... ; see also BrāṇP 33.

7) BhāgTN (p. 92,5-6):
Subject matter: False opinions on the reality of the world

harer avayavair lokāḥ sṛṣṭā iti vikalpanam /
sākṣāt satyam ato 'nyasmād vyāvahārikam ucyate /
iti mātsye (1)

(1) Cf. BhaviṣPV 1n. 7; MESQUITA 2000: 431ff.; 325ff. and MESQUITA 1990: 193ff.; 232ff.

8) BhāgTN (p. 95,4-5):
Subject matter: Viṣṇu's Heaven

trimūrdhā san harir dhatte dyutrayaṃ mūrdhabhis tribhiḥ /
anantāsanavaikuṇṭhanārāyaṇapurāṇi tu /
bahulakṣocchriteṣv eṣu sa vasaty amṛto hariḥ /
iti mātsye (1)

(1) Cf. ibid. l. 3: *sarvasya yathāvat sthitividaḥ* ... ; see also AgniP 12; 27 and BrāṇP 30.

9) BhāgTN (p. 105,1-2):
Subject matter: Hari, an ascetic and the Creator of the Universe

haris tāpasanāmāsau jātas tapasi vai manuḥ /
gajendraṃ mokṣayāmāsa sasarja ca jagad vibhuḥ /
iti ca mātsye (1)

(1) Cf. AgniP 12.

10) BhāgTN (p. 108,6):
Subject matter: Viṣṇu's Omnipotence

viṣṇor nānyena karmāṇi pareṣāṃ tannibandhanam /
iti mātsye (1)

(1) Cf. BhāgP II 7, 26cd: ... *kariṣyati janānupalakṣyamārgaḥ karmāṇi cātmamahimopanibandhanāni*; see also BhaviṣP 13.

11) BhāgTN (p. 236,7):
Subject matter: Viṣṇu's supreme transcendence

ananyādhīnaśaktitvād dhariḥ sva iti cocyate /
iti mātsye (1)

(1) Cf. AgniP 6; BhaviṣPV 13 and MESQUITA 2000: 424f.

12) BhāgTN (p. 294,2-3):
Subject matter: Viṣṇu's Sarvanāmatva

sarvaśabdābhidheyatvaṃ sarvāntaryāmakatvataḥ /
na tu sarvasvarūpatvāt sarvabhinno yato hariḥ /
iti mātsye (1)

(1) Cf. BhāgP 2; BrāṇP 2; MBh 2; NārP 42; PadP 81 and MESQUITA 2000: 162f; 456n. 567; 489f.

13) BhāgTN (p. 358,4-6):
Subject matter: Heaven of the Deities

devān atyuttamamunīn vinā ke śaiṃśumārakam /(1)
harer gṛhaṃ praviṣṭās tu dhruvo devāś ca tadgatāḥ /
iti mātsye (2)

(1) According to Madhva Śiṃśumāra is an Avatāra-manifestation of Viṣṇu, cf. ĀdiP 1; BrahP 38; BrāṇP 27; 52; 95[25].
(2) Cf. AgniP 27.

14) BhāgTN (p. 494,7-8):
Subject matter: Matsyāvatāra

anantaśaktir bhagavān matsyarūpī janārdanaḥ /
krīḍārthaṃ yācayāmāsa svayaṃ satyavrataṃ nṛpam /
iti mātsye (1)

(1) Cf. ĀdiP 1.

15) BhāgTN (p. 549,4-5):
Subject matter: Pāṇḍavas

jarāsandhaṃ nihatyaiva pāṇḍavais tu diśo jitāḥ /
prasādād vāsudevasya rājasūyaḥ kratuḥ kṛtaḥ /
iti mātsye (1)

(1) Cf. ibid. l. 1: *ajitaṃ jarāsandhaṃ bhagavata eva śrutvā / tathā hi sabhāparvaṇi / paścād digvijayokteḥ* ... ; see also BhaviṣPV 25; SkaP 22.

16) BhāgTN (p. 774,1-2):
Subject matter: Viṣṇu, the supreme Creator of the universe

antaḥsthaḥ puruṣo nāma jñānadaḥ sarvadehinām /
bahistha īśvaro nāma jñānādiphalado hariḥ /
iti mātsye (1)

(1) Cf. ibid. (p. 773,11): *janyajñānasya prākṛtatvaṃ sādhayati – prakṛter guṇasāmye tv ityādinā* ... ; see also AgniP 12; BrahP 53; MESQUITA 2000: 489n. 638 and MESQUITA 2000_1: 171n. 348 [= 1997: 139n. 335].

17) BSūBh (p. 134,2-3):
Subject matter: Indivisibility of Viṣṇu's nature

ekarūpaḥ paro viṣṇuḥ sarvatrāpi na saṃśayaḥ /
aiśvaryād rūpam ekaṃ ca sūryavad bahudheyate /
iti hi mātsye (1)

(1) Cf. ibid. (p. 133,25): *sthānāpekṣayāpi paramātmano na bhinnaṃ rūpam / sarveṣu bhūteṣu etam eva brahmety ācakṣate* (AiU II 3,4) ... ; see also BrāṇP 10; 69 and MESQUITA 2000: 429ff.

18) BSūBh (p. 134,22-23):
Subject matter: Viṣṇu's supreme transcendence

bhautikāni hi rūpāṇi bhūtebhyo 'sau paro yataḥ /
arūpavān ataḥ proktaḥ kva tadavyaktataḥ pare /
iti ca mātsye (1)

(1) Cf. ibid. l. 21: *prakṛtyādipravartakatvena taduttamatvān naiva rūpavad brahma / hiśabdāt asthūlam anaṇu ityādiśruteś ca* (BĀU III 8,8); see also AgniP 6; BrāṇP 69 and MatsyaP 5.

19) BSūBh (p. 135,13-14):
Subject matter: Viṣṇu, the object of Meditation

> *śuddhasphaṭikasaṅkāśaṃ vāsudevaṃ nirañjanam /*
> *cintayīta yatir nānyaṃ jñānarūpād ṛte hareḥ /*
> iti ca mātsye (1)

(1) Cf. ibid. l. 11: *darśayati cānandasya rūpatvam – tad vijñānena paripaśyanti dhīrā ānandarūpam amṛtaṃ yad vibhātīti* ... (MuU II 2,7); see also AgniP 20; NārP 5.

20) GīBh (p. 134,6-7):
Subject matter: Prakṛti / Mahad Brahman

> *mahatī brahmaṇī dve tu prakṛtiś ca maheśvaraḥ*
> iti tatraiva (1)

(1) Cf. ibid. (p. 133,17f.): *mahad brahma prakṛtiḥ sā ca śrīrbhūrdurgeti bhinnā ... avāpa svecchayā dāsyaṃ jagatāṃ prapitāmahītyādy* ānabhiṃlātaśrutiḥ (unknown source) / matsyapurāṇoktam *api svecchayaiva / mahadbrahmaśabdavācyā prakṛtir eva*; see also AgniP 25 and MESQUITA 2000: 477f.

Nāradīyapurāṇa (NārP)

[It is stated in the Purāṇa literature that Nārada was the proclaimer of NārP with twenty-five thousand Ślokas (cf. SkaP VII 1,2,43; AgniP 272,8; MatsyaP 53,23):

> *yatrāha nārado dharmān bṛhatkalpāśrayāṇi ca /*
> *pañcaviṃśatsahasrāṇi nāradīyaṃ tad ucyate //*

NārP appears not only in the list of the Mahāpurāṇas but also in most lists of the Upapurāṇas. BṛhannāradīyaP is mentioned together with NārP, which led to a confusion that they were different titles for the same text. BṛhannāradīyaP is evidently an Upapurāṇa. For the other details see (HAZRA 1987: 127f. and ROCHER 1986: 202f.). It is interesting to note that Madhva quotes once from (cf. below) UpanāradīyaP (= BṛhannāradīyaP.?). Perhaps the prefix *upa-* in this connection refers to its character as Upapurāṇa. Most of the quotes are cited in BhāgTN (twenty-one times), followed by GīBh (nineteen times) and GīT (nine times); BĀUBh (four times); BSūBh (four times) and IśUBh, VTN, each one time. NārP 48 [2ab] contains a verse from BhāgP XI 18,3. There is only one metrical lapse, namely in NārP 34[3cd].]

1) BĀUBh (p. 244,16-18):
Subject matter: Presiding Deities

parvatāḥ sikatāś caiva nadyaḥ kūpāḥ sarāṃsi ca /
haviḥkapālayūpādyā devatā eva sarvaśaḥ /
tattannāmaiva nāmaiṣāṃ bhinnānām abhimānataḥ /
nāmāni tāny api hareḥ sa hi sarvaguṇādhikaḥ /
iti nāradīye (1)

(1) Cf. BhavisPV 11; BrāṇP 2; GarP 34.

2) BĀUBh (p. 274,28+275,18):
Subject matter: Brahmā, the creator / Presiding God Vāyu / Caste system

vivasvadindravaruṇaviṣṇubhyo 'nye 'diteḥ sutāḥ /
rudrād anye tathā rudrā vāyor anye ca vāyavaḥ / [1]
agner anye ca vasavo vaiśyā ity eva kīrtitāḥ /
eka eva harer jātaḥ parivāravivarjitaḥ / [2]
vāyvādīn kṣatriyān sṛṣṭvā punar alpaparigrahaḥ /
icchan bahuparīvāraṃ vaiśyān devān sasarja ha / [3]
tato bahutarān icchan śūdrān devān sasarja ca /
aśvinau pṛthivī caiva kālā mṛtyava eva ca / [4]
śūdradevāḥ samuddiṣṭā devavarṇā iti smṛtāḥ /
sraṣṭā svayaṃ samuddiṣṭaḥ pālakā devatā imāḥ / [5]
dhāraṇaṃ katham asya syād gatiś cāsya kathaṃ parā /
iti matvā harer bhaktidharmarūpaṃ punar vibhuḥ / [6]
prāṇināṃ dhairyarūpaṃ ca vāyo rūpāntaraṃ punaḥ /
sasarja matimān brahmā viṣṇor ājñāpuraḥsaraḥ / [7]
tasmād vāyoḥ paro nāsti ṛte viṣṇuṃ sanātanam /
śeṣādīnāṃ kṣatriyāṇāṃ vāyur evādhipaḥ smṛtaḥ / [8]
dhāraṇād dharma ityāhur vāyur dhārayati prajāḥ / (1)
abalo 'pi tato vāyor viṣṇubhaktyādirūpiṇaḥ / [9]
prāptum icchati yuktaḥ san viṣṇuṃ subalavattaram /
yathaiva yuvarājena mahārājam abhīpsati / [10]
prāptuṃ dharmābhimānī sa vāyuḥ satyābhimānavān /
tasmād āhur dharmavidaṃ satyavetteti vedinaḥ / [11]
satyajñam atha dharmajñaṃ vāyur devo yatas tayoḥ / [12ab]
iti nāradīye (2)

(1) Cf.BrahVP 38.
(2) Cf. BhaviṣP 11; BrāṇP 29; VāmP 2 and MESQUITA 2003: 102f..

3) BĀUBh (p. 322,12-22):
Subject matter: Viṣṇu, the supreme Creator of the universe

vijitya sarvān papraccha yājñavalkya punar munīn /
yathā vanaspatau vṛkṣaśabda evaṃ yathārthataḥ / [1]
puruṣe 'pi hi tac chabdo nityatvād eva yujyate /
tasmān nāsya śarīreṇa nāśas tasmāt punar janiḥ / [2]
ā mukter bhavitā nityaṃ kutas tad iti cocyatām /
retaso jananaṃ yāvat pralayas tāvad eva hi / [3]
nirmūlasya ca vṛkṣasya pralaye puruṣasya ca /
punar utpādako yas taṃ vadantu mama kṛtsnaśaḥ / [4]
dhānājāta ivāyaṃ hi dṛśyate 'viduṣāṃ taruḥ /
asvātantryāt tu viduṣāṃ naiva tat kāraṇaṃ bhavet / [5]
añjasā pretya saṃbhūtikāraṇaṃ tad vadantu naḥ /
pretya saṃbhūtikartā hi svatantro ghaṭate yataḥ / [6]
iti pṛṣṭās tu munayo na vaktuṃ śekur añjasā /
tadvettāro 'pi tatpraśnanirmūlanabalojjhitāḥ / [7]
adhārṣṭyān matprabhāvena dharṣitā nāśakan yadā /
svayam eva tadovāca yājñavalkyo mahāmuniḥ / [8]
pūrṇānando harir nānyaḥ kāraṇaṃ sṛjyasarjane /
naivāsya janakaḥ kaścin nityajāto hy asau hariḥ / [9]
sa priyaḥ sarvadātṝṇāṃ jñāninām paramapriyaḥ /
ye tu tadbhāvitā nityaṃ teṣām eṣa parāyaṇam / [10]
iti nāradīye (1)

(1) Cf. ibid. (321,26+322,11): ... *vijñānam ānandaṃ brahmeti / tasyāpy anya utpādaka ity āśaṅkā mā bhūd iti* (ibid. p. 322,1f.) *jāta eva na jāyata ity āha puruṣāntarāpekṣayā punaḥśabdaḥ / na tu kriyābhyāsāpekṣayā / eka eva harir bandhuḥ punar anyo na vidyata itivat / rātir iṣṭaḥ / tiṣṭhamānasya tadvidaḥ parāyaṇam* ... ; see also AgniP 12.

4) BĀUBh (p. 344,15-16):
Subject matter: Immortality of spiritual Beings

anyeṣām amṛtatvaṃ tu bhaved viṣṇoḥ prasādataḥ /
nityāmṛtaḥ sa bhagavān śrīś ca nānyaḥ kathaṃcana /
iti nāradīye (1)

(1) Cf. ibid. ll. 13f.: *ayaṃ jīvaḥ / atha muktyanantaram evāśarīro bhavati / amṛtaḥ kadāpi na mṛtaḥ / praṇākhyaṃ brahmaiva* (= BĀU III 9,9) *ityādiśruteḥ / teja eva ca / teja iti śrīḥ* ... ; see also AgniP 25; BrāṇP 51; 71; MESQUITA 2000: 417ff. and MESQUITA 2003: 98n. 7.

5) BhāgTN (p. 46,5-7):
Subject matter: Meditation

suvidyamānam api yo dhyāyetaiva suniścitaḥ /
ucyate tasya karteti yathaiva munayo 'malāḥ /

jagad vilāpayāmāsur ity ucyante 'tha tatsmṛteḥ /
na ca tatsmṛtimātreṇa layo bhavati niścitam /
iti nāradīye (1)

(1) Cf. ibid. l. 4: *kāle tasya tatra layo bhaviṣyatīti dhyānamātraṃ vilāpanam* ... ; see also AgniP 20; MatsyaP 19.

6) BhāgTN (p. 49,4-5):
Subject matter: Viṣṇu's supreme transcendence

atyuttamānāṃ kuśalapraśno lokasukhekṣayā /
nityadāptasukhatvāt tu na teṣāṃ yujyate kvacit /
iti hi nāradīye (1)

(1) Cf. ibid. l. 3: *yathānyeṣāṃ sukhaṃ bhaviṣyati tathā / nityasukhatvād dhareḥ* ... ; see also AgniP 6 and MESQUITA 2000: 109n. 172; 463f.

7) BhāgTN (p. 94,11-12):
Subject matter: Viṣṇu's supreme transcendence

avyaktam ātmano 'nnaṃ ca mahadādi vināśi ca /
yadatītaḥ paro viṣṇuḥ sa evāto vimokṣadaḥ /
iti nāradīye (1)

(1) Cf. AgniP 6.

8) BhāgTN (p. 127,11-12):
Subject matter: Nirodha-Yoga / Liberation

anupraviśya paramaṃ jīvasya śayanaṃ tu yat /
sahaiva śaktibhiḥ svīyair icchādyair aprakāśitaiḥ /
sa nirodha iti prokto vimuktir yatra mokṣiṇām /
iti nāradīye (1)

(1) Cf. AgniP 16; GarP 53; NārP 38; PadP 42; SkaP 41.

9) BhāgTN (p. 141,10-11):
Subject matter: Reversion of normal course of time / Bewilderment of evil beings (*moha*)

eṣyac ca niścitaṃ yat tad atītatvena bhaṇyate /
cakravat parivṛtter vā duṣṭānāṃ mohanāya ca /
iti nāradīye (1)

(1) Cf. BrahP 9_1; MBh 42n. 6.

10) BhāgTN (p. 168,1-2):
Subject matter: Viṣṇu, the supreme Creator of the universe

svasāmarthyāt sa karmāṇi ramayā saha keśavaḥ /
kurute svayam evaiṣa kānicit puruṣottamaḥ /
iti nāradīye (1)

(1) Cf. AgniP 12 and 25.

11) BhāgTN (p. 183,2-3):
Subject matter: Viṣṇu, the supreme Creator of the universe

sṛṣṭvā devādidehān sa ātmānaṃ bahudhākarot /
tanniyantṛtayātmānaṃ prakṛtiṃ dehabhedataḥ /
iti nāradīye (1)

(1) Cf. ibid. n. 2: *etena ātmānaṃ sṛjatīty asyārthatrayam uktaṃ bhavati / ātmānam ity ātmīyāṃ prakṛtiṃ sṛjati / bhūtalokadehādisṛṣṭyā bahubhāva eva hi prakṛtisargaḥ / tataś ca tatra ātmānaṃ jīvaṃ bahudhā suranaratiryagādirūpeṇa sṛjati / tatas tatra niyāmakatayā svātmānaṃ bahudhā karotīti*; see also AgniP 6; 12 and MESQUITA 2000: 476f.

12) BhāgTN (p. 209,10-11):
Subject matter: Brahmaśapa

jayasya vijayasyāpi kadācid brahmaśāpataḥ /
kṛṣṇāvatāraparyantaṃ prātikūlyaṃ ca jāyate /
iti nāradīye (1)

(1) Cf. BhāgP III 16,26 (= III 17,26); IX 15,1; see also BrāṇP 59; SkaP 59 and RUKMANI 1970: 159.

13) BhāgTN (p. 231,6):
Subject matter: Svayaṃbhuva Manu

gatasāraṃ yātayāmaṃ yāmaḥ sāra ihocyate /
iti nāradīye (1)

(1) Cf. BrāṇP 90.

14) BhāgTN (p. 265,1-2):
Subject matter: Yama's world / death

tribhir muhūrtair dvābhyāṃ vā dinair daśabhir eva vā /
pakṣān māsena vā yāti yamalokam ito mṛtaḥ /
iti nāradīye (1)

(1) Cf. PadP 97.

15) BhāgTN (p. 322,6-7):
Subject matter: Pṛthu

devebhya ṛṣayo bhūpāś cocyante śaktimattayā /
kvacit kvacit tanmohārthaṃ kādācitkāc ca hetutaḥ /
iti nāradīye (1)

(1) Cf. BrāṇP 44; GarP 26; KūrP 13; PadP 10; VāmP 22; see also BrāṇP 42.

16) BhāgTN (p. 396,1-3):
Subject matter: Bhakti / Kīrtana

sarvathāghaharaṃ viṣṇor nāma tadbhaktipūrvakam /
abhaktyodāhṛtaṃ naiva phaladātṛ bhaviṣyati /
nāmasvāmitayā tasya smaraṇaṃ jāyate yataḥ /
bhaktasyāto nāmakīrtiḥ saṅketādāv apīḍitā /
ajāmilo 'pi smaraṇād bhaktyā mṛtyor amucyata /
iti nāradīye (1)

(1) Cf. ibid. (p. 395,11): *nārāyaṇo 'yam ity anya[helana]viṣayatvenoktam aghaharam* ... ; see also AgniP 20.

17) BhāgTN (p. 419,6-7):
Subject matter: Manas / Internal organ

manaso dveṣarāgābhyāṃ puṇyapāpasamudbhavaḥ /
putrādi puṇyapāpabhyāṃ tasmāt sarvaṃ manobhavam /
iti nāradīye (1)

(1) Cf. BhaviṣPV 17.

18) BhāgTN (p. 423,3-4):
Subject matter: Antaryāmin

anyāntaryāmiṇaṃ viṣṇum upāsyānyasamīpagaḥ /
bhaved yogyatayā tasya padaṃ vā prāpnuyān naraḥ /
iti nāradīye (1)

(1) Cf. ibid. n. 2: *yadantaryāmitayā viṣṇur upāsyate upāsakas tatsamīpaṃ prāpnoti / yogyaś cet tatpadaṃ vā prāpnoti / yathā śeṣāntaryāmiṇaṃ viṣṇum upāsya citraketuḥ śeṣasamīpam āpa / rudras tu tathopāsya śeṣapadavīm evāpa*; see also BhāgP 2 and BrahP 36.

19) BhāgTN (p. 447,3-5):
Subject matter: Path of liberation

jānatām api kartavyaṃ karmātmasadṛśaṃ sadā /
tatrātmasadṛśājñānād rāgāc caiva vimohitāḥ /
jānanto 'pi hy asadṛśaṃ karma kuryur ṛte vibhum /
caturāsyaṃ sa nāyogyaṃ karma kuryāt kathaṃcana /
iti nāradīye (1)

(1) Cf. ibid. n. 3: *ātmasadṛsājñānāt idam ātmasadṛśam idaṃ neti vivicyājānantaḥ kecid asadṛśaṃ karma kuryuḥ / yathā śaṃbūko rudrapadam icchan tapas tepe / kecid idam ātmāsadṛśam iti jānanto 'pi rāgād dveṣāc ca vimohitāḥ kuryuḥ / yathā hiraṇyakaśipuḥ*; see also AgniP 9; BrāṇP 53.

20) BhāgTN (p. 502,4-7):
Subject matter: Intrinsic aptitude (*yogyatā*) of Deities

devāditvaṃ yogyatayā tatsakāśas tv anusmṛteḥ /
śvetadvīpādi tatrāpi yogyatām apy apekṣya tu /
viṣṇoḥ sthānaṃ vinānyatra vāyuśakrādinām api /
trailokye deśabhedeṣu yogyatā na tv apekṣitā /
iti nāradīye (1)

(1) Cf. AgniP 27; BhaviṣPV 15; BrahP 36 and MESQUITA 2000: 506ff.

21) BhāgTN (p. 508,3-4):
Subject matter: Viṣṇu's attributes

sadā sarvaguṇāḍhyatvāt sattvavān harir ucyate /
na tu sattvaguṇātmatvād yatas triguṇavarjitaḥ /
iti nāradīye (1)

(1) Cf. BrahVP 5; see also BrāṇP 69.

22) BhāgTN (p. 530,1):
Subject matter: Viṣṇu, the supreme Creator of the universe

viṣṇuḥ pradhānataḥ sraṣṭā guṇasraṣṭā caturmukhaḥ /
iti nāradīye (1)

(1) Cf. ibid (p. 529,12f.): *dhātur guṇavisarjanam / hiraṇyagarbhasakāśād guṇabhūtā sṛṣṭir asya jagataḥ / prādhānyena viṣṇor eva ...* ; see also AgniP 12.

23) BhāgTN (p. 554,9-10):
Subject matter: Śrī

abhramā bhramatām attrī yā vedair adhigamyate /

tasyai namo 'stu te devyai viṣṇuvakṣaḥsthalāśraye /
iti nāradīye (1)

(1) Cf. ibid. ll. 7f.: *bhramantaḥ ti* (*at-ti* ?) *annaṃ yasyāḥ sā bhramattī tasyāḥ bhramattyāḥ* / *viparītajñāninām bhakṣakāyā ity arthaḥ* / *śrutibhiḥ śrutipramāṇena* ... ; see also AgniP 25.

24) BhāgTN (p. 564,6-7):
Subject matter: Pralaya

layasya tv aṣṭamo bhāgaḥ sṛṣṭikāla udāhṛtaḥ /
tatraiva vedasañcāro hy anyadā stutimātrakāḥ /
iti nāradīye (1)

(1) Cf. ibid. n. 4: ... *avaśiṣṭe 'ṣṭamabhāge sārdhadvādaśavarṣātmake sṛṣṭyārambhaḥ* / *tasminn evāvasare brahmādidevānāṃ sṛṣṭeḥ* / *tatra tu devānāṃ vidhiniṣedhātmanāpi sañcāro vartate kathaṃcit* / *anyadāvaśiṣṭapralayakāle tu kevalaṃ stutimātrakāḥ* ... ; see also BrāṇP 29; 46; SkaP 101; VarP 7; VāyuP 11.

25) BhāgTN (p. 638,3-4):
Subject matter: Attributes of Kṛṣṇa

ātmano 'vamatāṃ brūyur uttamā api sarvaśaḥ /
kadācid eva svaguṇān snigdheṣv eva hi sādhavaḥ /
iti nāradīye (1)

(1) Cf. ibid. n. 2: ... *tasyāpīdaṃ vivaraṇam – sarvaśa uttamāḥ sarvottamāḥ kṛṣṇādyā api svātmano 'vamatāṃ kvacit prakaṭaṃ brūyur iti* ... ; see also BrāṇP 69.

26) BSūBh (p. 6,2-6):
Subject matter: Hierarchy among the means of the liberation

karmaṇā tv adhamaḥ proktaḥ prasādaḥ śravaṇādibhiḥ /
madhyamo jñānasampattyā prasādas tūttamo mataḥ /
prasādāt tv adhamād viṣṇoḥ svargalokaḥ prakīrtitaḥ /
madhyamāj janalokādir uttamas tv eva muktidaḥ /
śravaṇaṃ mananaṃ caiva dhyānaṃ bhaktis tathaiva ca /
sādhanaṃ jñānasampattau pradhānaṃ nānyad iṣyate /
na caitāni vinā kaścij jñānam āpa kutaścana /
iti nāradīye (1)

(1) Cf. AgniP 9; BhaviṣPV 15; MESQUITA 2000: 519f. and MESQUITA 2007: 24n. 44 [= 2007$_1$: 441n. 43f.].

27) BSūBh (p. 33,9-10):
Subject matter: Indivisibility (*abheda*) of Viṣṇu's nature

yad yasmāj jāyate cāṅgāl lokadevādikaṃ hareḥ /
tannāmavācyam aṅgaṃ tad yathā brahmādikaṃ mukham /
iti nāradīyavacanān nābhedoktivirodhaḥ (1)

(1) Cf. BrāṇP 10 and MESQUITA 2000: 429ff.

28) BSūBh (p. 51,25-26):
Subject matter: Antaryāmin / Prakṛti

avikāro 'pi paramaḥ prakṛtiṃ tu vikāriṇīm /
anupraviśya govindaḥ prakṛtiś cābhidhīyate /
iti nāradīye (1)

(1) Cf. ibid. ll. 22f.: *prakarṣeṇa karotīti prakṛtir iti yogāc ca / prakṛtāv anupraviśya tāṃ pariṇāmya tatpariṇāmeṣu stitvātmano bahudhākaraṇāt* ... ; see also AgniP 25; BhāgP 2 and MESQUITA 2000: 476f.

29) BSūBh (p. 122,11-12):
Subject matter: Transmigration

svargāl lokād avāk prāpto vatsarāt pūrvam eva tu /
mātuḥ śarīram āpnoti paryaṭan yatra tatra ca /
iti ca nāradīye (1)

(1) Cf. ibid. ll. 8f.: *bahusthānagamanāt kalpāntam apy evaṃ syād ity ata āha ... tad ya iha ramaṇīyacaraṇā abhyāśo ha yat te ramaṇīyāṃ yonim āpadyante / iti* (ChU V 10,7) *viśeṣān nāticireṇa* ... ; see also BrāṇP 33.

30) GīBh (p. 3,2-3):
Subject matter: Pañcamaveda

brahmādyaiḥ prārthito viṣṇur bhārataṃ sa cakāra ha / (1)
yasmin daśārthāḥ sarvatra na jñeyāḥ sarvajantubhiḥ /
iti nāradīye (2)

(1) Cf. GīBh p. 1,1f.
(2) Cf. BhāgP II 10,1-2 (?):
atra sargo visargaś ca sthānaṃ poṣaṇam ūtayaḥ /
manvantareśānukathā nirodho muktir āśrayaḥ //
daśamasya viśudhyarthaṃ navānām iha lakṣaṇam /
varṇayanti mahātmānaḥ śrutenārthena cāñjasā //
see also BhaviṣP 10; SkaP 108 and MESQUITA 2000_1: 125ff.; 143ff. [= 1997: 101ff.; 115ff.].

31) GīBh (p. 19,1-4):
Subject matter: Viṣṇu's supreme transcendence

satyaṃ satyaṃ punaḥ satyaṃ śapathaiś cāpi koṭibhiḥ /
viṣṇumāhātmyaleśasya vibhaktasya ca koṭidhā /
punaś cānantadhā tasya punaś cāpi hy anantadhā /
naikāṃśasamamāhātmyāḥ śrīśeṣabrahmaśaṅkarāḥ /
iti nāradīye (1)

(1) Cf. AgniP 6; PadP 3 and MESQUITA 2000: 166n. 341; see also HOFSTÄTTER 2000: 228f.

32) GīBh (p. 29,5-6):
Subject matter: Difference between Jīvas and Viṣṇu

naiva tat prāpnuvanty ete brahmeśānādayaḥ surāḥ /
yat te padaṃ hi kaivalyam iti niṣedhāc ca nāradīye (1)

(1) Cf. AgniP 22.

33) GīBh (p. 35,13):
Subject matter: Transmigration / liberation

mahādeva pare janmaṃs tava muktir nirūpyate /
iti nāradīye (1)

(1) Cf. BrāṇP 33.

34) GīBh (p. 35,24-36,2):
Subject matter: Durāgamas / Sadāgamas

kutsitāni ca miśrāṇi rudro viṣṇupracoditaḥ /
cakāra śāstrāṇi vibhur ṛṣayas tatpracoditāḥ /
dadhīcyādyāḥ purāṇāni tacchāstrasamayena tu /
cakrur vedais tu brāhmāṇi vaiṣṇavān viṣṇuvedataḥ /
pañcarātraṃ bhārataṃ ca mūlarāmāyaṇaṃ tathā /
tathā purāṇaṃ bhāgavataṃ viṣṇuveda itīritaḥ /+1
ataḥ śaivapurāṇāni yojyāny anyāvirodhataḥ /
iti ca nāradīye (1)

(1) Cf. ibid. ll. 20f.: *yatra tu stutis tatra śivabhaktānāṃ stutiparatvam eva satyatvam / na hi teṣām apītaragranthaviruddhārthe prāmāṇyaṃ tathā hy uktam –*
eṣa mohaṃ sṛjāmy āśu yo janān mohayiṣyati /
tvaṃ ca rudra mahābāho mohaśāstrāṇi kāraya /
atatthyāni vitatthyāni darśayasva mahābhuja /
prakāśaṃ kuru cātmanam aprakāśaṃ ca māṃ kuru /
iti vārāhe = VarP 70,35-38.
= MBhTN I 48-50ab: ... iti vārāhavacanaṃ bramāṇḍoktam; see also BrāṇP 11 and MESQUITA 2000_1: 153f.; 165 [= 1997: 123f.; 133].

35) GīBh (p. 37,17-18):
Subject matter: Avatāras

kṛṣṇarāmādirūpāṇi paripūrṇāni sarvadā /
na cāṇumātraṃ bhinnāni tathāpy asmān vimohasi /
ityādeś ca nāradīye (1)

(1) Cf. ibid. ll. 16f.: *na cātra kiṃcid upacāratādi vācyam / acintyaśakteḥ padārtha-vaicitryāc cety uktam ... tasmād sarvadā sarvarūpeṣv aparigaṇitānantaguṇagaṇaṃ nityanirastāśeṣadoṣaṃ ca nārāyaṇākhyaṃ paraṃ brahmāparokṣajñānyṛcchatīti siddham*; see also ĀdiP 1 and MESQUITA 2000_1: 35ff. [= 1997: 29ff.].

36) GīBh (p. 44,5-7):
Subject matter: Beatific vision of Viṣṇu / Path of liberation

yathāha bhagavān –
yāni tīrthādivākyāni karmādiviṣayāṇi ca /
stāvakāny eva tāni syur ajñānāṃ mohakāni vā /
bhaven mokṣas tu maddṛṣṭer nānyatas tu kathaṃcana /
iti nāradīye (1)

(1) Cf. ibid. p. 43,23f.: ... *stutiparatā ca ... na ca tīrthastutivākyāni tatprastāve 'py uktaṃ jñānaniyamaṃ ghnanti / yathā kañcid dakṣaṃ bhṛtyaṃ pratyuktāny ayam eva hi rājā kiṃ rājñetyādīni ... ato 'parokṣajñānād eva mokṣaḥ / karma tu tatsādhanam eva*; BĀUBh (p. 267,3-7):
tulāpuruṣadānādyair aśvamedhādibhir makhaiḥ /
vārāṇasīprayāgāditīrthasnānādibhiḥ priye /
gayāśrāddhādibhiḥ pitryair vedapāṭhādibhir japaiḥ /
tapobhir ugrair niyamair yamair bhūtadayādibhiḥ /
guruśuṣruṣaṇaiḥ satyair dharmair varṇāśramoditaiḥ /
jñānadhyānādibhiḥ samyak caritair janmajanmani /
na yānti tat paraṃ śreyo viṣṇuṃ sarveśvareśvaram /
sarvabhāvair anāśritya purāṇapuruṣottamam /
iti pādme [= PadP Uttarakhaṇḍa 71,94-97];
see also AgniP 20; 24 and MESQUITA 2007: 21ff. [= 2007_1 441ff.].

36_1) GīBh (p. 58,10-13):
Subject matter: Saṃnyāsa

saṃnyāsas tu turīyo yo niṣkriyākhyaḥ sadharmakaḥ /
na tasmād uttamo dharmo loke kaścana vidyate /
tadbhakto 'pi hi yad gacchet tadgṛhastho na dhārmikaḥ /
madbhaktiś ca viraktis tadadhikāro nigadyate /
yadādhikāro bhavati brahmacāry api pravrajet /
iti nāradīye (1)

(1) Cf. ibid. ll. 8f.: *nāyaṃ saṃnyāso yatyāśramaḥ / dvandvatyāgāt tu saṃnyāsāt matpujaiva garīyasīti vacanāt* ... ; GīT (p. 59,23-28): ... *etasmān nyāsināṃ lokaṃ saṃyānti gṛhiṇo 'pi hi* ... iti vyāsasmṛteḥ (untraceable source-quotation); GīBh (p. 58,13-14): *brahmacaryād eva pravrajet / yad ahar eva virajed* iti ca (unknown source); see also AgniP 9; 21 and MESQUITA 2003_1: 206ff.

37) GīBh (p. 63,12-14):
Subject matter: Happiness / bliss

darśanasparśasaṃbhāṣād yat sukhaṃ jāyate nṛṇām /
ārāmaḥ sa tu vijñeyaḥ sukhaṃ kāmakṣayoditam /
iti nāradīye (1)

(1) Cf. ibid. ll. 9ff.: *ārāmaḥ paradarśanādinimittaṃ sukham / atra tu paramātmadarśanādinimittaṃ tat / sukhaṃ tūpadravakṣayavyaktam / atra kāmādikṣayavyaktam ātmasukham* ... *asaṃprajñātasamādhīnāṃ bāhyādarśanāt / darśane 'py akiṃcitkārād eva śabdaḥ / uktaṃ caitat* ... ; see also BhavișP 15.

38) GīBh (p. 68,14-15):
Subject matter: Meditation

nidrāśanabhayaśvāsaceṣṭātandryādivarjanam /
kṛtvā nimīlitākṣas tu śakto dhyāyan prasiddhyati /
iti nāradīye (1)

(1) Cf. ibid. l. 13: *anaśanādiniṣedho 'śaktasya / uktam hi* ... ; see also AgniP 9; 20; MatsyaP 19; NārP 5; 8.

39) GīBh (p. 72,5-6):
Subject matter: Beatific vision of Viṣṇu

atīva śraddhayā yukto jijñāsur viṣṇutatparaḥ /
jñātvā dhyātvātha dṛṣṭvā ca janmabhir bahubhiḥ pumān /
viśen nārāyaṇaṃ devaṃ nānyathā tu kathaṃcana /
iti nāradīye (1)

(1) Cf. ibid. ll. 3f.: *jijñāsur jñātvā prayatnaṃ karoti / evam anekajanmabhiḥ saṃsiddho 'parokṣajñānī bhūtvā parāṃ gatiṃ yāti / āha ca* ... ; see also AgniP 24 and MESQUITA 2007: 35n. 76 [= 2007_1: 448n. 75].

40) GīBh (p. 72,14-16):
Subject matter: Meditation / Beatific vision of Viṣṇu

ajñātvā dhyāyino dhyānāt jñānam eva viśiṣyate /
jñātvā dhyānaṃ jñānamātrād dhyānād api tu darśanam /

darśanāc caiva bhakteś ca na kiṃcit sādhanādhikam /
iti nāradīye (1)

(1) Cf. AgniP 24; NārP 38; 39.

41) GīBh (p. 74,4-9):
Subject matter: Śrī, conscious and unconscious Prakṛtis

prakṛtī dve tu devasya jaḍā caivājaḍā tathā /
avyaktākhyā jaḍā sā ca sṛṣṭyā bhinnāṣṭadhā punaḥ /
mahān buddhir manaś caiva pañcabhūtāni ceti ha /
aparā sā jaḍā śrīś ca pareyaṃ dhāryate tayā /
cidrūpā sā tv anantā ca anādinidhanā parā /
yatsamaṃ tu priyaṃ kiṃcin nāsti viṣṇor mahātmanaḥ /
nārāyaṇasya mahiṣī mātā sā brahmaṇo 'pi hi /
ābhyām idaṃ jagat sarvaṃ hariḥ sṛjati bhūtarāṭ /
iti nāradīye (1)

(1) Cf. ibid. l. 3: *aparā anuttamā vakṣyamāṇām apekṣya / jīvabhūtā śrīḥ / jīvānāṃ prāṇadhāriṇī cidrūpabhūtā sarvadā satī* ... ; see also AgniP 25; BrāṇP 51; MESQUITA 2000: 104f. nn. 163-165; 470ff. and HOFSTÄTTER 2000: 184f.

42) GīBh (p. 74,13-16):
Subject matter: Viṣṇu's supreme transcendence

sraṣṭā pātā ca saṃhartā niyantā ca prakāśitā /
yataḥ sarvasya tenāhaṃ sarvo 'sīty ṛṣibhiḥ stutaḥ /
sukharūpasya bhoktṛtvān na tu sarvasvarūpataḥ /
āgamiṣyat sukhaṃ cāpi tasyāsty eva sadāpi tu /
tathāpy acintyaśaktitvāj jātaṃ sukham atīva ca /
iti nāradīye (1)

(1) Cf. ibid. ll. 10f.: *prabhavādeḥ sattāpratītyādikāraṇatvāt tadbhoktṛtvāc ca prabhava ityādi / tathā śrutiḥ – sarvakāmaḥ sarvakarmā sarvagandhaḥ sarvarasaḥ sarvam idam abhyātto 'vākyanādara iti* / (ChU III 14,4) *āha ca* ... ; see also AgniP 12; BhāgP 2; BhaviṣP 13; BrāṇP 2; MBh 2; MatsyaP 12 and MESQUITA 2000: 141n. 274; 162ff.; 456n. 567.

43) GīBh (p. 77,12-14):
Subject matter: Viṣṇu's worship

āha ca nāradīye –
matsaṃpattyā tu gurvādīn bhajante madhyamā narāḥ /
madupādhitayā tāṃś ca sarvabhūtāni cottamāḥ /
iti (1)

(1) Cf. ibid. ll. 10f.: *anyat sarvaṃ parityajya mām eva ye prapadyante / gurvādivandanaṃ ca mayy eva samarpayanti / sa eva ca tatra sthitvā gurvādir bhavatītyādi paśyanti / āha ca* ... ; see also AgniP 20; SkaP 54.

44) GīBh (p. 77,23-24):
Subject matter: Deities / Demons

taccoktam nāradīye –
jñānapradhānā devās tu asurās tu ratā asau /
iti (1)

(1) Cf. ibid. l. 23: *asuṣu ratā asurāḥ / tac coktam* ... ; see also BhaviṣPV 12; BhaviṣP 5 and MESQUITA 2000: 527f.

45) GīBh (p. 78,15-16):
Subject matter: Liberation

uktaṃ ca nāradīye –
anto brahmādibhaktānāṃ madbhaktānām anantatā /
iti (1)

(1) Cf. ibid. l. 15: *yāṃ yāṃ brahmādirūpāṃ tanum / uktaṃ ca* ... ; see also AgniP 16.

46) GīBh (p. 84,26-27):
Subject matter: Viṣṇu, the supreme abode

gīyase padam ity eva munibhiḥ padyase yataḥ /
iti ca nāradīye (1)

(1) Cf. ibid. ll. 24f.: *prāpyate mumukṣubhir ity padaṃ svarūpam / 'padaḷ gatau' iti dhātoḥ / tad viṣṇoḥ paraṃ padam* iti śruteś *ca* /(KathU II 9) ... ; see also AgniP 27.

47) GīBh (p. 87,7-8):
Subject matter: Liberation / Kramamukti

tathāhi nāradīye –
agniṃ prāpya tataś cārcis tataś cāpy aharādikam /
iti (1)

(1) Cf. ibid. ll. 7f.: *jyotir arciḥ / te 'rciṣam abhisaṃbhavantīti hi* śrutiḥ (BĀU VI 2,15) ... *abhimānidevatāś cāgnyādayaḥ* ... ; see also AgniP 16; BhaviṣP 11 and BrahP 82.

48) GīT (p. 23,24-28):
Subject matter: Sadāgamas / Brahmatarka

brahmatarkas tarkaśāstraṃ viṣṇunā yat samīritam /
akṣapādakaṇādau ca sāṅkyayogau ca haitukāḥ /

bauddhapāśupatādyās tu pāṣaṇḍā iti kīrtitāḥ /
mīmāṃsā trividhā proktā brāhmī daivī ca kārmikī /
brahmatarkaṃ ca mīmāṃsāṃ seveta jñānasiddhaye /
vaidikajñānavairūpyān nānyat seveta paṇḍitaḥ /
ity anyasāṅkhyayogayor niṣiddhatvān nāradīye | (1)

(2) Cf. ibid. l. 23: *samyak khyātir jñānaṃ sāṅkhyam / yujyate 'neneti yogas tadupāyaḥ – samyak tattvadṛśiḥ sāṅkhyaṃ yogas tatsādhānaṃ smṛtam /* iti śabdanirṇaye (unknown source) and 2000_1: 91f. [= 1997: 72f.]; see also BrāṇP 11; PadP 2.

49) GīT (p. 25,24-31):
Subject matter: Heaven and hell

ye na jānanti taṃ viṣṇuṃ yāthārthyena sasaṃśayāḥ /
jijñāsavaś ca nitarāṃ śraddhāvantaḥ susādhavaḥ / [1]
nirṇetṝṇām abhāvena kevalaṃ jñānavarjitāḥ
te yājñikāḥ svargabhogakṣaye yānti manuṣyatām / [2]
yair niścitaṃ paratvaṃ tu viṣṇoḥ prāyo na yātanām /
brahmahatyādibhir api yānty ādhikye ciraṃ na tu / [3]
viśeṣa eṣa teṣāṃ tu tadanyeṣāṃ viparyayaḥ /
ye tu bhāgavatācāryaiḥ samyag yajñādi kurvate / [4]
bahirmukhā bhagavato 'nivṛttāś ca vikarmaṇaḥ /
dakṣiṇātarpitānāṃ tu ācāryāṇāṃ tu tejasā / [5]
yānti svargaṃ tataḥ kṣipraṃ tamo 'ndhaṃ prāpnuvanti ca /
tadanye naiva ca svargaṃ yānti viṣṇubahirmukhāḥ / [6]
iti nāradīye (1)

(1) Cf. ibid. ll. 15f.: *avyavasāyabuddhiḥ keṣām / yāṃ vācam avipaścitaḥ pravadanti tayāpahṛtacetasāṃ buddhir vyavasāyātmakatvena samādhāne na vartate ...* (MuU I 2,10; BhāgP XI 18,30) ... ; see also AgniP 27 and BhaviṣPV 19.

50) GīT (p. 28,27-31):
Subject matter: Punishment of sinful souls

ajñānāṃ jñāninām caiva muktānāṃ śaraṇaṃ hariḥ /
taṃ ye svaikyena manyante sarvabhinnaṃ guṇocchrayāt /
kṛpaṇās te tamasy andhe nipatanti na saṃśayaḥ /
na teṣām utthitiḥ kvāpi nityātiśayaduḥkhinām /
guṇabhedavidāṃ viṣṇor bhedābhedavidām api /
dehakarmādiṣu tathā prādurbhāvādike 'pi vā /
svodriktānāṃ tadīyānāṃ nindāṃ kurvanti ye 'pi ca /
sarveṣām api caiteṣāṃ gatir eṣā na saṃśayaḥ /
iti nāradīye (1)

(1) Cf. ibid. l. 26: *buddhau jātāyām api viṣṇum eva śaraṇam anviccha* ... ; see also BhavişPV 3n. 7; 12 and 19.

51) GīT (p. 41,22-29):
Subject matter: Āśrama-duties

jananāt parasasyādeḥ parjanyo meghasantatiḥ /
sa yajñāt karmaṇaḥ so 'pi samastaṃ karma keśavāt / [1]
sa nityo 'py akṣaratatirūpād vākyād dhi gamyate /
vākyam uccāryate bhūtais tāny annāt tac ca meghataḥ / [2]
tasmāt sarvagato viṣṇur nityaṃ yajñe pratiṣṭhitaḥ /
evaṃ pravartitaṃ cakraṃ nānuvartayatīha yaḥ / [3]
sa pāpo viśvahantṛtvān narake majjati dhruvam /
vāciko mānaso yajño nyāsināṃ tu viśeṣataḥ / [4]
vanasthasyākratur yajñaḥ kratvādir gṛhiṇo 'khilaḥ /
śuśrūṣādyātmako yajño vihito brahmacāriṇaḥ / [5]
vidyābhayādidānaṃ ca sarveṣām api saṃmatam /
gṛhiṇo vittadānaṃ ca vanasthasyānnapūrvakam / [6]
sarvaiḥ kāryaṃ tapo ghoram iti sarve trikarmiṇaḥ / [7ab]
iti nāradīye (1)

(1) Cf. ibid. ll. 21f.:
jño nāma bhagavān viṣṇus taṃ yāty uddeśa eṣa yaḥ /
sa yajña iti saṃprokto vihite karmaṇi sthitaḥ /
iti barkusruti (unknown source);
see also AgniP 9 and 20.

52) GīT (p. 53,25-27):
Subject matter: Intrinsic aptitudes (*yogyatā*) of the individual souls

svabhāviko brāhmaṇādiḥ śamādyair eva bhidyate /
yonibhedakṛto bhedo jñeya aupādhikas tv ayam /
viṣṇubhaktis tv anugatā sarvavarṇeṣu viśpatim /
ārabhya hīyate athāpi bhedaḥ svābhāvikas tataḥ /
iti nāradīye (1)

(1) Cf. ibid. (p. 52,29+53,24-25):
sattvasattvādhikarajorajobhis tamasā tathā /
varṇā vibhaktāś catvāraḥ sāttvikā eva vaiṣṇavāḥ /
iti ca (unknown source) ...
vaiṣṇavāḥ sāttvikā eva tāmasā eva cāpare /
daurlabhyasulabhatvena teṣāṃ varṇādibhinnatā /
iti ca (unknown source);
see also BrahP 36; SkaP 54 and MESQUITA 2000: 506ff.

53) GīT (p. 54,23-24):
Subject matter: Jīva's essential nature

karo 'smin mīyata iti karma jīva udāhṛtaḥ /
vidhiśabdenāmitatvād akarmā bhagavān hariḥ /
iti nāradīye (1)

(1) Cf. ibid. ll. 25f.: *kara iti sakārānto 'dṛṣṭavācī / kriyāvācī vā / tadadhīnatvāt / prasiddhaś ca jīve karmaśabdaḥ pañcarātre / kṛtsnaphalavatvāt kṛtsnakarmakṛt / anirāśrayo bhagavadāśrayatvāt / muktasya svāntryābhimānāt ... samādhir api tadadhīnety arthaḥ / ekaḥ svatantro bhagavāṃs tadīyaṃ tv anyad ucyate /* iti bhārate (= MBh 38). For the doctrine of Vidhi (= *kārya*) cf. NārP 58 and BrāṇP 71.

54) GīT (p. 64,22-23):
Subject matter: Liberation

amukto muktasādṛśyān mukta eva hi tattvadṛk /
kimu muktigatas tasmāj jñānam evādhikaṃ nare /
iti nāradīye (1)

(1) Cf. AgniP 16; 24.

55) GīT (p. 67,32-34):
Subject matter: Hierarchy among the human beings

animittasnehavāṃs tu suhṛj jñātvopakārakṛt /
mitraṃ vadhādikṛd arir dveṣyas tv apriyamātrakṛt /
udāsīnaḥ snehavato 'py asnehī tatkṛtānukṛt /
madhyastha iti vijñeyaḥ suhṛdeṣu viśiṣyate /
iti nāradīye (1)

(1) Cf. ibid. ll. 18f.: *pratyupakāranirapekṣyopakārakṛt suhṛt / kleśasthānaṃ nirūpya yo rakṣāṃ karoti* (*vidadhāti*) *samitram / arir vadhādikartā / kartavya upakāre 'pakāre ca ya udāste sa udāsīnaḥ / kartavyam ubhayam api yaḥ karoti sa madhyasthaḥ / avāsitakṛd dveṣyaḥ / āha caitat ...* ; see also BhaviṣPV 15; MBh 1.

56) GīT (p. 118,23-24):
Subject matter: Incomprehensibility of Viṣṇu and Srī

sūkṣmatvād aprasiddhatvād guṇabāhulyatas tathā /
anirdeśyau tathāvyaktāv acintyau śrīś ca mādhavaḥ /
iti nāradīye (1)

(1) Cf. AgniP 25 and BrāṇP 51.

57) IśUBh (p. 509,21-22):
Subject matter: Worship of Kṛṣṇa

ajñasya karma lipyeta kṛṣṇopāstim akurvataḥ /
jñānino 'pi yato hrāsa ānandasya bhaved dhruvam /
ato 'lepe 'pi lepaḥ syād ataḥ kāryaiva sā sadā /
iti nāradīye (1)

(1) Cf. ibid. l. 20: *akurvataḥ karma na lipyata iti nāsti* ... ; see also AgniP 20.

58) VTN (p. 15,20-23):
Subject matter: Veda, the only *pramāṇa* for Viṣṇu

uktaṃ ca nāradīye –
sarvajñaṃ sarvakartāraṃ nārāyaṇam anāmayam /
sarvottamaṃ jñāpayanti mahātātparyam atra hi /
sarveṣām api vedānām itihāsapurāṇayoḥ /
pramāṇanāṃ ca sarveṣāṃ tadarthaṃ cānyad ucyate /
iti (1)

(1) Cf. ibid. ll. 19f.: *prasiddhaṃ ca vyākaraṇaniruktādīnāṃ siddhamātre prāmāṇyaṃ sarvavādinām / tadanaṅgīkāre ca sarvaśābdavyavahārāsiddhiḥ* ... see also BrāṇP 11; 82; KūrP 20; PadP 3 and MESQUITA 2000: 75-78; 378ff.

Narasiṃhapurāṇa (NarsiṃP)

[This Purāṇa, the date of which is a matter of dispute among scholars – some dating it in the latter half of the fifth century, others in the ninth century, and still others in the middle of the thirteenth century (cf. ROCHER 1986: 205f.), is quoted by Madhva only twice. The quote in AiUBh (p. 177,21-23 = 67,17; see also PadP 1) is traceable.]

1) BĀUBh (p. 267,8):
Subject matter: Bhakti

bhāvo bhaktiḥ samuddiṣṭas tadvān bhāvuka ucyate /
iti nārasiṃhe (1)

(1) Cf. ibid. ll. 8f.: ... *srībhāgavatavacanaṃ ca* (= BhāgP VI 14,5) *parāyaṇa iti viśeṣaṇān na nārāyaṇāyanatvaṃ vinā muktidyotakam*; see also AgniP 20.

Padmapurāṇa (PadP)

[Some of the traceable quotes deviate slightly from the traditional wording, e.g. BĀUBh (p. 267,3-7) = PadP [Uttarakhaṇḍa] 71,94-97; cf. above NārP 36n. 1; BĀUBh (p. 276,29+278,11) = ibid. (71,101-104); MBhTN (I 53-55 = ibid. 71,114-116);

MBhTN (I 57-58 = ibid. 71,106-107). In one case there is only a general reference to PadP without a precise quotation (MBhTN XXII 423: uktaṃ pādmapurāṇe ca *tad etat sarvam añjasā / tasmān nāśaktir anayoḥ saṃbhāvyā bhīmapārthayoḥ //*). In GīBh (p. 19,19) it is referred to as a Śaiva Purāṇa: pādme śaive mārkaṇḍeyakathāprabandhe ... (cf. above MārkP 1, see also MBhTN (I 56ab): *uktaṃ pādmapurāṇe ca śaiva eva śivena tu* (cf. MESQUITA 2000: 156f. [= 1997: 126f.]). According to HAZRA (1987: 126), the Uttarakhaṇḍa is not a homogeneous work, since it contains additions and modifications belonging to a very recent date. He remarks in this connection: "The appearance of some of its parts in independent Mss shows that these parts did not originally belong to the Khaṇḍa. Further, in the marginal notes in a Ms of the Yathārthamañjarī ... it is written that according to a Purāṇācārya named Narasiṃha Ṭhakkura, Madhvācārya wrote three hundred verses on the denouncement of the ashes and the Rudrākṣas and added them to the Uttarakhaṇḍa ... Though the absence of such verses subjects the above information to doubts, there is a chapter (263) which seems to have been interpolated by some person belonging to the Śrī or Mādhva sect. In this chapter the Pāṣandins, including especially the Śiva-worshippers, have been described and the Māyāvāda (of Śaṅkarācārya) has been described as Pracchanna Bauddha ..."; see also Madhva's fictitious quotes attributed to NarP 48 and PadP 2 ... *bauddhapāśupatādyās tu pāṣaṇḍā iti kirtitāḥ* ... ; ... *śivaśaktimahāyānalokāyatapurasarāḥ / gāṇapatyās ca saurās ca sarve proktā durāgamāḥ* ... ; (cf. also MESQUITA 2000: 115n. 214 [= 1997: 92n. 204] and MESQUITA 2000: 528). Madhva attributes to PadP approximately one hundert and ten quotes, some of which refer also to the teaching of heretics. The lion's share has the BhāgTN, with fifty quotes, followed by BSūBh with twenty quotes; BĀUBh with seven; ChUBh with three, GīBh with seven; GīT thirteen, AiUBh and KhN with two quotes each, and KathUBh, MāṇUBh, MuUBh, ṚgBh, TaiUBh, VTN one each. PadP 2 and 41 have metrical lapses.]

1) AiUBh (p. 177,23-24):
Subject matter: Viṣṇu's Śakti

tāpanī pācikā caiva śeṣaṇī ca prakāśanī /
naiva rājan raveḥ śaktiḥ śaktir nārāyaṇasya sā /
iti ca pādme (1)

(1) Cf. ibid. ll. 8f.: *ya eṣa sūryamaṇḍale sthitvā tapati sa bhagavān nārāyaṇaḥ* ... ; see also a quote from NarsiṃP 67, 17 in AiUBh (p. 177,21-23) and BhaviṣP 13.

1_1) AiUBh (p. 214,3-4):
Subject matter: Viṣṇu's Sarvanāmatva

ātmabrahmādayaḥ śabdās tam ṛte viṣṇum avyayam /
na vartante tadanyatra śṛṅgibere 'gniśabdavat /
iti pādme (1)

(1) Cf. ibid. (p. 213,27f.): *nāmāni sarvāṇi yam āviśanti taṃ vai viṣṇuṃ paramam udāharanti* ... *indrasūryādayaḥ śabdā viṣṇāv eva hi mukhyataḥ / upacārāt tadanyeṣāṃ viṣṇunaiva kṛtāḥ puretyādinā tasyaiva sarvanāmavattvāc ca* ... ; see also BhāgP 1; BrahVP 19; 23; BrāṇP 2.

2) BĀUBh (p. 268,11-13):
Subject matter: Sadāgamas / Durāgamas

akṣapādakaṇādau ca sāṅkhyayogārhatās tathā /
śivaśaktimahāyānalokāyatapuraḥsarāḥ /
gāṇapatyās ca saurāś ca sarve proktā durāgamāḥ /
ṛgyajuḥsāmātharvāś cetihāsapurāṇakau /
svāgamā iti samproktā mīmāṃsā dharma eva ca /
iti pādme (1)

(1) Cf. ibid. l. 10: *na ca vedātmaketihāsapurāṇoktanyāyaṃ parityajya yena kenacit kḷptanyāyo yujyate* ... ; see also BrāṇP 11; NārP 48 and MESQUITA 2000_1: 156n. 325 [= 1997: 126n. 314].

3) BĀUBh (p. 268,18-19):
Subject matter: Viṣṇu's supreme transcendence

viṣṇoḥ sarvottamatvaṃ ca tadbhaktyā mokṣa eva ca /
śāstrārtha iti nirdiṣṭaḥ sarvaśāstrārthanirṇayāt /
iti pādme (1)

(1) Cf. BrāṇP 11; 82; NārP 31; 58; see also AgniP 6.

3_1) BĀUBh (p. 276,29+277,11):
Subject matter: Worship of Viṣṇu

kiṃtu brahmādibhir devaiḥ purā dṛṣṭvā niraṃhasaḥ /
nirbhayān viṣṇunāmnaiva yatheṣṭaṃ padam āgatān /
alabdhvā cātmanaḥ pūjāṃ samyagārādhito hariḥ /
mayā cāsmād api śraiṣṭhyaṃ vāñchatāhaṅkṛtātmanā /
tataḥ sākṣāj jagannāthaḥ prasanno bhaktavatsalaḥ /
aṃśāṃśenātmanaivaitān pūjayāmāsa keśavaḥ /
devān pitṝn dvijān havyakavyādyaiḥ karuṇāmayaḥ /
tataḥ prabhṛti pūjyante trailokye sacarācare /
iti ca pādme (1)

(1) Cf. AgniP 6; BhaviṣPV 4.

4) BĀUBh (p. 312,26-27):
Subject matter: Arjuna's arrow

karmāras tu tadā bāṇaṃ tīkṣṇam añjalikābhidham /
sandhadhānaḥ śare yāntaṃ rājānaṃ na dadarśa ha /
iti pādme (1)

(1) Cf. ibid. l. 26: *bāṇas tv ayomayaḥ proktaḥ śaro nālo 'sya kīrtita* ity abhidhānam (unknown source).

5) BĀUBh (p. 327,15):
Subject matter: Vṛndāraka

> *vṛndaiḥ prāpyatamatvāt tu vṛndāraka iti smṛtaḥ* /
> iti pādme (1)

(1) Cf. ibid. (p. 326,26f.): ... *svayogyajñānaṃ śrotuṃ siṃhāsanād avaruhyopasadanaṃ kṛtvovāca / yat svātmanā prāpyaṃ muktau tadupāsyaiva muktir bhavatīty ataḥ prāpyaṃ pṛcchati* ... .

6) BĀUBh (p. 327,26-27):
Subject matter: Viṣṇu's supreme transcendence

> *jīvabhogasya bhokteśo jīvas tadbhogabhuṅ na tu* /
> *viviktabhug ivāto 'sau bhagavān puruṣottamaḥ* /
> iti pādme (1)

(1) Cf. ibid. ll. 24f.: *tvatprasādād yadabhayam asmākaṃ prāptaṃ tad eva tava tṛptaye 'stu / nānyad vayaṃ praty upakartuṃ śaknuma ity arthaḥ sa bhagavān svakṛtena tuṣyed itivat / indho dīptaḥ* ... ; see also AgniP 6; 12; BhavişPV 8; SkaP 14; VāmP 5.

7) BĀUBh (p. 338,8-10):
Subject matter: The age of human beings

> *āmraṃ vālye 'pi patati pariṇāme hy uduṃbaram* /
> *samyak pāke tathāśvatthaphalaṃ jīvabhṛtis tathā* /
> *kalāv āmropamā jīvās tretāsv auduṃbaropamāḥ* /
> *kṛte 'śvatthasamāś caiva yānti brahmavaśāḥ sadā* /
> iti pādme

8) BhāgTN (p. 6,9-11):
Subject matter: Puruṣārtha

> pādme ca –
> *ākhyāyikāḥ pradṛśyante vedeṣv api hi sarvaśaḥ* /
> *dyotayantyas tu mahatāṃ tātparyaṃ tatra tatra ha* /
> *alābhaḥ puruṣārthasya proktam artham ṛte tv iti* /
> *dyotanāya mahārāja śraddhāvṛddhyartham eva ca* /
> iti (1)

(1) Cf. ibid. l. 8 : *prakārāntareṇāpi puruṣārthāśaṅkhānivṛttyartham ākhyāyikā* ... ; see also BhaviṣPV 21; GarP 9; MBh 46; 48; MESQUITA 2000: 107f. and MESQUITA 2000_1: 169n. 346 [= 1997: 137n. 333].

9) BhāgTN (p. 18,1-4):
Subject matter: The true and spurious proclaimer of Sāṅkhya

pādme ca –
kapilo vāsudevākhyas tantrasāṅkhyaṃ jagāda ha /
brahmādibhyaś ca devebhyo bhṛgvādibhyas tathaiva ca /
tathaivāsuraye sarvavedārthair upabṛṃhitam /
sarvavedaviruddhaṃ ca kapilo 'nyo jagāda ha /
sāṅkhyam āsuraye 'nyasmai kutarkaparibṛṃhitam /
iti (1)

(1) Cf. ibid. l. 18: *tantrasāṅkhyaṃ vedānusārī* ... ; see also NārP 48; PadP 2 and MESQUITA 2000_1: 156n. 325 [= 1997: 126n. 314].

10) BhāgTN (p. 18,12):
Subject matter: Pṛthu

āviveśa pṛthuṃ devaḥ śaṅkhī cakrī caturbhujaḥ /
iti hi pādme (1)

(1) Cf. ibid l. 11: *pṛthuśarīrāviṣṭaṃ rūpam* ... ; see also ĀdiP 1 and NārP 15.

11) BhāgTN (p. 21,2-3):
Subject matter: Viṣṇu's three-fold outward appearance

nārayaṇavarāhādyāḥ paramaṃ rūpam īśituḥ /
jaivaṃ tu pratibiṃbākhyaṃ jaḍam āropitaṃ hareḥ /
evaṃ hi trividhaṃ tasya rūpaṃ viṣṇor mahātmanaḥ /
iti pādme (1)

(1) Cf. ibid. l. 1: *etat jaḍarūpam* ... ; see also ĀdiP 1; AgniP 25; BhāgP 1; 3; AgniP 25; BrahP 52 and MESQUITA 2000: 33n. 12; 495f.

12) BhāgTN (p. 22,6-8):
Subject matter: Viṣṇu, the supreme Creator of the universe

aprayatnāt svatantratvāt phalānāṃ ca vivarjanāt /
kriyāyāś ca svarūpatvād akarteti ca taṃ viduḥ /
kartṛtvaṃ bhrāntijaṃ prāhur atattattvavido janāḥ /
aiśvaryajaṃ tu kartṛtvaṃ samyak tattattvavedinaḥ /
iti pādme (1)

(1) Cf. AgniP 12.

13) BhāgTN (p. 26,13-14):
Subject matter: Bewilderment of evil beings (*moha*)

jñānaśaktisvarūpo 'pi hy ajñāśaktaṃ vaded dhariḥ /
ajñānāṃ mohanāyeśas tena muhyanti mohitāḥ /
iti pādme (1)

(1) Cf. BrāṇP 33; PadP 29; 83; SkaP 12; 44; 115; 116; 119; Upagī 1; see also ĀdiP 1; HarV 8 and NārP 9.

14) BhāgTN (p. 40,4-14):
Subject matter: Prophecy of annihilation of Yadu-family (*yadukula-kṣayam*)

śāpaṃ śrutvā brāhmaṇānām uddhavaḥ khinnamānasaḥ /
udāsīnaṃ tathā kṛṣṇam iva suprītam eva ca / [1]
naśiṣyamāṇaṃ svakulaṃ svaryiyāsuṃ ca keśavam /
jñātvā prapaccha bhagavatsvarūpaṃ tam upahvare / [2]
maitreyo 'pi tadaivāgāj jijñāsus tattvam uttamam /
tayor adāt sa bhagavān jñānaṃ nirmalam añjasā / [3]
ṣaḍviṃśadvatsarāt pūrvaṃ svargateḥ puruṣottamaḥ /
preṣayāmāsa ca harir uddhavaṃ badarīm anu / [4]
kalāpagrāmiṇāṃ vaktum etat tattvam aśeṣataḥ /
viduraṃ tīrthayātrāstham antarāle sa uddhavaḥ / [5]
dṛṣṭvā naśiṣyamāṇaṃ ca kulaṃ jigamiṣuṃ harim /
kathayitvā badaryāṃ ca kalāpagrāmavāsinām / [6]
procya tattvam aśeṣeṇa vāsudevamukhodgatam /
ṣaḍviṃśadvarṣagamane punar āgatim ātmanaḥ / [7]
teṣām uktvā punaḥ kṛṣṇasannidhau vicacāra ha /
maitreyo vidurāyaitad ūcivān kṛṣṇacoditaḥ / [8]
viduraḥ pāṇḍavānāṃ ca vinā yaduvināśanam /
ṣaḍviṃśadvarṣataḥ pūrvaṃ jñātvāpy apriyam eva tat / [9]
nāvocad viduro dhīmāṃs tasmān nāpriyam āvadet / [10ab]
iti hi pādme (1)

(1) Cf. ibid. l. 3: *yadukulakṣayam eṣyat* ... ; see also BrāṇP 59; GarP 16; NārP 12; SkaP 34; 59; VarP 16.

15) BhāgTN (p. 57,1-2):
Subject matter: Virtuousness

śamaḥ priyādibuddhyujjhā kṣamā krodhādyanutthitiḥ /
mahāvirodhakartuś ca sahanaṃ tu titikṣaṇam /
iti pādme (1)

(1) Cf. ibid. (p. 56,10f.): *ekāntataḥ śubhabhāgitvaṃ saubhāgyam / śubhaikabhāgī subhago durbhagas tadviparyaya* iti gītākalpe (unknown source) ... ; see also BrahVP 35.

16) BhāgTN (p. 57,2-3):
Subject matter: Viṣṇu, the supreme Creator of the universe

svayaṃ sarvasya kartṛtvāt kutas tasya priyāpriye /
iti ca pādme (1)

(1) Cf. ibid. ll. 3f.:
priyam eva yataḥ sarvam apriyaṃ nāsti kutracit /
svayam eva yataḥ kartā śānto 'to harir īśvaraḥ /
iti brahmatarke (fictitious source);
see also AgniP 12.

17) BhāgTN (p. 81,9-10):
Subject matter: Bewilderment of evil beings (*moha*)

nityajñānena siddhaṃ ca punaḥ punar avekṣate /
līlayaiva harir devo duṣṭānāṃ mohanāya ca /
iti pādme (1)

(1) Cf. ibid. l. 8: *tad bhāgavataṃ purāṇam apaśyat* ... ; see also ĀdiP 1; MBh 42n. 6.

18) BhāgTN (p. 87,11-16):
Subject matter: Activity of sense organs

jñānendriyaiś ca manasā sattvaṃ badhnāti pūruṣam /
rajaḥ karmendriyair nityaṃ śarīreṇa tamas tathā /
āntaraṃ yat tu kartṛtvaṃ tat sattvenābhimanyate /
rajasā tv abhimanyeta karaṇaiḥ karmakāraṇaiḥ /
śarīraṃ vedanādyaṃ tu tamasā hy abhimanyate /
akartā karaṇair hīnaḥ śarīreṇa vivarjitaḥ /
nityajñānasvarūpo 'sau guṇair evābhimanyate /
evaṃ jīvaḥ pareṇaiva preritaḥ saṃsṛtiṃ vrajet /
na paraḥ saṃsṛtiṃ kvāpi svāntantryād adhikatvataḥ /
evaṃ jīvaparau bhinnau kim anyac chrotum icchasi /
iti pādme (1)

(1) Cf. BhaviṣPV 17; SkaP 119; see also MESQUITA 2000: 138n. 262; 258n. 49.

19) BhāgTN (p. 89,13-14):
Subject matter: Sense organs / Mahābhūtāni

viśiṣṭakāryaśaktitvād devā vaikārikāḥ smṛtāḥ /
atijājvalyamānatvāt taijasānīndriyāṇy api /
tāmasāni tu bhūtāni yatas tāvan na tūbhayam /
iti pādme (1)

(1) Cf. BhaviṣPV 17; see also MatsyaP 5 and SkaP 25.

20) BhāgTN (p. 93,3-4):
Subject matter: Virāṭ-Puruṣa

yājñikā romamūlasthā romāntasthās tu tatpare /
udbhijo vāsudevasya liṅgagās tu jarāyujāḥ /
iti pādme (1)

(1) Cf. AgniP 3.

21) BhāgTN (p. 100,6-7):
Subject matter: Avatāras / Deities

puruṣādyā hare rūpaṃ brahmādyās tatpriyāḥ smṛtāḥ /
svarūpabhūtā naivaite tatsannidhiyutā api /
iti pādme (1)

(1) Cf. ibid. 1.5: *puruṣa evādyo 'vatāraḥ / kālādayo rūpavat asvarūpam api priyatvāt*; see also AgniP 6; BhaviṣP 5 and BrāṇP 29.

21_1) BhāgTN (p. 100,13-15):
Subject matter: Viṣṇu's supreme transcendence / Presiding deity of sacrificial rite

yajñaśabdoditau dvau tu devau lokapuraskṛtau /
eko nārāyaṇas tatra rudra cchinnas tathāparaḥ /
sa tu yajñābhimānī syāt tatpatiḥ keśavaḥ smṛtaḥ /
iti pādme (1)

(1) Cf. Agni 6; BhāgP 2; BhaviṣP 11.

22) BhāgTN (p. 101,9-10):
Subject matter: Etymology of sacrificial rite / Presiding deity of sacrificial rite

kriyābhimānād yajño 'sāv indrasūnuḥ prakīrtitaḥ /

yajñeśatvāt svayaṃ viṣṇur yajño rucisutaḥ smṛtaḥ /
iti pādme (1)

(1) Cf. ibid. l. 11: *harir iti jñātvā īśāvāsyam ityādyādinānūktaḥ*; see also BhaviṣPV 11.

23) BhāgTN (p. 126,11-12):
Subject matter: Vyāsa, Viṣṇu's Avatāra

harir vyāsādirūpeṇa sarvajño 'pi svayaṃ prabhuḥ /
śṛṇoti nāradādibhyo mohāyaiṣāṃ prasiddhaye /
iti pādme (1)

(1) Cf. ĀdiP 1; BhaviṣPV 21: BrāṇP 14 and MESQUITA 1997: 35ff.

24) BhāgTN (p. 137,7-8):
Subject matter: Viṣṇu's supreme transcendence

lokānāṃ sukhakartṛtvam apekṣya kuśalaṃ vibhoḥ /
pṛcchyate satatānandāt kathaṃ tasyaiva pṛcchyate /
iti pādme (1)

(1) Cf. AgniP 6.

25) BhāgTN (p. 140,3):
Subject matter: Garuḍa

suparṇaḥ suparānandāt kākutstho vāci saṃsthiteḥ /
iti pādme (1)

(1) Cf. ibid. ll. 1f.: *bhīṣmakakanyāyā arthe savarṇamātrayogyatayā āhūtāḥ / eṣāṃ śriyo jihīrṣayāhvānabuddhir bhagavatā kṛtā* ... ; also ibid. n. 4; see also Ādi 1; BrāṇP 12[7]; SkaP 32[5]; VāmP 2.

26) BhāgTN (p. 141,3-4):
Subject matter: Viṣṇu's Avatāras

sarvadāpi viraktaḥ san bhāsayīta virāgavat /
kādācitkaḥ kutas tasya lokaśikṣārtham iṣyate /
iti pādme (1)

(1) Cf. ĀdiP 1; AgniP 6 and MESQUITA 2000_1: 40ff. [= 1997: 33f.].

27) BhāgTN (p. 144,1-2):
Subject matter: Eulogy of Mahābhārata

bhāratān nādhikaṃ viṣṇor mahimāvācakaṃ kvacit /

bhāratān na virāgāya bhāratān na vimuktaye /
iti pādme (1)

(1) Cf. ibid. (p. 143,13f.): *yasmin bhārate / hareḥ kathāyāṃ grāmyasukhānuvādair matir na gṛhitā ... sā grāmyasukhānuvādair na gṛhītā hareḥ kathāyāṃ vivardhamānā matiḥ*; see also KūrP 30_2 and MESQUITA 2000_1: 143f. [= 1997: 115f.].

28) BhagTN (p. 146,6):
Subject matter: Brahmā, the presiding Deity of Kāla and Jīva

kālajīvābhimānena rūpadvandvī caturmukhaḥ /
iti pādme (1)

(1) Cf. ibid. ll. 4f.: *kālamāyāṃśaliṅginaḥ tannimittaśarīrāḥ / hiraṇyagarbhasyaiva kālābhimāni jīvābhimāni ca dvividhaṃ rūpam* ... ; see also BhavişPV 11; BrahP 25 and BrāṇP 29.

29) BhāgTN (p. 153,5):
Subject matter: Etymology of *māyā*

māyā tu mahimā proktā prācurye tu mayaḍ yataḥ /
iti pādme (1)

(1) Cf. ibid. l. 4: *bhagavato māyāṃ mahimānam* ... and Aṣṭādhyāyī IV 3,82: *mayaṭ ca*; see also PadP 13.

30) BhāgTN (p. 157,10):
Subject matter: Creation

udakaṃ vāyunā śuṣkaṃ bhinnaṃ padmam abhūd dhareḥ /
iti pādme (1)

(1) Cf. BrāṇP 29.

31) BhāgTN (p. 162,2-3):
Subject matter: Brahmā's origin

yat tad divyaṃ hare rūpaṃ kṣīrasāgaramadhyagam /
sajjñānānandaikamātraṃ na tataḥ paramaṃ kvacit /
anādinityād avyaktāt tasmāj jajñe caturmukhaḥ /
iti pādme (1)

(1) Cf. ibid. (p. 161,13f.): *yan nābhipadmabhavanād aham āvirāsam yac cedaṃ bhagavataḥ svarūpam ānandamātraṃ paśyāmi yac cāśrito 'smi ataḥ paraṃ nāsti / ato na jñāyata ity avadyam atyuttamāpekṣayā / anādigṛhītam eva na gṛhyate* ... ; see also BrāṇP 29.

32) BhāgTN (p. 178,8-10):
Subject matter: Seat of thought and feeling of the organic world

tiraścīnāḥ sthāvarāś ca antaḥsparśā itīritāḥ /
yataḥ pratyakṣānumābhyāṃ hṛdgajñānaṃ na śāstragāḥ /
iti pādme (1)

(1) Cf. ibid. l. 11: *yad aprayatnād dhṛdayaṅgamaṃ tad eva jānanti na śāstrayukti-bhyām ity arthaḥ*; see also BrahP 24[6-7ab].

33) BhāgTN (p. 189,3+190,1):
Subject matter: Measuring and time-units

kākāṇikācatuṣkaṃ tu viṃśāṃśety abhidhīyate /
kṛṣṇalety api taṃ brūyus taiś caturbhis tu māṣakam /
caturaṅguladīrghe tu kṛte māṣacatuṣṭaye /
yāvat syāt pariṇāhena tāvad dvāraṃ vidhīyate /
prasthasya nāḍīpātrasya ṣaṭpalasya śubhe jale /
bhārādhikyenodakena kṣiprapūrtir bhaviṣyati /
atiśaitye kalaṅke ca māndye naiva tu pūraṇam /
tasmād vasantakāle ca prayāgasthodakena ca /
nāḍīśuddhiḥ parīkṣyā syād anyathā na samaṃ bhavet /
iti pādme (1)

(1) The measuring-units mentioned here depart from the rule and are therefore difficult to understand, cf. ViṣṇP VI 3,8f.:

...
unmānenāṃbhasas sā tu palāny ardhatrayodaśa /
hemamāṣaiḥ kṛtacchidraṃ caturbhiś caturaṅgulaiḥ /
māgadhena tu pramāṇena jalaprasthas tu sa smṛtaḥ /
nāḍikābhyām atha dvābhyāṃ muhūrto dvijasattama /
ahorātraṃ muhurtās tu triṃśanmāso dinais tathā /

see also the commentary of Viṣṇucitta: Viṣṇucittīya:
unmāneneti / tulayā mitasyāṃbhasaḥ palāni ardhatrayodaśa – ardhaṃ trayodaśaṃ yeṣāṃ tāni ardhatrayodaśa sārdhadvādaśety arthaḥ / sā nāḍikā – upacārāt tair nāḍikā jñātavyety arthaḥ / katham ityāha – hemeti / hemamāśaiḥ – māṣaḥ pañcaguñjāmānam / jalasyaitat sārdhaṃ paladvādaśakaṃ magadhadeśyaṃ prasthaṃ pūrayati / sa ca prasthaś caturguṇas san nāḍijñāpakaḥ iti śeṣaḥ / yathāha vāyuḥ (= VāyuP II 38,219f.)
[unmānenābhamsaś cāpi palāny ardhatrayodaśa]
...
muhūrtāś ca lavāś cāpi pramāṇajñaiḥ prakalpitāḥ /
tatsthānenāṃbhasāś cāpi palāny atha trayodaśa /
māgadhenaiva [*tu*] *mānena jalaprastho vidhīyate /*
ete [*evaṃ*] *cāpy udakaprasthāś catvāro nāliko* [°*kā*]*ghaṭaḥ /*
hemamāṣaiḥ kṛtacchidraiś [°*draś*] *caturbhiś caturaṅgulaiḥ /* [*iti*]

evaṃ caturmāṣasuvarṇaracitacaturaṅgulasūcīkṛtādhaś chidrādāḍhakajalapūrṇāt pañcāśatpalaparīmāṇād ghaṭāt tacchidreṇa pañcāśatpalaṃ jalaṃ yāvatā kālena niḥsarati tāvatkālo nāḍītyuktaṃ bhavati / athavāhorātre jalasya pūraṇaṃ niḥsaraṇaṃ vā ṣaṣṭivāraṃ yathā syāt tathā tatpātramānaṃ kāryam / anye tu caturmāṣahemanirmitayā caturaṅgulayā sūcyā kṛtacchidre sārdhadvādaśapale tāmrapātre tatpramāṇaṃ jalaṃ tacchidreṇa yāvatā kālena praviśati sa kāla ekā nāḍikā tāni palāni māgadhamānena jalaprastha iti varṇayanti / kṛtacchidrair iti ca paṭhanti / tatrāyam anvayaḥ – sā nāḍikā caturbhir hemamāṣaiḥ kṛtacchidrair niṣpannāny aṃbhaso 'rdhatrayodaśapalānīti.

34) BhāgTN (p. 228,7-9):
Subject matter: Viṣṇu's Sarvanāmatva / Antaryāmin

yatrāpi tu harer nāma tadanyatra prayujyate /
tadāntarahares tatra gṛhītir nānyathā bhavet /
svātantryād avaratvaṃ ca parasyāpi prayujyate /
sthitasyāpi yathā rājñaḥ svānāṃ jayaparājayau /
iti pādme (1)

(1) Cf. ibid. l. 10: *ato hṛṣīkeśo brahmāntaryāmī*; see also BhāgP 2; BrāṇP 2 and PadP 48.

35) BhāgTN (p. 234,13):
Subject matter: Avatāras

yugatraye 'vatāreṇa triyugaś ceti kathyate /
iti pādme

(1) Cf. ĀdiP 1; BrahP 9_1 and MESQUITA 2000_1: 48n. 73 [= 1997: 39n 65].

36) BhāgTN (p. 244,4):
Subject matter: Padārthasvarūpa

viśeṣaḥ kāryam uddiṣṭaṃ viśeṣād dṛśyate yataḥ /
iti pādme (1)

(1) Cf. HarV 9; MESQUITA 2000: 294ff.

37) BhāgTN (p. 309,9-10):
Subject matter: Viṣṇu, the Creator of Kalpas

cakre nārāyaṇaḥ sākṣāt kiṃstudhnaḥ kalpam ātmajam /
iti pādme (1)

(1) Cf. AgniP 12; see also BrahP 38; NārP 24.

38) BhāgTN (p. 315,4):
Subject matter: Avatāras

matsyarūpādinānātvadṛṣṭivad yan nirarthakam /
iti pādme (1)

(1) Cf. ibid. l. 3: *yalloke nirarthakaṃ tad bhagavadrūpeṣu pratītanānātvadṛṣṭāntena paśyanti santaḥ*; see also ĀdiP 1 and MESQUITA 2000_1: 35f. [= 1997: 29f.].

39) BhāgTN (p. 322,1-2):
Subject matter: Viṣṇu's Pūjā / Antaryāmin

bhūteṣu harir ity eva haryarpaṇadhiyā tathā /
sarvabhūteṣu ca hareḥ pūjā kāryātmavedibhiḥ /
iti pādme (1)

(1) Cf. AgniP 20; BhāgP 2 and ViṣP 9.

40) BhāgTN (p. 347,1-2):
Subject matter: Otherwordly trustworthy Scriptures / Sadāgamas

alaukikaṃ ca śāstrīyaṃ kartavyaṃ laukikaṃ kutaḥ /
lokārthaṃ śāstrahā yāti nirayaṃ tv itaraḥ surān /
iti pādme (1)

(1) Cf. BhaviṣP 10; BrāṇP 11; GarP 9; MESQUITA 2000: 51n. 13 MESQUITA 2000_1: 169n. 346 [= 1997: 137n. 333].

41) BhāgTN (p. 365,6-7):
Subject matter: Difference of Jīva from Hari

upapādayet parātmānaṃ jīvebhyo yaḥ pade pade /+1
bhede naiva na vai tasmāt priyo viṣṇos tu kaścana /
iti pādme
yo hareś caiva jīvānāṃ bhedavaktā hareḥ priya iti ca (1)

(1) Cf. ibid. l. 5: *viviktadṛṣṭiḥ jīvānāṃ dhiṣṇyatayā parameśvarasya bhedadṛṣṭiḥ*; see also AgniP 22.

42) BhāgTN (p. 370,8-9):
Subject matter: Liberation

nityodastā yogaśaktir anapekṣyaṃ phalaṃ yataḥ /
nityasvarūpabhūtāpi bahiḥphalavivarjanāt /
akarmety ucyate yadvan mokṣaḥ phalavivarjanāt /
iti pādme (1)

(1) Cf. ibid. l. 7: *yogamāyāṃ yogamāyāphalaṃ* [*bāhyam*]; see also Agni 16; NārP 8 and MESQUITA 2007: 14n. 19 [= 2007_1: 436n. 19].

43) BhāgTN (p. 442,4-5):
Subject matter: Bhakti

antarhiraṇyakādīnāṃ bhaktir asty eva keśave /
asurāveśatas tv anyān haristotṝn dviṣanti ca /
iti pādme (1)

(1) Cf. ibid. l. 3: *vivekasmṛtiḥ / avivekina eva vivekitvabhrāntiḥ*; see also AgniP 20; BrahVP 17; BrāṇP 53n. 4.

44) BhāgTN (p. 451,6-7):
Subject matter: Antaryāmin

parāpareṣu yasmāt tvaṃ vyāpto viṣṇo sanātana /
tasmān na vyatiriktaṃ tvad ityāhur vedavādinaḥ /
iti pādme (1)

(1) Cf. ibid. l. 3: *jīvānāṃ prāṇadhārakaḥ*; see also BhāgP 2.

45) BhāgTN (p. 500,1):
Subject matter: Etymology of Bharadvāja

bharadvājo marudbhiś ca bhṛto jāto dvayor yataḥ /
iti pādme (1)

(1) Cf. ibid. (p. 499,11-12): *dvājam imaṃ bhara / ucathyasya kṣetrajo bṛhaspater jāta iti dvayor jātatvād dvājaḥ / bṛhaspater vājaḥ prajāsantatir yena bhṛtā sa bṛhaspater bharadvājaḥ.*

46) BhāgTN (p. 504,5):
Subject matter: Etymology of Viṣṇu

svatantratvād sukhatvāc ca svanāmā viṣṇur ucyate /
iti pādme (1)

(1) Cf. ibid. l. 3:
paraḥ svo harir uddhāma iti nāmacatuṣṭayam /
viṣṇor guhaṃ tu yo veda sarvapāpaiḥ pramucyate /
iti prakāśikāyām (unknown source);
see also AgniP 6 and BrāṇP 68.

47) BhāgTN (p. 511,4-5):
Subject matter: Viṣṇu's graciousness

nāmarūpādi viṣṇos tu na śakyaṃ jñātum añjasā /
tathāpi tatprasādena jānanti paramarṣayaḥ /
iti pādme (1)

(1) Cf. ibid. l. 3: *devakriyāyāḥ pratiyanti / bhagavatpreraṇād jānanti*; see also AgniP 20; BrahP 83; BrahVP 14; KūrP 30_3; PadP 55; VāmP 25.

48) BhāgTN (p. 524,12-13):
Subject matter: Viṣṇu's supreme transcendence

prakṛtyādes tadvaśatvāt prakṛtyādir udīryate /
yathā rājā bhṛtyakṛtāt svayaṃ kartety udīryate /
yathā dehaṃ svatantratvāt svayam ity āhur añjasā /
iti pādme (1)

(1) Cf. AgniP 6; 25; PadP 34; 69 and MESQUITA 2000: 471ff.

49) BhāgTN (p. 526,8-9):
Subject matter: Liberation

apunarbhavamātrāt tu harisāmīpyam uttamam /
tatrāpi sparśayogyatvaṃ yathā vedavido viduḥ /
iti pādme (1)

(1) Cf. AgniP 16 and MESQUITA 2000: 524f.

50) BhāgTN (p. 536,7-8):
Subject matter: Āveśa / Avatāra

āveśo vasudevādau dehādānaṃ hareḥ smṛtam /
dehādānaṃ tadanyeṣāṃ janmeti kavayo viduḥ /
tathāpy asuramohāya grantheṣu bahudheva tu /
iti pādme (1)

(1) Cf. GĪ IV 5; 7-8; see also ĀdiP 1; BrahVP 17; BrāṇP 33; PadP 50; HACKER 1960: 48ff. and MESQUITA 2000_1: 35; 78 [= 1997: 29; 62].

51) BhāgTN (p. 538,6-9):
Subject matter: Bhakti, the means of liberation

bhaktyā hi nityakāmitvaṃ na tu bhaktiṃ vinā bhavet /
ataḥ kāmitayā vāpi muktir bhaktimatāṃ harau /
snehabhaktāḥ sadā devāḥ kāmitvenāpsaraḥstriyaḥ /
kāścit kāścin na kāmena bhaktyā kevalayaiva tu /
mokṣam āyānti nānyena bhaktiṃ yogyāṃ vinā kvacit /
iti pādme (1)

(1) Cf. ibid. ll. 4f.: *kāminaḥ kāmitvaṃ krodhinaḥ krodhitvam eva bhavatītyādi tanmayatā –*

vimuktāv api kāminyo viṣṇukāmā vrajastriyaḥ /
dveṣiṇaś ca harau nityadveṣiṇas tamasi sthitāḥ /
iti ca (unknown source) ... ;
see also AgniP 20.

52) BhāgTN (p. 586,5-6):
Subject matter: Viṣṇu's Sarvanāmatva / Viṣṇu, the supreme Creator of the universe

brahmeśendrādisannāmnāṃ ye 'rthabhūtā guṇā matāḥ /
pūrtīśitṛtvadraṣṭṛtvapramukhās te hareḥ sadā /
atas tu sarvanāmāsau sarvakartā ca keśavaḥ /
iti pādme (1)

(1) Cf. AgniP 12; BrāṇP 2.

53) BhāgTN (p. 779,9-10):
Subject matter: Prakṛti

ādhāraḥ prakṛter viṣṇur nādhāras tu hareḥ kvacit /
tathāpy avyaktago yadvad dṛśyate mandacetasām /
iti pādme (1)

(1) Cf. ibid. ll. 5f.: *yady api paramātmā prakṛtiś ca vilakṣaṇau / tathāpi tayor vailakṣaṇyaṃ na lakṣyate – antaraṃ ca bhidā ceti vailakṣaṇyaṃ prakīrtitam /* iti ca I (unknown source) *tadvailakṣaṇya kuto na dṛśyata iti praśnābhiprāyaḥ / anyonyādhāratvam eva dṛśyate / na tu parameśvarasyānanyādhāratvena prakṛtyādhāratvaṃ mandamatīnām ity arthaḥ* ... ; see also ĀdiP 1; AgniP 25; BrāṇP 51 and MESQUITA 2000: 474n. 606.

54) BhāgTN (p. 814,4-5):
Subject matter: Nidrā / Sunidrā

nidrā caiva sunidrā ca dvidhā nidrā prakīrtitā /
tatra nidrā bhaven nityā sunidrā mṛtikālagā /
iti pādme
manomātrasvarūpatvāt svapno māyeti kathyate /
iti ca (1)

(1) Cf. ibid. ll. 7f.: *tathā nanāviṣayadaṃ mana eva / manasā hi viṣayāḥ pratīyante*; see also BrāṇP 7. For Svapna cf. MESQUITA 1990: 249f.; 269f and MESQUITA 2000: 202n. 421.

55) BhāgTN (p. 827,4-5):
Subject matter: Bhakti

samāhite 'pi jīvena vikṣipte vā na tu kvacit /
viśeṣo vidyate viṣṇos tathāpi tu samāhite /
prīto bhavati vai nityaṃ sarvadharmakṛto 'pi ca /
iti pādme (1)

(1) Cf. ibid. l. 3: *bhagavato guṇadoṣābhāve 'pi jīvasya saṅgo 'varjanīya eva mukti-paryantam* ... ; see also AgniP 20.

55₁) BhāgTN (p. 836,8-10):
Subject matter: Doctrine of Avatāras

ajāto jātavad viṣṇur amṛto mṛtavat tathā /
māyayā darśayen nityam ajñānāṃ mohanāya ca /
iti pādme (1)

(1) Cf. ibid. l. 7: *tanubhṛdvat jananavad apy ayavac ca īhā tanubhajjananāpyayehā* ... ; see also ĀdiP 1 and MESQUITA 2000_1: 38f. [= 1997: 32f.].

56) BSūBh (p. 12,17-20):
Subject matter: Liberation / Ātman, Viṣṇu's specific appellation

cetanas tu dvidhā prokto jīva ātmeti ca prabho /
jīvā brahmādayaḥ proktā ātmaikas tu janārdanaḥ /
itareṣv ātmaśabdas tu sopacāro 'bhidhīyate /
tasyātmano nirguṇasya jñānān mokṣa udāhṛtaḥ /
saguṇās tv apare proktās tajjñānān naiva mucyate /
paro hi puruṣo viṣṇus tasmān mokṣas tataḥ smṛtaḥ /
iti pādme (1)

(1) Cf. ibid. l. 13: *na hi gauṇātmaniṣṭhasya mokṣaḥ* ... ; see also AgniP 16; BrahVP 19; 23 and MESQUITA 2000: 137n. 261.

57) BSūBh (p. 23,12-13):
Subject matter: Viṣṇu's Sarvanāmatva / Antaryāmin

tattannāmnocyate viṣṇuḥ sarvaśāstṛtvato hariḥ /
na kvāpi kiṃcin nāmāsti tam ṛte puruṣottamam /
iti ca pādme (1)

(1) Cf. ibid. l. 11: *śāstram antaryāmī* ... ; see also BhāgP 2; BrāṇP 2 and MESQUITA 2000: 162f.

58) BSūBh (p. 27,8-9):
Subject matter: Viṣṇu's supreme transcendence

śubhaṃ pibaty asau nityaṃ nāśubhaṃ sa hariḥ pibet /

pūrṇānandamayasyāsya ceṣṭā na jñāyate kvacit /
iti pādme (1)

(1) Cf. ibid. l. 5: *guhāṃ praviṣṭau pibantau viṣṇurūpe eva ... ātmāntarātmeti harir eka eva dvidhā sthitaḥ / niviṣṭo hṛdaye nityaṃ rasaṃ pibati karmajam /* iti bṛhatsaṃhitāyām (unknown source); see also AgniP 6 and MESQUITA 2000: 444n. 576.

59) BSūBh (p. 38,9-10):
Subject matter: Viṣṇu's supreme transcendence

nityatīrṇāśanāyādir eka eva hariḥ svataḥ /
aśanāyādikān anye tatprasādāt taranti hi /
iti pādme (1)

(1) Cf. ibid. l. 8f.: *yo aśanāyāpipāse śokaṃ mohaṃ jarāṃ mṛtyum atyeti* (BĀU III 5,1) *sa eṣa sarvebhyaḥ pāpmabhya udita* (ChU I 6,7) *ityādinā viṣṇor eva hi te guṇāḥ*; see also AgniP 6.

60) BSūBh (p. 50,2-3):
Subject matter: Viṣṇu's Sarvanāmatva

parasya vācakāḥ śabdāḥ samākṛṣyetareṣv api /
vyavahṛyante satataṃ lokavedānusārataḥ /
iti hi pādme (1)

(1) Cf. ibid. (p. 49,24): *paramātmavācinaḥ śabdā anyatra samākṛṣya vyavahṛyante ...* ; cf. Śābarabhāṣya *ad* MSū I 3, 30: *ya eva laukikāḥ śabdās ta eva vaidikā ta evaiṣām arthā iti / kutaḥ / prayogacodanābhāvāt / evaṃ prayogacodanā saṃbhavati yadi ta eva śabdās ta evārthā itarathā śabdānyatve 'rtho na pratīyeta*; cf. PadP 34; 62; 66; 69; see also BrāṇP 2, 72; 82 and MESQUITA 2000: 164n. 335.

61) BSūBh (p. 51,4):
Subject matter: Vyāsa's disciples

kṛṣṇadvaipāyanamatād ekadeśavidaḥ pare /
vadanty ete yathāprajñaṃ na virodhaḥ kathaṃcana /
iti pādme (1)

(1) Cf. ibid. l. 3: *sarvaṃ paramātmany avasthitam iti vaktuṃ tadvacanam* iti kāśakṛtsnaḥ; see also BhavisPV 21; BrāṇP 14 and MESQUITA 2000_1: 28n. 30 [= 1997: 23n. 23].

62) BSūBh (p. 75,7-8):
Subject matter: Viṣṇu, the supreme meaning of Śruti, Smṛti and Yukti

śrutayaḥ smṛtayaś caiva yuktayaś ceśvaraṃ param /

vadanti tadviruddhaṃ yo vadet tasmān na cādhamaḥ /
iti ca pādme (1)

(1) Cf. ibid. l. 6: *sakalaśrutismṛtiyuktiviruddhatvāc cānīśvaraṃ matam asamañjasam* ... ; see also BrāṇP 82; PadP 60 and MESQUITA 2000: 104n. 162; 166; 403n. 450; 405n. 456.

63) BSūBh (p. 94,9-11):
Subject matter: Viṣṇu's supreme transcendence

pratyakṣatvaṃ harer janma na vikāraḥ kathaṃcana /
puruṣaḥ prakṛtiḥ kālo mahān ityādiṣu kramāt /
vikāra eva jananaṃ puruṣe tadviśeṣaṇam /
paratantraviśeṣo hi vikāra iti kīrtitaḥ /
iti ca pādme (1)

(1) Cf. ibid. ll. 1f.: *sato 'py utpattir iti cen na / anutpattir eva sataḥ / tuśabdenoktavyasthām apākaroti / na hy asataḥ sad utpadyate / adṛṣṭatvād anupapatteḥ* ... ; see also AgniP 4; 6; 25 and MESQUITA 2000: 492n. 644-645.

64) BSūBh (p. 96,11-12):
Subject matter: Viṣṇu, the supreme Creator of the universe

anurūpaḥ kramaḥ sṛṣṭau pratirūpo laye kramaḥ /
iti krameṇa bhagavān sṛṣṭisaṃhārakṛd dhariḥ /
iti ca pādme (1)

(1) Cf. ibid. l. 9:
kramavacanam api viparītakramāpekṣayā /
kartā prāṇādikasyāsya hantā bhūmyādikasya ca /
yaḥ kramād vyutkramāc caiva sa hariḥ para ucyate /
ity ata eva bhāllaveyaśrutivacanāt (unknown source) ... ;
see also AgniP 12.

65) BSūBh (p. 99,17-19):
Subject matter: The Partlessness of the individual soul

acintyayeśaśaktyaiva hy eko 'vayavavarjitaḥ /
ātmānaṃ bahudhā kṛtvā krīḍate yogasaṃpadā /
iti pādme (1)

(1) Cf. ibid. l. 15: *yathā puṣpād gandhaḥ pṛthag gacchati evam aṃśino jīvād aṃśāḥ pṛthag gacchanti* ... ; see also BrāṇP 71; HarV 28 and MESQUITA 1989: 129-150.

66) BSūBh (p. 115,7-8):
Subject matter: Viṣṇu, the supreme Creator of the universe

sarvanāmnāṃ ca rūpāṇāṃ vyavahāreṣu keśavaḥ /
eka eva yataḥ sraṣṭā brahmādyās tadavāntarāḥ /
iti ca pādme (1)

(1) Cf. ibid. l. 4: *nāmarūpakḷptiḥ parād eva ... trivṛtkurvata iti hetugarbhaḥ / trivṛt-karaṇāpekṣatvān nāmarūpayoḥ* ... ; see also AgniP 12; BrāṇP 72 and PadP 60.

67) BSūBh (p. 121,18-20):
Subject matter: Three-fold division of the individual souls

nārāyaṇaprasādena samiddhajñānacakṣuṣā /
atyantaduḥkhasaṃllīnān niḥśeṣasukhavarjitān /
nityam eva tathābhūtān vimiśrāṃś ca gaṇān bahūn /
nirastāśeṣaduḥkhāṃś ca nityānandaikabhāginaḥ /
apaśyat trividhān brahmā sākṣād eva caturmukhaḥ /
iti darśanavacanāc ca pādme (1)

(1) Cf. AgniP 24; BrāṇP 71; PadP 86 and MESQUITA 2000: 510f.

68) BSūBh (p. 137,6-7):
Subject matter: Bhakti / Liberation

mahitvabuddhir bhaktis tu snehapūrvābhidhīyate /
tayaiva vyajyate samyag jīvarūpaṃ sukhādikam /
iti pādme (1)

(1) Cf. ibid. l. 4: *aṃbuvat snehena grahaṇaṃ jñānaṃ bhaktiṃ vinā na tatsādṛśyaṃ samyag abhivyajyate* ... (= KathU II 23); see also AgniP 16; 20; 24 and MESQUITA 2007: 29n. 59 [= 2007_1: 444n. 58].

69) BSūBh (p. 140,19-20):
Subject matter: Viṣṇu as topic of wordly language

alaukiko 'pi jñānādis tacchabdair eva bhaṇyate /
jñāpanārthāya lokasya yathā rājeva devarāṭ /
iti ca pādme (1)

(1) Cf. ibid. ll. 17f.: *jīveśvarasaṃbandhajñāpanārtham aprasiddho 'pi pādo yathā pādaśabdena vyapadiśyate pādo 'sya viśvā bhūtānīti* [Ṛg X 90,3] *tathā* ... ; Madhva follows the opinion of Mīmāṃsā-school that there is no diference between the vedic and wordly language, cf. Śābarabhāṣya (*ad* Sū I 1, 30); see also BrāṇP 2; PadP 34; 60; 62; SkaP 31.

70) BSūBh (p. 142,5-6):
Subject matter: Hierarchy among Deities

aiśvaryāt paramād viṣṇor bhaktyādīnām anāditaḥ /
brahmādīnāṃ sūpapannā hy ānandāder vicitratā /
iti hi pādme (1)

(1) Cf. BhaviṣPV 15 and MESQUITA 2000: 492ff.

71) BSūBh (p. 155,15-16):
Subject matter: Hierarchy of the released souls / Yogyatā

saṃpūrnopāsanād brahmā saṃpūrṇānandabhāg bhavet /
itare tu yathāyogaṃ samyag muktau bhavanti hi /
iti pādme (1)

(1) Cf. ibid. l. 14: *sarvaguṇayuktatvenopāsanād anyatraiva phale brahmādayo bhavanti* ... ; BhaviṣPV 15; BrahP 36 and MESQUITA 2000: 506f.

72) BSūBh (p. 179,6):
Subject matter: Liberation

na niṣiddhāni varteta pūrṇajñānaphalecchayā /
iti ca pādme (1)

(1) Cf. ibid. l. 5: *ata ity alpaphalatvaṃ sūcyati* ... ; see also AgniP 9.

73) BSūBh (p. 180,5-6):
Subject matter: Dharma as means of liberation

dharmasvarūpacitratvād yo yo devamanogataḥ /
sa eva dharmo vijñeyo na hy ete lokasaṃmitāḥ /
iti ca pādme (1)

(1) Cf. AgniP 9; 20 and BrahP 28.

74) BSūBh (p. 199,7-9):
Subject matter: Jīvanmukti

anabhīṣṭam anārabdhaṃ puṇyam apy asya naśyati /
kiṃtu pāpaṃ parabrahmajñānino nāsti saṃśayaḥ /
iti pādme (1)

(1) Cf. ibid. l. 5f.: *muktāv anubhavakāraṇād yadanyat tat puṇyam api vinaśyati / aprārabdham anabhīṣṭaṃ ca / tathā hy ekeṣāṃ pāṭha ubhayos tyāgena – tasya putrā dāyam upayanti suhṛdaḥ sādhukṛtyāṃ dviṣantaḥ pāpakṛtyām iti* (= Śaṅkaras BSūBh *ad* IV 1,16 and Rāmānujas BSūBh *ad* IV 1,17) ... ; see also ĀdityaP 1; AgniP 24 and MESQUITA 2007: 39f. [= 2007_1: 450f.].

75) BSūBh (p. 218,6-7):
Subject matter: Liberation as realization of all wordly wishes

yad upāste pumān jīvan yat prāptum abhivāñchati /
yac ca paśyati tṛptaḥ saṃs tat prāpnoti mṛter anu /
iti hi pādme (1)

(1) Cf. ibid. l. 5: *na hi kārye pratipattiḥ prāpnavānīty abhisandhiś ca* ... ; see also AgniP 16 and BhaviṣP 15.

76) ChUBh (p. 415,21-22):
Subject matter: King Pautrāyaṇa

rājā pautrāyaṇaḥ śokāc chūdreti muninoditaḥ /
prāṇavidyām avāpyāsmāt paraṃ dharmam avāptavān /
iti pādme

77) ChUBh (p. 445,8-9):
Subject matter: Rāma-Avatāra

svātmānaṃ paramaṃ viṣṇuṃ viditvāpi sa rāghavaḥ /
daityānāṃ mohanārthāya darśayāmāsa mūḍhatām /
iti pādme (1)

(1) Cf. AdiP 1 and MESQUITA 2000_1: 40 [= 1997: 33].

78) ChUBh (p. 453,7-9):
Subject matter: Devamānuṣa

devā manuṣyatāṃ prāptā vijñeyā devamānuṣāḥ /
dhyānaṃ kurvanta iva te naiva syur bahubhāṣiṇaḥ /
brūyur arthavatīṃ vācaṃ nānarthāṃ prāyaśo hi te /
iti pādme (1)

(1) Cf. BhaviṣP 5.

79) GīBh (p. 37,4-5):
Subject matter: Doctrine of Avatāras

na ca garbhe 'vasad devyā na cāpi vasudevataḥ /
na cāpi rāghavāj jāto na cāpi jamadagnitaḥ /
nityānando 'dvayo 'py evaṃ krīḍate moghadarśanaḥ /
iti pādme (1)

(1) Cf. ibid. l. 3: *tad eva līlayāsau paricchinādirūpeṇa darśayati māyayā* ... ; see also ĀdiP 1; MBh 42[74].

80) GīBh (p. 39,27-28):
Subject matter: Viṣṇu's worship by Deities and Kings

> *devādīnām ādirājñāṃ mahodyoge 'pi no manaḥ /*
> *viṣṇoś calati tadbhogo 'py atīva haritoṣaṇaḥ /*
> iti pādme (1)

(1) Cf. ibid. ll. 25f.: *ādhikārikās tu tatsthā eva prāyatye samarthāḥ / sa eva ca mahān bhagavatas toṣaḥ / tac coktam* ... ; see also BhaviṣP 5.

81) GīBh (p. 55,1-2):
Subject matter: Viṣṇu's supreme transcendence

> *tvadadhīnaṃ yataḥ sarvam ataḥ sarvo bhavān iti /*
> *vadanti munayaḥ sarve na tu sarvasvarūpataḥ /*
> iti pādme (1)

(1) Cf. ibid. (p. 54,20f.): *sarvam etad brahmety ucyate / tadadhīnasattāpratītitvāt / na tu tat svarūpatvāt / uktaṃ hi* ... ; Mesquita 2000: 455f.; see also AgniP 6; MatsyaP 12.

82) GīBh (p. 67,10-11):
Subject matter: Hierarchy in the worship

> *samānāṃ viṣamā pūjā viṣamāṇāṃ samā tathā /*
> *kriyate yena devo 'pi sa padād bhraśyate pumān /*
> iti pādme (1)

(1) Cf. ibid. l. 9: *na tu sādhupāpādīnāṃ pūjādisāmyam / tatra doṣasmṛteḥ* ... ; also (p. 62,24f.):

> *viṣameṣv api jīveṣu samo viṣṇuḥ sadaiva tu /*
> *yat tṛṇādigatasyāpi guṇāḥ pūrṇā hareḥ sadā /*
> iti ca (unknown source);

see also BhaviṣPV 15; BrahP 36; BrahPV 35.

83) GīBh (p. 79,12-14):
Subject matter: Māyā

> tathāha pādme –
> *ātmanaḥ prāvṛttiṃ caiva lokacittasya bandhanam /*
> *svasāmarthyena devyā ca kurute sa maheśvaraḥ /*
> iti (1)

(1) Cf. ibid. ll. 11f.: *yogena sāmarthyopāyena māyayā ca / mayaiva mūḍho nābhijānāti – tathāha* ... ; see also AgniP 25; PadP 13.

84) GīBh (p. 85,6):
Subject matter: Etymology of *hṛd*

> *hriyate tvayā jagad yasmād dhṛd ity eva prabhāṣyase* /
> iti hi pādme (1)

(1) Cf. ibid l. 5: *hṛdi nārāyaṇe* ... *na hi mūrdhni prāṇe hṛdi manasaḥ sthitiḥ saṃbhavati* ... .

84_1) GīBh (p. 137,6-7):
Subject matter: Śrī / Ramā

> *baddho vāpitu mukto vā na ramāvat priyo hareḥ* /
> iti pādme (1)

(1) Cf. ibid. l. 6: *brahmavat prakṛtivat bhagavatpriyatvaṃ brahmabhūyam / na tu tāvat priyatvam / kiṃtu priyatvamātram* ... ; see also AgniP 25.

85) GīT (p. 22,27-28):
Subject matter: *creatio ex nihilo*

> *tatra tatra sthito viṣṇur nityaṃ rakṣati nityadā* /
> *anityadaivānityaṃ ca nityānitye tatas tataḥ* /
> *bhāvābhāvaniyantā hi tad ekaḥ puruṣottamaḥ* /
> iti pādme (1)

(1) Cf. ibid. ll. 24f.: *dehī kuto 'vadhyaḥ / yasmād ayam īśvaraḥ sarvasya jīvasya sūkṣme sthūle ca dehe rakṣatvenāvasthitaḥ / ata evāvadhyaḥ / na svasāmarthyaṃ kasyāpi* /

> *dravyaṃ karma ca kālaś ca svabhāvo jīva eva ca* /
> *yadanugrahataḥ santi na santi yadupekṣayā* /
> iti hi bhāgavate (= BhāgP II 5,14 / II 10,12) ...

MESQUITA 2000: 461f.

86) GīT (p. 73,20-22):
Subject matter: Unlimited number of the individual souls / Tāratamya

> *anantānāṃ tu jīvānāṃ yatante kecid eva tu* /
> *muktyai teṣu ca mucyante kecin mukteṣu ca sphuṭam* /
> *kecanaiva hariṃ samyag brahmarudrādayo viduḥ* /
> *anyeṣāṃ yāvatā muktis tāvaj jñānaṃ harau param* /
> iti pādme (1)

(1) Cf. BrāṇP 71; PadP 67; SkaP 128 and MESQUITA 2000: 207n. 432.

87) GīT (p. 85,24-25):
Subject matter: Liberation

niyamāj janmano 'bhāvo muktasyaiva tathāpi tu /
maharlokam atītānāṃ na janmāṃśalayau vinā /
tatrāpy avaśyaṃ tat sthānaṃ taiḥ kṣipraṃ punar āpyate /
iti pādme (1)

(1) Cf. ibid. l. 18: *mahāmerusthabrahmasadanam ārabhya punarāvṛttiḥ* ... ; see also AgniP 16.

88) GīT (p. 87,27-28):
Subject matter: Liberation

vidvān brahma samāpnoti yatra tatra mṛto'pi san /
iti ca pādme (1)

(1) Cf. AgniP 16.

89) GīT (p. 95,29-30):
Subject matter: Bhakti

nāsya bhakto 'pi yo dveṣyo na cābhakto 'pi yaḥ priyaḥ /
kiṃtu bhaktyanusāreṇa phalado 'taḥ samo hariḥ /
iti pādme (1)

(1) Cf. AgniP 20 and MESQUITA 2007: 26 ff. [= 2007_1: 443ff.].

90) GīT (p. 107,30-31):
Subject matter: Location/seat of Deities in Viṣṇu's heaven

viṣṇuṃ samāśrito brahmā brahmaṇo 'ṅkagato haraḥ /
harasyāṅgaviśeṣeṣu devāḥ sarve 'pi saṃsthitāḥ /
iti pādme (1)

(1) Cf. ibid. l. 29: *kamalāsane brahmaṇi sthitaṃ rudram* ... ; see also BhaviṣP 5.

91) GīT (p. 115,21):
Subject matter: Viṣṇu's Sarvanāmatva

viśvanāmā sa bhagavān yataḥ pūrṇaguṇaḥ prabhuḥ /
iti pādme (1)

(1) Cf. BrāṇP 2.

92) GīT (p. 131,21-23):
Subject matter: Antaryāmin

duḥkhayogādirūpeṇa jīveṣu vinaśatsv api /
duḥkhayogādirahitaḥ sarvajīveṣv api sthitaḥ /

guṇaiḥ sarvaiḥ samo nityaṃ na hīno hīnago 'pi san /
iti paśyati yo viṣṇuṃ sa eva na tamo vrajet /
iti pādme (1)

(1) Cf. ibid. l. 20: *jīveṣu duḥkhayogādirūpeṇa vinaśyatsv apy atathābhūtam* ... ; see also BhāgP 2 and MESQUITA 2000: 489f.

93) GīT (p. 148,25-29):
Subject matter: Low-graded Deities / Tāratamya

yāgāt tu rājasāt svargaḥ sāṅkalpika udāhṛtaḥ /
lokaḥ sa dīnadevānāṃ sanāmnāṃ vāsavādibhiḥ /
viṣṇāv aśraddhayāyogyakāmāc caiṣāṃ punar bhavet /
narakaṃ ca vinā yajñaṃ rājasā naralokagāḥ /
niṣiddhakarma kuryuś ced īyus te narakaṃ dhruvam /
kadācit sāttvikāḥ kuryuḥ karma rājasatāmasam /
anye 'nyac ca tathāpy eṣāṃ sthitiḥ svābhāvike punaḥ /
svaṃ svaṃ karma tu sarveṣāṃ sadaiva syān mahatphalam /
anyad alpaphalaṃ caiva bāhulyaṃ teṣu lakṣaṇam /
iti pādme (1)

(1) Cf. BhaviṣPV 15; BhaviṣP 5.

93₁) GīT (p. 151,30+152,16):
Subject matter: Hell

svayajñādīn parityajya nirayaṃ yāty asaṃśayam /
iti pādme (1)

(1) Cf. ibid. ll. 29f.: *saṅgaphalatyāgam ṛte svarūpatyāgaḥ kārya iti mithyājñānākhya-mohāt* ... ; see also BhaviṣPV 19.

94) GīT (p. 154,20-29):
Subject matter: Sāttvika, Rājasa and Tāmasa doctrines

astitvād bhūtanāmabhyaḥ sarvajīvebhya eva yat /
muktebhyo 'pi pṛthaktvena viṣṇoḥ sarvatragasya ca / [1]
aikyena ca svarūpāṇāṃ prādurbhāvādikātmanām /
tāratamyena jīvānāṃ bhedenaiva parasparam / [2]
jaḍebhyaś caiva jīvānāṃ jaḍānāṃ ca parasparam /
tebhyo viṣṇoś ca samyak tallakṣaṇajñānapūrvakam / [3]
jñānaṃ sāttvikam uddiṣṭaṃ yat sākṣān muktikāraṇam /
viṣṇor anyasya yāthārthyajñānaṃ rājasam ucyate / [4]
yadi viṣṇuṃ na jānāti yadi vā miśratattvavit /

anyathākaraṇīyatvāt kāryākhyaṃ jīvam eva yaḥ / [5]
akāryaṃ brahma jānāti sa evākhilam ity api /
ekajīvaparijñānāt kṛtsnajño 'smīti manyate / [6]
yuktibhir jñānarāhityāt svapakṣasyālpayuktitaḥ /
ayuktatām eva guṇaṃ manyate cālpadarśanaḥ / [7]
atattvārthaṃ jagad brūte tattvārthajñānavarjanāt /
sa mukhyatāmasajñānī hy ekaikenāpi kiṃ punaḥ / [8]
sarvair etair viśeṣaiś ca yuktaḥ pāpatamādhikaḥ / [9ab]
iti pādme (1)

(1) Cf. ibid. ll. 30f.: *pṛthaktvena tu yajjnānam ity asya vyākhyā nānābhāvān ityādi / sarvagatam ekam īśvaraṃ na jānātīty etāvataiva rājasatvam / ekasya kṛtsnavajjñānam eva tāmasam / muktatvādirūpeṇānyathākaraṇīyatvāt parādhīnatvenālpasya jīvasya svāntantryādiguṇapūrṇatvāt kṛtsnena brahmaṇaikyajñānaṃ ca mahātamasam / kiṃ punas tāvan mātraṃ sarvam iti jñānam / kiṃ punas tatrāpy ekajīvād anyat kim api nāstīti / ahaitukaṃ jñānaṃ sarvam api tāmasam / kimu tad evoktalakṣaṇam / atattvārthavat sadasadvailakṣaṇyādyanyathārthakalpanāyuktam eva tāmasam / kimu tad evoktaviśeṣaṇair yuktam / prāyo 'lpajñānam api tāmasam / ajñānabahulyatvāt / kimu tadevoktamithyājñānabahulam ity apunaruktiḥ / ekasmin sarvajñānaṃ kārye jīve pūrṇabrahmeti saktaṃ jñānaṃ niryuktikaṃ cātattvārthakalpanāyuktam alpajñānaṃ ca pṛthak tāmasānīti vā / māyāvāde tv etāni samastāni / anyatrāpi tv ahaitukatvādikaṃ viruddhavādeṣu samaṃ sarveṣu*; see also BhaviṣPV 3n. 7; MESQUITA 2000: 468f.; 528f. and MESQUITA 2000_1: 104-120 [= 1997: 83-96].

95) GīT (p. 157,7-8):
Subject matter: Sāttvika-happiness

viṣṇoḥ prasādāt svamanaḥprasādāt sāttvikaṃ sukham /
iti pādme (1)

(1) Cf. Gī XVIII 37cd: *tat sukhaṃ sāttvikaṃ proktam ātmabuddhiprasādajam*; see also BhaviṣP 15.

96) GīT (p. 162,27-28):
Subject matter: True Bhakti

abhaktād api pāpaḥ syād asūyur doṣadṛg yataḥ /
iti ca pādme (1)

(1) Cf. ibid. ll. 25f.: *evam abhaktāya kadāpi na vācyam / kadācid alpatapaso 'lpaśuśruṣor api bhaktyādhikye vācyaṃ bhavatīti kadācaneti viśeṣaḥ / abhaktāc ca na vācyam asūyor iti tatrāpi caśabdaḥ samuccaye tathādhike nyūnatve ca prayujyate /* iti śabdanirṇaya (unknown source); see also AgniP 20.

97) KathUBh (p. 477,18-19):
Subject matter: Yama

yamo 'nuvādasantuṣṭo vahnes tannāmatām api /
sṛṅkāṃ svarṇamayīṃ caiva kaṇṭhamālām adād vibhuḥ /
iti pādme (1)

(1) Cf. ibid. ll. 17f.: *anekarūpāṃ suvarṇamayīm – bahurūpaṃ ca puraṭaṃ kārtsvaram itīryata* ity abhidhānāt (unknown source); see also NārP 14.

98) KhN (p. 227,4-6):
Subject matter: Brahmā

samīpato dūrato jñaṃ tvām uddiśyaiva madgatam /
ehi viṣṇo na me śaktis tvadāhvāne hi mām upa /
iti brahmāstuvad viṣṇuṃ tannābhyutthitapadmagaḥ /
iti pādme (1)

(1) Cf. ibid. ll. 2f.: *evaṃvidhaṃ madgataṃ tvām uddiśyaivopehi / viśvadha viśvadhāraka / samīpato dūrataś ca tvāṃ manyamānāya mahyaṃ manyave jñānāya mām upehīti vā* ... ; see also BrāṇP 29 and SkaP 121.

99) KhN (p. 241,7-8):
Subject matter: Indivisibility of Viṣṇu's nature

dehadehivibhāgaś ca na kvacit parameśvare /
guṇatadvadvibhāgo vā neha nāneti hi śrutiḥ /
iti pādme (1)

(1) Cf. BrāṇP 10 and MESQUITA 2000: 429ff.

100) MāṇUBh (p. 513,10-11):
Subject matter: Varuṇa

dhyāyan nārāyaṇaṃ devaṃ praṇavena samāhitaḥ /
maṇḍūkarūpī varuṇas tuṣṭāva hariṃ avyayam /
iti pādme (1)

(1) Cf. ibid. l. 9: *māṇḍūkarūpiṇā varuṇena catūrūpo nārāyaṇaḥ stūyate* ... ; BrahP 27; GarP 58.

101) MuUBh (p. 493,18-20):
Subject matter: Worship of Deities

agniṣṭomādibhir yajñaiḥ sarvadevasthitaṃ harim /
yajanti tāṃś ca kāritvād vasus tasmāt tathāyajat /
pṛthak pṛthak tu tretāyāṃ yajante devatā gaṇāḥ /
yathā kṛte tathā prājñās tretāyāṃ bahudhā tataḥ /
iti pādme (1)

(1) Cf. ibid. l. 17: *tretāyāṃ bahudhā santatāni* / *kṛte tv ekaprakāreṇaiva santatāni* ... ; see also AgniP 20 and BhaviṣP 5; BrāṇP 99.

102) ṚgBh (p. 7,1-2):
Subject matter: Vidyās

uktaṃ pādmapurāṇe ca –
kapilo bhagavān ajaḥ provāca brahmaṇe vidyāḥ / (1)

(1) Cf. ibid. (p. 6,10f.):
hayagrīvād imā vidyāḥ śvasitatvena niḥsṛtāḥ /
brahmaṇā svīkṛtās tāś ca rudraśeṣavipā api /
dakṣādyāḥ sanakādyāś ca śakrādyā manavas tathā /
jagṛhus te ca viśvasmiṃś cakrur vyāptās tato 'khilāḥ /
... ;
see also BrāṇP 101; PadP 9 and MESQUITA 2000: 71n. 63; 380f.

103) TaiUBh (p. 537,2-3):
Subject matter: Hierarchy in the state of liberation

kāmaḥ saṅkalpa ānando muktānāṃ tāratamyataḥ /
svarūpabhūtās te sarve nirdoṣā guṇarūpakāḥ /
iti pādme (1)

(1) Cf. ibid. ll. 1f.: *yaṃ yam antam abhikāmo bhavati so 'sya saṅkalpād eva bhavati* (ChU VIII 2,10) *iti muktānām api svarūpabhūtaḥ kāmaḥ pratīyate* ... ; see also BhaviṣPV 15; PadP 104.

104) VTN (p. 43,18-19):
Subject matter: Hierarchy in the state of liberation

nṛpādyāḥ śatadhṛtyantā muktigā uttarottaram /
guṇaiḥ sarvaiḥ śataguṇā modanta iti hi śrutiḥ /
iti pādme (1)

(1) Cf. BhaviṣPV 15; BrāṇP 29 and MESQUITA 2000: 234.

Skandapurāṇa (SkaP)

[Madhva describes SkaP sometimes as Śivaśāstra (MBhTN I 52c; cf. MESQUITA 2000: 156f. [= 1997: 126f.]). In one instance he quotes it as Śaivapurāṇa (cf. AiUBh (p. 219,27-28 = SkaP 6_1) and as *skānde śaive* or *skānde' py uktaṃ śivenaiva* (SkaP 80, 110 and 122). This remark is in agreement with NārP (I 104,1-213): *pravakṣyāmi purāṇaṃ skandasaṃjñakam*; ibid. (I 104,212b): *śivamāhātmyavarṇana*. This Adhyāya presents a synopsis of the Purāṇa (*skandapurāṇānukramaṇīvarṇana*). SkaP is neither a single nor a coherent text but it is "only a name to which extensive works, said to be the Saṃhitās or the Khaṇḍas of the original Purāṇa, and numerous Māhātmyas claim allegiance" (cf. ROCHER 1986: 228f.). The *vulgata*-SkaP is "merely a part of the bigger one, it is by no means a small work" (cf. HAZRA 1987: 157-166). It is nevertheless not identical with the oldest preserved text of SkaP, which was widespread in North India and considered as authoritative. Gradually it fell into oblivion and was replaced by other later versions of SkaP. The time of its origin is fixed between the 6th and 8th cent. A.D. It has only small textual connections with the Vulgata-Text (cf. The Skandapurāṇa, Volume I Adhyāyas 1-25, crit. edited ... by R. ADRIAENSEN et alii. Groningen 1998: 4f.; 24; see also H. BAKKER, Pārvatī's Svayaṃvara (Studies in the Skandapurāṇa I) WZKS 40 [1996]: 5-43 and R. ADRIAENSEN, H. BAKKER, H. ISAACSON, Towards a critical edition of the Skandapurāṇa, IIJ 37 [1994]: 325-331). This original text has been edited for the first time in 1988 [Skandapurāṇasya Ambikākāṇḍaḥ, saṃpādakaḥ Kṛṣṇaprasāda Bhaṭṭarāī. Kathmandu 1988 (Mahendraratnagranthamālā 2)]. The text references given below could not be traced in the vulgata-edition of SkaP. Since they are intimately related to the peculiar teachings of Madhva it is to be assumed that Madhva himself is their author, exactly as in the case of untraceable quotes from other Purāṇas and Itihāsas. Morever, with regard to the untraceable quotes which are ascribed to the SkaP, we might argue for their authenticity from the fact that Madhva claims to be a partial incarnation (*aṃśāvatāra*) of Viṣṇu, thereby becoming an authentic bearer of the revelation of Viṣṇu, an attribute usually ascribed to Vyāsa in the Hindu tradition (cf. MESQUITA 2000_1: 51-53f. [= 1997: 41-43f.]; see also above 'Introduction' n. 16).

According to Madhva, SkaP and PadP belong to the category of *mohaśāstrāṇi*, which have been composed by Rudra under the command of Hari in order to deceive the Asuras. The fact that Madhva accepts the authority of Śaiva Āgamas is based on the supposition that they contain textual passages, which are not in contradition with the Sadāgamas and also for the reason that they have been composed under the command of Viṣṇu. However, one should not reject on this ground that what is taught therein: *eṣāṃ yan na virodhi syāt tatroktaṃ tan na vāryate* (cf. MESQUITA 2000_1: 157f. [= 1997: 127f.]). It is striking that the highest number of quotes Madhva adduces in his different works belongs to SkaP, namely one hundred and thirty-two, followed by two other Śaivite Purāṇas, PadP, with one hundred and ten, and BrāṇP, with one hundred and seven quote-references. The highest share of quotes fall – as in the case of PadP and BrāṇP – to Madhva's commentary on BhāgP – BhāgTN (sixty-eight); BSūBh (twenty-eight); AiUBh (eight); GīBh (nine); BĀUBh; GīT; MBh and VTN (three each); ChUBh (two), and Anuv; IśUBh; KhN; MuUBh; ṚgBh one each.

The closing Śloka in SkaP 64 has been handed down also by later commentators. There are also verses in other metres than śloka, namely Vasantatilakā (SkaP 36[3ab]) and Upajāti (SkaP 79); SkaP 110 [1-6/4 with a surplus syllable] with Vaṃśasthavila-Metre together with two Śloka verses [7-8]. For metrical lapses, see SkaP 51[2cd]); SkaP 52[1ab, 3ab] and SkaP 54[3ab]) SkaP 129ab.]

1) AiUBh (p. 176,19-20):
Subject matter: Maṅgala-verse

aṅgeṣu yasya cchandāṃsi devā lokā makhā api /
tadvaśā niyatā nityaṃ namas tasmai parātmane /
iti ca skānde (1)

(1) Cf. ibid. ll. 15f.: *ad eva nārāyaṇākhyam adhikaṃ daivatam anyāni daivatamātrāṇi ... mukhyādhidaivataṃ nārāyaṇa eva ...* .

2) AiUBh (p. 186,29+187,10):
Subject matter: Bliss in liberation / Tāratamya

bhuñjate puruṣaṃ prāpya yathā caiva grahādayaḥ /
tathā muktāv uttamāyāṃ viṣṇum āviśya bhuñjate /
viṣṇor vaśāś ca te sarve sarvadā duḥkhavarjitāḥ /
na tu viṣṇuguṇān sarve bhuñjate te kadācana /
bāhyabhogān bhuñjate ca tāratamyena kāṃścana /
viṣṇor dehād bahiś cāpi nirgacchanti yatheṣṭataḥ /
ityādi ca skānde (1)

(1) Cf. ibid. ll. 27f: *na ca bhogarahitā muktir nāmānyāstīty atra kiṃcin mānam ...* ; see also AgniP 16; BhaviṣP 15; BrahVP 29.

3) AiUBh (p. 202, 28-29):
Subject matter: Lakṣamaṇa

lakṣmaṇaḥ pretyaḥ sugrīvaṃ babhāṣe rāmacoditaḥ /
iti ca skānde (1)

(1) Cf. ibid. ll. 26f.: *nātra pretyaśabdo maraṇavācī / kiṃtu pretām yajñāsya śaṃbhuvetyādivat prāptivācy eva / na hi mṛtaḥ punar eṣu lokeṣv eva rājati / ... yad vā – eti ca preti cetyādau* (BĀU V 3,1; KeU II 5) *prāptyarthe 'pi vedeṣu prasiddhatvāc ca ...* ; see also LORENZ 2003: 19f.

4) AiUBh (p. 213,26-27):
Subject matter: Viṣṇu's names

virūpākṣaḥ śivaḥ sūryaḥ surācāryo vināyakaḥ /
puṇḍarīkeṣaṇo viṣṇuḥ sahasrākṣaḥ surādhipaḥ /
iti ca skānde (1)

(1) Cf. ibid. ll. 23f.: ... *akārasya ca viṣṇāv eva prasiddhasyātrābhyāsāt / tasya yathā kapyāsaṃ puṇḍarīkam evam akṣiṇīti* (ChU I 6,7) *sūryamaṇḍale puṇḍarīkākṣatvena nirdiṣṭasyātrāpi ya eṣa tapatītyādinā* (BĀU I 2,7 / II 3,2) *bahuśo 'nusandhānāc ca / sūryo hi hiraṇyākṣaḥ savitā deva āgād iti piṅgākṣaḥ prasiddhaḥ ... nāmāni sarvāṇi yam āviśanti taṃ vai viṣṇuṃ paramam udāharanti ...* ; see also BrāṇP 68.

5) AiUBh (p. 215,22-25):
Subject matter: Viṣṇu's avatāras

nāyaṃ daśarathāj jāto na cāpi vasudevataḥ /
kvāsyājñānaṃ kuto duḥkhaṃ prādurbhāveṣv api prabhoḥ /

prādurbhūtaś cidānandaśarīro rāghavaḥ svayam |
stambhād vā naradehād vā naivāsya prākṛtā tanuḥ |
daityānāṃ mohanārthāya so 'jñānādyaṃ prakāśayet |
pūrṇacitsukharūpo 'pi sadā sarvāvatāragaḥ |
ityādi skānde (1)

(1) Cf. ibid. ll. 20f.: *aham eva svatantraḥ paripūrṇaguṇa iti kṛṣṇarāghavādisarvāvatārarūpo 'pi sarvadānubhavaty eva*; see also ĀdiP 1 and MESQUITA 2000_1: 37f. [= 1997: 31n. 39f.].

6) AiUBh (p. 217,15-18):
Subject matter: Kṛṣṇa's avatāra

kṛṣṇo hy atyaktadeho 'pi tyaktadehavad eva ca |
lokānāṃ darśayāmāsa svarūpasadṛśākṛtim |
yena rūpeṇa kaṃsādīn jaghne tadrūpa eva hi |
pūjyate 'dyāpi śarvādyair nirmitānyā śavākṛtiḥ |
svargārohaṇakāle hi janās tenaiva mohitāḥ |
yattad rūpaṃ nijaṃ viṣṇor dṛṣṭaṃ sarvanarair bhuvi |
adyāpi tad devaloke pūjyate sarvadaivataiḥ |
ityādi skānde (1)

(1) Cf. ibid. ll. 11f.: ... *jīvaśarīraṃ parityajyānyatra gamanamātraṃ viṣṇor apy astīti praitīty ukte apy avirodhaḥ | kṛṣṇarāghavādisvarūpam eva hy asau na parityajati* ... . ; see also ĀdiP 1.

6_1) AiUBh (p. 219,27-28):
Subject matter: Prajāpati and his epithets

prajāpatiḥ śivaḥ śeṣo liṅgam ity abhidhīyate |
liṅgābhimānī lokasya sraṣṭā giriśa eva hi |
iti śaivapurāṇe [= SkaP] (1)

(1) Cf. ibid. ll. 24f.: ... *prajāpatiḥ śivaḥ | liṅgābhimānitvāt* ... ; see also BhāgP 1; BhaviṣP 11; MBh 3.

7) AiUBh (p. 237,21-22):
Subject matter: Brahmā

yatra brahmā vedavākyaṃ vyācakṣāṇo makhair yajan |
somena ca suteneśam āste loke harer hi saḥ |
iti skānde (1)

(1) Cf. BrāṇP 29.

8) Anuv (p. 203,29-31):
Subject matter: Suffering (*duḥkha*) as means of bliss

yadendravairocanayor brahmāstrābhyāṃ sutāpitāḥ /
api naivājahur yuddharasāt te nāradādayaḥ /
iti skāndavacas [tasmāt sukhābhāvāya ko yatet] (1)

(1) Cf. ibid. ll. 28f.:
nāradādyāḥ sukhārthāya sahante duḥkham añjasā /
yuddhādidarśanaṃ yasmāt suduḥkhenāpi kurvate /
see also BhaviṣP 15; SkaP 63.

8_1) BĀUBh (p. 246,10-11):
Subject matter: Hierarchy among divine horses

patanti niyataṃ hantuṃ devāśvāḥ śatrumūrdasu /
vegādhikā āsurāśvā vegamātraṃ nṛvāhane /
iti skānde (1)

(1) Cf. ibid. (p. 245,27): *teṣāṃ teṣāṃ vāhaneṣu sthitvā tattatkarmakartṛvāt tattan nāmā.*

9) BĀUBh (p. 313,19-20):
Subject matter: Viṣṇu's supreme transcendence

dīpter ākāśaśabdoktā śrīr hi sarvāśrayā matā /
tadāśrayaḥ paro viṣṇuḥ so 'sthūlādiguṇo mataḥ /
iti skānde (1)

(1) Cf. AgniP 6; 25; 27; BrāṇP 51 and MESQUITA 2000: 105n. 164; 493f.

10) BĀUBh (p. 327,27-28):
Subject matter: Yājñavalkya

yājñavalkyo varaṃ datvā rājñā saṃvādakāmukaḥ /
vaidehanagaraṃ prāyāt santo yac chāstralolupāḥ /
iti skānde (1)

(1) Cf. BrāṇP 17.

11) BhāgTN (p. 5,8-10):
Subject matter: Etymology of Brahman

skānde ca –
vasanād vāsanād vastu nityāpratihataṃ yataḥ /

vāse nedaṃ yatas tunnam atas tad brahma śabdyate /
iti (1)

(1) Cf. ibid. l. 8: *vastu apratihatanityam* ... ; see also BhāgP 1 and 5.

12) BhāgTN (p. 7,9-10):
Subject matter: Māyā and its synonyms

mahāmāyety avidyeti niyatir mohanīti ca /
prakṛtir vāsanety evaṃ tavecchānanta kathyate /
iti hi skānde (1)

(1) Cf. ibid. ll. 8f.: *ātmamāyayā svarūpabhūtecchayā* ... ; see also BhaviṣP 13; HarV 8; PadP 13; VarP 18 and MESQUITA 2000: 158f.; 187f.

12$_1$) BhāgTN (p. 8,5-9):
Subject matter: Doctrine of Avatāras

uktaṃ ca skānde –
nityatṛptaḥ parānando yo 'vyayaḥ parameśvaraḥ /
yasya putraphalaṃ naiva yajjātaṃ jagad īdṛśam /
yadadhīnaśriyo 'pāṅgād brahmarudrādisaṃsthitiḥ /
sa putrārthaṃ tapas tepe vyāso rudrasya ceśvaraḥ /
kātaryaṃ darśayāmāsa viyoge laukikaṃ hariḥ /
kutaḥ kātaratā tasya nityānandamahodadheḥ /
iti (1)

(1) Cf. ibid. ll. 5f.: *anupetaṃ dehādibhiḥ* / *anabhimānāt* / *akātaraḥ kātaravad darśayāmāsa* ... also ll. 9f.:
īśann api hi lokasya sarvasya jagato hariḥ /
karmāṇi kurute nityaṃ kīnāśa iva durbala /
iti codyoge (unknown source);
see also ĀdiP 1; BhaviṣPV 21; ViṣDhP 1 and MESQUITA 2000$_1$: 37ff. [= 1997: 31ff.].

13) BhāgTN (p. 8,13):
Subject matter: Rudra and Śuka

ahaṅkārātmako rudraḥ śuko dvaipāyanātmajaḥ /
iti skānde (1)

(1) Cf. ibid. ll. 12f.: *sarvabhūtahṛdayo 'haṅkārātmakatvāt* ... ; see also BhaviṣPV 21; BrahP 22; GarP 20; SkaP 105.

14) BhāgTN (p. 14,6-8):
Subject matter: Viṣṇu's supreme transcendence

akḷptyā vai svatantratvād aśubhasya ca varjanāt /
abhoktā śubhabhoktṛtvād bhoktety eva ca taṃ viduḥ /
anyūnānadhikatvāc ca pūrṇaḥ svānandabhojanāt /
virāgāc ca parasyāsya bhoktṛtvapratiṣedhanam /
iti skānde (1)

(1) Cf. ibid. ll. 5f.: *anaśnan ity aśubhāpekṣayā paravaśatvāpekṣayā kḷptyapekṣayā ca* ... ; see also AgniP 6 and MESQUITA 2000: 458f.

15) BhāgTN (p. 21,7-8):
Subject matter: Viṣṇu's supreme transcendence

avijñāya paraṃ deham ānandātmānam avyayam /
āropayanti janimat pañcabhūtātmakaṃ jaḍam /
iti skānde (1)

(1) Cf. ibid. ll. 6f.: *dṛśyatvaṃ jaḍarūpatvam* ... ; see also AgniP 4; 6.

16) BhāgTN (p. 24,4-5):
Subject matter: Eulogy of Mahābhārata

bhārataṃ brāḥmaṇādīnāṃ vedārthapratipattaye /
tad eva vedas tv anyeṣāṃ narte tat kasyacit sukham /
iti skānde (1)

(1) Cf. KūrP 30_2 and MESQUITA 2000_1: 143ff. [= 1997: 117ff.]; see also GīBh (p. 1,3f.).

17) BhāgTN (p. 25,11-12):
Subject matter: Eulogy of Mahābhārata

yathā tu bhārate devo na tathānyeṣu keṣucit /
ucyate na tathāpīśaṃ jānanty ajñā janārdanam /
iti hi skānde (1)

(1) Cf. ibid. ll. 10f.: *punar apekṣitatvān na prāyena nirūpitāḥ* ... ; see also KūrP 30_2; and GīBh (p. 1,3f.).

18) BhāgTN (p. 30,3-4):
Subject matter: Definitions of different settlements

mṛgayājīvanaṃ kheṭo vāṭī puṣpopajīvinām /
grāmo bahujanākīrṇo rājarājāśrayaṃ puram /
jalasthalāyati sphītaṃ paṭṭanaṃ kīrtyate budhaiḥ /
iti skānde

19) BhāgTN (p. 32,1-2):
Subject matter: Drauṇi

pārthānuyātam ātmānaṃ drauṇiḥ svapne dadarśa ha /
bandhanaṃ cātmanas tatra draupadyā caiva mokṣaṇam /
iti skānde (1)

(1) Cf. ibid. ll. 11f.: *svātmana eva vipriyaṃ na bhartuḥ / prayojanābhāvād vipriyam iva / tasya priyam iti svāpoktam / svapno 'yam ... tasmān naiṣīkavirodhaḥ*; see also ibid. n. 8.; SkaP 37.

20) BhāgTN (p. 34,1-3):
Subject matter: Doctrine of Avatāras

asaṅgaś cāvyatho 'bhedyo 'nigrāhyo 'śoṣya eva ca /
viddho 'sṛgañcito baddha iti viṣṇuḥ pradṛśyate /
asurān mohayan devaḥ krīḍayaiva sureṣv api /
mānuṣān madhyayā dṛṣṭyā na mukteṣu kathaṃcana /
iti skānde (1)

(1) Cf. ĀdiP 1; BrahVP 20 and MESQUITA 2000_1: 40n. 51 [= 1997: 33n. 43].

21) BhāgTN (p. 41,8-9):
Subject matter: Viṣṇu, the Kāla

saṃhartā bhagavān viṣṇuḥ kāla ity abhidhīyate /
athavā guṇasarvasvaṃ kālaśabdo vyanakti hi /
iti ca skānde (1)

(1) Cf. BhāgP 1; BrahP 25; ViṣP 1.

22) BhāgTN (p. 42,6-10):
Subject matter: Sons of Pāṇḍu

skānde ca –
bhīmasantarjito rājñas tv anujñāṃ prāpya yatnataḥ /
dhṛtarāṣṭro vane vāsam akarod vatsaratrayam /
viduras taddidṛkṣārtham āgateṣu vanaṃ purā /
pāṇḍaveṣu tu rājānaṃ praviśyaikatvam āgataḥ /
tato dāvāgninā dagdhaṃ dhṛtarāṣṭraṃ ca saubalīm /
śrutvā kuntīṃ ca cintāṃ ta āpuḥ pāṇḍusutās tadā /
tāṃs tadā nārado vidvān śamayāmāsa dharmavit /
uktvottamām gatiṃ teṣāṃ niṣṭhāṃ tātkālikīṃ tathā /
ityādi (1)

(1) Cf. ibid. ll. 5f.: *pitarau kuntīdhṛtarāṣṭrau / na cāpaśyat tasya manasi teṣāṃ vipadbhāvo babhūva / anyathā mahābhāratavirodhāt* ... ; see also BhavişPV 25; MatsyaP 15.

23) BhāgTN (p. 65,10):
Subject matter: Vyāsa, the progenitor of Dhṛtarāṣṭra

> *vyāsaḥ ṣaṭśatavarṣīyo dhṛtarāṣṭram ajījanat /*
> iti skānde (1)

(1) Cf. ibid. l. 9: *dvāpare ca ādau ca kṛṣṇāvatārāpekṣayā* ... ; see also BhavişPV 21.

24) BhāgTN (p. 82,10-11):
Subject matter: Viṣṇu's worship as path to liberation

> *akāmo dharmakāmo vā mokṣakāmo 'pi yo bhavet /*
> *athavā sarvakāmo yaḥ sa viṣṇuṃ puruṣaṃ yajet /*
> iti skānde (1)

(1) Cf. AgniP 20; BrahP 28.

25) BhāgTN (p. 89,14-16):
Subject matter: Sense organs

> *jñānendriyāṇāṃ devānāṃ jñānaśaktir udīritā /*
> *kriyā karmendriyāṇāṃ ca bhūtānāṃ dravyaśaktitā /*
> iti skānde (1)

(1) Cf. BhavişPV 17; see also MatsyaP 5 and PadP 19.

26) BhāgTN (p. 91,14-15):
Subject matter: Etymology of Jīva

> *prāṇaṃ dhārayate yasmāt sa jīvaḥ parameśvaraḥ /*
> *ajīvo 'pi mahātejās tv athavā jīvayan jagat /*
> iti skānde (1)

(1) Cf. ibid. ll. 13f.: *jīva iti vā* ... ; see also BrāṇP 71.

27) BhāgTN (p. 92,1-2):
Subject matter: Cosmic egg

> *aṇḍe jātau pumāṃsau dvau harir brahmā tathaiva ca /*
> *anādis tu haris tatra brahmā sādir udāhṛtaḥ /*
> iti skānde (1)

(1) Cf. BrāṇP 29.

28) BhāgTN (p. 100,12-13):
Subject matter: Viṣṇu's nature and His sovereign power

sarvaṃ tu rūpavad viṣṇor viśeṣeṇa tu [vi]bhūtimat /
atipriyatvān naivaitat svarūpam api bhaṇyate /
iti skānde (1)

(1) Cf. ibid. ll. 15f.:
svato mahattvaṃ tu maho viśeṣaprāptiśaktitā /
vibhūtilakṣaṇonnāho lakṣmīśabdena bhaṇyate /
iti brahmatarke (ficitious source);
see also BhāgP 2; BrāṇP 51; MatsyaP 12 and MESQUITA 2000: 455f.

29) BhāgTN (p. 102,6-9):
Subject matter: Trimūrti

brahmaṇas tapataḥ pūrvaṃ viṣṇur jāta urukramaḥ /
sarvalokahitārthāya yena rūpaṃ prakāśitam /
yaś ca pāti sadā lokān ajito jayatāṃ varaḥ /
tasmād rudraḥ samutpannaḥ sarvasaṃhārakṛd vibhuḥ /
ete tripuruṣāḥ proktāḥ sṛṣṭisthityantakāriṇaḥ /
nimittamātraṃ tau devau viṣṇuḥ sarvasya kāraṇam /
iti skānde (1)

(1) Cf. ibid. ll. 5f.: *me tapataḥ sataḥ / saḥ naḥ arthe sanāt pūrvam ...* ; see also BrahP 52.

30) BhāgTN (p. 107,12-13):
Subject matter: Annihilation of Rāvaṇa

dhanurviṣphūrjitair naṣṭo rāvaṇaḥ pūrvam eva tu /
punaḥ śarai rāmamuktaiḥ sānubandho vineṣyati /
iti skānde (1)

(1) Cf. ibid. ll. 11f.: *vineṣyati vināśaṃ prāpnoti / dārahartuḥ bhagavataḥ ...* ; see also BhaviṣPV 12; BrahP 17; SkaP 73.

31) BhāgTN (p. 111,5-8):
Subject matter: Viṣṇu's Sarvanāmatva

rāmabhīmārjunādīni viṣṇor nāmāni sarvaśaḥ /
ramaṇābhayavarṇādyāḥ śabdavṛtter hi hetavaḥ /
harir hi tatratatrastho ramaṇādīn karoty ajaḥ /
atas tasyaiva nāmāni vyājād anyagatāni tu /
vyavahārapravṛttyarthaṃ duṣṭānāṃ mohanāya ca /
iti skānde (1)

(1) Cf. BrāṇP 2; PadP 60 and 69.

32) BhāgTN (p. 132,9-133,5):
Subject matter: Hierarchy (*tāratamya*) among rational beings

tāmasās tāmasā daityāḥ pradhānā devaśatravaḥ /
tāmasā rājasās teṣām anugās teṣu sāttvikāḥ / [1]
anākhyātāsurāḥ proktā mānuṣā duṣṭacāriṇaḥ /
rājasās tāmasāś caiva madhyā rājasarājasāḥ / [2]
rājasāḥ sāttvikās tatra mānuṣeṣūttamā gaṇāḥ /
devāḥ pṛthaganākhyātāḥ smṛtāḥ sāttvikatāmasāḥ / [3]
atāttvikās tathākhyātāḥ smṛtāḥ sāttvikarājasāḥ /
sāttvikāḥ sāttvikās tatra tāttvikāḥ parikīrtitāḥ / [4]
teṣāṃ ca sāttvikāḥ śeṣagarutmadrudratatstriyaḥ /
tato 'pi devī brahmāṇī brahmā caiva tataḥ svayam / [5]
sāttvikeṣu triṣu yadā tv ekasya pratibādhanam /
rajastamobhyāṃ viṣṇur hi tadā prādurbhavaty ajaḥ / [6]
rājasāṃs tāmasān hatvā sāttvikaṃ varddhayiṣyati / [7ab]
iti skānde (1)

(1) Cf. BhaviṣPV 15.

33) BhāgTN (p. 135,6-7):
Subject matter: Vidura

yuddhakāle tu viduras tīrthayātrāṃ gato 'pi san /
prāya āste gajapure pāṇḍavānāṃ vyapekṣayā /
iti skānde (1)

(1) Cf. SkaP 34; 37.

34) BhāgTN (p. 136,6-7):
Subject matter: Vidura

viduras tu prabhāsasthaḥ śāpaṃ saṅkṣepato 'śṛṇot /
yadūnāṃ vistarāt paścād uddhavād yamunām anu /
iti skānde (1)

(1) Cf. ibid. l. 5: *suhṛdvinaṣṭiṃ yaduvinaṣṭim eṣyām* ... ; see also BrāṇP 59; GarP 16; PadP 14; SkaP 33.

35) BhāgTN (p. 139,2-3):
Subject matter: Ignorance

ānandarūpaṃ dṛṣṭvā tu loko bhautikam eva tu /

manyate viṣṇurūpaṃ ca aho bhrāntir bahūtthitā I
iti skānde (1)

(1) Cf. ibid. l. 1: *trilokasyājñānaṃ bata* ... ; see also HarV 8; PadP 13.

36) BhāgTN (p. 142,11-143,1):
Subject matter: Avatāras

pṛthivīlokasantyāgo dehatyāgo hareḥ smṛtaḥ I
nityānandasvarūpatvād anyan naivopapadyate I
darśayej janamohāya sadṛśīṃ mṛtakākṛtim I
naṭavad bhagavān viṣṇuḥ parajñānātmako vibhuḥ I
iti skānde
rājan parasya tanubhṛjjananāpyayehā māyāviḍaṃbanam avaihi yathā naṭasya I iti ca (1)

(1) Cf. ibid. l. 10: *ākṛtiṃ pṛthivīm* I *śarīram ākṛtir dehaḥ kuḥ pṛthivī ca mahī tatheti hy* abhidhāne (unknown source) ... ; ibid. p. 836,7: *tanubhṛdvaj jananavad apyayavac cehā tanubhajjananāpyayehā*; see also ĀdiP 1; MBh 42n. 6; PadP 55_1 and MESQUITA 2000_1: 37-41 [= 1997: 31-34].

37) BhāgTN (p. 156,7-9):
Subject matter: Aṃśāvatāras

droṇadrauṇikṛpāḥ pārthā bhīṣmo vidurasañjayau I
ye cānye tatra devāṃśāḥ samyak tattvāparokṣiṇaḥ I
iti skānde (1)

(1) Cf. ĀdiP 1; BrāṇP 95; SkaP 19; 33 and MESQUITA 2000_1: 48f.; 53n. 86; 78n. 133-134 [= 1997: 39f.; 42n. 77; 62n. 122-123].

38) BhāgTN (p. 164,2):
Subject matter: Synonyms *of jñāna* and *ajñāna*

ajñānaṃ tu niśā proktā divā jñānam udīryate I
iti skānde (1)

(1) Cf. ibid. ll. 1f.: *arthair adhyāhṛtāni karaṇāṇi yeṣām* ... ; see also HarV 8; SkaP 35.

39) BhāgTN (p. 165, 5-7):
Subject matter: Heresies of the Advaita-Vedānta

īśasyāpūrṇatājñānaṃ viṣṇor anyasya ceśatā I
bhedas tasyāvatāreṣu jīvasyeśatvam eva ca I
tathā jīvatvaṃ īśasya jaḍābhedas tayor api I
bhedamoha iti proktaḥ sa sadā na harau kvacit I

anyeṣāṃ tatprasādena śanair yāti satām api /
iti skānde (1)

(1) Cf. BhaviṣPV 3n. 7; SkaP 40 and MESQUITA 2000: 528f.

40) BhāgTN (p. 173,1-6):
Subject matter: Heresies of the Advaita-Vedānta

sṛṣṭiś ca pralayaś caiva saṃhāro muktir eva ca /
devarṣiprabhṛtayo lokā bhūrādayas tathā /
anādyanantakālīnāḥ sarvadaikaprakārataḥ /
jagatpravāhaḥ satyo 'yaṃ naitan mithyā kathaṃcana /
ye tv etad anyathā brūyuḥ sarvahantāra eva te /
devair viṣṇvādibhiḥ śaptā ṛṣibhir mānuṣādibhiḥ /
setihāsais tathā vedaiḥ sarve yānty adharaṃ tamaḥ /
sarvabrahmatvavettāro jīvabrahmatvavedinaḥ /
anyasāmyavido viṣṇor viṣṇudveṣṭāra eva ca /
sarve yānti tamo ghoraṃ na teṣām utthitiḥ kvacit /
iti skānde (1)

(1) Cf. BhaviṣPV 3n. 7 and SkaP 39; see also MESQUITA 2000: 144f.; 156n. 312; 193f.; 326ff.; 467f.; 528.

41) BhāgTN (p. 180,7-8):
Subject matter: Liberation through Yoga

tattadākārasaṃyuktān sṛjyān sraṣṭāram eva ca /
yaḥ sadā saṃsmared yogī na sa bhūyo 'bhijāyate /
iti skāndavacanāt [prasiddhānām api dviśaphādīnāṃ smaraṇavidhānārthamuktiḥ] (1)

(1) Cf. AgniP 16; NārP 8.

42) BhāgTN (p. 205,1-2):
Subject matter: Bewilderment (*moha*) of evil beings

vyatyāsenāpi cocyanta avivekena kutracit /
duṣṭānāṃ mohanārthāya tatra tatra kathāḥ kvacit /
iti ca skānde (1)

(1) Cf. ibid. l. 3: *avivekenety asya vivicya nocyanta ity arthaḥ / na kartur avivekaḥ / sarvajñasya kuto 'jñānaṃ vyāsasyodārakarmaṇa ity uktatvāt / duṣṭāṇaṃ mohanārthāya* iti ca (unknown source); see also NārP 9; MBh 42n. 6.

43) BhāgTN (p. 206,3-4):
Subject matter: Bewilderment (*moha*) of demons

viṣṇuhastavadhāl loko bhaktasyānyasya na kvacit /
tathāpy asuramohāya na viviktaṃ kvacit kvacit /
iti skānde (1)

(1) Cf. ibid. ll. 4f.:
hiraṇyakaśipuś cāpi bhagavannindayā tamaḥ / iti ca (unknown source)
svataḥ sadgatiyogasya putrāder hetutā bhavet /
yogyatānādibhaktiḥ syād abhaktasya kuto gatiḥ //
iti brahmatarke (ficitious source);
see also ĀdiP 1; MBh 42n. 6; NārP 9.

44) BhāgTN (p. 216,6-8):
Subject matter: Viṣṇu's Yoga-Māyā

viprāṇāṃ cāpi bhaktānām anyeṣāṃ ca janārdanaḥ /
brahmaṇaḥ śaṅkarād vāpi devatābhyas tathaiva ca /
ātmanaś ca śriyaś caiva sakāśāt priyatām api /
pūjyatām atyayuktaṃ ca vadet kvāpi vimohayan /
iti skānde (1)

(1) Cf. ibid. ll. 4f.: *viprāṇāṃ caraṇapadmapavitrareṇoḥ sevayā pratilabdhaśīlaṃ śrīr na jahātīti yat / ataś chindyām –*
anuktāś ca guṇā viṣṇor uktā doṣā na tasya tu /
ajñānād doṣavijñānaṃ guṇajñānaṃ yathārthataḥ /
iti paiṅgiśruti (unknown source) ... ;
see also MBh 42n. 6; PadP 13.

45) BhāgTN (p. 231,1-2):
Subject matter: Varāha-Avatāra

jñānānandasvarūpebhyo romabhyo 'sya kuśādayaḥ /
vidhūnvataḥ prayāge tu varāhavapuṣo 'bhavan /
romāṇi tāni devasya rūpāṇy āsan sahasraśaḥ /
iti skānde (1)

(1) Cf. ibid. l. 3: *ta evāsan tebhya evāsan / saptasu prathameti* sūtrāt. This unknown Sūtra is quoted by Madhva very often, cf. e.g. AiUBh (p. 204,19); see also ĀdiP 1 and LORENZ 2005: 59n. 199.

46) BhāgTN (p. 244,7-8):
Subject matter: Definition of the internal organs of knowleldge

buddhir adhyavasānāya saṃśayaṃ kurute manaḥ /

abhimāne tv ahaṅkāraś cittaṃ smaraṇakāraṇam /
iti skānde (1)

(1) Cf. BhaviṣPV 17 and MESQUITA 2000: 253ff.

47) BhāgTN (p. 266,8-9):
Subject matter: Mukti / Jīvanmukti

tattvajñānaṃ tu devānāṃ garbhasthānāṃ bhaviṣyati /
uttamānām ṛṣīṇāṃ vāpy anyeṣāṃ bahujanmagam /
iti skānde (1)

(1) Cf. ibid. ll. 7f.: *aśarīravat paramātmavat / paramātmana eva deho 'pi tadvaśatvāt* ... ; see also ĀdityaP 1; VāmP 6; Śaṅkara (BSūBh *ad* Sū III 4,51) and MESQUITA 2007: 9n. 11 [= 2007_1: 434n. 11].

48) BhāgTN (p. 270,2-3):
Subject matter: Viṣṇu's supreme transcendence

yathāpūrvaṃ hareḥ sarvaguṇair nīcātmatā tathā /
brahmaṇaś ca tathānyeṣām anyeṣāṃ ca yathāpadam /
iti skānde (1)

(1) Cf. AgniP 6.

49) BhāgTN (p. 275,9-10):
Subject matter: Purāṇic accounts (written or oral) of the creation

sṛṣṭibhedād virūpaṃ ca tathā pañcottaraṃ śatam /
vairūpyam anyad vijñeyaṃ tātparyān mohanāya vā /
iti skānde (1)

(1) Cf. BrāṇP 9; VārP 15.

50) BhāgTN (p. 307,6-7):
Subject matter: Viṣṇu's *icchā* and its synonyms

mahāmāyety avidyeti niyatimohanīti ca /
prakṛtir vāsanety evaṃ tavecchānanta kathyate /
iti skānde (1)

(1) Cf. BhaviṣP 13; HarV 8; MESQUITA 2000: 159n. 322; 449n. 554f.

51) BhāgTN (p. 311,4-5):
Subject matter: Viṣṇu's supreme transcendence

sarvasya grahaṇād viṣṇuḥ sarvasaṅgraha ucyate /

vedasya tadvaktṛtvāt prādhānyaṃ tat trayīmayaḥ / -1
sarvaṃ tadviṣayatvena mukhyaṃ sarvamayas tataḥ /
iti skānde (1)

(1) Cf. ibid. l. 3: *lokādīn saṅgṛhṇātīti tatsaṅgrahaḥ* ... ; see also AgniP 6.

52) BhāgTN (p. 314,8-11):
Subject matter: Viṣṇu's *āveśa*

brahmaṇi anante garuḍe rudre kāme śacīpatau / +1
aniruddhe manau caiva pṛthau ca kṛtavīryaje /
nārade caivamādyeṣu viśeṣāt sannidhir hareḥ /
sudarśanādiṣv astreṣu tathā sannihito hariḥ /
naralakṣmaṇau balaś caiva śeṣasyāṃśāḥ prakīrtitāḥ / +1
tathā bharataśatrughnau cakraśaṅkhāv udāhṛtau /
pradyumnaś ca kumāraś ca skandaḥ kāmāṃśajāḥ smṛtāḥ /
iti skānde (1)

(1) Cf. ibid. l. 7: *tatra sannihitaḥ sākṣād bhagavān* ... ; see also ĀdiP 1; BrahVP 17; SkaP 37 and MESQUITA 2000_1: 49n. 76 [= 1997: 40n. 68].

53) BhāgTN (p. 318,9-12):
Subject matter: Hierarchy among the beings

praṇipātādikaṃ devair ṛṣyādiṣu janārdane /
kriyate 'to na teṣāṃ hi tejobhaṅgaḥ kathaṃcana /
atyuttamānām avare tejobhaṅgo na vidyate /
yathā narāṇāṃ tiryakṣu prāyaḥ sāmye hi sa smṛtaḥ /
iti skānde (1)

(1) Cf. BhaviṣPV 15 and BhaviṣP 5.

54) BhāgTN (p. 327,6-10):
Subject matter: Jīvopādhis

jīvopādhir dvidhā proktaḥ svarūpaṃ bāhyam eva ca /
bāhyopādhir layaṃ yāti muktāv anyasya tu sthitiḥ /
sarvopādhivināśe hi pratibiṃbaḥ kathaṃ bhavet /
kathaṃ cātmavināśāya prayatnaḥ setsyati kvacit /
apumarthatā ca mukteḥ syād abhāvāt puṃsa eva tu / +1
jñānajñeyādyabhāvāc ca sarvathā nopapadyate /
tasmād etan mataṃ yeṣāṃ tamoniṣṭhā hi te matāḥ /
iti skānde (1)

(1) Cf. ibid. l. 5: *abījaṃ hṛdayaṃ bījahṛdayaṃ vinā* ... ; see also BhāgP 3; BhaviṣPV 15[2]; BrahP 78; BrāṇP 71; MBh 50: NārP 43; 52; VāmP 12; VarP 14; 33; 34 and MESQUITA 2000: 495ff.

55) BhāgTN (p. 329,4-9):
Subject matter: Heresies

svapakṣapātas tv abhyāsād bhogārthaṃ vyāpṛtasya tu /
bhavet tato 'nekaśāstrayathārthasmaraṇeśitā /
naśyaty ataḥ smṛter nāśād bhagavatpakṣapātitā /
vinaśyet tena caivāsya bhavej jñānaviparyayaḥ /
na ca jñānaviparyāsād anyannāśakaraṃ kvacit /
sarvasyaitasya mūlaṃ hi duṣṭasaṃsarga eva tu /
duṣṭasaṅgo viraktasyāpy anyathājñānakāraṇam /
duṣṭasaṅgād dhi viṣṇoś ca svātmatvaṃ manyate 'budhaḥ /
abhāvaṃ svātmano 'nyasya muktiṃ cāpi nirātmatām /
iti skānde (1)

(1) Cf. BhaviṣPV 3n. 7; SkaP 39 and MESQUITA 2000: 528f.

56) BhāgTN (p. 397,2-3):
Subject matter: Viṣṇu, the resting place of the universe

yathā kathāpaṭāḥ sūtra otāḥ protāś ca saṃsthitāḥ /
evaṃ viṣṇāv idaṃ viśvam otaṃ protaṃ ca saṃsthitam /
iti skānde (1)

(1) Cf. ibid. ll. 1f.: *otaṃ protaṃ paṭavat* ... ; see also AgniP 6; SkaP 79; 91 and MESQUITA 2000: 457ff.

57) BhāgTN (p. 397,10-11):
Subject matter: Viṣṇu's worship

yathā rājñaḥ priyatvaṃ tu bhṛtyo veda na cātmanaḥ /
tathā jīvo na yatsakhyaṃ vetti tasmai namo 'stu te /
iti skānde (1)

(1) Cf. ibid. ll. 8f.: *guṇo yathā guṇinaḥ / kaścit purastho guṇabhūtaḥ pradhānabhūtasya rājñaḥ / mamāsau sakheti rājñā cintitam api na jānāti* ... ; see also AgniP 20.

58) BhāgTN (p. 420,12-13):
Subject matter: Indivisibility of Viṣṇu's nature

brahmeśānādibhir devair yat prāptuṃ naiva śakyate /

tad yatsvabhāvaḥ kaivalyaṃ sa bhavān kevalo hare /
iti ca skānde (1)

(1) Cf. BrāṇP 10.

59) BhāgTN (p. 427,7-428,3):
Subject matter: Curse / Śāpa

devā eva tadanyebhyaḥ śaktā nāsty atra saṃśayaḥ /
aśaktā api śaktānāṃ śaktāḥ śāpādiṣu sphuṭam / [1]
tathāpy aśaktair vihitāḥ śāpādyāḥ śaktimatsu tu /
atyalpāś cālpakālāś ca na samyak prabhavanti ca / [2]
yatnenāpohituṃ śakyā uttamais tu na saṃśayaḥ /
uttameṣu kṛtāḥ śāpāḥ kartṛṇāṃ jñānapuṇyayoḥ / [3]
niḥśeṣeṇa nihantāras tadanugraham antarā /
sadārayor brahmaviṣṇvor varaśāpādayo 'khilāḥ / [4]
tadanyena kṛtāḥ sarve niṣphalā eva niścayāt /
na cāpy avāntarāḥ śāpā bhavanty eṣāṃ tu kutracit / [5]
varā viṣṇoḥ śriyaś ca syur brahmaṇaś ca yathākramam /
uttamair adhamānāṃ tu varāḥ śāpā yathoditāḥ / [6]
saṃpūrṇaphaladā eva nātra kāryā vicāraṇā / [7ab]
iti skānde (1)

(1) Cf. ibid. l. 6: *pratiśaptum alaṃtamaḥ* ... ; see also BrāṇP 59; NārP 12; PadP 14; SkaP 34; VarP 16.

60) BhāgTN (p. 431,5-6):
Subject matter: Intrinsic aptitudes (*yogyatā*) of rational beings

na viṣṇor viṣamatvaṃ tu yogyatāpekṣayā kvacit /
yogyatāyās tanniyatyā viṣamatvaṃ bhaveta vā / (1)
iti skānde (2)

(1) Cf. ibid. n. 4: ... *tataḥ samo 'pi bhagavān anyeṣāṃ prākṛtānadṛṣṭyā viṣamaś ca pratīyate.*
(2) Cf. ibid. ll. 6f.: *viṣamatvaṃ tu doṣāya śubhāśubhaviparyaye / atas tādṛśavaiṣamyaṃ* brahmasūtre (= II 1,35-36) *nirākṛtam* ... ; see also BrahP 36; BrahVP 35 and MESQUITA 2000: 506ff.

61) BhāgTN (p. 449,1):
Subject matter: Hiraṇyakaśipu

brahmāṇam abhajad brahmapadārthaṃ sa hiraṇyakaḥ /
iti skānde (1)

(1) Cf. BhaviṣPV 12; GarP 29.

62) BhāgTN (p. 452,11-12):
Subject matter: Classes among the Deities

ādityā vasavo rudrās trividhā hi surā yataḥ /
marutaś caiva viśve ca sādhyādyāś caiva tadgatāḥ /
atas traya iti proktāś catvāro mānuṣāḥ smṛtāḥ /
iti skānde (1)

(1) Cf. BhaviṣPV 5; BrahP 22 and MESQUITA 2000: 495ff.

63) BhāgTN (p. 470,6-7):
Subject matter: Prahlāda

ṛte tu tāttvikān devān nāradādiṃs tathaiva ca /
prahlādād uttamaḥ ko nu viṣṇubhakto jagattraye /
iti skānde (1)

(1) Cf. BrāṇP 55; SkaP 8.

64) BhāgTN (p. 497,5-498,2):
Subject matter: Rāmāvatāra

nityapūrṇasukhajñaptisvarūpo 'sau yato vibhuḥ /
ato 'sya rāma ityākhyā tasya duḥkhaṃ kuto 'ṇvapi /
tathāpi lokaśikṣārtham aduḥkho duḥkhavartivat /
antarhitāṃ lokadṛṣṭyā sītām āsīt smarann iva /
jñāpanārthaṃ punar nityaṃ saṃbandhaṃ svātmanaḥ śriyā /
ayodhyāyā vinirgacchan sarvalokasya ceśvaraḥ /
pratyakṣaṃ tu śrīyā sārdhaṃ jagāmānādir avyayaḥ /
nākṣatramāsagaṇitaṃ trayodaśasahasrakam /
brahmalokasamaṃ cakre samastaṃ kṣitimaṇḍalam /
rāmo rāmo rāma iti sarveṣām abhavat tadā /
sarvo rāmamayo loko yadā rāmas tv apālayat /
iti skānde (1)

(1) Cf. ĀdiP 1; SkaP 73; 111 and MESQUITA 2000_1: 40f. [= 1997: 33f.]. According to TAGARE 1976 (Vol. IX, p. 1188) the last Śloka in the above quote has also been cited by the Advaitin Vaṃśīdhara in his commentary Bhāvārthadīpikāprakāśa. I was not able to check this information, but his second reference that this Śloka was also quoted by the Dvaita-author Vijayadhvajatīrtha (15th A.D.) in his commentary Padaratnāvalī (*ad* IX 11,23) is proved true.

65) BhāgTN (p. 537,7-14):
Subject matter: Paths of liberation / Liberation through hatred

kṛṣṇakāmās tadā gopyas tyaktvā dehaṃ divaṃ gatāḥ /
samyak kṛṣṇaṃ paraṃ brahma jñātvā kālāt paraṃ yayuḥ / [1]
pūrvaṃ ca jñānayuktās tās tatrāpi prāyaśas tathā /
atas tāsāṃ paraṃ brahma gatir āsīn na kāmataḥ / [2]
na tu jñānam ṛte mokṣo nānyaḥ pantheti hi śrutiḥ /
kāmayuktā sadā bhaktir jñānaṃ cāto vimuktigāḥ / [3]
ato mokṣe 'pi caitāsāṃ kāmo bhaktyānuvartate /
atodakatve na sadā dveṣiṇām adharaṃ tamaḥ / [4] (1)
muktiśabdoditaṃ caidyaprabhṛtau dveṣabhāginaḥ /
bhaktibhāgī pṛthaṅ muktim agād viṣṇuprasādataḥ / [5]
kāmas tv aśubhakṛc cāpi bhaktyā viṣṇoḥ prasādakṛt /
dveṣijīvayutaṃ cāpi bhaktaṃ viṣṇur vimocayet / [6]
aho 'tikaruṇā viṣṇoḥ śiśupālasya mokṣaṇāt / [7ab]
iti skānde (2)

(1) The reading adopted by the editor (65[4cd]): *atodakatvena* does not suit the context. For this reason I suggest a change in this reading: *atodakatve na*; see also BhāgTN (p. 433,8-10): *yasmād evaṃ ko 'py upadravo nāsti bhagavatas tasmād evaṃ dveṣādinā mano yoktuṃ śakyate / tad eva cintayati ca / anyathātmano duḥkhakāraṇaṃ dveṣādikaṃ kathaṃ sarvaniyāmako harir utpādayet*, cf. BrāṇP 53[5] and KūrP 22. BhāgP too accepts the doctrine of liberation through hatred (cf ibid. VII 1,30 [= VII 1,29]): ... *dveṣāt* ... *tadaghaṃ hitvā bahavas tadgatiṃ gatāḥ* (see BhāgP VII 1,31 (= VII 1,30):

gopyaḥ kāmād bhayāt kaṃso dveṣāc caidyādayo nṛpāḥ /
saṃbandhād vṛṣṇayaḥ snehād yūyaṃ bhaktyā vayaṃ vibho //

This is to be achieved only when a person seething with hatred fully concentrates his thoughts on Viṣṇu as God, as Śiśupāla, the Cedi-King did. Even in the throes of death, he looked upon Viṣṇu, striking him without hate, in His divine glory. As a result, all his sins were consumed, and he became absorbed into the supreme Viṣṇu. In case a person seething with hatred fails to think intensively of Viṣṇu, like Hiraṇyakaśipu, who did not recognize that the lion striking him to death was in reality Viṣṇu Himself, assuming the body of a lion (*nṛsiṃharūpa*), liberation is out of his reach (cf. ViṣP IV 15, 4f.): ... *tatra tu hiraṇyakaśipor viṣṇur ayam ity etan na manasy abhūt* ... *nātas tasminn anādinidhane parabrahmabhūte bhagavaty anālaṃbanīkṛte manasas tallayam tu* ... ; see specially HACKER 1959: 106f.

(2) Cf. BrāṇP 53; see also AgniP 9; BhaviṣPV 12; BrāṇP 38; GarP 29; 33; SkaP 61.

66) BhāgTN (p. 539,8-9):
Subject matter: Viṣṇu's names

mānavo badaraḥ sindhuḥ śaśinas tu trināmakam /
yo veda mucyate rogair viṣṇunāmneva saṃsṛteḥ /
iti skānde (1)

(1) Cf. BhāgP 1.

67) BhāgTN (p. 542,2-3):
Subject matter: Viṣṇu's supreme transcendence

ahaṃ paro hi madbhinnā jīvātmāno 'lpaśaktayaḥ /
madvaśāḥ sarva eveti brahmādīn manyate hariḥ /
iti skānde (1)

(1) Cf. ibid. l. 1: *anyātmatayā gṛhītāḥ / matto 'nye jīvātmāna eta iti bhagavatā gṛhītāḥ* ... ; see also AgniP 6; BrāṇP 61 and MESQUITA 2000: 371f.

68) BhāgTN (p. 545,13-14):
Subject matter: Viṣṇu's supreme transcendence

brahmastho brahmanāmāsau rudrastho rudranāmakaḥ /
tayor api niyantaikaḥ svayam eva janārdanaḥ /
iti skānde (1)

(1) Cf. AgniP 6.

69) BhāgTN (p. 547,9-548,2):
Subject matter: Heresies and their refutation by the best teachers

bhinnasyābhedato dṛṣṭir api bhedadṛśir matā /
vastuyāthātmyatas tasya bhinnatvād iti sūribhiḥ / [1] (1)
anyathājñānam evāto bhedajñānaṃ vininditam /
na vidyamānabhedasya darśanaṃ ninditaṃ kvacit / [2]
śilā deva iti jñānaṃ devo 'smīti ca yā dṛśiḥ /
uttamasyādhamatvena nīcasyoccatayā dṛśiḥ / [3]
asamasya samatvena samasyāsamadarśanam /
dravaṃ tīrtham iti jñānaṃ deho 'ham iti yā matiḥ / [4]
asadbhāryādiṣu svīyadarśanaṃ caivamādikam /
bhedajñānam iti proktaṃ yā cānyāpy ayathāmatiḥ / [5]
tasmāt tadapahānāya saṃsevyā guravo varāḥ /
tatrasthā devatāḥ sarvāḥ prīyante gurupūjayā / [6]
naivānyathaiṣāṃ prītiḥ syād gurūktim apahāya tu /
tasmāt pūjā viśeṣeṇa satāṃ kāryā nṛṇāṃ sadā / [7]
bhaktis tu tāratamyena viśiṣṭeṣv adhikā bhavet / [8ab]
iti skānde (2)

(1) Cf. MESQUITA 2000: 299ff.; 431f.
(2) Cf. ibid. ll. 3f.: *ammayādyabhimānino 'pi devā urukālenaiva punanti gurūpadeśaṃ prāpayitvā / bhedakṛtaḥ anyathājñāninaḥ / vipaścitas tu pratyakṣadarśanād anyathājñānam evāpagamayanti* ... ; see also BhaviṣPV 3n. 7; BhaviṣP 5; BrahVP 35; GarP 34.

70) BhāgTN (p. 582,5-6):
Subject matter: Viṣṇu, the cause of transmigration and liberation

satāṃ vimuktidād viṣṇor muktir yady abhyupeyate /
bandho 'pi tata eva syād yasmād ekas tayoḥ patiḥ /
iti skānde (1)

(1) Cf. ibid. ll. 1f.: ... (ŚvU III 8) iti śruter *muktis tasmād evety aṅgīkartavyam / ato bandho 'pi tata evety arthaḥ* ... ; see also BhaviṣP 3; SkaP 121 and MESQUITA 2000: 109n. 172; 489n. 638.

71) BhāgTN (p. 586,6-8):
Subject matter: Viṣṇu's Sarvanāmatva

ānandatvād anāmāsāv utkṛṣṭatvād unāmakaḥ /
etannāmadvayaṃ viṣṇor jñātvā pāpaiḥ pramucyate /
iti skānde (1)

(1) Cf. BrāṇP 2 and MESQUITA 2000: 158n. 318; 227n. 493.

72) BhāgTN (p. 589,11-12):
Subject matter: Liberation

mahābhāgyaṃ tu kaivalyam ajñānāṃ kaḥ pradāsyati /
ataḥ santo vijānanti hariṃ te tv anahaṅkṛtāḥ /
iti skānde (1)

(1) Cf. ibid. ll. 7f.: *iti loke dṛśyamānaprakāreṇa caratām vijane mokṣaviṣaye kaḥ sukhayati suṣṭhu anirastabhage / atas tvām eva santaṃ jñātvā bhavataḥ padāṃbujaṃ hṛdā niviśanti / harāvasatham ahaṅkāraṃ na kurvanti* ... ; see also AgniP 16; BrahVP 29.

73) BhāgTN (p. 593,7):
Subject matter: Rāmāvatāra

jihāti rāvaṇaṃ saṅkhye rāghavaḥ paramāstravit /
iti skānde (1)

(1) Cf. ibid. ll. 3f.: ... *pūrvoktāṃ dvividhāṃ kaṣṭāṃ prakṛtiṃ jahāti* [*jihāti*] *hanti ca / tad api tvam eva jahāsi jihāsi ca / utety tyāgavadhayoḥ samuccayārthe*; see also ĀdiP 1; SkaP 64.

74) BhāgTN (p. 626,5-6):
Subject matter: Sanatkumāra

kumāranāmā tu harir brahmacārivapuḥ svayam /

sanatkumārāya paraṃ provāca jagadīśvaraḥ /
iti skānde (1)

(1) Cf. ibid. ll. 6f.:
viṣṇoḥ sanatkumārākhyāc chuśruvur jñānam uttamam /
sanatkumārapramukhā yogeśāḥ parameśvarāt /
iti prakāśasaṃhitāyām (unknown source);
cf. BrahP 3.

75) BhāgTN (p. 702,9-10):
Subject matter: Sons of Brahmā

rudram indraṃ kumāraṃ ca vinaivānyāgrajo manuḥ /
brahmaputreṣv ādisṛṣṭāv anyathātvaṃ punarjaneḥ /
iti skānde (1)

(1) Cf. ibid. ll. 10f.:
ādisṛṣṭau pūrvajā ye te 'dhikāḥ sarvadā guṇaiḥ /
anādyanantakāleṣu muktāv api yathākramam /
iti nibandhe (unknown source);
see also BrāṇP 29.

76) BhāgTN (p. 752,1-5):
Subject matter: Law-field / The land of religion (*dharmakṣetra*)

nadīsamudragiraya āśramāś ca vanāni ca /
nagarāṇi ca divyāni śālagrāmādayas tathā /
teṣāṃ samīpagāś caiva deśā yojanamātrataḥ /
karmaṇyās tu samākhyātās tadanye kīkaṭāḥ smṛtāḥ /
tadanye 'pi tu ye deśāḥ kṛṣṇasāroṣitāḥ svataḥ /
karmaṇyā eva vijñeyā yadi nādhyuṣitāḥ khalaiḥ /
khalair adhyuṣitāś cāpi yadi sadbhir adhiṣṭhitāḥ /
karmaṇyā iti vijñeyā viṣṇuliṅgāni yatra ca /
iti skānde (1)

(1) Cf. ibid. ll. 5f.:
āntaraḥ sannidhir viṣṇor bāhyasannidhir eva ca /
dvividhaḥ sannidhiḥ proktaḥ kṛtrimo bāhya ucyate /
svābhāvikas tv āntaraḥ syāt pratimājīvago yathā /
iti ca (unknown source);
see also BrāṇP 49.

77) BhāgTN (p. 768,3-4):
Subject matter: Bhasmasnāna

bhasmasnānavidhānaṃ tu śrutyuktaṃ darśanānugam /

bhasmasnānaṃ tato 'grāhyaṃ vidhānaṃ tu nṛsiṃhagam /
iti skānde (1)

(1) Cf. ibid. n. 3: *śrutyuktaṃ nṛsiṃhapurāṇagataṃ ca bhasmasnānaṃ darśanānugatvād agrāhyam eva / śruter anuvāditvena tatra tātparyābhāvāt*; see ibid. p. 767,11f.:

...
darśanāny avalaṃbhyaiva paśupatyādināṃ tu yā /
bahuśrutiviruddhaṃ tu vadet sā darśanātmikā /
ante niṣedhasaṃyuktā bhasmasnānādikā ca sā /
yathāpradṛśyamānārthī samādhiḥ sā prakīrtitā /
viṣṇuḥ parama ityādyā sā ca vidvadbhir īritā /
ityādi bhāṣāviveke (unknown source);

see also MESQUITA 2000_1: 162f. [= 1997: 130f.].

78) BSūBh (p. 2,2-15):
Subject matter: Vyāsa, the author of Brahmasūtras

tac coktaṃ skānde –
nārāyaṇād viniṣpannaṃ jñānaṃ kṛtayuge sthitam /
kiṃcit tadanyathā jātaṃ tretāyāṃ dvāpare 'khilam / [1]
gautamasya ṛṣeḥ śāpāj jñāne tv ajñānatāṃ gate /
saṅkīrṇabuddhayo devā brahmarudrapuraḥsarāḥ / [2]
śaraṇyaṃ śaraṇaṃ jagmur nārāyaṇam anāmayam /
tair vijñāpitakāryas tu bhagavān puruṣottamaḥ / [3]
avatīrṇo mahāyogī satyavatyāṃ parāśarāt /
utsannān bhagavān vedān ujjahāra hariḥ svayam / [4]
caturdhā vyabhajat tāṃś ca caturviṃśatidhā punaḥ /
śatadhā caikadhā caiva tathaiva ca sahasradhā / [5]
kṛṣṇo dvādaśadhā caiva punas tasyārthavittaye /
cakāra brahmasūtrāṇi yeṣāṃ sūtratvam añjasā / [6]
alpākṣaram asandigdhaṃ sāravad viśvatomukham /
astobham anavadyaṃ ca sūtraṃ sūtravido viduḥ / [7]
nirviśeṣitasūtratvaṃ brahmasūtrasya cāpy ataḥ /
yathā vyāsatvam ekasya kṛṣṇasyānye viśeṣaṇāt / [8]
saviśeṣaṇasūtrāṇi hy aparāṇi vido viduḥ /
mukhyasya nirviśeṣeṇa śabdo 'nyeṣāṃ viśeṣataḥ / [9]
iti vedavidaḥ prāhuḥ śabdatattvārthavedinaḥ /
sūtreṣu yeṣu sarve 'pi nirṇayāḥ samudīritaḥ / [10]
śabdajātasya sarvasya yatpramāṇaś ca nirṇayaḥ /
evaṃvidhāni sūtrāṇi kṛtvā vyāso mahāyaśāḥ / [11]
brahmarudrādideveṣu manuṣyapitṛpakṣiṣu /
jñānaṃ saṃsthāpya bhagavān krīḍate parameśvaraḥ / [12]
ityādi (1)

(1) Cf. ibid. (p. 1,4-2,1): *dvāpare sarvatra jñāna ākulībhūte tannirṇayāya brahmarudrendrādibhir arthito bhagavān nārāyaṇo vyāsatvenāvatatāra / atheṣṭāniṣṭaprāptiparihārecchūnāṃ tadyogam avijānatāṃ tajjñāpanārthaṃ devam utsannaṃ vyañjayaṃś caturdhā vyabhajat / caturviṃśatidhaikaśatadhā sahasradhā dvādhaśadhā ca / tadarthanirṇayāya brahmasūtrāṇi cakāra* ... ; see also GīBh (1,4f.); BhaviṣPV 21 and BrāṇP 14.

79) BSūBh (p. 7,3-4):
Subject matter: Viṣṇu, the navel of the universe / the supreme Creator of the universe

ajasya nābhāv iti yasya nābher
abhūc chruteḥ puṣkaraṃ lokasāram /
tasmai namo vyastasamastaviśva-
vibhūtaye viṣṇave lokakartre /
iti skānde (1)

(1) Cf. ibid. (p. 6,13f.): *ajasya nābhāv iti* (Ṛg X 82,6) *tasya hi liṅgam / na ca prasiddārthaṃ vinānyo yujyate* ... ; see also AgniP 12; BhaviṣP 3; KūrP 14; SkaP 91.

80) BSūBh (p. 8,2-3):
Subject matter: Viṣṇu's supreme transcendence

śaive ca skānde –
śvapacād api kaṣṭatvaṃ brahmeśānādayaḥ surāḥ /
tadaivācyuta yānty eva yadaiva tvaṃ parāṅmukhaḥ /
iti (1)

(1) = BrahP 56; see also AgniP 6.

81) BSūBh (p. 8,11-12):
Subject matter: Viṣṇu, the supreme Creator of the universe

utpattisthitisaṃhārā niyatijñānam āvṛtiḥ /
bandhamokṣau ca puruṣād yasmāt sa harir ekarāṭ /
iti skānde (1)

(1) Cf. ibid. ll. 8f.: *brahmaṇo lakṣaṇam āha – sṛṣṭisthitisaṃhāraniyamanajñānājñānabandhamokṣā yataḥ* ... ; see also AgniP 12; BhaviṣP 3 and MESQUITA 2000: 489n. 638.

82) BSūBh (p. 10,8-10):
Subject matter: Definition of Śāstra

ṛgyajuḥsāmātharvāś ca bhārataṃ pañcarātrakam /
mūlarāmāyaṇaṃ caiva śāstram ity abhidhīyate /

yac cānukūlam etasya tac ca śāstraṃ prakīrtitam /
ato 'nyo granthavistāro naiva śāstraṃ kuvartma tat /
iti skānde (1)

(1) Cf. BhaviṣP 10; BrāṇP 11 and MESQUITA 2000: 51n. 13; 378ff.

83) BSūBh (p. 18,17-19):
Subject matter: The validity of inference is based on Veda

uktaṃ ca skānde –
yathākāmānumā yasmāt tasmāt sānapagā śruteḥ /
pūrvāparāvirodhāya ceṣyate nānyathā kvacit /
iti (1)

(1) Cf. ibid. l. 17: *yathākāmaṃ hy anumātuṃ śakyate / ato na tattve pṛthaganumānam apekṣyate* ... ; see also KūrP 20; VarP 31 and MESQUITA 2000: 368ff.

84) BSūBh (p. 22,17-18):
Subject matter: Puruṣasūkta / Rāmāvatāra

tasmin kāle mahārāja rāma evābhidhīyate /
yathā hi pauruṣe sūkte viṣṇur evābhidhīyate /
iti ca skānde (1)

(1) Cf. ibid. l. 15: *sa hi puruṣasūktābhidheyaḥ*; ... see also ĀdiP 1; SkaP 64.

85) BSūBh (p. 23,4-5):
Subject matter: Viṣṇu – *prāṇa*

viṣṇum evānayan devā viṣṇuṃ bhūtim upāsate /
sa eva sarvavedoktas tadratho deha ucyate /
iti skānde (1)

(1) Cf. ibid. ll. 4f.: ... *ityādyanugamād atrāpi prāṇo viṣṇur eva* ... ; MESQUITA 2003: 107ff.

86) BSūBh (p. 25,20-21):
Subject matter: Viṣṇu's Sarvanāmatva

sarvendriyamayo viṣṇuḥ sarvaprāṇiṣu ca sthitaḥ /
sarvanāmābhidheyaś ca sarvavedeḍitaś ca saḥ /
iti ca skānde (1)

(1) Cf. BrāṇP 2.

87) BSūBh (p. 26,12-13):
Subject matter: Viṣṇu, the supreme Creator of the universe

sraṣṭā pātā tathaivāttā nikhilasyaika eva tu /
vāsudevo varaḥ puṃsām itare 'lpasya vā na vā /
iti skānde (1)

(1) Cf. ibid. ll. 11f.: *na hi carācarasya sarvasyāttṛtvam aditeḥ* ... ; see also AgniP 12; SkaP 100.

88) BSūBh (p. 31,6-8):
Subject matter: Doctrine of three Akṣaras

aparaṃ tv akṣaraṃ yā sā prakṛtir jaḍarūpikā /
śrī parā prakṛtiḥ proktā cetanā viṣṇusaṃśrayā /
tām akṣaraṃ paraṃ prāhuḥ parataḥ param akṣaram /
harim evākhilaguṇam akṣaratrayam īritam /
iti skānde (1)

(1) Cf. SkaP 129; see also AgniP 6; 25 and MESQUITA 2000: 104f. (= Gī XV 16-20); 478; 506.

89) BSūBh (p. 33,17-18):
Subject matter: Vyāsa and his disciples

vyāsacittasthitākāśād avacchināni kānicit /
anye vyavaharanty etāny ūrīkṛtya gṛhādivat /
<u>iti skāndavacanān</u> *na matānāṃ parasparavirodhaḥ* / (1)

(1) Cf. ibid. ll. 5f.: *nāgnyādayaḥ śabdā agnyādivācakāḥ / tathāpi sākṣād evānanya-yogena brahmavācakair vyavahārārtham anabhijñānāc cānyatra vyavaharantīty abhy-upagame 'virodhaṃ jaiminir vakti* ... ; see also BhaviṣPV 21; BrāṇP 14; MESQUITA 2000_1: 28n. 30 [= 1997n. 23] and MESQUITA 2003_1: 206f.

90) BSūBh (p. 35,18-20):
Subject matter: Viṣṇu's names

skānde ca –
ṛte nārāyaṇādīni nāmāni puruṣottamaḥ /
prādād anyatra bhagavān rājevarte svakaṃ puram /
iti (1)

(1) Cf. BhāgP 1; BrahP 61 and BrāṇP 68.

91) BSūBh (p. 36,18-19):
Subject matter: Viṣṇu's supreme transcendence

pṛthivyādi prakṛtyantaṃ bhūtaṃ bhavyaṃ bhavac ca yat / (1)
viṣṇur eko bibhartīdaṃ nānyas tasmāt kṣamo dhṛtau /
iti ca skānde (2)

(1) = MBh 7[1b].
(2) Cf. ibid. ll. 15f.: *etasmin nu khalv akṣare gārgyākāśa otaś ca protaś ceti* (BĀU III 8,11) *ambarāntasya sarvasya dhṛter brahmaivākṣaram* ... ; see also AgniP 6; 25; PadP 53; SkaP 79 and MESQUITA 2000: 460n 579.

92) BSūBh (p. 38,12-13):
Subject matter: Viṣṇu's supreme transcendence

satyakāmo 'paro nāsti tam ṛte viṣṇum avyayam /
satyakāmatvam anyeṣāṃ bhavet tatkāmyakāmatā /
iti ca skānde (1)

(1) Cf. ibid. l. 11: *sāpekṣanirapekṣayoś ca nirapekṣaṃ svīkartavyam*; see also AgniP 6 and MESQUITA 2000: 519f.

93) BSūBh (p. 39,7-8):
Subject matter: Viṣṇu, the sovereign Ruler of the universe

sarveśo viṣṇur evaiko nānyo 'sti jagataḥ patiḥ /
iti ca skānde (1)

(1) Cf. ibid. ll. 3f.: ... *eṣa bhūtādhipatir eṣa bhūtapāla ityādyasya* (BĀU IV 4,22) *mahimno 'sminn upalabdheḥ ... ityādiśrutibhyas tasya hy eṣa mahimā* ... ; see also AgniP 6; 12.

94) BSūBh (p. 40,22-23):
Subject matter: Exegetical principles of the Veda

śrutir liṅgaṃ samākhyā ca vākyaṃ prakaraṇaṃ tathā /
pūrvapūrvaṃ balīyaḥ syād evam āgamanirṇayaḥ /
iti skānde (1)

(1) Cf. ibid. ll. 21f.: *vāmanaśabdād eva viṣṇur iti pramitaḥ / na hi śruter liṅgaṃ balavat* ... ; MīSū III 3,14; see also S. STARK, Vatsya Varadagurus Tattvanirṇaya, Teil 2: Übersetzung und Anmerkungen. Wien 1990: 68f. Madhva adduces in BSūBh (p. 10,17-18 *ad* Sū I 1,4) an anonymous fragment regarding six exegetical principles (*ṣaḍvidhatātparyaliṅga*), which had been cited already by Sudarśanasūri. Madhva ascribes this fragment to an unknown source called Bṛhatsaṃhitā, cf. MESQUITA 2000_1: 100n. 178 [= 1997: 80n. 167]; MESQUITA 2000: 85n. 95; see also BrahVP 30; SkaP 122; VarP 32.

95) BSūBh (p. 42,16-18):
Subject matter: Worship of Viṣṇu

yāvat sevā pare tattve tāvat sukhaviśeṣatā /
saṃbhavāc cāprakāśasya param ekam ṛte harim /
teṣāṃ sāmarthyayogāc ca devānāṃ apy upāsanam /
sarvaṃ vidhīyate nityaṃ sarvayajñādikarma ca /
iti skānde (1)

(1) Cf. ibid. ll. 14f.: *phalaviśeṣabhāvāt prāptapadānāṃ api devānāṃ madhvādiṣv apy adhikāraṃ bādarāyaṇo manyate / asti hi prakāsaviśeṣaḥ* ... ; see also AgniP 20.

96) BSūBh (p. 44,7-8):
Subject matter: Viṣṇu, the world-Ruler

nabhasvato 'pi sarvāḥ syuś ceṣṭā bhagavato hareḥ /
kimutānyasya jagato yasya ceṣṭā nabhasvataḥ /
iti hi skānde (1)

(1) Cf. ibid ll. 5f.: *ejatīti kampanavacanād udyatavajro bhagavān* ... (TaiU II 7; BĀU IV 4,18); see also BhāgP 2.

97) BSūBh (p. 48,4-5):
Subject matter: The individual soul is resting on Viṣṇu

yadadhīno guṇo 'nyasya tadguṇī so 'bhidhīyate /
yathā jīvaḥ parātmeti yathā rājā jayīty api /
iti ca skānde (1)

(1) Cf. ibid. ll. 3f.: *tadadhīnatvāc cāvyaktvādīnāṃ tasyaivāvyaktatvaparāvaratvādikam arthavat* ... ; see also AgniP 22; BrāṇP 71; SkaP 98; also MBh I 524* and MESQUITA 2000: 142n. 279; 371f.

98) BSūBh (p. 64,19-65,1):
Subject matter: Difference of Jīva from Viṣṇu

skānde ca –
udakaṃ tūdake siktaṃ miśram eva yathā bhavet /
na vai tad eva bhavati yato vṛddhiḥ pradṛśyate /
evam eva hi jīvo 'pi tādātmyaṃ paramātmanā /
prāpto 'pi nāsau bhavati svātantryādiviśeṣaṇāt /
iti (1)

(1) Cf. ibid. ll. 16f.: *yathā loka udaka udakāntarasyaikībhāvavyavahāre 'py antarbhedo 'sty eva evaṃ syād atrāpi / tathā ca* śrutir *yathodakaṃ śuddhe śuddham āsiktaṃ tādṛg eva bhavatīti* (KathU IV 15); see also AgniP 22; SkaP 97.

99) BSūBh (p. 65,15-16):
Subject matter: Pañcamaveda

anuktaṃ pañcabhir vedair na vastv asti kutaścana /
ato vedatvam eteṣāṃ yatas te sarvavedakāḥ /
iti skānde (1)

(1) Cf. ibid. l. 14: *svatantrasādhanabhāve pramāṇair upalabhyeta* ... ; see also BhaviṣP 10 and MESQUITA 2000_1: 126ff. [= 1997: 101ff.].

100) BSūBh (p. 95,24-26):
Subject matter: Viṣṇu, the supreme Creator of the universe

sraṣṭā pātā ca saṃhartā sa eko harir īśvaraḥ /
sraṣṭṛtvādikam anyeṣāṃ dāruyoṣavad ucyate /
ekadeśakriyā cātra na tu sarvātmaneritam /
sṛṣṭyādikaṃ samastaṃ tu viṣṇor eva parād bhavet /
iti ca skānde (1)

(1) Cf. ibid. ll. 20f.: ... (ŚvU I 10) *iti bandhalayasya tadabhidhyānanimittatvaliṅgāt tatkartṛtvaṃ pratīyate kimu sāder jagata ity etasmād eva saṃhārakartā viṣṇur iti pratīyate* ... ; see also AgniP 12; SkaP 87 and MESQUITA 2000: 470ff.

101) BSūBh (p. 96,21-24):
Subject matter: Origin of the universe / Creation

skānde ca –
parād avyaktam utpannam avyaktāt tu mahāṃs tathā /
vijñānatattvaṃ mahataḥ samutpannaṃ caturmukhāt /
vijñānatattvāt tu mano manastattvāc ca khādikam /
evaṃ bāhyā parā sṛṣṭir antas tadvyaktyapekṣayā /
viparītakramo jñeyo yasmād ante harer dṛśiḥ /
iti (1)

(1) Cf. ibid. ll.: 20f.: *manasaś ca vijñānam iti / vyapadeśaś carācareṣv ālocanād vijñānaṃ bhavatīti bhāgāpeṣayā syāt / na vijñānatattvāpekṣayā* ... ; see also AgniP 25; BrāṇP 29; NārP 24; VāyuP 11. Madhva dealt with the doctrine of evolution of Prakṛti in his work Tattvasaṃkhyāna.

102) BSūBh (p. 99,4-7):
Subject matter: Presiding Deities

skānde ca –
asamyak samyag iti ca hy avasthābhedataḥ surāḥ /
vyāptyavyāptiyutās tv anye cidguṇenaiva nānyathā /
cidguṇasya svarūpatvāt tadvyāptiś ceti yujyate /

śaktiyogāt surāṇāṃ tu vividhā ca vyavasthitiḥ /
iti (1)

(1) Cf. ibid. ll. 3-4: *yathālokasya prakāśaguṇena vyāptir jyotīrūpeṇāvyāptir evaṃ cidguṇena vyāptir jīvarūpeṇāvyāptir iti vā* ... ; see also BhavişP 11.

103) BSūBh (p. 110,2-3):
Subject matter: Number of the *prāṇas*

saptaiva mārutā bāhye prāṇāḥ sapta tathātmani /
adhidaive tathādhyātme saṅkhyāsāmyaṃ vido viduḥ /
iti ca skānde (1)

(1) Cf. ibid. ll. 1f.: *sapta prāṇāḥ prabhavanti tasmād* iti śrutiḥ (MuU II 1,8) ... ; see also BhavişPV 17; SkaP 114.

104) BSūBh (p. 181,8-11):
Subject matter: Liberation / Damnation

asurā āsureṇaiva svabhāvena ca karmaṇā /
jñānena viparītena tamo yānti viniścayāt /
devā daivasvabhāvena karmaṇā cāpy asaṃśayam /
samyagjñānena paramāṃ gatiṃ gacchanti vaiṣṇavīm /
nānayor anyathābhāvaḥ kadācit kvāpi vidyate /
mānuṣā miśramatayo vimiśragatayo 'pi ca /
iti skānde (1)

(1) Cf. ibid. ll. 6f.: *samyagjñānaviparītajñānayor antarā sthātānām api devāsura-bhāvayor dārḍhyadṛṣṭeḥ* ... ; see also AgniP 16 and BhavişPV 12; 19.

105) BSūBh (p. 208,5-6):
Subject matter: Umā / Rudra

umā vai vāk samuddiṣṭā mano rudra udāhṛtaḥ /
tad etan mithunaṃ jñātvā na dāṃpatyād vihīyate /
iti hi skānde (1)

(1) Cf. ibid. ll. 3f.: *vāgabhimāniny umā manobhimānini rudre vilīyate / vāco mano-vaśatvadarśanāt / tasya yāvan na vāṅ manasi saṃpadyata iti śabdāc ca* (ChU VI 15,1) ... ; see also BrahP 22; GarP 20; SkaP 13.

106) ChUBh (p. 401,16-17):
Subject matter: Three-fold worship of Viṣṇu

abhyased adhiyajñaṃ cāpy adhidaivaṃ viśeṣataḥ /

adhyātmaṃ tu viśeṣeṇa yasmād viṣṇus triṣūditaḥ /
iti skānde (1)

(1) Cf. ibid. ll. 14f.: *sarvāsu śākhāsv āraṇam āvartayed āraṇam āvartayed upaniṣadam āvartayed upaniṣadam āvartayed ity* (= ĀruṇyU II) *upaniṣadabhyāsasya satātparyaṃ vihitatvāt / abhagavadviṣayasya ninditatvāc ca nopaniṣatsv anyat ucyate* ... ; see also AgniP 20; KūrP 30_5; SkaP 114.

107) ChUBh (p. 456,13-14):
Subject matter: Viṣṇu = Ātman

ātmeti mukhyato viṣṇus tadanye tūpacārataḥ /
tathaiva sva iti proktas tasmād brahmātmabhūḥ svabhūḥ /
iti skānde (1)

(1) Cf. BhāgP 1; BrahVP 19; 23; BrāṇP 13[13f.]; VāmP 1; VarP 52 and MESQUITA 2000: 133ff.; 424n. 491; 530n. 707.

108) GīBh (p. 3,3-5):
Subject matter: Pañcamaveda

bhārataṃ cāpi kṛtavān pañcamaṃ vedam uttamam /
daśāvarārthaṃ sarvatra kevalaṃ viṣṇubodhakam /
parokṣārthaṃ tu sarvatra vedād apy uttamaṃ tu yat /
iti skānde (1)

(1) Cf. ibid. (p. 1,7): ... *kevalabhagavatsvarūpaparāṃ parokṣārthām mahābhārata-saṃhitām acīkḷpat*; see also BhaviṣP 10; BrāṇP 11; KūrP 30_2; NarP 30; SkaP 126 and Gautama XXVIII 48f.; Manu XII 110f.; MESQUITA 2000_1: 126ff. [= 1997: 101ff.].

109) GīBh (p. 4,29-30):
Subject matter: Jīvanmukti

yas tv evātmarato muktaḥ kāryaṃ tasyaiva nāsti hi /
tasmāt kurv eva karmāṇīty āha kṛṣṇo 'rjunaṃ smayan /
iti ca skānde (1)

(1) Cf. ibid. ll. 28f.: *yas tv ātmaratir eva syād ityādi tu muktiviṣayam* ... ; see also ĀdityaP 1 and MESQUITA 2007: 8n. 11; 16n. 25 [= 2007_1: 434n. 11; 437n. 25].

110) GīBh (p. 19,11-17):
Subject matter: Viṣṇu's absolute transcendence

tathā hi skānde śaive –
yadantaraṃ vyāghraharīndrayor vane
yadantaraṃ merugirīndravindhyayoḥ /

yadantaraṃ sūryasureḍyabiṃbayos
tadantaraṃ rudramahendrayor api /
yadantaraṃ siṃhagajendrayor vane
yadantaraṃ sūryaśaśāṅkayor divi /
yadantaraṃ jāhnavisūryakanyayos
tadantaraṃ brahmagirīśayor api /
yadantaraṃ pralayajavāriviplușor / +1
yadantaraṃ staṃbahiraṇyagarbhayoḥ /
sphuliṅgasaṃvartakayor yadantaraṃ
tadantaraṃ viṣṇuhiraṇyagarbhayoḥ /
anantatvān mahāviṣṇos tadantaram anantakam /
māhātmyasūcanārthāya hy udāharaṇam īritam /
tatsamo 'bhyadhiko vāpi nāsti kaścit kadācana /
etena satyavākyena tam eva praviśāmy aham /
ityādy āha (1)

(1) Cf. ibid. ll. 6f. ... :
nāsti nārāyaṇasamaṃ na bhūtaṃ na bhaviṣyati /
etena satyavākyena sarvārthān sādhayāmy aham //
... ;
cf. MBh = MESQUITA 2000: 190n. 394; 406n 461; see also AgniP 6.

111) GīBh (p. 37,9-12):
Subject matter: Rāmāvatāra

pūrter acintyavīryo yo yaś ca dāśarathiḥ svayam /
rudravākyam ṛtaṃ kartum ajito jitavat sthitaḥ /
yo 'jito vijito bhaktyā gāṅgeyaṃ na jaghāna ha /
na cāṃbāṃ grāhayāmāsa karuṇaḥ ko 'paras tataḥ /
ityādibhyaś ca skānde na tatra saṃsārasamānadharmā nirūpyāḥ /(1)

(1) Cf. ibid. l. 3: *tad eva līlayā cāsau paricchinnādirūpeṇa darśayati māyayā* ... ; see also ĀdiP 1; SkaP 64; VarP 22 and MESQUITA 2000_1: 37ff. [= 1997: 31ff.].

112) GīBh (p. 51,22-23):
Subject matter: Omniscience in liberation

ekaṃ ca tattvato jñātuṃ vinā sarvajñatāṃ naraḥ /
na samartho mahendro 'pi tasmāt sarvatra jijñaset /
iti skānde (1)

(1) Cf. ibid. ll. 20f.: *'tattvataḥ'* (Gī IV 9b) *iti viśeṣaṇāc ca sarvajñānam āpatati / yatraivaṃ bhavati tatra tattvata iti viśeṣaṇe na virodhaḥ / uktaṃ ca* ... ; see also AgniP 16 and 24.

113) GīBh (p. 82,2):
Subject matter: Modification (derivative of the Prakṛti)

vikāro 'vyaktajanma hi /
iti ca skānde (1)

(1) Cf. AgniP 25 and MESQUITA 2000: 151n. 304; 323f.

114) GīBh (p. 82,17-19):
Subject matter: Definitions of Adhyātman, Adhidaivata and Adhibhūta

skānde ca –
ātmābhimānādhikārasthitam adhyātmam ucyate /
dehād bāhyaṃ vinātīva bāhyatvād adhidaivatam /
devādhikāragaṃ sarvaṃ mahābhūtādhikāragam /
tatkāraṇaṃ tathā kāryam adhibhūtaṃ tadantikāt /
iti (1)

(1) Cf. ibid. ll. 13f. āha ca gītākalpe (unknown source):
dehasthaviṣṇurūpāṇi adhiyajña itīritaḥ /
karmeśvarasya sṛṣṭyākhyaṃ tac cāpīcchādyam ucyate /
adhibhūtaṃ jaḍaṃ proktam adhyātmaṃ jīva ucyate /
hiraṇyagarbho 'dhidaivaṃ devaḥ saṅkarṣaṇo 'pi vā /
brahma nārāyaṇo devaḥ sarvadeveśvareśvaraḥ /
iti;
see also BrāṇP 68; KūrP 30_5; SkaP 106.

115) GīBh (p. 83,8):
Subject matter: Videhamukti / Bewilderment

tyajan dehaṃ na kaścit tu moham āpnoty asaṃśayam /
iti skānde (1)

(1) Cf. HarV 8; PadP 13.

116) GīBh (p. 87,23-88,2):
Subject matter: Annihilation of bewilderment (*moha*)

tac cāha skānde –
sṛtī jñātvā tu sopāye anuṣṭhīya ca sādhanam /
na kaścin moham āpnoti na cānyā tatra vai gatiḥ /
iti (1)

(1) Cf. ibid. ll. 23f.: *ete sṛtī sopāye jñātvānuṣṭhāya na muhyati* ... ; see also BhavisP 3; HarV 8; PadP 13.

117) GīT (p. 11,26-27):
Subject matter: Birth / Death

svadehayogavigamanāmajanmamṛtī purā /
iṣyete hy eva jīvasya mukter na tu hareḥ kvacit /
iti skānde (1)

(1) Cf. AgniP 4; BrāṇP 33 and MESQUITA 2000: 493n. 645.

118) GīT (p. 131,26-28):
Subject matter: Viṣṇu, the supreme Creator of the universe

svayaṃ prakṛtya bhagavān karoti nikhilaṃ jagat /
naiva kartā hareḥ kaścid akartā tena keśavaḥ /
iti skānde (1)

(1) Cf. ibid. ll. 24f.: *prakṛtya svayam eva prārabhya viṣṇunā kriyamāṇāni / viṣṇor nānyaḥ pūrvapreraka iti* ... ; see also AgniP 12 and MESQUITA 2000: 491.

119) GīT (p. 136,24-25):
Subject matter: Definition of happiness and sorrow

karmaṇo rājasasyoktaṃ duḥkhamiśraṃ sukhaṃ phalam /
ajñānajaṃ tāmasasya nityaduḥkhaṃ phalaṃ viduḥ /
iti skānde (1)

(1) Cf. ibid. ll. 22f.: *rajasas tu phalaṃ duḥkham ity atra duḥkham iti duḥkhamiśraṃ sukham / duḥkhaṃ dur iti saṃproktaṃ khaṃ nāma sukham ucyata* iti śabdanirṇaye (unknown source); see also PadP 13 and 18.

120) ĪśUBh (p. 512,17-18):
Subject matter: Prayer for liberation

yad asmān kurute 'tyalpāṃs tad eno 'smad viyojaya /
naya no mokṣavittāyety astaud yajñaṃ manuḥ svarāṭ /
iti skānde (1)

(1) Cf. ibid. l. 15: *juhurāṇaṃ asmān alpaṃ kurvat / yuyodhi viyojaya* ... ; see also AgniP 9.

121) KhN (p. 227,6-7):
Subject matter: Viṣṇu, the grantor of liberation

samīpe dūrataś caiva dhyāyantaṃ tvāṃ sadā vibho /
mām ehi jñānadānāyety āha gādhisuto harim /
iti skānde (1)

(1) Cf. ibid. ll. 2f.: *evaṃvidhaṃ madgataṃ tvām uddiśyaivopehi / viśvadha viśvadhāraka / samīpato dūrataś ca tvāṃ manyamānāya mahyaṃ manyave jñānāya mām upehīti vā* ... ; see also AgniP 9; BhaviṣP 3; PadP 98; SkaP 70 and MESQUITA 2000_1: 171n. 348 [= 1997: 139n. 335].

122) MBhTN (I 50cd-51):
Subject matter: Satsiddhāntas = *nirṇayāḥ*

amohāya guṇā viṣṇor ākāraś ciccharīratā /
nirdoṣatvaṃ tāratamyaṃ muktānām api cocyate /
etadviruddhaṃ yat sarvaṃ tanmohāyeti nirṇayaḥ / [iti]
skānde 'py uktam śivenaiva ... (1)

(1) Cf. BhaviṣPV 3n. 7; BrāṇP 94; SkaP 94 and MESQUITA 2000_1: 156f.; 169f. [= 1997: 126f.; 137f.].

123) MBhTN (XXII 332-333):
Subject matter: Requital for actions

kvacit pāpaṃ ca puṇyānāṃ vṛddhaye bhavati sphuṭam /
vṛtrahatyā yathendrasya jātā dharmasya vṛddhaye /
devānāṃ vā munīnāṃ vā bhaved evaṃ na vai nṛṇām /
pāpaṃ yat puṇyam evaitad asurāṇāṃ vilomataḥ /
evaṃ skānde *hi vacanaṃ na pāpaṃ tac chacīpateḥ /* [iti] (1)

(1) Cf. ibid. v. 330f.:
indro 'py avāpa svaṃ sthānam iṣṭvā viṣṇuṃ vipāpakaḥ /
dharmavṛddhyartham evaitat pāpam āsīc chacīpateḥ /
na hi lokāvanaṃ pāpaṃ trailokyeśasya vajriṇaḥ /
vṛtraṃ hatvā mahānāsetyādi vedapadaṃ ca yat /
also BhaviṣP 12.

124) MBhTN (XXXII 66):
Subject matter: Bhīma
ṛṇāny unmucya doṣoktyā svānāṃ bhīmaḥ svakāṃ tanum /
tatyāja paramaṃ dhyāyann āpa ca sthānam uttamam /
iti skāndapurāṇoktaṃ vyāsavākyam ṛṣīn prati | (1)

(1) Cf. MBh 46.

125) MuUBh (p. 499,21-22):
Subject matter: Dependence of Jīvas on Viṣṇu

brahmatvaṃ bṛṃhitatvaṃ syāj jīvānāṃ na parātmatā /
asvatantrasya jīvasya kuto nityasvatantratā /
iti skānde (1)

(1) Cf. AgniP 22; BrāṇP 71; SkaP 97 and MESQUITA 2000: 166-168; 456f.

126) ṚgBh (p. 10,13-14):
Subject matter: Sadāgamas

trayo 'rthāḥ sarvavedeṣu daśārthāḥ sarvabhārate /
viṣṇoḥ sahasranāmāpi nirantaraśatārthakam /
iti skāndavaco yasmād arthabhedavyapekṣayā |
nirdoṣatvaṃ harer vakti doṣam anyeṣv api kramāt (1)

(1) Cf. ibid. ll. 12f.:
ato doṣavaco yatra tad vākyam avaraṃ vadet /
nirdoṣataiva viṣṇos tu kramān madhyagateṣv api /
also BhaviṣP 10; BrāṇP 11; 86; SkaP 108; UpanārP 1.

127) VTN (p. 20,6-8):
Subject matter: Viṣṇu, the supreme Creator of the universe
utpattisthitisaṃhārā niyatir jñānam āvṛttiḥ /
bandhamokṣau ca puruṣād yasmāt sa harir ekarāṭ /
iti ca skānde (1)

(1) Cf. ChUBh (p. 442,21-23):
sṛṣṭiḥ sthitiś ca saṃhāro niyatir jñānam āvṛttiḥ /
bandhamokṣau ca kathyante yasyotkarṣaprasiddhaye /
yasyotkarṣaprasiddhyarthaṃ sarvavedāś ca yuktayaḥ /
jñatvaiva ca yadutkarṣaṃ mucyante sa hariḥ paraḥ /
iti ca (unknown quote);
see also AgniP 12; SkaP 81 and MESQUITA 2000: 109; 470ff. and MESQUITA 2000_1: 171n. 348 [= 1997: 139n. 335].

128) VTN (p. 37,19-20):
Subject matter: Endless number of the individual souls
sahasrayojanasabhāṃ prabhāvād viśvakarmaṇaḥ /
anantā rāśayo 'nantāḥ prajānām adhisaṃsthitāḥ /
iti skānde (1)

(1) Cf. BrāṇP 71; PadP 86 and MESQUITA 2000: 207.

129) VTN (p. 40,8-9):
Subject matter: Viṣṇu's supreme transcendence

brahmaśeṣasuparṇeśaśakrasūryaguhādayaḥ /
sarve kṣarā akṣarā tu śrīr ekā tatparo hariḥ /
iti skānde (1)

(1) Cf. GīT (p. 141,26+142,25 [iti nārāyaṇaśruti (unknown source)]; see also AgniP 6; 25; BrāṇP 51 and MESQUITA 2000: 104f.; 223f. and 489n. 638.

Upagītā (Upagī)

1) (GīBh p. 33,10):
Subject matter: Bewilderment (*moha*)

tathā hi mohaśabdārtha ukta upagītāsu –
mohasañjñitam adharmalakṣaṇaṃ caiva niyataṃ pāpakarmasv iti (1)

(1) Cf. HarP 8; MBh 42n. 6; PadP 13.

Upanāradīyapurāṇa (UpanārP)

1) (GīBh p. 3,1-2):
Subject matter: Pañcamaveda

brahmāpi tan na jānāti īṣat sarvo 'pi jānate /
bahvartham ṛṣayas tat tu bhārataṃ pravadanti hi /
ity upanāradīye (1)

(1) Cf. BhaviṣP 10; KūrP 30_2; SkaP 126.

Vahnipurāṇa (VahniP)

[VahniP is not identical with AgniP, although sometimes it is confused with the latter (cf. HAZRA 1987: 139f.; ROCHER 1986: 63f.). There is one metrical lapse (2ab).]

1) BhāgTN (p. 90,11-13):
Subject matter: Doctrine of Avatāras

anādyananto 'pi harir vaikārikagaṇeṣv ajaḥ /
avatīrṇaḥ padāṅguṣṭham adhyāste viśvabhug vibhuḥ /
pādadevas tu yajño 'nyastaṃ praviśya hariḥ svayam /
sarvaṃ vidhārayan dehaṃ vartate sarvaśaktidhṛk /
iti vahnipurāṇe (1)

(1) Cf. BhāgP VII 8,18-19; see also ĀdiP 1 and MESQUITA 2000_1: 37 [= 1997: 31].

Vāmanapurāṇa (VāmP)

[NārP (I 105,1-22) provides a summary of VāmP. Only the first part (1-13ab) corresponds with the traditional VāmP. There is no sectarian spirit in this Purāṇa (cf. HAZRA 1987: 76-92; ROCHER 1986: 238f.). Most quotes from this Purāṇa are to be found in BhāgTN (thirty-one), followed by BSūBh (seven), BĀUBh and GīBh (two each); ĪŚuBh (one). VāmP 14ab has one metrical lapse.]

1) BĀUBh (p. 272,14-15):
Subject matter: Viṣṇu = Ātman

devānāṃ vyāpakatvāt tu teṣām ātmā hariḥ sadā /
tajjñaḥ priyas tatas teṣāṃ tasya nābhūtidās tataḥ /
iti vāmane (1)

(1) Cf. ibid. l. 13: *sa īśvara eṣāṃ devānām ātmā bhavati / puṃlliṅgaṃ ca tat satyaṃ sa ātmetyādivat* (ChU VI 8,7) *bhavati* ... ; BhāgP 1; BrahVP 22; SkaP 107 and MESQUITA 2000: 142f.

2) BĀUBh (p. 274,12-19):
Subject matter: Classification of the castes

viṣṇor brāhmaṇajātiḥ san brahmā jajñe caturmukhaḥ /
ito 'gre jagatas tasmāt kṣatrajātir ajāyata / [1]
vāyuḥ sadāśivo 'nanto garuḍaḥ śakra eva ca /
kāmaś ca varuṇaś caiva somasūryau yamas tathā / [2]
evam ādyāḥ kṣatriyās tu devānāṃ brahmanirmitāḥ /
śreyasī sarvajātibhyaḥ kṣatrajātir iti śrutiḥ / [3]
naiva kṣatrāt parā jātir brahmajātiṃ vinā kvacit /
brāhmaṇāc ca paro rājā rājasūyāśvamedhayoḥ / [4]
upāste rājasūye 'to brāhmaṇo rājasūyinam /
āsīna āsanādhastāt tathāpi brāhmaṇo guruḥ / [5]
tasmāt sa rājasūyānte brāhmaṇān vandayīta ca /
yaḥ kṣatriyo brāhmaṇahā pitṛhā sa prakīrtitaḥ / [6]
pāpīyān eva bhavati hatvā svapitaraṃ yathā / [7ab]
iti vāmane (1)

(1) Cf. AgniP 2; 20; BhaviṣP 11; NārP 2 and MESQUITA 2003: 99n. 8; see also BrāṇP 12[7]; PadP 25; SkaP [5].

3) BhāgTN (p. 5,16-17):
Subject matter: Author of BhāgP

vāmane ca –
adhikāraṃ phalaṃ caiva pratipādyaṃ ca vastu yat /

smṛtvā prārabhato granthaṃ karotīśo mahat phalam /
<u>iti</u> (1)

(1) Cf. ibid. (p. 4,11): *adhikāriviṣayaphalāny ucyante*; (p. 5,14f.): *sadyaḥśabda āpekṣika iti tatkṣaṇād iti / na cāsaṃpūrṇādhikāriṇāṃ tatkṣaṇād avaruddhyata iti sadyaśabdaḥ / adhikāriviṣayaphalānāṃ smaraṇāt phalādhikyaṃ bhavati* ... ; see also GarP 8.

4) BhāgTN (p. 12,7-9):
Subject matter: Three-fold outward appearances of Viṣṇu

vāmanapurāṇe ca –
brahmaviṣṇvīśarūpāṇi trīṇi viṣṇor mahātmanaḥ /
brahmaṇi brahmarūpaḥ sa śivarūpī śive sthitaḥ /
pṛthag eva sthito devo viṣṇurūpo janārdanaḥ /
iti (1)

(1) Cf. ibid. ll. 7f.: *viṣṇor eva trisañjñāḥ* ... *trayo 'pi guṇā viṣṇvāśrayāḥ / tathāpi sattvatanau jīve śreyāṃsi syuḥ*; BrahP 52 and MESQUITA 2000: 33n. 12.

5) BhāgTN (p. 14,4):
Subject matter: Viṣnu, the possessor of flawless qualities

sarvatra sārabhug devo nāsāraṃ sa kadācana /
iti vāmanapurāṇe (1)

(1) Cf. ibid. l. 3: *tadguṇān eva bhuṅkte / na doṣān* ... ; see also BrāṇP 69; PadP 6.

6) BhāgTN (p. 77,14-15):
Subject matter: Liberation

viṣṇor lokaṃ tadaivaike yānti kālāntare pare /
ājñayaiva hareḥ kecid apūrteḥ kecid añjasā /
vihṛtyaivānyalokeṣu mucyante brahmaṇā saha /
iti vāmane (1)

(1) Cf. ibid. l: 13: *ṛte satyaloke / anidaṃvidāṃ abrahmavidām / durantaduḥkhaṃ ca prabhavaś ca* ... ; see also AgniP 16; 27 and SkaP 47; VarP 4.

7) BhāgTN (p. 80,12-13):
Subject matter: Antaryāmin

pañcabhūtaiś ca śabdādyair indriyair jīvarāśibhiḥ /
yukta ākāśago viṣṇur manastham upagacchati /
iti vāmane (1)

(1) Cf. ibid. l. 11: *bhūtasūkṣmāṇi pañcabhūtāni jīvāś ca* ... ; see also BhāgP 2.

8) BhāgTN (p. 83,6-7):
Subject matter: Upāsanā / Liberation

āpteḥ sarvaguṇānāṃ ya ātmanāmatayā harim /
upāste nityaśo vidvān āptakāmas tadā bhavet /
iti vāmane (1)

(1) Cf. AgniP 16; 20.

9) BhāgTN (p. 85,3-5):
Subject matter: Viṣṇu, the basis / navel of the Universe

adhiṣṭhānam iti proktaṃ mūlādhāraṃ vicakṣaṇaiḥ /
yatsthitaṃ dṛśyate vastu saṃsthānaṃ tadudīritam /
ubhayaṃ harir evāsya jagato munipuṅgava /
iti vāmane (1)

(1) Cf. ibid. l. 3: *tadvaśatvād idaṃ rūpaṃ harer naiva svarūpata* iti mānasaṃhitāyāṃ (unknown source); see also AgniP 6; BhaviṣPV 6 and MESQUITA 2000: 301f.; 464n. 584f.; 455f.

10) BhāgTN (p. 93,15):
Subject matter: Viṣṇu, the origin of the Deities

kumārabrahmarudrādyā harer madhyāt samudgatāḥ /
iti vāmane (1)

(1) Cf. BhaviṣP 5; BrahP 22; 52.

11) BhāgTN (p. 94,7-8):
Subject matter: Antaryāmin

paśyan svadhiṣṇyaṃ dehaṃ sa bahiṣṭhān viṣayān api /
evam aṇḍāntaraṃ paśyan bahiḥ sarvaṃ ca paśyati /
iti vāmane (1)

(1) Cf. BhāgP 2.

12) BhāgTN (p. 95,1-2):
Subject matter: Viṣṇu, the *svarūpāṃśa / svarūpāṃsī*

svarūpāṃśo vibhinnāṃśa iti dvedhāṃśa iṣyate /
anantāsanavaikuṇṭhapadmanābhāḥ svayaṃ hariḥ /
jīvā ime vibhinnāṃśā dharmādharmādisaṃyutāḥ /
iti vāmane (1)

(1) Cf. AgniP 22; 27; SkaP 54; VarP 33 and MESQUITA 2000: 445f; 497f.

13) BhāgTN (p. 123,13-14):
Subject matter: Liberation

> *yena yena yathā jñātvā niyataṃ muktir āpyate* /
> *tad vijñānam iti proktaṃ jñānaṃ sādhāraṇaṃ smṛtam* /
> iti vāmane (1)

(1) Cf. GīBh *ad* VI,8: *vijñānaṃ viśeṣajñānam aparokṣajñānaṃ vā*; see also *ad* VII 2; AgniP 16 ; 24 and ViṣP 6n. 1.

14) BhāgTN (p. 133,8-9):
Subject matter: Trimūrti

> *matsyādirūpī poṣayati nṛsiṃho rudrasaṃsthitaḥ* /+1
> *vilāyayed viriñcasthaḥ sṛjate viṣṇur avyayaḥ* /
> iti vāmane (1)

(1) Cf. BrahP 52.

15) BhāgTN (p. 166,3-4):
Subject matter: Avatāras

> *brahmādibhāvo viṣṇos tu tanniyāmakatā bhavet* /
> *matsyāditā svabhāvas tu nānyathā kvacid iṣyate* /
> iti vāmane
> *anantāsanavaikuṇṭhakṣīrābdhistho haris tripāt* /
> iti ca (1)

(1) Cf. ĀdiP 1; AgniP 27 and MESQUITA 2000_1: 35ff. [= 1997: 29ff.].

16) BhāgTN (p. 170,9):
Subject matter: Liberation

> *muktasyāpi hareḥ prītiḥ sarvato 'py anurajyate* /
> iti vāmane (1)

(1) Cf. ibid. l. 8: *niḥśreyasam rājyam* / *mokṣe 'pi rañjanīyā matprītir eva* ... ; see also AgniP 16.

17) BhāgTN (p. 225,7-8):
Subject matter: Hierarchy among Deities

> *sṛṣṭau laye tāratamyaṃ devānāṃ jñāyate sphuṭam* /
> *tāratamyaparijñāne mahātātparyam iṣyate* /

atas tad bahuśas tūktam anyac caitat prakāśakam /
iti vāmane (1)

(1) Cf. BhavişPV 15 and BhavişP 11.

18) BhāgTN (p. 234,7):
Subject matter: Sattva

mahāguṇābhipūrṇatvaṃ sattvam ity ucyate budhaiḥ /
iti vāmane (1)

(1) Cf. MatsyaP 1.

19) BhāgTN (p. 268,8-9):
Subject matter: Heaven and hell

īṣadbhakto bhagavati sukarmā svargam eṣyate /
abhakto nirayaṃ yāti sukarmāpi na saṃśayaḥ /
iti vāmane (1)

(1) Cf. BhavişPV 19.

20) BhāgTN (p. 271,12-14):
Subject matter: Presiding Deities / Viṣṇu's supreme transcendence

ekādaśendriyātmā ca pañcabhūtātmakas tathā /
sarvābhimānī bhagavān svarāḍindraḥ purandaraḥ /
idam aṇḍaṃ jagat sarvaṃ śakradehaṃ vidur budhāḥ /
tatpatis triguṇo rudras tasya brahmā tato hariḥ /
iti vāmane (1)

(1) Cf. AgniP 6; BhavişP 11; BrahP 22.

21) BhāgTN (p. 278,7-8):
Subject matter: Mukhyaprāṇa

giriḥ prāṇaḥ samuddiṣṭhas tatsutā vedavāk smṛtā /
puṣpaṃ svargādayaḥ proktāḥ phalaṃ mokṣa udāhṛtaḥ /
iti vāmane (1)

(1) Cf. BrahVP 13; VāyuP 8; see also BhavişPV 17 and SkaP 85.

22) BhāgTN (p. 310,7-9):
Subject matter: Pṛthu

anapatyo 'pi saddharmā lokajin nātra saṃśayaḥ /
devais tu pṛthujanmārthe havir aṅgasya no hṛtam /
anapatyatvakarmāsau bālahatyākṛteḥ purā /
ato duṣṭo 'bhavat putra iṣṭo viṣṇur ataḥ pṛthuḥ /
iti vāmane (1)

(1) Cf. BrāṇP 42; NārP 15.

23) BhāgTN (p. 443,1):
Subject matter: Hari's supreme transcendence

suviruddhasvabhāvatvāj jīvād anyatamo hariḥ /
iti vāmane (1)

(1) Cf. ibid. p. 442,12f.: *anyatama ātmā paramātmā ... bhagavanmāhātmyakathanena sarvasya tadvaśatvāt sa eva bhajanīyo na śokena prayojanam iti phalitārthaḥ*; see also AgniP 6 and BrāṇP 69.

24) BhāgTN (p. 504,9-10):
Subject matter: Daiva / Transmigration

yathā kuṇḍasthitasyāgner daivād dārūpasan namet /
dehayogo viyogaś ca tathā daivān na cānyathā /
iti vāmane (1)

(1) Cf. ibid. ll. 8f.: *kuṇḍādisthāgner dāruyogādau svataḥ pravṛttyabhāvāt* ... ; see also BrāṇP 33.

25) BhāgTN (p. 508,7-8):
Subject matter: Viṣṇu's graciousness

bhagavatpādapoto 'sau nānyapotasamo bata /
sannidhāyāpi śiṣyeṣu tam eva prāpnuyur ataḥ /
iti vāmane (1)

(1) Cf. BrahP 46; PadP 47.

26) BhāgTN (p. 524,4-5):
Subject matter: Viṣṇu's nature

rūpyatvāt tu jagad rūpaṃ viṣṇoḥ sākṣāt sukhātmakam /
nityapūrṇaṃ samuddiṣṭaṃ svarūpaṃ paramātmanaḥ /
iti vāmane (1)

(1) Cf. AgniP 6; BrāṇP 69; VarP 52.

27) BhāgTN (p. 548,2-5):
Subject matter: Worship of the Deities

uttamā api deveśā avarān viduṣo nṛṇām /
pūjāyai saṃprayacchanti parokṣatvapriyā yataḥ /
teṣu sthitvā svayaṃ pūjāṃ gṛhṇanty anupamāṃ sadā /
jñānāni ca prayacchanti tasmād evaṃvidā sadā /
pūjitāḥ syuḥ suravarāḥ sabrahmāṇaḥ sakeśavāḥ /
iti vāmane (1)

(1) Cf. AgniP 20.

28) BhāgTN (p. 581,10-11):
Subject matter: Viṣṇu's supreme transcendence

viṣṇunā devatā baddhā viṣṇave ca balipradāḥ /
viṣṇur āsāṃ patir nityaṃ na viṣṇor bandhakaḥ kvacit /
iti vāmane (1)

(1) Cf. AgniP 6.

29) BhāgTN (p. 584,13-14):
Subject matter: Liberation

samyagjñānavadācāryān mucyate puruṣo bhavāt /
dvāv eva nityamuktau tu paramaḥ prakṛtis tathā /
iti vāmane (1)

(1) Cf. ibid. ll. 7f.: *anantam aduṣṭayā jānatācāryeṇa santatād bhavāt parimucyate / abaddhaś ca prakṛtipareśau vinānyo na vidyate / yatas tayor evodbhavo na ghaṭate / tayor ajayor asubhṛta udbhavanti / deśataḥ kālataś ca yatra paramas tatra prakṛtir yatra prakṛtis tatra parama ity ubhayayujoḥ* ... ; see also AgniP 16; BrāṇP 51; MESQUITA 2000: 105n. 164; 417f.; MESQUITA 2007: 42n. 96 [= 2007_1: 451n. 94] and Gī XV 16.

30) BhāgTN (p. 600,7-9):
Subject matter: Viṣṇu's supreme transcendence

sarvottamo 'pi bhagavān guṇabhāvaṃ janārdanaḥ /
darśayed vasudevāder ātmano jīvatām api /
ajñāśaktādibhāvas tu kutas tasyākhileśituḥ /
kutaś ca jīvatā tasya pradhānapuruṣeśituḥ /
kuto doṣāḥ sarvaguṇapūrṇasyānandavāridheḥ /
iti vāmane (1)

(1) Cf. AgniP 6.

31) BhāgTN (p. 627,8-9):
Subject matter: Viṣṇu as Vāmana-Avatāra

upendrarūpī bhagavān pratimanvantaraṃ vibhuḥ /
asurān hanti niyataṃ śrāddhadeve ca vāmanaḥ /
iti vāmane (1)

(1) Cf. ĀdiP 1; VāmP 36.

32) BhāgTN (p. 633,5-6):
Subject matter: Śrī

aspardhinī spardhanīva śrīr āste vanamālayā /
na hi spardhādayo doṣāḥ saṃvidrūpāṃ spṛśanti tām /
iti vāmane (1)

(1) Cf. AgniP 25.

33) BhāgTN (p. 844,1-4):
Subject matter: Viṣṇu's supreme transcendence

svasantānodbhavaṃ kīrtyā yojayan janamejayam /
śakto 'py aśaktavad yaṣṭur indra āsīd upckṣakaḥ /
evam eva ṛṣīṇāṃ ca kīrtiṃ yojayatāmunā /
kṛtopekṣā mahendreṇa kimu viṣṇuḥ parātparaḥ /
tasmād viṣṇor aśakyaṃ na bhūtabhavyabhavatsv api /
na cāniṣṭaṃ guṇair eṣa pūrṇo nārāyaṇaḥ sadā /
iti vāmane (1)

(1) Cf. AgniP 6.

34) BSūBh (p. 12,7-9):
Subject matter: Definition of *ātman / anātman*

yo guṇaiḥ sarvato hīno yaś ca doṣavivarjitaḥ /
heyopādeyarahitaḥ sa ātmety abhidhīyate /
etad anyasvabhāvo yaḥ so 'nātmeti satāṃ mataḥ /
anātmany ātmaśabdas tu sopacāraḥ prayujyate /
iti vāmane (1)

(1) Cf. ibid. ll. 6f.: *na ca gauṇa ātmā dṛśyo vācyaś ca nirguṇa iti yuktam / ātmaśabdāt* ... ; see also BrahVP 19; BrāṇP 71; SkaP 107; VāmP 1; VarP 52 and MESQUITA 2000: 142f.

35) BSūBh (p. 22,7-8):
Subject matter: Viṣṇu's Sarvanāmatva

sarvacchandobhidho hy eṣa sarvadevābhidho 'py asau /
sarvalokābhido 'py eṣa teṣāṃ tadupacārataḥ /
iti vāmane (1)

(1) Cf. BrāṇP 2.

36) BSūBh (p. 28,21-22):
Subject matter: Vāmana-Avatāra

yatsthānatvād idaṃ cakṣur asaṅgaṃ sarvavastubhiḥ /
sa vāmanaḥ paro 'smākaṃ gatir ity eva cintaya /
iti ca vāmane (1)

(1) Cf. ibid. ll. 19f.: *sa īśaḥ so 'sapatnaḥ sa hariḥ sa paraḥ parovarīyān yad idaṃ cakṣuṣi sarpir vodakaṃ vā siñcati vartmanī eva gacchati sa bhāmanaḥ sa vāmanaḥ sa ānandaḥ so 'cyuta* iti caturvedaśikhāyāṃ (unknown source); see also ĀdiP 1 and KūrP 30_1; VāmP 31.

37) BSūBh (p. 35,15-17):
Subject matter: Viṣṇu's Sarvanāmatva

vāmane ca –
na tu nārāyaṇādīnāṃ nāmnām anyatra saṃbhavaḥ /
anyanāmnāṃ gatir viṣṇur eka eva prakīrtitaḥ /
iti (1)

(1) Cf. BrāṇP 2; 68 and MESQUITA 2000: 33n. 12.

38) BSūBh (p. 63,15-16):
Subject matter: Definition of Pramāṇa

yāvad eva pramāṇena siddhaṃ tāvad ahāpayan /
svīkuryān naiva cānyatra śaṅkyaṃ mānam ṛte kvacit /
iti vāmane (1)

(1) Cf. ibid. ll. 12f.: ... *ato yāvat pramāṇasiddhaṃ tāvad evāṇgīkartavyam / nāto 'nyacchaṅkyam* ... ; see also KūrP 20.

39) BSūBh (p. 94,27-29):
Subject matter: Viṣṇu's almighty power

vāmane ca –
tatra tatra sthito viṣṇus tattacchaktīḥ prabodhayan /
eka eva mahāśaktiḥ kurute sarvam añjasā /
iti (1)

(1) Cf. BhaviṣP 13; MESQUITA 2000: 484f.

40) BSūBh (p. 96,13-15):
Subject matter: Antaryāmin

vāmane ca –
pūrve pūrve yato viṣṇoḥ sannidhānaṃ kramādhikam /
sāmarthyādhikyam eteṣāṃ paścād eva layas tathā /
vyāptiś cābhyadhikā teṣām ata eva na saṃśayaḥ /
iti (1)

(1) Cf. ibid. ll. 12f.: *pūrveṣāṃ pūrveṣāṃ sāmarthyādhikyād upapadyate ca* ... ; see also BhāgP 2.

41) GīBh (p. 67,11-12):
Subject matter: Tāratamya

vittaṃ bandhur vayaḥ karma vidyā caiva tu pañcamī /
etāni mānyasthānāni garīyo hy uttarottaram /
iti vāmane (1)

(1) Cf. BhaviṣPV 15.

42) GīBh (p. 129,8):
Subject matter: Ahaṃgrahopāsana

tadīyo 'ham iti jñānam ahaṃgraha itīritaḥ /
iti vāmane (1)

(1) Cf. ibid. ll. 6f.: *ahaṃgrahopāsane ca phalādhikyam* āgniveśyaśrutisiddham (unknown source) *'ahaṃgrahopāsakas tasya sāmyam abhyāso havā aśnute nātra śaṅkā' iti ... tadvaśatvāt tu so'smīti bhṛtyair eva na tu svata* iti ca (unknown source) *prātibiṃbyena so'smi bhṛtyaś ceti bhāvanā* ... ; see also AgniP 20; BhāgP 3.

43) ĪśUBh (p. 509,24+510,8):
Subject matter: Asuras

mahāduḥkhaikahetutvāt prāpyatvād asurais tathā /
asuryā nāma te lokās tān yānti vimukhā harau /
iti vāmane (1)

(1) Cf. ibid. ll. 23f.: *suṣṭhu ramaṇaviruddhatvād asurāṇāṃ prāpyatvāc ca asuryāḥ* ... ; see also BhaviṣPV 12 and MESQUITA 2000: 527f.

Varāhapurāṇa (VarP)

[According to NārP (I 103,1-17) VarP consists of two parts. Like VāmP, the VarP too consists only of the first part. With regard to its contents VarP is said to be "a religious manual, almost wholly occupied with forms of prayer, and rules for devotional observances addressed to Viṣṇu" (cf. ROCHER 1986: 242; HAZRA 1987: 96-107). Three references ascribed to this Purāṇa are traceable: VarP 75,44 [with deviations] in BhāgTN (p. 15,8-9); in BĀUBh (p. 314,17-19); VarP 66,18 in Anuv (p. 88,23-24); in MuUBh (p. 491,22-23) slightly deviating; (see also below VarP 59 and VarP 70,35f. also deviating) in GīBh (p. 35,22-24); BSūBh (p. 7,12-8,1); KhN (p. 247,26-27 and in MBhTN (I 48-50ab: iti vārāhavacanaṃ brahmāṇḍoktam also ibid. XXII 151f.; cf. MESQUITA 2000_1: 153f. [= 1997: 123f.]). The majority of references is quoted in BhāgTN (twenty-nine), BSūBh (nineteen); GīT (five); BĀUBh; ĪśUBh and MāṇUBh (one); KathUBh; MuUBh and VTN (two each). Metrical lapses in VarP 2[5cd]; 26[2ab]; 32ab; 51[8cd].]

1) BĀUBh (p. 244,10-12):
Subject matter: Brahmā, the proclaimer of BĀU

yathā tuṣṭāva lakṣmīśaṃ sargādau caturānanaḥ /
tathā jagāda sūryāya yājñavalkyāya so 'bravīt /
vājirūpeṇa sūryeṇa proktaṃ vājasaneyakam /
kaṇvāya yājñavalkyo 'dāt kāṇvaṃ tena prakīrtitam /
iti vārāhe (1)

(1) Cf. ibid. ll. 5f.:

...
sarvajñaṃ sarvaśaktiṃ suramunim anujādyaiḥ sevyamānaṃ
viṣṇuṃ vande sadāhaṃ sakalajagadanādyantam ānandadaṃ tam //
see also BrāṇP 29; 51.

2) BhāgTN (p. 15,8-16,1):
Subject matter: Viṣṇu's bodies

sarve nityāḥ śāśvatāś ca dehās tasya parātmanaḥ /
hānopādānarahitā naiva prakṛtijāḥ kvacit /
paramānandasandohā jñānamātrāś ca sarvaśaḥ /
sarve sarvaguṇaiḥ pūrṇāḥ sarvadoṣavivarjitāḥ /
anyūnānadhikāś caiva guṇaiḥ sarvaiś ca sarvataḥ /
dehidehabhidā cātra neśvare vidyate kvacit /
tatsvīkārādiśabdas tu hastasvīkāravat smṛtaḥ /
vailakṣaṇyān na vā tatra jñānamātrārtham īritam /
kevalaiśvaryasaṃyogād īśvaraḥ prakṛteḥ paraḥ /
jāto gatas tv idaṃ rūpaṃ tad ityādi vyavahriyate /+1
iti mahāvarāhe (1)

(1) Cf. ibid. ll. 7f.:
na tasya prākṛtā mūrtir māṃsamedo 'sthisaṃbhavā /
na yogitvād īśvaratavāt satyarūpācyuto vibhuḥ //
iti vārāhe (= VarP 75,44) ... ;
see also AgniP 4; MESQUITA 2000$_1$: 35f. [= 1997: 29f.] and MESQUITA 2000: 429ff.; 440ff.

3) BhāgTN (p. 19,8-9):
Subject matter: Balarāma-Avatāra

śaṅkhacakrabhṛd īśeśaḥ śvetavarṇo mahābhujaḥ /
āviṣṭaḥ śvetakeśātmā śeṣāṃśaṃ rohiṇīsutam /
iti vārāhe (1)

(1) Cf. ibid. ll. 7f.: *āveśo balabhadre*; see also ĀdiP 1; BrahP 17 and MESQUITA 2000$_1$: 35f. [= 1997: 29f.].

4) BhāgTN (p. 77,13-14):
Subject matter: Liberation

sarvaduḥkhavihīnā ye muktāḥ prāyas tu tādṛśāḥ /
amuktāś ca janādyeṣu viśeṣeṇa tu satyagāḥ /
iti vārāhe (1)

(1) Cf. ibid. ll. 12f.: *ṛte satyaloke / anidaṃvidāṃ abrahmavidām / durantaduḥkhaṃ ca prabhavaś ca* ... ; see also AgniP 16; 27 and VāmP 6.

5) BhāgTN (p. 80,9-10):
Subject matter: Antaryāmin

manasthito harir nityaṃ sarvadeveṣu saṃsthitaḥ /
devapradhānakān lokān karoty anugataḥ sadā /
iti vārāhe (1)

(1) Cf. ibid. ll. 8f.: *vividhakāryayuktaṃ vikāryam / devamayaṃ devapradhānam* ... ; see also BhāgP 2.

6) BhāgTN (p. 87,2-3):
Subject matter: Viṣṇu's supreme transcendence

gamyejyajñeyavācyeṣu yojyeṣu ca paro hariḥ /
tapasā pūjyamānānāṃ sarvalokebhya eva ca /
iti vārāhe (1)

(1) Cf. ibid. ll. 1f.: *vedapratipādyeṣu sa para ityādi* ... ; see also AgniP 6.

7) BhāgTN (p. 193,4-195,2):
Subject matter: Pralaya

yugaikasaptater ūrdhvaṃ sārddhāṣṭādaśalakṣakam /
vatsarāṇāṃ manor bhuktiḥ sahasraṃ caturuttaram /
śatānāṃ pralayaś caiva pañcottaram athāpi ca /
ādyeṣu ṣaṭsu prathame dvisāhasraṃ prakīrtitam /
vatsarāṇāṃ manor anta evam indrādināṃ bhavet /
iti mahāvarāhe (1)

(1) Cf. ibid. (p. 192,10): *dinastho bhagavān bhoktā* ... ; see also KūrP 30_6; NārP 24.

8) BhāgTN (p. 205,9-10):
Subject matter: Viṣṇu's *līlā*

piśācacaryām acarad rudro viṣṇvājñayaiva tu /
garbhiṇīvadhanodārtham aho viṣṇur viḍaṃbakṛt /
iti vārāhe (1)

(1) Cf. BhavişP 13; BrahVP 20 and MESQUITA 2000_1: 37f. [= 1997: 31f.].

9) BhāgTN (p. 225,1-3):
Subject matter: *līlā*

yathecchayaiva sarvaṃ tu manasā dehato 'pi vā /
kartuṃ śakto 'pi cāstrādyā līlaivānantaśaktinaḥ /
iti vārāhe (1)

(1) Cf. BrahVP 20; VarP 8.

10) BhāgTN (p. 225,8-12):
Subject matter: Presiding Deities and their hierarchy

mahato brahmavāyū ca tadbhārye cābhimāninaḥ /
ahamaḥ śeṣavīndrau ca rudrendrau kāmatatstriyaḥ /
manasas tv aniruddhaś ca candraś cānye yathoditam /
evaṃ kramo vyatyayas tu sūkṣmasthūlādibhedataḥ /
sṛṣṭau guṇe ca jñānādau muktisthe cāpy ayaṃ kramaḥ /
niyamenānyathoktis tu mohāyāsurajanmanām /
iti vārāhe (1)

(1) Cf. BhavişPV 15; BhavişP 11.

11) BhāgTN (p. 234,1-3):
Subject matter: The bodies of Avatāras

nāvatāreṣv api harer dehaḥ śuklādisaṃbhavaḥ /
tathāpi śuklasaṃsthaḥ san mātṛdehaṃ praviśya ca /
vilāpya śuklaṃ tatraiva kevalajñānarūpakaḥ /
udeti bhagavān viṣṇuḥ kāle lokaṃ vimohayan /
iti mahāvarāhe (1)

(1) Cf. ĀdiP 1; AgniP 4 and MESQUITA 2000_1: 36f. [= 1997: 30f.].

12) BhāgTN (p. 267,8-9):
Subject matter: Good behaviour

satpuṃsu ca tathā strīṣu na saṅgo doṣam āvahet /
yathāyogye guṇāyaiva doṣakṛd duṣṭajantuṣu /
iti vārāhe (1)

(1) Cf. also HarV 31.

13) BhāgTN (p. 272,10):
Subject matter: Viṣṇu / Śrī

tvaṃ pradhānamayo deva pradhānād adhiko yataḥ /
iti vārāhe (1)

(1) Cf. ibid. ll. 9f.: *bhūtendriyārthātmamayaṃ tebhyaḥ pradhānam* ... ; BrāṇP 51 and MESQUITA 2000: 421f.

14) BhāgTN (p. 273,5-6):
Subject matter: Jīvopādhi

jīvopādhiprabhṛtaya āmukteḥ sarvadehinām /
niyamāt santy abhāvas tu niṣphalatvād udīryate /
iti vārāhe (1)

(1) Cf. BrāṇP 71; SkaP 54 and MESQUITA 2000: 497ff.

15) BhāgTN (p. 275,10-276,3):
Subject matter: Viṣṇu, the supreme meaning of the epic literature

ṛte tu pāṇḍavakathāṃ kārṣṇaṃ rāmāyaṇaṃ tathā /
viṣṇor brahmādināṃ caiva kramād vyatyastaśaktitām /
etadāpādakaṃ cānyad ṛte kalpādibhedataḥ /
kathābhedas tu vijñeyo mohāyaiteṣu bhinnatā /
iti vārāhe (1)

(1) Cf. BrāṇP 82; SkaP 49.

16) BhāgTN (p. 278,1-3):
Subject matter: Yogyatā of the individual souls

ye jñānaviṣayāḥ śāpā muktigāś cādhikāriṇām /
kādācitkās te bhavanti naiva te sārvakālikāḥ /
teṣāṃ jñānasya mukteś ca tāratamyasya caiva ha /
bhagavanniyatatvāt tu śāpādir nātra kāraṇam /
iti vārāhe (1)

(1) Cf. BrahP 36; BrāṇP 59; NārP 12; PadP 14; SkaP 59; MESQUITA 2000: 506ff. and MESQUITA 2007: 34n. 73 [= 2007_1 447n. 72].

17) BhāgTN (p. 307,5-6):
Subject matter: Eternity and transitoriness of the world

anyathātvāt kṣipranāśāj jagat svapnādivat smṛtam /
vartamānaṃ niyatyaiva sadaiva paramātmani /
iti vārāhe (1)

(1) Cf. BrāṇP 103; GarP 6; SkaP 40; VarP 21; 27; 55; see also BhaviṣPV 1; MESQUITA 2000_1: 104ff. [= 1997: 84ff.] and MESQUITA 2000: 460ff.

18) BhāgTN (p. 316,3):
Subject matter: Māyādeha

brahmādijīvadehās tu māyādehāḥ prakīrtitāḥ /
iti vārāhe (1)

(1) Cf. AgniP 4; HarV 8; SkaP 12; VarP 21 and MESQUITA 2000: 158f.; 187f.

19) BhāgTN (p. 317,1-2):
Subject matter: Viṣṇu's unconceivable almighty power (*acintyaśakti*)

viruddhaśaktayo yasya nityā yugapad eva ca /
tasmai namo bhagavate viṣṇave sarvajiṣṇave /
iti vārāhe (1)

(1) Cf. BhaviṣP 13; BrāṇP 69 and MESQUITA 2000: 449f.; 477f.

20) BhāgTN (p. 322,10):
Subject matter: Prakāśavadbhuva / Kramamukti

prakāśavadbhuvo devā mānuṣāś cāpi kecana /
iti vārāhe (1)

(1) Cf. ĀdityaP 1; BrahP 82.

21) BhāgTN (p. 332,9-10):
Subject matter: Māyā

māyeti jñānanāma syān māyeti prakṛtis tathā /
jñānaṃ svarūpaṃ viṣṇos tu prakṛtir na hares tanuḥ /
evaṃ vivekino viśvaṃ brahmarūpeṇa neṣyate /
iti vārāhe (1)

(1) Cf. ibid. ll. 11f.: ... *jñānaprakṛtyākhyamāyādvayasya vivekajñānāt sadasator viṣṇvātmatayā pratītiḥ srajyahibuddhir iva vidhūyata ity arthaḥ*; see also AgniP 4; HarV 8; PadP 13; VarP 18 and MESQUITA 2000: 158f.; 187f.

22) BhāgTN (p. 334,8-9):
Subject matter: Rāmāvatāra

na gurur na ca dharmo 'sti rāmadevasya kutracit /
tathāpi dharmarakṣārthaṃ gurubhaktim adarśayat /
iti vārāhe (1)

(1) Cf. ĀdiP 1; SkaP 64; 111.

23) BhāgTN (p. 347,9-10):
Subject matter: Difference of Jīva from Viṣṇu

svapno yato na svatantras tatas taddarśakaḥ paraḥ /
jīvād anyas tu vijñeyaḥ sa viṣṇur iti dhāryatām /
iti vārāhe (1)

(1) Cf. ibid. ll. 6f.: ... (BĀU IV 3,11) *iti śrutiprasiddhaṃ svapna iveti dṛṣṭāntatvenocyate / svapne hi jīvasyāsvātantryaṃ prasiddham / atas tatra parameśvarādhīnatvaṃ siddham eva / ato jīvavyatirikta īśvaraḥ siddhaḥ* ... ; see also AgniP 22; BrāṇP 7.

24) BhāgTN (p. 350,4-6):
Subject matter: Veda

vedo vadann api hariṃ na samyag vakti kutracit /
nārohayaty anubhavam aprasiddhasvarūpataḥ /
tathāpy anubhavārohaḥ prasanne keśave bhavet /
kiṃcid eva susamyak ca svayaṃ tv anubhavaty amum /
iti vārāhe (1)

(1) Cf. ibid. ll. 3f.: *mantraliṅgair vyavacchinnaṃ vedaśabdoktamātram* ... and BSūBh (p. 11,12f.); see also BhaviṣP 10; BrahPV 30; BrāṇP 11; VarP 30; 61 and MESQUITA 2000_1: 164 [= 1997: 132].

25) BhāgTN (p. 361,8-9):
Subject matter: Doctrine of Avatāra / Bewilderment (*moha*) of evil beings

duṣṭānāṃ mohanārthāya yajña indrapade sthitaḥ /
paspardha vṛṣabheṇaiva svarūpeṇa hariḥ svayam /
iti vārāhe (1)

(1) Cf. ĀdiP 1 and MBh 42n. 6.

26) BhāgTN (p. 538,14-539,3):
Subject matter: Viṣṇu's Upāsana

patitvena śriyopāsyo brahmaṇā me piteti ca /
pitāmahatayānyeṣāṃ tridaśānāṃ janārdanaḥ /
prapitāmaho me bhagavān iti sarvajanasya tu /+1
guruḥ śrībrahmaṇor viṣṇuḥ surāṇāṃ ca guror guruḥ /
mūlabhūtaguruḥ sarvajanānāṃ puruṣottamaḥ /
gurur brahmāsya jagato daivaṃ viṣṇuḥ sanātanaḥ /
ity evopāsanaṃ kāryaṃ nānyathā tu kathaṃcana /
iti vārāhe (1)

(1) Cf. AgniP 20; BrāṇP 51.

27) BhāgTN (p. 592,18-20):
Subject matter: Viṣṇu's supreme transcendence / Eternity of the world

jīvasya jagataś caiva yad īśābhedato vacaḥ /
atāttvikaṃ jagac ceti viṣṇvadhīnatvavācakam /
abhedas tu kutas tasya paramasyāvareṇa tu /
mithyātvaṃ ca kutas tasya jagato nityavartanāt /
iti vārāhe (1)

(1) Cf. AgniP 6; BhavisPV 1; VarP 17; 55 also MESQUITA 2000_1: 102ff. [= 1997: 83ff.] and MESQUITA 2000: 158n. 317; 186n. 386f.; 467ff.

28) BhāgTN (p. 602,7-8):
Subject matter: Three types of Bhaktas

kecid unmādavad bhaktā bāhyaliṅgapradarśakāḥ /
kecid āntarabhaktāḥ syuḥ kecic caivobhayātmakāḥ /
mukhaprasādād dārḍhyāc ca bhaktir jñeyā na cānyataḥ /
iti vārāhe (1)

(1) Cf. AgniP 20 and MESQUITA 2007: 9n. 11; 28n. 58; 37n. 82 [= 2007_1: 434n. 11; 444n. 57.; 449n. 81]; see also ViṣP 2.

29) BhāgTN (p. 607,5-6):
Subject matter: Viṣṇu's supreme transcendence

naivaṃ tvayā nu mantavyaṃ jīvātmāham iti kvacit /
sarvair guṇaiḥ susaṃpannaṃ daivaṃ māṃ jñātum arhasi /
iti vārāhe (1)

(1) Cf. ibid. ll. 3f.:
naivaṃ tvayā nu mantavyaṃ dṛṣṭo jīvo mayeti ha /
sarvabhūtaguṇair yuktaṃ devaṃ tvaṃ jñātum arhasi //
iti ca mokṣadharmeṣu (= MBh XII 326,43/45); see also AgniP 6 and MESQUITA 2000: 133ff.

30) BhāgTN (p. 765,8):
Subject matter: Origin of the Vedas

meyatvān maya uddiṣṭo vedaḥ prāṇādibhiḥ sadā /
iti vārāhe (1)

(1) Cf. ibid. l. 7: *prāṇendriyamanobhir mīyate* ... ; see also BrāṇP 11; 101; VarP 24 and MESQUITA 2000: 71n. 63.

31) BSūBh (p. 10,3-4):
Subject matter: The validity of inference is based on Veda

sarvatra śakyate kartum āgamaṃ hi vinānumā /
tasmān na sā śaktimatī vināgamam udīkṣitum /
iti vārāhe (1)

(1) Cf. ibid. (9,8+10,2): *na cānumānasya niyataprāmāṇyam* ... *śakyatvāc cānumānāṃ sarvatra* ... ; see also KūrP 20; SkaP 83 and MESQUITA 2000: 56n. 24; 336n. 261; 369f.

32) BSūBh (p. 52,17-18):
Subject matter: Vinirṇaya (final settlement of the meaning / conclusive argument)

avadhāraṇārthaṃ sarvasyāpy uktasyādhyāyamūlataḥ /+1
dviruktiṃ kurvate prājñā adhyāyānte vinirṇaye /
iti vārāhe (1)

(1) Cf. ibid. ll. 16f.: *etena tadadhinatvādyuktayuktisamudāyena* ... ; see also BrahVP 30; GarP 41; SkaP 94.

33) BSūBh (p. 105,9-12):
Subject matter: Bhedābheda (*jīva* = *aṃśa*)

vārāhe ca –
putrabhrātṛsakhitvena svāmitvena yato hariḥ /
bahudhā gīyate vedair jīvo 'ṃśas tasya tena tu /
yato bhedena tasyāyam abhedena ca gīyate /
ataś cāṃśatvam uddhiṣṭaṃ bhedābhedau na mukhyataḥ /
iti (1)

(1) Cf. ibid. ll. 7f.: tathācāgniveśyaśrutiḥ – *aṃśo hy eṣa parasya bhinnaṃ hy enam adhīyire 'bhinnaṃ hy enam adhīyira* iti ... (unknown source); see also BrāṇP 71; VāmP 12; SkaP 54 and MESQUITA 2000: 497f.

34) BSūBh (p. 106,17-20):
Subject matter: Transmigration and liberation

vārāhe ca –
aṃśāś ca dehayogyatvāj jīvā bandhādisaṃyuktāḥ /
anugrāhyāś ceśvareṇa na tu matsyādiko hariḥ /
adehabandhayogyatvād yathā sūryaprabhākṣiṇī /
yathāmṛtasamudrasya śleṣmādeś ca dvirūpatā /
anugrāhyatvam anyasya tenaivāvṛttirodhanam /
iti (1)

(1) Cf. ibid. ll. 4f.: *parānujñayā pravṛttiḥ parato bandhanivrittiś ca jīvasya pratīyete aṃśatve 'pi dehasaṃbandhāt / ya ātmānam antaro yamayati* (BĀU III 7,9) *tam evaṃ vidvān amṛta iha bhavati* (TaiĀr III 1,3 [?] *ityādinā / na tu parasya ... apūrṇaśaktitvāc ca jīvasya na matsyādisāmyam* / tathā ca caturvedaśikhāyām (ibid. l. 22) ... (unknown source); see also AgniP 16; BrāṇP 33; 71; SkaP 54; VarP 37.

35) BSūBh (p. 107,3-6):
Subject matter: Difference between Jīvas and Avatāras

vārāhe ca –
dvirūpāv aṃśakau tasya paramasya harer vibhoḥ /
pratibiṃbāṃśakaś cātha svarūpāṃśaka eva ca /
pratibiṃbāṃśakā jīvāḥ prādurbhāvāḥ pare smṛtāḥ /
pratibiṃbeṣv alpasāmyaṃ svarūpāṇītarāṇi tu /
iti (1)

(1) Cf. ibid. l. 3: *rūpaṃ rūpaṃ pratirūpo babhūva* (KathU V 5,9) *iti pratibiṃbatvāc ca na sāmyam* ... ; see also ĀdiP 1; AgniP 22; BhāgP 3; BrāṇP 71; MESQUITA 2000_1: 35ff. [= 1997: 29ff.] and MESQUITA 2000: 416ff.; 497ff.

36) BSūBh (p. 113,15-18):
Subject matter: Viṣṇu, the prime cause of the universe

karaṇaiḥ kāraṇaṃ brahma puruṣāpekṣayākhilam /
śrotrādibhiḥ kārayati karaṇānīty ato viduḥ /
na jīvāpekṣayā mukhyaṃ kārayet parameśvaraḥ /
kevalātmecchayā tasmān mukhyatvaṃ tasya niścitam /
iti ca vārāhe (1)

(1) Cf. ibid. ll. 13f.: *jīvenaiva karaṇaiḥ kārayati paramātmā / ato na virodhaḥ / eṣa hy anenātmanā cakṣuṣā darśayati śrotreṇa śrāvayati manasā mānayati buddhyā bodhayati tasmād etāv āhuḥ sṛtir asṛtir* itīti <u>bhāllaveyaśruteḥ</u> (unknown source); see also AgniP 12 and MESQUITA 2000: 470ff.; 497ff.

37) BSūBh (p. 117,3):
Subject matter: Transmigration / Liberation

bhūtabandhas tu saṃsāro muktis tebhyas vimocanam /
iti ca vārāhe (1)

(1) Cf. ibid. ll. 2f.: ... *bhūtabandho hi bandhaḥ* ... ; see also AgniP 16; BrāṇP 33; VarP 34.

38) BSūBh (p. 122,21-22):
Subject matter: Bondage / Kramamukti

svargād avāg gato dehī vrīhyāditaradehagaḥ /
abhuñjaṃs tu krameṇaiva deham āpnoti kālataḥ /
iti ca vārāhe (1)

(1) Cf. ibid. ll. 17f.: *anyādhiṣṭhate vrīhyādiśarīre* (ChU V 10,6) *praveśaḥ / na tu bhogo 'sya / dhūmo bhūtvābhraṃ bhavati* (ChU V 10,5) *ityādipūrvoktavat / so 'vāg gataḥ sthāvarān praviśaty abhogenaiva vrajan sthūlaṃ śarīram eti sthūlāc charīrād bhogān anubhuṅkta ity abhilāpāt* <u>kauṣāravaśrutau</u> (unknown source); see also BrahP 82; BrāṇP 33; VarP 37.

39) BSūBh (p. 122,24-25):
Subject matter: Sacrificial victims (animals) / *hiṃsā*

hiṃsā tv avaidikā yā tu tayānartho dhruvaṃ bhavet /
vedoktayā hiṃsayā tu naivānarthaḥ kathaṃcana /
iti hi vārāhe (1)

(1) Cf. ibid. ll. 23f.: *hiṃsārūpatvāt pāpasyāpi saṃbhavād duḥkhaṃ ca bhavatv iti cet / na / śabdavihitavāt* ... ; BrāṇP 35 and HOUBEN 1999: 157.

40) BSūBh (p. 133,16-18):
Subject matter: Four stages / states of consciousness

hṛdayasthāt parāj jīvo dūrastho jāgrad eṣyati /
samīpasthas tathā svapnaṃ svapity asmin layaṃ vrajan /
yata evaṃ trayo 'vasthā mohas tu pariśeṣataḥ /
ardhaprāptir iti jñeyo duḥkhamātrapratismṛteḥ /
iti vārāhe (1)

(1) Cf. ibid. ll. 15f.: *mohāvasthāyāṃ parameśvare 'rdhaprāptir jīvasya* ... ; see also BrāṇP 7; KūrP 28 and HACKER 1985: 131f.

41) BSūBh (p. 142,2-3):
Subject matter: Hierarchy among individual souls

brahmādiguṇavaiśeṣyād ānandaḥ paramasya ca /
pratibiṃbatvam āyāti madhyoccādivibhedataḥ /
iti ca vārāhe (1)

(1) Cf. ibid. (p. 140,24f.): *yathādityasya darpaṇādisthānaviśeṣāt pratibiṃbaviśeṣaḥ / evam ānandāder api* ... ; see also BhāgP 3; BhaviṣPV 15 and MESQUITA 2000: 497ff.

42) BSūBh (p. 155,26-27):
Subject matter: Hierarchy among released souls

naiva sarvaguṇāḥ sarvair upāsyā muktibhedataḥ /
viriñcasyaiva yan muktāv ānandasya supūrṇatā /
iti hi vārāhe (1)

(1) Cf. ibid. ll. 25f.: *phalabhedārtham upacayāpacayayor bhāvān na sarveṣāṃ priyaśirastvādiguṇopāsāprāptiḥ* ... ; see also BhaviṣP 15 and MESQUITA 2000: 522f.

43) BSūBh (p. 161,22-24):
Subject matter: Means of liberation: Śravaṇa etc.

vārāhe ca –
guruprasādo balavān na tasmād balavattaram /
tathāpi śravaṇādiś ca kartavyo mokṣasiddhaye /
iti (1)

(1) Cf. ibid. ll. 20f.: ... (ChU IV 9,3) *ity anujñānād upakosalavacanāc ca liṅgabhūyastvād gurupradānam eva balavat / tarhi tāvatālam iti ca na mantavyam / śrotavyo mantavya ityādes* (BĀU II 4,5) *tad api kartavyam* ... ; see also AgniP 9 and MESQUITA 2007: 24n. 45 [= 2007_1: 442n. 44f.].

44) BSūBh (p. 189,7-11):
Subject matter: Teachers of the human beings: Devas and Ācāryas

vārāhe ca –
jñānādidānaṃ devānāṃ viṣṇunā sādhu coditam /
vede ca teṣāṃ vihitaṃ tatrācāryo mahattaraḥ /
vihitaḥ sahakāritve sahakāryantaraṃ prajāḥ /
pātratvena yathā rājño yathā śiṣyā guror api /
tasmāc chrutaṃ phalaṃ tāsām ācāryāṇāṃ mahattaram /
tato mahattaraṃ proktaṃ devānām uttarottaram /
iti (1)

(1) Cf. ibid. ll. 6f.: *devānāṃ jñāpanādikarmaṇi sahakāryantaratvena prajā vidhīyante / yathā prajāvato rājñaḥ prajāḥ sahakāritvena vidhīyante / yathā cācāryasya śiṣyāḥ* ... ; see also BhaviṣP 5.

45) BSūBh (p. 197,16-18):
Subject matter: Body postures in meditation

tam eva deśaṃ seveta taṃ kālaṃ tām avasthitam /
tān eva bhogān seveta mano yatra prasīdati /
na hi deśādibhiḥ kaścid viśeṣaḥ samudīritaḥ /
manaḥprasādanārthaṃ hi deśakālādicintanā /
iti hi vārāhe (1)

(1) Cf. ibid. ll. 15f.: *deśakālāvasthādiṣu yatraikāgratā bhavati tatraiva sthāvyam* ... ; see also BrāṇP 79.

46) BSūBh (p. 212,13-14):
Subject matter: Hierarchy among the rational beings

matsyakūrmavarāhādyāḥ samā viṣṇor abhedataḥ /
brahmādyas tv asamāḥ proktāḥ prakṛtiś ca samāsamā /
iti ca vārāhe (1)

(1) Cf. ĀdiP 1; BhaviṣPV 15 and MESQUITA 2000: 498ff.

47) BSūBh (p. 224,4-6):
Subject matter: Viṣṇu, the divine Ruler of the released souls / Tāratamya

paramo 'dhipatis teṣāṃ viṣṇur eva na saṃśayaḥ /
brahmādimānuṣāntānāṃ sarveṣām aviśeṣataḥ /
tataḥ prāṇādināmāntāḥ sarve 'pi patayaḥ kramāt /
ācāryāś caiva sarve 'pi yair jñānaṃ supratiṣṭhitam /

etebhyo 'nyaḥ patir naiva muktānāṃ nātra saṃśayaḥ /
iti hi vārāhe (1)

(1) Cf. ibid. (p. 223,2+224,1): *na teṣāṃ bhogādiṣu prayatnāpekṣā* ... (ChU VIII 2,1) ityādi śruteḥ / *satyasaṅkalpatvād eva* ... ; see also AgniP 6; BhaviṣPV 15 and MESQUITA 2000: 519ff.

48) BSūBh (p. 226,13-16):
Subject matter: Hierarchy among the released souls

vārāhe ca –
svādhikānandasaṃprāptau sṛṣṭyādivyāpṛtiṣv api / (1)
muktānāṃ naiva kāmaḥ syād anyān kāmāṃs tu bhuñjate /
tadyogyatā naiva teṣāṃ kadācit kvāpi vidyate /
na cāyogyaṃ vimukto 'pi prāpnuyān na ca kāmayet /
iti (2)

(1) Cf. BhaviṣPV 15; VarP 49; VāyuP 1 and 2_1.
(2) Cf. ibid. l. 13: *jīvaprakaraṇatvāj jīvānāṃ tādṛksāmarthyavidūratvāc ca* ... ; MESQUITA 2000: 170n. 353; see above VarP 42.

49) BSūBh (p. 228,4-7):
Subject matter: Released deities

vārāhe ca –
svādhikāreṇa vartante devā muktāv api sphuṭam /
baliṃ haranti muktāya viriñcāya ca pūrvavat /
sabrahmakās tu te devā viṣṇave ca viśeṣataḥ /
na vikārādhikāras tu muktānām anya eva tu /
vikārādhikṛtā jñeyā ye niyuktās tu viṣṇunā /
iti (1)

(1) Cf. ibid. ll. 3f.: *vikāravarti vyāpāro muktānāṃ na vidyate* / *imaṃ mānavam āvartaṃ nāvartanta iti* hi śrutiḥ (ChU IV 15,5); see also VāyuP 1; BhaviṣP 5 and VarP 48.

50) GīT (p. 13,24-25):
Subject matter: Definition of transient / limited existence – Viṣṇu's supreme transcendence

anityatvaṃ dehahānir duḥkhaprāptir apūrṇatā /
nāśaś caturvidhaḥ proktas tadabhāvo hareḥ sadā /
tadanyeṣāṃ tu sarveṣāṃ nāśāḥ kecid bhavanti hi /
iti mahāvarāhe (1)

(1) Cf. ibid. l. 23: *yady api nityatvaṃ jīvasyāpy asti* / *tathāpi sarvaprakāreṇāvināśitvaṃ viṣṇor eveti tuśabdaḥ* / *deśataḥ kālataś caiva guṇataś ca tridhā tatiḥ* / *sā samastā*

harer eva na hy anye pūrṇasadguṇā iti paramaśrutiḥ (unknown source); see also AgniP 4; 6 and MESQUITA 2000: 425f.; 416f.

51) GīT (p. 21,17-29):
Subject matter: Avatāras / Aṃśāvatāras

matsyakūrmādirūpāṇāṃ guṇānāṃ karmaṇām api /
tathaivāvayavānāṃ ca bhedaṃ paśyati yaḥ kvacit / [1]
bhedābhedau ca yaḥ paśyet sa yāti tama eva tu /
paśyed abhedam evaiṣāṃ bubhūṣuḥ puruṣas tataḥ / [2]
abhede 'pi viśeṣo 'sti vyavahāras tato bhavet /
viśeṣiṇāṃ viśeṣasya tathā bhedaviśeṣayoḥ / [3]
viśeṣas tu sa evāyaṃ nānavasthā tataḥ kvacit /
prādurbhāvādirūpeṣu mūlarūpe ca sarvaśaḥ / [4]
na viśeṣo 'sti sāmarthye guṇeṣv api kadācana /
matsyakūrmavarāhāś ca nṛsiṃhavaṭubhārgavāḥ / [5]
rāghavaḥ kṛṣṇabuddhau ca kalkivyāsaitareyakāḥ /
datto dhanvantarir yajñaḥ kapilo haṃsatāpasau / [6]
śiṃśumāro hayāsyaś ca hariḥ kṛṣṇaś ca dharmajaḥ /
nārāyaṇas tathetyādyāḥ sākṣān nārāyaṇaḥ svayam / [7]
brahmarudrau śeṣaviṣau śakrādyā nāradas tathā /
sanatkumāraḥ kāmabhavo 'py aniruddho vināyakaḥ / [8] +1
sudarśanādyāyudhāni pṛthvādyāś cakravartinaḥ /
ityādyā viṣṇunāviṣṭā bhinnāḥ saṃsāriṇo hareḥ / [9]
teṣv eva lakṣmaṇādyeṣu triṣv evaṃ ca balādiṣu /
narārjunādiṣu tathā punar āveśa ucyate / [10]
svalpas tu punar āveśo dharmaputrādiṣu prabhoḥ /
etaj jānāti yas tasmin prītir abhyadikā hareḥ / [11]
saṅkarajñāninas tatra pātas tamasi ca dhruvaḥ / [12ab]
iti ca mahāvarāhe (1)

(1) Cf. ĀdiP 1; BrāṇP 10; 95[11cd-48]; MESQUITA 2000_1: 35f.; 46ff.; 72ff. [= 1997: 29f.; 38ff.; 58ff.] and MESQUITA 2000: 440f.

52) GīT (p. 61,14-16):
Subject matter: Definition of *svayaṃbhū*

svātantryād bhagavān viṣṇuḥ svabhāva iti kīrtitaḥ /
tat svātantryaṃ kadāpy eṣa nānyasya sṛjati kvacit /
svātantryāḍ eva pāpādisaṃbandhaḥ kurvato 'pi na /
ajñānāvṛtabuddhitvād īdṛśaṃ taṃ na jānate /
iti mahāvarāhe (1)

(1) Cf. ibid. l. 12: *svayam eva bhavati bhāvayati ceti svabhāvaḥ bhagavān / svabhāvatvāt svayam eva kartṛtvādiṣu pravartate*; (l. 32f.:) *hariḥ svabhāvataḥ kartā sarvam anyat tadīritam / ataḥ sā kartṛtā tasya na kadācid vinaśyatīti* paiṅgiśrutiḥ (unknown source); see also AgniP 6; BhāgP 1; BrahP 23; BrāṇP 32; SkaP 107; VarP 55[4ab] and MESQUITA 2000: 424f.; 491; 530.

53) GīT (p. 112,26-27):
Subject matter: Viṣṇu is Kāla

kālaḥ kalitasaṃpūrṇasadguṇatvāj janārdanaḥ /
saṃhārāt sarvavittvād vā sarvavidrāvaṇena vā /
iti mahāvarāhe (1)

(1) Cf. BhāgP 1; BrahP 25; see also MESQUITA 2000: 492n. 644.

54) GīT (p. 160,20-23):
Subject matter: Videhamukti / Kramamukti / Jīvanmukti

sarvapāpakṣayād dehaṃ tyaktvā devān kramād vrajan /
prāpya lakṣmīṃ tatprasādāt punaḥ svṛddhā harau yadā /
bhaktis tayā punar jñāne svṛddhe viṣṇuṃ prapadyate /
aparokṣadṛśo viṣṇoḥ śarīre 'pi sataḥ purā /
tyaktadehādikasyāpi yāvad viṣṇuṃ prapadyate /
tāvad guṇā vivardhante sthitāḥ syuḥ prāpya keśavam /
iti mahāvarāhe (1)

(1) Cf. ibid. (p. 159,30f.): ... *tadanantaram naiṣkarmayasiddhiṃ prāpto bhūtvā brahmākhyāyā mahālakṣmyāḥ sakāśaṃ yathāpnoti tathā nibodha* ... ; see also ĀdityaP 1; AgniP 16; BrahP 82 and MESQUITA 2007: 12n. 15 [= 2007_1: 435n. 15].

55) ĪśUBh (p. 510,24+511,16):
Subject matter: Viṣṇu's supreme transcendence / Eternity of the world

śukraṃ tacchokarāhityād avraṇaṃ nityapūrṇataḥ /
pāvanatvāt sadā śuddham akāyaṃ liṅgavarjanāt / [1]
sthūladehasya rāhityād asnāviram udāhṛtam /
evaṃbhūto 'pi sārvajñyāt kavir ity eva śabdyate / [2]
brahmādisarvamanasāṃ prakṛtyā manaso 'pi ca /
īśitṛtvān manīṣī sa paribhūḥ sarvato varaḥ / [3]
sadānanyāśrayatvāc ca svayaṃbhūḥ parikīrtitaḥ /
sa satyaṃ jagad etādṛṅ nityam eva pravāhataḥ / [4]
anādyanantakāleṣu pravāhaikaprakārakam /
niyamenaiva sasṛje bhagavān puruṣottamaḥ / [5]
sajjñānānandaśīrṣo 'sau sajjñānānandabāhukaḥ /
sajjñānānandadehaś ca sajjñānānandapādavān / [6]

evaṃbhūto mahāviṣṇur yathārthaṃ jagad īdṛśam /
anādyanantakālīnaṃ sasarjātmecchayā prabhuḥ / [7]
iti vārāhe (1)

(1) Cf. AgniP 4; 6; BhaviṣPV 1; VarP 17 and MESQUITA 2000_1: 38f.; 137n. 278 [= 1997: 32f.; 110n. 267].

56) KathUBh (p. 480,15-16):
Subject matter: Liberation

muktajīve sthitaṃ viṣṇuṃ viditvā jīvataḥ pṛthak /
modate modanīyaṃ taṃ prāpya muktaḥ sadaiva ca /
iti mahāvārāhe (1)

(1) Cf. ibid. ll. 14f.: ... *gahvare muktajīve sthitam / pravṛhya jīvāt pṛthakkṛtya* ... ; see also HEIMANN 1922: 34 and AgniP 16.

57) KathUBh (p. 486,25-27):
Subject matter: Liberation

brahmādīnāṃ ca muktānāṃ sukhaṃ viṣṇusukhasya tu /
pratibiṃbas tu vipluṭko viṣṇor eva paraṃ sukham /
samyag bhāti na bhātīti jānīyāṃ tat kathaṃ nv aham /
tatprasādam ṛte divyam anirdeśyaṃ paraṃ sukham /
iti ca mahāvārāhe (1)

(1) Cf. ibid. ll. 24f.: *etad eva bhagavadrūpaṃ paramaṃ sukham / jñānisukhaṃ tu tadvipluṇmātram* ... ; see also AgniP 16; BhāgP 3; BhaviṣP 15.

58) MāṇUBh (p. 514,13):
Subject matter: Dream-state

jāgraddarśanasaṃskārarūpatvāt svapnagaṃ tu yat /
praviviktaṃ tu tajjñānakāraṇo 'ntarjña ucyate /
iti vārāhe (1)

(1) Cf. BrāṇP 7 and MESQUITA 2000: 202; 250n. 27.

59) MuUBh (p. 491,22-23):
Subject matter: Means of liberation

vedaiś ca pañcarātraiś ca bhaktyā yajñais tathaiva ca /
dṛśyo 'haṃ nānyathā dṛśyo varṣakoṭiśatair api /
ityādi vārāhe (1)

(1) A divergent reading of this quote is handed down in VarP 66,18:
vedena pañcarātreṇa bhaktyā yajñena ca dvija /

prāpyo 'haṃ nānyathā vatsa varṣakoṭyāyutair api //

cf. Anuv (p. 88,23-24):

vedena pañcarātreṇa bhaktyā yajñena caiva hi /
dṛśyo 'haṃ nānyathā dṛśyo varṣakoṭiśatair api /
iti vārāhavacanam;

see also AgniP 9 and BhaviṣP 1.

60) MuUBh (p. 497,26-27):
Subject matter: Liberation

sarvaṃ tīrtvā hariṃ śukraṃ prati vṛttir bhavet punaḥ /
jñāninaḥ sā hi muktiḥ syāt tan naivātyeti kaścana /
iti mahāvārāhe (1)

(1) Cf. ibid. l. 25: *etac chukraṃ praty anyad ativartante* ... ; see also AgniP 16.

61) VTN (p. 15,7-8):
Subject matter: Definitions of the Veda

vedās te nityavinnitvāc chrutayaś cākhilaiḥ śruteḥ /
āmnāyo 'nanyathāpāṭhād īśabuddhisthitaḥ sadā /
iti mahāvārāhe (1)

(1) Cf. ibid. ll. 6f.: *na cānityatve śrutir veda ityādiviśeṣaśabdo yujyate* ... ; see also BrāṇP 11; 101;VarP 24 and MESQUITA 2000: 73n. 70f.; 378ff.

62) VTN (p. 19,15-16):
Subject matter: Viṣṇu, the supreme meaning of the Veda

mukhyaṃ ca sarvavedānāṃ tātparyaṃ śrīpateḥ param /
utkarṣe tu tadanyatra tātparyaṃ syād avāntaram /
iti mahāvarāhe (1)

(1) Cf. ibid. ll. 17f.: *yuktaṃ ca viṣṇoḥ sarvotkarṣe mahātātparyaṃ sarvāgamānāṃ* / *mokṣo hi sarvapuruṣārthottamaḥ*; see also BrāṇP 51; 82 and MESQUITA 2000: 107n. 167; 402f.

Vāyupurāṇa (VāyuP)

[The designation 'Vāyuprokta', as synonym for Vāyupurāṇa, is not known to tradition. In MBh (III 189,14cd and also in Vācaspati's Tattvavaiśāradī *ad* YSū I 19), however, there is mention of a *vāyuproktaṃ purāṇam* in quite general terms. It is not clear what Madhva had in mind while he used the designaton *vāyuprokta*. It remains a mystery whether he really meant Vāyupurāṇa with this term or something else. It is interesting to note that Madhva always closes these quotes with iti vāyuprokte. It is also worthy of note that most of these quotes refer to *prāṇa* or *mukhyaprāṇa*, which is intimately connected with the god Vāyu in the philosophy of Madhva (cf. MESQUITA 2003).

It looks as though VāyuP and BrāṇP were originally one and the same, and that only at a later date they went their own ways. This should be the reason why Brahmāṇḍa is called Vāyavīya, (KūrmP I 1,15) as *vāyavīyam ... / aṣṭādaśaṃ samuddiṣṭaṃ brahmāṇḍam iti saṃjñitam.* Besides, in all the colophons of BrāṇP-Adhyāyas the BrāṇP is designated *vāyuprokta.* On the contrary, not a single quote attributed by Madhva to BrāṇP is specified by him as *vāyuprokta.* In several lists of Purāṇas the characterization of VāyuP as an independent and separate work is absent (cf. ROCHER 1986: 33). In some lists, ŚivaP is replaced by VāyuP. SkaP (V 3,1,33) explains it as follows:

caturthaṃ vāyunā proktaṃ vāyavīyam iti smṛtaṃ /
śivabhaktisamāyogāc chaivaṃ tac cāparākhyayā //

To put it simply: all the quotes given below are assigned to Vāyupurāṇa. Not all the quotes could be identified. There is an evident contradiction between VāyuP 1 (in longer diction) and VāyuP 2_1 (in shorter diction). Most of these quotes are found in BSūBh (nine), BhāgTN (five); BĀUBh (four) and MBhTN (one). Metrical lapse in VāyuP 3_3ab.]

1) BĀUBh (p. 260,20-25):
Subject matter: Qualities of the released souls

ādhipatyam ṛte caiva ānandena ca karmaṇā /
sarve te brahmaṇas tulyā bhogena viṣayeṇa ca /
nānātvenābhisaṃbudhās tadā tatkālabhāvinā /
prakṛtau karaṇātītāḥ svātmany eva vyavasthitāḥ /
pradarśayitvā hy ātmānaṃ prakṛtis teṣu sarvaśaḥ /
puruṣānyabahutvena pratītā na pravartate /
pravartati punaḥ sarge teṣāṃ sā na pravartate /
saṃyogaḥ prakṛter naiṣāṃ muktānāṃ tattvadarśanāt /
samā duḥkhanivṛttis tu muktānām api sarvaśaḥ /
mānuṣādiviriñcāntaṃ sukhaṃ muktau śatottaram /
ityādi vāyuprokte (1)

(1) Surprinsingly, this quote, in almost identical wording, is cited again in BĀUBh (p. 293,18-21; below VāyuP 2_1), which however is in clear contradiction to it. A variant reading indicated by the editor (*ādhipatyaṃ na caiva hi*) attempts to clear up this contradiction; see also AgniP 16; BhaviṣP 4; 5; 15; VarP 45; 48; 49; VāyuP 2_1.

2) BĀUBh (p. 268,5-7)
Subject matter: Āgama, the best among the best Pramāṇas

anumāyā virodhaś cet pratyakṣeṇāgamena vā /
saivāprāmāṇatāṃ gacched āgamadviṭ tathākṣajam /
tasmād āgama evaiko mānānām uttamottamaḥ /

dharmārthakāmamokṣāṇāṃ sākṣād eva pradāyakaḥ /
<u>iti vāyuproktavacanān</u> nānumānavirodho vaktuṃ yujyate (1)

(1) Cf. ibid. ll. 3f.: *tārkikāṇāṃ tūktavacanānāṃ prāmāṇyaṃ siddham eva / atas tadvirodhi kathanaṃ mohate eva* ... GarP 9; KūrP 20; MBh 8 and MESQUITA 2000: 355f.; see also VāyuP II 8,342:

dharmārthakāmamokṣāṇāṃ mānuṣāḥ sādhakās tu vai /
tato 'dhaḥ srotasas te vai utpadyante surāsurāḥ //

MESQUITA 2000_1: 169n. 346 [= 1997: 137n. 333].

2_1) BĀUBh (p. 293,18-21)
Subject matter: Qualities of the released souls

nānātvenābhisaṃbudhās tadā tatkālabhāvinā /
saṃyogaḥ prakṛter naiṣāṃ muktānāṃ tattvadarśanāt /
pravartati punaḥ sarge teṣāṃ sā na pravartate /
ānandena vinā caiva bhogena viṣayeṇa ca /
sarve te brahmaṇas tulyā ādhipatyena caiva hi /
iti vāyuprokte (1)

(1) This quote in abridged version deviates, in two crucial points, from the longer version Madhva used in BĀUBh (p. 260,20-25 = VāyuP 1), namely that the released individual souls are without happiness and secondly that they have the power of sovereignty over the world, in the same way as Brahmā. Both these views are in flagrant contradiction to the teachings of Madhva, namely that the released souls are entirely happy: *tatrānandādīnāṃ vṛddhir hrāsaś ca na vidyate / ekaprakāreṇaiva sarvadā sthitiḥ* (cf. BSūBh p. 228,10f., see also MESQUITA 2000: 520ff.) and that Brahmā is the only being who possesses the sovereignty over the world; cf. BrahVP 30; KūrP 16; VarP 48; 49.

3) BĀUBh (p. 321,16-17):
Subject matter: Mahāpuruṣalakṣaṇa

ṣaṇṇavatyaṅgulo yas tu nyagrodhaparimaṇḍalaḥ /
daśatālaś caturhastaḥ sa devair api pūjyate /
iti vāyuprokte (1)

(1) Cf. BrāṇP 103_3; VāyuP 3_4 (slightly deviating); MESQUITA 2000: 63; 382n. 395 and LORENZ 2005: 53f.

3_1) BhāgTN (p. 11,2-3):
Subject matter: Jīva is absolutely different from Viṣṇu

bhedadṛṣṭyābhimānena paśyanto yānti tatpadam /
ityādi vāyuprokte (1)

(1) Cf. ibid. (p. 10,6f.): *yasmāt paramātmaiva tattvaṃ tasmāt tam eva paśyanti munayaḥ ... ātmanīśvara iti na jīvaikyam ucyate / pareṣām api brahmādīnāṃ yato 'varatvaṃ sa parāvaraḥ*; see also AgniP 22 and MESQUITA 2000: 165ff.

3_2) BhāgTN (p. 59,10-11):
Subject matter: Liberation

samyak svarūpasyāvyaktir abhāvo jananasya ca /
alpayatnāt tato vṛddhihetoḥ satsaṅgatir varā /
iti vāyuprokte (1)

(1) Cf. Yogasūtra I 3: *tadā draṣṭuḥ svarūpe 'vasthānam*; (Bhāṣya): *svarūpapratiṣṭhā tadānīṃ citiśaktir yathā kaivalye ...* ; see also AgniP 16; MESQUITA 1994: 473f. and MESQUITA 1995: 244f.

3_3) BhāgTN (p. 91,9-10):
Subject matter: Definition of Jīva

yaḥ prāṇadhāraṇaṃ prāṇaprasādāt kurute 'niśam /
sa jīva iti saṃdiṣṭas tadanyo 'jīva ucyate /
yatprasādāt sa tu prāṇaḥ kurute svasya dhāraṇam /
iti vāyuprokte (1)

(1) Cf. ibid. ll. 7f.: *kālakarmasvabhāvastho 'jīvaḥ parameśvaro 'jīvaṃ svātmānam ajījanat / tadaṇḍaṃ yathā svātmānaṃ prasūte tathā cakāra ...* ; see also BrahVP 19; BrāṇP 71 and HarV 26.

3_4) BhāgTN (p. 364,2-3):
Subject matter: Mahāpuruṣalakṣaṇa

ṣaṇṇavatyaṅgulo yas tu nyagrodhaparimaṇḍalaḥ /
saptapādaś caturhastaḥ sa devair api pūjyate /
iti vāyuprokte (1)

(1) Cf. ibid. (p. 363,10f.).:
jñānaṃ viṣṇor uttamatve tad eva pratipūruṣam /
viśeṣeṇa tu vijñānaṃ tac ca jānāti sarvavit /
dvātriṃśallakṣaṇair yuktas tīkṣṇadaṃṣṭraś ca saumyaruk /
ghoraruktve 'pi puruṣaḥ sa sarvajñā udāhṛtaḥ /
ity adhyātme ... *nyagrodhamaṇḍalo vyāmo bāhū nyagrodha ucyata* iti ca; (unknown sources); cf. above VāyuP 3 (slightly deviating).

3_5) BhāgTN (p. 767,5-6):
Subject matter: Prāṇa

bhuṅkte yad akhilān sparśān āsparśo viṣṇur ucyate /
tasya prakāśakaṃ nityaṃ namasye prāṇam ekalam /

prāṇasyaiva mano nityaṃ vāsudevaṃ prakāśayet /
iti vāyuprokte (1)

(1) Cf. ibid. ll. 3f.: *āsparśarūpiṇā* / *āsparśo viṣṇus taṃ rūpayati prakāśayatīty āsparśarūpi prāṇasya manaḥ* / *ā samantāt sparśā bhogā asyaivety āsparśaḥ* ... ; see also BhavişPV 17 and MESQUITA 2000: 135n. 254-267.

4) BSūBh (p. 109,12-13):
Subject matter: Manas

pūrvaṃ manaḥ samutpannaṃ tato 'nyeṣāṃ samudbhavaḥ /
tadanutpattivacanam alpopacayakāraṇāt /
iti vāyuproktavacanaṃ caśabdena gṛhītam (1)

(1) Cf. ibid. ll. 11f.: *manaḥ sarvendriyāṇi ceti* (= MuU I 1,2) *pūrvoktatvān nānutpattir manaso yujyate* ... ; see also BhavişPV 17.

5) BSūBh (p. 109,20-21):
Subject matter: Sense organs

vāgindriyasya nityatvaṃ śrutisannidhiyogyatā /
utpattir manaso yasmān na nityatvaṃ kutaścana /
iti vāyuprokte (1)

(1) Cf. ibid. ll. 19f.: *tasmān mana eva pūrvarūpaṃ vāguttararūpam iti* (AiU I 1,2) *manaḥpūrvakatvād vāco nānutpattiḥ* ... ; see also BhavişPV 17.

6) BSūBh (p. 110,13-14):
Subject matter: Definition of Transmigration / Mokṣa

saṃsārasthitihetutvāt sthitaṃ karma vido viduḥ /
tasmād udgatihetutvāj jñānaṃ gatir ihocyate /
iti ca vāyuprokte (1)

(1) Cf. ibid. ll. 12f.: *hastādīnāṃ karmaviṣayatvān na sahapāṭhaḥ* ... ; see also AgniP 16 and BrāṇP 33; VarP 34.

7) BSūBh (p. 110,23-24):
Subject matter: Prāṇa

yatprāptir yatparityāga utpattir maraṇaṃ tathā /
tasyotpattir mṛtiś caiva kathaṃ prāṇasya yujyate /
iti yuktir vāyuprokte (1)

(1) Cf. ibid. ll. 22f.: *naiṣa prāṇa udeti nāstam ety ekala eva madhye sthātāthainam āhur madhyama itīti mukhyaprāṇasyānutpattiḥ śruyate* ... ; see also BhavişPV 17 and MESQUITA 2003: 105f.

8) BSūBh (p. 111,9-10):
Subject matter: Mukhyaprāṇa / Viṣṇu's absolute transcendence

bhūtāni ceṣṭā mantrāś ca mukhyaprāṇād idaṃ jagat /
mukhyaprāṇaḥ parasmāc ca na paraḥ kāraṇānvitaḥ /
iti vāyuprokte (1)

(1) Cf. ibid. ll. 8f.: *khaṃ vāyuḥ / tapo mantrāḥ karma iti* (PraśU VI 4) *pṛthagupadeśāt* ... ; see also AgniP 6; BhaviṣPV 17; MatsyaP 5; VāmP 21 and VāyuP 7 and MESQUITA 2003: 102n. 14.

9) BSūBh (p. 112,8-9):
Subject matter: Prāṇa

prāṇāpānādayaḥ sarve mukhyadāsā yato 'niśam /
atas tadājñāyā nityaṃ svāni karmāṇi kurvate /
iti yuktir vāyuprokte (1)

(1) Cf. ibid. ll. 7f.: *sarve vā ete mukhyadāsāḥ prāṇo 'pāno vyāna udānaḥ samāna ity atha prāṇo vāva samrāḍ* iti kauṇḍinyaśrutiḥ (unknown source); see also BhaviṣPV 17 and MESQUITA 2003: 103n. 16.

10) BSūBh (p. 112,21-22):
Subject matter: Prāṇa, the base of the Universe

yataḥ sarvaṃ jagad vyāpya tiṣṭhati prāṇa eva tu /
ato dhṛtaṃ jagat sarvam anyathā kena dhāryate /
iti ca yuktir vāyuprokte (1)

(1) Cf. ibid. ll. 20f.: *prāṇa evādhastāt prāṇa upariṣṭāt prāṇo madhyataḥ prāṇaḥ sarvataḥ prāṇa evedaṃ sarvam iti prāṇasya vyāptiḥ pratīyate*; see also BhaviṣPV 17 and MESQUITA 2003: 101f.

11) BSūBh (p. 115,20-22):
Subject matter: Origin of the Universe out of *mahābhūtāni*

pañcabhūtātmakaṃ sarvaṃ tathāpy ekavivakṣayā /
ekabhūtātmakatvena vyavahāras tu vaidike /
bhaumam ity eva kāṭhinyāc chauklyād audakam ity api /
tejiṣṭhatvāt taijasaṃ ca yathāsthnāṃ vacanaṃ śrutau /
iti vāyuprokte (1)

(1) Cf. ibid. ll. 17f.: *yat kaṭhinaṃ sā pṛthivī yad dravaṃ tadāpo yaduṣṇaṃ tat teja iti śruter* (SārīrakaU I) *māṃsādyeva bhaumam na sarvaśarīram aptejasoś ca kāryaṃ yathāśabdam aṅgīkartavyam* ... ; For accumulation-Theory cf. FRAUWALLNER 1973: 97; see also BhaviṣPV 1; BrāṇP 29; MBh 24; MatsyaP 5; SkaP 101.

12) BSūBh (p. 158,12-14):
Subject matter: Videhamukti

vāyuprokte ca
sthitaprajñatvam āptā ye jñānena paramātmanaḥ /
brahmalokaṃ gatāḥ sarve brahmaṇā ca paraṃ gatāḥ /
tīrṇatartavyabhāgāś ca svecchayopāsate param /
iti (1)

(1) Cf. ibid. ll. 10f.: *svecchayety aṅgīkartavyam / muktasya tīrṇatvāt / tīrṇo hi tadā sarvāñ chokān hṛdayasya bhavatīti hy anye paṭhanti* (BĀU IV 3,22) ... ; see also ĀdityaP 1; AgniP 16 and MESQUITA 2007: 12n. 15; 13n. 18f. [= 2007_1: 435n. 15; 436n. 18f.].

13) MBhTN (II 51):
Subject matter: Eulogy of Mahābhārata

vāyuprokte 'pi tat proktaṃ bhāratasya praśaṃsanam /
kṛṣṇadvaipāyanaṃ vyāsaṃ viddhi nārāyaṇaṃ prabhum /
ko hy anyaḥ puṇḍarīkākṣān mahābhāratakṛd bhavet /
[iti] (1)

(1) This quote appears also in PadP (I 1,43cd-44ab), ViṣṇP (III 4,5) and in MBh (XII 334,9), see also MESQUITA 2000_1: 42ff. [= 1997: 35ff.] and BrāṇP 14; KūrP 30_2.

Viṣṇudharmapurāṇa (ViṣDhP)

[Although this text of the Bhāgavatas calls itself a *śāstra* it is rather a Purāṇa. It is dated between A.D. 200 and 300 A.D. (cf. ROCHER 1986: 249f.). Of late, GRÜNENDAHL (1983f.) convincingly proved that this text is wrongly called Purāṇa, and that it supplied textual basis to other Purāṇas as AgniP and ViṣḍhUP. In the tradition, Viṣṇudharmāḥ and ViṣḍhUP have been very often confused with each other. In Madhva's works it appears only once.]

1) BhāgP (p. 8,10-11):
Subject matter: Divine and human behaviour

devatve devavacceṣṭā mānuṣatve ca mānuṣī / (1)
iti ca śrīviṣṇudharme (2)

(1) This quotation has similarities with Viṣṇudharmāḥ 66,36:
devatve devikā ceṣṭā tiryaktve mama tāmasī /
icchayā mānuṣatve vicarāmi nṛceṣṭayā //
(2) Cf. BhagTN (p. 8,9):
īśann api hi lokasya sarvasya jagato hariḥ /

karmāṇi kurute nityaṃ kīnāśa iva durbala /
iti codyoge (unknown source);
cf. MBh 42n. 5 and SkaP 12₁; see also BhaviṣP 5.

Viṣṇudharmottarapurāṇa (ViṣDhUP)

[ViṣDhUP, which is very often confused with Viṣṇudharmāḥ, is a Pañcarātra-Text. It has been mentioned by Madhva only once in his works. Its date is between 6 and 9 cent. A.D. (cf. ROCHER 1986: 250f.).]

1) BhāgP (p. 16,7-11):
Subject matter: Flawlessness of Viṣṇu

viṣṇudharmottare ca
guṇāḥ sarve 'pi yujyante hy aiśvaryāt puruṣottame /
doṣāḥ kathaṃcin naivātra yujyante paramo hi saḥ /
guṇadoṣau māyayaiva kecid āhur apaṇḍitāḥ /
na tatra māyā māyī vā tadīyau tau kuto hy ataḥ /
tasmān na māyayā sarvaṃ sarvam aiśvaryasaṃbhavam /
amāyo hīśvaro yasmāt tasmāt taṃ paramaṃ viduḥ /(1)

(1) Cf. ibid. l. 3: *tasyaivāsthūlatvādyaiśvaryogāt* ... ; see also BhaviṣP 13; BrāṇP 69 and KūrP 1.

Viṣṇupurāṇa (ViṣP)

[Although the ViṣṇP "is the best representative of the whole class of sectarian Purāṇas, since it is purely Vaiṣṇava in its teaching from beginning to end ..." (cf. HAZRA: 1987: 19ff.; ROCHER 1986: 245f.), Madhva very seldom cites from it, in fact, only (four times) in GīBh and (six times) in GīT. One of them is traceable: MBhTN XI 2 = ViṣP IV 10,6. Metrical lapses in ViṣP 2 (Prosa?) and ViṣP 4.]

1) GīBh (p. 12,14-15):
Subject matter: Prakṛti / Puruṣa

prakṛtiḥ puruṣaś caiva nityau kālaś ca sattama /
iti vacanāc chrīviṣṇupurāṇe (1)

(1) Cf. ibid. ll. 14f.: *asataḥ kāraṇasya sato brahmaṇaś ca abhāvo na vidyate* ... ; see also AgniP 25; SkaP 21.

2) GīBh (p. 96,11-12):
Subject matter: Definition of Abhaktas

śaṭhamatir upāyati yo 'rthatṛṣṇāṃ tam

adhamaceṣṭam avaihi nāsya bhaktam /
iti hi śrīviṣṇupurāṇe (1)

(1) Cf. ibid. ll. 6f.: uktaṃ ca śāṇḍilyaśākhāyām (unknown source) –
nāvirato duścaritān nābhakto nāsamāhitaḥ /
samyag bhakto bhavet kaścid vāsudeve 'malāśayaḥ /
devarṣayas tadaṃśāś ca bhavanti kva ca jñānataḥ /
iti;
cf. BhavisPV 12; see also VarP 28.

3) GīBh (p. 107,25):
Subject matter: Viṣṇu's unconceivable almighty power (*acintyaśakti*)

acintyāḥ khalu ye bhāvā na tāṃs tarkeṇa yojayet /
iti śrīviṣṇupurāṇe (1)

(1) Cf. ibid. ll. 19f.: *tāni caikaikāni rūpāṇy anantāni caikatra bhavanti* ... *nacaitad ayuktam* / *acintyaśaktitvād īśvarasya* ... ; see also BhaviṣP 13 and BrāṇP 69.

4) GīT (p. 17,21-23):
Subject matter: The characteristic features of Jīva and Viṣṇu / Viṣṇu's supreme transcendence

alpaśaktir asārvajñaṃ pāratantryam apūrṇatā /
upajīvakatvaṃ jīvatvam īśatvaṃ tadviparyayaḥ /+ 1
svābhāvikaṃ tayor etan nānyathā syāt kathaṃcana /
vadanti śāśvatāv etāv ata eva mahājanāḥ /
iti mahāviṣṇupurāṇe (1)

(1) Cf. ibid. ll. 19f.: *ayaṃ jīvo 'pi ajo nityaś ca* / *anyathā punarukteḥ* / *śāśvataś ca* / *na kadācid asvātantryādikaṃ jīvasvarūpaṃ jahāti* ... ; see also ibid. (p. 15,30-31):
...
sa jīvanāmā bhagavān prāṇadhāraṇahetutaḥ /
upacāreṇa jīvākhyā saṃsāriṇi nigadyate /
tadadhīnam idaṃ sarvaṃ nānyadhīnaḥ sa īśvaraḥ /
[iti];
see also AgniP 6; 22; BrāṇP 71 and MESQUITA 2000: 137-140; 166n. 342-343; 372n. 359.

5) GīT (p. 19,31-32):
Subject matter: Viṣṇu's omnipresence

nityaṃ sarvagate viṣṇāv aṇur jīvo vyavasthitaḥ /
na cāsya tadadhīnatvaṃ hetuto 'pi vicālyate /
niṣedhavidhipātratvāt sanātana iti smṛtaḥ /
iti mahāviṣṇupurāṇe (1)

(1) Cf. ibid. (p. 18,31f.): *nityaṃ sarvagate sthito 'ṇuś cāyam iti sarvagatasthāṇuḥ / sarvagato viṣṇuḥ / tadadhīnatvādikaṃ tatsthatvam / hetuto 'pi tatsthatvān na calatīty acalaḥ / nādena śabdena saha vartata iti sanādana eva sanātanaḥ* ... ; see also BhāgP 2; BrāṇP 71 and MESQUITA 1989: 129ff.

6) GīT (p. 67,31-32):
Subject matter: Equanimity

yasya yatra yathā vṛttir vihitā vartanaṃ tathā /
jñānaṃ vāpi samatvaṃ tad viṣamatvam ato 'nyathā /
iti mahāviṣṇupurāṇe (1)

(1) Cf. ibid. (p. 66,31):
sarvatra viṣṇor utkarṣajñānaṃ jñānam itīryate /
tadviśeṣaparijñānaṃ vijñānam iti gīyate /
iti (unknown source);
see also BrahVP 35 and VāmP 13.

7) GīT (p. 98,25-29):
Subject matter: Mahārṣis

manavo bodhavaiśeṣyād devā brahmādayaḥ smṛtāḥ /
viprādivarṇabhedena catvāro bahavo 'pi te /
dīnatvād devanāmānas tv anye brahmādināmakāḥ /
avaiṣṇavakṛto yajño dīnair devais tu bhujyate /
vaiṣṇavais tu kṛto yajño devair hi manunāmakaiḥ /
marīcyādyās tu tatputrā mānavā nāmataḥ smṛtāḥ /
tatputrapautrā munayas tathā mānavamānavāḥ /
tebhyo manuṣyā ity eṣā sṛṣṭir viṣṇoḥ samutthitāḥ /
iti mahāviṣṇupurāṇe (1)

(1) Cf. ViṣP III 2,54:
manavo bhūbhujaḥ sendrā devāḥ saptarṣayas tathā /
sattviko 'ṃśaḥ sthitikaro jagato dvijasattama //
cf. also GīT (p. 146,22+147,25:
...
śrīś ca sādhyakṣavidyākhyā brahmendrādyāś ca devatāḥ /
vibudhatvāt tu manvākhyā bhuñjate prītipūrvakam /
...
dīnatvād devanāmāno brahmendrādisanāmakāḥ /
...
ityādi ca (unknown source);
see also BrahP 83; KūrP 30$_3$.

8) GīT (p. 135,23+136,22):
Subject matter: Viṣṇu's supreme transcendence

mahālakṣmīr iti parā bhāryā nārāyaṇasya yā /
prakṛtir nāma sā jñeyā prakarṣeṇa karoti yat / [1]
tasyās tu trīṇi rūpāṇi sattvaṃ nāma rajas tamaḥ /
sṛṣṭikāle vibhajyante sattvaṃ śrīḥ sadguṇaprabhā / [2]
rajo rañjanakartṛtvād bhūḥ sā sṛṣṭikarī yataḥ /
yadāveśād iyaṃ pṛthvī bhūmir ity eva kathyate / [3]
jīvānāṃ glapanād durgā tama ity eva kīrtitā /
etābhis tisṛbhir jīvāḥ sarve baddhā amuktigāḥ / [4]
sarvān badhnanti sarvāś ca tathāpi tu viśeṣataḥ /
śrīr devabandhikā nṛṇāṃ bhūr daityānām athāparā / [5]
etābhyo 'nyaṃ paraṃ caiva viṣṇuṃ jñātvā vimucyate /
sāmarthyātiśayād āsām naitābhyo vidyate paraḥ / [6]
iti yāvad vijānāti tāvat taṃ nṛpaśuṃ viduḥ /
tasmād ābhyo 'dhikaguṇo viṣṇur jñeyaḥ sadaiva ca / [7]
iti mahāviṣṇupurāṇe (1)

(1) Cf. ibid. ll. 20f.: *etebhyaḥ sattvādiguṇebhyo 'nyaṃ kartāram īśaṃ yadā paśyati tadaivāyaṃ nā puruṣaḥ / anyathā paśusamaḥ / na kevalam anyatvena paśyan nā taṃ kartāraṃ viṣṇum / kiṃtu guṇebhya uttamatvena ca* ... ; also GīBh (p. 133,18-20: *tathā ca* kāṣāyaṇaśrutiḥ – (unknown source)

śrīr bhūr durgā bhagavatī tu māyā sā lokasūtir jagato bandhikā ca /
umāvāgādyā anyajīvās tadaṃśās tadātmanā sarvavedeṣu gītāḥ /
iti;

ibid. (p. 51,1-2):

mahadādes tu mātā yā śrīr bhūmir iti kalpitā /
vimohikā ca durgākhyā tābhir viṣṇur ajo 'pi hi /
jātavat prathate hy ātmacidbalān mūḍhacetasām /
iti (unknown source);

cf. also GīT (p. 73,24-27) and BhāgTN (p. 35,13f.):

śrīrbhūrdurgeti yā bhinnā jīvamāyā mahātmanaḥ /
ātmamāyā tadicchā syāt guṇamāyā jaḍātmikā /
iti mahāsaṃhitāyām (unknown source);

ViṣP I 8,18:

sraṣṭā viṣṇur iyaṃ sṛṣṭiḥ śrīr bhūmir bhūdharo hariḥ /
saṃtoṣo bhagavāṃl lakṣmīs tuṣṭir maitreya śāsvatī //

see also AgniP 6; 25; BrāṇP 51 and MESQUITA 2000: 473ff.

9) GīT (p. 162,20-22):
Subject matter: Pūjā

sarvottamatvavijñānapūrvaṃ tatra manaḥ sadā /
sarvādhikapremayuktaṃ sarvasyātra samarpaṇam /
akhaṇḍā trividhā pūjā tadratyaiva svabhāvataḥ /
rakṣatīty eva viśvāsas tadīyo 'yam iti smṛtiḥ /

śaraṇāgatir eṣā syād viṣṇau mokṣaphalapradā |
iti mahāviṣṇupurāṇe (1)

(1) Cf. AgniP 20; PadP 39 and MESQUITA 2007: 24n. 46f. [= 2007_1: 442n. 45f.].

INDICES

1. Pāda-Index of the Untraceable Source-quotations from the Purāṇas and the Māhabhārata

The first number refers to the sequence of the Purāṇa and Mahābhārata quotes. The brackets refer to parts of the Ślokas when the quote is longer than five Ślokas.

aṃśa ity eva cocyate	BrahP 20d
aṃśāṃśenātmanaivaitān	PadP 3_1a
aṃśāś ca dehayogyatvāj	VarP 34a
aṃśo naivāmbarīṣake	GarP 31b
akarod aṇḍam udvṛddham	BrāṇP 29c
akarod vatsaratrayam	SkaP 22d
akartā karaṇair hīnaḥ	PadP 18c
akartā tena keśavaḥ	SkaP 118d
akartṛtvaṃ tathā hareḥ	BrāṇP 12 (= 4b)
akarteti ca taṃ viduḥ	PadP 12d
akarmā bhagavān hariḥ	NārP 53d
akarmety ucyate yadvan	PadP 42a
akāmo dharmakāmo vā	SkaP 24a
akāyaṃ liṅgavarjanāt	VarP 55 (= 1d)
akāraḥ sarvavāgātmā	GarP 38 (= 7a)
akāryaṃ brahma jānāti	PadP 94 (= 6a)
akḷptyā vai svatantratvād	SkaP 14a
akṣataḥ kṣatavad viṣṇur	BrāṇP 39a
akṣadvādaśakaṃ purā	BrāṇP 46b
akṣapādakaṇādau ca	PadP 2a
akṣapādakaṇādau ca	NārP 48c
akṣayāv iṣudhī divye	MBh 47 (= 168a)
akṣaratrayam īritam	SkaP 88d
akṣānumāgamānāṃ ca	BrahVP 42 (= 4c)
akhaṇḍā trividhā pūjā	ViṣP 9a
agaṇyya padākramya	GarP 34_1a
agamad vaiṣṇave rathe	GarP 5 (= 5d)
agamyaṃ tat surair api	BrāṇP 91d
agād viṣṇuprasādataḥ	GarP 47
agād viṣṇuprasādataḥ	SkaP 65 (= 5d)
aguṇatvam adehatvam	BrāṇP 12 (= 4a)

aguṇo 'guṇadehatvāt	AgniP 11a
agniṃ prāpya tataś cārcis	NārP 47a
agniputrā mahātmānas	KūrP 4a
agnir aṅgapraṇetṛtaḥ	BrāṇP 92d
agnir yathaiko lokeṣu	KūrP 31 (= 9a)
agniviprārcako 'py evaṃ	BrāṇP 13 (= 10a)
agniṣṭomādibhir yajñaiḥ	PadP 101a
agnisomaguhādinām	BrāṇP 12 (= 7b)
agner anye ca vasavo	NārP 2 (= 2a)
agnau kriyāvatāṃ viṣṇur	BrahP 58a
agnyādiśaktisaṃstambhas	KūrP 19a
aṅgaṃ ced viṣṇukāryeṣu	BrāṇP 95c (= 16c)
aṅgaṃ bhīmavad īśituḥ	BrāṇP 95d (= 40d)
aṅgabhūtāḥ krameṇa tu	BhaviṣPV 32 (= 123d)
aṅgāni harisevāyāṃ	BhaviṣPV 30 (= 99c)
aṅgīkurvanti tatpakṣaḥ	BhaviṣPV 2 (= 4a)
aṅgīkṛtaṃ ca prāmāṇyaṃ	BhaviṣPV 2 (= 3a)
aṅgeṣu yasya cchandāṃsi	SkaP 1a
acalaṃ cec charīraṃ syān	BrāṇP 79
acalā tasya bhaktiḥ syād	GarP 52c
acalā śrīs tato matā	AgniP 25b
acintyayeśaśaktyaiva	PadP 65a
acintyaśaktitaś caiva	BrāṇP 91c
acintyāḥ khalu ye bhāvā	ViṣP 3a
acintyāḥ śaktayas tāsāṃ	BhaviṣP 11 (= 1c)
acintyau śrīś ca mādhavaḥ	NārP 56d
acetanaṃ prākṛtam etad āhur	MBh 49c
acetanaḥ sparśagamyo	KūrP 32 (= 11c)
acchidrasevanāc caiva	BhaviṣPV 30 (= 97a)
acchedyatvaṃ ca sarvaśaḥ	BrāṇP 12 (= 17d)
ajasya nābhāv iti yasya nābher	SkaP 79a
ajāto jātavad viṣṇur	PadP 55_1a
ajānann iva keśavaḥ	BrāṇP 60b
ajānan pṛcchati smānyāṃs	MBh 42 (= 78c)
ajāmilo 'pi smaraṇād	NārP 16a
ajito jayatāṃ varaḥ	SkaP 29b
ajito jitavac caiva	BrāṇP 39c
ajito jitavat sthitaḥ	SkaP 111d
ajīvo 'pi mahātejās	SkaP 26c
ajeyatvam abhedyatvam	BrāṇP 12c (= 17c)
ajñatvaṃ pāravaśyaṃ vā	BhaviṣPV 29 (= 38a)

ajñasya karma lipyeta	NārP 57a
ajñāto jagadīśvaraḥ	BrāṇP 13 (= 11d)
ajñātvā dhyāyino dhyānāt	NārP 40a
ajñānaṃ tu niśā proktā	SkaP 38a
ajñānaṃ nāśitā vāpi	BrāṇP 12 (= 2c)
ajñānaṃ suptiśabdoktaṃ	MBh 13a
ajñānajaṃ tāmasasya	SkaP 119c
ajñānāṃ kaḥ pradāsyati	SkaP 72b
ajñānāṃ jñāninām caiva	NārP 50a
ajñānāṃ mohakāni vā	NārP 36d
ajñānāṃ mohanāya ca	KūrP 3d
ajñānāṃ mohanāya ca	PadP 55_1d
ajñānāṃ mohanāyeśas	PadP 13c
ajñānābhibhavaspṛṣṭās	BrāṇP 2 (= 2c)
ajñānābhibhavāspṛṣṭau	BrāṇP 2 (= 1c)
ajñānāvṛtabuddhitvād	VarP 52c
ajñāśaktādibhāvas tu	VāmP 30a
añjasā pretya saṃbhūti-	NārP 3 (= 6a)
aṇumātro 'py ayaṃ jīvaḥ	BrāṇP 71a
aṇur jīvo vyavasthitaḥ	ViṣṇP 5b
aṇḍasthānāṃ ca sā gatiḥ	MatsyaP 6d
aṇḍe jātau pumāṃsau dvau	SkaP 27a
ata ātmavivṛddhis tu	BrahVP 19c
ata eva na saṃśayaḥ	VāmP 40b
ata eva mahājanāḥ	ViṣP 4d
ata eva samagratvaṃ	BhaviṣPV 3 (= 4a)
ataḥ kāmitayā vāpi	PadP 51c
ataḥ kāryaiva sā sadā	NārP 57b
ataḥ ko 'nyo hareḥ prabhuḥ	BrāṇP 90d
ataḥ paramahaṃso 'ham	GarP 36 (= 10a)
ataḥ prāptir iti prāhur	BrahVP 13c
ataḥ śatruvivṛddhau ca	BrahVP 19c
ataḥ śāstrād vinirṇayaḥ	MBh 8d
ataḥ śaivapurāṇāni	NārP 34a
ataḥ śrutitvam etāsāṃ	BrāṇP 104 (= 2c)
ataḥ santo vijānanti	SkaP 72c
ataḥ sarvo bhavān iti	PadP 81b
ataḥ svarūpataḥ samyak	MatsyaP 4c
atattattvavido janāḥ	PadP 12b
atattvārthaṃ jagad brūte	PadP 94 (= 8a)
atatthyāni vitatthyāni	BrāṇP 94a

atarkyaṃ tarkyam ajñeyaṃ	GarP 39c
ataś ca pūrvam uccāryāḥ	GarP 38 (= 8a)
ataś ca vyatyayād etad	BrahP 9_1c
ataś ca sarvalokānām	BhaviṣPV 4 (= 7a)
ataś cāṃśatvam uddhiṣṭaṃ	VarP 33c
atas tatsādhakaṃ śāstraṃ	BrāṇP 11c
atas tat sraṣṭum aicchata	BrāṇP 34d
atas tadājñāyā nityaṃ	VāyuP 9c
atas tad eva mantavyaṃ	BhaviṣPV 29 (= 30c)
atas tad bahuśas tūktam	VāmP 17a
atas tad brahma śabdyate	SkaP 11d
atas tasmin parājayaḥ	BrāṇP 16b
atas tasyaiva nāmāni	SkaP 31c
atas tāsāṃ paraṃ brahma	SkaP 65 (= 2c)
atas tu sarvanāmāsau	PadP 52a
atas tu saubhareḥ śāpaṃ	BrāṇP 59a
atas tṛptiś ca māṃsataḥ	MBh 24b
atas teṣūktam agrāhyam	BhaviṣPV 29 (= 34c)
atas traya iti proktāś	SkaP 62a
atāttvikaṃ jagac ceti	VarP 27c
atāttvikās tathākhyātāḥ	SkaP 32 (= 4a)
atijājvalyamāṇatvāt	PadP 19c
atipriyatvād bhagavān	BrāṇP 3 (= 7c)
atipriyatvān naivaitat	SkaP 28c
atipriye yathā rājā	BrahP 68a
atibhinnasvarūpau tau	GarP 30 (= 8a)
atiśaitye kalaṅke ca	PadP 33a
atītatvena bhaṇyate	NārP 9b
atītānāgatajñānī	HarV 31a
atītānāgate tathā	BrahP 9_1b
atītya ca janārdanaḥ	KūrP 23d
atīva śraddhayā yukto	NārP 39a
atuṣṭā tadatuṣṭiṃ ca	BrāṇP 89c
atuṣṭir aprasādaś ca	BrahP 6a
atṛptasyaiva bhogārthaṃ	HarV 33 (= 10c)
ato 'gnisūryasomānām	BrāṇP 9 (= 4c)
ato 'gnisūryasomānām	BrāṇP 9 (= 5a)
ato 'gnāv eva devānām	BrāṇP 13 (= 7c)
ato jñānād vinaśyati	BrāṇP 33b
atodakatve na sadā	SkaP 65 (= 4c)
ato duṣṭo 'bhavat putra	VāmP 22c

ato dehādivṛttaye	BhavişPV 13b
ato daihikavṛddau vā	BrahVP 19c
ato dhṛtaṃ jagat sarvam	VāyuP 10c
ato nānyaṃ prayācayet	BrahP 84d
ato nāmnaś ca rūpasya	BrāṇP 72a
ato 'nutpattir iṣyate	BhavişPV 17b
ato 'nyo granthavistāro	SkaP 82c
ato 'pi sa svecchayā kiṃcid eva	BrāṇP 100c
ato brahmapade yogyā	GarP 36 (= 11a)
ato bhayānako jātas	GarP 29c
ato 'bhāvaṃ vadanty enaṃ	KūrP 22c
ato bhrāntyā hi saṃbandho	BrāṇP 33a
ato mano 'bhimānena	MBh 21c
ato mayy aparādhas tu	BrāṇP 53 (= 5c)
ato mānaṃ na tat smṛtam	BhavişPV 2 (= 13b)
ato mukhyāśrayo viṣṇuś	KūrP 32 (= 8c)
ato mokṣam avāpsyasi	BrāṇP 9 (= 13b)
ato mokṣe 'pi caitāsāṃ	SkaP 65 (= 4a)
ato yady asurāveśāt	BrāṇP 53 (= 6a)
ato 'rcato yato jātā	BrāṇP 8c
ato 'lepe 'pi lepaḥ syād	NārP 57a
ato 'vittvā paraṃ devaṃ	BrahP 76c
ato vimohanāyaiva	BrāṇP 41a
ato viṣṇubalāśrayam	BrahVP 44d
ato vedatvam eteṣāṃ	SkaP 99c
ato 'sya rāma ityākhyā	SkaP 64c
ato hi vaiṣṇavā lokā	AgniP 27c
atyantaduḥkhasaṃllīnān	PadP 67c
atyannaś cātithiḥ prokto	KūrP 32 (= 3a)
atyapriye sukham api	BrahP 68c
atyalpāś cālpakālāś ca	SkaP 59 (= 2c)
atyuttamānāṃ kuśala-	NārP 6a
atyuttamānām avare	SkaP 53a
atra manonāmā mahābalaḥ	GarP 5 (= 6b)
atra ślokā bhavantīti	GarP 58a
atraiva ca sthitis teṣām	GarP 45 (= 2a)
atroktaṃ sarvaśāstreṣu	BrāṇP 95 (= 48a)
atroktam astīty ekā tu	BrāṇP 64 (= 3c)
atha tatkṛpayā viṣṇuḥ	BrahVP 21c
-atha tatrasthaḥ prādahaj jagat	BrahP 43 (= 2b)
atharvā brahmaṇo 'jani	BrāṇP 98b

athavā guṇasarvasvaṃ	SkaP 21c
athavā nirarthakāt pāṭhād	BrahVP 38 (= 14c)
athavā rudradehastho	BrahP 30c
athavā sarvakāmo yaḥ	SkaP 24c
athaśabdas tv ataḥśabdo	GarP 38 (= 4a)
athātaḥ śabdapūrvāṇi	GarP 38 (= 1a)
athātaḥśabdayor evaṃ	GarP 38 (= 8c)
athāpi cāsurāveśāt	BrāṇP 59c
adarśayet svakaṃ lokaṃ	HarV 1_1a
adāyadās tu putrāṇām	BrāṇP 30a
aduḥkho duḥkhavartivat	SkaP 64b
adṛśyaḥ san paraḥ svayam	KūrP 22b
adṛśyoktau tatas teṣām	BhavişP 10 (= 4c)
adṛṣtam eva jñānena	BhavişPV 21 (= 3a)
adṛṣṭāśrutapūrvatvād	BrāṇP 55a
adehabandhayogyatvād	VarP 34a
adehasthā iti dvidhā	KūrP 17d
adoṣatvād guṇāc caiva	BhavişPV 2 (= 16c)
adoṣatvān mahāviṣṇor	BrāṇP 3 (= 13a)
adyāpi tad devaloke	SkaP 6a
adhamā nirayāyaiva	BhavişPV 30 (= 87c)
adhamā mānuṣotkṛṣṭās	GarP 37 (= 2a)
adharaṃ yāti ca tamaḥ	BhavişPV 26c
adharasya yato bhavet	KūrP 26d
adharmalakṣaṇaṃ caiva	Upagītā 1a
adhastād yatra notthitiḥ	BrāṇP 78d
adhārṣṭyān matprabhāvena	NārP 3 (= 8a)
adhikaṃ yaiḥ kṛtaṃ tatra	BrāṇP 95 (= 45a)
adhikaṃ vā mumukṣuṇām	GarP 53b
adhikajñānalabdhyarthaṃ	BrāṇP 3 (= 15a)
adhikasya samasyāpi	KūrP 18a
adhikāraṃ phalaṃ caiva	VāmP 3a
-adhikāro nigadyate	NārP 36_1d
adhijyam api yat kartuṃ	MBh 47 (= 166a)
adhidaivaṃ prāpnuvanti	BrahP 67c
adhidaivaṃ viśeṣataḥ	SkaP 106b
adhidaive tathādhyātme	SkaP 103c
adhidaive tathādhyātme	GarP 5 (= 2c)
adhibhūtaṃ tadantikāt	SkaP 114d
adhibhūtaṃ tu māyāntaṃ	KūrP 30_5a
adhiṣṭhānaṃ ca sadṛśaṃ	BrahVP 44a

anādinidhanā parā	NārP 41b
anādipratibimbāś ca	KūrP 32 (= 13c)
anādibhakto yasmān me	BrāṇP 53 (= 6c)
anādis tu haris tatra	SkaP 27c
anādyanantakālīnaṃ	VarP 55 (= 7c)
anādyanantakālīnāḥ	SkaP 40a
anādyanantakāleṣu	GarP 37 (= 8c)
anādyanantakāleṣu	VarP 55 (= 5a)
anādyananto 'pi harir	VahniP 1a
anādyānandacidghanaḥ	GarP 13d
anāmā so 'prasiddhatvād	BrahP 65a
anāraṃbhamanantaṃ ca	BrahVP 38 (= 16a)
anārabdhaphalānāṃ ca	BrāṇP 6a
anāśaṃ prārthayanti hi	BhaviṣPV 4 (= 8d)
anityatvaṃ dehahānir	VarP 50a
anityatvaṃ sthirātmanām	BrāṇP 104 (= 8b)
anityatvāt saduḥkhatvān	MBh 48a
anityadaivānityaṃ ca	PadP 85c
anityanarakāṇi tu	MBh 26d
anityāni tu bhūtāni	KūrP 23a
animittasnehavāṃs tu	NārP 55a
aniruddhasukhānāṃ ca	BrāṇP 15 (= 5c)
aniruddhas tathecchati	BrāṇP 12 (= 30b)
aniruddhākhyarūpeṇa	BrāṇP 12 (= 29c)
aniruddhe manau caiva	SkaP 52c
anirdeśyaṃ paraṃ sukham	VarP 57d
anirdeśyau tathāvyaktāv	NārP 56c
anīśatvaṃ ca duḥkhitvaṃ	BhaviṣPV 29 (= 39a)
anīho 'kliṣṭakāritvāt	BrahP 47a
anuktaṃ pañcabhir vedair	SkaP 99a
anuktānāṃ pramāṇānāṃ	GarP 41a
anugacchanti sarvaśaḥ	BrāṇP 73d
anugās teṣu sāttvikāḥ	SkaP 32 (= 1d)
anugrāhyatvam anyasya	VarP 34a
anugrāhyāś ceśvareṇa	VarP 34c
anujñāṃ prāpya yatnataḥ	SkaP 22b
anujñāto rauhiṇeyāt	MBh 47 (= 164a)
anuddhāryo 'parair martyaiḥ	BrāṇP 105 (= 3c)
anupraviśya govindaḥ	NārP 28c
anupraviśya paramaṃ	NārP 8a
anupraviśya brahmāṇaṃ	GarP 17a

anumānaṃ na kutracit	KūrP 20b
anumāyā virodhaś cet	VāyuP 2a
anuyātā tamo viśet	BrāṇP 57b
anurūpaḥ kramaḥ sṛṣṭau	PadP 64a
anuvratā yatra surāsurārcitāḥ	BhāgP 2b
anuṣṭhāya ca śāstrārthaṃ	BhavişPV 2 (= 7c)
anuṣṭhīya ca sādhanam	SkaP 116b
anusāritayā brūyuḥ	BrāṇP 39c
anekayugaparyantam	KūrP 30_6a
anejan nirbhayatvāt tad	BrāṇP 91a
antaḥsthaḥ puruṣo nāma	MatsyaP 16a
antaḥsparśā itīritāḥ	PadP 32b
antatas tv eva viṣṇave	BrahVP 38 (= 8b)
antaraṃ kiṃcid eva hi	BhavişPV 25d
antaraṅgaṃ hanūmāṃś ca	BrāṇP 95 (= 33c)
antarāle sa uddhavaḥ	PadP 14 (= 5d)
antarikṣaś ca vāyujaḥ	BrāṇP 15 (= 3b)
antarikṣe tu kecana	GarP 45 (= 2b)
antarbahiś ca sauptaṃ ca	BrāṇP 97a
antaryāmiṇam īśeśam	KūrP 21a
antaryāmisvarūpeṇa	BhavişP 6 (= 1a)
antaryāmyādirūpāṇi	KūrP 17a
antarhitāṃ lokadṛṣṭyā	SkaP 64c
antarhiraṇyakādīnāṃ	PadP 43a
antaś cakṣur devatā tu	KūrP 32 (= 15a)
antaś cakṣur na lipyate	KūrP 32 (= 14d)
antas tadvyaktyapekṣayā	SkaP 101d
antasthasya bahiṣṭhe tu	BrahVP 6a
anto brahmādibhaktānāṃ	NārP 45a
antyadeho yathā nijaḥ	BhavişPV 27b
andhaṃ yasmān na cothitiḥ	BrahVP 38 (= 15d)
andhe tamasi ye niṣṭhās	HarV 30c
annatvena puraiva yat	BhavişPV 4 (= 6b)
annābhimāninī sākṣāc	BrāṇP 3 (= 21a)
annābhimānī rudraś ca	BrāṇP 83c
anyakarmakṛter api	BrahVP 38 (= 10b)
anyac caitat prakāśakam	VāmP 17b
anyatra kṛtyāpekṣā syād	BhavişPV 13c
anyatra pūryate kvāpi	BrāṇP 95b (= 46c)
anyatra brāhmaṇānāṃ tu	BrāṇP 95 (= 22a)
anyatra bhīmapārthābhyāṃ	MBh 47 (= 166c)

anyatra sarvavākyānāṃ	BrāṇP 84a
anyathākaraṇīyatvāt	PadP 94 (= 5c)
anyathākartum īśo 'pi	BrāṇP 8a
anyathā kurvataḥ karma	BrāṇP 45c
anyathā kena dhāryate	VāyuP 10d
anyathājñānakāraṇam	SkaP 55b
anyathājñānam evāto	SkaP 69 (= 2a)
anyathājñāninām ca te	GarP 34d
anyathā tūttamānāṃ hi	BrāṇP 59c
anyathātvaṃ punar janeḥ	SkaP 75d
anyathā tv asatāṃ bhavet	HarV 33 (= 1d)
anyathātvāt kṣipranāśāj	VarP 17a
anyathā dṛśyamānaṃ tu	BrāṇP 64 (= 8c)
anyathā na samaṃ bhavet	PadP 33b
anyathā pratipattyā tu	BrahP 48 (= 7a)
anyathā pratipadyanta	BrahP 48 (= 7c)
anyathālpaphalaṃ bhavet	AgniP 15b
anyathā so ātmahā smṛtaḥ	BrāṇP 25d
anyathaiṣāṃ sthitiḥ kṛtiḥ	BrāṇP 12 (= 9d)
anyathopāsakā ye tu	KūrP 31 (= 1a)
anyad alpaphalaṃ caiva	PadP 93a
anyadaivatapūjāpi	AgniP 20a
anyanāmnāṃ gatir viṣṇur	VāmP 37c
anyannāśakaraṃ kvacit	SkaP 55b
anyan naivopapadyate	SkaP 36d
anyasāmyavido viṣṇor	SkaP 40a
anyātulyair atiśayair	KūrP 17a
anyān kāmāṃs tu bhuñjate	VarP 48d
anyān jigāya prayayau	BrahP 35c
anyāntaryāmiṇaṃ viṣṇum	NārP 18a
anyārthaṃ ca svayaṃ viṣṇur	GarP 31c
anyāveśanimittaṃ ced	BrāṇP 95 (= 17c)
anyāveśād yadi dviṣan	BrāṇP 53 (= 3d)
anyūnānadhikatvāc ca	SkaP 14a
anyūnānadhikāś caiva	VarP 2a
anye kramād abahalās	HarV 34c
anye ca prārthayan samam	BrāṇP 47d
anye caiva mitaiḥ śabdair	BrāṇP 2 (= 4a)
anye 'nyac ca tathāpy eṣāṃ	PadP 93a
anye vyavaharanty etāny	SkaP 89a
anyeṣāṃ ca janārdanaḥ	SkaP 44b

apekṣya kuśalaṃ vibhoḥ	PadP 24b
apekṣyāhaṃ tvam ity api	KūrP 21b
apauruṣeyavedeṣu	GarP 50a
apy ānande mitho hy uktas	HarV 2a
aprakāśaṃ ca māṃ kuru	BrāṇP 94d
apratīkā devatās tu	GarP 44a
apratīkāśrayā ye hi	GarP 44a
aprameyo 'niyojyaś ca	MBh 42 (= 72a)
aprayatnāt svatantratvāt	PadP 12a
aprasiddhasvarūpataḥ	VarP 24d
aprasiddher avācyaṃ tad	GarP 39a
aprāmāṇyaṃ na saṃsayaḥ	BhaviṣP 10 (= 4d)
apsṛṣṭyarthaṃ janārdanaḥ	BrāṇP 8d
abalo 'pi tato vāyor	NārP 2 (= 9c)
abjagojādrijeṣv eva	KūrP 32 (= 5c)
abhaktād api pāpaḥ syād	PadP 96a
abhakto nirayaṃ yāti	VāmP 19c
abhaktyodāhṛtaṃ naiva	NārP 16c
abhavat sārathir viṣṇor	GarP 5 (= 6c)
abhāvaṃ svātmano 'nyasya	SkaP 55a
abhāvāt puṃsa eva tu	GarP 54b
abhāvāt svecchayā bhavet	BrāṇP 76d
-abhāvān na sukhī bhavet	BrāṇP 9 (= 17b)
abhāve pṛthagarthāṇāṃ	MBh 8_1a
abhāvo janasya ca	VāyuP 3_2a
abhidhāgocarāḥ surāḥ	BrāṇP 9 (= 3d)
abhipede paraṃ sthānaṃ	BhaviṣP 9 (= 3a)
abhiprāyadvayaṃ hy asti	BrāṇP 3 (= 26a)
abhiprāyadvayasyāpi	BrāṇP 3 (= 28c)
abhimanyamānasahitās	BrāṇP 9 (= 2a)
abhimānavato dehe	HarV 3c
abhimānāt tu jīvānāṃ	HarV 32c
abhimānī caturmukhaḥ	BrahP 20b
abhimāne tv ahaṅkāraś	SkaP 46c
abhuñjaṃs tu krameṇaiva	VarP 38c
abhūc chruteḥ puṣkaraṃ lokasāram	SkaP 79b
abhedaḥ sarvarūpeṣu	BhaviṣPV 29 (= 45a)
abhedapratipādakam	BrahP 43 (= 8b)
abhedam īśarūpāṇāṃ	BhaviṣP 1a
abhedas tu kutas tasya	VarP 27a
abhedena ca gīyate	VarP 33b

asamasya samatvena	SkaP 69 (= 4a)
asamyak samyag iti ca	SkaP 102a
asargā kevalāvyaktā	HarV 9c
asādhyaṃ vā tato vedāḥ	BhavişPV 2 (= 18c)
asurā api ye viṣṇuṃ	BrahVP 10a
asurā āsureṇaiva	SkaP 104a
asurāḥ pratipadyante	BrahP 48 (= 4c)
asurāṇāṃ tamaḥprāptis	BhavişPV 30 (= 90a)
asurāṇāṃ tamogateḥ	BhavişPV 29 (= 34d)
asurāṇāṃ rakṣasāṃ ca	BrahP 24 (= 6c)
asurāṇāṃ vilomataḥ	SkaP 123d
asurādes tathā doṣā	BrahP 78a
asurān damayan viṣṇuḥ	BhavişPV 22a
asurān mohayan devaḥ	SkaP 20a
asurān hanti niyataṃ	VāmP 31c
asurā bahulā yasmāt	BrahP 73a
asurā rākṣaśāś caiva	BhavişP 7 (= 2a)
asurā vāyasāḥ smṛtāḥ	GarP 36 (= 15b)
asurāveśatas tv anyān	PadP 43c
asurāś caiva vāyasāḥ	GarP 36 (= 9b)
asurās tu ratā asau	NārP 44b
asurās te 'pi vijñeyā	BrahVP 10c
asuryā nāma te lokās	VāmP 43c
asūyur doṣadṛg yataḥ	PadP 96b
asau sūryagato viṣṇur	BrāṇP 85c
astitvād bhūtanāmabhyaḥ	PadP 94 (= 1a)
astobham anavadyaṃ ca	SkaP 78 (= 7c)
astaud yajñaṃ manuḥ svarāṭ	SkaP 120d
asthūlaś cānaṇuś caiva	KūrP 1a
asthūlānaṇurūpo 'sau	BrahP 62a
asnāviram udāhṛtam	VarP 55 (= 2b)
aspardhinī spardhanīva	VāmP 32a
asmi nityāstitāmānāt	BrāṇP 92c
asy asmītyādibhiḥ śabdair	BrahVP 2c
asvatantrasya jīvasya	KūrP 32 (= 16a)
asvatantrasya jīvasya	SkaP 125c
asvātantryaṃ ca vedādāv	BrāṇP 65a
asvātantryāt tadanyeṣām	MBh 20c
asvātantryāt tu jīvasya	HarV 19a
asvātantryāt tu viduṣāṃ	NārP 3 (= 5c)
ahaṃgraha itīritaḥ	VāmP 42b

ājñayaiva hareḥ kecid	VāmP 6c
āṇḍakośas tu sāvṛtiḥ	BrahVP 8b
ātmanaḥ kartṛtābhrāntyā	MBh 16c
ātmanaḥ prāvṛttiṃ caiva	PadP 83a
ātmanaś ca śriyaś caiva	SkaP 44a
ātmanāmatayā harim	VāmP 8b
ātmano jīvatām api	VāmP 30d
ātmano dehagehādi	HarV 20a
ātmano bahudhābhāve	AgniP 7c
ātmano 'vamatāṃ brūyur	NārP 25a
ātmaprasavakāraṇam	BrāṇP 29d
ātmabrahmādayaḥ śabdās	BrahVP 23a
ātmabrahmādayaḥ śabdās	PadP 1_1a
ātmavat sā harer vibhoḥ	BrahP 25d
ātmaśabdaḥ pare viṣṇau	BrāṇP 4a
ātmā teṣām agocaraḥ	HarV 32d
ātmānaṃ bahudhākarot	NārP 11b
ātmānaṃ bahudhā kṛtvā	PadP 65c
ātmānaṃ muktidaṃ viṣṇur	BrahP 50a
ātmānando 'kṣaraḥ svarāṭ	BhāgP 1b
ātmābhimānādhikāra-	SkaP 114a
ātmāmeyaḥ paraṃ brahma	KūrP 25a
ātmā viṣṇur iti dhyānaṃ	BrahP 74a
ātmā hi viṣṇur devānāṃ	BhaviṣPV 3 (= 16a)
ātmeti mukhyato viṣṇus	SkaP 107a
ātmety upāsanaṃ kāryaṃ	BhaviṣPV 23a
ātmety eva paraṃ devam	GarP 45 (= 1a)
ātmety evocyate budhaiḥ	BhaviṣPV 4 (= 1d)
ātmeśabrahmasaṃbhavān	BhāgP 1b
ātmaikas tu janārdanaḥ	PadP 56d
ātmopāsādike vidhau	HarV 6d
ādānādanakartṛtvād	HarV 32c
ādāyāntaradhād dāna-	BrahP 41c
ādityamaṇḍalasthas tu	BrāṇP 30c
ādityasaṃsthito viṣṇur	BrāṇP 3 (= 25a)
ādityādyāḥ samāśritāḥ	BrāṇP 52d
ādityā vasavo rudrās	SkaP 62a
-ādidoṣayutatvataḥ	BhaviṣPV 12d
ādino rākṣasāḥ proktās	BrahP 49a
ādau tu teṣām api ca	GarP 37 (= 3c)
ādyanta iti vijñeyaḥ	BrahP 49c

ābrahmaṇo janādyās tu	BrahP 12c
ābrahmā sthitadhīr jīvan-	BhaviṣP 5 (= 1a)
ābhāsābhāsarūpās tu	BhaviṣPV 28c
ābhyām idaṃ jagat sarvaṃ	NārP 41c
āmukteḥ sarvadehinām	VarP 14b
ā mukter bhavitā nityaṃ	NārP 3 (= 3a)
ā mokṣān mahatī tṛptir	BrāṇP 21c
āmnāyo 'nanyathāpāṭhād	VarP 61c
āmraṃ vālye 'pi patati	PadP 7a
āyudhānāṃ yathā vajram	MārkP 2c
āraṇyake viśeṣeṇa	BrāṇP 82c
āraṇyakeṣvṛte viṣṇuṃ	BrāṇP 82a
ārabhya hīyate athāpi	NārP 52c
ārāmaḥ sa tu vijñeyaḥ	NārP 37c
āropayanti janimat	SkaP 15c
-āroho 'thāvarohaṇam	MBh 26b
ārdrīkṛtāni tānīha	BrāṇP 21a
āvartantīṃ pradakṣiṇam	BrahP 41b
āvartayed vedatantrān	HarV 23c
ā vimukter vidhir nityaṃ	BrāṇP 80a
āviveśa pṛthuṃ devaḥ	PadP 10a
āviṣṭaḥ śvetakeśātmā	VarP 3c
āviṣṭaḥ sarvabhūteṣu	HarV 14c
āviṣṭagrahavad bhavet	BrāṇP 28d
āviṣṭā hariṇā jīvā	BrahVP 17a
āviṣṭo viṣṇunāthendro	BrāṇP 3 (= 4c)
āveśo vasudevādau	PadP 50a
āśramāś ca vanāni ca	SkaP 76b
āśrayaṃ sarvajīvānāṃ	BrāṇP 13 (= 10c)
āśrayaḥ svāśrayaṃ yataḥ	BrāṇP 15 (= 10d)
āśrayo viṣṇur eva saḥ	BhaviṣPV 4 (= 7b)
āsīna āsanādhastāt	VāmP 2 (= 5c)
āsurā niyataṃ janāḥ	BrahP 48 (= 7d)
āsurīnāṃ varādes tu	BrāṇP 95 (= 38a)
āste abjādikas tataḥ	KūrP 32d (= 5d)
āste loke harer hi saḥ	SkaP 7d
āste sa vāsudevātmā	BrahP 43 (= 3c)
āsthāya vyāpnute jagat	GarP 14b
āsthito bhagavān hariḥ	GarP 34_1b
āsparśo viṣṇu ucyate	VāyuP 3_5b
āha kṛṣṇo 'rjunaṃ smayan	SkaP 109d

iti vedavaco 'khilam HarV 33 (= 7b)
iti vedavidaḥ prāhuḥ SkaP 78 (= 10a)
iti vedavido viduḥ GarP 22b
iti saṅgavinirṇayaḥ BhavişPV 13d
iti sapta pradhānāni MBh 26c
iti sarvajanasya tu VarP 26b
iti sarve trikarmiṇaḥ NārP 51 (= 7cd)
iti sāmānyato janiḥ BrahP 69b
itihāsapurāṇayoḥ NārP 58b
ito 'gre jagatas tasmāt VāmP 2 (= 1c)
ittham satām niścayaḥ syād HarV 33 (= 1c)
ity anyasāṅkhyayogayor NārP 48b
ity anyā tatra pūrvā tu BrāṇP 64 (= 4a)
ity abhiprāyam asyaiva BrāṇP 3 (= 28a)
ity avādīd dharir bhūpā HarV 1a
ityādi kathitaṃ sarvaṃ BrāṇP 95 (= 49a)
ityādi darśayed viṣṇur BrāṇP 60a
ityādibhedato vācya HarV 24a
ityādyam ūhanaṃ tarkaḥ KūrP 20c
ityādyasuramohāya MBh 42 (= 79a)
ityādyāḥ kevalo viṣṇur BrāṇP 95 (= 27a)
ityādyā viṣṇunāviṣṭā VarP 51 (= 9c)
ityādy uktaṃ bhagavatā BhavişPV 29 (= 47c)
ity āpaś cakravartinaḥ BrāṇP 15 (= 1b)
ity āhur vedavādinaḥ PadP 44d
ity ucyate tadīśatvān MBh 7c
ity ucyate śrutau viṣṇuḥ MBh 7c
ity ucyante 'tha tatsmṛteḥ NārP 5b
ity etat sūtragaṃ tathā BhavişPV 31 (= 129b)
ity etad akhilaṃ param BhavişPV 30 (= 99d)
ity eva viddhi satatam BrāṇP 9 (= 13a)
ity evopāsanaṃ kāryaṃ VarP 26a
idaṃ jagat sarvam athedṛśāni BrāṇP 57a
idaṃ satyaṃ na saṃśayaḥ BrāṇP 12 (= 22c)
idaṃ satyam idam satyam BrāṇP 12 (= 22c)
idam aṇḍaṃ jagat sarvaṃ VāmP 20a
idam annaṃ taveti saḥ BrāṇP 3 (= 5b)
idānīṃ muktim eṣyasi MārkP 1b
idānīm api jānāti BhavişPV 3 (= 15a)
indra āsīd upekṣakaḥ VāmP 33d
indrasūnuḥ prakīrtitaḥ PadP 22b

ubhayaṃ veda īryate BrāṇP 18d
ubhayaṃ harir evāsya VāmP 9a
ubhayatrāpi tātparyam HarV 6c
ubhayātmakasūtitvād BrāṇP 70a
ubhayoḥ pakṣayoḥ sthitvā GarP 5 (= 4c)
ubhayor apy abaddhatvaṃ BhavişPV 24c
umā vāci samāsthitā GarP 5 (= 5b)
umā vai vāk samuddiṣṭā SkaP 105a
ūcivān kṛṣṇacoditaḥ PadP 14 (= 8b)
ūce sa prathame tv eva BrāṇP 3 (= 9a)
ūnavācī hi viṭśabdaḥ BrāṇP 13 (= 2a)
ūnasāmyādhikāḥ kramāt BrahP 9d
ūrīkṛtya gṛhādivat SkaP 89d
ūrjaṃ sārānnam uddiṣṭham BrahP 29a
ūrṇanābhyādiko viṣṇor BrahP 9a
ūrdhvaṃ madhyaṃ tathādharam KūrP 26b
ūrdhvalokeṣu saṃvyāpta BrāṇP 52c
ūrdhvasrotasa ity eva BrahP 24 (= 5b)
ṛksahasraṃ hareḥ priyam GarP 1b
ṛksahasrātmakaṃ matam BrāṇP 3 (= 23d)
ṛksāhasraṃ śaśaṃsātra BrāṇP 3 (= 5c)
ṛgādayaś ca catvāraḥ BhavişPV 29 (= 30a)
ṛgādyā bhārataṃ caiva BrāṇP 103_1a
ṛgyajuḥsāmātharvākhyā BhavişP 10 (= 1a)
ṛgyajuḥsāmātharvāś PadP 2c
ṛgyajuḥsāmātharvāś ca SkaP 82a
ṛjūn yogyān vinā kvacit BrāṇP 54d
ṛṇāny unmucya doṣoktyā SkaP 124a
ṛtaprāptiviruddhatvāt GarP 34_1c
ṛtam ity eva cocyate KūrP 32 (= 6d)
ṛtarūpe tathā vede KūrP 32 (= 4c)
ṛtūnāṃ pañcaviṃśakam BhavişP 9 (= 1b)
ṛte kalpādibhedataḥ VarP 15b
ṛte tu tāttvikān devān SkaP 63a
ṛte tu pāṇḍavakathāṃ VarP 15a
ṛte namati no rudraṃ GarP 20c
ṛte nārāyaṇādīni SkaP 90a
ṛte brahmāṇam avyayam HarV 19_1d
ṛte viṣṇuṃ sanātanam NārP 2 (= 8b)
ṛte satyavatīsūnoḥ MBh 42 (= 71c)
ṛṣabhatvena saṅgopya BrahP 43 (= 3a)

ekadeśavidaḥ pare	PadP 61b
ekadeśasvabhāvena	GarP 42a
ekadehagatā api	GarP 33b
ekaprakārā bahuśo	GarP 3a
ekabhaktiḥ sa ucyate	GarP 55b
ekabhūtātmakatvena	VāyuP 11c
ekam aṇḍaṃ bahutvena	BrāṇP 37a
ekam eva paraṃ padam	GarP 9b
ekarūpaḥ paro viṣṇuḥ	MatsyaP 17a
ekaśabdaiś dviśabdaiś ca	BhavisP 14a
ekasthānagatād vā syuḥ	MBh 18c
ekasmāt siddhayo viṣṇoḥ	MBh 18a
ekasyāpi bhaviṣyati	BhaviṣPV 3 (= 22b)
ekādaśendriyātmā ca	VāmP 20a
ekādvitīyaśrutayaḥ	BrāṇP 62c
ekā viṣṇuparāyaṇā	BrahVP 38 (= 17b)
ekenāpi bhaven muktis	HarV 13c
ekaikaśās triṣu pṛthag	BhaviṣPV 32 (= 119c)
eko nārāyaṇas tatra	PadP 21_1c
eko 'pi bahugā yathā	BhaviṣPV 3 (= 21b)
eko 'pi sthānanānātvān	BrahVP 11a
eko hi kartā jagato	BrahP 66c
ejobāhulyato 'janiḥ	BrāṇP 3d
etac catuṣṭayaṃ viṣṇuḥ	KūrP 23a
etaj jānāti yas tasmin	VarP 51 (= 11c)
etat tattvam aśeṣataḥ	PadP 14 (= 5b)
etat sarvaṃ turīyeṇa	BrāṇP 97c
etat sarvaṃ sarvavedair	BrāṇP 12 (= 21a)
etadanyat tu yac chāstraṃ	HarV 5 (= 7a/11a)
etad anyasvabhāvo yaḥ	VāmP 34a
etad ākhyāhi me brahman	GarP 38 (= 2c)
etadāpādakaṃ cānyad	VarP 15a
etad vinā na kasyāpi	BhaviṣPV 30 (= 80c)
etadviruddhaṃ yat tu syān	BhaviṣPV 29 (= 31c)
etadviruddhaṃ yat sarvam	BrāṇP 94c
etadviruddhaṃ yat sarvam	SkaP 122a
etannāmadvayaṃ viṣṇor	SkaP 71c
etan mayam idaṃ jagat	BrāṇP 9 (= 1d)
etayor eva kiṃkarāḥ	MBh 42 (≐ 69d)
etasmād brahmaśabdo 'yaṃ	BrahP 59a
etāṃs tvam āsūrān viddhi	HarV 26a

evaṃ vilakṣaṇaṃ devam	BhaviṣPV 3 (= 18a)
evaṃ vivekino viśvaṃ	VarP 21a
evaṃ viṣṇāv idaṃ viśvam	SkaP 56c
evaṃ sadrūpakaṃ brahma	HarV 24a
evaṃ samā nṛjīvās tu	BrahP 78a
evaṃ sarvapadānāṃ ca	BhaviṣPV 30 (= 94c)
evaṃ sarvasya jagataḥ	BrāṇP 9 (= 8c)
evaṃ sukarmaṇaś cāpi	AgniP 16c
evaṃ suptāv api sphuṭam	HarV 25d
evaṃ surāsuranareṣv	GarP 34_1a
evaṃ hi trividhaṃ tasya	PadP 11a
evam agner abhivyaktas	BrahP 43 (= 2c)
evam aṇḍāntaraṃ paśyan	VāmP 11c
evam anye 'pi tādṛśāḥ	BrahVP 42 (= 5b)
evam anyeṣu tu dvayam	BrāṇP 48b
evam apy etayor eka	HarV 13a
evam āgamanirṇayaḥ	SkaP 94d
evamādyāḥ kṣatriyās tu	VāmP 2 (= 3a)
evam indrādināṃ bhavet	VarP 7
evam ukto nāradena	GarP 38 (= 3a)
evam eva ṛṣīṇāṃ ca	VāmP 33a
evam eva ca devānāṃ	BrāṇP 12 (= 16c)
evam eva ca saṃsāre	BrāṇP 15 (= 10a)
evam eva tu niḥsīmā	HarV 28c
evam eva tu sarvatra	BrāṇP 60a
evam eva mahāśakti	HarV 24c
evam eva śamādīnāṃ	BrahVP 40a
evam eva hi jīvo 'pi	SkaP 98a
eva tāny āpnuvanti ca	BrāṇP 30d
eva viṣṇos tu gacchati	BhaviṣPV 28d
evāsti kvacana prabhoḥ	GarP 4b
eṣa ity abhidhīyate	BrāṇP 3 (= 19d)
eṣa eva na saṃśayaḥ	BrāṇP 12 (= 24b)
eṣa kārtayugo dharmaḥ	BrahVP 38 (= 2c)
eṣa dharmo 'tiphalado	BrahVP 38 (= 6a)
eṣa bhāgavato mukhyas	BrahVP 38 (= 5c)
eṣa me saṃśayo brahman	BrāṇP 105 (= 3a)
eṣa mohaṃ sṛjāmy āśu	BrāṇP 94a
eṣa rāmaḥ sa lāṅgalī	MBh 47 (= 162d)
eṣa śāstrasya nirṇayaḥ	ĀdityaP 1d
eṣāṃ yan na virodhi syāt	BhaviṣPV 29 (= 35c)

eṣām īśvaratāpi vā	BrāṇP 12 (= 10b)
eṣām eva prakīrtitā	BrāṇP 9 (= 3b)
eṣo 'ham iti cāsmṛteḥ	BrāṇP 9 (= 15b)
eṣyac ca niścitaṃ yat tad	NārP 9a
ehi viṣṇo na me śaktis	PadP 98c
aikātmyajñānato yānti	BrahVP 19_1a
-aikātmyajñānam ucyate	BrāṇP 40d
aikyena ca svarūpāṇāṃ	PadP 94 (= 2a)
aichad viṣṇur adehaḥ san	BrāṇP 8a
aitadātmyam ato viduḥ	BrāṇP 9 (= 10b)
aitareyo hariḥ prāha	BrahP 16a
aiśvaryajaṃ tu kartṛtvaṃ	PadP 12c
aiśvaryayogād bhagavān	KūrP 1a
aiśvaryāt paramād viṣṇor	PadP 70a
aiśvaryāt puruṣottamaḥ	BrahP 62d
aiśvaryāt puruṣottamaḥ	BrāṇP 66d
aiśvaryāt pūrṇaśaktitaḥ	BrahP 47d
aiśvaryādiguṇatvād vā	AgniP 11c
aiśvaryād indra ucyate	BrāṇP 68d
aiśvaryād indra ucyate	GarP 1b
aiśvaryād eka eva tu	BrahVP 4d
aiśvaryād rūpam ekaṃ	MatsyaP 17c
oṃkāraś cāthaśabdaś ca	GarP 38 (= 6a)
ojas tv anabhibhāvyatvāt	MBh 12c
otaṃ protaṃ ca saṃsthitam	SkaP 56d
otāḥ protāś ca saṃsthitāḥ	SkaP 56b
om ātmā bhagavān viṣṇur	BhāgP 1a
oṣadhīnāṃ yathā yavā	MārkP 2d
ka eva puruṣārthabhāk	GarP 20d
kaṃsapūtanikādyāś ca	BrahVP 10a
kaḥ prasanno bhaved divyāṃ	MatsyaP 3c
kakṣīvati samāsthitaḥ	BhaviṣPV 3 (= 11d)
kaṇṭhamālām adād vibhuḥ	PadP 97d
kaṇvāya yājñavalkyo 'dāt	VarP 1c
kathaṃ cātmavināśāya	SkaP 54c
kathaṃcit kenacit kvacit	BrāṇP 59b
kathaṃcid ajayat param	BrāṇP 60d
kathaṃ tasyaiva pṛcchyate	PadP 24d
kathaṃ prāṇasya yujyate	VāyuP 7d
katham uttamatā tayoḥ	GarP 38 (= 2b)
kathayitvā badaryāṃ ca	PadP 14 (= 6c)

-kalpanaṃ bhrama iṣyate	BrahVP 44b
kalpayen naiva tadbhāve	MBh 8_1c
kavir ity eva śabdyate	VarP 55 (= 2d)
-kavyādyaiḥ karuṇāmayaḥ	PadP 3_1d
kaś cārthas tu tayor vidvan	GarP 38 (= 2a)
kaścid asti dvijottama	GarP 36 (= 16b)
kaścid vyaktīkariṣyati	BrahVP 26b
kaśyapaḥ sanakādyāś ca	BrāṇP 95 (= 30a)
kasmin rūpe 'pi vidyate	HarV 7b
kasyacin mokṣa iṣyate	BrahP 74b
kasya syān mukhyanityatā	BhaviṣPV 18b
kākāṇikācatuṣkaṃ tu	PadP 33a
kākutstho vāci saṃsthiteḥ	PadP 25b
kāṇvaṃ tena prakīrtitam	VarP 1d
kātaryaṃ darśayāmāsa	SkaP 12_1 (= 3a)
kādācitkaḥ kutas tasya	PadP 26c
kādācitkaviśeṣas tu	KūrP 30c
kādācitkāc ca hetutaḥ	NārP 15d
kādācitkās te bhavanti	VarP 16c
kānicit puruṣottamaḥ	NārP 10d
kānicid darśayāmāsa	BrāṇP 21a
kāma icchati sarvadā	BrāṇP 12 (= 29b)
kāmaḥ saṅkalpa ānando	PadP 103a
kāmadevaṃ ratiś cāpi	BrāṇP 51c
kāmadevasthitaṃ viṣṇum	BrāṇP 51a
kāmapallavasaṃyutaḥ	BrāṇP 21b
kāmaputro 'niruddhaś ca	BrāṇP 95 (= 28c)
kāmam eva viveśa saḥ	BrāṇP 12 (= 28d)
kāmayuktā sadā bhaktir	SkaP 65 (= 3c)
kāmaś ca varuṇaś caiva	VāmP 2 (= 2c)
kāmas tv aśubhakṛc ca	SkaP 65 (= 6a)
-kāmāc caiṣāṃ punar bhavet	PadP 93b
kāmānukūlakāmatvaṃ	BrahP 75c
kāmitvenāpsaraḥstriyaḥ	PadP 51b
kāmo bhaktyānuvartate	SkaP 65b
kāyatyāgakṣaṇo yadā	GarP 48 (= 4b)
-kāyika mahārājika	MBh 33b
-kāraṇaṃ tad vadantu naḥ	NārP 3 (= 6b)
kāraṇaṃ bandhamokṣayoḥ	BrahVP 34
kāraṇaṃ sṛjyasarjane	NārP 3 (= 9b)
kāraṇaṃ syāt parājaye	BrāṇP 16d

kumāro nāma bhagavān	BrahP 3 (= 1a)
kurute sa maheśvaraḥ	PadP 83d
kurute sarvam añjasā	VāmP 39d
kurute svayam evaiṣa	NārP 10c
kurute svasya dhāraṇam	VāyuP 3_3b
kuryāc chaṅkām api kvacit	BrahVP 38 (= 4b)
kuryāt kṣayiṣṇuphalavān	BrāṇP 13 (= 12c)
kuryur na tu vighātane	BrāṇP 41d
kuryuś ca na sa duḥkhabhāk	BrāṇP 39d
kurvanty eva surās tatra	BrāṇP 64 (= 6a)
kurvāṇo 'pi trayīkriyāḥ	BrahVP 38 (= 12d)
kulaṃ jigamiṣuṃ harim	PadP 14 (= 6b)
kuśāstraṃ sarvavedānāṃ	BrahP 43 (= 8c)
kuhakaṃ tad viduḥ surāḥ	MBh 42d (= 79d)
kūṭasthaṃ cākṣaraṃ ca tām	BrāṇP 89b
kṛcchrāder api yajñāder	GarP 53a
kṛtakṛtyas tyajet saṅgaṃ	BhaviṣPV 13a
kṛtam anena duṣkṛtam	BrāṇP 53 (= 6b)
kṛtāny evājñayā hareḥ	BhaviṣPV 29 (= 34b)
kṛte māṣacatuṣṭaye	PadP 33b
kṛte 'śvatthasamāś caiva	PadP 7c
kṛtopekṣā mahendreṇa	VāmP 33c
kṛto viṣṇuvaśatvaṃ hi	BrāṇP 95 (= 11c)
kṛttivāsās tato devo	BrāṇP 68a
kṛttyātmakam imaṃ dehaṃ	BrāṇP 68c
kṛtvā nimīlitākṣas tu	NārP 38c
kṛtvā yuddhāya daṃsitaḥ	AgniP 10d
kṛtvā vyāso mahāyaśāḥ	SkaP 78 (= 11d)
kṛtsnajño 'smīti manyate	PadP 94 (= 6d)
kṛpaṇās te tamasy andhe	NārP 50a
kṛṣṇaṃ cakrādilakṣaṇaiḥ	GarP 29b
kṛṣṇakāmās tadā gopyas	SkaP 65 (= 1a)
kṛṣṇadvaipāyanaṃ vyāsaṃ	VāyuP 13a
kṛṣṇadvaipāyanamatād	PadP 61a
kṛṣṇadvaipāyanas tathā	BrāṇP 95 (= 24d)
kṛṣṇadvaipāyanena tu	BrāṇP 21b
kṛṣṇarāmādirūpāṇi	NārP 35a
kṛṣṇarāmādirūpeṣu	BrāṇP 95 (= 23a)
kṛṣṇalety api taṃ brūyus	PadP 33c
kṛṣṇasāroṣitāḥ svataḥ	SkaP 76b
kṛṣṇasyānye viśeṣaṇāt	SkaP 78 (= 8d)

kṛṣṇād vā devakīsutāt	MBh 42 (= 71d)
kṛṣṇāyā bhīmarāmayoḥ	AgniP 24d
kṛṣṇāvatāraparyantaṃ	NārP 12c
kṛṣṇena ca mahātmanā	MBh 47 (= 164d)
kṛṣṇo dvādaśadhā caiva	SkaP 78 (= 6a)
kṛṣṇopāstim akurvataḥ	NārP 57b
kṛṣṇo hy atyaktadeho 'pi	SkaP 6a
ke ca tittirayas tatra	GarP 36 (= 7c)
kecanaiva hariṃ samyag	PadP 86a
ke ca pārāvatā gaṇāḥ	GarP 36 (= 7b)
kecic caivobhayātmakāḥ	VarP 28d
kecit kālata evaitāṃ	HarV 33 (= 7c)
kecit teṣāṃ jñānaṃ na jāyate	BrahVP 43d
kecit satye mahājñānā	GarP 45 (= 3a)
kecit svarge maharloke	GarP 45 (= 2c)
kecid ajñā janā viduḥ	HarV 33 (= 4b)
kecid atraiva mucyante	GarP 45 (= 1c)
kecid āntarabhaktāḥ syuḥ	VarP 28c
kecid āhur anaipuṇāḥ	HarV 33 (= 10b)
kecid āhur apaṇḍitāḥ	ViṣDhUP 1b
kecid unmādavad bhaktā	VarP 28a
kecid bhedaṃ vinindanti	GarP 23a
kecid rudrād brahmaṇaś ca	HarV 33 (= 8a)
kecin nivṛttam ityāhur	BhaviṣP 5 (= 4a)
kecin mukteṣu ca sphuṭam	PadP 86d
kenacit puruṣottamaḥ	KūrP 22b
kevalaṃ jñānavarjitāḥ	NārP 49 (= 2b)
kevalaṃ tattvanirṇayam	BrāṇP 86 (= 5d)
kevalaṃ niraye niṣṭhā	HarV 30a
kevalaṃ viṣṇubodhakam	SkaP 108d
kevalaṃ sukhabhoginaḥ	GarP 6b
kevalajñānarūpakaḥ	VarP 11b
kevalāgamavijñeyo	BrāṇP 103_1a
kevalātmecchayā tasmān	VarP 36c
kevalātmopakārakṛt	KūrP 30_2b
kevalābhedataḥ sphuṭam	GarP 34_1d
kevalaiśvaryasaṃyogād	VarP 2a
keśavapratibiṃbakaḥ	BhāgP 3d
keśavo vāyusaṃyutaḥ	BrāṇP 3 (= 6c)
keśavo vedanārtavat	ĀdiP 1a
ke śukāḥ ke ca vāyasāḥ	GarP 36 (= 7d)

khyāpayanti durātmāno	BhaviṣP 7 (= 4a)
khyāpayāmāsa sarvavit	BrāṇP 48d
gaṅgāyām udaka eva	MBh 10a
gacchato mriyamāṇasya	HarV 3a
gacchanti kṣīrasāgaram	GarP 45 (= 3b)
gacchanti ca sadā tamaḥ	BrahVP 10d
gacched brahmasalokatām	GarP 44d
gajendraṃ mokṣayāmāsa	MatsyaP 9c
gaṇyate śāstravedibhiḥ	BrāṇP 35d
gatasāraṃ yātayāmaṃ	NārP 13a
gatās te viṣṇum ity ṛtāḥ	KūrP 32 (= 6b)
gatiṃ gacchanti vaiṣṇavīm	SkaP 104d
gatiṃ śaśaṃsa kuntyāś ca	BrāṇP 23c
gatidvayajigīṣavaḥ	BrahVP 10d
gatir āsīn na kāmataḥ	SkaP 65 (= 2d)
gatir ity eva cintaya	VāmP 36d
gatir eṣā na saṃśayaḥ	NārP 50d
gatiś cāsya kathaṃ parā	NārP 2 (= 6b)
gatis teṣāṃ yathānijam	BrahVP 10d
gatvā dakṣam atha avadhīt	BrahP 35d
gandharvāṇāṃ tathā rājnāṃ	BrāṇP 48[8a]
gandharvādiśataṃ tathā	GarP 44d
gamayet kṣipram eva tu	BrāṇP 89b
gamyejyajñeyavācyeṣu	VarP 6a
gayaś ca lakṣmaṇādyāś ca	BrāṇP 95 (= 31a)
garīyo hy uttarottaram	VāmP 41d
garuḍaḥ śakra eva ca	VāmP 2 (= 2b)
garuḍendrasūryavighnāder	BrāṇP 12 (= 7a)
-garutmadrudratatstriyaḥ	SkaP 32 (= 5b)
garbhasthānāṃ bhaviṣyati	SkaP 47b
garbhiṇīvadhanodārtham	VarP 8c
garbhe vā bahir evātha	BrahP 69c
gāṅgeyaṃ na jaghāna ha	SkaP 111b
gāṇapatyās ca saurāś ca	PadP 2a
gāṇḍīvaṃ dhanuṣāṃ śreṣṭham	MBh 47 (= 168c)
gāndhārīdhṛtarāṣṭrayoḥ	BrāṇP 23d
gāyatrībhaṣyarūpo 'sau	GarP 8c
gāyatryopāsako hi saḥ	BrāṇP 3 (= 31b)
giriḥ prāṇaḥ samuddiṣṭhas	VāmP 21a
giriśasya balaṃ marut	MBh 45b
gītāyāṃ tad udāhṛtam	BrahVP 39 (= 4d)

gīyate na tu bādhyatva-	BhaviṣPV 12c
gīyate puruṣottamaḥ	BrāṇP 68d
gīyase padam ity eva	NārP 46a
guṇatadvadvibhāgo vā	PadP 99c
guṇadoṣau mānuṣāṇāṃ	BrahP 78c
guṇadoṣau māyayaiva	ViṣDhUP 1a
guṇapūrter ātmaśabdo	BrahP 22a
guṇapūrtyabhidhāyī sa	BrāṇP 4c
guṇabāhulyatas tathā	NārP 56b
guṇabhāvaṃ janārdanaḥ	VāmP 30b
guṇabhedavidāṃ viṣṇor	NārP 50a
guṇamātrasvarūpiṇaḥ	BrahVP 28d
guṇarūpaṃ janārdanam	KūrP 31 (= 7d)
guṇalabdhiṃ tato brūte	KūrP 7c
guṇavyatikarābhāve	GarP 19a
guṇasāmye 'pi kimuta	BhaviṣPV 2 (= 14a)
guṇasraṣṭā caturmukhaḥ	NārP 22b
guṇahetuḥ kathaṃcana	BrāṇP 95 (= 37d)
guṇāḥ santy eva sarvaśaḥ	GarP 46b
guṇāḥ sarve 'pi yujyante	ViṣDhUP 1a
guṇāḥ svarūpabhūtāś ca	BrahP 40a
guṇātmikā ca sā devī	GarP 36 (= 3a)
guṇādhikavirodhi yat	BhaviṣPV 2 (= 14b)
guṇānāṃ karmaṇām api	VarP 51 (= 1b)
guṇānusāriṇīṃ pūjāṃ	BrahVP 35a
-guṇān eva pracakṣate	BrāṇP 2d
guṇā viruddhā api tu	KūrP 1a
guṇeṣv api kadācana	VarP 51 (= 5b)
guṇaiḥ sarvaiḥ śataguṇā	PadP 104c
guṇaiḥ sarvaiḥ samo nityaṃ	PadP 92a
guṇaiḥ sarvair udīrṇatā	BhaviṣPV 29 (= 44d)
guṇaiḥ sarvair upāsyo 'sau	BhaviṣPV 20a
guṇaiḥ sarvair harir yataḥ	BhaviṣPV 3 (= 26d)
guṇaiḥ sarvaiś ca sarvataḥ	VarP 2b
guṇaiḥ sarvais tathaiva ca	HarV 5 (= 10b)
guṇaikamātrarūpās tu	BrahP 78a
guṇair evābhimanyate	PadP 18b
-guṇair nīcātmatā tathā	SkaP 48b
guṇair sarvair na saṃśayaḥ	BrahVP 12_1d
guruḥ śrībrahmaṇor viṣṇuḥ	VarP 26c
guruprasādo balavān	VarP 43a

janmamṛtyādivivarjitaḥ	BrāṇP 105 (= 1d)
janmamṛtyādisaṅgatiḥ	KūrP 10d
janmamṛtyuvihīnāś ca	GarP 6c
janmāntare śrutās tās tu	BrāṇP 104 (= 3a)
janmeti kavayo viduḥ	PadP 50d
janyādiṃ mānuṣā janāḥ	BrahP 48 (= 4d)
jayasya vijayasyāpi	NārP 12a
jayed buddhibalo naras	BrahVP 34b
jarāsandhaṃ nihatyaiva	MatsyaP 15a
jalajāḥ pakṣiṇas tathā	BrāṇP 35b
jalasthalāyati sphītaṃ	SkaP 18a
jāgarti svapiteṣv api	BrāṇP 93d
jāgraddarśanasaṃskāra-	VarP 58a
jāgradvat tu yathā svapnaḥ	HarV 20a
jāgrādiṣv avasthiteḥ	GarP 54b
jātaṃ sukham atīva ca	NārP 42b
jātas tapasi vai manuḥ	MatsyaP 9b
jātāḥ krodavaśā bhuvi	BhaviṣP 7 (= 3d)
jātā dharmasya vṛddhaye	SkaP 123d
-jātābhyo nijasatstriyaḥ	BhaviṣPV 27d
jātismaro dvidhā śāstraṃ	BrahP 43 (= 5a)
jātismṛtipramāṇāc ca	BhaviṣPV 2 (= 7a)
jāto gatas tv idaṃ rūpaṃ	VarP 2c
jāto 'smi varddhe dhanavān	BrahP 48 (= 1c)
jānakī rugmiṇī tathā	BrāṇP 95 (= 39b)
jānatām api kartavyaṃ	NārP 19a
jānanti paramarṣayaḥ	PadP 47d
jānanto 'pi viśeṣārtha	AgniP 19a
jānanto 'pi hy asadṛśaṃ	NārP 19a
jānanto 'py ṛṣayaḥ sadā	BrāṇP 47b
jānanty ajñā janārdanam	SkaP 17d
jānan sālvakṛtāṃ māyām	BrāṇP 60a
jānāti jīvaḥ sa jñeyaḥ	HarV 11c
jānīto lokavanditau	BrāṇP 31b
jānīyāṃ tat kathaṃ nv aham	VarP 57b
jānīyāṃ tvām iti prāha	BrāṇP 3 (= 15c)
jānīyāt tadadhīnaṃ ca	BrahVP 38 (= 4c)
jānīyad viṣṇum añjasā	BrāṇP 105 (= 8b)
jānīyān na guṇānāṃ ca	KūrP 31 (= 8a)
jāyate naiva kutrāpi	MBh 42 (= 75a)
jāyante nātra saṃśayaḥ	MBh 16d

jñānamātrārtham īritam	VarP 2d
jñānamātrāś ca sarvaśaḥ	VarP 2b
jñānam āpa kutaścana	NārP 26b
jñānam eva viśiṣyate	NārP 40b
jñānam evādhikaṃ nare	NārP 54d
jñānarūpād ṛte hareḥ	MatsyaP 19d
jñānavyaktaṃ nijaṃ sukham	GarP 19d
jñānaśaktir udīritā	SkaP 25b
jñānaśaktisvarūpo 'pi	PadP 13a
jñānasāhāyyakārakam	BrāṇP 45b
jñānasya mukhyavācitvān	MārkP 3a
jñānasyāpi samagrataḥ	BhavisPV 3 (= 5d)
jñānasyaivaṃ vyavasthitiḥ	BhaviṣPV 15d
-jñānāt tadvyaktim āvrajet	KūrP 31 (= 7b)
jñānātmakam udāhṛtam	BrahVP 18d
jñānādayo guṇā yasmāj	BrāṇP 95 (= 20a)
jñānādidānaṃ devānāṃ	VarP 44a
jñānādiphalado hariḥ	MatsyaP 16d
jñānādivyaktir avyaktiḥ	BrahVP 7a
-jñānād eva vimuktigāḥ	BrahVP 42 (= 6b)
jñānād bhedasya darśanāt	BhaviṣPV 2 (= 6b)
-jñānād viṣṇoḥ sadocyatām	BrāṇP 9 (= 19b)
jñānādhikyāt samīpagāḥ	GarP 45d
jñānānandaguṇeṣv api	BrahVP 12_1b
jñānānandasvarūpebhyo	SkaP 45 (= 3d)
jñānānandātmake viṣṇau	BrāṇP 52a
jñānānandātmako deha	BrahP 43 (= 1a)
jñānāni ca prayacchanti	VāmP 27c
jñānān mokṣa udāhṛtaḥ	PadP 56d
jñānān mokṣo bhavaty eva	BrāṇP 77a
-jñānāya sthāpanāya vā	AgniP 19b
jñānārthaṃ śāstram iṣyate	BrāṇP 11b
jñāninaḥ sā hi muktiḥ syāt	VarP 60c
jñāninām karmayuktānāṃ	GarP 48a
jñāninām gṛhiṇāṃ padam	BrāṇP 30d
jñāninām paramapriyaḥ	NārP 3 (= 10b)
jñāninām bramacāriṇām	BrāṇP 30d
jñānino 'jñāninas tathā	HarV 33 (= 2d)
-jñānino nāsti saṃśayaḥ	PadP 74d
jñānino 'pi yato hrāsa	NārP 57c
jñāne tv ajñānatāṃ gate	SkaP 78 (= 2b)

tac ceśvarakṛtaṃ svayam	BhavișPV 16d
tacchaktyekāṃśabhāginaḥ	BrahVP 20b
tacchatāṃśādidarśinaḥ	BrāṇP 88d
tacchatāṃśena rudras tu	BrāṇP 88c
tacchatāṃśena vāsavaḥ	BrāṇP 88d
tacchabdair api kathyate	GarP 4d
tacchabdair eva bhaṇyate	PadP 69b
tacchāstrasamayena tu	NārP 34b
tacchrutvā tuṣṭim agamat	BrāṇP 3 (= 6a)
tajjanmani varāḥ pāpa	BhavișPV 27c
tajjīvābhinnaṃ tadāsurāḥ	BrāṇP 9b
tajjñaḥ priyas tatas teṣāṃ	VāmP 1c
tajjñānān naiva mucyate	PadP 56b
tajjñānān mucyate 'ñjasā	BrāṇP 86 (= 1d)
tajjñāpanāya lokānām	BrāṇP 47c
tajjño yasmāc ca sādhakaḥ	BhavișPV 3 (= 16d)
tata eveti setsyati	BrahP 50d
tataḥ paryaṅkaśayana	BrāṇP 57c
tataḥ paścāc ca phalgunaḥ	BrāṇP 95 (= 42b)
tataḥ paścād draupadī ca	BrāṇP 95 (= 40a)
tataḥ prabhṛti pūjyante	PadP 3_1c
tataḥ prāṇādināmāntāḥ	VarP 47a
tataḥ śreyāṃsi vāñchanti	BrāṇP 54a
tataḥ saṃmohayāmāsa	BrāṇP 22a
tataḥ sanaka eva ca	GarP 7d
tataḥ sākṣājjagannāthaḥ	PadP 3_1c
tataḥ sūkte tathovāca	BhavișPV 3 (= 14a)
tataś cāpy aharādikam	NārP 47b
tataś cottamapuruṣāḥ	BhavișPV 3 (= 9b)
tatas taddarśakaḥ paraḥ	VarP 23b
tatas tām aharad vibhuḥ	BrāṇP 60d
tatas tu devadeveśaḥ	HarV 25c
tatas teṣāṃ na durlabham	BrahVP 42 (= 4b)
tato jayed buddhibalo naras	BrahVP 34
tato 'tituṣṭo bhagavān	BrāṇP 3 (= 8c)
tato dāvāgninā dagdhaṃ	SkaP 22a
tato dehaṃ yathākramam	BrahP 69d
tato 'dhikam iva vyaktaṃ	KūrP 31 (= 1c)
tato 'nyeṣāṃ samudbhavaḥ	VāyuP 4b
tato 'pi devī brahmāṇī	SkaP 32 (= 5c)
tato bahutarān icchan	NārP 2 (= 4a)

tato bharatavālinau	BrāṇP 95 (= 43d)
tato mahattaraṃ proktaṃ	VarP 44c
tato māṃ pratipadyate	BrahP 80b
tato viṣṇoḥ parotkarṣaṃ	KūrP 32 (= 10a)
tato vetteti ca tvaṃ sa	BrāṇP 3 (= 17c)
tat karoti svayaṃ prabhuḥ	BrāṇP 8d
tatkarmaiva sadā bhavet	BrahVP 38 (= 9d)
tatkāraṇaṃ tathā kāryam	SkaP 114d
tatkālasthitabhakteṣu	GarP 28a
tat kim atra niyāmakam	GarP 38 (= 1d)
tat kuryāt karma vaiṣṇavam	AgniP 26d
tatkrameṇa ca tair varṇais	BrāṇP 104 (= 2a)
tattacchaktīḥ prabodhayan	VāmP 39b
tattacchaktyā vikalpyate	HarV 24b
tattacchabdābhidheyatā	KūrP 22b
tattadākārasaṃyuktān	SkaP 41a
tat tad ity eva bhaṇyate	BhaviṣPV 6b
tattadvividhabhūtis tu	HarV 33 (= 3c)
tattantratvān na tatsaṃstha-	BrahVP 8c
tattannāmaiva nāmaiṣāṃ	NārP 1a
tattannāmnocyate viṣṇuḥ	PadP 57a
tat tu pūrṇatvataḥ pūṣā	BrāṇP 92a
tattvajñaḥ puruṣas tadvad	BhaviṣPV 3 (= 21a)
tattvajñānaṃ tu devānāṃ	SkaP 47a
tattvajñānaṃ vināpi tu	BrāṇP 12 (= 6b)
tattvajñāne viṣṇubhaktau	MBh 46a
tattvanirṇayavailomyaṃ	BrāṇP 16c
tattvavādiṣu kopāc ca	BrahVP 42 (= 4a)
tattvavid devagauḥ prokto	AgniP 1a
tattvārthajñānavarjanāt	PadP 94 (= 8b)
tatthyavastudvayaṃ vinā	BrahVP 44b
tatpatiḥ keśavaḥ smṛtaḥ	PadP 21_1b
tatpatis triguṇo rudras	VāmP 20c
tatpāramyāt sarasvatī	BrāṇP 15 (= 8d)
tatputrapautrā munayas	ViṣP 7a
tatputraś cāniruddhakaḥ	BrāṇP 95 (= 31d)
tatpratīpaṃ tu yad dṛśyen	BhaviṣPV 32 (= 113c)
tatpraśiṣyaḥ krumur nāma	BrahP 43 (= 7a)
tatprasādam ṛte divyam	VarP 57c
tatprasādāc ca gacchati	BrāṇP 58d
tatprasādāt taranti hi	PadP 59d

tathāpy arāgākṛṣṭatvāt	GarP 4c
tathāpy avyaktago yadvad	PadP 53c
tathāpy aśaktair vihitāḥ	SkaP 59 (= 2a)
tathāpy asuramohāya	BrāṇP 105 (= 5c)
tathāpy asuramohāya	PadP 50a
tathāpy asuramohāya	SkaP 43c
tathāpy asmān vimohasi	NārP 35d
tathāpy ekavivakṣayā	VāyuP 11b
tathāpy eṣu hariḥ sthitaḥ	BrahP 15b
tathā prākṛtadehatvaṃ	BhaviṣPV 29 (= 38c)
tathā prāṇo ramā caiva	BrāṇP 62a
tathā bharataśatrughnau	SkaP 52c
tathā bhāgavataṃ bhuvi	BrāṇP 21d
tathā bhedaviśeṣayoḥ	VarP 51 (= 3d)
tathā mānavamānavāḥ	ViṣP 7b
tathā muktāv uttamāyāṃ	SkaP 2c
tathārthaḥ kalpya etayoḥ	KūrP 24d
tathāvikṛta eva san	BrahP 47b
tathā vipre ca mānuṣe	BrāṇP 13 (= 8b)
tathā śabdasya kālasya	BrahVP 12_{1}a
tathā saṃhārakartṛtām	KūrP 32 (= 5b)
tathā sannihito hariḥ	SkaP 52d
tathā siddhimatām api	BhaviṣPV 2 (= 17b)
tathā svagatabhedasya	BrāṇP 62a
tathā svaviṣayaṃ jñānaṃ	GarP 2a
tathā harau jagad idaṃ	BrahP 33c
tathā hi karuṇo viṣṇur	BrāṇP 53 (= 3c)
tathaiko bahurūpavān	BrāṇP 66b
tathaiteṣāṃ matāni tu	BhaviṣPV 21 (= 5b)
tathaiva ca sahasradhā	SkaP 78 (= 5d)
tathaiva tena gītāyā	BrahVP 39 (= 5c)
tathaiva paramātmānam	BrāṇP 58c
tathaiva parameśvaraḥ	BrahP 68d
tathaiva baḍavāvaktraḥ	BrāṇP 95 (= 26c)
tathaiva bhagavadbhaktiṃ	BrāṇP 49c
tathaiva me mano nityaṃ	BrahP 60c
tathaivarteṣu mukteṣu	KūrP 32 (= 6a)
tathaiva sarvaśāstrāṇāṃ	MārkP 2a
tathaiva sva iti proktas	SkaP 107c
tathaivānyasvarūpeṣu	BrahP 53a
tathaivānvīkṣikī parā	MatsyaP 2b

tathaivāvayavānāṃ ca	VarP 51 (= 1c)
tathaivāśramabhedataḥ	GarP 45 (= 5d)
tathaivāśvataro 'paraḥ	BrāṇP 35d
tathaivāsuraye sarva-	PadP 9a
tathau prāṇātmakau proktau	GarP 38 (= 7c)
tadaṅgajāni tattvāni	HarV 10c
tadaṅgānāṃ mukhādinām	BrāṇP 10d
tadatantraniṣedhakāḥ	BrāṇP 62b
tadatantrasya varjanāt	BrahP 1_2b
tadadhīnapravṛttitvāt	BrahP 84a
tadananyam udīryate	HarV 21d
tadanugraham antarā	SkaP 59 (= 4b)
tadanutpattivacanam	VāyuP 4c
tadanuvratāś ca ye	BrahVP 43c
tadantatvāj janārdanaḥ	BrahP 49b
tadantaraṃ brahmagirīśayor api	SkaP 110d
tadantaraṃ rudramahendrayor api	SkaP 110d
tadantaraṃ viṣṇuhiraṇyagarbhayoḥ	SkaP 110d
tadantaram anantakam	SkaP 110b
tadantaryāmyapekṣayā	BrahP 36b
tadanyagatam ucyate	BrahP 25b
tadanyatra prayujyate	PadP 34b
tadanyā devatāḥ sarvāḥ	HarV 25a
tadanyābhāvato nānyad	BrāṇP 34c
tadanyārthān na tu smaret	BrāṇP 25b
tadanye kīkaṭāḥ smṛtāḥ	SkaP 76d
tadanye kramayogena	BrāṇP 88c
tadanye cetanāḥ sarve	BrāṇP 2 (= 2a)
tadanye tadvaśā matāḥ	BrāṇP 40b
tadanye tūpacārataḥ	SkaP 107b
tadanyena kṛtāḥ sarve	SkaP 59 (= 5a)
tadanye naiva ca svargaṃ	NārP 49 (= 6c)
tadanye 'nye 'pi cartvijaḥ	BrāṇP 3 (= 3b)
tadanye 'pi tu ye deśāḥ	SkaP 76a
tadanyeṣāṃ tamo bhavet	BrāṇP 64 (= 6b)
tadanyeṣāṃ tu sarveṣāṃ	VarP 50a
tadanyeṣāṃ viparyayaḥ	BhaviṣPV 30 (= 93b)
tadanyo 'jīva ucyate	VāyuP 3_3d
tadanyo viṣṇur ity api	BhaviṣPV 3 (= 24b)
tadabandhaḥ parātmanaḥ	BhaviṣPV 24d
tadabhāvo hareḥ sadā	VarP 50d

tadarthaṃ cānyad ucyate NārP 58d
tadarthaṃ tv anyasādhanam HarV 13d
tadarthāḥ pūrvasargavat BrāṇP 104 (= 6d)
tadarthās tu kathāḥ sarvā BhavisPV 32 (= 113a)
tadaheyaṃ paraṃ brahma BhavisPV 3 (= 4c)
tadāṃśā hi sureṣv api BrahP 21b
tadā tatkālabhāvinā VāyuP 1b
tadā tatkālabhāvinā VāyuP 2 $_1$b
tadā tadabhimāni tu GarP 30 (= 7c)
tadā te 'pi tathā neyā GarP 37 (= 4c)
tadādiṣṭaphalāṃ gatim MBh 28c
tadā doṣo na jāyate GarP 37 (= 5b)
tadādhāro yato viṣṇuḥ BrāṇP 68c
tadā niyamato bhavet BhaviṣPV 30 (= 90b)
tadāntarahares tatra PadP 34c
tadā prādurbhavaty ajaḥ SkaP 32 (= 6d)
tadā muktiś ca devānāṃ BhaviṣPV 30 (= 91a)
tadā mukto bhavaty asau BhaviṣP 2 (= 6b)
tadāvasthāprabodhādi- HarV 19c
tadā vāsavam āviśat BrāṇP 3 (= 4b)
tadāveśāṃs tathā samyag BhaviṣPV 30 (= 82c)
tadāśrayaḥ paro viṣṇuḥ SkaP 9c
tadā sañcintayed devaṃ HarV 3a
tadāsuravimohanam HarV 5 (= 11b)
tadāsau virurāva ha BrahVP 21b
tadicchayā yato hy asya KūrP 27c
tad ityādi vyavahriyate VarP 2d
tadīyaṃ tv anyad ucyate MBh 38b
tadīyaṃ sarvam eva yat BrahP 84b
tadīyo 'yam iti smṛtiḥ ViṣP 9d
tadīyo 'ham iti jñānam VāmP 42a
tadīyau tau kuto hy ataḥ ViṣDhUP 1d
tadukter anusārataḥ KūrP 7b
tad uktham iti saṃproktaṃ GarP 1c
taduccasaṅgateḥ kvāpi GarP 37 (= 5a)
tadutpattivacaś caiva BrāṇP 104 (= 5a)
tadupādhikṛtaṃ matam BhaviṣPV 15b
tad ekaḥ puruṣottamaḥ PadP 85b
tad etad vāsudevasya BhaviṣPV 4 (= 9c)
tad etan mithunaṃ jñātvā SkaP 105c
tad eno 'smad viyojaya SkaP 120b

tadvān bhāvuka ucyate	NarasimP 1b
tad vijñānam iti proktaṃ	VāmP 13c
tadvidhaś cāparo nāsti	MBh 42 (= 70c)
tadviśiṣṭatvavittaye	BrāṇP 82d
tadvettāro 'pi tatpraśna	NārP 3 (= 7c)
tadvyāptiś ceti yujyate	SkaP 102b
tanuṃ tyaktvā divaṃ gataḥ	MBh 42 (= 78d)
tantrasāṅkhyaṃ jagāda ha	PadP 9b
tannābhyutthitapadmagaḥ	PadP 98b
tannāmabhiś ca strīrūpaiḥ	GarP 5 (= 1c)
tannāmavācyam aṅgaṃ tad	NārP 27c
tanniyantṛtayātmānaṃ	NārP 11c
tanniyāmakatā bhavet	VāmP 15b
tan naivātyeti kaścana	VarP 60d
tanmataṃ na virudhyate	BrahP 63d
tan manyante bhautikaṃ tu	BrahP 32
tanmātvaṃ kveti taṃ vadet	BhavişPV 2 (= 1d)
tanmūlatvād ahaṃ tridhā	GarP 12d
tanmohāyeti nirṇayaḥ	BrāṇP 94d
tanmohāyeti nirṇayaḥ	SkaP 122b
tanvā tadyogyayā tathā	BhavişPV 30 (= 91d)
tapantaṃ veda so 'pi hi	BrāṇP 3 (= 30d)
tapann asmīti cocivān	BrāṇP 3 (= 25b)
tapann evāsmīty avadat	BrāṇP 3 (= 30c)
tapasā pūjyamānānāṃ	VarP 6c
tapasā vāpy upāyair vā	BrāṇP 12 (= 9a)
tapasā śaktito 'pi vā	BhavişPV 3 (= 30b)
tapasā strītvam āpire	KūrP 4b
tapasvī bahuvedavit	BrāṇP 103_2b
tama ity eva kīrtitā	VişP 8 (= 4b)
tam attuṃ vyādadād āsyaṃ	BrahVP 21a
tam adhamaceṣṭam avaihi nāsya bhaktam	VişṇP 2b
tamaś cāpi kathaṃcana	BhavişPV 30 (= 88d)
tamasā hy abhimanyate	PadP 18b
tamasi sthasya daivataiḥ	BrāṇP 15 (= 11d)
tamas tu śārvaraṃ vidyān	MBh 39a
tamasy eva vinikṣipet	GarP 36 (= 5d)
tam ṛte naiva cāvasthā	HarV 25a
tam ṛte puruṣottamam	PadP 57b
tam ṛte viṣṇum avyayam	BrahVP 23b
tam ṛte viṣṇum avyayam	PadP 1_1b

tasmai namo bhagavate	KūrP 30_1c
tasmai namo vyastasamastaviśva-	SkaP 79c
tasya tarkasya satyatvam	BrāṇP 3 (= 27a)
tasya tasminn abhedataḥ	BrahVP 6b
tasya darśanato yāti	HarV 5 (= 4a)
tasya duḥkhaṃ kuto 'ṇvapi	SkaP 64d
tasya nābhūtidās tataḥ	VāmP 1d
tasya prakāśakaṃ nityaṃ	VāyuP 3_5a
tasya prasādād icchanti	MBh 28b
tasya prītāś ca devatāḥ	BhavişPV 3 (= 17b)
tasya brahmā tato hariḥ	VāmP 20d
tasya viṣṇuḥ prasīdati	BrahVP 35d
tasya viṣṇor adehinaḥ	BrāṇP 8d
tasya viṣṇor vaśe rudro	BrahVP 16c
tasya śāntyādayo 'ṇgāni	AgniP 15c
tasyā ino hi viṣṇuḥ sa	BrāṇP 3 (= 22c)
tasyāṅgaṃ prathamaṃ vāyuḥ	BhavişPV 32 (= 118a)
tasyātmano nirguṇasya	PadP 56c
tasyādhyarddhatanutvataḥ	BrāṇP 82b
tasyāpi jñātṛmantṛtvaṃ	GarP 30 (= 3c)
tasyāpi priyatāṃ hariḥ	BrahVP 12b
tasyāpi muktir niyatā	BhavişPV 9a
tasyāpi viṣṇoḥ sṛṣṭiṃ tu	HarV 33 (= 10a)
tasyāpy anugrahārthāya	GarP 31c
tasyāvatārā dehasthā	KūrP 17c
tasyāvirodhato yojyaṃ	BrāṇP 50c
tasyāśrayo 'sti vety evaṃ	BrāṇP 15 (= 11a)
tasyāsanavidhānārthaṃ	MBh 12a
tasyās tu trīṇi rūpāṇi	ViṣP 8 (= 2a)
tasyās tu paramo viṣṇur	BrāṇP 89c
tasyāsty eva sadāpi tu	NārP 42d
tasyecchanty avināśitām	BhavişPV 4 (= 8b)
tasyetthaṃ vaḥ kutaḥ kṛtam	BrahVP 16b
tasyai namo 'stu te devyau	NārP 23c
tasyaiva tadavasthatvāt	GarP 34_1c
tasyaiva darśanapatham	KūrP 30_1b
tasyotpattir mṛtiś caiva	VāyuP 7c
tā evāpo dadau tasya	KūrP 30_3a
tāṃ dvaitadṛṣṭiṃ me deva	BrahP 10a
tāṃ brahma mahad ity āhuḥ	BrāṇP 89a
tāṃ vinā na hi kiṃcana	BhavişP 2 (= 1d)

tebhyo manuṣyā ity eṣā	ViṣP 7c
tebhyo yāti tamo ghoram	BrahVP 38 (= 5c)
tebhyo viṣṇoś ca samyak tal-	PadP 94 (= 3c)
te mukhyasrotasas tataḥ	BrahP 24 (= 1d)
te mucyante na caivānye	GarP 36 (= 12a)
te yājñikāḥ svargabhoga	NārP 49 (= 2c)
te yānti param eva tu	GarP 44b
te vai tāmasatāmasāḥ	HarV 30d
teṣāṃ karmeti niścayaḥ	BrahP 77d
teṣāṃ ca sāttvikāḥ śeṣa-	SkaP 32 (= 5a)
teṣāṃ jñānaṃ na jāyate	BrahVP 43d
teṣāṃ jñānaṃ hi tādṛśa	BhaviṣPV 3 (= 6b)
teṣāṃ jñānasya mukteś ca	VarP 16a
teṣāṃ tadupacārataḥ	VāmP 35d
teṣāṃ dharmajñāpanārthaṃ	BrāṇP 48a
teṣāṃ paraṃparāprāptaṃ	GarP 36 (= 11c)
teṣāṃ bhaktyādibhir guṇaiḥ	GarP 31b
teṣāṃ bhītir na cābhavat	AgniP 24b
teṣāṃ bhūtair upacayaḥ	BhaviṣPV 18c
teṣāṃ yad anyathā dṛśyaṃ	BhaviṣPV 15a
teṣāṃ yaśasa ādirāṭ	GarP 31b
teṣāṃ śaktyā vikalpyate	HarV 24b
teṣāṃ saṃpātajo bhāvo	BhaviṣP 2 (= 2c)
teṣāṃ saṅgaṃ parityajet	GarP 37 (= 3b)
teṣāṃ satyaṃ hariḥ sākṣād	BrāṇP 9 (= 6a)
teṣāṃ samīpagāś caiva	SkaP 76a
teṣāṃ sā na pravartate	VāyuP 1b
teṣāṃ sā na pravartate	VāyuP 2_1b
teṣāṃ sāmarthyayogāc ca	SkaP 95a
teṣām antargato hariḥ	MBh 6b
teṣām anye tu yoginaḥ	BrahP 34b
teṣām artho 'nvavekṣyate	BrahP 85d
teṣām aśaktatoktiś ca	BrāṇP 41c
teṣām ātmā hariḥ sadā	VāmP 1b
teṣām uktvā punaḥ kṛṣṇa-	PadP 14a (= 8a)
teṣām uttamasaṅgasya	GarP 37 (= 3a)
teṣām eva ca vārṣṇeyaḥ	BrahVP 39 (= 2a)
teṣām eva bhaven muktir	GarP 50c
teṣām eṣa parāyaṇam	NārP 3 (= 10d)
teṣām aiśvaryabhogo hi	BrāṇP 48c
teṣu caivottamottamāḥ	GarP 45 (= 7b)

dakṣabhāge sthitaḥ sadā BrāṇP 3 (= 22d)
dakṣavāmaśrutisthitau GarP 5 (= 4b)
dakṣādyāḥ sanakādyāś ca BrāṇP 101a
dakṣādyā manavas tathā BrāṇP 95 (= 29b)
dakṣiṇaṃ nāma socyate BrāṇP 3 (= 22b)
dakṣiṇātarpitānāṃ tu NārP 49 (= 5c)
dakṣinābhiḥ sahaivaitan HarV 1a
dattaṃ durvāsasaṃ somam BhāgP 1c
dattaṃ vā bāhyam eva tu BrāṇP 59d
dattavyāsādirūpeṣu BrāṇP 95 (= 23c)
datto 'to brahmarāteti BrahP 18c
datto dhanvantarir yajñaḥ VarP 51 (= 6c)
datto varo mayāsyeti BrāṇP 19c
dadarśa varuṇaḥ svayam HarV 32b
dadāti narasañcayāt BrahVP 35b
dadāni varam ity amum BrāṇP 3 (= 8d)
dadyān nirāśī ca sadā BrahVP 38 (= 3c)
dadhīcyādyāḥ purāṇāni NārP 34a
darpanāśārtham eva ca GarP 31d
-darśanaṃ caivamādikam SkaP 69 (= 5b)
darśanaṃ tad udāhṛtam BhavişPV 32 (= 116d)
-darśanaṃ na kvacid bhavet BrāṇP 103b
darśanaṃ ninditaṃ kvacit SkaP 69 (= 2d)
darśanasparśasaṃbhāṣād NārP 37a
darśanāc caiva bhakteś ca NārP 40a
darśanāntarasiddhaṃ ca BhavişPV 32 (= 117a)
darśanābhyāsato dṛṣṭir AgniP 24c
-darśanāya harer api BrāṇP 55b
-darśane 'nye na tu kvacit GarP 44b
darśanoktaṃ ca gṛhyate BhavişPV 32 (= 116b)
darśayanty anyathaiva tu MBh 42 (= 80d)
darśayann api mohāya ĀdiP 1b
darśayasva mahābhuja BrāṇP 94b
darśayāmāsa nāṭyavat MBh 42b (= 79b)
darśayāmāsa mūḍhatām PadP 77d
darśayec chuddasadguṇaḥ BrāṇP 105 (= 6b)
darśayej janamohāya SkaP 36a
darśayet tāny ajo hariḥ 105 (= 7b)
darśayed vasudevāder VāmP 30c
darśayen naravad dhariḥ BhavişPV 29 (= 37b)
darśayeyur aśaktavat GarP 26_1b

davāgnim anupraviśya-	BrahP 43 (= 2a)
daśatālaś caturhastaḥ	VāyuP 3c
daśārthāḥ sarvabhārate	SkaP 126b
daśāvarārthaṃ sarvatra	SkaP 108c
-dātā sa bhagavān hariḥ	GarP 30 (= 4b)
dānatīrthatapoyajña-	BhavişPV 30 (= 99a)
dānavās tu tamolayāḥ	BhavişPV 30 (= 87d)
dāruyoṣavad ucyate	SkaP 100d
dideśa brahmaṇe brahma	BrahP 3 (= 1c)
dinair daśabhir eva vā	NārP 14b
divā jñānam udīryate	SkaP 38b
divādidevatābhis tu	BrahP 82a
diśaḥ śrotreṇa caiva hi	MBh 29b
dīnatvād devanāmānas	ViṣP 7a
dīnair devais tu bhujyate	ViṣP 7d
dīpter ākāśaśabdoktā	SkaP 9a
duḥkhaprāptir apūrṇatā	VarP 50b
-duḥkhabhogena tu kvacit	BrahVP 8d
duḥkhamātrapratismṛteḥ	VarP 40d
duḥkhamiśraṃ sukhaṃ phalam	SkaP 119b
duḥkhayug dṛśyate katham	BrāṇP 105 (= 2d)
duḥkhayogādirahitaḥ	PadP 92c
duḥkhayogādirūpeṇa	PadP 92a
duḥkhasya cāpy āyatanaṃ śarīram	MBh 49b
duḥkhājñānaśramādīn sa	BrāṇP 105 (= 6a)
duḥkhājñānādirūpiṇaḥ	KūrP 31 (= 3b)
duḥkhājñānādisantīrṇāḥ	KūrP 31 (= 3c)
duḥkhitvaṃ bhinnatāpi vā	BrāṇP 12 (= 1d)
duḥkhī bhavati nānyathā	MBh 21d
duḥkhī sītā ca mārgate	MBh 42 (= 77b)
duḥkhair naiva hi lipyate	KūrP 32 (= 16b)
duḥkhopalabdhimātrās te	BhavişPV 15c
duḥśāstraṃ tadvirodhi yat	BrāṇP 11d
dugdhadohāṃ tu gāṃ rakṣet	HarV 27a
durāgamās tadanye ye	BrāṇP 103$_1$c
durduḥkham iti vijñeyaṃ	HarV 12a
duryodhanavadhād api	BrāṇP 95 (= 15d)
durvāsāś ca svayaṃ rudras	GarP 31a
duṣṭatvaṃ teṣu saṃsthitam	BhavişPV 2 (= 8d)
duṣṭasaṃsarga eva tu	SkaP 55d
duṣṭasaṅgād dhi viṣṇoś ca	SkaP 55c

devarṣiprabhṛtayo	SkaP 40c
devavarṇā iti smṛtāḥ	NārP 2 (= 5b)
-devaviprāḥ kramāt sadā	HarV 5 (= 9d)
devaviprādinām api	BrāṇP 12 (= 7d)
devasya pratirūpakāḥ	KūrP 32 (= 9d)
devaṛṣiprabhṛtayo	SkaP 40c
devā eva tadanyebhyaś	SkaP 59 (= 1a)
devā eva sadā matāḥ	BrahP 78b
devāḥ pṛthaganākhyātāḥ	SkaP 32 (= 3c)
devāḥ śaktāś ca mohāya	GarP 26_1b
devāḥ sarve 'pi saṃsthitāḥ	PadP 90d
devā gāvaḥ sarasvatī	GarP 10b
devāditvaṃ yogyatayā	NārP 20a
devādīnām ādirājñāṃ	PadP 80a
devā daivasvabhāvena	SkaP 104a
devādhikāragaṃ sarvaṃ	SkaP 114a
devān atyuttamamunīn	MatsyaP 13a
devānām adhidaivatam	KūrP 30_5b
devānām apy upāsanam	SkaP 95b
devānām apriyaṃ jñānaṃ	BhaviṣPV 3 (= 24c)
devānām aśruteṣv api	HarV 28d
devānām aṣṭasiddhayaḥ	HarV 28d
devānām uttarottaram	VarP 44d
devānāṃ karmaṇaivaite	BrāṇP 1a
devānāṃ ca viśeṣataḥ	BhaviṣPV 28b
devānāṃ jñāyate sphuṭam	VāmP 17b
devānāṃ tattvavedini	BhaviṣPV 3 (= 23b)
devānāṃ nāśubhād ghrāsaḥ	BrāṇP 48c
devānāṃ nirayo nāsti	BhaviṣPV 30 (= 88c)
devānāṃ paśuvac cāsau	BhaviṣPV 3 (= 20a)
devānāṃ brahmanirmitāḥ	VāmP 2 (= 3b)
devānāṃ vā munīnāṃ vā	SkaP 123a
devānāṃ vā vyapekṣayā	BrāṇP 104 (= 7d)
devānāṃ vyāpakatvāt tu	VāmP 1a
devā naivaṃ tu dānavāḥ	BhaviṣPV 15b
devān pitṝn dvijān havya	PadP 3_1a
devān bhojayati jñāna-	BhaviṣPV 3 (= 21c)
devā brahmādayaḥ smṛtāḥ	VarP 7b
devā bhāryāsamanvitāḥ	GarP 5 (= 2b)
devā manuṣyatāṃ prāptā	PadP 78a
devā muktāv api sphuṭam	VarP 49b

dveṣād āgrahiṇo harau HarV 19_1b
dveṣijīvayutaṃ cāpi SkaP 65 (= 6c)
dveṣiṇāṃ ca ramāpatau BrahP 77b
dveṣiṇāpakṛtaṃ bhavet BrāṇP 53 (= 4d)
dveṣiṇām adharam tamaḥ SkaP 65 (= 4d)
dveṣyas tv apriyamātrakṛt NārP 55d
dvaipāyanena yad buddhaṃ BrahP 1_5a
dvau nityau saṃprakīrtitau MBh 26b
dvau panthānau prakīrtitau MBh 27b
dvau prāṇau dvau ca cetanau BrāṇP 2 (= 1b)
dhanurviṣphūrjitair naṣṭo SkaP 30a
dhanyāścaryo 'ham evaiko HarV 1c
dhanyo 'sīty udito mayā HarV 1b
dharma eṣāṃ tathā bhāryā BrāṇP 95 (= 29a)
dharmaḥ satya iti prokto BrahP 28a
dharmatattvasya keśavaḥ BrāṇP 48b
dharmadehāvatārāder BhaviṣPV 26a
dharmaputrādiṣu prabhoḥ VarP 51 (= 11b)
dharmapuṣpas tv arthapattraḥ BrāṇP 21a
-dharmarūpaṃ punar vibhuḥ NārP 2 (= 6d)
dharmaś cāpi hareḥ priyaḥ BrahP 28b
dharmaś cārthaś ca kāmaś ca MBh 46a
dharmasvarūpacitratvād PadP 73a
dharmādharmaphalaṃ mṛtau MBh 15b
dharmādharmavihīno 'pi BrāṇP 48c
dharmādharmādisaṃyutāḥ VāmP 12b
dharmān adyāpi tatragaḥ BrahP 43 (= 3b)
dharmārthakāmamokṣāṇām GarP 9a
dharmārthakāmamokṣāṇāṃ VāyuP 2c
dharmopamas tv adharmo ya HarV 16a
dharṣitā nāśakan yadā NārP 3 (= 8b)
dhānājāta ivāyaṃ hi NārP 3 (= 5a)
dhānyāni yadvat khalagāni martyaḥ BrāṇP 57c
dhārako 'nyo na vidyate KūrP 32 (= 10d)
dhāraṇaṃ katham asya syād NārP 2 (= 6a)
dhāraṇād dharma ityāhur NārP 2 (= 9a)
dhārayaty aniśaṃ devo KūrP 23a
dhūmādibhāvaprāptiś ca GarP 42a
dhṛtarāṣṭraṃ ca saubalīm SkaP 22b
dhṛtarāṣṭram ajījanat SkaP 23b
dhṛtarāṣṭre mṛte sūtaḥ BrāṇP 23a

na gurur na ca dharmo 'sti VarP 22a
na ca kevalatarkeṇa BrāṇP 103_{1}c
na ca garbhe 'vasad devyā PadP 79a
na ca jñānaviparyāsād SkaP 55a
na ca tatpadam iṣyate GarP 42b
na ca tatsmṛtimātreṇa NārP 5c
na ca dadyād dharis tādṛg BrāṇP 59c
na ca māyāvinā māyā BrāṇP 103a
na calet svāt padād yasmād AgniP 25a
na ca śatrur udīritaḥ BrahVP 19b
na ca sṛṣṭyādikaṃ bhrāntir BrāṇP 33c
na ca hāpyaḥ kathaṃcana GarP 37 (= 8d)
na cāṃbāṃ grāhayāmāsa SkaP 111
na cāṇumātraṃ bhinnāni NārP 35c
na cāniṣṭaṃ guṇair eṣa VāmP 33c
na cānyadharmākaraṇād AgniP 17c
na cānyas tādṛśo vettā BrāṇP 31c
na cānyā tatra vai gatiḥ SkaP 116d
na cāpi jamadagnitaḥ MBh 42 (= 74d)
na cāpi jamadagnitaḥ PadP 79d
na cāpi rāghavāj jāto PadP 79c
na cāpi vasudevataḥ PadP 79b
na cāpi vasudevataḥ SkaP 5b
na cāpy abhedo jagatā HarV 21a
na cāpy avāntarāḥ śāpā SkaP 59 (= 5c)
na cābhakto 'pi yaḥ priyaḥ PadP 89b
na cāyogyaṃ vimukto 'pi VarP 48c
na cāsya tadadhīnatvaṃ ViṣP 5c
na caitāni vinā kaścij NārP 26a
na janmāṃśalayau vinā PadP 87d
na jānaṃs tanmataṃ param BrahP 43 (= 7b)
na jānīto hariṃ param BrahP 23d
na jigīṣukathāyāṃ tu BrāṇP 16c
na jīvam avasādayet BrahVP 34b
na jīvāpekṣayā mukhyaṃ VarP 36a
na jīveṣu guṇāḥ pūrṇā BrahP 36c
na jñāyate ca tadrūpam GarP 34c
na jñeyāḥ sarvajantubhiḥ NārP 30d
naṭavad bhagavān viṣṇuḥ SkaP 36c
na tacchāstraṃ kuvartma tat HarV 5 (= 7b)
na tataḥ paramaṃ kvacit PadP 31d

na teṣāṃ yujyate kvacit	NārP 6d
na teṣām utthitiḥ kvacit	SkaP 40d
na teṣām utthitiḥ kvāpi	NārP 50c
na tāv anye vijānanti	GarP 36 (= 4a)
na dāṃpatyād vihīyate	SkaP 105d
nadīsamudragiraya	SkaP 76a
na duḥkhaṃ kvacid iṣyate	MBh 21b
na duḥkhaṃ sahate kvacit	BrahP 68b
na duḥkhādīn kadācana	BrahVP 28d
na dṛṣṭyādau sa īśvaraḥ	GarP 30 (= 2d)
na devapadam anvicchet	BrāṇP 78a
na devotpattikāraṇam	BrāṇP 1b
na dehayogo hi janir	AgniP 4a
na dehasthāni hṛtpateḥ	KūrP 17d
na daivaṃ keśavāt param	MBh 41d
nadyaḥ kūpāḥ sarāṃsi ca	NārP 1b
na dravaṃ tīrtham ucyate	GarP 34b
na dharmādhyāḥ paraṃ sukham	MBh 48b
na nityatvaṃ kutaścana	VāyuP 5d
na niyamyaniṣedhikāḥ	BrāṇP 62b
na niṣiddhāni varteta	PadP 72a
na paraḥ kāraṇānvitaḥ	VāyuP 8d
na paraḥ saṃsṛtiṃ kvāpi	PadP 5a
na parabrahmaṇaḥ kaścid	BrāṇP 15 (= 10c)
na pāṣaṇḍī na haitukī	BrahVP 38 (= 15b)
na pramātuṃ mahābāhuḥ	MBh 42 (= 73a)
na bādhaḥ kvāpi dṛśyate	BhaviṣPV 2 (= 17a)
na bādhyaṃ dṛśyate kvacit	BhaviṣPV 2 (= 18b)
na bhayaṃ keśavasya ca	BrāṇP 63b
nabhasvato 'pi sarvāḥ syuś	SkaP 96a
na bhāratasamaṃ śāstraṃ	BrāṇP 86 (= 2a)
na bhītir brahmadarśinām	AgniP 24d
na bhedo vidyate kvacit	BrahVP 11d
na bhrāntikalpitaṃ viśvam	BrahVP 44c
na bhrāntir bhavati kvāpi	BrahVP 44c
na matsamo 'dhiko vāpi	GarP 36 (= 16a)
namas tasmai parātmane	SkaP 1d
namaste śārṅgadhāriṇe	MBh 40d
namasye prāṇam ekalam	VāyuP 3_5b
na mānatvaṃ gamiṣyati	BhaviṣPV 2 (= 15b)
na mānī mānadaḥ paraḥ	GarP 30 (= 8d)

na śakyaṃ jñātum añjasā PadP 47b
na śakyante 'mitatvataḥ BrahP 59b
na śākalyo viveda tam BrāṇP 17d
na śāsyajanavarjanāt KūrP 18d
naśiṣyamāṇaṃ svakulam PadP 14 (= 2a)
naśyaty ataḥ smṛter nāśād SkaP 55a
na śleṣaṃ yānti kānicit BhavişPV 31 (= 128b)
na saṃbhavanti yasmāt tair BrahVP 23c
na saṅgo doṣam āvahet VarP 12b
na sa bhūyo 'bhijāyate SkaP 41d
na samartho mahendro 'pi SkaP 112c
na samyak prabhavanti ca SkaP 59 (= 2d)
na samyak phalado viṣṇur BrāṇP 13 (= 11c)
na samyag vakti kutracit VarP 24b
na sa veda paraṃ viṣṇuṃ BhavişPV 3 (= 19a)
na sāmānyavacāṃsy api BrāṇP 3 (= 13b)
na sāmyaṃ jīvakṛṣṇayoḥ BrāṇP 61d
na striyo yānti puṃstvaṃ tu BhavişPV 27c
na snehabhaṅgo devyās tu BrāṇP 63a
na svataḥ śakyate kvacit GarP 30 (= 3d)
na svatas tu kathaṃcana BhavişP 10 (= 4b)
na svarūpaṃ harer etat BrahP 15a
na harer īśitā tv anyaḥ HarV 25a
na harer balam anyataḥ MBh 45d
na hi te devatāsamāḥ GarP 26_1d
na hi deśādibhiḥ kaścid VarP 45a
na hi dehādir ātmā syān BrahVP 19a
na hi doṣābhidhāyini BrāṇP 3 (= 12c)
na hi samyag udāhṛtaṃ BrāṇP 95 (= 49b)
na hi spardhādayo doṣāḥ VāmP 32c
na hīno hīnago 'pi san PadP 92b
na hy akāmaḥ kvacit kaścid BrāṇP 102c
na hy anyasyānyathābhāvo GarP 42a
na hy ānantyāt karmāṇāṃ bhoganāśaḥ BrāṇP 100d
na hy ete lokasaṃmitāḥ PadP 73d
na hrāso na ca vṛddhir vā BrahVP 29a
nākāmahatatā parā MBh 5b
nākṣajena na kenacit BrāṇP 103_1d
nākṣatramāsagaṇitaṃ SkaP 64c
nāgākāraiva raśmitvam GarP 5 (= 5c)
nāṅgīkurvanti te 'py evaṃ KūrP 31 (= 5c)

nityaṃ viṣṇum upāsate	GarP 23d
nityaṃ sarvagate viṣṇāu	ViṣP 5a
nityaṃ hīno 'khilair doṣaiḥ	KūrP 32 (= 1a)
nityaḥ paramanityaś ca	KūrP 23a
nityacaitanyarūpavān	BhaviṣP 2 (= 5b)
nityajāto hy asau hariḥ	NārP 3 (= 9d)
nityajñānasvarūpatvān	BrāṇP 76c
nityajñānasvarūpo 'sau	PadP 18a
nityajñānena siddhaṃ ca	PadP 17a
nityatīrṇāśanāyādir	PadP 59a
nityatṛptaḥ parānando	SkaP 12_1a
nityatvaṃ pūrṇatām api	BhaviṣPV 3 (= 25b)
nityatvād eva yujyate	NārP 3 (= 2b)
nityadāptasukhatvāt tu	NārP 6c
nityaduḥkhaṃ phalaṃ viduḥ	SkaP 119d
nityaduḥkhaṃ sukhojjhitam	BrahVP 38 (= 16b)
nityadṛk paramātmāsau	HarV 11a
nityanaimittikāḥ kriyāḥ	HarV 5 (= 4d)
nityapūrṇaṃ samuddiṣṭaṃ	VāmP 26c
nityapūrṇaguṇo 'pi san	KūrP 7d
nityapūrṇasukhajñapti-	SkaP 64a
nityapūrṇāni sarvaśaḥ	KūrP 17d
nityapūrṇo 'khilaguṇo	BrāṇP 105 (= 1a)
nityam eva tathābhūtān	PadP 67a
nityam eva pravāhataḥ	VarP 55 (= 4d)
nityasūryāṃśuvāriṇā	BrāṇP 36b
nityasvarūpabhūtāpi	PadP 42c
nityāḥ svābhāvikā api	BrahP 78b
nityātiśayaduḥkhinām	NārP 50d
nityānandajñānabalā	BhaviṣPV 15a
nityānandamahodadheḥ	SkaP 12_1 (= 3d)
nityānandasvarūpatvād	SkaP 36c
nityānandasvarūpiṇaḥ	BrāṇP 53 (= 4b)
nityānande ca bhoge ca	GarP 45 (= 7c)
nityānandaikabhāginaḥ	PadP 67d
nityānandaikabhoginām	HarV 2d
nityānandaikarūpiṇaḥ	MBh 42 (= 75d)
nityānandaikalakṣaṇaḥ	KūrP 23b
nityānando 'dvayo 'py evaṃ	PadP 79a
nityānitye tatas tataḥ	PadP 85d
nityāny etāni saukṣmyeṇa	BhaviṣPV 18a

nityāpratihataṃ yataḥ	SkaP 11b
nityāmṛtaḥ sa bhagavān	NārP 4c
nityā yugapad eva ca	VarP 19b
nityārūḍhaṃ cidātmakam	BhaviṣP 3d
nityāviṣṭo yatas tataḥ	BrahVP 13b
nityā vedāḥ samastāś ca	BrāṇP 104 (= 1a)
nityāvyakto yato devaḥ	BrahVP 26c
nityāstijñānagocaram	BhaviṣPV 3 (= 7d)
nityās te cetanā api	AgniP 27d
nityāheyatvahetutaḥ	BrāṇP 85b
nityāheyas tathaivānyas	BhaviṣPV 3 (= 24a)
nityodastā yogaśaktir	PadP 42a
nityoditajñānatanoḥ	GarP 18c
nityopādhyā svarūpayā	BhāgP 3b
nityo vāyur udāhṛtaḥ	KūrP 23b
nityau kālaś ca sattama	ViṣP 1b
nityau nityasukhaṃ caiva	GarP 19c
nityau svābhāvikau matau	BrahP 78d
nidrākāmādyabhāvena	BhaviṣP 2 (= 4a)
nidrā caiva sunidrā ca	PadP 54a
nidrāśanabhayaśvāsa-	NārP 38a
nindāṃ kurvanti ye 'pi ca	NārP 50b
nindāyām anyad eva tu	GarP 21b
nindyante yatrakutracit	GarP 21b
nipatanti na saṃśayaḥ	NārP 50b
nimittamātraṃ tau devau	SkaP 29c
niyataṃ cāpi tatpadam	BhaviṣPV 9b
niyataṃ pāpakarmaṣu	Upagītā 1b
niyataṃ muktidāyinī	GarP 36 (= 6d)
niyataṃ muktir āpyate	VāmP 13b
niyatā naiva kenāpi	BhaviṣPV 24a
niyatā hi harer guṇāḥ	BhaviṣPV 24b
niyatijñānam āvṛtiḥ	SkaP 81b
niyatimohanīti ca	SkaP 50b
niyatir jñānam āvṛttiḥ	SkaP 127b
niyatir mohanīti ca	SkaP 12b
-niyatyajñānabandhanān	BhaviṣPV 30 (= 83b)
niyantā ca prakāśitā	NārP 42b
-niyantā tadvaśāḥ pare	BhaviṣPV 30 (= 79d)
niyantānya itīrite	BrahVP 42 (= 2d)
niyantā rakṣitā hariḥ	BrāṇP 9 (= 9d)

nirbījas tv anyadaivataḥ	KūrP 11b
nirbhayān viṣṇunāmnaiva	PadP 3_1b
nirbhedo 'pi hariḥ svayam	GarP 13b
nirmame 'ṇḍaṃ mahattaram	BrahVP 21b
nirmalena samoṣṇena	BrāṇP 36a
nirmitānyā śavākṛtiḥ	SkaP 6d
-nirmūlanabalojjhitāḥ	NārP 3 (= 7d)
nirmūlasya ca vṛkṣasya	NārP 3 (= 4a)
nirvāṇaṃ cābhidhīyate	BrahP 14b
nirviśeṣitasūtratvaṃ	SkaP 78 (= 8a)
nivṛttaṃ muktaye tu yat	BhaviṣP 5 (= 2d)
nivṛttasarvadoṣās te	BrahVP 28a
'nivṛttāś ca vikarmaṇaḥ	NārP 49 (= 5b)
niśā sā parikīrtitā	KūrP 6b
niścayāt sādhayed arthaṃ	KūrP 20c
niścitya paramaṃ vrajet	HarV 5 (= 11d)
niṣādas tāmaso 'bhavat	KūrP 13d
niṣādo venadehataḥ	GarP 26b
niṣiddhakarma kuryuś ced	PadP 93a
niṣiddhatvān nāradīye	NārP 48
niṣedhavidhipātratvāt	ViṣP 5a
niṣedhavidhyutkramaṇāt	GarP 36 (= 5c)
niṣkāmatvāc ca yogyataḥ	BhaviṣPV 30 (= 97b)
niṣkriyākhyaḥ sadharmakaḥ	NārP 36_1b
niṣṭhāṃ tātkālikīṃ tathā	SkaP 22d
niṣphalaṃ tat tayā vinā	HarV 5 (= 6b)
niṣphalatvād udīryate	VarP 14d
niṣphalā eva niścayāt	SkaP 59 (= 5b)
niṣphalā saphalā caiva	GarP 36 (= 6a)
niṣphalaivāsure tasmāc	GarP 36 (= 5a)
nihatā yena dānavāḥ	MBh 40b
nīcatā nāsya tatkṛtā	BrahVP 13d
nīcamadhyavidāsinaḥ	BrahP 4b
nīcasyoccatayā dṛśiḥ	SkaP 69 (= 3d)
nīcānāṃ nānyathā bhavet	BhaviṣPV 30 (= 79b)
nītā harisarūpatām	BrāṇP 53 (= 3b)
nītīḥ kavayati svayam	BhaviṣPV 3 (= 12b)
nṛkarmotpattikāraṇam	BrāṇP 1d
nṛṇāṃ vedaḥ pradarśayet	BrahP 1_3 (= 1b)
nṛpādyāḥ śatadhṛtyantā	PadP 104a
nṛpāś ca manupūrvakāḥ	BrahVP 39 (= 3d)

naivānyasya ca kasyāpi GarP 31c
naivānyaiḥ sādhanair api BhavișPV 30 (= 94b)
naivāptā guṇapūrṇatā BrahVP 23d
naivāsya janakaḥ kaścin NārP 3 (= 9c)
naivāsya prākṛtā tanuḥ SkaP 5d
naivāhāryāḥ kathaṃcana KūrP 1d
naivaitad dvayam āpyate BhavișPV 30 (= 89d)
naiśvaryāṇi svakīyāni BrāṇP 48c
naiṣa bhāvayituṃ yogyaḥ KūrP 22a
naiṣāṃ bhedaḥ kathaṃcana BrāṇP 95 (= 27b)
noce rugmivadhe hariḥ BrāṇP 63d
notkrāmanti kadācana GarP 45 (= 1d)
nodabinduṃ na taṇḍulam BrahVP 38 (= 3b)
nopādānaṃ hīndriyāṇām BhavișPV 17a
nollaṅghyaḥ sarvacetanaiḥ BhavișPV 30 (= 98b)
nyagrodhaparimaṇḍalaḥ VāyuP 3b/ 3_4b
nyāsināṃ tu viśeṣataḥ NārP 51 (= 4d)
nyūnādhikyādikaṃ tathā BrāṇP 16b
pakṣān māsena vā yāti NārP 14c
pañcatvaṃ samudīritam KūrP 15d
pañcadhaiṣa hariḥ sthitaḥ GarP 5 (= 1b)
pañcapañcaiva te sarve BrahP 42c
pañcaprāṇāś ca karmaṇaḥ BhavișPV 18_1b
pañcabhūtātmakaṃ jaḍam SkaP 15d
pañcabhūtātmakaṃ sarvaṃ VāyuP 11a
pañcabhūtātmakas tathā VāmP 20b
pañcabhūtāni ceti ha NārP 41b
pañcabhūtaiś ca śabdādyair VāmP 7a
pañcabhedāṃś ca vijñāya BhavișPV 30 (= 81a)
pañcamaṃ vedam uttamam SkaP 108b
pañcarātraṃ ca bhāratam BhavișPV 29b
pañcarātraṃ ca vedāś ca BrāṇP 64 (= 6c)
pañcarātraṃ bhārataṃ ca NārP 34a
pañcarātraṃ yato 'khilam BrahVP 39 (= 6b)
pañcarātram athākhilam BrāṇP 103_1b
pañcarātravirodhiṣu BrāṇP 64 (= 4d)
pañcarātrātmakaṃ jñānaṃ BrahVP 39 (= 1c)
pañcarātrātmakatvataḥ BhavișPV 29 (= 32b)
pañcendriyābhimeyatvān MatsyaP 5a
pañcottaram athāpi ca VarP 7b
paṭṭanaṃ kīrtyate budhaiḥ SkaP 18b

pārāśaryo jātukarṇyaḥ	BrāṇP 14a
pārthānuyātam ātmānaṃ	SkaP 19a
pārtho 'pīṣat tadātmakaḥ	BhavișPV 32 (= 122b)
pālakā devatā imāḥ	NārP 2 (= 5d)
pālitāvyāhatendriyaiḥ	BrāṇP 46d
pāvanatvāt sadā śuddham	VarP 55 (= 1c)
pāṣaṇḍaṃ nirmame nṛpaḥ	BrahP 43 (= 5b)
pāṣaṇḍā iti kīrtitāḥ	NārP 48b
piṅgalāyāṃ ca vartataḥ	MBh 11b
piṇḍaṃ putrajaniṃ tathā	BhavișPV 4 (= 4b)
pitaro 'psarasāṃ śatam	BrāṇP 48d
pitāto bhagavān prabhuḥ	BrāṇP 72d
pitāmahatayānyeṣāṃ	VarP 26c
pitṛśatrusuteṣu ca	GarP 51b
pitṛhā sa prakīrtitaḥ	VāmP 2 (= 6d)
pitrā dattaṃ mahābalaḥ	BrahP 38d
pitrādiś ca yato bhavet	BrahP 48 (= 3d)
pinākīti tataḥ śrutaḥ	BrāṇP 68d
pibanti ye narā nākaṃ	BrāṇP 68a
piśācacaryām acarad	VarP 8a
piśācānāṃ tathaiva ca	BrahP 24 (= 6d)
piśācās tatpathi sthitāḥ	BhavișP 7 (= 2d)
puṃśaktyā brahmavittaye	AgniP 14d
puṃsāṃ svābhāvikā api	BhavișPV 27b
puṃsā sahaiva puṃdeha-	BhavișPV 27a
puṃso 'śubhasya kiṃ bhadraṃ	MBh 22c
puṃstvaṃ vidvadbhir ucyate	BrāṇP 70b
puṇḍarīkeṣaṇo viṣṇuḥ	SkaP 4c
puṇyapāpasamudbhavaḥ	NārP 17b
puṇyapāpādikaṃ viṣṇuḥ	BhavișP 12a
puṇyapāpādivarjitāḥ	BrahVP 28b
puṇyam apy asya naśyati	PadP 74b
putraṃ taṃ kalpayāmāsa	BrāṇP 22c
putrabhrātṛsakhitvena	VarP 33a
putrādikaṃ viparyeti	BrahP 48 (= 3c)
putrādi puṇyapāpabhyāṃ	NārP 17c
putrān prādāj janārdanaḥ	BrahVP 14d
punaḥ kaliyuge prāpta	BhavișP 7 (= 3a)
punaḥ kuryāt punaḥ svargaṃ	BrahVP 38 (= 9a)
punaḥ punaḥ kathāḥ prāhur	AgniP 9a
punaḥ punar avekṣate	PadP 17b

puruṣo 'nantaśayanaḥ	GarP 45 (= 5a)
puruṣo niyamena tu	BrahP 76b
puruṣo hṛdisthaḥ para[ma]ḥ	BrahP 30a
pulastyaḥ pulahaḥ kratuḥ	BrahP 83b
puṣpaṃ svargādayaḥ proktāḥ	VāmP 21c
pūjayāmāsa keśavaḥ	PadP 3_1d
pūjā kāryātmavedibhiḥ	PadP 39d
pūjāyā viṣamā dṛṣṭiḥ	BrahVP 35c
pūjāyai saṃprayacchanti	VāmP 27c
pūjitaḥ keśavaṃ vrajet	BrahVP 37d
pūjitas tv ayanenāsau	GarP 57a
pūjitāḥ syuḥ suravarāḥ	VāmP 27a
pūjito brahma yāti hi	BrahP 82b
pūjyatām atyayuktaṃ ca	SkaP 44c
pūjyate 'dyāpi śarvādyair	SkaP 6c
pūjyate sarvadaivataiḥ	SkaP 6b
pūjyante cāvarais te tu	GarP 45 (= 8c)
pūtanākaṃsanaraka-	GarP 33a
pūrayanti diśaḥ somaṃ	GarP 10a
pūrṇaṃ sarvottamaṃ mayā	GarP 36 (= 9d)
pūrṇaḥ svānandabhojanāt	SkaP 14b
pūrṇacitsukharūpo 'pi	SkaP 5c
pūrṇajñānaphalecchayā	PadP 72b
pūrṇajñānasvarūpataḥ	MārkP 3d
pūrṇajñānāmṛtasyāsya	BrahP 51a
pūrṇatvaṃ ca sadā viṣṇoḥ	HarV 32c
pūrṇatvaṃ sūcayed vibhoḥ	MārkP 3d
pūrṇatvāt sarvanāmakaḥ	BrāṇP 3 (= 17d)
pūrṇatvād asmināmāsau	BrāṇP 85c
pūrṇapūrṇatvahetutaḥ	BrāṇP 85d
pūrṇaprajñas tṛtīyas tu	BhaviṣPV 32 (= 118a)
pūrṇaśaktitvato hareḥ	BhaviṣPV 16b
pūrṇaśakteḥ kuto māyā	HarV 33 (= 5c)
pūrṇas tu harir evaiko	HarV 32a
-pūrṇasyānandavāridheḥ	VāmP 30b
pūrṇākhilaguṇo hy asau	BhaviṣPV 29 (= 40b)
pūrṇānandamayasyāsya	PadP 58c
pūrṇānandamayāni tu	MārkP 3b
pūrṇānando harir nānyaḥ	NārP 3 (= 9a)
pūrṇo nārāyaṇaḥ sadā	VāmP 33d
pūrṇo nityam apūrṇāś ca	BhaviṣPV 3 (= 27)

pūrtiśitṛtvadraṣṭṛtva	PadP 52c
pūrter acintyavīryo yo	SkaP 111a
pūrvaṃ ca jñānayuktās tās	SkaP 65 (= 2a)
-pūrvaṃ tatra manaḥ	ViṣP 9b
pūrvaṃ tu pauṇḍrako nāma	BrahP 43 (= 4c)
pūrvaṃ manaḥ samutpannaṃ	VāyuP 4a
pūrvaṃ layodake magnāṃ	BrāṇP 38a
pūrvakarma prayatnaṃ ca	BhaviṣPV 16a
pūrvakarmātra kāraṇam	BhaviṣP 10 (= 3b)
pūrvapūrvaṃ balīyaḥ syād	SkaP 94c
pūrvam eva janārdanaḥ	GarP 16b
pūrvam eva svabhāvataḥ	BrāṇP 91b
pūrvam evopadiṣṭo 'pi	GarP 16c
pūrvavat samudīritā	GarP 45 (= 9b)
pūrvasṛṣṭān rathāvṛttyā	GarP 27a
pūrvasmād uttarottaram	BrāṇP 9 (= 2b)
pūrvasmād uttarottaram	GarP 45 (= 8b)
-pūrvāḥ sarve 'pi sarvadā	BhaviṣPV 30 (= 99b)
pūrvāparāvirodhāya	SkaP 83c
pūrve pūrve yato viṣṇoḥ	VāmP 40a
pūrve saptarṣayaḥ smṛtāḥ	BrahP 83d
pūrvoktasyāvadhāraṇe	GarP 41d
pūrvoktau brahmakṛṣṇayoḥ	BrahVP 6d
pūrvottarāvirodhena	KūrP 20a
pṛcchato 'pi śiraḥ sadā	BrāṇP 15 (= 11b)
pṛcchanti sādhavo yasmāt	AgniP 19c
pṛcchyate satatānandāt	PadP 24c
pṛthaktvajñānavarjanāt	BrāṇP 9 (= 18d)
pṛthak pṛthak tu tretāyāṃ	PadP 101a
pṛthak sthitvā jagat pāti	BrahP 52c
pṛthag eva sthito devo	VāmP 4a
pṛthag evāham atyalpa-	BrāṇP 9 (= 12c)
pṛthagjñānaṃ tad ity āhur	GarP 23a
pṛthagdṛṣṭiḥ sa vijñeyo	BhaviṣP 8c
pṛthag vaktuṃ guṇās tasya	BrahP 59a
pṛthag vakṣye na tān aham	GarP 9d
pṛthaṅnāmāni yasmāt tad-	BrāṇP 2 (= 6c)
pṛthivī dharmamūrdhani	MBh 31a
pṛthivīlokasantyāgo	SkaP 36a
pṛthivyāṃ nānyavarṣagāḥ	BrāṇP 49
pṛthivyādi prakṛtyantaṃ	SkaP 91a

pṛthivyādyabhimāninyo	BhaviṣP 11 (= 1a)
pṛthunā svargatiṃ gataḥ	BrāṇP 42b
pṛthū rāmam anuvrataḥ	BrāṇP 44d
pṛthau ca kṛtavīryaje	SkaP 52d
pṛthvādyāś cakravartinaḥ	VarP 51 (= 9b)
peśaskṛdrūpatāṃ kīṭo	BrāṇP 53 (= 2a)
paurvāparyaṃ yato naiva	BrahP 9_1a
'py atīva haritoṣaṇaḥ	PadP 80d
'py aniruddho vināyakaḥ	VarP 51 (= 8d)
'py asnehī tatkṛtānukṛt	NārP 55b
'py uccanīcādi pūrvavat	GarP 19b
'py etāvan naiva vismaret	BhaviṣPV 23d
prakarṣeṇa karoti yat	ViṣP 8 (= 1d)
prakārāṇāṃ ca kāraṇam	BhaviṣPV 11b
prakāśaṃ kuru cātmānam	BrāṇP 94c
prakāśayate saiveyaṃ	BrāṇP 105 (= 5a)
prakāśavadbhuvo devā	VarP 20a
prakṛtiṃ tu vikāriṇīm	NārP 28b
prakṛtiṃ dehabhedataḥ	NārP 11d
prakṛtiḥ kāla eva ca	KūrP 23d
prakṛtiḥ puruṣaś ceti	BrāṇP 70c
prakṛtiḥ puruṣaś caiva	ViṣP 1a
prakṛtiḥ prāṇa eva ca	BrahP 15b
prakṛtir jaḍarūpikā	SkaP 88b
prakṛtir na hares tanuḥ	VarP 21d
prakṛtir nāma sā jñeyā	ViṣP 8 (= 1c)
prakṛtir vāsanety evam	SkaP 50c
prakṛtir vāsanety evam	SkaP 12c
prakṛtiś ca maheśvaraḥ	MatsyaP 20b
prakṛtiś ca samāsamā	VarP 46d
prakṛtiś cābhidhīyate	NārP 28d
prakṛtis teṣu sarvaśaḥ	VāyuP 1b
prakṛtis trividhā matā	HarV 9b
prakṛtī dve tu devasya	NārP 41a
prakṛteḥ prākṛtasyāpi	BhaviṣPV 24c
prakṛter deśakālataḥ	BrahVP 12_1b
prakṛter vikāratā vā-	BrāṇP 12 (= 2a)
prakṛtes tu svatantratā	AgniP 7d
prakṛtau karaṇātītāḥ	VāyuP 1c
prakṛtyabhinnatā vāpi	BrāṇP 12 (= 3a)
prakṛtyā ca vivarjitāḥ	GarP 6b

praviśya ca bahirgatāḥ GarP 45 (= 9d)
praviśya sarge tu punaḥ GarP 19c
praviśya hariḥ svayam VahniP 16
praviśyaikatvam āgataḥ SkaP 22d
praviṣṭatvāc charīreṣu BrāṇP 57a
praviṣṭo 'nyo na vidyate KūrP 32 (= 9b)
pravṛttaṃ karma ceṣyate BhaviṣP 5 (= 1d)
pravṛttaye prakṛtigaṃ BrahP 84c
pravṛtto duṣṭanidhane BrāṇP 95 (= 22a)
pravṛttyādiprakāśanam BrahP 10b
praveśād yatibhiḥ kāryā BrāṇP 64 (= 2c)
praveśo nirgamaś caiva BrāṇP 87a
-praśno lokasukhekṣayā NārP 6b
praśrayeṇa ca kīrtyā ca BrāṇP 44c
prasanne keśave bhavet VarP 24b
prasanno bhaktavatsalaḥ PadP 3_1b
prasādaḥ śravaṇādibhiḥ NārP 26b
prasādas tūttamo mataḥ NārP 26d
- prasādāt kurute 'niśam VāyuP 3_3b
prasādāt tv adhamād viṣṇoḥ NārP 26a
-prasādāt sāttvikaṃ sukham PadP 95b
prasādād iti vā bhavet GarP 38 (= 4d)
prasādād vāsudevasya MatsyaP 15c
prasiddhaṃ sarvavedataḥ HarV 32d
prasiddho 'bhūta eva ca BrahP 8b
prasthasya nāḍīpātrasya PadP 33a
prahetir hetir eva ca BrāṇP 98d
prahlādaṃ preṣayat tadā BrāṇP 55d
prahlādād uttamaḥ ko nu SkaP 63c
prahlāde caiva vātsalya- BrāṇP 55a
prahlādo nityabhaktimān BrāṇP 56d
prākṛtair dṛśyamānaṃ tu GarP 34a
prācurye tu mayaḍ yataḥ PadP 29b
prāṇaṃ daśavidhaṃ tathā GarP 17b
prāṇaṃ dhārayate yasmāt SkaP 26a
prāṇaḥ prāṇeśvaro hariḥ HarV 25d
prāṇavidyām avāpyāsmāt PadP 76c
prāṇas tv ababhimānavān BrāṇP 83b
prāṇasyāpi balapradam HarV 24d
praṇasyaiva mano nityaṃ VāyuP 3_3a
prāṇasyaiva vaśe 'sthitāḥ HarV 25b

priyaś ca viṣṇoḥ sarvebhyas	BrāṇP 95 (= 14c)
priyo viṣṇos tu kaścana	PadP 41d
prītiyogān naiva tasya	BhaviṣPV 3 (= 17c)
prītir abhyadikā hareḥ	VarP 51 (= 11d)
prītir mama mahīyasī	BrahP 77b
prīto bhavati vai nityaṃ	PadP 55a
prītyā muktau sukhonnatiḥ	BhaviṣP 5 (= 3d)
prītyaiva śakram āviṣṭo	BrāṇP 3 (= 7a)
prīyante gurupūjayā	SkaP 69 (= 6d)
pretya saṃbhūtikartā hi	NārP 3 (= 6c)
-prerakaḥ samudāhṛtaḥ	GarP 38 (= 5b)
preraṇād uśanā smṛtaḥ	BhaviṣPV 3 (= 12d)
prerayaty atra kañcana	BrahP 1_3 (= 1d)
prerayan manumānasam	BhaviṣPV 3 (= 10d)
preritaḥ saṃsṛtiṃ vrajet	PadP 18d
prerito viṣṇulokaṃ ca	BrāṇP 6c
preṣayāmāsa ca harir	PadP 14 (= 4c)
proktaṃ vājasaneyakam	VarP 1b
proktam artham ṛte tv iti	PadP 8b
procya tattvam aśeṣena	PadP 14 (= 7a)
procyate bhagavān viṣṇur	BrāṇP 66c
procyate viṣṇur evaikaḥ	BrahP 57c
procyante jñānibhis tataḥ	BrahP 24 (= 3b)
procyante brahmarūpeṇa	BhaviṣPV 14c
procyamānaṃ nibodha me	BrahP 69d
provāca jagadīśvaraḥ	SkaP 74d
provāca brahmaṇe vidyāḥ	PadP 102b
phalaṃ kuryād viphalaṃ prāyaśaś ca	BrāṇP 100d
-phalaṃ jīvabhṛtis tathā	PadP 7d
phalaṃ mokṣa udāhṛtaḥ	VāmP 21d
phalakartṛtvato hariḥ	MBh 9b
phaladātṛ bhaviṣyati	NārP 16d
phaladātrā tu bāhyena	BrahP 53c
phalado 'taḥ samo hariḥ	PadP 89d
phalabhogasya darśanāt	BhaviṣPV 2 (= 7d)
phalānāṃ ca vivarjanāt	PadP 12b
phenena vadham asya tu	AgniP 10d
phene vajraṃ samāveśya	AgniP 10a
baddhaḥ śakrajitetyādi	MBh 42 (= 77c)
baddhānāṃ muktigānāṃ vā	BrāṇP 12 (= 14a)
baddhyate naiva kenacit	MBh 42 (= 75b)

bṛhattvāt sarvavarṇānāṃ BrāṇP 13a (= 1a)
bṛhat pūrṇaguṇatvāc ca KūrP 32 (= 7a)
bṛhatpūrṇo yataḥ sadā BrāṇP 85b
bauddhapāśupatādyās tu NārP 48a
brahmacaryam apālayat BrahP 3 (= 2b)
brahmacarye sthito vibhuḥ BrahP 3 (= 1d)
brahmacārivapuḥ svayam SkaP 74b
brahmacāryapy pravrajet NārP 36_1d
brahmajas tu hiraṇyākhyaḥ BrāṇP 38a
brahmajātiṃ vinā kvacit VāmP 2 (= 4b)
brahmajñānasutarpitāḥ BhavişPV 25b
brahmajñānāt samagratvaṃ BhavişPV 3 (= 1c)
brahmaṇaḥ padmabhūr iti BrahP 61b
brahmaṇaḥ prathame kalpe BrāṇP 98a
brahmaṇaḥ śaṅkarād vāpi SkaP 44c
brahmaṇaḥ sannidhir bhavet BrāṇP 13 (= 7b)
brahmaṇaḥ sarvadevatāḥ GarP 36 (= 13b)
brahmaṇaś ca tathānyeṣāṃ SkaP 48c
brahmaṇaś ca yathākramam SkaP 59 (= 6b)
brahmaṇas tapataḥ pūrvaṃ SkaP 29a
brahmaṇā kālanāmnā tu BrahP 26a
brahmaṇā ca paraṃ gatāḥ VāyuP 12d
brahmaṇāttam idaṃ sarvaṃ BrahP 55a
brahmaṇā nāradāya ca BrāṇP 96
brahmaṇā parameśvaraḥ BhavişPV 20b
brahmaṇā me piteti ca VarP 26b
brahmaṇā vātha rudreṇa BrāṇP 12 (= 15a)
brahmaṇā saha saṃprāpte GarP 44a
brahmaṇā svīkṛtās tāś ca BrāṇP 101c
brahmaṇi brahmarūpaḥ sa VāmP 4c
brahmaṇi stho 'sṛjad viṣṇuḥ BrahP 52a
brahmaṇe viṣṇur avyayaḥ HarV 1b
brahmaṇo 'ṅkagato haraḥ PadP 90b
brahmaṇo 'nantarudrayoḥ BrāṇP 12 (= 6d)
brahmaṇo 'pi hy amuktasya MBh 5a
brahmaṇo vidhicoditā BrahP 72b
brahmaṇo 'heyatāṃ sadā BrahP 1_4b
brahmaṇy anante garuḍe SkaP 52a
brahmatarkaṃ ca mīmāṃsāṃ NārP 48a
brahmatarkas tarkaśāstraṃ NārP 48a
brahmatvaṃ bṛṃhitatvaṃ syāj SkaP 125a

brahmā caiva tataḥ svayam	SkaP 32 (= 5d)
brahmā jajñe caturmukhaḥ	VāmP 2 (= 1b)
brahmāṇaṃ prāviśad viṣṇuḥ	BrahP 22_1a
brahmāṇam abhajad brahma	SkaP 61a
brahmāṇam asṛjat prabhuḥ	BrahVP 21d
brahmāṇḍe hariṇa svayam	BrāṇP 95 (= 49b)
brahmā tac cāharāditvaṃ	KūrP 8c
brahmā tuṣṭava sāmaraḥ	BhaviṣP 96 (= 2b)
brahmātmako yato vāyuḥ	BrāṇP 95 (= 34a)
brahmā dakṣo manuḥ pṛthuḥ	BrahVP 17b
brahmā dadarśa tapasā	GarP 15c
brahmādayaḥ krameṇaiva	BrahP 70c
brahmādayaś ca tatkīrtiṃ	GarP 31c
brahmādayo hi bhūtāni	MBh 6a
brahmādiguṇavaiśeṣyād	VarP 41a
brahmādijīvadehās tu	VarP 18a
brahmādibhaktikoṭyaṃśād	GarP 31a
brahmādibhāvo viṣṇos tu	VāmP 15a
brahmādibhiḥ sargakarī	BhaviṣPV 8a
brahmādibhyaś ca devebhyo	PadP 9c
brahmādimānuṣāntānāṃ	VarP 47c
brahmādisarvamanasāṃ	VarP 55 (= 5a)
brahmādisthāvarāntakaiḥ	BrāṇP 64 (= 5b)
brahmādīnāṃ ca muktānāṃ	VarP 57a
brahmādīnāṃ prakāśitam	BrāṇP 95 (= 11d)
brahmādīnāṃ viśeṣataḥ	GarP 24d
brahmādīnāṃ sūpapannā	PadP 70c
brahmādīn manyate hariḥ	SkaP 67d
brahmādeḥ sāmyam eva vā	KūrP 31 (= 9b)
brahmādeḥ sāmyam eva vā	BrāṇP 12 (= 12d)
brahmāder nindanāya ca	GarP 31b
brahmāder viṣṇvadhīnatva-	GarP 31c
brahmā devaiḥ parivṛtaḥ	GarP 19a
brahmādyabhedaḥ sāmyaṃ vā	BhaviṣPV 29 (= 41a)
brahmādyas tv asamāḥ proktāḥ	VarP 46c
brahmādyāḥ sarva eva hi	BrāṇP 4b
brahmādyā bodhitāḥ sarve	BrāṇP 12 (= 26a)
brahmādyā muktabandhanāḥ	BrāṇP 28b
brahmādyāś ca nirāśiṣaḥ	GarP 31d
brahmādyāś caiva tanmateḥ	BrāṇP 39b
brahmādyāś caiva devatāḥ	BrāṇP 95 (= 30b)

brahmādyās tatpriyāḥ smṛtāḥ PadP 21b
brahmādyās tadavāntarāḥ PadP 66d
brahmādyās tūrdhvalokagāḥ BrāṇP 15 (= 6d)
brahmādyaiḥ prārthito viṣṇur NārP 30a
brahmādyair arthitaḥ prādāt BhaviṣPV 4 (= 6c)
brahmādyaiś caiva saṃyutam GarP 15b
brahmādyais tan na buddhyate BrahP 1_5b
brahmādhikaś ca devebhyaḥ BrāṇP 95c
brahmādhir muktigāminām BrāṇP 15 (= 9b)
brahmā nārāyaṇasya ca BrahP 34d
brahmāpaśyac caturmukhaḥ BrāṇP 88b
brahmāpaśyat tathātmānaṃ BrāṇP 37c
brahmāpi tan na jānāti UpanārP 1a
brahmāpi sarvadātmānam BhaviṣPV 3 (= 3a)
brahmā provāca sattamaḥ GarP 38 (= 3b)
brahmā brahmābhavat svayam BrāṇP 3 (= 22b)
brahmā śubhacaturmukhaḥ BrāṇP 13 (= 3d)
brahmā sādir udāhṛtaḥ SkaP 27d
brahmāstrābhyāṃ sutāpitāḥ SkaP 8b
brahmā sthānu [ity ārabhya] MBh 28a
brahmāsmīti vicintanam BrahP 48 (= 5b)
brahmāsmīty ucyate viṣṇur BrāṇP 85a
brahmā hi sthiracidrūpo HarV 34a
brahmāhīnatvato haraḥ BrahP 22b
brahmedaṃ jagad ity api GarP 42d
brahmeśānādayaḥ surāḥ BrahP 56b
brahmeśānādayaḥ surāḥ NārP 32b
brahmeśānādayaḥ surāḥ SkaP 80b
brahmeśānādibhiḥ sarvaiḥ MBh 43a
brahmeśānādibhir devair SkaP 58a
brahmeśendrādisannāmnāṃ PadP 52a
brahmainaṃ paśyati sphuṭam HarV 34d
brahmaiva ca caturmukhaḥ BrahP 66d
brāhmaṇaḥ parikīrtitaḥ BrāṇP 13 (= 13b)
brāhmaṇāc ca paro rājā VāmP 2 (= 4c)
brāhmaṇānām apīḍāyai BrāṇP 59c
brāhmaṇān vandayīta ca VāmP 2b
brāhmaṇena sahaivāste BrāṇP 13 (= 3c)
brāhmaṇeṣv api kathyate BrāṇP 82d
brāhmaṇo mukham ity eva BrahP 13a
brāhmaṇo rājasūyinam VāmP 2 (= 5b)

brāhmā viṣṇoḥ suto ’grajaḥ BrāṇP 98d
brāhmī daivī ca kārmikī NārP 48d
brūyur arthavatīṃ vācaṃ PadP 78a
brūyur nānyaṃ kataṃcana BrāṇP 81d
brūyuś cānye kvacit tat tu KūrP 7a
bhaktaṃ viṣṇur vimocayet SkaP 65 (= 6d)
bhaktaḥ kutra ca mucyate BrahVP 36b
bhaktasyāto nāmakīrtiḥ NārP 16c
bhaktasyānyasya na kvacit SkaP 43b
bhaktiṃ yogyāṃ vinā kvacit PadP 51b
bhaktijñāne na cānyathā BrāṇP 95 (= 18b)
bhaktijñānena ye harim BrahVP 31b
bhaktidveṣayutāś ca syur BrahVP 10c
bhaktipūrvam avekṣante BrahVP 10c
bhaktibhāgī pṛthaṅ muktim SkaP 65 (= 5c)
bhaktimadbhiḥ suniṣṭhitaiḥ BrāṇP 103_1b
bhaktimān sa vimucyate BhaviṣP 1d
bhaktir asty eva keśave PadP 43b
bhaktir jñeyā na cānyataḥ VarP 28b
bhaktiś cānantakālīnā BrāṇP 80c
bhaktis tayā punar jñāne VarP 54a
bhaktis tu tāratamyena SkaP 69 (= 8a)
bhaktis tv ekā vimuktaye BhaviṣPV 30 (= 99b)
bhaktair eva na cānyathā BrāṇP 103_1b
bhaktyā kevalayaiva tu PadP 51d
bhaktyādīnām anāditaḥ PadP 70b
bhaktyādyā iti niścayaḥ BrāṇP 95 (= 36d)
bhaktyādyāḥ strīṣu nityaśaḥ BrāṇP 95 (= 36b)
bhaktyādyāḥ strīṣu yat tataḥ BrāṇP 95d
bhaktyā mṛtyor amucyata NārP 16b
bhaktyā yajñais tathaiva ca VarP 59b
bhaktyā viṣṇoḥ prasādakṛt SkaP 65 (= 6b)
bhaktyā hi nityakāmitvaṃ PadP 51a
bhaktyudrekād akāmanāt AgniP 23b
bhagavatkāryasādhakaḥ BhaviṣPV 32 (= 118d)
bhagavatpakṣapātitā SkaP 55b
bhagavatpadanaukā yā BrahP 46a
bhagavatpādapoto ’sau VāmP 25a
bhagavaddarśanād yasya BhaviṣP 8a
bhagavantaṃ vinānyatra BrahP 10a
bhagavantaṃ hariṃ prabhum GarP 15d

bhārataṃ cāpi kṛtavān SkaP 108a
bhārataṃ pañcarātraṃ ca BhaviṣP 10 (= 1c)
bhārataṃ pañcarātrakam SkaP 82b
bhārataṃ pravadanti hi UpanārP 1d
bhārataṃ brāhmaṇādīnāṃ SkaP 16a
bhārataṃ sa cakāra ha NārP 30b
bhārataṃ sarvavedāś ca BrāṇP 86 (= 2c)
bhārataṃ sarvavedāś ca BrāṇP 95 (= 9a)
bhārataṃ sarvaśāstreṣu KūrP 30_2a
bhāratākhyāni yānīha BrāṇP 21c
bhāratān na vimuktaye PadP 27d
bhāratān na virāgāya PadP 27c
bhāratān nādhikaṃ viṣṇor PadP 27a
bhāratārthavinirṇayaḥ GarP 8b
bhārate gītikā varā KūrP 30_2b
bhārate nirṇayoditaḥ BhaviṣPV 32 (= 112d)
bhārate yaśa ūcivān BrāṇP 95 (= 13b)
bhāratokto yathārthataḥ BhaviṣPV 32 (= 117d)
bhārahārārtham udyamāt AgniP 24b
bhārādhikyenodakena PadP 33c
bhāryā nārāyanasya yā ViṣP 8 (= 1b)
bhāvarūpasthiratvāder BhaviṣPV 2 (= 6a)
bhāvāt sa parameśvaraḥ HarV 15d
bhāvābhāvaniyantā hi PadP 85a
bhāvābhāvamataṃ tathā BhaviṣPV 2 (= 12b)
bhāvābhāvātmatā sākaṃ BhaviṣPV 2 (= 5a)
bhāvitvāc caiva kāryasya BrahVP 14a
-bhāve 'nyaniyater dhruvam HarV 13b
bhāvo bhaktiḥ samuddiṣṭas NrasiṃhaP 1a
bhāvyo hi taṃ vinā naiva GarP 37 (= 6c)
bhāṣās tu trividhās tatra BhaviṣPV 32 (= 114a)
bhāsate kiṃcid aśrutam HarV 28b
bhāsayīta virāgavat PadP 26b
bhidā yadi na dṛśyeta BrāṇP 43a
bhidyate parvatair andhe BrāṇP 15 (= 11c)
bhinnaṃ padmam abhūd dhareḥ PadP 30b
bhinnatvagrudhirasravaḥ MBh 42 (= 78b)
bhinnatvād iti sūribhiḥ SkaP 69 (= 1d)
bhinnasyābhedato dṛṣṭir SkaP 69 (= 1a)
bhinnasvarūpaṃ brahmādyā GarP 25c
bhinnasvarūpam abhidaṃ GarP 25a

bhūmir ity eva kathyate ViṣP 8 (= 3d)
bhūmau tat pṛthunā sarvaṃ BhaviṣP 7 (= 2c)
bhūyād viṣṇuparāyaṇam BrahP 60d
bhūrādyāś ca mukhatrayāt BrahP 27b
bhūrīṇi vā mām abhiyānti saṅkhye BrāṇP 57b
bhūr daityānām athāparā ViṣP 8 (= 5d)
bhṛgur adhvaryur abhavad BrāṇP 3 (= 2a)
bhṛgvādibhyas tathaiva ca PadP 9d
bhṛto jāto dvayor yataḥ PadP 45b
bhṛtyo veda na cātmanaḥ SkaP 57b
bhedaṃ jīveśayor api BhaviṣP 1b
bhedaṃ paśyati yaḥ kvacit VarP 51 (= 1d)
bhedaṃ brahmānyavastunoḥ GarP 23b
bhedaḥ svābhāvikas tataḥ NārP 52d
bhedajñānaṃ vininditam SkaP 69 (= 2b)
bhedajñānam iti proktaṃ SkaP 69 (= 5c)
bhedadṛṣṭiś ca saṅkaraḥ BhaviṣPV 26b
bhedadṛṣṭyābhimānena BrāṇP 28c
bhedadṛṣṭyābhimānena VāyuP 3_1a
bhedamoha iti proktaḥ SkaP 39c
bhedavaktā harer priyaḥ PadP 41b
bhedas tasyāvatāreṣu SkaP 39c
bhedasya paramārthatām GarP 23d
bhedābhedavidām api NārP 50b
bhedābhedena darśanāt BrāṇP 10b
bhedābhedau ca yaḥ paśyet VarP 51 (= 2a)
bhedābhedau na mukhyataḥ VarP 33d
bhedena jīvān anyonyaṃ GarP 6c
-bhedena trividhaṃ matam BrahP 42b
bhedena darśanād vāpi BrāṇP 10a
bhedeneśaṃ guṇaiḥ saha GarP 6b
bhedenaiva jagat sarvaṃ GarP 6a
bhede naiva na vai tasmāt PadP 41c
bhedenaiva parasparam PadP 94 (= 2d)
bhede 'pi viśeṣo 'sti VarP 51a
bhedo jīveśayor api BrāṇP 12 (= 19d)
bhedo vā viṣṇurūpeṣu BrāṇP 12 (= 12a)
bheryā khyāpayato 'niśam BhaviṣP 7 (= 1d)
bhoktā tayoś cetanakaḥ śarīrī MBh 49d
bhoktṛtvaṃ sukhaduḥkhānāṃ BhaviṣPV 8c
bhoktṛtvapratiṣedhanam SkaP 14d

madanantaram eva tu	GarP 36 (= 10b)
madupādhitayā tāṃś ca	NārP 43c
maddeha iti darśanāt	BhavişPV 5 (= 5d)
madbhaktānām anantatā	NārP 45b
madbhaktiś ca viraktis tad-	NārP 36_1c
madvaśāḥ sarva eveti	SkaP 67c
madhukaiṭabhayoś caiva	BrāṇP 54a
madhutvaṃ prāpitaḥ saṃvid-	BrāṇP 9 (= 17a)
madhyamāṃ gatim evāpur	GarP 33a
madhyamāj janalokādir	NārP 26c
madhyamā mānuṣā ye tu	BhavişPV 30 (= 87a)
madhyamo jñānasaṃpattyā	NārP 26c
madhyamo vāyur evaika	BrāṇP 2 (= 3a)
madhyastha iti vijñeyaḥ	NārP 55a
madhyā rājasarājasāḥ	SkaP 32 (= 2d)
madhyoccādivibhedataḥ	VarP 41d
mana eva na saṃśayaḥ	BrahVP 34d
mana eva manuṣyāṇāṃ	BrahVP 34a
manaḥ paraṃ kāraṇam āmananti	BrahVP 34a
manaḥprasādanārthaṃ hi	VarP 45c
manaḥ saktiṃ vrajed yadi	BrāṇP 48d
manavo bodhavaiśeṣyād	ViṣP 7a
manaś ca pañca bhūtāni	BrahP 15c
manasaś cāpy acālanam	BrāṇP 79b
manasas tv aniruddhaś ca	VarP 10a
manasā dehato 'pi vā	VarP 9b
manasā samudīrayet	HarV 5 (= 3d)
manasā saha tat punaḥ	BrahP 42d
manasi vyaktatāṃ yāmi	MBh 17a
manasi sthitaḥ śivaś ca	GarP 5 (= 6a)
manaso dveṣarāgābhyāṃ	NārP 17a
manaso niyamādibhiḥ	KūrP 17b
manastattvāc ca khādikam	SkaP 101b
manastham upagacchati	VāmP 7d
manasthito harir nityaṃ	VarP 5a
manuputrāś ca ṛṣayaḥ	BrāṇP 95 (= 29c)
manur eṣo 'vabodhatvān	BhavişPV 3 (= 10a)
manuṣyapitṛpakṣiṣu	SkaP 78 (= 12b)
manuṣyāṇāṃ vimiśritam	BhavişPV 15b
manogatāṃs tu saṃskārān	BrāṇP 74a
mano jitaṃ tadā bandhuḥ	BrahVP 34d

mām ehi jñānadānāyety	SkaP 121c
māyayā darśayen nityam	PadP 55_1c
māyā cāsmād api sraiṣṭhyaṃ	PadP 3_1c
māyā tu mahimā proktā	PadP 29a
māyādehāḥ prakīrtitāḥ	VarP 18b
māyāviḍaṃbanam avaihi yathā naṭasya	SkaP 36 (= 3c)
māyeti jñānanāma syān	VarP 21a
māyeti prakṛtis tathā	VarP 21b
māruty eva yataś ceṣṭā	BrāṇP 91c
mārkaṇḍeyasamāsyayā	BrāṇP 95 (= 48b)
māsaiḥ parivṛtena ha	GarP 57b
māhātmyajñānapūrvas tu	BhavișPV 30 (= 85a)
māhātmyasūcanārthāya	SkaP 110c
mitākṣaraṃ ślokavācyam	BrāṇP 18c
mitraṃ me dakṣiṇā rāmā	HarV 1d
mitraṃ vadhādikṛd arir	NārP 55c
mitram ity abhidhīyate	MBh 1b
mitraś ca varuṇaś cātho	BrāṇP 98c
mitho nityaṃ svarūpataḥ	BhavișPV 6d
mithyā jagad idaṃ sarvaṃ	BrahVP 42 (= 1c)
mithyājñānaṃ pṛthagjñānam	GarP 22a
mithyātvaṃ ca kutas tasya	VarP 27c
mithyātvaṃ jagato 'pi vā	BrāṇP 12 (= 3d)
mithyātvān neśvaro 'syāsti	BrahVP 42 (= 2a)
mithyādarśanadoṣena	BrāṇP 105 (= 7c)
minoti trāyate ceti	MBh 1a
miśram eva yathā bhavet	SkaP 98b
mīmāṃsā trividhā proktā	NārP 48c
mīmāṃsā dharma eva ca	PadP 2b
mīmāṃsābhiś ca niścitam	BhavișPV 4 (= 10b)
mukta eva hi tattvadṛk	NārP 54b
muktajīve sthitaṃ viṣṇuṃ	VarP 56a
muktavāyvādibhir viṣṇum	BrāṇP 34a
-muktaś cety abhidhīyate	BhavișP 5b
muktas tasya ca muktas tu	BrāṇP 15 (= 2a)
muktasya tu vikarmaṇaḥ	AgniP 16b
muktasyāpi hareḥ prītiḥ	VāmP 16a
muktasyaiva tathāpi tu	PadP 87b
muktasyaiva turīyakaḥ	BrāṇP 97b
muktā api yato 'khilāḥ	BrāṇP 6d
muktāḥ paśyanti sarvaśaḥ	GarP 6d

mokṣe 'dhikasukhāptaye	BrāṇP 3 (= 15b)
mokṣo jñānaṃ ca kramaśo	BhaviṣPV 30 (= 78c)
mokṣopāyo yoga iti	AgniP 21a
mokṣo brahmādinām api	BrāṇP 12 (= 19b)
mocayiṣye tatas tv aham	BrāṇP 53 (= 6d)
modate modanīyaṃ taṃ	VarP 56c
modaty eṣa sadā bhūtair	MBh 42 (= 72c)
modanta iti hi śrutiḥ	PadP 104d
mohanāya ca daityānāṃ	GarP 31a
mohanārthaṃ dānavānāṃ	BrāṇP 22a
mohanārthaṃ durātmanām	BrahP 9_1d
moham āpnoty asaṃśayam	SkaP 115b
mohayan māyayā jagat	BrāṇP 60b
mohaśāstrāṇi kāraya	BrāṇP 94d
mohaś caiva viparyayaḥ	MBh 39b
mohas tu pariśeṣataḥ	VarP 40b
mohād yanmāyayā nityaṃ	BrahP 48 (= 2c)
-mohāya tad udāhṛtam	BhaviṣPV 29 (= 46d)
mohāyānyad vaco bhavet	BrahVP 10d
mohāyāsurajanmanām	VarP 10d
mohāyaiteṣu bhinnatā	VarP 15d
mohāyaiva vinirdiśet	BrāṇP 64 (= 8d)
mohāyaiṣāṃ prasiddhaye	PadP 23d
mohārthānāṃ ca saṃśayam	BhaviṣPV 29 (= 43b)
mohārthāny anyaśāstrāṇi	BhaviṣPV 29 (= 34a)
moho 'nye tu tadāgrahāḥ	HarV 8b
mauktānāṃ deva āśrayaḥ	BrāṇP 15 (= 7b)
mauktānām antarikṣagāḥ	BrāṇP 15 (= 2d)
mauktānām indra āśrayaḥ	BrāṇP 15 (= 5d)
mausalaṃ jñānasantatyā	GarP 16c
mriya ityādikaḥ sadā	BrahP 48 (= 1d)
mriyate kuta eva tu	MBh 42b (= 75b)
mriyamāṇaśarīriṇam	BrāṇP 93b
ya īśena bhidāṃ vadet	BrahP 53d
ya etadanyathā brūyus	BhaviṣPV 1a
ya evaṃ veda tattvavit	MBh 6d
yaḥ kṣatriyo brāhmaṇahā	VāmP 2 (= 6c)
yaḥ paśyati surādiṃś ca	HarV 22c
yaḥ paśyet sthirayā buddhyā	BhaviṣP 1c
yaḥ prāṇadhāraṇaṃ prāṇa-	VāyuP 3_3a
yaḥ sadā saṃsmared yogī	SkaP 41c

yaḥ sthāṇoḥ sthāṇutāṃ prādād BrahP 3 (= 1c)
yac ca paśyati tṛptaḥ saṃs PadP 75c
yac cānukūlam etasya SkaP 82a
yacchaktyekāṃśasaṃbhūtaṃ BrahP 2a
yacchatv ity atrir aicchata BrahVP 14d
yajanti tāṃś ca kāritvād PadP 101c
yajanti devaiḥ saha ye kṛte janāḥ BrāṇP 99b
yajante devatāḥ gaṇāḥ PadP 101b
yajante 'nyadevatāḥ BrahVP 42 (= 5d)
yajjātaṃ jagad īdṛśam SkaP 12_1 (= 1d)
yajña indrapade sthitaḥ VarP 25b
yajñaśabdoditau dvau tu PadP 21_1a
yajñāṃś ca kurute vibhuḥ BhavișPV 4 (= 2d)
yajñāṅgatvena bhaktitaḥ BrāṇP 3 (= 5d)
yajñādīn devatādīnām BhavișPV 4 (= 6a)
yajñeśatvāt svayaṃ viṣṇur PadP 22c
yajñeṣūpakṛtaṃ yataḥ BrāṇP 35b
yajñopayogaṃ ca satām BrahP 24 (= 2c)
yajño rucisutaḥ smṛtaḥ PadP 22d
yata evaṃ trayo 'vasthā VarP 40a
yata eva janārdanaḥ KūrP 29d
yata eva tadājñāyā BhavișP 13d
yata eva pravartate KūrP 28b
yataḥ kaviḥ sa kāmasya BhavișPV 3 (= 12c)
yataḥ kṛṣṇavaśe sarve BrāṇP 95 (= 12a)
yataḥ pūrṇaguṇaḥ prabhuḥ PadP 91b
yataḥ pratyakṣānumābhyāṃ PadP 32c
yataḥ prāptam ivāśeṣaṃ GarP 36 (= 10c)
yataḥ sarvaṃ jagad vyāpya VāyuP 10a
yataḥ sarvasya tenāhaṃ NārP 42c
yataḥ svapakṣaprāmāṇyaṃ BhavișPV 2 (= 3c)
yatante kecid eva tu PadP 86b
yatante śubhakarmasu GarP 11d
yatas tasyāpi kāmasya MBh 5c
yatas tāvan na tūbhayam PadP 19b
yatas tā hariṇā dṛṣṭāḥ BrāṇP 104 (= 4a)
yatas teṣāṃ niyāmakaḥ BrāṇP 9 (= 6b)
yatas te sarvavedakāḥ SkaP 99d
yatas triguṇavarjitaḥ NārP 21d
yatīnāṃ gatir uttamā BhavișPV 9d
yatīnāṃ dhruvalokastho BrāṇP 30a

yāti tat paramaṃ padam	BrāṇP 20d
yāti nānyaḥ kathaṃcana	HarV 5 (= 6d)
yāti yāvad dharer vaśe	BrahVP 38 (= 9b)
yādāṃsi sāgare yadvat	BrahVP 6c
yāni tīrthādivākyāni	NārP 36a
yāni vedavacāṃsy api	BhavișPV 29 (= 36b)
yānti kālāntare pare	VāmP 6b
yānti kiṃstughnakeśavam	BrāṇP 26d
yānti teṣām anindakāḥ	KūrP 31 (= 1d)
yānti pūrvāṇy uttarāṇi	BhavișPV 31 (= 128a)
yānti brahmavaśāḥ sadā	PadP 7d
yānti viṣṇubahirmukhāḥ	NārP 49 (= 6d)
yānti strītvaṃ pumāṃso 'pi	BhavișPV 27a
yānti svargaṃ tataḥ kṣipraṃ	NārP 49 (= 6a)
yānty ādhikye ciraṃ na tu	NārP 49 (= 3d)
yānty eva sṛṣṭikartṛtvaṃ	KūrP 31 (= 4c)
yāmaḥ sāra ihocyate	NārP 13b
yā mārutād garbham adhatta pūrvaṃ	BrāṇP 96a
yāmi nānyasya kasyacit	KūrP 30_1d
yāvac chvetaṃ na gacchati	ĀdityaP 1b
yāvaj jñānena mokṣaḥ syāt	BrāṇP 3 (= 14c)
yāvat sukṣīrasāgare	GarP 45 (= 4d)
yāvat sevā pare tattve	SkaP 95a
yāvad eva pramāṇena	VāmP 38a
yāvaddehasthito viṣṇus	GarP 30 (= 6a)
yāvad viṣṇuṃ prapadyate	VarP 54b
yāvad viṣṇuḥ supūrṇabhuk	HarV 28b
yāvad vetti hariḥ svayam	BrāṇP 31d
yā vedair adhigamyate	NārP 23b
yāsāṃ rūpaṃ guṇās tāsāṃ	BrāṇP 95 (= 36c)
yukta ākāśago viṣṇur	VāmP 7c
yuktaḥ pāpatamādhikaḥ	PadP 94 (= 9b)
yuktayaś ceśvaraṃ param	PadP 62b
yuktibhir jñānarāhityāt	PadP 94 (= 7a)
yuktīnāṃ ca viśeṣataḥ	BrāṇP 84d
yugatraye 'vatāreṇa	PadP 35a
yugapat kramaśaś caiva	BrahVP 9c
yugaikasaptater ūrdhvaṃ	VarP 7a
yujyante paramo hi saḥ	ViṣDhUP 1d
yuddhakāle tu viduras	SkaP 33a
ye gacchanty adharaṃ tamaḥ	BrahP 32

vāyur evādhipaḥ smṛtaḥ	NārP 2 (= 8d)
vāyur devo yatas tayoḥ	NārP 2 (= 12b)
vāyur dhārayati prajāḥ	NārP 2 (= 9b)
vāyur nārāyaṇaś ca tau	BrāṇP 2 (= 1d)
vāyuśakrādinām api	NārP 20b
vāyuś ca tadanujñayā	BhavişPV 30 (= 78b)
vāyuś cābabhimānavān	BrāṇP 9 (= 1b)
vāyusthaḥ śuciṣan mataḥ	KūrP 32 (= 1d)
vāyor anyasya na brāḥmam	BrāṇP 95 (= 34c)
vāyor anye ca vāyavaḥ	NārP 2 (= 1d)
vāyo rūpāntaraṃ punaḥ	NārP 2 (= 7b)
vāyor devasya sarvaśaḥ	BhavişPV 28d
vāyvādīn kṣatriyān sṛṣṭvā	NārP 2 (= 3a)
vāsudeva udīryate	AgniP 11d
vāsudevaṃ nirañjanam	MatsyaP 19b
vāsudevaṃ prakāśayet	VāyuP 3_3b
vāsudevaḥ paraḥ pumān	BrāṇP 29b
vāsudevaḥ paraḥ pumān	BrāṇP 70b
vāsudevaḥ sudurmatiḥ	BrahP 43 (= 4d)
vāsudevapratīpataḥ	BrāṇP 95 (= 21b)
vāsudevaprasādataḥ	BrāṇP 104 (= 3b)
vāsudevaprasādena	BhavişP 2 (= 6a)
vāsudevam ajaṃ vibhum	KūrP 4d
vāsudevamukhodgatam	PadP 14 (= 7b)
vāsudevam upāśritāḥ	MBh 44d
vāsudevasya mahimā	BhavişPV 32 (= 112c)
vāsudevākhyarūpeṇa	BrāṇP 12 (= 27a)
vāsudevātmatāṃ sarva-	BrahP 43 (= 7c)
vāsudevād anantarau	MBh 47 (= 167b)
vāsudevāśritā devā	BrāṇP 28a
vāsudeve ratiḥ sthirā	BrahVP 19d
vāsudevaikasaṃśrayāḥ	BhavişP 11 (= 2b)
vāsudevo varaḥ puṃsām	SkaP 87c
vāsudevo 'ham ity ajaḥ	BrahP 43 (= 3d)
vāsudevo 'ham ity api	BrahP 43 (= 5d/9d)
vāsenedaṃ yatas tunnam	SkaP 11c
viṃśad anyāsu jātiṣu	BrāṇP 48b
viṃśad eva sahasrāṇi	BhavişPV 2 (= 11c)
viṃśallakṣaṇato 'nūnas	BrāṇP 103_2a
vikarmakaraṇād vrajet	BrāṇP 48b
vikāra iti kīrtitaḥ	PadP 63d

-śarīro rāghavaḥ svayam	SkaP 5b
śarvaḥ viriñcaś ca virocanāt	BrāṇP 68b
śaśinas tu trināmakam	SkaP 66b
śākhādyā anyadevatāḥ	KūrP 11d
śātitāni phalānīha	BrāṇP 21a
śāpaṃ śrutvā brāhmaṇānām	PadP 14 (= 1a)
śāpaṃ saṅkṣepato 'śṛṇot	SkaP 34b
śāpādir nātra kāraṇam	VarP 16d
śāpādyāḥ śaktimatsu tu	SkaP 59 (= 2b)
śāpād vyaiti tapo 'khilam	BrāṇP 59b
śārīraṃ vedanādyaṃ tu	PadP 18a
śārīras tu tridhā bhinno	GarP 54a
śārīrād vācikābhyāso	BrahVP 3a
śāśvatā viṣṇubuddhigāḥ	BrāṇP 104 (= 1b)
śāstram ity abhidhīyate	SkaP 82d
śāstrārtha iti nirdiṣṭaḥ	PadP 3c
śāstrārtho nānyathā kvacit	BrāṇP 12 (= 23d)
śāstreṣu bhāratam sāraṃ	BrāṇP 86 (= 1a)
śiṃśumāravapuṣy atha	BrāṇP 52b
śiṃśumārānugaḥ sthitaḥ	BrahP 38b
śiṃśumāro rūceḥ sutaḥ	BrāṇP 95 (= 25b)
śiṃśumāro hayāsyaś ca	VarP 51 (= 7a)
śiṃśumāro hariḥ paraḥ	BrāṇP 27b
-śilā deva iti jñānaṃ	SkaP 69 (= 3a)
śilālohā nakhāśrayāḥ	AgniP 3b
śilāvat tasya deho 'yam	BrahVP 8a
śivaḥ prathamajaḥ sutaḥ	BrāṇP 98b
śivaḥ sukhātmakatvena	BrāṇP 68a
śivabrahmādisāmyaṃ ca	HarV 5 (= 8a)
śivarūpī śive sthitaḥ	VāmP 4d
śivaśaktimahāyāna-	PadP 2c
śivaśaktyādikaṃ yac ca	BhaviṣPV 2 (= 12c)
-śivādidhyānato hareḥ	GarP 53d
śivād indrādibhis tathā	KūrP 12b
śivānāṃ cānyathāsvare	AgniP 8b
śivo hīśvaranāmā syāt	BrāṇP 15 (= 8c)
śiśupālasya mokṣaṇāt	SkaP 65 (= 7b)
-śiśupālādiṣu dvidhā	GarP 33b
śukaprabhṛtibhir janaiḥ	BrāṇP 21b
śukā iti samuddhiṣṭā	GarP 36 (= 14c)
śuko drauṇiś ca tat tanū	BhaviṣPV 32 (= 122b)

sa eva śukrasaṃsthas tu	BhaviṣPV 3 (= 12a)
sa eva sarvavedoktas	SkaP 85c
sa eva sūribhiḥ prāpyaḥ	BhaviṣPV 3 (= 11a)
sa eva sūryasaṃsthaḥ san	BrāṇP 3 (= 20a)
sa eva sūryasaṃsthaś ca	HarV 3a
sa eva sūryasaṃsthena	HarV 3a
sa eva hi vimucyate	BrahVP 38d
sa evākhilam ity api	PadP 94 (= 6b)
sa evāto vimokṣadaḥ	NārP 7d
sa evānyasvarūpeṇa	BrāṇP 30a
sa evāpy antarikṣagaḥ	KūrP 32 (= 2b)
sa evārtho na cāparaḥ	BrāṇP 64 (= 8b)
sa eṣa musalāyudhaḥ	MBh 47 (= 163d)
saṃnyāsas tu turīyo yo	NārP 36_1a
saṃnyāse tu turīye vai	BrahP 77a
-saṃpattyā viṣṇusaṃśrayāt	BhaviṣP 3 (= 21d)
saṃpādya teṣāṃ phalam icchayaiva	BrāṇP 100b
saṃpūrṇaguṇahīnatā	BrāṇP 12 (= 11d)
saṃpūrṇaphalatā tathā	GarP 41d
saṃpūrṇaphaladā eva	SkaP 59 (= 7a)
saṃpūrṇānandabhāg bhavet	PadP 71b
saṃpūrṇopāsanād brahmā	PadP 71a
saṃpradāyāgatāś ca ye	GarP 50d
saṃprāptam api jīveṣu	BrāṇP 93c
saṃbandhaṃ svātmanaḥ śriyā	SkaP 64b
-saṃbandhaḥ kurvato 'pi na	VarP 52b
saṃbhavāc cāprakāśasya	SkaP 95c
saṃbhūtaḥ keśavājñayā	BhaviṣPV 32 (= 119b)
saṃbhogo neśajīvayoḥ	GarP 40d
saṃyogaḥ prakṛter naiṣāṃ	VāyuP 1c
saṃyogaḥ prakṛter naiṣāṃ	VāyuP 2_1c
saṃvatsaradvayaṃ caiva	BhaviṣP 9c
saṃvic chāstraṃ paraṃ padam	BhāgP 2a
saṃvidrūpāṃ spṛśanti tām	VāmP 32d
saṃśayaṃ kurute manaḥ	SkaP 46b
saṃśrayas tata eva saḥ	BhaviṣPV 4 (= 4d)
saṃsāraṃ niyamaṃ tathā	BrāṇP 75b
saṃsāranirṛteḥ śiraḥ	GarP 34_1b
saṃsāraś cādivarjitaḥ	BrahP 76b
saṃsārasāgarāt tīrṇo	BrāṇP 9 (= 15c)
saṃsārasthitihetutvāt	VāyuP 6a

samyak snehayutā matiḥ	HarV 5 (= 1b)
samyak svarūpasyāvyaktir	VāyuP 3_2a
samyagārādhito hariḥ	PadP 3_1b
samyag guṇagaṇajñānād	AgniP 23a
samyag jñātum aśakyatvād	BrāṇP 91c
samyag jñātvā vimucyate	KūrP 32 (= 10b)
samyagjñānaṃ tu devānāṃ	BhavisPV 15a
samyagjñānavadācāryān	VāmP 29a
samyagjñānena paramāṃ	SkaP 104c
samyagbhaktim ṛte muktir	BrāṇP 12 (= 4c)
samyag bhāti na bhātīti	VarP 57a
samyag bhedena yaḥ paśyet	BrāṇP 58a
samyag muktau bhavanti hi	PadP 71d
samyag yajñādi kurvate	NārP 49 (= 4d)
sa yajñāt karmaṇaḥ so 'pi	NārP 51 (= 1c)
sa yāti tama eva tu	VarP 51 (= 2b)
sayujaḥ paramātmānaṃ	GarP 45 (= 9c)
sargādau caturānanaḥ	VarP 1b
sarge sarge 'nyathaiva tu	BrāṇP 104 (= 6b)
sarge sarge 'munaivaita	BrāṇP 104 (= 1c)
sarva ete satāṃ matāḥ	GarP 38 (= 8b)
sarvaṃ kṛṇoti tad yuktam	BrahP 47c
sarvaṃ ceśvaratas teṣāṃ	BrahP 78a
sarvaṃ tat tattvavit sadā	BrahVP 38 (= 4d)
sarvaṃ tadviṣayatvena	SkaP 51a
sarvaṃ tīrtvā hariṃ śukraṃ	VarP 60a
sarvaṃ tu rūpavad viṣṇor	SkaP 28a
sarvaṃ bhaktyartham uddiṣṭaṃ	HarV 5 (= 6a)
sarvaṃ moghaṃ śubhaṃ tasya	BhavisPV 26a
sarvaṃ mohārtham uddiṣṭaṃ	BrāṇP 12 (= 14c)
sarvaṃ vidhārayan dehaṃ	VahniP 1c
sarvaṃ vidhīyate nityaṃ	SkaP 95c
sarvaṃ harer vaśatvena	HarV 21a
sarvakartā ca keśavaḥ	PadP 52b
sarvakartāraṃ īśeśaṃ	KūrP 31 (= 6a)
sarvakartā sarvaśaktir	HarV 33 (= 9a)
sarvakarmā sa eva hi	BhavisPV 3 (= 13d)
sarvagatvāc ca tat param	BrāṇP 91d
sarvagranthāntarasthitam	BrāṇP 50d
sarvaceṣṭayitṛtvāt tu	MBh 12a
sarvacchandobhidho hy eṣa	VāmP 35a

sarvadāstīti meyaṃ ca	BhavişPV 3 (= 3c)
sarvaduḥkhavihīnā ye	VarP 4a
sarvadevasthitaṃ harim	PadP 101b
sarvadevābhidho 'py asau	VāmP 35b
sarvadeveṣu saṃsthitaḥ	VarP 5b
sarvadehastharūpeṣu	BhavişPV 29 (= 40c)
sarvadaikaprakārataḥ	SkaP 40b
sarvadaiva bubhūṣibhiḥ	BrāṇP 12 (= 24d)
sarvadaiva vyavasthitam	BhavişPV 3 (= 29d)
sarvadoṣanivṛttās te	BrahVP 28a
sarvadoṣavinirmuktaṃ	KūrP 31 (= 7c)
sarvadoṣavivarjitaḥ	BrāṇP 13 (= 15d)
sarvadoṣavivarjitāḥ	BrahP 78b
sarvadoṣavivarjitāḥ	VarP 2d
sarvadoṣavihīnatvaṃ	BhavişPV 29 (= 44c)
sarvadoṣavyatītasya	HarV 33 (= 6a)
sarvadoṣavyapetatvaṃ	BrāṇP 12 (= 20c)
sarvadharmakṛto 'pi ca	PadP 55b
sarvanāmatva eva tu	BrāṇP 3 (= 12b)
sarvanāmavatas tasya	BrāṇP 3 (= 20c)
sarvanāmābhidheyaś ca	SkaP 86c
sarvanāmā yato viṣṇus	BrāṇP 25a
sarvanāmāham asmy eka	BrāṇP 3 (= 11c)
sarvanāmnāṃ ca rūpāṇāṃ	PadP 66a
sarvapāpakṣayād dehaṃ	VarP 54a
sarvapāpāni bhasmasāt	BhavişPV 31 (= 127d)
sarvapāpaiḥ pramucyate	BrāṇP 86 (= 4d)
sarvapāpaiḥ pramucyate	BrāṇP 95 (= 11b)
sarvapūjyaś caturmukhaḥ	GarP 45 (= 8d)
sarvaprāṇiśarīragaḥ	MārkP 3b
sarvaprāṇiṣu ca sthitaḥ	SkaP 86b
sarvabuddhaṃ sa vai veda	BrahP 1$_5$c
sarvabrahmatvavettāro	SkaP 40c
sarvabhinnaṃ guṇocchrayāt	NārP 50d
sarvabhinno yato hariḥ	MatsyaP 12d
sarvabhūtāni cottamāḥ	NārP 43
sarvabhūteṣu kurute	BrahVP 35c
sarvabhūteṣu ca hareḥ	PadP 39c
sarvam aiśvaryasaṃbhavam	ViṣDhUP 1b
sarvayajñādikarma ca	SkaP 95d
sarvarūpaprabhūtataḥ	BrāṇP 3 (= 18d)

sa viṣṇur āptakāmatvād	BhaviṣPV 4 (= 1c)
sa viṣṇur iti dhāryatām	VarP 23d
saviṣvā cāyanenāsau	BrahVP 37c
sa vedo jñānadarśanāt	BrāṇP 103_2d
sa śrotriya udāhṛtaḥ	BrāṇP 102b
sa satyaṃ jagad etādṛṅ	VarP 55 (= 4c)
sa sadā na harau kvacit	SkaP 39d
sa sa yāti samagratām	BhaviṣPV 3 (= 5b)
sasarja ca jagad vibhuḥ	MatsyaP 9d
sasarja matimān brahmā	NārP 2 (= 7c)
sasarjātmecchayā prabhuḥ	VarP 55 (= 7d)
sa sarvabhūtasamadṛg	HarV 22a
sa sūkṣmaḥ sarvagaḥ sadā	BrāṇP 9 (= 10)
sa sūryaḥ sūryabhāryā ca	GarP 5 (= 3a)
sa sraṣṭā caiva saṃhartā	BrāṇP 9 (= 9c)
sa svapna iti gīyate	BrāṇP 74d
sahakāryantaraṃ prajāḥ	VarP 44b
sahanaṃ tu titikṣaṇam	PadP 15d
sa hanty ajñānasaṃbhavāḥ	BrāṇP 58b
saha viṣṇur jagatpatiḥ	BrahVP 14b
saha śete harir niśi	BrahP 26b
sahaś ca svecchayā kṛteḥ	MBh 12d
sahasraṃ caturuttaram	VarP 7d
sahasrayojanasabhāṃ	SkaP 128a
sahasrākṣaḥ sahasrapāt	BrahP 22_1b
sahasrākṣaḥ surādhipaḥ	SkaP 4d
sahāpūpaṃ prabhakṣayet	BrāṇP 7b
sa hi kāmair na hanyate	BrāṇP 102d
sa hi kāmair na hanyate	BrāṇP 102b
sa hi jīveṣu saṃviṣṭhaḥ	BhaviṣPV 4 (= 4a)
sa hi jīveṣu saṃsthitaḥ	BhaviṣPV 4 (= 2b)
sa hi nāśaṃ na gacchati	BrahVP 19b
sa hi brahmātmavin mataḥ	BrahP 55d
sa hi mukto 'kāmahataḥ	BrāṇP 102c
sa hi sarvaguṇādhikaḥ	NārP 1d
sa hi sarvamanovṛtti-	GarP 38 (= 5a)
sa hi sarvādhiko mataḥ	HarV 25b
sahaiva śaktibhiḥ svīyair	NārP 8c
sa hy ācārān uvāceśaḥ	BhaviṣPV 3 (= 10c)
sākṣāc ca pitaraṃ punaḥ	AgniP 2b
sākṣāt satyam ato 'nyasmād	MatsyaP 7c

sūryavad bahudheyate	MatsyaP 17d
sūryaś candro bṛhaspatiḥ	BrāṇP 95 (= 28d)
sūryasaṃsthād dhi rūpāt sa	HarV 3c
sūryasomau ca vidyutam	BrāṇP 20b
sūryāntastho mumukṣubhiḥ	BhavisPV 3 (= 11b)
sūrye vā deha eva vā	BrāṇP 26b
sūryo yathāntaraś cakṣuḥ	KūrP 32 (= 14a)
sṛjate viṣṇur avyayaḥ	VāmP 15d
sṛjyān sraṣṭāram eva ca	SkaP 41b
sṛṅkāṃ svarṇamayīṃ caiva	PadP 97c
sṛṭāv āvartayaty asau	BhaviṣPV 22d
sṛtiyogyāḥ sadaiva hi	BhaviṣPV 30 (= 87b)
sṛtı jñātvā tu sopāye	SkaP 116a
sṛṣṭā iti vikalpanam	MatsyaP 7b
sṛṣṭā brahmādayo devā	MBh 40a
sṛṣṭiṃ ca pālanaṃ caiva	BrāṇP 75a
sṛṣṭiḥ proktā hy apaṇḍitaiḥ	HarV 33 (= 3d)
sṛṣṭikarma nyayojayat	BrahVP 21d
sṛṣṭikāla udāhṛtaḥ	NārP 24b
sṛṣṭikāle vidhīyate	BhaviṣPV 18d
sṛṣṭikāle vibhajyante	ViṣP 8 (= 2c)
sṛṣṭibhedād virūpaṃ ca	SkaP 49a
sṛṣṭim āhur akovidāḥ	HarV 33 (= 7d)
sṛṣṭirakṣāhṛtijñāna	BhaviṣPV 30 (= 83a)
sṛṣṭir viṣṇoḥ samutthitāḥ	ViṣP 7d
sṛṣṭiś ca pralayaś caiva	SkaP 40a
sṛṣṭisaṃhārakṛd dhariḥ	PadP 64d
sṛṣṭisthityantakāriṇaḥ	SkaP 29b
sṛṣṭau guṇe ca jñānādau	VarP 10a
sṛṣṭau bhogās tathottamāḥ	GarP 19d
sṛṣṭau laye tāratamyaṃ	VāmP 17a
sṛṣṭyādikaṃ samastaṃ tu	SkaP 100c
sṛṣṭyādivyāpṛtiṣv api	VarP 48b
sṛṣṭyā bhinnāṣṭadhā punaḥ	NārP 41d
sṛṣṭvā devādidehān sa	NārP 11a
sṛṣṭvā viṣṇuḥ purā prabhuḥ	BrahVP 1b
setihāsapurāṇakān	BhaviṣPV 30 (= 84b)
setihāsais tathā vedaiḥ	SkaP 40a
senayor ubhayor api	MBh 46b
senāmadhye 'rjunāya ca	BrahVP 39 (= 2b)
seveta jñānasiddhaye	NārP 48c

sevyo viṣṇuḥ sadaiva hi	BhaviṣPV 30 (= 96d)
saiva ca draupadī nāma	BhaviṣPV 32 (= 120c)
saiva viṣṇuṃ vijānāti	GarP 36 (= 3c)
saivāpramāṇatāṃ gacched	VāyuP 2c
saiṣa saṃsṛtir ucyate	HarV 20b
so 'jñānādyaṃ prakāśayet	SkaP 5b
so 'tmano manasāsrākṣīd	BrahVP 21c
so 'tmānam arcann acarad	BrāṇP 8c
so 'nantaguṇa īritaḥ	BrāṇP 2 (= 6b)
so 'nātmeti satāṃ mataḥ	VāmP 34b
so 'niruddhaṃ viveśa ha	BrāṇP 12 (= 29d)
so 'nyaṃ katham upāśrayet	MBh 23b
sopacāraḥ prayujyate	VāmP 34d
sopacāro 'bhidhīyate	PadP 56b
so 'pi yanmokṣaniyataṃ	HarV 5 (= 3c)
so 'pi viṣṇur ameyātmā	HarV 17c
somaś ca rohiṇī caiva	GarP 5 (= 4a)
somasūryau yamas tathā	VāmP 2 (= 2d)
somena ca suteneśam	SkaP 7c
so 'yaṃ viṣṇū ramābrahma-	HarV 32a
so 'yaṃ sarveṣu jīveṣu	BhaviṣPV 4 (= 1a)
so 'sṛjad bhuvanaṃ sarvam	BrahVP 21a
so 'sthūlādiguṇo mataḥ	SkaP 9d
so 'haṃ cāsāv aheyataḥ	HarV 3d
saugatādyā durāgamāḥ	BhaviṣPV 2 (= 8b)
saurāṇāṃ cāpi muktānām	BrāṇP 15 (= 4a)
skandaḥ kāmāṃśajāḥ smṛtāḥ	SkaP 52b
skhalanaṃ saṃbhaved yataḥ	BrāṇP 16b
staṃbhād vā naradehād vā	SkaP 5c
stāvakāny eva tāni syur	NārP 36c
stutyarthaṃ tasya devasya	BrahP 51c
stuvann api janārdanam	BrāṇP 56b
stotraṃ śrutvaiva yajñena	BrāṇP 90c
strītvam āhur manīṣiṇaḥ	BrāṇP 70d
strīpuṃmalābhiyogātma-	BrāṇP 105 (= 4a)
strīpuṃrūpadvayī viṣṇor	BrāṇP 5a
strīrūpaś caiva puṃrūpo	GarP 4a
strīrūpo hayaśīrṣavān	BrāṇP 95 (= 26b)
strī vāpy anūnadaśakaṃ	BrahP 76c
sthānabhedāt pṛthagvidhāḥ	MBh 18b
sthāvarāṇi divaḥ prāptaḥ	BrahP 69a

sthāvarebhyaś ca pūruṣam	BrahP 69b
sthāsnubhir niyamān mukhyā	BrahP 24 (= 1a)
sthāsnuṣv athāpi puruṣe	BrahP 69a
sthita ukto duroṇasat	KūrP 31 (= 3d)
sthitaṃ karma vido viduḥ	VāyuP 6b
sthitaṃ brahmāpi sarvagam	BrahP 25b
sthitaprajñatvam āptā ye	VāyuP 12a
sthitaprajñā hi te matāḥ	GarP 21d
sthitaprajño 'pi yas tūrdhvaḥ	GarP 47a
-sthitam adhyātmam ucyate	SkaP 114b
sthitas tannāmako 'pi saḥ	BrāṇP 15 (= 5b)
sthitasyāpi yathā rājñaḥ	PadP 34c
sthitāḥ syuḥ prāpya keśavam	VarP 54d
-sthitiḥ syād varadānataḥ	BhavişPV 27b
sthitiḥ svābhāvike punaḥ	PadP 93b
sthiter gatir avāpyate	BrahP 24 (= 1b)
sthitau sthitiḥ praveśaś ca	GarP 42c
sthityādiṣu viśeṣataḥ	BrahVP 9b
sthitvā rudre tv abhakṣayat	BrahP 52b
sthūladehasya rāhityād	VarP 55 (= 2a)
sthūlasūkṣmaviśeṣo 'tra	GarP 43a
sthūlāṃś cakre priyavrataḥ	GarP 27b
sthūlo 'ṇuś caiva sarvataḥ	KūrP 1b
snigdheṣv eva hi sādhavaḥ	NārP 25d
snehapūrvābhidhīyate	PadP 68b
snehabhīta ivāthāpi	BrāṇP 63c
snehād annaṃ dadātīti	BrāṇP 53 (= 1a)
sneho bhaktir iti proktas	BhavişPV 30 (= 85c)
sphuliṅgasaṃvartakayor yadantaraṃ	SkaP 110c
sma bhrāntis tatra tatkṛtā	BrāṇP 74b
smaraṃs tu yāvad arthaḥ syād	BrāṇP 25c
smaraṇaṃ jāyate yataḥ	NārP 16b
smartavyaḥ satataṃ viṣṇur	MBh 42 (= 69a)
smīti jīvaḥ samuddiṣṭaḥ	BrāṇP 85a
smītyalpaṃ sumitatvataḥ	BrāṇP 85b
smṛtayo 'py anukūlataḥ	BhavişPV 29 (= 32d)
smṛtāḥ sāttvikatāmasāḥ	SkaP 32 (= 3d)
smṛtāḥ sāttvikarājasāḥ	SkaP 32 (= 4b)
smṛtvā prārabhato granthaṃ	VāmP 3c
syād abhāvāt puṃsa eva tu	SkaP 54b
syād eva mokṣo nānyasmād	BhavişPV 21 (= 1c)

syād dhi bhāgavatasyaiva	AgniP 23a
syān na hy evaṃ kvāpi tat kenacit syāt	BrāṇP 100b
syuḥ svatantrasya kiṃ punaḥ	KūrP 10b
sraṣṭā pātā ca saṃhartā	NārP 42a
sraṣṭā pātā ca saṃhartā	SkaP 100a
sraṣṭā pātā tathaivāttā	SkaP 87a
sraṣṭā svayaṃ samuddiṣṭaḥ	NārP 2 (= 5c)
sraṣṭṛtvāc caiva pātṛtvān	MBh 2a
sraṣṭṛtvādikam anyeṣāṃ	SkaP 100c
svaṃ svaṃ karma tu sarveṣāṃ	PadP 93c
svakīyāny api keśavaḥ	BrahP 61b
svaguṇasyānusāreṇa	GarP 32a
svajagadvyāpṛtis teṣāṃ	GarP 45c
svata eva tataḥ param	BrāṇP 80b
svata eva pareśasya	BhaviṣPV 24a
svata eva hares tathā	BrahVP 13b
svata evāsya sarvadā	BhaviṣPV 3b
svataḥ pravṛttyaśaktatvād	BrahP 84a
svataḥ prāmāṇyam eteṣāṃ	BhaviṣP 10 (= 2c)
svataḥ sarve 'pi cidrūpāḥ	BrahP 78a
svatantraḥ sa paro viṣṇur	BrāṇP 105 (= 1c)
svatantratvāt sukhatvāc ca	PadP 46a
svatantratvāt svatantro hi	KūrP 31 (= 17a)
svatantrasya ca varjanāt	KūrP 18b
svatantrācintya sadguṇe	BrāṇP 105 (= 6d)
svatantro ghaṭate yataḥ	NārP 3 (= 6d)
svatantro jagati kvacit	BrāṇP 62d
svatantro nāparaḥ kaścid	BrāṇP 62a
svato jñātā ca mantā ca	GarP 30 (= 4c)
svato 'dhikaguṇaṃ hatvā	AgniP 2a
svato manasthitir viṣṇau	BrāṇP 24a
svadehaṃ vyāpya tiṣṭhati	BrāṇP 71b
svadehayogavigama-	SkaP 117a
svadehe brahmadṛṣṭyaiva	GarP 44c
svanāmā viṣṇur ucyate	PadP 46b
svanāśe śocanaṃ kutaḥ	BrahVP 19d
svanīceṣu tu deveṣu	GarP 37 (= 7c)
svapakṣapātas tv abhyāsād	SkaP 55a
svapakṣasyālpayuktitaḥ	PadP 94 (= 7b)
svapadaṃ ca surān nayan	BhaviṣPV 22b
svapity asmin layaṃ vrajan	VarP 40d

2. Index of Other Untraceable Source-quotations

The three lists mentioned here had been put together first by GLASENAPP 1923 (*21f.) [=1992:24]. I have used them with some decisive changes. First of all, I have supplemented his lists with further details, such as with several new source-titles which GLASENAPP had overlooked. Unlike GLASENAPP, I have ordered all these titles in alphabetical sequence, pointing out their precise location in the different works of Madhva.

Madhva ascribes some of the Śruti-sources expressly to Sāmaveda (indicated below with an asterisk *); other sources, like sauparṇa-śākhā, are attributed to Ṛgveda (GīBh p. 21,14). The first list comprises source-titles with Śruti-names; the titles of the second list are very similar to the sources of Āgama literature (cf. O. SCHRADER, Introduction to the Pañcarātra and the Ahirbudhnya Saṃhitā, Madras 1973). On the basis of this similarity, I have added to this list several new titles. Among them are also some, which have escaped the notice of GLASENAPP. The third list contains the remaining source-titles. In some cases, this classification may appear arbitrary.

2.1. Index of Untraceable Śruti-quotes

[with titles like °brāhmaṇa; °khila; °śākhā; °saṃhitā; °śikhā; °śruti; °upaniṣad]

Ācāyāṣyaśruti (GīBh p. 153,3-4)
Āgneyaśākhā (GīBh p. 102,8-11)
Āgniveśyaśākhā* (GīBh p. 117, 9-10; 120,14-15)
Āgniveśyaśruti* (BSūBh p. 102,6-7; 22-23; 105,7-8; 111,12-13; 114,23-25; GīBh p. 146,18-19)
Aitareyasaṃhitā (AiUBh p. 187,18+188,15; 189,31+190,10; 190,17+191, 29; 208,12-25; 209,20+213,16; 216,16-28; 218,24-219,21; 221,24+222,14; 238,18+239,25)
Ānabhiṃlātaśākhā* (GīBh p. 121,7-9)
Ānabhiṃlātaśruti* (GīBh p. 134,5-6)
Antaryāmisaṃhitā (BhāgTN p. 690,19-691,3)
Āruṇiśruti (BhāgTN p. 581,8-9)
Auddālakāyaṇaśruti (BSūBh p. 225,3-5; BhāgTN p. 567,7-8)
Āyāsyaśākhā* (GīBh p. 120,6-9; 129,2-3/10-11)

2.2. Index of Untraceable Quotes from the Āgamas

[with titles like Saṃhitā and Tantra]

617,1-11; 620,1-2; 646,6-7; 665,6-666,6; 687,6-688,1; 694,10-15; 756,1-757,4; 771,4-7; 810,9-811,1; 819,9-10; 830,5-6; 836,1-4)
Tantramālā (BĀUBh p. 354,26+355,18; BhāgTN p. 108,11; 109,10; 137,4; 273,2; 414,4-6; 423,8-9; 425,10-11; 474,5-7; 354,26+355,18)
Tantranirṇaya (BhāgTN p. 399,7-9; 431,6-9)
Tantranirukta (BhāgTN p. 371,8-372,2; 652,3-5; 662,2-3; 722,11-13)
Tantraprakāśikā (BhāgTN p. 192,6-7)
Tantrasāra (BhāgTN p. 164,8; 166,9-10; 291,1-2; 293,7-9; 295,11-13; 319, 7-9; 325,9-10; 330,1-5; 334,13-14; 388,4-5; 406,10-11; 408,10-11; 437,15-18; 472,11-12)
Tattvasaṃhitā (BĀUBh p. 302,26+303,16; BhāgTN p. 840,4-841,1; ChUBh p. 418,23-27; ĪśUBh p. 410,16-17; TaiUBh p. 526,15-17)
Udārasaṃhitā (BhāgTN p. 72,11-13)
Uddāmasaṃhitā (BhāgTN p. 601,7-10)
Vaihāyasasaṃhitā (BĀUBh p. 245,19-26; GīT p. 115,20-21; KhN p. 240, 8-10)
Vāsudevādhyātma (BhāgTN p. 36,1-2)
Vibhūti (BhāgTN p. 724,9-10)
Vibhūtitattva (GīT p. 25-28; 103,25-27)
Vimalasaṃhitā (BhāgTN p. 560,7-9)
Vimuktisaṃhitā (BĀUBh p. 247,17-18)
Viṣṇusaṃhitā (BhāgTN p. 7,10-11; 90,3-4; 352,5-6; 661,3-5)
Viṣṇutantra (BhāgTN p. 754,9-10)
Viśvasaṃhitā (BhāgTN p. 690,9-11)
Vyāsanirukta (BĀUBh p. 247,3-4; BhāgTN p. 120,3-4; 588,3)
Vyāsasaṃhitā (KhN 242,7-8)
Vyāsasmṛti (BĀUBh p. 268,15-17; BhāgTN p. 58,9-10; 201,1; 479,3-4; 765, 8-10; BSūBh p. 20,8-10; GīBh p. 23,15; 151,18-19; GīT p. 59,23- 28; KhN p. 239,3-4; MBhTN XXXII 69; MuUBh p. 492,17-18; 492, 22-23 [= GīBh 39,15-16]; Vāda p. 45,13-46,2; 47,10-13)
Vyāsatantra (BhāgTN p. 627,1-2)
Vyāsavākya (MBhTN II 131-141ab)
Vyāsayoga (GīBh p. 85,4)
Vyomasaṃhitā (BhāgTN p. 70,8-9; 99,9-100,4; 101,3-5; 127,6-8; 145,1-2; 150,2-4; 165,13-14; 170,3-6; 180,16-17; 358,4; 371,2-3; 400,6-7; BSūBh p. 4,11-5,4; 95,12-15; 97,17-18)
Yādavādhyātma (BhāgTN p. 704,7-10)

2.3. Index of Untraceable Source-quotes from Other Works

Dhyānayoga (BhāgTN p. 709,4-10; 799,3-11)
Gāndharva (BhāgTN p. 110,4; 462,7)
Gatisāra (KathUBh p. 476,13-19)
Gītākalpa (BhāgTN p. 57,1; 724,5-7; 727,7-9; GīBh p. 75,6-10/12-14; 76, 2-4/8; 80,10-13; 82,13-16)
Guṇaparama (BĀUBh p. 352,26+353,15)
Gurutattva (ṚgBh p. 12,9)
Guruviveka (BhāgTN p. 588,10-15; 659,1-4)
Guruvṛttābhidha (Anuv p. 191,23-192,4)
Jīvanirṇaya (BhāgTN p. 631,1-5)
Jīvatattva (BhāgTN p.663,1-2)
Jīveśabheda (BhāgTN p. 516,3-4)
Jñānaviveka (BhāgTN p. 332,6-7)
Kālakīya (ChUBh p. 411,14-23)
Kālanirṇaya (BĀUBh p. 302,24-25)
Kālaviveka (BhāgTN p. 562,7-8)
Kāpileya (BhāgTN p. 10,11; 234,10; 238,5-6; 240,1-2; 242,9-11; 245,6-10; 249,2-5; 252,4/8-9; 261,9-10; 262,11-263,2; 264,3; 558,9-559,2; 716,4-6)
Karaṇaviveka (BĀUBh p. 248,22-25)
Karmānupūrvī (ChUBh p. 423,21-22)
Karmatattva (TaiUBh p. 527,15-16/23-24)
Karmaviveka (BhāgTN p. 684,6-8; KhN p. 247,18-20)
Kriyāvidhāna (BhāgTN p. 629,1-7)
Kriyāyoga (BhāgTN p. 511,9-10)
Lakṣaṇa (BhāgTN p. 661,8-9)
Liṅganirṇaya (ChUBh p. 456,16-18)
Mahāmīmāṃsā (BĀUBh p. 323,20; 310,18-28; 313,25+314,17; 315,25+ 317,20; 328,18+329,21; 332,19-27; 335,13-15; 339,15-19; 341,27+ 342,18; BhāgTN p. 9,6)
Mahātattvaviveka (BhāgTN p. 561,5-562,4)
Mahāvyākaraṇa (BhāgTN p. 45,4-6; 229,3; 566,1-2; ṚgBh p. 206,2)
Mānasa (ChUBh p. 379,25-26; 468,18-20)
Māyāvaibhava (BhāgTN p. 652,5-8; 668,19-12; BSūBh p. 168,2-4)
Muktitattva (BhāgTN p. 655,5-6; 662,5-6)
Muktiviveka (BhāgTN p. 672,20; MuUBh p. 498,23-25)
Nairguṇya (MāṇUBh p. 513,14-15)
Nāmamahodadhi (BhāgTN p. 47,3-4; 48,2-3; 55,8; 61,3; 93,15-17; BSūBh p. 119,20)
Nāmanirṇaya (AiUBh p. 213,19-21)
Nāmanirukta (KathUBh p. 477,15-16)
Nārāyaṇagopālakalpa (GīBh p. 85,18-20)
Nārāyaṇarāmakalpa (GīBh p. 32,4-5)

3. Thematic Classification of the Untraceable Source-quotations

This classification comprises references which are related in each case to a particular topic in its different variations. To simplify matters, all references to a particular topic (v.g. Asuras/Demons) have been gathered under one single textual quote (v.g. BhavişPV 12). This quotation is referred to in every other unknown quotation broaching the same or similar subject. When this quotation has more than five entries it has been italicized.

Abhyāsa	GarP 3
Adhibhūta	SkaP 114
Adhidaiva	SkaP 114
Adhikadṛṣṭānta	BrahP 9
Adhikāra of Gods	KūrP 16
Adhyātma	SkaP 114
Agni's sons	KūrP 4
Ajāmila	NarP 16
Akṣaratraya	SkaP 88
Ānvīkṣikī	MatsyaP 2
Arjuna's arrow	PadP 4
Aṣṭadaśasiddhi (Yoga)	HarV 28
Asuras / Demons	BhavişPV 12
Athātas (*pratīka*: BSū I 1.1.)	GarP 38
Ātman, Viṣṇu's specific appellation	BrahVP 19
Āveśa	BrahVP 17
Badarī (the sacred place of Viṣṇu's instruction)	GarP 16
Bali	BrāṇP 56
Beatific vision of Viṣṇu / Liberation	AgniP 24
Bewilderment of evil beings / demons	MBh 42n. 6
BhāgP (analytical account)	GarP 8
Bhakti / Pujā / Upāsana	AgniP 20
Bharadvāja (etymology)	PadP 45
Bhārata-Karmabhūmi / Dharmakṣetra	BrāṇP 49
Bhāṣās trividhās (categories of speech)	BhavişPV 32[114f.]
Bhasmasnāna	SkaP 77
Bhīma's virtues	MBh 46

Heaven of Brahmā	BhaviṣPV 9
Hell / Heaven	BhaviṣPV 19
Heresies of Advaita	SkaP 39-40
Hierarchy among divine horses	SkaP 81
Hierarchy of the spiritual beings	BhaviṣPV 15
Hiraṇyakaśipu	GarP 29
Hiraṇyākṣa	AgniP 8
Human age	PadP 7
Hṛd (etymology)	PadP 84
Idols / Tīrtha	GarP 34
Ignorance	HarV 8
Indivisibility (abheda) of Viṣṇu's nature	BrāṇP 10
Intrinsic aptitude (yogyatā) of Jīvas	BrahP 36
Jainas	BrahP 43
Janārdana (etymology)	BrahP 49
Jīva's nature	BrāṇP 71
Jīvopādhi	SkaP 54
Kāla	BrahP 25
Kāma	MBh 37
Kapila (Sāṃkhya)	PadP 9
King Ambarīṣa	GarP 31
King Parīkṣit	MBh 10
King Pautrāyana	PadP 76
King Yama	NārP 14
Kramamukti	BrahP 82
Kṛṣṇadvaipāyana	BrāṇP 14
Lakṣamaṇa / Rāma	SkaP 3
Liberation / Emancipation	AgniP 16
Liberation through hatred	BrāṇP 53
Liberation while still alive (jīvanmukti)	ĀdityaP 1
Mahāpuruṣalakṣaṇa	BrāṇP 103_2
Mahārṣis	ViṣṇP 7
Mahidāsa	BrāṇP 67
Māyā	VarP 18
Meaning of a sentence (*siddhārtha*) against *karyārtha*	BrahP 13
Means and ways of liberation	AgniP 9
Measuring and time-units	PadP 33
Mind (bad states)	BrahP 6
Mitra (etymology)	MBh 1
Moha	PadP 13
Mokṣa (synonyms)	BrahP 14

Saṃnyāsa	NārP 36_1
Sanatkumāra	BrahP 3
Śāpa	BrāṇP 59
Saptarṣi	BrahP 83
Śāstra (definition)	SkaP 82
Satkāryavāda	BrahP 31
Sattva	MatsyaP 1
Saubhariśāpa	BrāṇP 59
Sense organs / Breath of life / vāyū / prāṇa	BhaviṣPV 17
Seven hells	MBh 26
Śiṃśumārāvatāra	BrāṇP 27
Śiśupāla	BrāṇP 53
Śiva's epithets	BrahP 61
Soma	GarP 10
Sons of Brahmā	SkaP 75
Spies (in the secret service)	BrahP 7
Śraddhā	BrāṇP 64
Śrotriya (definition)	BrāṇP 102
States of consciousness	BrāṇP 7
Śuka	SkaP 13
Śukī	BrahP 41
Svarūpa of a wordly object	PadP 36
Svayaṃbhū	VarP 52
Svāyaṃbhuva Manu	NārP 13
Śvetadvīpa	ĀdityaP 1
Syllabus of the right and heretical doctrines	BhaviṣPV 3n.7
Symbols/ Hari's marks	AgniP 3
Theory of error	BrahVP 44
Tīrtha/Idols	BrahP 58
Transmigration (*saṃsāra*)	BrāṇP 33
Trimūrti	BrahP 52
Uddhava	GarP 16
Umā/Rudra	SkaP 105
Upadharma	HarV 16
Ur-Elemente	MatsyaP 5
Vairāgya	BhāgP 4
Vāmadeva	BhaviṣPV 3[8f.]
Varuṇa	GarP 58
Vasu	PadP 101
Veda tree	BrāṇP 21
Vedic ritual	BhaviṣPV 7

Yadu-Family (prophecy of annihilation)	PadP 14
Yājñavalkya	BrāṇP 17
Yama	NārP 14
Yoga-meditation	NārP 8
Yogic powers	HarV 28